MACROECONOMICS

MACROECONOMICS

SECOND EDITION

ROGER A. ARNOLD
CALIFORNIA STATE UNIVERSITY, SAN MARCOS

WEST PUBLISHING COMPANY
ST. PAUL   NEW YORK   LOS ANGELES   SAN FRANCISCO

To
SHEILA, DANIEL, AND DAVID

■

Production Credits
Production, Prepress, Printing, and
Binding by West Publishing Company
Copy Editing: Elaine Levin
Composition: Parkwood Composition Service
Indexing: Pat Lewis

Photo Credits
All photographs are supplied courtesy of the
individual economists featured in the interviews.

Acknowledgments
15 Friedman, Milton, "The Methodology of Positive Economics," *Essays in Positive Economics.* (Chicago: The University of Chicago Press, 1953), p. 15. Reprinted with permission. **95** Leijonhufvud, Axel. "Effective Demand Failures," *Swedish Journal of Economics* 75 (1973), p. 28. Reprinted with permission. **497–498** Smith, Adam. *The Theory of Moral Sentiments.* (Oxford: Oxford University Press, 1976), p. 234. Reprinted with permission. Material from *The New Palgrave: A Dictionary of Economics* reprinted with permission from Macmillan Press Ltd.

Library of Congress Cataloging-in-Publication Data

Arnold, Roger A.
   Macroeconomics / Roger A. Arnold.—2nd ed.
     p.   cm.
ISBN 0-314-88425-4 (soft)
1. Macroeconomics.   I. Title.
HB172.5.A76 1992
339—dc20

91-34763
CIP ∞

CONTENTS IN BRIEF

THE WORLD ECONOMY   409

CONTENTS

ECONOMICS IN OUR TIMES
■
Economic Growth: An Expanding PPF Ends the Political Tug-of-War, for a While 40

ECONOMICS IN OUR TIMES
■
Interview: Vernon Smith 65

CONTENTS
■

ECONOMICS IN OUR TIMES
▪
What Does Price Have to Do with
Being Late to Class? 84

MACROECONOMICS 89
▪

ECONOMICS IN OUR TIMES
∎
The Underground Economy 119

ECONOMICS IN OUR TIMES
∎
No Communication with the Outside World: The BEA at Work 125

ECONOMICS IN OUR TIMES
∎
How Do You Know if You're Beating Inflation or If Inflation is Beating You?

ECONOMICS IN OUR TIMES
∎
Can Economics Pick the Winner? 143

CONTENTS
∎
xii

ECONOMICS IN OUR TIMES
■
Interview: Alice Rivlin 237

ECONOMICS IN OUR TIMES
■
The Savings and Loan
Crisis 264

ECONOMICS IN OUR TIMES
■
Everything You Wanted to Know
About Federal Reserve Notes but
Were Too Busy Spending Them
to Ask 272

xv

ECONOMICS IN OUR TIMES
■
**A Lot of Finger Pointing Goes on
During a Rapid Inflation 292**

ECONOMICS IN OUR TIMES
■
**Does Dog Racing Cause
Continued Inflation? 294**

ECONOMICS IN OUR TIMES
■
**Does the Fed Think in Terms of
MV = PQ? 307**

CONTENTS
■
xvi

CONTENTS

ECONOMICS IN OUR TIMES
■
Proposals to Deal with the
Deficit   405

THE WORLD ECONOMY   409
■

ECONOMICS IN OUR TIMES
■
Interview: Lester Thurow   433

CONTENTS
■
xix

CONTENTS
■
xx

In the second edition of *Macroeconomics*, I have tried to retain the strengths of the first edition, eliminate any weaknesses, and continue in my endeavor to write a text that is both exciting and pedagogically sound. It is a cliche, perhaps, but nevertheless true: one of the major motivating factors for my writing a principles text is to convey to students the excitement, richness, and power of economic analysis that I, and thousands of economics professors across the country, experience daily.

The second edition of *Macroeconomics* is a cleaner, better organized, more innovative text than the first edition. I have listened to the constructive comments of numerous reviewers and colleagues, hundreds of students, the editorial staff of West Publishing Company, and the little voice inside of me, to write a book that I trust you will find worth your time.

ORGANIZATION OF THE SECOND EDITION

Section I. Economics: The Science of Scarcity.   This book is organized into three sections. Section I discusses the key concepts and tools in economics. Two of the four chapters are devoted to supply-and-demand analysis. Upon completion of this section, the student should have a solid understanding of the economic way of thinking.

Section II. Macroeconomics.   The organization of macroeconomics is different than in the first edition. Adopters of the second edition will find a smoother macroeconomics to teach. First, a new introductory chapter, Chapter 5, introduces the student to the key players in macroeconomics (consumers, businesses, government, foreigners, the Fed, and so on) and presents an organizational scheme that can be used as he or she reads the 13 remaining macroeconomic chapters.

Overall, macroeconomics is presented in terms of major topics. The first topic is macroeconomic measurements. Gross national product (GNP), real GNP, price indices, and unemployment and employment rates are discussed. The second topic is theory and fiscal policy. Here the origins of Keynesian theory, both old and new Keynesian theory, and fiscal policy are discussed. The third topic is theory, money, and policy. Money and banking, the Federal Reserve System, classical and monetarist theory, inflation, and monetary policy are discussed. The fourth topic is theory, expectations, and policy. Phillips curve analysis, job search theory, new classical theory, adaptive and rational expectations, business cycles, and monetary and fiscal policy are discussed. There are other items discussed under each of the four major topics, but the major ones have been noted here. Also, the defining framework of the macroeconomics section is the aggregate demand-aggregate supply (*AD-AS*) framework, although the income-expenditure (*I-E*) framework and $MV = PQ$ framework are used, too.

Three Organizational Categories.   Offices can be cluttered without file cabinets and bookshelves, and minds can be cluttered without methods of organizing information. The macroeconomics student is better able to understand all the information that comes her way in a macroeconomics course if she has a way of "processing" and "filing" the information as it is obtained. With this in mind, three organizational categories have been developed for the student studying macroeconomics. (See Chapter 5 for a complete discussion of the three organizational categories.) The first organizational category is the P-Q category, where P stands for the price level and Q stands for real GNP. The student learns that P and Q are two very important variables in macroeconomics and that much of what he or she studies is either directly or indirectly related to these variables. For example, GNP is P times Q, inflation is a rising P, deflation is a falling P, economic growth is related to an increasing Q, a recessionary gap is the condition in the economy when Q is below its natural level, the business cycle consists of recurrent swings (up and down) in Q, and so on. Seeing topics in terms of either directly or indirectly relating to P and/or Q helps the student to see the common denominator of much that is discussed in macroeconomics.

The second organizational category is the *inherently stable-inherently unstable* category. The student learns that much of the debate in macroeconomics centers around whether or not the economy is self-equilibrating, or self-regulating, and inherently stable. There are those economists who believe that it is (e.g., monetarists and new classical economists), and those economists that do not (e.g., Keynesians). The view of the economy an economist has is implicit in the theory in which he believes is true and in his policy proposals. The uses of this category are numerous for the student. For example, upon learning, say, that Keynesians believe the economy is inherently unstable, the student is led to ask: But why do Keynesians believe the economy is inherently unstable? This brings the student to a discussion of inflexible wages, monopoly elements in the economy, and more.

The third organizational category is the *effective-ineffective* category. Here the words *effective* and *ineffective* describe fiscal and monetary policy. The student learns that an economist can take one of several positions within this category. She can believe that monetary policy is effective and fiscal policy is not, or that fiscal policy is effective and monetary policy is not, or that neither is effective, and so on. Also, the student learns that one's view of the economy (as being inherently stable or inherently unstable) also is tied to whether or not one advocates trying to use policy to stabilize the economy.

In short, the three categories are there to help the student categorize and organize the many details he is asked to learn. They are there to help him keep the big picture, or the fundamental issues, of macroeconomics in front of him as proceeds to work through the technical aspects of macroeconomic problems, theories, and policies.

International Coverage in Macroeconomics. Every author of a principles text says that it is imperative to integrate international economics into macroeconomics, and every author is correct. But it is important *how* it is integrated. Is it integrated to such an extent that domestic macroeconomic issues take second place? Is it integrated to such an extent that the macroeconomics course is a completely new course to teach? Is it integrated in a non-substantive way, such as throwing in, here and there, a phrase or two that mentions, say, the international value of the dollar? I have tried to integrate international economics into macroeconomics in, what I consider, a substantive, complete, but not overtaxing way. Mainly, it has been added to the theoretical and policy discussions in the text. To cite only three of the many examples, there is a theoretical discussion of the relationship between the budget deficit and the trade deficit, and a policy discussion of both fiscal and monetary policy in an open economy.

THINKING LIKE AN ECONOMIST: A NEW FEATURE

■

The authors of principles books are quick to point out that their books teach students how to think like an economist—but they never tell us how they accomplish this feat. Supposedly, students will read the book and simply figure out how economists think. It is true that some students do pick up how economists think by using this method, but too many do not. I believe that it is the author's responsibility to explicitly point out, where possible, how economists think. I have done this throughout this book, at appropriate places. These places are easily identifiable throughout the text.

ECONOMICS IN OUR TIMES: APPLICATIONS

■

Gary Becker, in his interview in this book, said that the way to give students a good feel for economics is to show them "how to use it to understand the world about them." I believe Becker is exactly right. In the classroom, I have found that students get unusually excited over economics when I use it to provide them with insights into their world. After all, the student is rational; raise the benefits of learning economics relative to the costs, and he will want to learn more economics. I have tried to make the applications in this book as exciting and relevant to the student as I could. Some people may feel that a few of the applications are a little offbeat, and are not ordinary. Well, I hope so. I don't think that we have to continually use the same old applications to illustrate economic analysis to our students. We can break out of the mold sometimes, get a little daring, and just have some fun.

INTERSPERSED QUESTIONS: ANTICIPATING WHAT THE READER WANTS TO ASK

■

Often when I read books I wish the author were around so that now and then I could ask a question. I think students feel the same way when they are reading an economics textbook such as this one. That is why I have interspersed throughout the text questions that the reader might have come up with as he or she is reading along. Then, I have answered these questions.

INTERVIEWS: SOME NEW, MANY UPDATED

■

It is one thing to have the author of a text discuss monetarism, and it is quite another to read what Milton Friedman has to say about it. It is one thing to have the author of a text discuss Phillips curve analysis, and it is quite another to have Robert Solow discuss it. There are 12 interviews with well-known economists in this text. The economists interviewed include Gary Becker, Paul Samuelson, Alice Rivlin, Milton Friedman, Allan Meltzer, Robert Solow, Thomas Sargent, George Akerlof, Charles Plosser, Lester Thurow, Irma Adelman, and Vernon Smith. Many of the interviews are new and many are updated from the first edition.

INTERNATIONAL COVERAGE

■

With international economic news making front-page headlines, it is imperative to present students with a book that clearly identifies how international economic events affect the U.S. economy and how U.S. economic events affect the world economy. This edition of *Macroeconomics* has international economics thoroughly integrated throughout.

A MODERN BOOK

■

The second edition of *Macroeconomics* continues in the tradition of the first edition: to present the reader with a truly modern book. Topics added to the second edition include an expanded and updated discussion of new Keynesian economics, economic changes in Eastern Europe and the Soviet Union, and the Japanese economy, among others.

SUPPLEMENTS: PRINTED, COMPUTERIZED, AND LASER TECHNOLOGY

■

The supplements that go along with this book include:

■ Study Guides
■ MicroGuide Computerized Study Guide
■ Instructor's Manual
■ Enrichment Lectures
■ Test Bank (over 6,000 questions)
■ WestTest Microcomputer Testing
■ Study Wizard Software Package (Computer Software for Microeconomics and Macroeconomics)
■ Transparencies
■ Video disc/Videotape

Study Guide. The Study Guide was principally written by Thomas Wyrick of Southwest Missouri State University. Each chapter explains, reviews, and tests the student on important facts, concepts, and diagrams found in corresponding chapters in this book. Chapter parts include an introduction to and purpose of each chapter, a review of concepts from earlier chapters, a fill-in-the-blank review of concepts to be learned, and problems and exercises. I wrote the self-test that ends each chapter.

MicroGuide Computerized Study Guide. The computerized study guide allows students to sit at the computer and quiz themselves on text material chapter by chapter. The questions are taken from the printed study guide. Students can choose any chapter or combination of chapters and the program will provide multiple-choice, true/false, matching, and fill-in-the-blank questions. Special features include: feedback on the correct answer and page-referencing to the main text, grading at the end of each session, the option to print quiz questions and results. MicroGuide is available for IBM PCs/compatibles with 512K or Macintoshes with Hypercard.

Instructor's Manual. The Instructor's Manual was written by Keith A. Rowley, formerly of Baylor University. It offers detailed lecture assistance for this book. Chapter parts include an overview of each text chapter, a list of chapter objectives, a list of key terms, a detailed chapter outline with lecture notes, and answers to end-of-chapter questions.

Enrichment Lectures. Twenty-five lectures with accompanying transparencies are included in the supplement package. The lectures are on current topics of high interest to instructors and students alike. The lectures were prepared by Keith Rowley and Thomas Wyrick.

Test Bank. The double-size test bank contains more than 6,000 test questions. Approximately 1,000 questions are new, with special emphasis on graphing-related problems. The test bank was prepared by Patricia Freeman of University of Southern Louisiana and Dusan Stojanovic of Washington University.

WestTest Microcomputer Testing. The new WestTest 2.0 testing system for either IBM PCs and compatibles or Macintoshes allows you to choose, create, edit, store, and print exams and answer keys. The system is menu-driven with a new desktop format and the options of using keystrokes or a mouse, accelerators, and function keys.

The New Economics Study Wizard 2.0 Software Package. There is a macroeconomic software package that comes with this book. The software package was developed by Dennis Muraoka of California State University at Long Beach. The software package has the following components: a graphics tutorial that is animated and annotated and contains a quiz on the graphs; terms and definitions in the form of a game; and a quiz that provides a review for the exam. Hardware requirements: IBM PC/compatibles, DOS 2.0 or higher with minimum 256K available in RAM. Graphics tutorials require CGA, EGA, or VGA with color monitor. At the end of each chapter in the text, students will find questions and problems. A few of the questions and problems have a logo next to them, indicating that the material in these questions and problems can be used in conjunction with the software package.

Transparencies. 150 transparencies (many in color) of key exhibits in the text are available for classroom use.

Video Disc/Videotape. I am excited about the fact that the second edition of *Economics* comes with a supplement like this one. Laser technology now makes it possible, with a touch of a button, to access key diagrams from the text. Not only that but the illustrations are presented in such a way that students can clearly and in proper time sequence see how the diagrams are built. Suppose the instructor wants to show students the intricacies of supply-and-demand analysis. He or she pushes the button, and there is a demand curve. Push the button again, and a supply curve appears. Push again, and the equilibrium point is identified. Push again, there is equilibrium price. And so on. For students this is a way to understand diagrams by seeing how they are built. For instructors, this is a way to offer step-by-step explanations and diagrammatics with simply a push of a button.

    The new video disc also makes it possible to access footage from the popular

Economics U$A* series which was funded by the Annenberg/CPB project. This is a way to bring real-world economic events (sights, sounds, and analysis) into the classroom. Economics has never been more real and relevant to students. (All the video segments which appear on the disc are also available on videotape presented as clips in the same order in which they appear on the disc.)

IN APPRECIATION
■

This book could not have been written and published without the generous and expert assistance of many people. A deep debt of gratitude is owed to the reviewers of the first edition, the reviewers of the second edition, and the numerous persons who have offered constructive comments and suggestions on one or both of the editions.

First Edition Reviewers and Others I Wish to Thank

Jack Adams
University of Arkansas, Little Rock

William Askwig
University of Southern Colorado

Michael Babcock
Kansas State University

Dan Barszcz
College of DuPage, Illinois

Robert Berry
Miami University, Ohio

George Bohler
Florida Junior College

Tom Bonsor
Eastern Washington University

Michael D. Brendler
Louisiana State University

Baird Brock
Central Missouri State University

Kathleen Bromley
Monroe Community College, New York

Kathleen Brook
New Mexico State University

Douglas Brown
Georgetown University

Ernest Buchholz
Santa Monica Community College, California

Gary Burbridge
Grand Rapids Junior College, Michigan

Maureen Burton
California State Polytechnic University, Pomona

Carol Carnes
Kansas State University

Paul Coomes
University of Louisville, Kentucky

Eleanor Craig
University of Delaware

Diane Cunningham
Glendale Community College, California

Wilford Cummings
Grosmont College, California

Douglas C. Darran
University of South Carolina

Edward Day
University of Central Florida

Johan Deprez
University of Tennessee

James Dietz
California State University, Fullerton

Stuart Dorsey
University of West Virginia

Richard Douglas
Bowling Green State University, Ohio

Natalia Drury
Northern Virginia Community College

Lu Ann Duffus
California State University, Hayward

John Eckalbar
California State University, Chico

John Elliott
University of Southern California

Charles Fischer
Pittsburg State University, Kansas

John Gemello
San Francisco State University

Carl Guelzo
Cantonsville Community College, Maryland

Jan Hansen
University of Wisconsin, Eau Claire

John Henderson
Georgia State University

Ken Howard
East Texas Baptist University

Mark Karscig
Central Missouri State University

Stanley Keil
Ball State University, Indiana

Richard Kieffer
State University of New York, Buffalo

Gene Kimmett
William Rainey Harper College, Illinois

Luther Lawson
University of North Carolina

Frank Leori
College of San Mateo, California

Kenneth Long
New River Community College, Virginia

Michael Magura
University of Toledo, Ohio

Bruce McCrea
Lansing Community College, Michigan

*Economics U$A was produced by Educational Film Center. Copyright © 1986 by Educational Film Center.

Gerald McDougall
Wichita State University, Kansas

Kevin McGee
University of Wisconsin, Oshkosh

Francois Melese
Auburn University, Alabama

Herbert Miliken
American River College, California

Richard Miller
Pennsylvania State University

Ernest Moser
Northeast Louisiana University

Farhang Niroomand
University of Southern Mississippi

Eliot Orton
New Mexico State University

Marty Perline
Wichita State University, Kansas

Harold Petersen
Boston College

Douglas Poe
University of Texas, Austin

Joseph Rezny
St. Louis Community College, Missouri

Terry Ridgway
University of Nevada, Las Vegas

Thomas Romans
State University of New York, Buffalo

Robert Ross
Bloomsburg State College, Pennsylvania

Keith A. Rowley
Baylor University, Texas

Anandi Sahu
Oakland University, Michigan

Richard Scoggins
California State University, Long Beach

Alan Sleeman
Western Washington University

John Sondey
University of Idaho

Shahram Shafiee
North Harris County College, Texas

Paul Seidenstat
Temple University, Pennsylvania

Robert W. Thomas
Iowa State University

Roger Trenary
Kansas State University

Richard L. Tontz
California State University, Northridge

Bruce Vanderporten
Loyola University, Illinois

Richard O. Welch
University of Texas at San Antonio

Thomas Weiss
University of Kansas

Donald A. Wells
University of Arizona

John Wight
University of Richmond, Virginia

Thomas Wyrick
Southwest Missouri State University

Second Edition Reviewers and Others I Wish to Thank

Scott Bloom
North Dakota State University

Thomas Carroll
University of Nevada, Las Vegas

Larry Cox
Southwest Missouri State University

Diane Cunningham
Los Angeles Valley College

Emit Deal
Macon College

Charles Van Eaton
Hillsdale College

Michael Fabritius
University of Mary Hardin Baylor

Frederick Fagal
Marywood College

Ralph Fowler
Diablo Valley College

Bob Gillette
Texas A&M University

Lynn Gillette
Indiana University, Indianapolis

Simon Hakim
Temple University

Lewis Karstensson
University of Nevada, Las Vegas

Abraham Kidane
California State University, Dominguez Hills

W. Barbara Killen
University of Minnesota

J. David Lages
Southwest Missouri State University

Anthony Lee
Austin Community College

Marjory Mabery
Delaware County Community College

Bernard Malamud
University of Nevada, Las Vegas

Michael Marlowe
California Polytechnic State University, San Louis Obisto

Phil J. McLewin
Ramapo College of New Jersey

Tina Quinn
Arkansas State University

Terry Ridgway
University of Nevada, Las Vegas

Paul Snoonian
University of Lowell

Paul Taube
Pan American University

Roger Trenary
Kansas State University

Mark Wheeler
Bowling Green State University

Thomas Wyrick
Southwest Missouri State University

I offer my sincerest thanks to the twelve (12) economists who appear in the interviews in this book. Each was generous with his or her time, genuinely interested in reaching students, and always gracious. Their contributions have greatly added to the range and richness of views found in this book.

I offer my sincerest gratitude to Thomas Wyrick (Southwest Missouri State University), who, besides writing the study guide, read the entire manuscript and provided detailed comments and invaluable suggestions. My thanks to Keith Row-

PREFACE

xxix

ley (formerly of Baylor University), who wrote the instructor's manual and enrichment lectures. My heartfelt appreciation to Patricia Freeman (University of Southwestern Louisiana) who wrote questions for and organized the test bank and to Dusan Stojanovic (Washington University) who wrote questions for the test bank.

My deepest debt of gratitude goes to Clyde Perlee, Jr., editor-in-chief of West's college division. He continues to be my inspiration for writing the best book I know how to write. He is one of those persons who you know has made your life better just by being who he is. I am extremely fortunate that he is my editor and my friend. My many thanks to Bill Stryker, production editor, who has the ability to produce a book that is better than an author has a right to hope for. My belief—that he is the best at what he does—continues to be confirmed. I am also grateful to Theresa O'Dell, developmental editor. She worked hard and capably supervising all the details of the supplement package and she continues to make working on this project fun.

My thanks also go to Kristin J. McCarthy and Ellen Stanton for their work on the marketing program and to Beth Hoeppner for her work on the video disc. In addition, my gratitude to Elaine Levin for her excellent copy-editing.

My deepest appreciation goes to my wife, Sheila. She is always there with her support, encouragement, understanding, and love. Finally, I want to thank my two sons: Daniel, who is four years old, and David, who is 17 months old. Watching them, in everything they do, from sleeping to tearing the house apart, is one of the great pleasures of life.

MACROECONOMICS

AN INTRODUCTION TO ECONOMICS

PART

I

ECONOMICS: THE SCIENCE OF SCARCITY

WHAT ECONOMICS IS ABOUT

WHAT THIS CHAPTER IS ABOUT

We begin this chapter by answering some of the questions you may have about the study of economics. Next, we discuss what many economists consider to be the most important concept in economics—scarcity. Then, we discuss the role and nature of theory in economics and the scientific way of thinking. Finally, we discuss the several categories into which economics can be divided.

Scarcity is the basic economic problem that all individuals and societies face.

■

Scarcity
The condition where our wants are greater than the limited resources available to satisfy those wants.

Economics
The science of scarcity: the science of how individuals and societies deal with the fact that wants are greater than the limited resources available to satisfy those wants.

Economic Analysis
The process of applying economic tools and the economic way of thinking to real-world problems.

Here are the answers to five questions about economics that students are likely to ask.

What Is Economics?

Without matter and motion, there would be no physics; without living things, there would be no biology; and without **scarcity,** there would be no economics.

Scarcity is the condition where our wants are greater than the limited resources available to satisfy those wants. Scarcity is the basic economic problem that all individuals and societies face.

Since there would be no economics without scarcity, **economics** is defined as the *science of scarcity.* Specifically, *it is the science of how individuals and societies deal with the fact that wants are greater than the limited resources available to satisfy those wants.*

What Do Economists Study?

Economists study markets, prices, costs, production, inflation, unemployment, interest rates, business cycles, budget deficits, trade deficits, exchange rates, and so on. These are many of the subjects discussed in this book.

But economists increasingly study other areas of human activity as well—such things as crime, family relationships, war, politics, psychology, the law, and much more.[1]

Economists today do not have a preconceived notion of what they should and should not study. They may simply observe the world until something captures their attention or piques their curiosity. They then apply **economic analysis**—composed of the tools of economics and the economic way of thinking—to whatever it is that they are interested in.

This may seem like an odd way to proceed. Some noneconomists think it would be better if economists decided on the 30 or so topics they feel they are best equipped to study and then study these and no more. But economists believe this approach grossly underestimates the power of economic analysis. Although economists do not believe that economics can explain everything about the world, they do believe it can explain much about it. An objective of this text is to show you that economic analysis is more powerful at explaining your world to you than you may have believed was possible.

What Is the Economic Way of Thinking?

In general, the economic way of thinking refers to the way economists view, interpret, and analyze the world. Consider an analogy from the field of architecture. Suppose you see a skyscraper in New York City. To your untrained eye, you see only a building that rises high into the sky. An architect sees much more. She sees a certain form and style; she sees the way that geometric shapes have come together to create an atmosphere and a mood. She sees things that others are blind to.

So it is with the economist. In a grocery store you may see shelves of food and drink. An economist sees more. He sees buyers and sellers having come together to determine what goods will be produced and at what prices the goods will be

[1]The subjects listed in this paragraph are not usually covered in a principles of economics course.

sold; he sees costs and production. He sees buyers and sellers trying to make themselves better off; he sees profit and loss. The economist sees the *process* that has resulted in the shelves of food and drink in much the same way that the architect sees the process of the creation of the skyscraper.

Why Study Economics?

Not everyone studies economics for the same reasons. Some people study it because of its relevance to problem solving in the real world. For example, the economist Alfred Marshall (1842–1924) was greatly concerned with poverty, which he believed was at the root of many social problems. He hoped that the study of economics would enable him to better understand the causes of poverty and to find a solution to it.

Some people study economics because of its explanatory and predictive power. For them, economics answers many of their questions—it explains why things are as they are and it predicts what is likely to happen under certain conditions. This can be a heady experience. The economist Paul Samuelson (b. 1915) said that setting out to explore the exciting world of economics for the first time is a unique thrill. Many undergraduate economics students agree.

Other people study economics because of their desire to learn about certain ideas that have shaped the world. The economist John Maynard Keynes (1883–1946) said that "the ideas of economists and political philosophers, both when they are right and when they are wrong, are more powerful than is commonly understood. Indeed, the world is ruled by little else. Practical men, who believe themselves to be quite exempt from any intellectual influences, are usually slaves of some defunct economist."

In this text, we hope to show you that your study of economics can enrich and broaden your life and provide you with much stimulating thought along the way.

Why Study Economics in the 1990s?

An understanding of economics is your ticket to some of the most exciting events in the world.

Many of the big news stories of the early 1990s were economics stories. For example, in 1990, the eyes of the world turned to the Soviet Union and many Eastern European nations as they began to move away from a highly controlled economy to one that placed greater emphasis on individual initiative and market forces.

In 1990, Iraq moved into Kuwait and the world began to worry about the future oil supply. In the United States, economists and others wondered how a sharp rise in the price of oil would affect the U.S. economy. Would it mean higher prices, a cutback in production, and an increase in unemployment?

In 1991, an unsuccessful coup attempt against Soviet President Mikhail Gorbachev resulted in his banning many of his colleagues from rule, forming a political alliance with Russian President and economic reform advocate, Boris Yeltsin, and resuming the move towards greater economic and political freedom. The world watched as a once tightly closed command-economy nation opened itself, albeit shakily at times, to the forces of democracy and free enterprise. The stage was set for the unfolding of an economic and political event that would have repercussions throughout the world and had the potential to change the character of the world economy.

In 1992, many European nations moved toward further economic integration in what has been termed a "United States of Europe." In the United States and Japan, people wondered what a United States of Europe would mean in terms of international trade (Will an economically united Europe promote or retard international trade?), international competitiveness, domestic jobs, and much more.

In the United States, in 1990, the longest peacetime economic expansion in U.S. history halted. People worried about the oncoming economic recession. They asked, how long will the recession last, how deep will it be, how high will unemployment rise, and what will it mean to U.S. competitiveness in the world?

The days when the people of different nations could live lives isolated from one another are gone forever. The world is getting smaller, but individuals' consciousness of global events and their impact is increasing. We think the catalyst for this increased international awareness is economic in nature. Americans are interested in the Japanese because Japanese economic decisions affect American lives. The Japanese are interested in Europe because European economic unification affects Japan.

The one language that bids to become universal is the language of economics. The American businessperson may not speak Japanese, and the Japanese businessperson may not speak English, but both of them know the language of supply and demand, profits, production, costs, international trade, and competition. Both of them know the language of economics. It is becoming an increasingly important language for you to know, too.

SCARCITY, CHOICE, AND OPPORTUNITY COST

In this section, we discuss the basics of economics, which include scarcity, choice, and opportunity cost. We look at several questions. What are the consequences of scarcity? What is the relationship between scarcity and choice? And what is the relationship between choice and opportunity cost?

Scarcity

Good
Anything from which individuals receive utility or satisfaction.

Bad
Anything from which individuals receive disutility or dissatisfaction.

Utility
The satisfaction one receives (from the consumption of a good).

Disutility
The dissatisfaction one receives (from the consumption of a bad).

Free Good
A good where the amount available is greater than the amount people want at zero price.

Economic Good
A scarce good. A good where the amount available is less than people would want if it were given away at zero price.

As noted earlier, *scarcity* is the condition where our wants outstrip the limited resources available to satisfy those wants. Bluntly put, given the unlimited wants of people, there is never enough.

But never enough of what? Do we mean that there are never enough resources to produce *everything* in the world—from computers to pollution? Might there be too much of some things—pollution, for example? Economists break down "things" into two categories: **goods** and **bads.** A good is anything from which individuals receive **utility** or satisfaction. A bad is anything from which individuals receive **disutility** or dissatisfaction. Goods are such things as clothing, education, leisure time, food, television sets, and houses. Bads are such things as pollution and garbage.

The category *goods* is broken down further into **free goods** and **economic goods.** A free good is a good sufficiently available from nature to satisfy all possible desires. More formally, a free good is a good where the amount available is greater than the amount people want at zero price. An example would be clean air before the days of air pollution or sunshine in a sunny climate (such as in Phoenix, Arizona.)

An economic good is scarce: It is a good for which the quantity available is less than people would want if it were given away at zero price. For example, a car is an economic, or scarce, good. Even if cars were given away at zero price, still people would want more cars than there would be cars available.

So when we ask, Never enough of *what?* the answer is that there are never enough resources to produce enough *economic goods* to satisfy peoples' unlimited wants. This is the **economic problem** in a nutshell. It is a problem for people in the United States, the Soviet Union, France, Brazil, or any other place in the world.

Economic Problem
The fact that there are not enough resources to produce enough goods to satisfy peoples' unlimited wants.

Question:

It was stated earlier that "clean air before air pollution" is an example of a free good. Does this mean than clean air today is not a free good? People don't pay for the air they breathe today; doesn't it follow that it must be a free good?

Answer:

Consider the air in Los Angeles County today. Some of the air is dirty, some is very dirty, some is clean. For example, the air in Malibu is relatively clean compared with the air in Pasadena and Riverside. The people who live in Malibu are "buying" clean air by paying a higher price for Malibu property—that is, the price of clean air in Malibu is included in the purchase price of Malibu property. Stated differently, people are prepared to pay a higher price for Malibu property than Riverside property because Malibu residents have relatively clean air.

Before pollution, when all air was equally clean, individuals would not have paid for clean air either directly or indirectly through the purchase price of property. But now that Malibu has an environmental advantage, property values have risen there relative to Pasadena and Riverside. We conclude that (1) a free good at one time may be an economic good at another, and (2) people may pay for something even if there is no explicit charge.

To understand that people may pay for something even if there is no explicit charge for it is to think like an economist. As we explained, individuals who purchase homes in Malibu "pay" for the relatively clean air although they are not explicitly charged for it. An understanding of this point prevents us from incorrectly thinking that they are getting something for nothing.

THINKING LIKE AN ECONOMIST

Scarcity Implies Choice

Because scarcity exists, people must make **choices,** that is, they must select among restricted alternatives. The logic is straightforward: Because of scarcity, because our infinite wants bump up against limited resources, some wants must go unsatisfied. We must therefore choose which wants we will satisfy and which we will not. For example, Valerie wants a one-month vacation in Hawaii, new clothes, and a down payment for a car. She cannot satisfy all her wants; she chooses the one-month vacation in Hawaii.

We are always either making choices or living the consequences of choices we have made. At this moment you are living the consequence of a choice you made earlier. That choice was to read this chapter. You could have been doing something else. Daily, you make choices about what to buy, how much to buy, what to do, and so on. There is no way to avoid making choices because (you guessed it) there is no way to avoid scarcity.

Consider how choice operates in the following scenario: Three U.S. senators are having a discussion. "We need more schools," says the senator from Florida.

Choice
The act of selecting among restricted alternatives.

What Does Scarcity Have to Do with the Number of Friends You Have?

At first glance, scarcity and the number of friends you have probably seem unrelated. But scarcity implies choice, and choice implies opportunity cost; thus if a person incurs an opportunity cost when he or she makes a friend, the link between the number of friends a person has and scarcity is established.

But does a person incur an opportunity cost when he or she makes a friend? The answer is yes. First, you have to meet someone (could you be doing something else?), you have to talk to this person (could you be doing something else?), you may have to drive over to this person's house for a party (could you be doing something else?), you may have to invite this person over to your house for dinner (could you be doing something else?), you have to be there for this person when he or she needs your help (could you be doing something else?). In short, making friends comes at a cost. (It comes with benefits, too.)

Now the higher the opportunity cost of making friends, the fewer friends you will have, all other things held constant. For example, the average five-year-old may say she has 10 friends and that she plays with each of them every week. The average 40-year-old may say he has four friends and that he talks to, or gets together with, maybe one or two every two weeks. Are adults less friendly than children, or do adults simply face higher opportunity costs of making friends than children do? We suggest it is the latter. An adult who spent as much time a week making and keeping friends as a child does would have to forfeit the opportunity to work at a job and earn an income.

Pursuing the analysis, would there be any difference between the number of friends a person would have in a large city than in a small town? In large cities there are museums, plays, numerous restaurants, great libraries, concerts, sports events, and usually better opportunities to earn a large income than exist in small towns. There are more things competing for a person's time in a large city than in a small town. We conclude that the opportunity cost of making friends is higher in a large city than in a small town and that the "average" person will have fewer friends in a large city than in a small town. Perhaps this is why large cities are so often said to be cold and impersonal and small towns are said to be friendly.

"Indeed we do," says the senator from South Carolina, "but not at the expense of a stronger national defense. First we must rebuild our defenses, and then later we will build more schools."

"You are both misguided," says the senator from Kansas. "What we need to do first is to take better care of the unfortunate among us: the old, the sick, and the poor."

Words to this effect are spoken daily in the U.S. Congress, on college campuses, in state legislatures, in homes, and on news programs. You may not have paid much attention to such talk, viewing it as simply part of life. People always disagree, don't they?

Notice, though, that the disagreements concern choices. The senator from Florida chooses education over national defense and other options. The senator from South Carolina chooses national defense over education and other things. The senator from Kansas chooses helping the poor over education, defense, and other things. They are involved in a political tug-of-war because not all the senators can get what they want. More resources for education mean fewer resources for defense. Why? The answer is: *scarcity.*

Choice and Opportunity Cost

Choices imply opportunities or alternatives forfeited. For example, when you chose to read this chapter, you forfeited the opportunity to do something else—

watch television, talk on the telephone, or sleep. The most highly valued opportunity or alternative forfeited when a choice is made is known as **opportunity cost.** If watching television is what you would have done had you not chosen to read this chapter—if it was your *next best alternative*—then the opportunity cost of reading this chapter is watching television.

Opportunity Cost
The most highly valued opportunity or alternative forfeited when a choice is made.

Can you make a choice without incurring a cost? (Economists often leave off the word *opportunity* before the word *cost.* We occasionally follow this accepted practice.) Can you choose to attend class tomorrow without giving something up? Can you choose to buy a Toyota without giving up the opportunity to buy a Ford? Can the United States choose to build more roads without giving up the opportunity to build more schools? The answer to all these questions is no. To capture the idea that there are always opportunity costs to making choices, economists say *"there is no such thing as a free lunch."*

Economics has the ability to make the invisible visible. Consider how the three words "no free lunch" can do this.

Suppose the federal government builds a new interstate highway system. It hires thousands of people to work on the project. The newspapers in the towns the interstate highway passes through report on all the increased job activity. It looks as if there are more people working on road construction and no fewer people than formerly working at anything else; it looks as if there are more highways and nothing less of anything else (no fewer cameras, cars, computers, and so on). But say the words "no free lunch" and see if the picture changes.

"No free lunch" reminds us that something must have been given up to build the new interstate highway system. First, the taxpayers give up dollars, so we add taxpayers to our picture.

But what specifically did the taxpayers give up by paying taxes? They gave up the opportunity to buy more clothes, cars, books, and so on. So we add to our picture all the goods and services that would have been produced and consumed had the highway not been built. And if, say, more clothes would have been produced had the highway not been built, it follows that more people would have worked in the clothing industry than worked in it when the highway system was built. We add them to our picture. When we remind ourselves that there is no such thing as a free lunch, we begin to see things that *might have been.* And that, we think, is something worth seeing.

Economists understand that "there is no such thing as a free lunch." Obtaining any desirable good or service requires giving up the opportunity to have others. A consequence of this way of thinking is the ability to see things that might have been.

THINKING LIKE AN ECONOMIST

Opportunity Cost and Behavior

Look around your class. Are there any rock stars between the ages of 18 and 25 in the class? Any movie stars? Any fashion models? Probably not. The reason is that, for these people, the opportunity cost of attending college is much higher than it is for most 18-to-25-year-olds.

What do you give up to go to college? Most people say the tuition money. If you pay $1,000 a semester for eight semesters, this is $8,000. But, of course, as long as you could be earning income working at a job, this $8,000 is not the full cost of your attending college. For example, if you weren't in college you might be working at a full-time job earning $25,000 annually. Certainly, this $25,000, or at least a part of it if you are currently working part-time, is forfeited because you attend college. It is part of the cost of your attending college.

Even if the tuition cost is the same for everyone who attends your college, the opportunity cost of attending is not the same for everyone. What would an 18-year-old rock star be forfeiting in unearned income if he decided to attend your college? What would a 17-year-old top fashion model be giving up in income? Such persons rarely attend college—although the tuition cost would be easy for them to pay—because of the relatively high opportunity costs. They might say that they "can't afford to attend college." This doesn't mean that they can't afford the tuition, but that they don't want to do without the large income they would earn if they do not attend college. An economist would put it this way: The benefits of attending college are outweighed by the costs.

Let us consider another example. Two economists at Michigan State University, Daniel Hamermesh and Jeff Biddle, have found that people reduce their sleep time (up to the biological limit) the higher their wages. For example, if the wages of an average worker are doubled, that person will spend approximately 20 minutes less in bed. The reason has to do with opportunity cost: The higher one's wages, the higher the opportunity cost of not working. "Not working" takes into account sleeping, since sleeping is one of the things people do when they are not working. In short, higher wages come with higher opportunity costs of sleeping and it turns out that people end up sleeping less.

THE NATURE AND ROLE OF THEORY

Economics is a field replete with theories. In this section, we explain why and how theories are used in economics.

Why Build Theories?

Economists build theories in order to explain and predict real-world events. Not only do economists build theories, but you do, too. Almost anytime you want to explain something to yourself or to others—for example, why you prefer to read fiction than nonfiction, why your brother got a divorce, why you consistently gain weight during the holiday season—you build a theory. In seeking an explanation, you are not doing anything different from the economist who wants to explain the behavior of, say, consumers, or the sociologist who wants to explain the behavior of adult males reared in slums.

What Is a Theory?

Theory
An abstract representation of the real world designed with the intent to better understand that world.

A **theory** is an abstract representation of the real world designed to better understand that world. It is built on the factors, or variables, that the theorist believes are most important to explain and predict the phenomenon under consideration. Thus, the essence of good theory building is separating the wheat from the chaff.

For example, suppose a criminologist's objective is to explain why some people turn to crime. Before actually building the theory, she considers a number of variables that may explain why some people turn to crime. These variables include (1) the ease or difficulty of getting a gun, (2) parental childrearing practices, (3) the neighborhood a person grew up in, (4) whether a person was abused as a child, (5) family education, (6) the type of friends a person has, (7) a person's IQ, (8) climate, and (9) a person's diet.

The criminologist may think that some of these variables greatly affect the chance that a person will become a criminal, whereas some affect it only slightly, and others do not affect it at all. A theory emphasizes only those variables that the theorist believes are the main or critical variables that explain an event. The process of focusing on a limited number of variables to explain or predict an event is called **abstraction.** Thus, if the criminologist in our example thinks that parental childrearing practices and family education are likely to explain much more about criminal behavior than the other variables, her (abstract) theory will emphasize these two variables only. Such variables as IQ, climate, and a person's diet will be ignored by her theory.

Abstraction
The process (used in building a theory) of focusing on a limited number of variables to explain or predict an event.

"Leaving certain variables out," or a greater degree of abstraction, is sometimes the best thing to do even when you are not building theories. Suppose you are walking across campus and someone asks you how to get to the president's office. How much detail would you give? We expect that it would be just enough to get the person from where she is to where she wants to go. You might say, "Go straight until you come to the big red building, turn right, walk about 100 yards, and then turn left. The president's office is in the circular building."

You would probably not say, "Go straight for 556 yards, during which time you will pass the English building, in which Dr. Quirk teaches English 101 in Room 156, and the music building, which, by the way, was constructed in 1899 . . . and on and on.

The simple, direct set of instructions leaves out certain information, such as where Dr. Quirk teaches English and when the music building was constructed. But if the objective is to get the person to the president's office rather than to give a tour of the campus, this information is unnecessary. Too much information simply clutters and makes accomplishing the objective at hand more difficult.

Question:

Suppose a person criticizes a theory because it doesn't consider all the variables that might explain the phenomenon it seeks to explain. Is this a weak or strong criticism of the theory?

Answer:

It is a weak criticism. No theory considers all the variables that might explain a given phenomenon. All theories are abstractions from reality. But it doesn't follow that (abstract) theories *cannot* explain reality. The objective in theory building is to ignore those variables that are essentially irrelevant to the case at hand, so that it becomes easier to isolate the important variables that the untrained observer would probably miss.

Building and Testing a Theory

There is a procedure to do scientific work—whether in biology, chemistry, or economics. We outline this approach next.

1. Decide on what it is you want to explain or predict. For example, you may want to explain or predict interest rates, the exchange rate between the U.S. dollar and the Japanese yen, and so on.

2. Identify the variables that you believe are important to what you want to explain or predict. Variables are magnitudes that can change. For example, price is a variable. One day the price of a good may be $10 and a week later it may be $12.

An economist who wants to explain or predict the buying behavior of consumers may build his "theory of buying behavior" on the variable *price*.

3. State the assumptions of the theory. An assumption is a critical or key element of a theory. It is a statement that one *supposes* to be true. The difference between an assumption and a fact is that a fact represents objective truth. It is a fact that you are reading this book this moment; no one doubts this. With an assumption, objective truth does not necessarily exist; there is room for doubt. An economist may make the assumption that the only motive that the owners of business firms have is to earn as much money as possible—that is, to maximize their profits. But, of course, this may not be the truth. The owners of business firms may not be *only* motivated by profits, or they may not be motivated by profits at all. We discuss how important the realism of assumptions is to a theory in the next section.

4. State the hypothesis. A hypothesis is a conditional statement specifying how two variables relate. Typically, hypotheses follow the "if–then" form: For example, *if* you smoke cigarettes, *then* you will increase the probability of getting lung cancer. In effect, the hypothesis is a *prediction* as to what will happen to one thing as something else changes.

5. Test the theory by comparing its predictions against real-world events. Suppose the theory predicts that, as taxes are raised, there will be less investment and lower economic growth. We then look at the data on investment and economic growth to see if the evidence fails to reject the theory that produced that specific prediction.

6. If the evidence fails to reject the theory, then no further action is necessary, although it is a good idea to continue to examine the theory closely. If a theory predicts that, say, orange prices will rise within two weeks of a cold snap in Florida, and this actually happens, then the evidence fails to reject the theory.

7. If the evidence rejects the theory, then either formulate a new theory, or amend the old theory in terms of its variables, assumptions, and hypotheses. For example, if a theory predicts that interest rates will rise within two months of an increase in the money supply, and this does not happen, then it is time to either formulate a new theory or amend the old theory.

Question:

In the preceding points 5 and 6, the phrase "fails to reject" was used instead of the word "prove." Why not simply say that "we look at the data to see if the evidence proves the theory," instead of saying "we look at the data to see if the evidence fails to reject the theory"?

Answer:

The following example explains why. Suppose a theory predicts that all swans are white. Researchers go out into the field and record the color of all the swans they see. Every swan they see is white. The evidence does not prove the theory is correct because there may be swans that are not white that the researchers did not see. How can the researchers be certain they saw all the swans? Thus, it is more accurate to say that the evidence *fails to reject* the theory than to say it *proves* the theory. (See Exhibit 1–1 for a schematic summary of the scientific process.)

How Do We Judge Theories?

Many people think the assumptions in many theories are unrealistic. In fact, countless jokes have been made about economists theorizing on the basis of unrealistic assumptions.

EXHIBIT 1–1
Building and Testing a Theory

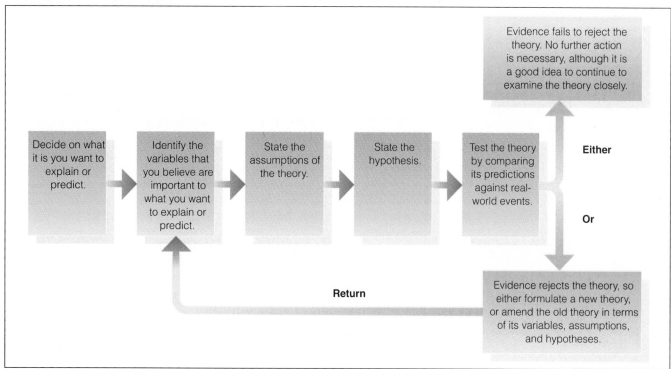

In one of the more popular jokes, a physicist, a chemist, and an economist are shipwrecked on a desert island. A few days pass and a can of beans is washed up on the shore.

The physicist, explaining to the others how the can may be opened, says, "I've calculated that the terminal velocity of this can thrown to a height of 27 feet is 204 feet per second. If we place a rock under the can, the impact will burst the seams without splattering the beans."

The chemist says, "That's risky since we can't be sure we will throw the can to exactly 27 feet high. Here's a better idea. We can start a fire and heat the can over it for 88 seconds. According to my calculations, the heat should just burst the seams."

The economist thinks about it a minute and then says, "Both of your methods for opening the can may work, but they are too complicated. My approach is much simpler. Assume a can opener."

Are there unrealistic assumptions in economics? The answer is yes, but many economists maintain that arguing about assumptions is a waste of time ("My assumptions are more nearly realistic than yours") because *a theory is better judged by its predictive power than by its assumptions.* In short, the better the theory predicts, the better the theory—no matter the degree of realism of its assumptions. Economist Milton Friedman argues that

> the relevant question to ask about the "assumptions" of a theory is not whether they are descriptively "realistic," for they never are, but whether they are sufficiently good approximations for the purpose in hand. And this question can be answered only by seeing whether the theory works, which means whether it yields sufficiently accurate predictions.[2]

[2]Milton Friedman, "The Methodology of Positive Economics in *Essays in Positive Economics* (Chicago: The University of Chicago Press, 1953), p. 15. Reprinted with permission.

WHAT ECONOMICS IS ABOUT
■
15

To illustrate, Friedman cites Newton's law of falling bodies, which assumes, unrealistically, that bodies fall in a vacuum. Does the theory predict well, even though it is based on an unrealistic assumption? For many falling bodies, such as a rubber ball dropped off a roof, it does. Friedman would argue that the theory is useful because it predicts well for numerous falling bodies, even though in the real world bodies do not always fall in a vacuum. We could say that for many falling bodies it is *as if* they were falling in a vacuum. Friedman would say that the assumption of a vacuum is a "sufficiently good approximation for the purpose in hand."

The Friedman position can be summarized as follows: If the theory works, if the evidence fails to reject the theory, then it is a good and useful theory, and the assumptions of the theory, no matter what anyone might think of them, are a sufficiently good approximation for the purpose in hand. Some economists accept Friedman's position, along with all its implications.[3] Other economists, many of them well respected, do not. As you will soon find out, there are not only numerous theories in economics, but there are also numerous debates.

SCIENTIFIC THINKING
■

The economic way of thinking is a subset of the scientific way of thinking. In this section, we discuss a few of the fundamentals of scientific thinking. The topics include the association–causation issue, the fallacy of composition, and the *ceteris paribus* condition. The first two topics describe obstacles to thinking scientifically, whereas the third is an important component of scientifically describing relationships between things.

The Association–Causation Issue

Association is one thing, causation is another. A problem arises when we confuse the two.

Two events are associated if they are linked or connected in some way. For example, suppose you wash your car at 10:00 A.M. and at 10:30 A.M. it starts to rain. Since it rains shortly after you wash your car, the two events are associated (linked, connected) in time. Does it follow that the first event (your washing the car) *caused* the second event (the rain)? The answer is no. *Association is not causation.* If A occurs before B, it does not necessarily follow that A is the cause and B the effect.

In the car–rain example it is obvious that association was not causation, but consider a case where it is not as apparent. Suppose Jones tells you that the U.S. trade deficit got bigger in January and 11 months later economic activity had turned down. She then states that the first event (the growing trade deficit) caused the second event (the downturn in economic activity). You may be tempted to accept this as truth. But, of course, a simple statement of cause and effect is not enough to establish cause and effect. Without any evidence, we can't be certain that we haven't stumbled onto a disguised version of the car–rain example.

Question:

If two events are associated, can one of the events be the cause of the other?

[3]All parts of this position are not original with Friedman. However, he is given credit for refining the position and arguing its merits.

Answer:

Yes. For example, suppose that on Monday evening James comes into close contact with a person who has the measles. A few days later he comes down with the measles. The two events are associated, and it is the case that the first event (coming into close contact with a person who has the measles) is the cause of the second event (coming down with the measles). So there can be causation where there is association. The main point, though, is that causation doesn't necessarily follow association.

The Fallacy of Composition

The **fallacy of composition** is the erroneous view that what is good or true for the individual is *necessarily* good or true for the group. In fact, what is good for the individual may be good for the group, but not necessarily. For example, John stands up at a soccer game and sees the game better. Does it follow that if *everyone* stands up at the soccer game *everyone* will see better? No. Mary moves to the suburbs because she dislikes crowds in the city. Does it follow that if *everyone* moves from the city to the suburbs for the same reason as Mary *everyone* will be better off? No. Bob does his holiday shopping early so he can beat the crowds. Does it follow that if *everyone* does his holiday shopping early that *everyone* can beat the crowds? No.

Fallacy of Composition
The erroneous view that what is good or true for the individual is necessarily good or true for the group.

The Ceteris Paribus Condition: Taking One Thing at a Time

Ceteris Paribus is a Latin term that means "all other things held constant." Individuals use the term when they are trying to separate out effects. To illustrate, assume that both good nutrition and moderate exercise *increase* the number of years people live and that bad nutrition and little-to-no exercise *decrease* the number of years people live. Suppose now that a person eats well. Will he or she live longer or not? We would answer, "If a person eats well, that person will live longer, *ceteris paribus.* We add the condition that "all other things are held constant" because, as we have already pointed out, another factor, little-to-no exercise, can decrease the number of years a person lives. Thus, a person who eats well but doesn't exercise may end up living a shorter life. If this were the case, would it mean that good nutrition does not increase the number of years a person lives? Not at all. It would only mean that the lack of exercise reduced the person's life by more than the good nutrition added to it, *making it appear as if* good nutrition does not increase the number of years a person lives. To convey the correct relationship between good nutrition and years lived, we must use the *ceteris paribus* condition.

Ceteris Paribus
The Latin term meaning "all other things held constant."

ECONOMIC CATEGORIES

Economics is sometimes broken down into different categories, according to the type of questions economists ask. Four common economic categories include positive economics, normative economics, macroeconomics, and microeconomics. We discuss each in turn.

Positive and Normative Economics

Positive economics attempts to determine *what is*. **Normative economics** addresses *what should be.* Essentially, positive economics deals with *cause–effect relation-*

Positive Economics
The study of "what is" in economic matters.

Normative Economics
The study of "what should be" in economic matters.

Interview: Gary Becker

Gary Becker has been described as "one of the most original minds in modern economics" and as an "economic imperialist" because of his work in extending the economic way of thinking into traditionally non-economic areas. He is currently at the University of Chicago.

How and when did you first come to the realization that economic theory could be used to analyze behavior outside the marketplace? And was it a gradual realization, or did it occur suddenly?

It was gradual on my part. A couple of things I did early in my career involved applications outside the traditional areas. One was on racial discrimination. No economist had been looking at that problem although it has been a major social problem. About the same time I did a shorter piece on the application of economic thinking to political behavior. Then I worked on such topics as human capital, population, and allocation of time. Only gradually did I begin to see that the economic way of thinking provided a unified way to approach many subjects in the social sciences.

Is there a difference between the way an economist thinks about problems and the way, say, a sociologist does? For example, would the economist and the sociologist approach the problem of welfare in a different way?

The economist instinctively thinks in terms of the paradigm of rationality. Specifically, economists assume that people are maximizing, say, utility or profit. From here they reason that people respond to changes in prices and costs. For example, the economist will argue that if you increase welfare benefits, this will increase the number of people who will go on welfare. And in turn this will have other effects. It will increase the birth rates of unmarried

mothers, and so on. This is the economist's line of attack.

Many sociologists deemphasize the importance of the assumption of rationality. They look more at social or aggregate influences on people. They might ask questions such as, Does what other people are doing influence what I want to do? How does peer pressure operate on people? In short, sociologists will stress the social structure and social forces, and economists will stress individual variables. Both are relevant and both should be merged and in some of my recent work I am trying to do this.

Along the same lines, it appears that the tools of economics have been applied to areas in sociology but that the reverse is not true to any great extent. Is this correct?

On the whole you are correct, but things are beginning to change. The influence of some sociologists is being felt in economics in regard to bringing in more social influences on individual behavior. As I mentioned, economists have been lax in not paying attention to this. We all live in society and we all are greatly influenced by what people around us are doing. The question is how to analyze this. We are learning now how to do so, and in recent years

economists have written papers examining how social forces influence different phenomena—such as underclass behavior. I have a paper coming out on restaurant prices that addresses why restaurants may not raise prices even in the face of excess demand.

Do you think the tools of economics can explain things in psychology—such as phobias, neurosis, and so on.

I believe some of those things can be illuminated with the tools of economics. For example, drug addiction and other addictive behavior is usually thought of as simply a psychological or biological problem, but there is a very important economic component there. The economic component helps us to understand how people get addicted, and how the addiction might change when various life events, employment, or prices change. So, yes, in many areas of psychology the economic way of thinking has value. And some psychologists use very similar ways of thinking to analyze behavior.

You are actively involved in economics research. What questions are you currently trying to answer?

I am working on problems of habitual and addictive behavior—drugs and alcohol. But also ordinary habits, too. For example, we may get accustomed to a particular view or a standard of living as a habit. I am also trying to analyze in a systematic manner how social factors influence behavior. For example, if other people like to go to a restaurant that might influence whether I go. Or if other people in my neighborhood are going to college, or if their children are going to college, this might influence my own behavior or my family's behavior. These are some of the types of issues I am currently working on.

What are the consequences of economic

illiteracy on the individual's level? on society's level?

Economic literacy helps people make better decisions for themselves. Consider a simple problem like buying a house. Economics helps people understand mortgages and interest rates. It helps them understand how mortgage rates will be affected if there is inflation. There are many circumstances under which individuals would benefit significantly if they had greater command of very simple tools of economic analysis.

On the social level it has important consequences for how voters or citizens react to different policy proposals. For example, economists are quick to point out the undesirable effects of rent controls. However rent controls exist in some places of the U.S.—such as New York City and Berkeley, California. There are many reasons for this—pressure groups supporting certain policies and so on. But it also comes down to what the average citizen is going to support and vote for. Economic literacy would help enormously in evaluating these and many other policy proposals. So at a social level it is very important to upgrade economic literacy as it would improve policies—although it is important to remind ourselves that illiteracy is not the only reason we get most of these policies.

What do you predict will be a major economic problem the United States will have to face in the mid-1990s?

I think that the quality of our human capital, especially at the elementary and high school levels, has deteriorated quite a bit lately. We are educating a lot of people but we are educating them poorly. This deterioration in human capital is also showing up in the data. For example, the earnings of high school graduates has declined in real terms in the past decade. This is something of great concern. Not only on the domestic front, but in the international arena as well, since international com-

petition is becoming more and more important. The issue of how we go about increasing the quality of our human capital is very serious and surely it will be with us to the end of this century.

What got you interested in economics?

I got interested when I was an undergraduate in college. I came into college with a strong interest in mathematics, and at the same time with a strong commitment to do something to help society. I learned in the first economics course I took that economics could deal rigourously, a la mathematics, with social problems. That stimulated me because in economics I saw that I could combine both the mathematics and my desire to do something to help society. There was a rigor in economics, a theoretical framework of analysis, that I found very appealing.

What do you think a good principles of economics text should do?

I think it should put less emphasis on dotting all the i's and crossing all the t's of formal theory, and try to give the reader a good feel for economics and how to use it to understand the world about him or her. I find that this is the way to stimulate graduate students and it is even truer of undergraduate students. A textbook should help students interpret the economic and social world.

Suppose you could ask a student who had just completed a microeconomics principles course only one or two questions in order to determine if he or she understood the way economists think. What would the question(s) be and how would you answer it (them)?

I was recently in Moscow and I was asked by the Vice Dean of Moscow State University to interview some of their students who would come to the University of Chicago to do graduate work. I only had an hour to interview six students so I had to be very quick. I was told what courses they had had, and so I decided to ask them one or two

microeconomic questions. My questions were simple ones: First, What determines a shortage in a competitive market? Second, What does your answer imply about black market prices? The answers are that a shortage is caused by preventing prices from equilibrating, and black market prices tend to exceed what market prices would be in a competitive market because supply is restricted. Some of them did quite well and some did not do well. But those would be two of the questions I would ask and there is nothing fancy about them. But the way they answered told me if someone had learned by rote, or had learned to think like an economist.

What persons have had the greatest influence on your thinking and how would you summarize what you learned from each of them?

The four most influential economists were Milton Friedman, T. W. Schultz, H. G. Lewis, who were all teachers of mine at the University of Chicago, and George Stigler, who came to Chicago after I left, but who I have had as a colleague for many years now.

I learned many things from all of them. Milton Friedman was my teacher in the first year and he solidified my belief that economics is not for playing games but that it is a powerful tool for understanding the world. All the others stressed the same thing. Lewis taught me that labor economics didn't simply have to be institutional, that it could rely on economic analysis—which labor economics had not done up until that point. Ted Schultz put stress on looking at the big picture—economic development, human capital and many other areas. George Stigler has taught me many things about industrial organization and the value of economics in understanding regulation and other problems. From all of them I got some things in common, yet each had unique insights. I feel enormously indebted that I was fortunate enough to study in one way or another with such people.

ships that can be tested. Normative economics, however, deals with *value judgments* and *opinions* that cannot be tested.

Many topics in economics can be discussed within both a positive and a normative framework. Consider the minimum wage. An economist practicing positive economics would want to know the effect of the minimum wage on, say, teenage unemployment. An economist practicing normative economics would address issues that directly or indirectly relate to whether the minimum wage should exist.

This book mainly deals with positive economics. For the most part, we discuss the economic world as it is, not the way someone might think it should be. As you read, there are two points to keep in mind. First, although we have taken pains to keep our discussions within the boundaries of positive economics, at times we may operate perilously close to the normative border. If, here and there, we drop a value judgment into the discussion, recognize it for what it is. It would be wrong for you to accept as true something that we simply state as an opinion. Second, keep in mind that, no matter what your normative objectives, positive economics can shed some light on how they might be accomplished.

For example, suppose you believe that absolute poverty *should* be eliminated and the unemployment rate *should* be lowered. No doubt you have ideas as to how these goals can be accomplished. But are they correct? For example, will a greater redistribution of income eliminate absolute poverty? Will lowering taxes lower the unemployment rate? There is no guarantee that the means you *think* will bring about certain ends will do so. This is where sound positive economics can help. It helps us see *what is.* As someone once said, It is not enough to want to do good, it is important also to know how to do good.

Macroeconomics and Microeconomics

It has been said that the tools of microeconomics are microscopes, the tools of macroeconomics telescopes. Macroeconomics stands back from the trees in order to see the forest. Microeconomics gets up close and examines the tree itself, its bark, its limbs, and the soil in which it grows. **Microeconomics** is the branch of economics that deals with human behavior and choices as they relate to relatively small units—the individual, the firm, the industry, a single market. **Macroeconomics** is the branch of economics that deals with human behavior and choices as they relate to the entire economy. In microeconomics economists discuss a single price; in macroeconomics they discuss the price level. Microeconomics deals with the demand for a particular good or service; macroeconomics deals with aggregate or total demand for goods and services. Microeconomics examines how a tax change affects a single firm's output; macroeconomics looks at how a tax change affects the entire economy's output.

Microeconomics
The branch of economics that deals with human behavior and choices as they relate to relatively small units—the individual, the firm, the industry, a single market.

Macroeconomics
The branch of economics that deals with human behavior and choices as they relate to the entire economy.

CHAPTER SUMMARY

Economics

■ Economics is the science of scarcity: It is the science of how individuals and societies deal with the fact that wants are greater than the limited resources available to satisfy those wants.

Goods and Bads

■ A good is anything from which individuals receive utility or satisfaction. A bad is anything from which individuals receive disutility or dissatisfaction.

■ Economists usually speak of two types of goods: economic goods and free goods. A free good is a good where the amount available is greater than the amount people want at zero price. An economic good is scarce: It is a good where the quantity available is less than people would want if it were given away at zero price.

Scarcity, Choice, Opportunity Cost

■ Scarcity implies choice. In a world of limited resources, we must choose which wants will be satisfied and which will go unsatisfied.

■ Choice implies opportunity cost. Opportunity cost is the most highly valued opportunity or alternative forfeited when a choice is made. Cost implies sacrifice and can have both a money and a nonmoney dimension.

Theory

■ Economists build theories in order to explain and predict real-world events. Theories are necessarily abstractions from, as opposed to descriptions of, the real world.

■ All theories abstract from reality; they focus on the critical variables that the theorist believes explain and predict the phenomenon at hand.

Here are the steps in building and testing a theory:

1. Decide on what it is you want to explain or predict.
2. Identify the variables that you believe are relevant to what you want to explain or predict.
3. State the assumptions of the theory.
4. State the hypothesis.
5. Test the theory by comparing its predictions against real-world events.
6. If the evidence fails to reject the theory, then no further action is necessary, although it is a good idea to continue to examine the theory closely.
7. If the evidence rejects the theory, then either formulate an entirely new theory, or amend the old theory in terms of its variables, assumptions, and hypotheses.

■ Economists commonly judge a theory according to how well is predicts, not the degree of realism of its assumptions.

Scientific Thinking

■ Association is one thing, causation is another. Simply because two events are associated (in time, for example), it does not necessarily follow that one is the cause and the other is the effect.

■ The fallacy of composition is the erroneous view that what is good or true for the individual is necessarily good or true for the group.

■ *Ceteris paribus* is a Latin term that means "all other things held constant." The *ceteris paribus* condition is used to separate out effects.

Economic Categories

■ Positive economics attempts to determine *what is;* normative economics addresses *what should be.*

■ Microeconomics deals with human behavior and choices as they relate to relatively small units—the individual, the firm, the industry, a single market. Macroeconomics deals with human behavior and choices as they relate to the entire economy.

Key Terms and Concepts

Scarcity	Free Good	Fallacy of Composition
Economics	Economic Good	*Ceteris Paribus*
Economic Analysis	Economic Problem	Positive Economics
Good	Choice	Normative Economics
Bad	Opportunity Cost	Microeconomics
Utility	Theory	Macroeconomics
Disutility	Abstraction	

QUESTIONS AND PROBLEMS

1. Give two examples for each of the following: (a) a free good, (b) an economic good, (c) a bad.

2. The United States is considered a rich country because Americans have an abundance of goods and services to choose from. How can there be scarcity in a land of abundance?

3. Explain the links between scarcity, choice, and opportunity cost.

4. If someone were to say that there is zero opportunity cost to your doing homework, what would this mean?

5. Give an example that illustrates that a person can incur a cost without spending dollars.

6. Which of the following statements would Milton Friedman agree with and why?

   Statement 1: The theory does not work because its assumptions are false.
   Statement 2: The assumptions are false because the theory does not work.

7. Do a simple exercise that will help you understand the concept of opportunity cost. On one side of a sheet of paper, list all the goods you buy and the activities you undertake in a single day. On the other side, note the opportunity cost of each purchase or activity.

8. Discuss the opportunity costs of attending college for four years. Is college more or less costly than you thought it was? Explain.

9. How would your life be different if you didn't live in a world characterized by scarcity?

10. Explain the relationship between changes in opportunity costs and changes in behavior.

11. Think of a few examples that illustrate that association is not causation.

12. Think of a few examples that illustrate the fallacy of composition.

13. Some employees remark that they receive free health insurance from their employers. Is this truly free health insurance?

APPENDIX
A

WORKING WITH GRAPHS

A picture is worth a thousand words. With this familiar saying in mind, economists construct their graphs. A few lines, some curves, a few points, and much can be conveyed.

HOW TO READ GRAPHS

Most graphs look like one-half of a picture frame with something inside. For example, take a look at Exhibit 1A–1a. It has two axes: the vertical axis and the horizontal axis. On the vertical axis we have written "Y" and on the horizontal

EXHIBIT 1A–1
A Downward-Sloping Line: What It Says, How to Calculate Its Slope

In (a) each point represents a given quantity of both X and Y. Since the downward-sloping line indicates that as X rises (falls), Y falls (rises), the two variables are inversely related. In (b) the slope is calculated as ΔY/ΔX.

axis "X". As we move up the vertical axis and to the right on the horizontal axis, the numbers become larger.

Inside the area marked off by the two axes is a downward-sloping line with four points, A, B, C, and D. Each point corresponds to so much X and so much Y. For example, point A corresponds to 10X and 40Y and B corresponds to 20X and 30Y. The downward-sloping line indicates the relationship between the two variables. It tells us that as X rises, Y falls; and as X falls, Y rises. If one variable goes up as the other goes down, the two variables are **inversely related.**

Consider now the lines in Exhibit 1A–2. In (a) X and Y move in the same direction: As X rises, Y rises; as X falls, Y falls. The two variables are **directly re-**

Inversely Related
Two variables are inversely related if they move in opposite directions.

EXHIBIT 1A–2
Different Relationships

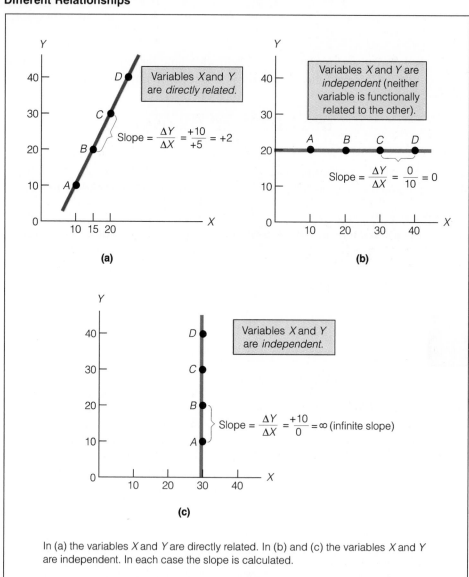

In (a) the variables X and Y are directly related. In (b) and (c) the variables X and Y are independent. In each case the slope is calculated.

lated.[1] In (b) as X increases, Y does not change. The two variables are **independent.** In (c) as Y increases, X does not change. Again the two variables are *independent.*

SLOPE OF THE LINE

It is often not only important to know *how* two variables are related but also to know *how much* one variable changes as the other variable changes. To find out, we need only calculate the **slope** of the line. The slope is the ratio of the change in the variable on the vertical axis to the change in the variable on the horizontal axis. For example, if Y is on the vertical axis and X on the horizontal axis, the slope is equal to $\Delta Y/\Delta X$. (The symbol "Δ" means "change in.")

$$\text{Slope} = \frac{\Delta Y}{\Delta X}$$

Suppose we calculate the slope between point A and B in Exhibit 1A–1b. The change in Y is equal to -10 (from 40 down to 30); the change in X is equal to $+10$ (from 10 up to 20). The slope therefore is $-10/+10 = -1$.[2] We have also calculated the slopes of the lines in Exhibit 1A–2.

THE SLOPE OF A CURVE

Economic graphs use both lines and curves. The slope of a curve is not constant throughout as it is for a straight line. The slope of a curve varies from one point to another.

Calculating the slope of a curve at a given point requires two steps as illustrated for point A in Exhibit 1A–3. First, draw a line tangent to the point (a tangent line is one that just touches the curve but does not cross it). Second, pick any two points on the tangent line and determine the slope. In Exhibit 1A–3 the slope of the line between points B and C is $+.67$. It follows that the slope of the curve at point A (and only at point $A)$ is $+.67$.

THE 45° LINE

Economists sometimes make use of the *45° line.* This is a straight line that bisects the right angle formed by the intersection of the vertical and horizontal axes. (See Exhibit 1A–4.) As a result, the 45° line divides the space enclosed by the two axes into *two equal parts.* We have illustrated this by shading the two equal parts in different colors. The major characteristic of the 45° line is that any point that lies on it is equidistant from both the horizontal and vertical axes. For example, point A is exactly as far from the horizontal axis as it is from the vertical axis. It follows that point A represents as much X as it does Y. Specifically, in the exhibit we see that point A represents 20 units of X and 20 units of Y.

---

[1]Instead of the term *inversely related,* some economists speak of two variables that move in opposite directions as being *negatively related.* Inversely related = negatively related. Similarly, instead of the term *directly related,* some economists speak of two variables that move in the same direction as being *positively related.* Directly related = positively related.

[2]A minus sign before the number signifies that the two variables, X and Y, are *inversely related.* A plus sign signifies that the two variables are *directly related.*

EXHIBIT 1A–3
Calculating the Slope of a Curve (at a Particular Point)

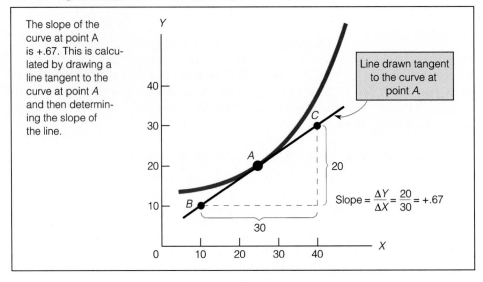

The slope of the curve at point A is +.67. This is calculated by drawing a line tangent to the curve at point *A* and then determining the slope of the line.

Line drawn tangent to the curve at point *A*.

$$\text{Slope} = \frac{\Delta Y}{\Delta X} = \frac{20}{30} = +.67$$

PIE CHARTS

In numerous places in this text you will come across a *pie chart.* A pie chart is a convenient way to represent the different parts of something which when added together equal the whole. Suppose we consider a typical 24-hour weekday for Charles Myers. On a typical weekday, Charles spends 8 hours sleeping, 4 hours taking classes at the university, 4 hours working at his parttime job, 2 hours doing homework, 1 hour eating, 2 hours watching television, and 3 hours doing really nothing (we'll call it "hanging around"). It is easy to represent the breakdown of a typical weekday for Charles in pie chart form. We have done this in Exhibit 1A–5. As you will notice, pie charts give you a quick visual message as to rough percentage breakdowns and relative relationships. For example, in Exhibit 1A–5

EXHIBIT 1A–4
The 45° Line

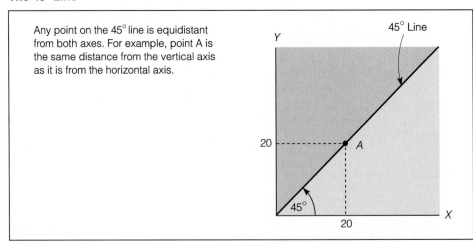

Any point on the 45° line is equidistant from both axes. For example, point A is the same distance from the vertical axis as it is from the horizontal axis.

EXHIBIT 1A–5
A Pie Chart

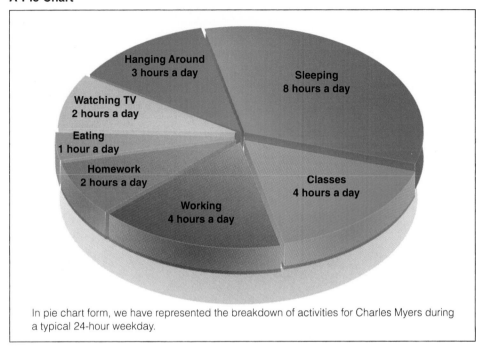

In pie chart form, we have represented the breakdown of activities for Charles Myers during a typical 24-hour weekday.

it is easy to see that Charles spends twice as much time working as doing homework.

BAR GRAPHS

The bar graph is another visual aid that economists use to convey relative relationships. For example, suppose we wanted to represent the **gross national product** (GNP) for different countries in a single year, say, 1988. Gross national product is the total market value of all final goods and services produced annually in an economy. In a bar chart we not only can note the actual GNP for each country but also provide a quick picture of the relative relationships between the GNPs of different countries. For instance, in Exhibit 1A–6 it is easy to see that the GNP of Japan was slightly over three times the GNP of France in 1988.

Gross National Product
The total market value of all final goods and services produced annually in an economy.

LINE GRAPHS

Sometimes information is best and most easily displayed in a line graph. Line graphs are particularly useful when illustrating changes in a variable over some time period. Suppose we want to illustrate the variations in "average points per game" for a college basketball team in different years. As you can see from Exhibit 1A–7a, the basketball team has been on a roller coaster during the years 1977–90. Perhaps the message that is transmitted here is that there is a lack of consistency in the performance of the team from one year to the next.

Suppose now we were to plot the data presented in (a) of Exhibit 1A–7 in (b) of the exhibit, except this time we use a different measurement scale on the vertical axis. As you can see, there appears much less variation in the performance of the

EXHIBIT 1A–6
A Bar Graph

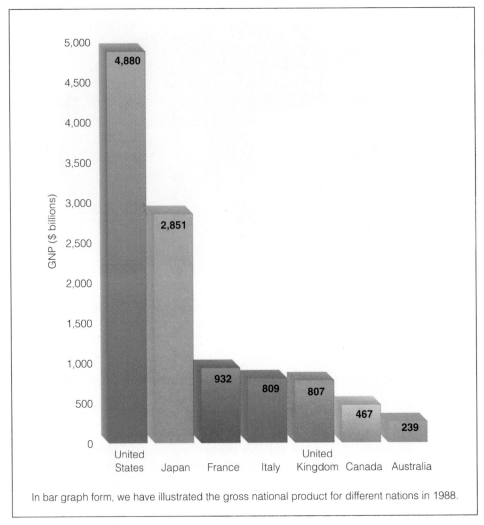

In bar graph form, we have illustrated the gross national product for different nations in 1988.

SOURCE: U.S. Bureau of the Census, Statistical Abstract of the United States, 1990 (Washington, D.C.: U.S. Government Printing Office, 1990).

basketball team than appeared in (a). In fact, we could choose some scale such that if we were to plot the data we would end up with close to a straight line. Our point is simple: Data plotted in line graph form may convey different messages depending on the measurement scale used.

Sometimes economists will present two line graphs in one exhibit. This is usually done when someone either (1) wants to draw attention to the relationship between the two variables, or (2) the difference between the two variables is noteworthy. In Exhibit 1A–8, we use line graphs to note the variation and trend in federal government expenditures and tax receipts for the years 1975–90 and to draw attention to what has been happening to the "gap" between the two. Since, for the years noted, expenditures were greater than receipts, the "gap" is the **budget deficit.** (If expenditures are greater than receipts, there is a budget deficit; if expenditures are less than receipts, there is a budget surplus.)

Budget Deficit
Occurs when government expenditures outstrip tax receipts.

PART I
ECONOMICS: THE SCIENCE OF
SCARCITY

■

EXHIBIT 1A–7
The Two Line Graphs Plot the Same Data

Year	Average Points per Game
1977	50
1978	40
1979	59
1980	51
1981	60
1982	50
1983	75
1984	63
1985	60
1986	71
1987	61
1988	55
1989	70
1990	64

In (a) we plot the average points per game for a college basketball team in different years. The variation between the years is pronounced. In panel (b) we plot the same data as were plotted in (a) and there appears much less variation in the performance of the team than appeared in (a).

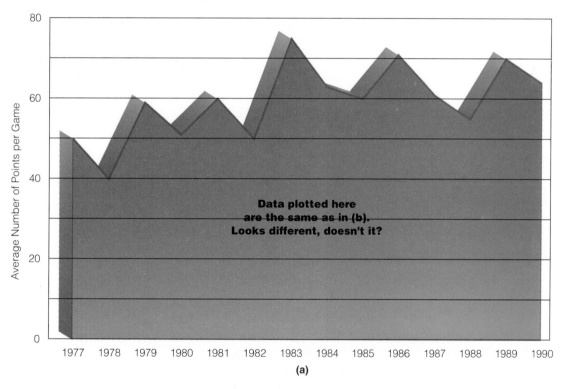

Data plotted here are the same as in (b). Looks different, doesn't it?

(a)

Data plotted here are the same as in (a). Looks different, doesn't it?

(b)

EXHIBIT 1A–8
Federal Government Expenditures and Tax Receipts, 1975–90.

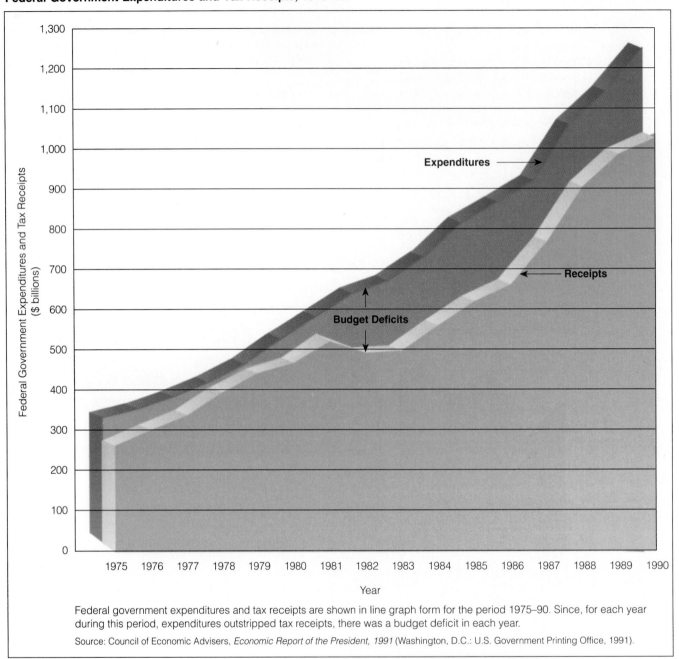

Federal government expenditures and tax receipts are shown in line graph form for the period 1975–90. Since, for each year during this period, expenditures outstripped tax receipts, there was a budget deficit in each year.

Source: Council of Economic Advisers, *Economic Report of the President, 1991* (Washington, D.C.: U.S. Government Printing Office, 1991).

APPENDIX SUMMARY

■ If one variable rises as the other falls, the two variables are inversely related.
■ A downward-sloping line (left to right) represents two variables that are inversely related.

- If one variable rises as the other rises, the two variables are directly related.
- An upward-sloping line (left to right) represents two variables that are directly related.
- If one variable rises as the other remains constant, the two variables are independent.
- The slope of a line is the ratio of the change in the variable on the vertical axis to the change in the variable on the horizontal axis.
- To determine the slope of a point on a curve, draw a line tangent to the point and then determine the slope of the line.
- Any point on a 45° line is equidistant from the two axes.
- A pie chart is a convenient way to represent the different parts of something which when added together equal the whole. A pie chart gives a visual message as to rough percentage breakdowns and relative relationships.
- A bar graph is a convenient way to represent relative relationships.

QUESTIONS AND PROBLEMS

1. What type of relationship would you expect between the following: (a) hot dogs and hot dog buns, (b) the price of winter coats and sales of winter coats, (c) the price of personal computers and the production of personal computers, (d) sales of toothbrushes and sales of cat food, (e) number of children in a family and the number of toys in a family.

2. Represent the following data in bar graph form.

Year	U.S. Money Supply ($ Billions)
1980	408.9
1981	436.5
1982	474.5
1983	521.2
1984	552.1
1985	620.1
1986	724.7
1987	750.4
1988	787.5
1989	794.8
1990	825.5

3. Plot the following data and specify the type of relationship between the two variables. (Place "price" on the vertical axis and "quantity demanded" on the horizontal axis.)

Price of Apples ($)	Quantity Demanded of Apples
0.25	1000
0.50	800
0.70	700
0.95	500
1.00	400
1.10	350

4. In Exhibit 1A–1a, determine the slope between points B and C.

5. In Exhibit 1A–2a, determine the slope between points A and B.

6. What is the special characteristic of a 45° line?

7. What is the slope of a 45° line?

8. When would it be preferable to illustrate data using a pie chart instead of a bar chart?

9. Plot the following data and specify the type of relationship between the two variables. (Place "price" on the vertical axis and "quantity supplied" on the horizontal axis.)

Price of Apples ($)	Quantity Supplied of Apples
0.25	350
0.50	400
0.70	500
0.95	700
1.00	800
1.10	1000

FUNDAMENTALS OF ECONOMIC THINKING

WITHIN THE PRODUCTION POSSIBILITIES FRONTIER (PPF) FRAMEWORK

WHAT THIS CHAPTER IS ABOUT

In economics, there are frameworks that provide the "environment" within which certain topics are discussed. Probably the best-known framework in economics is the supply-and-demand framework (see Chapter 3). Here, we introduce you to the production possibilities frontier framework (the PPF framework). Within it, we discuss a few key economic concepts. Then we describe the efficiency criterion, a tool that economists can use to evaluate policies. Finally, we look at three economic questions that every society must answer.

THE PRODUCTION POSSIBILITIES FRONTIER FRAMEWORK

■

In this section, we begin by defining the four categories of resources and developing the *production possibilities frontier framework* (the PPF framework). Next, we use the framework to discuss and illustrate the key economic concepts of scarcity, choice, opportunity cost and the law of increasing costs, economic growth, efficiency and inefficiency, and unemployed resources.

Resources

Goods are produced with *resources* (sometimes resources are referred to as *inputs* or *factors of production*). Economists commonly divide resources into four categories: **land, labor, capital,** and **entrepreneurship.** *Land* includes all natural resources, such as minerals, forests, water, and unimproved land. *Labor* refers to the physical and mental talents that people contribute to the production process. *Capital* consists of produced goods that can be used as inputs for further production, such things as machinery, tools, computers, trucks, buildings, and factories. *Entrepreneurship* refers to the particular talent that some people have for organizing the resources of land, labor, and capital into the production of goods and to the search for new business opportunities and the development of new ways of doing things.

The Production Possibilities Frontier

The **production possibilities frontier (PPF)** represents the possible combinations of two goods that an economy can produce in a certain period of time, under the conditions of a given state of **technology,** no unemployed resources, and efficient production. Within this context, there can exist (1) constant opportunity costs between the two goods or (2) changing opportunity costs between the two goods. We discuss each in turn.

Constant Opportunity Costs between Goods: The Case of the Straight-Line Production Possibilities Frontier.   Assume three things: (1) Only two goods can be produced in an economy, computers and television sets. (2) The opportunity cost of 1 television set is 1 computer. (3) The opportunity cost between television sets and computers is *constant* as more of one good is produced.

In Exhibit 2–1a, we have identified six combinations of computers and television sets that can be produced. For example, combination *A* is 50,000 computers and 0 television sets; combination *B* is 40,000 computers and 10,000 television sets, and so on.[1] We plotted these six combinations of computers and television sets in Exhibit 2–1b. Each combination represents a different point. For example, the combination of 50,000 computers and 0 television sets is represented by point *A*. The line that connects the points *A–F* is called the production possibilities frontier.

Notice that the production possibilities frontier is a straight line. This is because the opportunity cost of producing computers and television sets is constant. For example, if the economy were to move from point *A* to *B,* or from *B* to *C,* and so on, the opportunity cost of each good would remain constant at 1 for 1. For example, at point *A,* 50,000 computers and 0 television sets are produced. At *B,*

---

[1]If zero television sets are produced, which is the case for combination A, we are implicitly assuming that zero resources are used in the production of television sets.

Land
All natural resources, such as minerals, forests, water, and unimproved land.

Labor
The physical and mental talents people contribute to the production process.

Capital
Produced goods that can be used as inputs for further production, such things as machinery, tools, computers, trucks, buildings, and factories.

Entrepreneurship
The particular talent that some people have for organizing the resources of land, labor, and capital into the production of goods, seeking new business opportunities, and developing new ways of doing things.

Production Possibilities Frontier
Represents the possible combinations of two goods that an economy can produce in a certain period of time, under the conditions of a given state of technology, no unemployed resources, and efficient production.

Technology
The body of skills and knowledge concerning the use of resources in production. An advance in technology commonly refers to the ability to produce more output with a fixed amount of resources or the ability to produce the same output with fewer resources.

EXHIBIT 2–1
Production Possibilities Frontier (Constant Opportunity Costs)

COMBINATION	COMPUTERS AND TELEVISION SETS (number of units per year)		POINT IN PANEL (b)
A	50,000 and	0	A
B	40,000 and	10,000	B
C	30,000 and	20,000	C
D	20,000 and	30,000	D
E	10,000 and	40,000	E
F	0 and	50,000	F

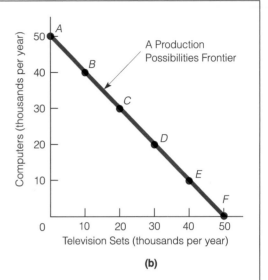

(a)

(b)

We assume that the opportunity cost of producing either good does not change as more of the other good is produced. Under the conditions of a given state of technology, no unemployed resources, and efficient production, the economy can produce

any of the six combinations of computers and television sets in panel (a). We have plotted these combinations in panel (b). The line connecting these points is a production possibilities frontier.

40,000 computers and 10,000 television sets are produced. We conclude that for every 1 computer not produced, 1 television set is produced.

Changing Opportunity Costs between Goods: The Case of the Bowed Outward (Concave) Production Possibilities Frontier. Assume two things: (1) Only two goods can be produced in the economy, computers and television sets. (2) The opportunity cost between computers and television sets changes as more of one good is produced.

In Exhibit 2–2a, we have identified four combinations of computers and television sets that can be produced. For example, combination A is 50,000 computers and 0 television sets; combination B is 40,000 computers and 20,000 television sets; and so on. We plotted these four combinations of computers and television sets in Exhibit 2–2b. Each combination represents a different point. The curved line that connects the points A–D is called the production possibilities frontier.

Notice that the production possibilities frontier is bowed outward, or *concave.* This is because the opportunity cost of television sets changes (increases) as more sets are produced. For example, when the economy moves from producing 0 television sets to 20,000 television sets, the opportunity cost comes in the form of 10,000 fewer computers (computer production falls by 10,000, from 50,000 to 40,000). This means for every 1 television set produced, ½ computer is not produced; thus, the opportunity cost of 1 television set is ½ computer.

Notice, though, that when the economy moves from producing 20,000 television sets to producing 40,000 television sets, the opportunity cost comes in the form of 15,000 fewer computers (computer production falls by 15,000, from 40,000 to 25,000). This means for every 1 television set produced, ¾ computer is not produced. In short, the opportunity cost of producing television sets increases as more television sets are produced.

EXHIBIT 2–2
Production Possibilities Frontier (Changing Opportunity Costs)

COMBINATION	COMPUTERS AND TELEVISION SETS (number of units per year)			POINT IN PANEL (b)
A	50,000	and	0	A
B	40,000	and	20,000	B
C	25,000	and	40,000	C
D	0	and	60,000	D

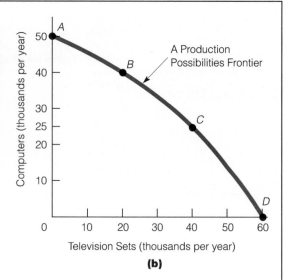

(a)

(b)

We assume that the opportunity costs change as more of one good is produced. Under the conditions of a given state of technology, no unemployed resources, and efficient production, the economy can produce any of the four combinations of computers and television sets in panel (a). We have plotted these combinations in panel (b). The curve connecting these points is a production possibilities frontier.

Scarcity

Recall from Chapter 1 that scarcity is the condition where wants outstrip the resources available to satisfy those wants. The finiteness of resources is graphically portrayed by the production possibilities frontier itself (Exhibit 2–3). The frontier tells us, "At this point in time, that's as far as society can go. It is limited to choosing any combination of two goods on the frontier or below it."

The frontier separates two regions: (1) an **attainable region,** which consists of the points on the PPF and all points below it, and (2) an **unattainable region,** which consists of the points above the PPF. Scarcity implies that some things are attainable and some things are unattainable.

Attainable Region
Includes those points on and below the production possibilities frontier.

Unattainable Region
Includes those points above the production possibilities frontier.

Choice

Choice is visible in Exhibit 2–3 once we realize that an economy can operate at only one point at a time. For example, an economy cannot operate at points A *and* B in Exhibit 2–3, producing 10 apples and 6 potatoes *and* producing 9½ apples and 7 potatoes, too. It must *choose* one.

Opportunity Cost

Opportunity cost becomes visible as we move from one point to another. Suppose we are at point *D* in Exhibit 2–3 and choose to move to point *E.* At *D* the economy produces 11 potatoes and 5 apples. At *E* it produces 12 potatoes and 3 apples. In moving from *D* to *E,* what is the opportunity cost of the addition (the 12th) potato? It is what must be forfeited to obtain that potato—which is 2 apples.

EXHIBIT 2–3
Economic Concepts within a PPF Framework

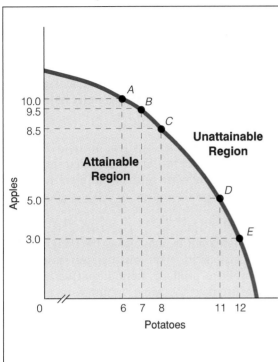

Within the production possibilities frontier framework, we illustrate four economic concepts: scarcity, choice, opportunity cost, and the law of increasing opportunity costs. First, the finiteness of resources implicit in the condition of *scarcity* is illustrated by the *PPF* itself. Second, since the economy can operate at only one of many points, it must make a *choice*. Third, *opportunity cost* is illustrated by a movement from point *D* to point *E*: to produce the 12th potato, the cost is 2 apples. Fourth, the *law of increasing opportunity costs* is illustrated as we move down the *PPF* from point *A* to *B* to *C* and so on. As the economy produces more potatoes, the cost in terms of forfeited apple production rises. (Note: We have not identified the "time period" of production on either the vertical or horizontal axis, as we did in Exhibits 2–1 and 2–2. Within the *PPF*-framework, this is implicit.)

Law of Increasing Opportunity Costs.   A resource is *specialized* if it is better suited to the production of one good than others. A resource is *nonspecialized* if it is equally suited to the production of all goods.

When resources are specialized, increased production of one good comes at increased opportunity costs. This is the **law of increasing opportunity costs,** which is illustrated in Exhibit 2–3. Notice that moving from the production of 6 to 7 potatoes (point *A* to *B)* requires giving up ½ apple. Moving from 7 to 8 potatoes (point *B* to *C)* requires giving up 1 apple, however. And moving from 11 to 12 potatoes (point *D* to *E)* requires giving up 2 apples. We conclude that as more potatoes are produced, the opportunity cost of producing potatoes rises: hence, the law of increasing opportunity costs.

It is easy to see that increasing costs give the production possibilities frontier its curvature. But since a production possibilities frontier need not be curved, but can be a straight line, increasing costs need not occur.

Are most production possibilities frontiers curved? Do increasing costs occur often? The answer is yes. The reason is that most resources are simply better suited for the production of some goods than others. For example, some land is better suited for the production of wheat than corn. Some individuals are better suited for producing cars than tomatoes. Also, in the early stages of the production of a good, it is likely that the resources best suited to its production are used and that as production increases, more and more less-well-suited resources are used.

Consider the production of houses. In the early stages of house production, no doubt the persons most skilled at house building are employed. If house production increases, though, less skilled individuals will enter the house-building in-

Law of Increasing Opportunity Costs
As more of a good is produced, the higher the opportunity costs of producing that good.

EXHIBIT 2–4
**Economic Growth within a PPF
Framework**

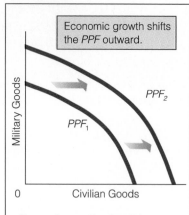

Economic growth shifts
the *PPF* outward.

PPF₂

PPF₁

Military Goods

0   Civilian Goods

Economic growth refers to an
increase in the productive capabilities of an economy, resulting in a
shift outward in the production
possibilities frontier.

dustry. Where three skilled house builders could build a house in a month, as
many as seven unskilled builders may be required to build it in the same time.

Economic Growth

Economic growth refers to the increased productive capabilities of an economy; it
is illustrated by a shift outward in the production possibilities frontier. Two major
factors that affect economic growth are (1) an increase in the quantity of resources
and (2) an advance in technology.

An Increase in the Quantity of Resources. With an increase in the quantity of
resources (say, through a new discovery of resources), it is possible to produce a
greater quantity of output. In Exhibit 2–4, an increase in the quantity of resources
makes it possible to produce more military goods and more civilian goods, thus
shifting the PPF outward from PPF_1 to PPF_2.

An Advance in Technology. Earlier we defined technology as the body of skills
and knowledge concerning the use of resources in production. An advance in
technology commonly refers to the ability to produce more output with a fixed
quantity of resources or the ability to produce the same output with a smaller
quantity of resources.

   Suppose there is an advance in technology such that more military goods and
more civilian goods can be produced with the same quantity of resources. As a
result, the PPF shifts outward in Exhibit 2–4 from PPF_1 to PPF_2. The outcome is
the same as in the first condition, increasing the quantity of resources.

Efficiency

Efficiency
In terms of production, the condition
where the maximum output is produced with given resources and technology. Efficiency implies the impossibility of gains in one area without
losses in another.

Economists speak about different types of **efficiency.** Here we discuss *efficiency in
production* (productive efficiency). We say that the economy is *efficient* if it is
producing the maximum output with given resources and technology. In Exhibit
2–5, points *A, B, C, D,* and *E* are all efficient points. Notice that each point lies *on*
the production possibilities frontier instead of below it; each point represents the
outer limit of the attainable region. In other words, we are getting the most (in
terms of output) out of what we have (in terms of available resources and
technology).

   It follows that the economy is exhibiting **inefficiency** if it is producing less than
the maximum output with given resources and technology. In Exhibit 2–5, point
F is an inefficient point. It lies below the production possibilities frontier; it is
below the outer limit of the attainable region. In other words, we could do better
with what we have.

Inefficiency
In terms of production, the condition
where less than the maximum output
is produced with given resources and
technology. Inefficiency implies the
possibility of gains in one area without losses in another.

   Consider another way of viewing efficiency and inefficiency. Start at efficient
point *A* in Exhibit 2–5 and move to efficient point *B*. We go from a position of
more television sets (55,000) and fewer cars (5,000) to a position of fewer television
sets (50,000) and more cars (15,000). Move now from point *B* back to *A*. We go
from a position of fewer television sets (50,000) and more cars (15,000) to a position of more television sets (55,000) and fewer cars (5,000). Notice that if we start
at an efficient point—such as *A* or *B*—it is impossible to get more of one good
without getting less of another good. Once again, we can move from *A* to *B* and

get more cars, but not without getting fewer television sets. *Efficiency implies that gains are impossible in one area without losses in another.* This is common sense. If efficiency exists, we already are getting the most we can out of what we have; therefore we cannot do better in one area (getting more of one good) without necessarily doing worse in another (getting less of another good).

Now consider inefficient point *F*, a point at which the economy is *not* producing the maximum output with given resources and technology. Move from point *F* to *C*. We get more television sets and no fewer cars. What if we move from *F* to *D*? We get more television sets and more cars. Finally, move from *F* to *E*. We get more cars and no fewer television sets. We can only conclude that moving from *F* can give us more of at least one good and no less of another good. (Moving from *F* to *D*, we got more of both goods.) *Inefficiency implies that gains are possible in one area without losses in another.* This is also common sense. If inefficiency exists, we are *not* getting the most out of what we have; therefore we can do better in one area without necessarily doing worse in another.

Efficiency implies that gains are impossible in one area without losses in another. Inefficiency implies that gains are possible in one area without losses in another.

Question:

Suppose we move from point F *to* B. *More television sets are produced but fewer cars—in other words, more of one good but less of another. Doesn't this mean* F *is an efficient point although it was labeled an inefficient point?*

Answer:

Efficiency implies that gains are impossible in one area without losses in another. Point *F* does not fit this definition, since from *F* we *could* move to *C*, *D*, or *E*—all these moves are possible—and get gains in one area without getting losses in another. It follows that *F* is an inefficient point. Simply because a move from *F* to

EXHIBIT 2–5
Efficiency, Inefficiency, and Unemployed Resources within a PPF Framework

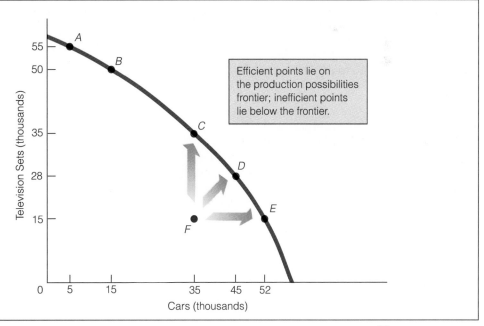

Points *A*, *B*, *C*, *D*, and *E* are efficient points. They lie on the production possibilities frontier. It is *impossible* to move away from these points and get more of one good without getting less of another good. Point *F* is an inefficient point. It lies below the production possibilities frontier. It is *possible* to move away from it and get more of (at least) one good and no less of another. At efficient points, all resources are being used in the production of goods. At inefficient points, some resources are not being used to produce goods, that is, there are some unemployed resources.

Efficient points lie on the production possibilities frontier; inefficient points lie below the frontier.

Economic Growth: An Expanding PPF Ends the Political Tug-of-War, for a While

Liberals and conservatives of both political parties often pull in different economic directions. To illustrate, suppose we are currently at point A in Exhibit 2–6, with X_2 of good X and Y_2 of good Y. Conservatives prefer C to A and thus try to convince the liberals and the rest of the nation to move to C. The liberals, however, prefer B to A and try to convince the conservatives and the rest of the nation to move to B. Thus, we have a political tug-of-war.

Is there a way that both groups can get what they want? There is, but the production possibilities frontier must shift outward from PPF_1 to PPF_2. This can occur if there is economic growth. With a new production possibilities frontier, PPF_2, point D represents the quantity of X that the conservatives want and the quantity of Y that the liberals want. At point D, conservatives have X_3 units of good X, which is what they would have had at C; and liberals have Y_3 units of good Y, which is what they would have had at B. Through economic growth, both conservatives and liberals can get what they want; the political tug-of-war will cease, at least for a while.

We say "for a while" because even at point D there is scarcity: The wants of liberals and conservatives are both greater than the resources available to satisfy those wants. Starting at point D, liberals might push for a movement up the production possibilities frontier and conservatives for a movement down it.

A question to think about: Would you expect to see more intense political battles in a growing economy or in a stagnant economy, *ceteris paribus*? Why?

EXHIBIT 2–6
Economic Growth Ends Political Battles, for a While

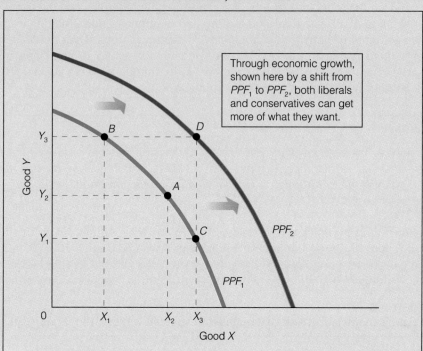

Through economic growth, shown here by a shift from PPF_1 to PPF_2, both liberals and conservatives can get more of what they want.

The economy is at point A, but conservatives want to be at C and liberals want to be at B. As a result, there is a political tug-of-war. Both conservatives and liberals can get the quantity of the good they want through economic growth. This is represented by point D on PPF_2.

B brings gains in one area and losses in another, it does not necessarily follow that a move from *F* to some other point would always bring the same results. In short, as long as it is *possible* to move from *F* to some point and get gains in one area without getting losses in another, then *F* is an inefficient point.

Unemployed Resources

When the economy exhibits inefficiency, it is not producing the maximum output with the available resources and technology. One reason may be that it is not using all its resources—that is, some of its resources are unemployed, such as at point *F* in Exhibit 2–5.

When the economy exhibits efficiency, it is producing the maximum output with the available resources and technology. This means it is using all its resources to produce goods—all its resources are employed, none are unemployed. At the efficient points *A–E* in Exhibit 2–5, there are no unemployed resources.

The Efficiency Criterion

Besides evaluating production, economists also evaluate policies, programs, and institutions in terms of efficiency. Here they employ the **efficiency criterion,** which, broadly speaking, addresses the question of whether an alternative arrangement of resources or goods exists that can make at least one person better off without making anyone else worse off.

Efficiency Criterion
Addresses the question of whether an alternative arrangement exists that can make at least one person better off without making anyone else worse off.

Suppose it is wartime and the government rations gasoline. The rationing scheme works this way: (1) Each person is given 10 ration tickets per week. (2) Each ticket permits the holder to buy 1 gallon of gasoline. (3) People are prohibited from selling their ration tickets. Is this gasoline rationing system efficient or inefficient?

Consider Johnson and Brown. Johnson is a traveling salesman who usually buys 50 gallons of gasoline a week. Brown is a writer, who usually works at home and buys 3 gallons of gasoline a week. Currently Brown uses 3 of his 10 (rationed) gallons of gasoline for work purposes and he uses the remaining 7 gallons for simply leisure driving. Since Brown places a low priority on leisure driving, he agrees to illegally sell Johnson seven ration tickets at a price of $1 per ticket.

Who is better off? Who is worse off? Both Johnson and Brown expect to be better off (they wouldn't have traded otherwise), and it appears that no one is worse off. We conclude that the specific gasoline rationing system—where buying and selling rationing tickets is prohibited—is an inefficient system. An alternative system used by Johnson and Brown, in which ration tickets are bought and sold, helps at least one person (in this example it helped two) and makes no one worse off.

Question:

A legal gasoline rationing system has been labeled inefficient, and it is strongly implied that an illegal gasoline rationing system is preferable to it. Is this the type of conclusion that we want?

Answer:

When we do positive economic analysis, there is no specific type of conclusion that we want. The question is simply whether an alternative arrangement would permit a more highly valued use of the nation's resources than rationing.

THREE ECONOMIC QUESTIONS EVERY SOCIETY MUST ANSWER

These are the economic questions that every society must answer.

First, **What goods will be produced?** We know that in a world of efficiently utilized scarce resources, more of one good necessarily means less of something else. Should we have more cars and fewer subways or more subways and fewer cars. More generally, should we have more military goods and fewer civilian goods?

Second, once it has been decided which goods will be produced, **How will the goods be produced?** For example, will farmers using modern tractors produce food, or will farmers using primitive tools produce it? Will the food be produced on private farms, where production decisions are made by individual farmers, or will it be produced on collective farms, where production decisions are made by government bureaucrats?

Third, **For whom will the goods be produced?** Will it be anyone who is able and willing to pay the prices for the goods, or will government decide who will have the goods?

In the late-1980s and early-1990s, numerous socialist societies began to look at different answers (from those formerly held to) for some or all of the questions. The Soviet Union, the People's Republic of China, and the nations of Eastern Europe commenced, to different degrees, to allow the market forces of supply and demand to play a larger role in everyday economic affairs. We shall see just how the market forces of supply and demand operate in Chapters 3 and 4.

The layperson looks at nations and sees differences. For example, people speak French in France and English in the United States; the crime rate is higher in the United States than it is in England; and so on. The economist looks at nations and sees similarities. For example, the United States has to decide which goods to produce and so does China. The economist sees similarities because scarcity—the defining feature of economics—and its consequences are common to all nations—the United States, France, China, and so on. The English language may ''disappear'' at a nation's border, but scarcity doesn't.

Resources

■ Economists divide resources into four categories: land, labor, capital, and entrepreneurship.

■ Land includes all natural resources, such as minerals, forests, water, and unimproved land.

■ Labor refers to the physical and mental talents that people contribute to the production process.

■ Capital consists of produced goods that can be used as inputs for further production, such things as machinery, tools, computers, trucks, buildings, and factories.

- Entrepreneurship refers to the particular talent that some people have for organizing the resources of land, labor, and capital into the production of goods and to the search for new business opportunities and the development of new ways of doing things.

The Production Possibilities Frontier

- The production possibilities frontier (PPF) represents the possible combinations of two goods that an economy can produce in a certain period of time, under the conditions of a given state of technology, no unemployed resources, and efficient production.

Economic Concepts within a PPF Framework

- The finiteness of resources implicit in the scarcity condition is represented by the production possibilities frontier itself. The frontier separates what is attainable from what is unattainable.
- Choice is visible in the PPF framework once we realize that society cannot operate at more than one point at a time: thus, it must choose.
- Opportunity cost is visible in the PPF framework when we move from one point on the PPF to another point on the PPF.
- A curved (bowed outward) PPF illustrates the law of increasing costs: Increased production of one good comes at increased opportunity costs.
- Economic growth is illustrated by a shift outward in the PPF. Two major factors that affect economic growth are (1) an increase in the quantity of resources and (2) an advance in technology.

Efficiency and Inefficiency

- All points on the production possibilities frontier are efficient points; all points below it are inefficient.
- Efficiency implies that gains are impossible in one area without losses in another. Inefficiency implies that gains are possible in one area without losses in another.
- When the economy is efficient, it is employing all its resources. When the economy is inefficient, some resources are unemployed.

The Efficiency Criterion

- Economists sometimes use the efficiency criterion to evaluate policies, programs, and institutions. The efficiency criterion addresses the question of whether an alternative arrangement exists that can make at least one person better off without making anyone else worse off. If the answer is no, then the (existing) policy–program–institution is said to be efficient. If the answer is yes—that is, if an alternative exists that can make at least one person better off without making anyone else worse off—then the (existing) policy–program–institution is inefficient.

Three Economic Questions

- Every society must answer three economic questions: (1) What goods will be produced? (2) How will the goods be produced? (3) For whom will the goods be produced?

Key Terms and Concepts

Land

Labor

Capital

Entrepreneurship

Production Possibilities
 Frontier

Technology

Attainable Region

Unattainable Region

Law of Increasing
 Opportunity Costs

Efficiency

Inefficiency

Efficiency Criterion

QUESTIONS AND PROBLEMS

1. How would each of the following affect the U.S. production possibilities frontier: (a) an increase in the number of illegal aliens entering the country; (b) a war; (c) the discovery of a new oil field; (d) a decrease in the unemployment rate; (e) a law that requires individuals to enter lines of work for which they are not suited?

2. Suppose the economy can produce cars and computers only. Write out six attainable combinations of the two goods, holding the opportunity cost (between the two goods) constant at something other than 1 for 1. Draw the production possibilities frontier.

3. Suppose the economy can produce cars and computers only. Write out six attainable combinations of the two goods in which you represent the law of increasing opportunity costs. Draw the production possibilities frontier.

4. Explain how the following can be represented in a production possibilities framework: the finiteness of resources implicit in the scarcity condition, choice, and opportunity cost.

5. What condition must hold before the production possibilities frontier is bowed outward? a straight line?

6. Within the PPF framework, explain each of the following: (a) a disagreement between a person who favors more domestic welfare spending and one who favors more national defense spending; (b) an increase in the population; and (c) a technological change that makes resources less specialized.

7. Some people have said that the Central Intelligence Agency (CIA) regularly estimates (a) the total quantity of output produced in the Soviet Union and (b) the total quantity of civilian goods produced in the Soviet Union. Of what interest would this data, or the information that perhaps could be deduced from it, be to the CIA? (Hint: Think in terms of a PPF).

8. Suppose the United States can produce the following efficient combinations of cars and tanks.

	Possible Combinations				
	A	B	C	D	E
Cars (in millions)	0	10	20	30	40
Tanks (in thousands)	60	55	45	30	0

a. Are there constant or increasing opportunity costs associated with tank production?

b. Draw the production possibilities frontier based on the data in the table.

c. Suppose there is a change in technology that allows the United States to produce more tanks with the same resources, but does not allow it to produce more cars with the same resources. Draw and label the new PPF in relation to the old PPF.

9. Suppose a nation's PPF shifts inward as its population grows. What happens, on average, to the material standard of living of the people? Explain your answer.

10. "A nation may be able to live beyond its means, but the world cannot." Do you agree or disagree? Explain your answer.

SUPPLY, DEMAND, AND PRICE: THEORY

WHAT THIS CHAPTER IS ABOUT

Psychologists sometimes play a game called *word association* to learn more about their patients. The psychologist says a word, and the patient says the first word that comes into his or her head. Morning, night. Girl, boy. Sunrise, sunset. If the patient were an economist and the psychologist said "supply," the economist would undoubtedly answer "demand." To economists, supply and demand go together. (Thomas Carlyle, the historian and philosopher, said that "it is easy to train economists. Just teach a parrot to say 'Supply and Demand.'" Not funny, Carlyle.) Supply and demand have been called the "bread and butter" of economics. In this chapter, we discuss them, first separately and then together.

DEMAND

A **market** is any arrangement by which people exchange goods and services. There are two sides to a market: a buying side and a selling side. *Demand* is relevant to the buying side, *supply* is relevant to the selling side. We start with a discussion of demand.

Market
Any arrangement by which people exchange goods and services.

About Demand

The word **demand** has a specific meaning in economics. It refers to (1) the willingness and ability of buyers to purchase different quantities of a good (2) at different prices (3) during a specific time period (per day, week, and so on).[1]

There is no demand, and a person is not a buyer, unless there is both willingness and ability to buy. For example, Josie may be willing to buy the computer but be unable to pay the price; Tanya may be able but unwilling. Neither Josie nor Tanya demand a computer.

If you think that people will buy more units of a good at lower than higher prices, you instinctively understand the **law of demand,** which holds that *as the price of a good rises, the quantity demanded of the good falls, and as the price of a good falls, the quantity demanded of the good rises, ceteris paribus.* Simply put, the law of demand states that the price of a good and the quantity demanded of the good are inversely related, *ceteris paribus:*

$$P\uparrow \qquad Q_d\downarrow$$
$$P\downarrow \qquad Q_d\uparrow \qquad ceteris\ paribus$$

where P = price, and Q_d = quantity demanded.

Quantity demanded is the number of units of a good that individuals are *willing* and *able to buy* at a particular price during some time period. For example, suppose individuals are willing and able to buy 100 TV dinners per week at the price of $4 per unit. One hundred units is therefore the quantity demanded of TV dinners at $4.

Demand
The willingness and ability of buyers to purchase different quantities of a good at different prices during a specific time period.

Law of Demand
As the price of a good rises, the quantity demanded of the good falls, and as the price of a good falls, the quantity demanded of the good rises, *ceteris paribus.*

Question:

If a person is willing and able to buy a particular car at $40,000, will she actually make this purchase?

Answer:

Not necessarily. Willingness and ability to buy refers to the buyer, but it takes both a buyer *and* a seller before an exchange can be made. A person may be willing and able to buy a particular car for $40,000, but that car may not currently exist, or it may exist and a seller may not be willing to sell it for $40,000.

When Bill says, "The more money a person has, the more expensive cars— Porsches, Corvettes, Jaguars, and so on—he will buy," he is *not* thinking like an economist. An economist knows that the ability to buy something does not necessarily imply the willingness to buy it.

THINKING LIKE AN ECONOMIST

[1]Demand takes into account *services* as well as goods. Goods are tangible and include such things as shirts, books, and television sets. Services are intangible and include such things as dental care, medical care, and an economics lecture. To simplify the discussion, however, we refer to only *goods.*

From the Law of Demand to a Demand Schedule to a Demand Curve

Demand Schedule
The numerical tabulation of the quantity demanded of a good at different prices.

A **demand schedule** is one way of representing the inverse relationship between price and quantity demanded specified by the law of demand. It is the numerical tabulation of the quantity demanded of a good at different prices. A demand schedule for good X is illustrated in Exhibit 3–1a.

In Exhibit 3–1b, the four price–quantity combinations are plotted and the points connected, giving us a **(downward-sloping) demand curve.** A (downward-sloping) demand curve is the graphical representation of the inverse relationship between price and quantity demanded specified by the law of demand. In short, the demand curve is a picture of the law of demand.

(Downward-sloping) Demand Curve
The graphical representation of the law of demand.

The Market Demand Curve

An *individual demand curve* represents the price–quantity combinations for a single buyer. A *market demand curve* represents the price–quantity combinations for all buyers of a particular good. For example, we could speak about Jones's demand for honey. Here an individual demand curve would be relevant. Or we could speak about all buyers' demand for honey. Here a market demand curve would be relevant.

In Exhibit 3–2, we have derived a market demand curve by "summing up" the individual demand curves. A demand schedule for Jones, Smith, and "all other buyers" is shown in (a). The market demand schedule is then obtained by adding up the quantity demanded by each party at each price. In (b) the data points are plotted, giving us a market demand curve.

How Much of a Good Buyers Are Willing to Buy Depends on Price, Among Other Things

How many car stereos are people willing to buy? How many 16-year-olds on summer vacation are local businesses willing to hire? Are people willing to buy 5,000

EXHIBIT 3–1
Demand Schedule and Demand Curve

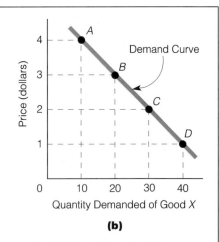

DEMAND SCHEDULE FOR GOOD _X_

PRICE (dollars)	QUANTITY DEMANDED	POINT IN PANEL (b)
4	10	A
3	20	B
2	30	C
1	40	D

(a)

(b)

(a) A demand schedule for good _X_. (b) A demand curve, obtained by plotting the different price–quantity combinations and connecting the points. On a demand curve the price (in dollars) represents price per unit of the good; and the quantity demanded, on the horizontal axis, is always relevant for a specific time period (a week, a month, and so on).

car stereos and hire 3,300 16-year-olds? Is there one specific number in each case? No. People might be willing to buy anywhere from 0 to 50,000 car stereos. It depends on the price of car stereos. At $50 they will probably buy more car stereos than at $200.

This is an obvious point, perhaps. But think of how often we mistakenly believe that the quantity demanded of a good is independent of the price of the good. For example, some people often speak as if there are a fixed number of jobs in the United States. You might have heard someone say, "We've got to protect U.S. jobs from foreign competition, because if foreign firms outcompete U.S. firms, U.S. workers will lose their jobs, and it is unlikely they will find work elsewhere because there are *only so many jobs.*"

But it is not true that there are only so many jobs. There are only so many jobs at a *particular wage rate* (just as people are willing to buy only so many car stereos

EXHIBIT 3–2
Deriving a Market Demand Schedule and Market Demand Curve

In (a), the market demand schedule is derived by adding up the quantity demanded by each party at each price. In (b), the data points are plotted, giving us a market demand curve. Only two points on the market demand curve are noted.

	Quantity Demanded			
PRICE	JONES	SMITH	OTHER BUYERS	ALL BUYERS
$15	1	2	20	23
14	2	3	45	50
13	3	4	70	77
12	4	5	100	109
11	5	6	130	141
10	6	7	160	173

(a)

(b)

49

at a particular price). The lower the wage rate, the greater the quantity demanded of labor, and the more jobs there are, *ceteris paribus.*

Question:

The history department at the university has hired additional history professors during the past five years, even though salaries have stayed constant. The additional professors were hired because of an increase in student enrollment. Doesn't this indicate that the number of jobs in the history department depends on how many students want to take history classes, not on the salaries of history professors?

Answer:

Recall that how much of a good people are willing to buy depends on price, *among other things.* Student enrollment is one of the *other things.* But simply because student enrollment affects the number of job openings for history professors, it does not follow that professors' salaries do not.

Look at it this way. Suppose *all other things* (student enrollment and so forth) are held constant while history professors' salaries go down. What would the university do? It might hire more history professors and have smaller classes (classes averaging 30 students instead of 40 students, for example). Now suppose salaries rise. What would the university do? It might not be as willing to grant permanent positions to its history faculty, and it probably will have bigger history classes.

Factors That Can Cause the Demand Curve to Shift

We constructed the demand schedule in Exhibit 3–1a and plotted the demand curve in (b) with the condition that all other things are held constant. But what if any of those other things change? Obviously, the demand schedule will change, and the demand curve will shift. Here we discuss what these other things are and how changes in them can affect (shift) the demand curve.

Income. As a person's income rises, he or she *can* buy more of any particular good (say, blue jeans) at given prices. But the ability to buy more blue jeans does not necessarily imply the willingness to do so.

Let's consider two cases. First, suppose a person's income increases and she buys more blue jeans. In this case, the demand curve for blue jeans shifts rightward, or, as economists also say, the demand for blue jeans increases. In this case, blue jeans are a **normal good.** The demand for a normal good rises as income rises and falls as income falls. The demand for a normal good and income are directly related.

Now suppose a person's income increases and she buys fewer jeans. In this case, the demand curve for blue jeans shifts leftward, or demand decreases; this time blue jeans are an **inferior good.** The demand for an inferior good falls as income rises and rises as income falls. The demand for an inferior good and income are inversely related. Hotdogs and used cars might be inferior goods because many people buy less of these goods as their incomes rise.

Exhibit 3–3a illustrates a rightward shift in the demand curve (implying that people are willing to buy larger quantities of the good at each price), and Exhibit 3–3b illustrates a leftward shift in the demand curve (implying that people are willing to buy smaller quantities of the good at each price).

Normal Good
A good the demand for which rises (falls) as income rises (falls).

Inferior Good
A good the demand for which falls (rises) as income rises (falls).

Preferences. Peoples' preferences affect the amount of a good they are willing to buy at a particular price. A change in preferences in favor of a good shifts the demand curve rightward. A change in preferences away from the good shifts the demand curve leftward. For example, if people begin to favor spy novels to a greater degree than previously, the demand for spy novels increases, and the demand curve shifts rightward.

Prices of Related Goods. There are two types of related goods: **substitutes** and **complements.** Two goods are substitutes if they satisfy similar needs or desires. With substitutes, the demand for one rises as the price of the other rises, and the demand for one falls as the price of the other falls. For example, for many people Coca-Cola is a substitute for Pepsi-Cola; thus, higher Coca-Cola prices will increase the demand for Pepsi-Cola as people substitute Pepsi for the higher priced Coke (Exhibit 3–4a). Other examples of substitutes include coffee and tea, corn chips and potato chips, two brands of margarine, and foreign and domestic cars.

Two goods are complements if they are consumed jointly. For example, tennis rackets and tennis balls are used together to play tennis. With complements, the demand for one rises when the price of the other falls and the demand for one falls as the price of the other rises. For example, as the price of tennis rackets rises, the demand for tennis balls falls, as Exhibit 3–4b shows. Other examples of complements include cars and tires, shirts and trousers, lightbulbs and lamps, and golf clubs and golf balls.

Number of Buyers. The demand for a good in a particular area is related to the number of buyers in the market area. The more buyers, the higher the demand; the

> **Substitutes**
> Two goods that satisfy similar needs or desires. With substitutes, the demand for one rises as the price of the other rises (or the demand for one falls as the price of the other falls).
>
> **Complements**
> Two goods that are used jointly in consumption. With complements, the demand for one rises as the price of the other falls (or the demand for one falls as the price of the other rises).

EXHIBIT 3–3
Shifts in the Demand Curve

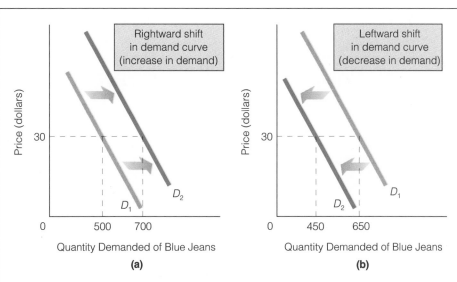

(a) The demand curve shifts rightward from D_1 to D_2. This represents an increase in demand for blue jeans: At each price the quantity demanded of blue jeans is greater than before. For example, 700 units instead of 500 is the quantity demanded at $30. (b) The demand curve shifts leftward from D_1 to D_2. This represents a decrease in demand for blue jeans: At each price the quantity demanded of blue jeans is less. For example, 450 units instead of 650 is the quantity demanded at $30.

EXHIBIT 3–4
Substitutes and Complements

If Coca-Cola and Pepsi-Cola are substitutes, a higher price for Coca-Cola leads to . . .

SUBSTITUTES

. . . a rightward shift in the demand curve for Pepsi-Cola.

(a)

(a) Coca-Cola and Pepsi-Cola are substitutes: The price of one and the demand for the other are directly related.

If tennis rackets and tennis balls are complements, a higher price for tennis rackets leads to . . .

COMPLEMENTS

. . . a leftward shift in the demand curve for tennis balls.

(b)

(b) Tennis rackets and tennis balls are complements: The price of one and the demand for the other are inversely related.

fewer buyers, the lower the demand. The number of buyers may increase owing to a higher birthrate, increased immigration, the migration of people from one region of the country to another, and so on. The number of buyers may decrease owing to a higher deathrate, war, the migration of people from one region of the country to another, and so on.

Expectations of Future Price. Buyers who expect the price of cars to be higher next month may buy cars now, increasing the current demand for cars. Buyers who expect the price of cars to be lower next month may put off buying cars now, decreasing the current demand for cars and increasing the future demand for cars.

A Change in Quantity Demanded versus a Change in Demand

A *change in demand* refers to a shift in the demand curve, as illustrated in Exhibit 3–5a. For example, saying that the demand for apples has increased is the same as saying that the demand curve for apples has shifted rightward. As we have seen, the factors that can change demand (shift the demand curve) include income, preferences, prices of related goods, number of buyers, and expectations of (future) price.

A *change in quantity demanded* refers to a movement along a demand curve as in Exhibit 3–5b. What can cause a change in the quantity demanded of a good? A change in the price of the good, or (its) **own price.** For example, a change in the price of computers brings about a change in the quantity demanded of computers.

It is important to distinguish between a *change in demand* (shift in the demand curve) and a *change in quantity demanded* (movement along a demand curve), as the following exercise illustrates.[2]

[2]Note to students: Economics professors are sticklers when it comes to your knowing the difference between a change in demand and a change in quantity demanded. Consequently, you can expect a question or two that relate to the difference on the next test. A typical true-or-false question might be, "A rise in the price of oranges will lead to a fall in the demand for oranges, *ceteris paribus.*" The correct answer is False. A rise in the price of oranges will lead to a fall in the *quantity demanded* of oranges, *ceteris paribus.* Remember, own price directly changes quantity demanded.

A change in demand refers to a shift in the demand curve; a change in quantity demanded refers to a movement along a demand curve.

Own Price
The price of a good. For example, if the price of oranges is $1, this is (its) own price.

EXHIBIT 3–5
A Change in Demand versus a Change in Quantity Demand

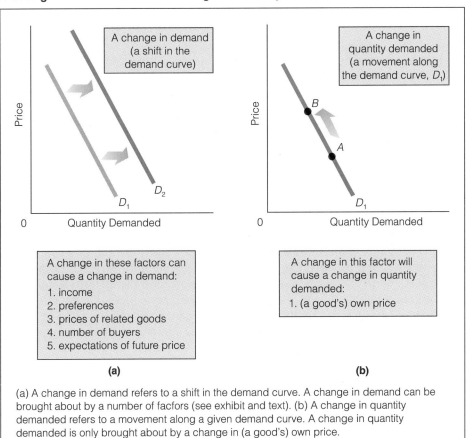

(a) A change in demand refers to a shift in the demand curve. A change in demand can be brought about by a number of factors (see exhibit and text). (b) A change in quantity demanded refers to a movement along a given demand curve. A change in quantity demanded is only brought about by a change in (a good's) own price.

An Exercise: Learning to Keep the Law of Demand Straight

Your friend says, "I've noticed that the price of dining out at restaurants has gone up. I've also noticed that more people are dining out at restaurants. But the law of demand predicts the opposite. It holds that if the price of a good rises, less of that good will be consumed. Obviously, the law of demand must be wrong."

Suppose we accept as truth that the price of dining out at restaurants has gone up and that more people are eating out at restaurants. Does it follow that the law of demand does not hold? Not at all. The inverse relationship between price and quantity demanded holds if *all other things are held constant.* What your friend has observed is a case where all other things were not constant.

To illustrate, consider Exhibit 3–6a. Your friend may initially have observed two points, *A* and *B*, where *B* represents a higher price and a greater consumption of meals than *A*. From this he concluded that people buy more restaurant meals at higher prices than lower prices. In short, your friend sees the demand curve as upward sloping as in Exhibit 3–6b.

But the important point is that the 14 million meals consumed at point *B* is *not the result of a higher price but the result of a higher demand curve,* as in Exhibit 3–6c. In short, the consumption of meals has increased from 10 million to 14 million because the demand curve has shifted rightward from D_1 to D_2 (owing perhaps to a rise in incomes or a change in preferences), not because price has increased from \$10 to \$15 (as your friend mistakenly thought was the case).

SUPPLY

■

We turn now to the other side of the market: supply. Using a format similar to our discussion of demand, we first define the law of supply, then discuss the factors that can cause the supply curve to shift. Finally, we distinguish between a change in quantity supplied and a change in supply.

What Is Supply?

Supply
The willingness and ability of sellers to produce and offer to sell different quantities of a good at different prices during a specific time period.

The word **supply** has a specific meaning in economics. It refers to (1) the willingness and ability of sellers to produce and offer to sell different quantities of a good (2) at different prices (3) during a specific time period (per day, week, and so on).

The Law of Supply

Law of Supply
As the price of a good rises, the quantity supplied of the good rises, and as the price of a good falls, the quantity supplied of the good falls, *ceteris paribus.*

The **law of supply** states that *as the price of a good rises, the quantity supplied of the good rises, and as the price of a good falls, the quantity supplied of the good falls, ceteris paribus.* Simply put, the price of a good and the quantity supplied of the good are directly related, *ceteris paribus.*[3] (*Quantity supplied* is the number of units of a good sellers are willing and able to produce and offer to sell at a particular price.) The *upward-sloping* **supply curve** is the graphical representation of the law of supply (Exhibit 3–7).

(Upward-sloping) Supply Curve
The graphical representation of the law of supply.

The law of supply can be summarized as

$$P\uparrow \qquad Q_s\uparrow$$
$$P\downarrow \qquad Q_s\downarrow \qquad \textit{ceteris paribus}$$

where P = price and Q_s = quantity supplied.

[3]The law of supply, like the law of demand, holds for services as well as goods.

EXHIBIT 3–6
Keeping the Law of Demand Straight

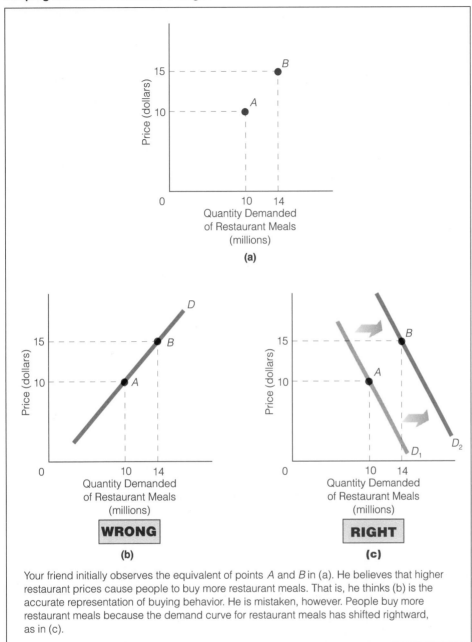

(a)

(b) **WRONG**

(c) **RIGHT**

Your friend initially observes the equivalent of points *A* and *B* in (a). He believes that higher restaurant prices cause people to buy more restaurant meals. That is, he thinks (b) is the accurate representation of buying behavior. He is mistaken, however. People buy more restaurant meals because the demand curve for restaurant meals has shifted rightward, as in (c).

The law of supply holds for the production of most goods. It does not hold when there is *no time to produce more units of a good.* For example, a theater in Atlanta is sold out for tonight's play. Even if ticket prices were to increase from $30 to $40, there would be no additional seats in the theater. There is no time to produce more seats. The supply curve for theater seats is illustrated in Exhibit 3–8a. It is fixed at the number of seats in the theater, 500.[4]

[4]The vertical supply curve is said to be *perfectly inelastic.*

EXHIBIT 3–7
A Supply Curve

The upward-sloping supply curve is the graphical representation of the law of supply, which holds that price and quantity supplied are directly related *ceteris paribus*. On a supply curve the price (in dollars) represents price per unit of the good; and the quantity supplied, on the horizontal axis, is always relevant for a specific time period (a week, a month, and so on).

The law of supply also does not hold *for goods that cannot be produced over any period of time.* For example, since the violin maker Antonio Stradivari died in 1737, a rise in the price of Stradivarius violins does not affect the number of Stradivarius violins supplied, as Exhibit 3–8b illustrates.

Question:

The law of supply holds that price and quantity supplied are directly related. The upward-sloping supply curve is the graphical representation of this law. But then, what do the vertical supply curves in panels (a) and (b) of Exhibit 3–8 represent? It can't be the law of supply.

EXHIBIT 3–8
Supply Curves When There Is No Time to Produce More or No More Can Be Produced

The supply curve is not upward sloping when there is no time to produce additional units or when additional units cannot be produced. In those cases, the supply curve is vertical.

Answer:

They represent an independent relationship between price and quantity supplied.

Why Most Supply Curves Are Upward Sloping

Most supply curves are upward sloping. The fundamental reason for this involves the *law of diminishing marginal returns,* which we discuss at length in Chapter 23. Here, it suffices to say that an upward-sloping supply curve reflects the fact that, under certain conditions, a higher price is an incentive to producers to produce more of a good. This incentive comes in the form of higher profits. For example, if the price of computers rises, and all other things (for example, per-unit costs) are held constant, computer companies will earn higher profits per computer, which encourages them to increase the quantity of computers they supply to the market.

Generally, though, producing more of good does not come with constant per-unit costs. As we learned in Chapter 2, the law of increasing costs is usually operable. The law states that increased production of a good comes at increased opportunity costs. Thus, an upward-sloping supply curve reflects the fact that per-unit production costs rise when more units of a good are produced, so a higher price is necessary to elicit more output.

The Market Supply Curve

An *individual supply curve* represents the price–quantity combinations for a single seller. The *market supply curve* represents the price–quantity combinations for all sellers of a particular good. In Exhibit 3–9, we have derived a market supply curve by "summing up" the individual supply curves. In (a) a **supply schedule,** the numerical tabulation of the quantity supplied of a good at different prices, is given for Brown, Alberts, and "all other suppliers." The market supply schedule is then obtained by adding up the quantity supplied by each party at each price, *ceteris paribus.* In (b), the data points are plotted, giving us a market supply curve.

Supply Schedule
The numerical tabulation of the quantity supplied of a good at different prices.

Factors That Can Cause the Supply Curve to Shift

The supply curve in Exhibit 3–7 is based on the condition that all other things are held constant. But what if any of these other things change? Obviously, the supply curve will shift rightward or leftward, as in Exhibit 3–10. Here we discuss what these other things are and how changes in them can affect (shift) the supply curve.

Prices of Relevant Resources. Resources are necessary to produce goods. For example, wood is necessary to produce doors. If the price of wood falls, the supply curve of doors shifts rightward; if the price of wood rises, the supply curve of wood shifts leftward. Another example: Farmland, fertilizer, and tractors are necessary to produce corn. A fall in the price of one of these resources decreases the per-unit cost of producing corn, and therefore increases the quantity of corn that farmers will be willing and able to sell at each price; it shifts the supply curve of corn rightward. A rise in the price of one of these resources increases the per unit cost of producing corn and shifts the supply curve leftward.

Technology. In Chapter 2, we defined *technology* as the body of skills and knowledge relevant to the use of inputs or resources in production. We also said that an advance in technology refers to the ability to generate more output with a fixed amount of resources, thus reducing per-unit production costs. If this occurs, the quantity supplied of a good at each price increases. Why? The reason is that lower costs increase profitability and therefore provide producers with an incentive to produce more. For example, if corn growers develop a way to grow more corn using the same amount of water and other resources, it follows that per-unit production costs fall, profitability increases, and growers will want to grow and sell more corn at each price. The supply curve of corn shifts rightward.

Number of Sellers. If more sellers begin producing a particular good, perhaps because of high profits, the supply curve shifts rightward. If some sellers stop producing a particular good, perhaps because of losses, the supply curve shifts leftward.

EXHIBIT 3–9
Deriving a Market Supply Schedule and Market Supply Curve

(a) The market supply schedule is derived by adding up the quantity supplied by each party at each price. (b) The data points are plotted, giving us a market supply curve. Only two points on the market supply curve are noted.

PRICE	Quantity Supplied			
	BROWN	ALBERTS	OTHER SUPPLIERS	ALL SUPPLIERS
$10	1	2	96	99
11	2	3	98	103
12	3	4	102	109
13	4	5	106	115
14	5	6	108	119
15	6	7	110	123

(a)

(b)

EXHIBIT 3–10
Shifts in the Supply Curve

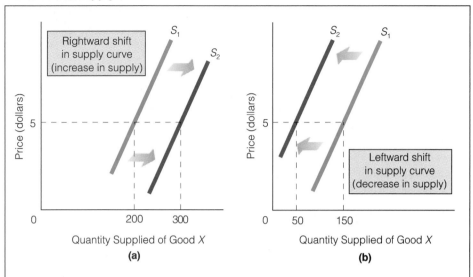

(a) The supply curve shifts rightward from S_1 to S_2. This represents an increase in the supply of good X: At each price the quantity supplied of good X is greater. For example, 300 units instead of 200 is the quantity supplied at $5. (b) The supply curve shifts leftward from S_1 to S_2. This represents a decrease in the supply of good X: At each price the quantity supplied of good X is less. For example, 50 units instead of 150 is the quantity supplied at $5.

Expectations of Future Price. If the price of a good is expected to be higher in the future, producers may hold back some of the product today (if possible—for example, perishables cannot be held back) to have more to sell at the higher future price. Therefore, the current supply curve shifts leftward. For example, if oil producers expect the price of oil to be higher next year, some may hold oil off the market this year to be able to sell it next year. Similarly, if they expect the price of oil to be lower next year, they might pump more oil this year than previously planned.

Taxes and Subsidies. Some taxes increase per-unit costs. Suppose a shoe manufacturer must pay a $2 tax per pair of shoes produced. This would lead to a leftward shift in the supply curve, indicating that the manufacturer would want to produce and offer to sell fewer pairs of shoes at each price. If the tax is eliminated, the supply curve would shift rightward.

Subsidies have the opposite effect. Suppose the government subsidizes the production of corn. It promises to pay corn farmers $2 for every bushel of corn they produce. Because of the subsidy, the quantity supplied of corn is greater at each price, and the supply curve of corn shifts rightward. Removal of the subsidy shifts the supply curve of corn leftward. A rough rule of thumb is that we get more of what we subsidize and less of what we tax.

Government Restrictions. Sometimes government acts to reduce supply. Consider a U.S. import quota on Japanese television sets. An import quota, or quantitative restriction on foreign goods, reduces the supply of Japanese television sets. It shifts the supply curve leftward. The elimination of the import quota allows the supply of Japanese television sets in the United States to shift rightward.

Licensure has a similar effect. With licensure, individuals must meet certain requirements before they can legally carry out a task. For example, owner-operators of day-care centers must meet certain requirements before they are allowed to sell their services. No doubt this reduces the number of day-care centers and shifts the supply curve of day-care centers leftward.

A Change in Supply versus a Change in Quantity Supplied

A *change in supply* refers to a shift in the supply curve, as illustrated in Exhibit 3–11a. For example, saying that the supply of oranges has increased is the same as saying that the supply curve for oranges has shifted rightward. As we discussed earlier, the factors that can change supply (shift the supply curve) include prices of relevant resources, technology, number of sellers, expectations of future price, taxes and subsidies, and government restrictions.

A *change in quantity supplied* refers to a movement along a supply curve as in Exhibit 3–11b. What can cause a change in the quantity supplied of a good? The answer is a change in the price of the good, or own price.

EXHIBIT 3–11
A Change in Supply versus a Change in Quantity Supplied

(a) A change in supply refers to a shift in the supply curve. A change in supply can be brought about by a number of facfors (see exhibit and text). (b) A change in quantity supplied refers to a movement along a given supply curve. A change in quantity supplied is only brought about by a change in (a good's) own price.

THE MARKET: PUTTING SUPPLY AND DEMAND TOGETHER

The English economist Alfred Marshall (1842–1924) compared supply and demand to the two blades of a pair of scissors. It is impossible to say which blade does the actual cutting. In the same way, it is impossible to say whether demand or supply is responsible for the market price we observe: Price is determined by both sides of the market.

Supply and Demand at Work at an Auction

Think of yourself at an auction where bushels of corn are bought and sold. In this auction, the auctioneer will adjust the corn price to sell all the corn offered for sale. The supply curve of corn is vertical as is Exhibit 3–12. It cuts the horizontal axis at 40,000 bushels; that is, quantity supplied is 40,000 bushels. The demand curve for corn is downward sloping. Furthermore, suppose each potential buyer of corn is sitting in front of a computer that registers the number of bushels he or she wants to buy. For example, if Nancy Bernstein wants to buy 5,000 bushels of corn, she simply types the number "5,000" into her computer.

The auction begins. (Follow along in Exhibit 3–12 as we relay to you what is happening at the auction.) The auctioneer calls out the price:

$6.00. The potential buyers think for a second, and then each registers the number of bushels he or she wants to buy at that price. The total is 10,000 bushels, which is the quantity demanded of corn at $6.00. The auctioneer, realizing that 30,000 bushels of corn (40,000 − 10,000 = 30,000) will go unsold at this price, decides to lower the price per bushel to:

$5.00. The quantity demanded increases to 20,000 bushels, but still the quantity supplied of corn at this price is greater than the quantity demanded. The auctioneer calls out:

EXHIBIT 3–12
Supply and Demand at Work at an Auction

Q_d = quantity demanded; Q_s = quantity supplied. The auctioneer calls out different prices, and buyers record how much they are willing to buy. At prices $6.00, $5.00, and $4.00, quantity supplied is greater than quantity demanded. At prices $1.25 and $2.25, quantity demanded is greater than quantity supplied. At $3.10, quantity demanded equals quantity supplied.

■ $4.00. The quantity demand increases to 30,000 bushels, but the quantity supplied at $4.00 is greater than the quantity demanded. The auctioneer drops the price down to:

■ $1.25. At this price, the quantity demanded jumps to 60,000 bushels and is greater than quantity supplied by 20,000 bushels. The auctioneer calls out a higher price:

■ $2.25. The quantity demanded drops to 50,000 bushels, but still buyers want to buy more corn at this price than there is corn to be sold. The auctioneer calls out:

■ $3.10. At this price, the quantity demanded of corn is 40,000 bushels, and the quantity supplied of corn is 40,000 bushels. The auction stops. The 40,000 bushels of corn are bought and sold at $3.10 per bushel.

Learning the Language of Supply and Demand: A Few Important Terms

If quantity supplied is greater than quantity demanded, a **surplus** or **excess supply** exists. If quantity demanded is greater than quantity supplied, a **shortage** or **excess demand** exists. In Exhibit 3–12, a surplus exists at $6.00, $5.00, and $4.00. A shortage exists at $1.25 and $2.25. The price at which quantity demanded equals quantity supplied is the **equilibrium price** or **market-clearing price.** In our example, $3.10 is the equilibrium price. The quantity that corresponds to the equilibrium price is the **equilibrium quantity.** In our example, it is 40,000 bushels of corn. Any price at which quantity demanded is not equal to quantity supplied is a **disequilibrium price.** A market that exhibits either a surplus ($Q_s > Q_d$) or a shortage ($Q_d > Q_s$) is said to be in **disequilibrium.** A market in which quantity demanded equals quantity supplied ($Q_d = Q_s$) is said to be in **equilibrium.** *Equilibrium* is identified by the letter *"E"* in Exhibit 3–12.

Question:

Some people use the words shortage *and* scarcity *as synonyms. Do they refer to the same thing?*

Answer:

No. Scarcity is the condition where wants are greater than the resources available to satisfy those wants. Shortage is the condition where quantity demanded is greater than quantity supplied. A shortage occurs at *some* prices: specifically, at any disequilibrium price that is *below* equilibrium price (for example, $2.25 in Exhibit 3–12). Scarcity occurs at *all* prices. Even at equilibrium price ($3.10 in Exhibit 3–12), where quantity demanded equals quantity supplied, scarcity exists.

Moving to Equilibrium: What Happens to Price When There Is a Surplus or a Shortage?

What did the auctioneer do when the price was $6.00 and there was a surplus of corn? He lowered the price. What did the auctioneer do when the price was $2.25 and there was a shortage of corn? He raised the price. The behavior of the auctioneer can be summarized this way: If a surplus exists, lower price; if a shortage exists, raise price. This is how the auctioneer moved the corn market into equilibrium.

Surplus (Excess Supply)
A condition in which quantity supplied is greater than quantity demanded. Surpluses only occur at prices above equilibrium price.

Shortage (Excess Demand)
A condition in which quantity demanded is greater than quantity supplied. Shortages only occur at prices below equilibrium price.

Equilibrium Price (Market-clearing Price)
The price at which quantity demanded of the good equals quantity supplied.

Equilibrium Quantity
The quantity that corresponds to equilibrium price. The quantity at which the amount of the good buyers are willing and able to buy equals the amount sellers are willing and able to sell, and both equal the amount actually bought and sold.

Disequilibrium Price
A price other than equilibrium price. A price at which quantity demanded does not equal quantity supplied.

Disequilibrium
A state of either surplus or shortage in a market.

Equilibrium
Equilibrium means "at rest." Equilibrium is the price–quantity combination in a market from which there is no tendency for buyers or sellers to move away. Graphically, equilibrium is the intersection point of the supply and demand curves.

Not all markets have auctioneers. (When was the last time you saw an auctioneer in the grocery store?) But many markets act *as if* an auctioneer were calling out higher and lower prices until equilibrium price is reached. In many real-world auctioneerless markets, prices fall when there is a surplus and rise when there is a shortage. Why?

Why Does Price Fall When There Is A Surplus? With a surplus, suppliers will not be able to sell all they had hoped to sell at a particular price. As a result, their inventories grow beyond the level they hold in preparation for demand changes. Sellers will want to reduce their inventories. Some will lower prices to do so; some will cut back on production; others will do a little of both. As we show in Exhibit 3–13, there is a tendency for price and output to fall until equilibrium is achieved.

Why Does Price Rise When There Is A Shortage? With a shortage, buyers will not be able to buy all they had hoped to buy. Some buyers will bid up the price to get sellers to sell to them instead of to other buyers. Some sellers, seeing buyers clamor for the goods, will realize that they can raise the price on the goods they have for sale. Higher prices will also call forth added output. Thus, there is a tendency for price and output to rise until equilibrium is achieved (see Exhibit 3–13).

Not all markets have auctioneers, but many markets act as if an auctioneer were calling out higher and lower prices until equilibrium price is reached.

EXHIBIT 3–13
Moving to Equilibrium

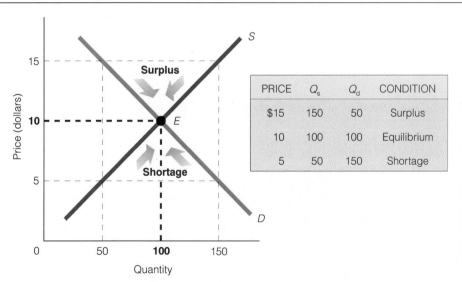

PRICE	Q_s	Q_d	CONDITION
$15	150	50	Surplus
10	100	100	Equilibrium
5	50	150	Shortage

If there is a surplus, sellers' inventories rise above the level they hold in preparation for demand changes. Sellers will want to reduce their inventories. As a result, price and output fall until equilibrium is achieved. If there is a shortage, some buyers will bid up price to get sellers to sell to them instead of to other buyers. Some sellers will realize they can raise the price on the goods they have for sale. Higher prices will call forth added output. Price and output rise until equilibrium is achieved. (Note: Recall that price, on the vertical axis, is price per unit of the good; and quantity, on the horizontal axis, is for a specific time period. In this text we do not specify this on the axes themselves, but consider it to be understood.)

Moving to Equilibrium: Maximum and Minimum Prices

Our discussion of surpluses and shortages has illustrated how a market moves to equilibrium, but there is another way to show this. Exhibit 3–14 depicts the market for good *X*. Look at the first unit of good *X*. What is the *maximum price buyers would be willing and able to pay for it?* The answer is $7. This can be seen by following the dotted line up from the first unit of the good to the demand curve.

What is the *minimum price sellers need to receive before they would be willing and able to produce and offer to sell* this unit of good *X*? It is $1. This can be seen by following the dotted line up from the first unit to the supply curve. Since the maximum price buyers are willing and able to pay is greater than the minimum price sellers need to receive, we can be sure that the first unit of good *X* will be exchanged.

What happens to the second unit? Here the maximum price buyers are willing and able to pay is $6, and the minimum price sellers need to receive is $2. We can be sure that the second unit of good *X* will be exchanged. In fact, we can be sure exchange will occur as long as the maximum price buyers are willing and able to pay is greater than the minimum price sellers need to receive. The exhibit shows that a total of four units of good *X* will be exchanged. The fifth unit will not be exchanged because the maximum price buyers are willing and able to pay ($3) is less than the minimum price suppliers need to receive ($5).

In the process just described, buyers and sellers exchange money for goods as long as both benefit from the exchange. The market converges on a quantity of 4 units of good *X* and a $4 price per unit. This is equilibrium. This way of explaining the movement to equilibrium illustrates two points that were hidden from view when we discussed it in term of surpluses and shortages: (1) *At equilibrium, all the mutually beneficial gains from the exchange have been obtained.* (2) *At equilibrium price, maximum price (for the buyer) and minimum price (for the seller) are the same.*

EXHIBIT 3–14
Moving to Equilibrium in Terms of Maximum and Minimum Prices

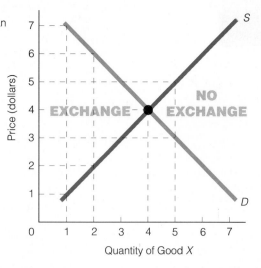

As long as the maximum price buyers are willing and able to pay is greater than the minimum price suppliers need to receive, an exchange will occur. This condition is met for units 1–4. The market converges on equilibrium through a process of making mutually beneficial exchanges.

Interview: Vernon Smith

On the blackboard, the economics instructor draws a downward-sloping demand curve. She then draws an upward-sloping supply curve. A small dot is placed at the intersection of the two curves. "This is the equilibrium point," the instructor says. The instructor then identifies equilibrium price—the price at which quantity demanded equals quantity supplied. "This is how many markets work," the instructor comments. "Supply and demand determine price." But is this right? Do supply and demand determine price? They do on the blackboard, but do they in real life, too?

Some economists have begun to study economic behavior and test economic theories under *laboratory conditions.* This new area of research is called *experimental economics.* One of the pioneers in this area is Vernon L. Smith. Professor Smith is at the University of Arizona, Tucson.

What is experimental economics?

There are two kinds of experiments in economics: field and laboratory experiments. In field experiments the investigator seeks to measure the demand, supply or incentive response of subjects in a particular institutional setting in the economy. For example, proposals to introduce peak load pricing rules into the pricing of electric power, or to modify welfare or unemployment insurance programs to include incentive payments for seeking employment, have been evaluated by comparing the responses of samples of households with and without the proposed incentives.

Laboratory experiments are used to study the performance of markets using reward motivated subjects under controlled laboratory conditions. Every laboratory experiment has three elements.

(1) A value/cost *environment.* Thus buyers are assigned redemption values, and sellers costs, for units of an abstract commodity to be exchanged. This environment defines the conditions of demand and supply in a competitive market experiment or the market structure of an oligopoly experiment. Buyers are paid in cash the difference between the assigned (demand) values and the prices at which they buy; sellers receive the difference between selling price and assigned unit costs. Thus, buyers are motivated to buy as cheaply as they can, and sellers to sell as high as they can. This control over the supply/demand environment distinguishes the laboratory from the field experiment.

(2) An *institution,* defining the rules of communication or message transfer among market participants. It is these rules that determine the incentives and strategies of market participants. For example, in a progressive auction buyers announce bids in sequence until there is only one outstanding bid, which is declared the winner. In a stock exchange buyers freely announce bids to buy, sellers announce offers to sell, and contracts for exchange occur whenever a bid or an offer is accepted. In retail markets, sellers post take-it-or-leave-it price offers, and buyers accept or reject units at these prices.

(3) The *behavior* of the participants. Elements (1) and (2) are controlled by the experimenter, who then observes (3).

Among the many objectives of an experiment are to use observations for the following. (a) Test a received theory. (b) Discriminate among theories. (c) Evaluate policy proposals. (d) Compare environments. (e) Compare institutions. (f) Evaluate new institutional designs using the laboratory as a testbed.

In your experiments, have you found that supply and demand forces work like economists say they work?

Generally, yes. But there are many features of these forces that are not adequately addressed in traditional theory. For example, there are variations in the speed of a market's response to these forces depending upon the trading institutions: posted price and sealed-bid auction markets do not respond as quickly as the open outcry double (two-sided) auction used in commodity and stock exchanges. In the case of the double auction institution the forces of supply and demand actually work *better* than economists have said they do. Thus convergence to the supply and demand equilibrium occurs quickly even when numbers are very small—2 to 4 buyers and as many sellers are usually sufficient to guarantee the predicted supply and demand equilibrium. If anything, traditional economics has underestimated the power of supply and demand under some institutional implementations.

What are a few of the questions you have answered using experimental methods?

(1) A key contestable market hypothesis: If entry and exit are free will competitive pricing result even where costs show increasing returns to scale and the industry can support only one firm? In research conducted by R. Mark Issac (University of Arizona) and myself we have experimental results that are consistent with this hypothesis.

(2) Do laboratory stock markets support the hypothesis that asset market prices reflect the underlying fundamental value of the asset; that is, are expectations rational in such markets? Work with a number of coauthors using software developed by Arlington Williams (Indiana University) provides only weak support for this hypothesis. In asset markets current demand depends strongly on the expectations of the participants. If the participants have bullish expectations that prices will rise yielding capital gains, this fact alone can cause rising prices (expectations are self-fulfilling). In experimental markets with fundamental value known by all trades (the dividend structure is common information), we observe large departures of asset prices from asset value (price booms, followed by crashes), but this discrepancy is reduced when the same subjects return for a second experiment, and is largely eliminated when they return for a third. Eventually, in a stationary environment, subjects come to have common rational expectations by learning that sustainable profits cannot be made at prices that depart from fundamental value.

(3) Do market regulations or restraints sometimes perversely affect the competitive performance of markets? Yes. For example in pioneering work by R. Mark Issac and Charles Plott (Cal Tech) it has been shown that price ceilings, even when they are not binding (are above

the equilibrium supply and demand price) tend to depress prices in double auction markets. This is because the price controls interfere with the institutional dynamics of trade by restricting the strategies of sellers more severely than buyers. Consequently, convergence is slower and more erratic than in unrestrained markets. In collaboration with Don Coursey (Washington University, St. Louis) we have found that these results extend to posted price markets.

What questions are you currently trying to answer?

(1) Can some of the discrepancies between the predictions of standard theory and experimental observations be explained or modelled by introducing decision cost; that is, by hypothesizing that there is an effort cost (of thinking, analyzing and deciding) to be weighed against value in choosing a best response?

(2) Are subjects more likely to engage in self-interested behavior at the expense of an opponent, when they feel that any advantage they enjoy has been earned, and is therefore justified? This question is central to the role of "property rights" in markets. The pioneers in this research were Elizabeth Hoffman (University of Arizona) and Matthew Spitzer (USC).

(3) How can the computer make possible new forms of exchange? With my colleague, Stephen Rassenti, and Kevin McCabe (University of Minnesota) we are studying new "smart" computer assisted market institutions. In these institutions a computer helps coordinate technologically interdependent markets by applying algorithms for maximizing the gains from exchange to the bids and offers of decentralized agents. For example, we are applying such computerized trading institutions to pricing and allocation among producers, wholesalers and transporters in complex natural gas pipeline networks. This market

combines the information advantages of decentralized ownership with the coordination advantages of central (computerized) pricing.

Have you ever been surprised by one of your research findings?

Many times. My education left me completely unprepared for the discovery that quite small numbers can yield competitive equilibrium outcomes under double auction trading rules. The finding that price controls affect market dynamics, even though they are non-binding at the static equilibrium was a surprise; although a study of experimental data has made it entirely understandable. I was also surprised to find it so easy to observe stock market price bubbles in the laboratory.

What impact has experimental economics had on the economics profession? Do you think a larger percentage of the profession will be experimental economists in the next two decades?

I first began doing experiments, as classroom exercises, at Purdue University, in early 1956. At about this same time Reinhard Seltan ran some oligopoly experiments in Germany. But the output of research papers was modest until about the mid-1970s when Charles Plott and I, and soon many others, became much more active in experimentation. Interest and research accelerated greatly in the 1980s. The University of Arizona has had a computerized laboratory for experimental economics since 1976, but there are now many more laboratories: Cal Tech, Texas A&M, Indiana University, University of Houston, University of Pittsburgh, Virginia Commonwealth University, Carnegie-Mellon University, University of Michigan, University of Iowa, New York University, University of Colorado, in German and British universities, and others in the making. This growth in experimental economics laboratories suggests a larger percentage of economists may be experimentalists in the next two decades. Professional and foundation support has been excellent.

What got you interested in economics?

My father's influence (he was a tool and die maker) started me in science and engineering at Cal Tech, but my mother, who was active in socialist politics, probably accounts for the great interest I found in economics when I took my first introductory course. Although I completed my BS degree at Cal Tech, I went on to graduate study in economics at the University of Kansas and Harvard. But it was my experimental subjects who taught me that markets work, under weaker conditions than were traditionally thought to be necessary, and are much more trustworthy in promoting efficient allocations than are the central planning and regulation systems of government. But government is important in defining and enforcing property rights and fostering free institutions of exchange.

Changes in Equilibrium Price and Quantity

Equilibrium price and quantity are determined by supply and demand. Anytime either demand or supply changes or both change, equilibrium price and quantity change. Exhibit 3–15 illustrates 14 different cases where this occurs. Cases (a)–(d) illustrate the four basic changes in supply and demand, where either supply *or* demand changes. Cases (e)–(n) are combinations of (a)–(d), where both supply *and* demand change.

- (a) Demand rises (the demand curve shifts rightward), and supply is constant (the supply curve does not move). Equilibrium price rises, equilibrium quantity rises, too.
- (b) Demand falls, supply is constant. Equilibrium price falls, equilibrium quantity falls.
- (c) Supply rises, demand is constant. Equilibrium price falls, equilibrium quantity rises.
- (d) Supply falls, demand is constant. Equilibrium price rises, equilibrium quantity falls.
- (e) Demand rises and supply falls by an equal amount. Equilibrium price rises, equilibrium quantity is constant.
- (f) Demand falls and supply rises by an equal amount. Equilibrium price falls, equilibrium quantity is constant.
- (g) Demand rises by a greater amount than supply falls. Equilibrium price and quantity rise.
- (h) Demand rises by a lesser amount than supply falls. Equilibrium price rises, equilibrium quantity falls.
- (i) Demand falls by a greater amount than supply rises. Equilibrium price and quantity fall.
- (j) Demand falls by a lesser amount than supply rises. Equilibrium price falls, equilibrium quantity rises.
- (k) Demand rises by a greater amount than supply rises. Equilibrium price and quantity rise.
- (l) Demand rises by a lesser amount than supply rises. Equilibrium price falls, equilibrium quantity rises.
- (m) Demand falls by a greater amount than supply falls. Equilibrium price and quantity fall.
- (n) Demand falls by a lesser amount than supply falls. Equilibrium price rises, equilibrium quantity falls.

EXHIBIT 3–15
Equilibrium Price and Quantity Effects of Supply-Curve and Demand-Curve Shifts

The exhibit illustrates the effects on equilibrium price and quantity of a change in demand, a change in supply, or a change in both. Below each diagram the condition leading to the effects are noted, using the following symbols: (1) a bar over a letter means *constant* (thus, $\bar{S}$ means that supply is constant);

(2) a downward-pointing arrow ($\downarrow$) indicates a fall; (3) an upward-pointing arrow ($\uparrow$) indicates a rise. A rise (fall) in demand is the same as a rightward (leftward) shift in the demand curve. A rise (fall) in supply is the same as a rightward (leftward) shift in the supply curve.

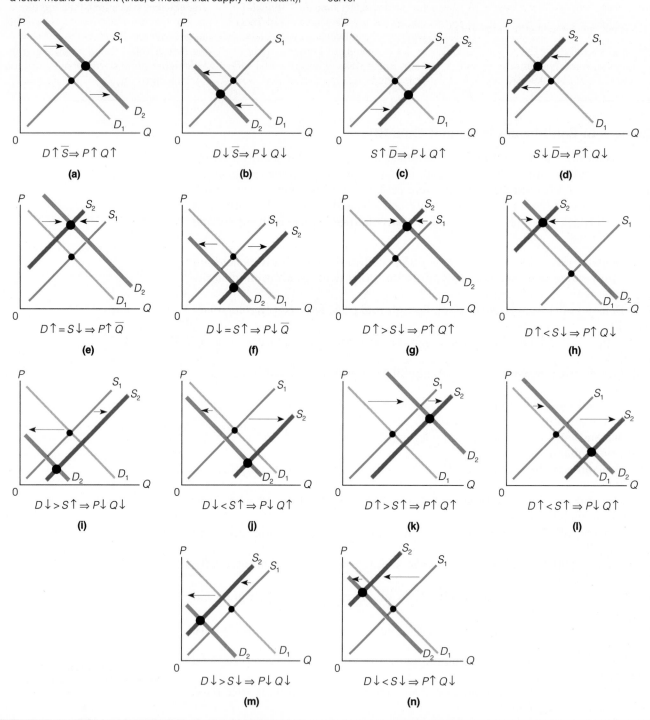

$D\uparrow \bar{S} \Rightarrow P\uparrow Q\uparrow$

(a)

$D\downarrow \bar{S} \Rightarrow P\downarrow Q\downarrow$

(b)

$S\uparrow \bar{D} \Rightarrow P\downarrow Q\uparrow$

(c)

$S\downarrow \bar{D} \Rightarrow P\uparrow Q\downarrow$

(d)

$D\uparrow = S\downarrow \Rightarrow P\uparrow \bar{Q}$

(e)

$D\downarrow = S\uparrow \Rightarrow P\downarrow \bar{Q}$

(f)

$D\uparrow > S\downarrow \Rightarrow P\uparrow Q\uparrow$

(g)

$D\uparrow < S\downarrow \Rightarrow P\uparrow Q\downarrow$

(h)

$D\downarrow > S\uparrow \Rightarrow P\downarrow Q\downarrow$

(i)

$D\downarrow < S\uparrow \Rightarrow P\downarrow Q\uparrow$

(j)

$D\uparrow > S\uparrow \Rightarrow P\uparrow Q\uparrow$

(k)

$D\uparrow < S\uparrow \Rightarrow P\downarrow Q\uparrow$

(l)

$D\downarrow > S\downarrow \Rightarrow P\downarrow Q\downarrow$

(m)

$D\downarrow < S\downarrow \Rightarrow P\uparrow Q\downarrow$

(n)

68

Absolute and Relative Prices

The **absolute price** of a good is its price in money terms. For example, the absolute price of a car might be $20,000. The **relative price** of a good is its price in terms of another good (not in terms of money). Suppose the absolute price of a car is $20,000 and the absolute price of a computer is $2,000. The relative price of the car (in terms of computers) is 10 computers. A person necessarily gives up the opportunity to buy 10 computers when he or she buys a car.

What happens to the relative price of a good as its absolute price increases (decreases) *ceteris paribus.* Suppose the absolute price of the car rises to $22,000. The relative price of the car rises to 11 computers. If the absolute price of the car falls to $18,000, the relative price of the car falls to 9 computers. We conclude that as the absolute price of a good rises, the relative price of the good rises; as the absolute price of a good falls, the relative price of a good falls, *ceteris paribus.* (If we had omitted *"ceteris paribus,"* the statement would not necessarily be true.)

Absolute Price
The price of a good in money terms.

Relative Price
The price of a good in terms of another good.

Question:

Is it possible for the absolute price of a good to rise while its relative price falls?

Answer:

Yes. Suppose there are two goods, houses and cars, whose absolute prices are $100,000 and $20,000, respectively. The relative price of 1 house is 5 cars. Now suppose the absolute price of houses rises to $120,000 and the absolute price of cars rises to $30,000. This is a 20 percent increase in the absolute price of houses and a 50 percent increase in the absolute price of cars. Now the relative price of a house is 4 cars. We conclude that even though the absolute price of houses has increased (from $100,000 to $120,000), its relative price has decreased (from 5 to 4 cars). This is because the absolute price of cars increased by a greater percentage than the absolute price of houses.

Using Relative Price to Think Like An Economist

Let us use relative price to think through a problem. Suppose that both high-quality and medium-quality apples are grown in the state of Washington. Their prices are 10 cents and 5 cents, respectively. The cost of transportation to New York City per apple, regardless of quality, is 5 cents. In New York City, a high-quality apple is 15 cents and a medium-quality apple is 10 cents. In which place, Washington or New York, would you predict that *relatively* more high-quality apples are consumed, *ceteris paribus?*

An economist would predict that relatively more high-quality apples would be consumed in the place where high-quality apples are relatively cheaper. And this is in New York.

The relative price of a high-quality apple in Washington is 2 medium-quality apples; the relative price of a high-quality apple in New York is 1.5 medium-quality apples. We show the simple arithmetic here.

Washington

1 high-quality apple = 10 cents
1 medium-quality apple = 5 cents
1 high-quality apple = 2 medium-quality apples

New York

1 high-quality apple = 15 cents
1 medium-quality apple = 10 cents
1 high-quality apple = 1.5 medium-quality apples

Question:

If the higher the price of a good, the lower the quantity demanded of that good, why do New Yorkers buy more high-quality apples than Washingtonians when New Yorkers pay 15 cents per high-quality apple and Washingtonians pay 10 cents per high-quality apple?

Answer:

We did not say that New Yorkers buy *more* high-quality apples than Washingtonians, but that New Yorkers buy *relatively more* high-quality apples than Washingtonians. There is a difference between *more* and *relatively more. More* indicates a larger absolute number; *relatively more* indicates a greater share of the total.

To illustrate, let's say that Washingtonians buy 10,000 high-quality apples and 30,000 medium-quality apples, and New Yorkers buy 5,000 high-quality apples and 7,500 medium-quality apples. Washingtonians buy *more* high-quality apples, but New Yorkers buy *relatively more* high-quality apples. Of all the apples New Yorkers buy, 40 percent are high-quality apples (5,000 is 40 percent of 12,500). Of all the apples Washingtonians buy, 25 percent are high-quality apples (10,000 is 25 percent of 40,000).

The apple example illustrates that relative price, *not* absolute price, is what matters in predicting consumer behavior. In fact, people only care about absolute price to the degree that it relates to relative price. For example, if Jackie's college tuition rises from $35 to $70 a credit, *ceteris paribus,* this means she *forfeits more of other things*—more movies on Friday, more dinners out, more new clothes—as a result, it is this forfeiture of other things that matters to Jackie; it is the relative price of her education that matters to her.

Demand

■ The law of demand states that as the price of a good rises, the quantity demanded of the good falls, and as the price of a good falls, the quantity demanded of the good rises, *ceteris paribus.* The law of demand holds that price and quantity demanded are inversely related.

■ Quantity demanded is the total number of units of a good that buyers are willing and able to buy at a particular price.

■ A (downward-sloping) demand curve is the graphical representation of the law of demand.

■ Factors that can shift the demand curve include income, preferences, prices of related goods (substitutes and complements), number of buyers, and expectations of future price.

■ A change in quantity demanded is directly brought about by a change in a good's own price.

Supply

■ The law of supply states that as the price of a good rises, the quantity supplied of the good rises, and as the price of a good falls, the quantity supplied of the good falls, *ceteris paribus.* The law of supply asserts that price and quantity supplied are directly related.

■ The law of supply does not hold when there is no time to produce more units of a good, or for goods that cannot be produced (over any period of time).

■ The upward-sloping supply curve is the graphical representation of the law of supply. More generally, a supply curve (no matter how it slopes) represents the relationship between price and quantity supplied.

■ Factors that can shift the supply curve include prices of relevant resources, technology, number of sellers, expectations of future price, taxes and subsidies, and government restrictions.

■ A change in quantity supplied is directly brought about by a change in a good's own price.

The Market

■ Both demand and supply establish equilibrium price and quantity.

■ A surplus exists in a market if, at some price, quantity supplied is greater than quantity demanded. A shortage exists if, at some price, quantity demanded is greater than quantity supplied.

Absolute and Relative Prices

■ The absolute price of a good is its price in money terms. The relative price of a good is its price in terms of another good.

■ As the absolute price of a good rises, its relative price may rise or fall. What happens depends on the percentage increase in the absolute price of other goods. For example, if the absolute price of apples rises by a greater percentage than the absolute price of oranges, the relative price of oranges falls, even though its absolute price has risen.

Key Terms and Concepts

Market	Complements	Equilibrium Price (Market-clearing Price)
Demand	Own Price	
Law of Demand	Supply	Equilibrium Quantity
Demand Schedule	Law of Supply	Disequilibrium Price
Demand Curve	Supply Curve	Disequilibrium
Normal Good	Supply Schedule	Equilibrium
Inferior Good	Surplus (Excess Supply)	Absolute Price
Substitutes	Shortage (Excess Demand)	Relative Price

1. True or false? As the price of oranges rises, the demand for oranges falls, *ceteris paribus.* Explain your answer.

2. "The price of a bushel of wheat was $3.00 last month and is $3.70 today. The demand curve for wheat must have shifted rightward between last month and today." Discuss.

3. "Some goods are bought largely because they have 'snob appeal.' For example, the residents of Palm Beach gain prestige by buying expensive items. In fact, they won't buy some items unless they are expensive. The law of demand, which holds that people buy more at lower prices than higher prices, obviously doesn't hold for Palm Beachers. In short, the following rule applies in Palm Beach: high prices, buy; low prices, don't buy." Discuss.

4. "The price of T-shirts keeps rising and rising, and people keep buying more and more. T-shirts must have an upward-sloping demand curve." Identify the error.

5. "Demand is more important to the determination of price than supply." Discuss.

6. Predict what would happen to the equilibrium price of marijuana if it were legalized.

7. Compare the ratings for television shows with prices for goods. How are ratings like prices? How are ratings different from prices? (Hint: How does rising demand for a particular television show manifest itself?)

8. In this chapter, we showed that because the relative price of high-quality apples is lower in New York than in Washington State, New Yorkers consume relatively more high-quality apples. Apply this principle in different areas. For example, ask yourself if you would consume relatively more expensive meals on vacation in Mexico than at home. (Hint: Might there be a transportation cost of going on vacation that is analogous to the transport cost of moving apples from Washington State to New York?)

9. Discuss whether you think the law of demand holds for criminal activity? Do potential criminals "buy" less (more) crime, the higher (lower) the "price" of crime, *ceteris paribus?* Explain your answer.

10. Many movie theaters charge a lower admission price for the first show on weekday afternoons than for a weeknight or weekend show. Explain why.

11. The current price for good *X* is $10, the quantity demanded is 150 and the quantity supplied is 190. For every one dollar decrease in price, quantity supplied falls by 5 units and quantity demanded rises by 7 units. What is the equilibrium price and quantity of good *X?*

12. In year 1 the price of a television set is $400 and the price of a computer is $2,000. In year 2 the price of a television set is $450 and the price of a computer is $2,100. What is the relative price of a television in both years? What is the relative price of a computer in both years?

CHAPTER

4

SUPPLY, DEMAND, AND PRICE: APPLICATIONS

WHAT THIS CHAPTER IS ABOUT

Price has two tasks: It is a rationing device and a transmitter of information. We begin this chapter with a discussion of these two tasks. Next, we discuss what happens when price controls prevent price from performing its two tasks. Finally, we give some real-world examples of supply, demand, and price at work.

73

Price serves as a ration-ing device.

Price as a Rationing Device

Because scarcity exists, a *rationing device* is needed to determine who gets what of the available limited resources and goods. Price serves as a rationing device. It rations *scarce resources* to those producers who pay the price for the resources. It rations *scarce goods* to those buyers who pay the price for the goods. It is as simple as this: Pay the price, and the resources or goods are yours. Don't pay the price, and they aren't.

Resources and goods do not have to be rationed by price. They could be rationed by *political power, ethnic background, physical appearance, religion, favoritism, brute force,* or on a *first-come-first-served* basis, to name only a few possibilities. All these are means that could be used to decide who gets what. Therefore, all could be rationing devices.

Consider a world where brute force is the only rationing device. There the only way you could get what you want is by physically taking it from someone else. Of course, other people would be trying to take things away from you. Suppose you build a canoe to go fishing in, but your next-door neighbor, a burly fellow, hits you over the head and takes the canoe. He gets what he wants, not by paying a price, but through brute force. The strongest persons most willing to use their muscle to get what they want would rule. How would you fare in this world?

Consider a world where religion backed up by the power of the state is used as a rationing device. If you want a car, or food, or an education, you must be a member of the "right" religion as determined by the persons that rule.[1]

Consider a world where ethnic background is used as a rationing device. Who gets what is decided by whether a person is the "right" ethnic background.[2]

Rationing Device
Something that is used to decide who gets what of available goods and resources. Price is a rationing device.

Question:

Clearly, rationing devices such as brute force, religion, and ethnic background work to the disadvantage of the weak and people of the "wrong" religion and ethnic background. But price as a rationing device also works to the disadvantage of some people: specifically, the poor. Isn't this correct?

Answer:

Undoubtedly, if price is the rationing device, poor people will not be able to buy some goods that rich people can buy. It is similar, in this sense, to using ethnic background as the rationing device and prohibiting the Chinese, for example, from buying some goods that the non-Chinese can buy. However, a poor person can sometimes earn the income to pay the price, but a Chinese person can never change his or her ethnic background. There are thousands of examples of poor people becoming rich people, but there is not one example of a Chinese person becoming English, Spanish, or French.

---

[1]Even recently, in some countries religion has been used to ration goods. For example, in Ayatollah Khomeini's Iran, buying many goods was illegal unless you were a Moslem. Members of the Baha'i and Jewish faiths were discriminated against in this regard.

[2]There are numerous cases throughout history where persons of a particular ethnic background could not legally buy certain goods. In the United States, the most notable example is that blacks were at one time prohibited from buying food in "white" restaurants.

Finally, we need to understand that no matter what rationing device is used, it will be of greater benefit to some people than others. This is a consequence of living in a world of inherently unequal individuals.

Follow-up Question:

Why not use need *as the rationing device?*

Answer:

There are problems here. First, who would determine which groups are in need? Republicans? Democrats? Social workers? Second, what is it that people really need? We might agree that all people need a certain amount of food, water, clothing, and shelter. But what else? Do people need television sets, VCRs, trips to Aspen in the winter, personal computers, and so forth? Third, if need were the rationing device, would there be an incentive to work? With price as a rationing device, people have to produce goods and services to earn the income necessary to buy goods. If they could obtain these goods and services without working—by simply expressing a "need"—would anything be produced? Would anyone actually work under such a system?

Price as a Transmitter of Information

On the surface, price is a number with a dollar sign ($) in front of it. Below the surface, price is a transmitter of information, much as telephones, letters, and smoke signals are transmitters of information. To illustrate, consider the following set of events.

On Saturday, Noelle walks into a local grocery store and purchases a half-gallon of orange juice for $2.50. On Sunday, unknown to her, a cold spell hits Florida and wipes out one-quarter of the orange crop. The cold spell shifts the supply curve of oranges leftward and leads to a rise in the equilibrium price of oranges. Higher orange prices shift the supply curve of orange juice leftward and drive up its equilibrium price. Next Saturday, Noelle returns to the grocery store and notices that the price of a half-gallon of orange juice is $3.50. She decides to buy a quart of orange juice for $1.75 instead of a half-gallon for $3.50. (Her demand curve for orange juice is downward sloping; she buys less at higher prices than at lower prices.)

What kind of information does price transmit? By moving up and down, it transmits information on the *relative scarcity* of a good. The higher price for orange juice is saying (once we translate its message into English): "There has been a cold spell in Florida resulting in less orange juice. The gap between people's wants for orange juice and the amount of orange juice available to satisfy those wants has widened."

Notice, too, that because Noelle directly responded to the higher price of orange juice by cutting back on her consumption, she indirectly responded to the information of the increased relative scarcity of orange juice, even without being informed about Florida weather conditions. Because the price increase has encouraged Noelle to help conserve orange juice, it has worked to promote social cooperation.

Price serves as a transmitter of information.

PRICE CONTROLS

■

Price is not always permitted to be a rationing device and transmitter of information. Sometimes it is controlled. There are two types of price controls: price ceilings and price floors. In our discussion of price controls, we use the word *price* in the generic sense. It refers to the price of an apple, for example, the price of labor (wage), the price of credit (interest rate), and the price of a rental unit (rent).

Price Ceiling: Definition and Effects

Price Ceiling
A government-mandated maximum price above which legal trades cannot be made.

A **price ceiling** is a government-mandated maximum price above which legal trades cannot be made. For example, suppose the government mandates that the maximum price at which good X can be bought and sold is $8. It follows that $8 is a price ceiling. If $8 is below the equilibrium price of good X, as in Exhibit 4–1, any or all of the following effects may arise.[3]

Shortages. At the $12 equilibrium price in Exhibit 4–1, the quantity demanded of good X (150) is equal to the quantity supplied (150). At the $8 price ceiling, a

[3]If a price ceiling is above the equilibrium price (say, $8 is the price ceiling and $4 is the equilibrium price), it has no effects. Usually, however, a price ceiling is below the equilibrium price.
The price ceiling effects we discuss here hold for a particular market structure and not necessarily for all market structures. The relevant market structure is usually referred to as a perfectly competitive market, a price-taker market, or a perfect market. No matter what the term, we are assuming enough buyers and sellers so that no single buyer or seller can influence price.

EXHIBIT 4–1
A Price Ceiling

The price ceiling is $8 and the equilibrium price $12. At $12, quantity demanded = quantity supplied. At $8, quantity demanded > quantity supplied. (Recall that price, on the vertical axis, always represents price per unit; and quantity, on the horizontal axis, always holds for a specific time period.)

shortage exists: The quantity demanded (190) is greater than the quantity supplied (100). In Chapter 3, we learned that when a shortage exists, there is a tendency for price and output to rise to equilibrium. But when a price ceiling exists, this tendency cannot be realized since it is unlawful to trade at the equilibrium price.

Fewer Exchanges.   At equilibrium price, 150 units of goods *X* are bought and sold. At the price ceiling in Exhibit 4–1, 100 units of good *X* are bought and sold. (Buyers would prefer to buy 190 units, but only 100 are supplied.) We conclude that price ceilings cause fewer exchanges to be made.

Nonprice Rationing Devices.   If an equilibrium price of $12 *fully* rationed good *X* before the price ceiling was imposed, it follows that a (lower) price of $8 can only partly ration it. In short, price ceilings prevent price from rising to the level sufficient to ration goods fully. What then helps price do what it once did alone? The answer is some other (nonprice) rationing device, such as first-come-first-served (FCFS).

In Exhibit 4–1, 100 units of good *X* will be sold at $8 although buyers are willing to buy 190 units at this price. What happens? Possibly, good *X* will be sold on a FCFS basis for $8 per unit. In other words, to buy good *X* a person needs not only to pay $8 per unit but also to be one of the first persons in line.

Black Market.   A black market is an illegal market. There are principally two varieties: one in which illegal goods are bought and sold (for example, cocaine in this country) and one in which goods are bought and sold at illegal prices (for example, buying and selling goods above a price ceiling). The latter type of black market is relevant here. Buyers and sellers will regularly get around a price ceiling by making their exchanges "under the table." For example, some buyers of good *X* may offer some sellers more than $8 per unit in order to buy the good. No doubt some sellers will accept the offers.

Black Market
An illegal market. There are two varieties: one in which illegal goods are bought and sold and one in which goods are bought and sold at illegal prices.

Question:

Why would some buyers offer more then $8 per unit when they can buy good X for $8?

Answer:

Not all buyers can buy the amount of good *X* they want at $8. As Exhibit 4–1 shows, there is a shortage: Buyers are willing to buy 190 units at $8, but sellers are only willing to sell 100 units. In short, 90 fewer units will be sold than buyers would like to buy. Some buyers will go unsatisfied. How, then, does any *one* buyer make it more likely that sellers will sell to him or her instead of to someone else? The answer is by offering to pay a higher price. Since it is illegal to pay a higher price, however, the transaction must be made "under the table." It is a black market transaction.

Tie-in Sales.   In Exhibit 4–1, what is the maximum price buyers would be willing and able to pay per unit for 100 units of good *X*? As we can see, it is $18. The maximum *legal* price, however, is $8. This difference between the two prices often prompts a **tie-in sale,** a sale whereby one good can be purchased *only if* another good is also purchased. For example, if Ralph's Gas Station only sells gasoline to customers if they buy a car wash, the two goods are linked together in a tie-in sale.

Tie-in Sale
A sale whereby one good can be purchased only if another good is also purchased.

Suppose that the sellers of good X in Exhibit 4–1 also sell good Y. They might offer to sell buyers good X at $8 only if the buyers agree to buy good Y at, say, $10. We choose $10 as the price for good Y because that is the difference between the maximum per-unit price buyers are willing and able to pay for 100 units of good X (specifically, $18) and the maximum legal price ($8).

In New York City and other communities with rent-control laws, tie-in sales sometimes result from rent ceilings on apartments. Occasionally, in order to rent an apartment, an individual must agree to buy the furniture in the apartment.

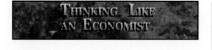

Economists understand that government policy sometimes has unintended effects. For example, a price ceiling policy that may be intended to lower prices for the poor ends up causing shortages, the use of nonprice rationing devices, black markets, and tie-in sales. It is not clear that once we consider both the price ceiling *and* its effects that the poor are helped. The economist knows that wanting to do good (for others) is not sufficient. It is important to know *how* to do good, too.

Do Buyers Prefer Lower Prices to Higher Prices?

"Of course," someone might say, "buyers prefer lower prices to higher prices. What buyer in his right mind would want to pay a higher price for anything?" But wait a minute. Price ceilings are often lower than equilibrium prices. Does it follow that buyers prefer price ceilings to equilibrium prices? Not necessarily. As explained earlier, price ceilings have effects that equilibrium prices do not: shortages, use of first-come-first-served as a rationing device, tie-in sales, and so on. It could be that a buyer would prefer to pay a higher price (an equilibrium price) and avoid the effects of a price ceiling than pay a lower price and have to deal with them. All we can say for certain is that *if all other things are held constant,* buyers prefer lower prices to higher prices. As in many cases, the *ceteris paribus* condition makes all the difference.

Price Ceilings and False Information

Let's go back to the orange juice example we discussed previously. Suppose there is a price ceiling on orange juice at $2.50 per half-gallon, which happens to be the equilibrium price of orange juice before the cold spell in Florida. Further, suppose the price ceiling is maintained even after the cold spell and subsequent fall in the supply of orange juice. Price is not permitted to rise to its new equilibrium level, $3.50, even though the supply curve of orange juice has shifted leftward. Can the information about the increased relative scarcity of orange juice (due to the cold spell) get through to orange juice buyers? No. Since price is prohibited from rising, it obviously cannot transmit this information. As far as buyers are concerned, nothing has changed, and they mistakenly think that they can go on drinking orange juice at the same rate as before. But this is a delusion. One way or the other, some people must curtail their consumption of orange juice, now that fewer oranges are available.

The lesson is simple. Price ceilings (below equilibrium price) distort the flow of accurate information to buyers. Buyers end up thinking that reality is something other than it is; they base their buying expectations on false information. Problems follow, buyers soon feel the unintended, unexpected, and undesirable effects of price ceilings.

Price Floor: Definition and Effects

A **price floor** is a government-mandated minimum price below which legal trades cannot be made. For example, suppose the government mandates that the minimum price at which good X can be sold is $20. It follows that $20 is a price floor (Exhibit 4–2). If the price floor is above the equilibrium price, the two following effects arise.[4]

Surpluses. At the $15 equilibrium price in Exhibit 4–2, the quantity demanded of good X (130) is equal to the quantity supplied (130). At the $20 price floor, a surplus exists; the quantity supplied (180) is greater than the quantity demanded (90). In Chapter 3, we learned that a surplus is a temporary state of affairs. When a surplus exists, there is a tendency for price and output to fall to equilibrium. But when a price floor exists, this tendency cannot be realized since it is unlawful to trade at the equilibrium price.

Fewer Exchanges. At equilibrium price in Exhibit 4–2, 130 units of good X are bought and sold. At the price floor, 90 units are bought and sold. (Sellers want to sell 180 units, but buyers buy only 90.) We conclude that price floors cause fewer exchanges to be made.

Two Cases of Price Floors

We turn now to two real-world examples of price floors. The first is *agricultural price supports;* the second is the *minimum wage law.*

[4]If a price floor is below the equilibrium price (say, $20 is the price floor and $25 is the equilibrium price), it has no effects. Usually, however, a price floor is above the equilibrium price.
As with price ceilings, the price floor effects we discuss here hold for a perfectly competitive market. See footnote 3.

Price Floor
A government-mandated minimum price below which legal trades cannot be made.

EXHIBIT 4–2
A Price Floor

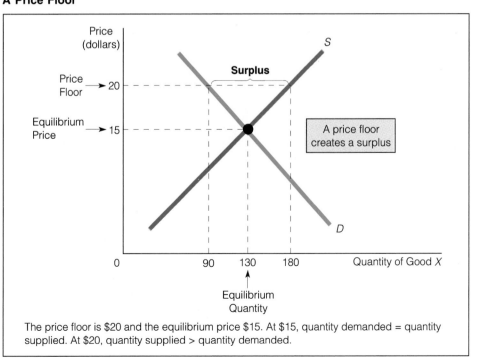

The price floor is $20 and the equilibrium price $15. At $15, quantity demanded = quantity supplied. At $20, quantity supplied > quantity demanded.

Price Support
The minimum price government determines farmers will receive for their
products. Not all agricultural products
have price supports.

Case 1: Agricultural Price Supports. A price support (in agriculture) is an example of a price floor. It is a government-guaranteed minimum price. Some of the
agricultural products that either have or have had price supports include wheat,
cotton, feed grains, dairy products, peanuts, and tobacco. Suppose the price support for wheat is set above the equilibrium price at $6 per bushel, as in Exhibit
4–3. At this price, quantity supplied is greater than quantity demanded and there
is a surplus of wheat. Also, the number of bushels of wheat bought by *private
citizens* is less (10) at the price support (price floor) than at equilibrium price (18).[5]
We would expect wheat buyers to dislike the price support program since they
end up paying higher than equilibrium price for the wheat they buy.

What happens to the surplus? Under supply-and-demand conditions, farmers
could get rid of the surplus of wheat by lowering price. But, of course, there is no
need to lower price. The price is supported by *government,* which buys the surplus
at the price support. Since the government's purchase of surplus wheat needs to
be stored, it sometimes must pay huge storage costs. For example, in the 1950s
and early 1960s, storage costs for wheat rose rapidly, reaching over $1 million per
day at one period. For the taxpayers who ultimately had to pay the bill, this was
not a happy state of affairs.

Thus, the effects of agricultural price supports are (1) a surplus, (2) fewer exchanges (less wheat bought by private citizens), (3) higher prices paid by consumers of wheat, and (4) government purchase and storage of the surplus wheat
(for which taxpayers end up paying).[6]

[5]We specify *private citizens* here because some of the wheat crop is purchased by the government.
[6]For more on agriculture and government policies that affect this industry, see Chapter 30.

EXHIBIT 4–3
Effects of an Agricultural Price Support

At a price support of $6 per bushel (as compared to the $4 per bushel equilibrium price),
consumers of wheat pay higher prices, a surplus results, fewer bushels of wheat are bought
by private citizens, and government buys and stores the surplus (which taxpayers pay for).

Case 2: The Minimum Wage Law. The *minimum wage* is a price floor—a government-mandated minimum price for labor. It affects the market for unskilled labor. In Exhibit 4–4, the minimum wage is $4.25 an hour and the equilibrium wage is $3.25. At the equilibrium wage, N_1 workers are employed. At the higher minimum wage, N_3 workers want to work, but only N_2 actually do work. There is a surplus of workers equal to $N_3 - N_2$ in this unskilled labor market. In addition, fewer workers are working at the minimum wage (N_2) than at the equilibrium wage (N_1). Overall, the effects of the minimum wage are (1) a surplus of unskilled workers and (2) fewer workers employed.[7]

Question:

Isn't the minimum wage necessary to guarantee everybody a decent wage? If the minimum wage didn't exist, wouldn't employers hire workers for next to nothing?

Answer:

Employers may want to hire workers for "next to nothing," but the wages workers receive depend on the demand for and supply of labor. In other words, employers

[7]We remind the reader that the effects of the minimum wage are determined for a perfectly competitive (price-taker or perfect) market.

EXHIBIT 4–4
Effects of the Minimum Wage

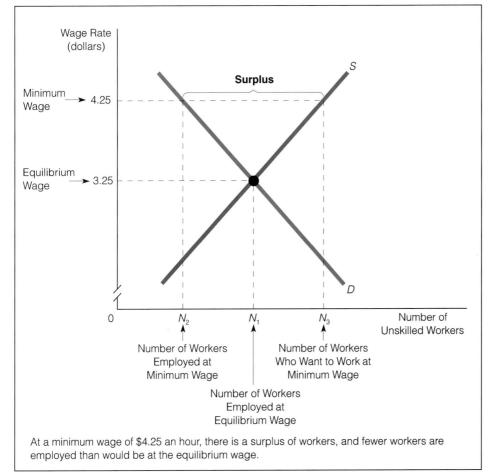

At a minimum wage of $4.25 an hour, there is a surplus of workers, and fewer workers are employed than would be at the equilibrium wage.

do not set wages at whatever level they like: In a competitive market setting, the forces of supply and demand determine equilibrium wages.

As to the minimum wage guaranteeing a decent wage, suppose Johnny Bates, a 17-year-old in Chicago, finds that his labor is worth $3.25 an hour to employers. If the government mandates that Johnny must be paid $4.25 an hour ($1 more an hour than he's currently worth to employers), no employer will hire him. So the minimum wage does not guarantee Johnny a decent wage; in fact, it may guarantee him no wage.

APPLICATIONS OF SUPPLY AND DEMAND

■

Do the tools of supply and demand help us to understand more about the real world? We think they do, and we hope you agree. But if, by chance, you remain an unbeliever, then this section is for you. In it we present more applications of supply and demand. They all illustrate how price serves as a rationing device.

Freeway Congestion

What does a traffic jam on a busy freeway in any large city have to do with supply and demand? Actually, it has quite a bit to do with supply and demand. Look at it this way: There is a demand for driving on the freeway and a supply of freeway space. The supply of freeway space is fixed (freeways do not expand and contract over a day, week, or month). The demand, however, fluctuates. Sometimes it is higher than at other times. For example, we would expect the demand for driving on the freeway to be higher at 8 A.M. (rush hour) than at 11 P.M. But even though this may be the case, the money price for driving on the freeway is always the same—always zero. A zero money price means that no tolls are paid to drive on the freeway.

Exhibit 4–5 shows two demand curves for driving on the freeway: $D_{8A.M.}$ and $D_{11P.M.}$ We have assumed the demand at 8 A.M. is greater than at 11 P.M. We have also assumed that at $D_{11P.M.}$ and zero money price the freeway market clears: Quantity demanded of freeway space equals quantity supplied of freeway space. At the higher demand, $D_{8A.M.}$, however, this is not the case. At zero money price, a shortage of freeway space exists: The quantity demanded of freeway space is greater than the quantity supplied of freeway space. The shortage appears in the form of freeway congestion, bumper-to-bumper traffic. One way to eliminate the shortage is through an increase in the money price of driving on the freeway at 8 A.M. For example, as Exhibit 4–5 shows, a toll of 70 cents would clear the freeway market at 8 A.M.

If charging different prices (tolls) at different times of the day on freeways sounds like an unusual idea, consider how Miami Beach hotels price their rooms. They charge different prices for their rooms at different times of the year. During the winter months when the demand for vacationing in Miami Beach is high, the hotels charge higher prices than when the demand is (relatively) low. If different prices were charged for freeway space at different times of the day, freeway space would be rationed the same way Miami Beach hotel rooms are rationed.

EXHIBIT 4–5
Freeway Congestion and Supply and Demand

The demand for driving on the freeway is higher at 8A.M. than at 11P.M. At zero money price and $D_{11P.M.}$, the freeway market clears. At zero money price and $D_{8A.M.}$, there is a shortage of freeway space, which shows up as freeway congestion. At a price (toll) of 70 cents, the shortage is eliminated and freeway congestion disappears.

Question:

If this is correct, and freeway congestion can be eliminated by charging different tolls at different times of the day, why isn't this done?

Answer:

First, simply because a certain action will eliminate a problem, it does not necessarily follow that it is desirable to carry out that action. A system of tolls will reduce, if not eliminate, freeway congestion, but it may not be worth the cost to build and staff the toll booths. As technology for monitoring usage and billing improves, however, it's possible that we'll institute such a system. In some places in Hong Kong, this has already been done.

Second, freeways are "owned" by the taxpayers and managed by government, not privately owned and managed. The present owner–management team (taxpayers and government officials) is less likely to propose and implement a toll system than a privately owned and managed team that seeks to maximize profits.

Finally, some people argue that rationing freeway space by money price would hurt the poor by making it more expensive for them to get to work and to travel; a few traffic jams are preferable.

Tipping at a Las Vegas Show

To get a good seat at a Las Vegas show, you have to tip (in advance) the person who seats you. Tourists in Las Vegas usually complain, "I don't know why I have to pay that guy $10 to walk me to my seat. It is ridiculous." But is it? Supply and demand explain what is going on.

In Las Vegas, all tickets for the same show sell for the same price (unlike tickets for a play in New York, say, where some tickets sell for higher prices than others). There are no seat assignments, however; buying a ticket guarantees you a seat, but it could be *any* seat from a good seat, center stage, to a bad seat, far in the back.

The show, therefore, has two markets: a market for good seats and a market for bad seats. In each market there is a demand for and a supply of seats. The bad

EXHIBIT 4–6
Good and Bad Seats at a Las Vegas Show

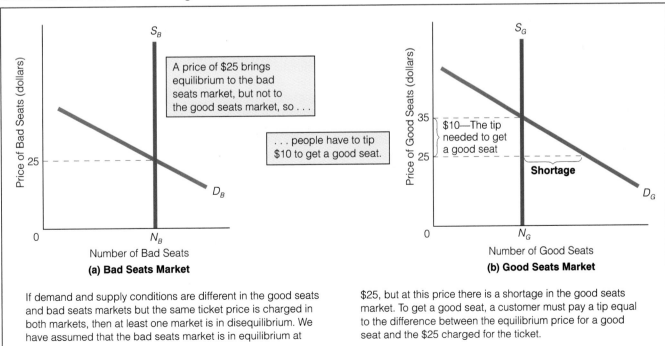

If demand and supply conditions are different in the good seats and bad seats markets but the same ticket price is charged in both markets, then at least one market is in disequilibrium. We have assumed that the bad seats market is in equilibrium at

$25, but at this price there is a shortage in the good seats market. To get a good seat, a customer must pay a tip equal to the difference between the equilibrium price for a good seat and the $25 charged for the ticket.

What Does Price Have to Do with Being Late to Class?

Class starts at 10 o'clock in the morning. At 10:09, Pam Ferrario walks in late. She apologizes to the instructor, saying, "I've been on campus for 20 minutes, but I couldn't find a parking space." Her classmates nod, knowing full well what she is talking about. Here at the university, especially between the hours of 8 A.M. and 2 P.M., parking spaces are hard to come by.

This scene is replayed every day at many universities and colleges across the country. Students are late for class because on many days there isn't a parking space to be found.

What can be done about this? Students could start for class earlier. Suppose you have a class at 10 A.M., and you live in an apartment 5 miles from the campus. If you are lucky enough to find an open parking space as soon as you enter the campus parking lot, then you need only leave home at 9:35. However, you can't count on such good luck, so you'd better leave at 9:15, just to be on the safe side.

Who pays for the shortage of parking spaces under this scheme? The student does. He or she doesn't pay in money but in time.

Or, if you choose not to leave home earlier, then you might pay in being late to class, as we saw earlier.

Are there alternatives to the pay-in-time and pay-in-being-late-to-class schemes for rationing campus parking spots? Some economists have suggested a pay-in-price scheme. For example, the university could install meters in the parking lot and raise the fee high enough so that between the hours of 8 A.M. and 2 P.M., the quantity demanded for parking spaces equals the quantity supplied.

Such suggestions are sometimes criticized because students must pay the fee, no matter how high, in order to attend classes. Well, that's not exactly true. Parking off campus and using public transportation are sometimes alternatives. But this is not really the main point. The issue isn't paying or not paying, but choosing the form in which payment is made—dollar price, time, or being late for class.

Some economists have taken the pay-in-price scheme farther and have argued that parking spots should be auctioned on a yearly basis. In other words, a student would rent a parking spot for a year. This way the student would always know that a parking spot would be open when he or she arrived at the campus. People who parked in someone else's spot would be ticketed by campus police.

Additionally, under this scheme, a student who rented a parking spot and chose not to use it between certain hours of the day could rent it out to someone else during this period. So we would expect to see notices like this on campus billboards:

Parking Spot for Rent

Near Arts Building and Student Union. Ideal for liberal arts students. Available on a 2–12 hour basis between 12 noon and 12 midnight. Rate: 50 cents per hour. Call 471-3564.

The argument is often heard that allocating campus parking spots according to price may be all right for rich and middle-income students, but that it hurts poor students. This is not a trivial argument, but it is often misleading. Poor students are not necessarily students without an income; they are simply students with relatively lower incomes than others. Poor students may choose to rearrange their purchases and buy more of one thing (a parking spot) and less of another (clothes, entertainment, and so on). We shouldn't jump to the conclusion that the poor would always prefer a nonmoney rationing scheme to a money rationing scheme.

Give price rationing for campus parking spots some thought. Consider what you believe to be its advantages and disadvantages. Perhaps the next time you're late for class and your instructor looks at you disapprovingly, you might say, "Is it my fault that we don't ration campus parking spots by price?"

seats market is shown in Exhibit 4–6a, the good seats market in Exhibit 4–6b. Notice that the demand is greater for good seats than bad seats (as we would expect).[8]

Normally, different market conditions (different demand and supply curves)

[8]We have drawn a vertical supply curve in both the good seats and bad seats markets. We are assuming here that the time period under consideration is so short that the quantity supplied of both good seats and bad seats cannot change even if price does. However, even with an upward-sloping supply curve in each market, the analysis is the same.

would bring about different equilibrium prices. The (manager of the) show, however, sells all tickets for the same price, $25. This is the equilibrium price in the bad seats market, but, as Exhibit 4–6b shows, it is a disequilibrium price (below equilibrium price) in the good seats market. The results is a shortage of good seats.

How are the "too few" good seats rationed? That is done by price in the form of a tie-in sale. To get a good seat, it is necessary to tip (in advance) the person who decides where you will sit. First tip the person who does the seating, then get a good seat (assuming, of course, you tipped enough). The necessary tip to get a good seat is equal to the difference between the equilibrium price for a good seat and the $25 charged. In Exhibit 4–6, we have assumed the equilibrium price is $35; thus, the tip is $10.

GPAs, ACTs, and SATs

In many colleges and universities, students pay less than the equilibrium tuition (price) to attend. Usually, the student pays part of the price of his or her education (by way of tuition payments), and taxpayers and private donors pay part (by way of tax payments and charitable donations, respectively). To illustrate, suppose the student at University X pays the tuition, T_1 (Exhibit 4–7a). As we can see, this is below the equilibrium tuition, T_E. At T_1, the number of students who want to

EXHIBIT 4–7
University Admissions

$N_1 - N_2$ = shortage due to T_1 being charged instead of T_E. GPAs, ACTs, and SATs enter the picture as nonprice rationing devices.

(a)

$N_1 - N_2$ = shortage at T_1 when demand is D_1.

$N_3 - N_2$ = shortage at T_1 when demand is D_2.

(b)

(a) If T_1 is charged when T_E is the equilibrium tuition, there will be a shortage of university openings. The university will use GPAs, ACTs, and SATs as admission criteria (nonprice rationing devices). (b) If the demand for the university falls, and T_1 is still charged, the shortage will become smaller, and, we predict, admission standards will be lowered.

attend the university (N_1) is greater than the number of openings at the university (N_2): that is, quantity demanded is greater than quantity supplied. A shortage of university space exists. The university receives more applications for admission to the freshman class than there are places. Something has to be done. But what? The way the university rations its openings is by some combination of money price and other selected nonprice rationing devices. The student must pay the tuition, or have someone else pay it, *and* meet the standards of the nonprice rationing devices, which usually include such things as GPAs (grade point average), ACTs (American College Test), and SATs (Scholastic Aptitude Test).

Question:

Suppose the demand for University X falls, but tuition T_1 is still charged. Would admission requirements be reduced?

Answer:

The theory predicts that admission requirements would be reduced. To illustrate, suppose the demand for university openings falls from D_1 to D_2, as in Exhibit 4–7b. The shortage of university openings falls from $N_1 - N_2$ to $N_3 - N_2$. As the shortage falls, the GPA, ACT, and SAT requirements do not need to be as stringent as before. We would predict that if the demand for University X falls, university admission standards would be reduced, *ceteris paribus*.

Chapter Summary

Price as a Rationing Device

■ Scarcity implies the need for a rationing device. Possible rationing devices include price, political power, first-come-first-served, ethnic background, physical appearance, religion, favoritism, and brute force.

Price as a Transmitter of Information

■ In a market in which price is permitted to rise and fall according to supply and demand, price transmits information on the relative scarcity of a good. A higher (lower) price informs us that the gap between people's wants and the amount of resources or goods available to satisfy those wants has widened (narrowed).

Price Ceilings

■ A price ceiling is a government-mandated maximum price. If a price ceiling is below the equilibrium price, some or all of the following effects arise: shortages, fewer exchanges, nonprice rationing devices, black markets (of the variety in which it is illegal to sell at particular prices), and tie-in sales.
■ Consumers do not necessarily prefer (lower) price ceilings to (higher) equilibrium prices. They may prefer higher prices and none of the effects of price ceilings to lower prices and some of the effects of price ceilings. All we can say for sure is that consumers prefer lower to higher prices, *ceteris paribus*.

- Freely flexible prices (prices that are allowed to respond to the forces of supply and demand) transmit accurate information about relative scarcities. Controlled prices transmit inaccurate or false information about relative scarcities.

Price Floors

- A price floor is a government-mandated minimum price. If a price floor is above the equilibrium price, the following effects arise: surpluses and fewer exchanges.
- Both agricultural price supports and the minimum wage are examples of price floors. The effects of agricultural price supports are surpluses, fewer exchanges, higher prices for consumers, and government purchase and storage (or other disposal) of the surplus (that is, taxpayers pay). The effects of the minimum wage are a surplus (of unskilled labor) and fewer workers employed.

Key Terms and Concepts

Rationing Device	Black Market	Price Floor
Price Ceiling	Tie-in Sale	Price Support

QUESTIONS AND PROBLEMS

1. "If price were outlawed as the rationing device used in markets, there would be no need for another rationing device to take its place. We would have reached utopia." Discuss.

2. Many of the proponents of price ceilings argue that government-mandated maximum prices simply reduce producers' profits and do not affect the quantity supplied of a good on the market. What must the supply curve look like before a price ceiling does not affect quantity supplied?

3. The minimum wage hurts some unskilled workers because it prices them out of the labor market. For example, if the minimum wage is $4.25 per hour, and employers are only willing to pay a person $2.90 per hour, that person cannot legally be hired. Since the minimum wage largely applies to unskilled workers, would you expect all unskilled workers to be against the minimum wage?

4. Some people argue that the minimum wage, by pricing many unskilled teenagers out of the labor market, causes these individuals to turn to selling drugs. After all, if a person can't get a job legally, he or she will get one illegally. The alternative is to starve. Other people disagree. They state that some teenagers would still sell drugs even if all could be hired at the minimum wage—because of the monetary difference between clerking for $4.25 an hour and selling drugs for hundreds of dollars a week. What do you think?

5. What kind of information does price transmit?

6. Suppose the price of IBM stock rises by $2 a share. Does the price rise transmit any information to you? What does it say?

7. Should grades in an economics class be "rationed" according to money price instead of how well a student does on the exams? If they were, and potential employers learned of this, what effect might this have on the value of your college degree?

8. The money price of driving on a freeway is always the same—zero. Is the (opportunity) cost always the same and zero, too? Explain your answer.

9. Think about ticket scalpers at a rock concert, a baseball game, or an opera. Might they exist because the tickets to these events were originally sold for less than the equilibrium price? Why? In what way is a ticket scalper like and unlike your retail grocer, who buys food from a wholesaler and turns around and sells it to you?

10. How might we go about determining the equilibrium toll on a freeway at a particular time of day?

MACROECONOMICS

MACROECONOMIC FUNDAMENTALS

AN INTRODUCTION TO MACROECONOMICS

WHAT THIS CHAPTER IS ABOUT

This chapter is a preview of later macroeconomics chapters. First, it presents a way to categorize much of what you will learn in macroeconomics. Second, it describes the major players in the macroeconomic arena. Third, it discusses some of the facts and questions macroeconomists find interesting. Fourth, it provides a roadmap to our study of macroeconomics.

Macroeconomics has two major variables— the price level (P) and real GNP (Q).

Macroeconomics
The branch of economics that deals with human behavior and choices as they relate to highly aggregated markets (such as the goods and services market) or the entire economy.

Price Level
The weighted average of the prices of all goods and services.

Real GNP
The value of the entire output produced annually in an economy, adjusted for price changes. It also can be defined as GNP (gross national product) valued in prices prevailing in the base year.

Macroeconomics is the branch of economics that deals with human behavior and choices as they relate to highly aggregated markets (such as the goods and services market) or the entire economy. The subject matter in macroeconomics includes (1) macroeconomic problems, (2) macroeconomic theories, (3) macroeconomic policies and, (4) different views of how the economy works. To help you categorize what you learn in macroeconomics, we develop three macroeconomic organizational categories. We call these categories (1) the P–Q category, (2) the inherently stable–inherently unstable category, and (3) the effective–ineffective category.

The *P–Q* Category

Macroeconomics has two major variables—the **price level** and **real GNP.** The price level is the weighted average of the prices paid for goods and services. Real GNP is the total market value of the entire output produced annually in an economy, adjusted for price changes. We discuss both the price level and real GNP in depth in Chapter 7, but for now you may simply want to view the price level as an average price and real GNP as the quantity of output produced.

The symbol we use for the price level is P; the symbol we use for the real GNP is Q. Thus, we can talk about the P–Q category.

Here is a list of topics in macroeconomics. Notice how each of the topics is defined, or partly defined, by price level (P), real GNP (Q), or both.

Gross national product (GNP). P times Q.
Real GNP. Q.
Price level. P.
Unemployment. Changes in unemployment are related to changes in Q.
Inflation. A rising P.
Deflation. A falling P.
Economic growth. Related to increasing Q.
Stagflation. A rising P combined with rising unemployment.
Business cycle. Recurrent swings (up and down) in Q, among other things.
Recessionary gap. The condition of the economy when Q is below its natural level.
Inflationary gap. The condition of the economy when Q is above its natural level.
Fiscal policy. Concerned with stabilizing P, achieving low unemployment (which is related to Q), and promoting economic growth (which is also related to Q), among other things.
Monetary policy. Concerned with stabilizing P, achieving low unemployment (which is related to Q), and promoting economic growth (which is also related to Q), among other things.

Question:

How should the P–Q category be used by a student of macroeconomics?

Answer:

When the student comes across a macroeconomics topic, she should ask herself if it relates directly or indirectly to either P, Q, or both. In many cases, she will see that it does. This realization helps the student to see the *common denominator* of much that is discussed in macroeconomics.

Some economists argue that the economy is inherently stable *and others argue that it is* inherently unstable.*

The Inherently Stable–Inherently Unstable Category

In Chapter 3, we showed that an unhampered market tends toward equilibrium. If price is above its equilibrium level, a surplus develops and price falls. If price is below its equilibrium level, a shortage develops and price rises. A market is self-equilibrating, or self-regulating, and inherently stable. No one directs it to equilibrium, the point at which quantity supplied equals quantity demanded. It moves there under its own forces.

Does the same hold true for the economy? Does the economy as a whole tend toward equilibrium and stability? Economists are divided. Some argue that it does, and some argue that it does not.

Consider the Great Depression of the 1930s. During this period in U.S. history, unemployment skyrocketed, the production of goods and services plummeted (*Q* fell), prices fell (*P* fell), banks closed, savings were lost, and companies went bankrupt. What does this period indicate about the inherent properties of a market economy? Some observers argue that the Great Depression is proof of the *inherent instability* of a market (or capitalist) economy, and demonstrates that natural economic forces, if left to themselves, may bring on human suffering.

Other observers see things differently. They argue that left to itself, the economy would never have nosedived into the Great Depression. The Depression, they believe, was largely caused and made worse by government tampering with the *inherently stable,* self-equilibrating, and wealth-producing properties of a market economy.

Which came first? Did the market economy turn down under the weight of its own forces, producing massive unemployment, with government later stepping in to restrain the destructive market forces? Or was the market economy pushed into depression, and held there, by government economic tampering? The answer largely depends on how the inherent properties of a market economy are viewed. As economist Axel Leijonhufvud notes:

> The central issue in macroeconomic theory is—once again—the extent to which the economy, or at least its market sectors, may properly be regarded as a self-regulating system. . . . How well or badly, do its "automatic" mechanisms perform?[1]

Question:

It sounds as if one person simply "views the economy" one way and another person simply views it another way—much as one person likes chocolate ice cream and another person likes vanilla. Is there more to it than preference or likes and dislikes?

Answer:

Yes. A person may come to hold a particular view of things in a number of different ways: through his or her reading of the facts, through a leap of faith, and so on. But we are not focusing our attention on the course one travels to come to a particular view of the economy, only on the view itself. Furthermore, we believe that a difference in views can and does generate debate, which is valuable. The interviews with economists in this text present a number of views.

[1]Axel Leijonhufvud, "Effective Demand Failures," *Swedish Journal of Economics* 75 (1973): 28.

The **effectiveness** *of fis-*
cal and monetary policy
is a key issue of eco-
nomic debate.

Fiscal Policy
Changes in government expenditures
and taxation in an effort to achieve
particular macroeconomic goals, such
as low unemployment, stable prices,
economic growth, and so on.

Monetary Policy
The deliberate control of the money
supply and credit conditions in an effort to achieve particular macroeconomic goals, such as low unemployment, stable prices, economic growth,
and so on.

Follow-up Question:

Can't positive economic analysis settle all debates?

Answer:

There are times when positive economic analysis may not be enough to settle
debates. Deep-seated differences in the way people view the world may cause them
to view the same facts in a different light.

The Effective–Ineffective Category

Here the words *effective* and *ineffective* describe **fiscal policy** and **monetary policy.**
Fiscal policy relates to changes in government expenditures and taxation in an
effort to achieve particular macroeconomic goals, such as low unemployment, stable prices, economic growth, and so on. Monetary policy refers to the deliberate
control of the money supply and credit conditions in an effort to achieve the same
macroeconomic goals.

An economist can take one of several positions within the effective–ineffective
category. She can believe that fiscal and monetary policy are always effective (at
meeting their goals), or that both fiscal and monetary policy are ineffective, or that
fiscal policy is effective and monetary policy is ineffective, and so on.

Often, an economist's position on the effectiveness–ineffectiveness of policy is
implicit in his or her view of how the economy works—that is, whether the economy is inherently stable or unstable.

Question:

*How should the effective–ineffective category be used by a student of
macroeconomics?*

Answer:

The effective–ineffective category is sometimes useful in turning the implicit into
the explicit, or pushing what is below the surface up to the surface. For example,
a student may read what economist Jones says on, say, unemployment and inflation without being aware of the common thread that runs between the two topics.
At times like this, he should ask himself if and how what is being said either
supports or invalidates a particular position on policy. For example, does what
economist Jones says support the position that fiscal policy is effective at achieving
the macroeconomic goal of low unemployment?

A Final Word on the Three Organizational Categories

One or more of the three macroeconomic organizational categories can be used in
much of what we discuss in macroeconomics. They are there to help you categorize
and organize the many details you will be asked to learn. Moreover, they are there
to help you keep the big picture, or the fundamental issues, of macroeconomics
in front of you as you proceed to work through the technical aspects of macroeconomic problems, theories, and policies.

THE MACROECONOMIC PLAYERS

The principal players in macroeconomics are (1) households, (2) businesses,
(3) government at all levels, (4) the federal government, in particular the president

of the United States, the U.S. Congress, and the U.S. Treasury, (5) foreigners as buyers of U.S. goods, (6) Americans as buyers of foreign goods, and (7) the Federal Reserve System. We briefly discuss each of them in turn. You will learn much more about each in subsequent chapters.

Households

Economists usually divide the economy into four sectors: the household sector, the business sector, the government sector, and the foreign sector. The household sector consists of persons like you and your family. These are people who buy consumer goods—such goods as television sets, carpets, lamps, cars, refrigerators, toothpaste, and much more. Household expenditures are referred to as **consumption.** The total amount of, and changes in, consumption may influence economic events.

Consumption
Household spending on consumer goods.

Businesses

Gross private domestic investment, (or simply **investment**) is the sum of all purchases made by businesses on newly produced capital goods plus changes in business inventories. It also includes expenditures on new residential housing. The total amount of, and changes in, investment may influence economic events.

Gross Private Domestic Investment, or Investment
The sum of all purchases of newly produced capital goods plus changes in business inventories. It also includes expenditures on new residential housing.

Government at All Levels

Expenditures made by government at all levels—local, state, and federal—are referred to as **government expenditures,** or **government spending.** The total amount of, and changes in, government expenditures may influence economic events.

Government Expenditures, or Government Spending
The total dollar amounts spent by federal, state, and local governments on final goods and services.

The Federal Government

The federal government—in particular, the president of the United States, the U.S. Congress, and the U.S. Treasury—is important to the working of the economy. Together, the president and the Congress decide on matters of government spending and taxation—that is, *fiscal policy.* The U.S. Treasury is important because it finances federal budget deficits. The actions of these three institutions may influence economic events.

Foreigners as Buyers of U.S. Goods

Foreigners buy goods produced by Americans. The total foreign spending on domestic (U.S.) goods is called **exports.** How much foreigners spend on American goods may influence economic events in the United States.

Exports
Total foreign spending on domestic (U.S.) goods.

Americans as Buyers of Imported Goods

Americans buy goods from the residents of foreign nations. The total domestic (U.S.) spending on foreign goods is called **imports.** How much Americans spend on foreign goods may influence economic events in the United States.

Imports
Total domestic (U.S.) spending on foreign goods.

The Federal Reserve System

The **Federal Reserve System,** popularly called **the Fed,** is the central bank of the United States. Its principal components are the Board of Governors, which is the

The Federal Reserve System (the Fed)
The central bank of the United States; its primary duty is to control the money supply.

governing body of the Federal Reserve System, the 12 Federal Reserve District Banks, and the approximately 6,000 member commercial banks. The primary duty of the Federal Reserve System is to control the money supply, or implement *monetary policy.* You will learn in later chapters that the Fed can increase and decrease the money supply and that such actions may influence economic events.

A FEW FACTS AND QUESTIONS IN MACROECONOMICS

■

An economist, like any scientist attempting to understand the world, deals with facts. Facts are often interesting in themselves, but they usually don't stand alone. Facts often lead to questions.

What follows are some macroeconomic facts and some of the questions economists have asked about those facts. Together, the facts and the questions define some of the issues of macroeconomics and ultimately lead to the development of theories (to explain the facts and predict what will happen) and policies.

The Price Level

Exhibit 5–1 shows the price level in the United States for the years 1800–1990. As you can see, the price level went up in some years and down in other years. This fact leads us to ask, What causes the price level to rise? to fall?

EXHIBIT 5–1
The Price Level, 1800–1990

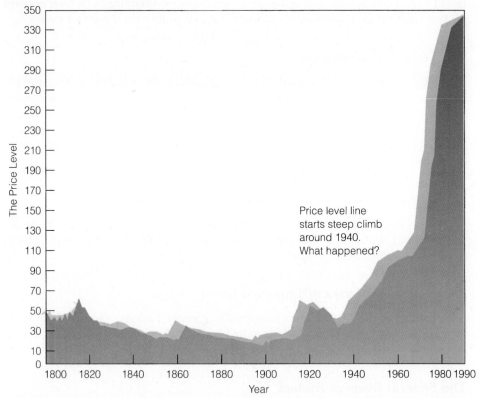

Price level line starts steep climb around 1940. What happened?

SOURCE: U.S. Bureau of the Census, *Historical Statistics of the United States* (Washington, D.C.: U.S. Government Printing Office, 1960); Council of Economic Advisers, *Economic Report of the President, 1991* (Washington, D.C.: U.S. Government Printing Office, 1991).

The Unemployment Rate

Exhibit 5–2 shows the unemployment rate in the United States for the years 1800–1990. We notice an unusually high unemployment rate during the Great Depression years (1929–33). Overall, we notice that the unemployment rate rises in some years and falls in other years. The facts lead us to ask, What caused the skyrocketing unemployment rate during the Great Depression? What causes the unemployment rate to rise? to fall?

Unemployment and Inflation

Over the short run, there sometimes is a **trade-off** between unemployment and inflation. A trade-off exists between unemployment and inflation if as one rises the other falls, that is, they move in opposite directions, or are *inversely related*.[2]

Trade-off
A situation in which the attainment of something desirable necessarily implies the loss of something else desirable.

[2]We remind the reader that if two variables move in the same direction, they are *directly related;* if they move in the opposite directions, they are *inversely related.* See Chapter 1, Appendix A.

EXHIBIT 5–2
The Unemployment Rate, 1990–1990

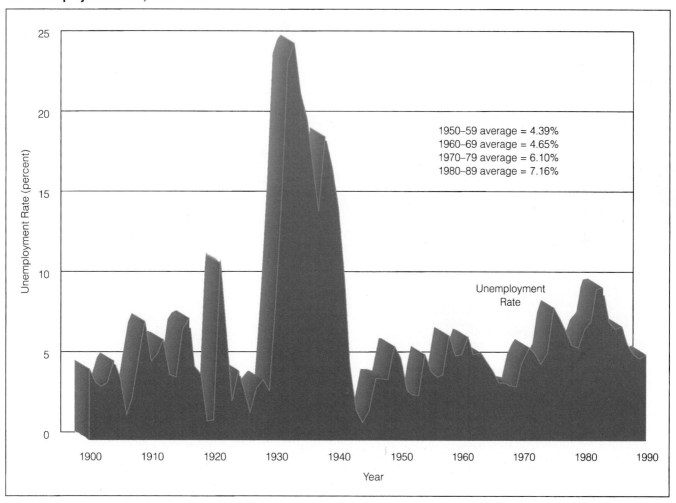

SOURCE: U.S. Bureau of the Census, *Historical Statistics of the United States* (Washington, D.C.: U.S. Government Printing Office, 1960); Council of Economic Advisers, *Economic Report of the President, 1991* (Washington, D.C.: Government Printing Office, 1991).

For example, in 1965, the unemployment rate was 4.5 percent and the inflation rate was 1.6 percent. One year later, in 1966, the unemployment had dropped to 3.8 percent, but the inflation rate had risen to 2.8 percent.

The same trade-off between inflation and unemployment existed between 1972 and 1973, 1976 and 1977, 1981 and 1982, 1986 and 1987, to name only four other sets of years. Exhibit 5–3a illustrates the inflation and unemployment rates for *selected years only*.

If we look at periods longer than one year, however, such as 1966 to 1970, 1972 to 1977, or 1973 to 1981 (Exhibit 5–3b), we notice that inflation and unemployment didn't move in the *opposite* direction, they moved in the *same* direction. For example, both inflation and unemployment were higher in 1970 than 1966. In short, there was no trade-off. We ask, Why is there sometimes a trade-off between inflation and unemployment over the short run? Why isn't there a trade-off in the long run?

Inflation and Interest Rates

High inflation rates are associated with high interest rates, and low inflation rates are associated with low interest rates[3] (Exhibit 5–4). This apparent relationship raises several questions: Do high inflation rates cause high interest rates? Or do

[3]The interest rate we are talking about here is the *nominal* (or *market*) interest rate, as measured by three-month U.S. Treasury bill rate. In a later chapter, you will learn that economists sometimes distinguish between the nominal interest rate and the real interest rate.

EXHIBIT 5–3
Unemployment and Inflation Rates, Selected Years

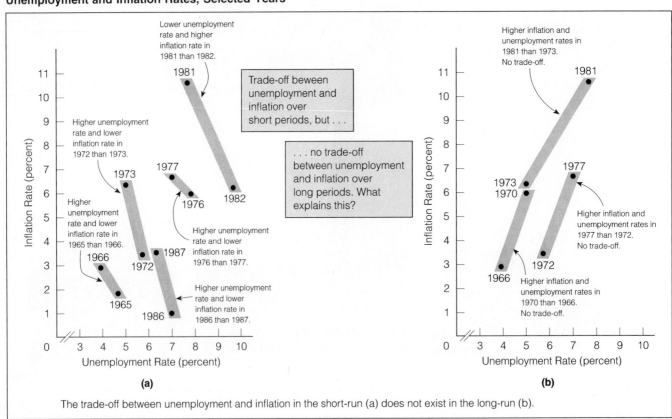

The trade-off between unemployment and inflation in the short-run (a) does not exist in the long-run (b).

SOURCE: Council of Economic Advisers, *Economic Report of the President, 1991* (Washington, D.C.: U.S. Government Printing Office, 1991).

EXHIBIT 5–4
Inflation and Interest Rates, 1960–90

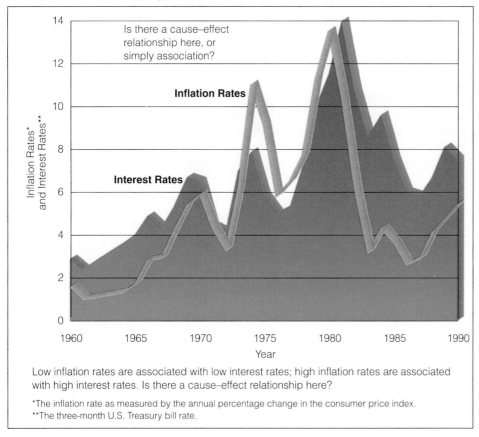

Is there a cause–effect relationship here, or simply association?

Inflation Rates

Interest Rates

Low inflation rates are associated with low interest rates; high inflation rates are associated with high interest rates. Is there a cause–effect relationship here?

*The inflation rate as measured by the annual percentage change in the consumer price index.
**The three-month U.S. Treasury bill rate.

SOURCE: Council of Economic Advisers, *Economic Report of the President, 1991* (Washington, D.C.: U.S. Government Printing Office, 1991).

high interest rates cause high inflation rates? Or is neither the cause nor the effect of the other?

Budget Deficits and Surpluses

Between 1946 and 1969, a run of federal government **budget deficits** was usually followed fairly closely by a run of federal **budget surpluses** (Exhibit 5–5). Beginning in 1970, however, a budget deficit has occurred each year. This raises the questions, What happened in or around the 1960s and 1970s to change things? What is the effect of budget deficits on the economy?

Recessions and Politics

Between the end of the Civil War in 1865 and 1990, the United States experienced 28 **recessions.** The most severe downturn in economic activity occurred during the years of the Great Depression. Some people have argued that the economic hardships encountered during this time led to major political changes. In particular, they mention the New Deal of President Franklin D. Roosevelt with its political restructuring of social and economic institutions. This raises the questions, Were these major political developments merely coincidental to the Great Depres-

Budget deficit
Occurs when government expenditures (G) are greater than tax receipts (T): G > T.

Budget surplus
Occurs when government expenditures (G) are less than tax receipts (T): G < T.

Recession
A decline in real GNP (real output) that lasts for two consecutive quarters (six months) or more.

101

EXHIBIT 5–5
The Status of the Federal Budget, 1946–90

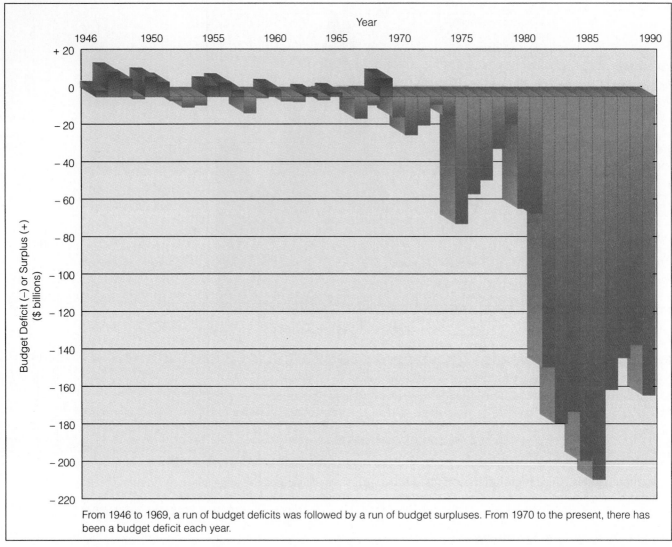

From 1946 to 1969, a run of budget deficits was followed by a run of budget surpluses. From 1970 to the present, there has been a budget deficit each year.

Source: Council of Economic Advisers, *Economic Report of the President, 1991* (Washington, D.C.: U.S. Government Printing Office, 1991).

sion, or were they a consequence of it? More generally, what is the relationship between economic events and political change? Finally, what causes recessions?

Business Cycles

Over long periods, the U.S. economy has fluctuated between expansionary and contractionary phases in economic activity, like a roller coaster. The roller coaster rises to the top, and then it comes down, then it goes up again, and then down. These upward and downward fluctuations in economic activity are referred to as **business cycles.** There are four stages to a business cycle: (1) the *expansion,* (2) the *peak* of the expansion, (3) the *contraction,* and (4) the *trough* or bottom of the contraction. The typical business cycle—from the beginning of the expansion through the trough of the contraction—is approximately four to five years, although

Business cycle
Recurrent swings in general economic activity, usually measured in terms of the unemployment rate and real GNP.

a few have been shorter and some longer. This pattern leads to a question: Why doesn't economic activity stay on a steady course instead of moving upward and downward in a seemingly endless cycle?

Deficits and Inflation Rates

Some economists argue that bigger budget deficits (as a percentage of total output) cause higher inflation rates. They point to the periods 1961–65, 1966–70, 1971–75, and 1976–80 as evidence. In each of these five-year periods, as the average annual deficit grew, the average annual inflation rate rose.

But other economists argue that bigger budget deficits do not cause higher inflation rates. They cite the 1981–85 period, in which the average annual deficit grew and the average annual inflation rate fell.

The evidence is mixed bag. Is there a cause–effective relationship between deficits and inflation or not? Under what conditions might there be?

Net Exports

For most of this century, United States exports were greater than its imports—that is, **net exports** (or the difference between exports and imports) were positive. Beginning in 1983, though, the situation began to reverse (see Exhibit 5–6). This raises the question, How has this turnabout affected the U.S. economy?

Net Exports
Exports – imports.

A ROADMAP TO MACROECONOMICS

When beginning a long trip by car, it is customary to have a roadmap in front of you so that you know where you are going and what you can expect along the way. Similarly, when beginning a course of study, such as macroeconomics, it is nice to have a roadmap in front of you to know where you are headed and what you will learn on the way. Let's now outline our roadmap to learning macroeconomics. (As you follow the roadmap, note the times our discussion relates either directly or indirectly to P, the price level, or Q, real GNP).

In Chapter 6, we discuss a key economic measurement, **gross national product (GNP)**. Gross national product is the total market value of all final goods and services produced annually in an economy. In P–Q terms, GNP is P times Q. For example, if a tiny economy produces, say, only 12 oranges the whole year, and the price of each orange is $2, then the GNP for the economy is $2 times 12 oranges, or $24.

In Chapter 7, we take the two components of GNP—P and Q—and look at each separately. We study the price level, then we study real GNP. Finally, we discuss unemployment, which is related to changes in real GNP.

In Chapter 8, we develop a framework of analysis, called the aggregate demand–aggregate supply framework (AD–AS framework), in which we can graphically represent changes in the key variables we have studied up to this point—that is, changes in GNP, the price level, real GNP, and to a lesser extent, unemployment. Chapter 8 puts into pictures much of what we have been discussing in Chapters 6 and 7.

Next, we begin our discussion of economic theory. The theory we discuss in Chapter 9 emphasizes unemployment. In Chapter 10, we discuss fiscal policy, in particular, how it may be used to deal with unemployment.

Gross national product (GNP)
The total market value of all final goods and services produced annually in an economy.

EXHIBIT 5–6
Net Exports, 1970–1990

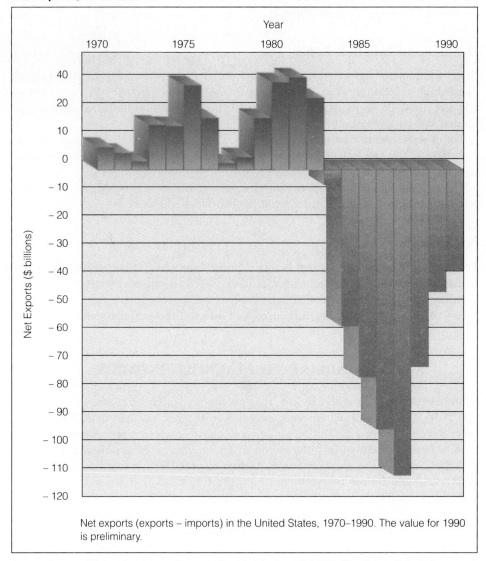

Net exports (exports – imports) in the United States, 1970–1990. The value for 1990 is preliminary.

SOURCE: Council of Economic Advisers, *Economic Report of the President, 1991* (Washington, D.C.: U.S. Government Printing Office, 1991).

Chapters 11–15 introduce money into the macroeconomics picture. Chapters 11 and 12 deal with money and banking and the Federal Reserve System, respectively.

In Chapter 13, we discuss a major macroeconomic problem, inflation, in terms of the *AD–AS* framework developed earlier.

In Chapter 14, we turn again to economic theory and discuss a theory that emphasizes the price level and a theory that emphasizes GNP.

In Chapter 15, our focus is monetary policy, in particular, how it may be used to deal with inflation and unemployment.

In Chapter 16, both inflation and unemployment is our theme. We introduce the important concept of expectations to the macroeconomics discussion, as well as a new macroeconomic theory.

In Chapter 17, we bring together a number of points developed in earlier chapters and discuss them within the context of business cycle theory.

In our last macroeconomics chapter, Chapter 18, we discuss budget deficits and debt, two topics of current interest.

Familiarity Does Not Equal Knowledge

As you study macroeconomics, we urge you to be open minded. Partly because economics is, in part or wholly, the subject of so many stories reported in magazines and newspapers, on the radio and television, laypersons often think they know more about it than they really do. In other words, familiarity with, not knowledge of, economics sometimes prompts people to hold ideas that may not be correct. Perhaps you already have some ideas about the causes of high inflation rates or high unemployment rates. Maybe your ideas are correct, and maybe not. Whatever mindset you bring to the study of macroeconomics, we hope you will be open to new ideas. This does not mean that you should accept everything you read in this text or everything your economics professor tells you. Both the text and the professor need to be questioned (undoubtedly, at times your professor will question the text). But remember that just as you question the text and the professor, you should question your own preconceived ideas, too. Your attitude is as important to understanding the subject as reading the text and taking notes.

CHAPTER SUMMARY

Three Macroeconomic Organizational Categories

■ The *P–Q* category: Macroeconomics emphasizes two major economic variables—the price level (*P*), the weighted average of prices paid for goods and services, and real GNP (*Q*), the total market value of economic output, adjusted for price changes. Many of the topics discussed in macroeconomics are directly or indirectly related to *P, Q,* or both.

■ The inherently stable–inherently unstable category: Some economists view the economy as self-equilibrating, or inherently stable, and some view it as inherently unstable (and therefore in need of manipulation).

■ The effective–ineffective category: Some economists believe that macroeconomic policy, such as fiscal policy, is effective at accomplishing its goals; some economists believe it is ineffective.

Macroeconomic Players

■ The key macroeconomic players are (1) households, (2) businesses, (3) government at all levels, (4) the federal government, in particular the president of the United States, the U.S. Congress, and the U.S. Treasury, (5) foreigners as buyers of U.S. goods, (6) Americans as buyers of foreign goods, and (7) the Federal Reserve System.

Facts and Questions

■ Economists often proceed from facts to questions to theories. For example, an economist might note that the price level was stable over one period of time and rising over another. He might then ask, Why? What factors affect the price level?

Naturally, the economist tries to find an answer. At this level of analysis, theories are formed, explanations offered, predictions made, and later, policies suggested.
■ Macroeconomic facts and questions relate to some of the following topics: the price level, unemployment, inflation, interest rates, budget deficits, recessions, and business cycles.

Key Terms and Concepts

Macroeconomics

Price Level

Real GNP

Fiscal Policy

Monetary Policy

Consumption

Gross Private Domestic Investment (Investment)

Government Expenditures

Exports

Imports

Federal Reserve System (the Fed)

Trade-Off

Budget Deficit

Budget Surplus

Recession

Business Cycle

Net Exports

Gross National Product

QUESTIONS AND PROBLEMS

1. Explain how each of the following is related to *P, Q,* or both: (a) inflation, (b) unemployment, (c) stagflation, (d) monetary policy, (e) fiscal policy.
2. What does it mean to say a person believes the economy is inherently unstable? inherently stable?
3. Suppose economist Jones says that fiscal policy is ineffective. Ineffective at what?
4. What is the Fed and what is its primary duty?
5. What is the difference between monetary policy and fiscal policy?
6. According to economist Axel Leijonhufvud, what is the central issue in macroeconomic theory?
7. Some persons are likely to argue that since the data show rising inflation rates and rising budget deficits over some time periods, and falling inflation rates and rising budget deficits over other time periods, there is obviously no connection between deficits and interest rates. What might be incorrect about this conclusion?
8. In the text, it was noted that economists do not all share the same view as to the inherent nature of a market economy. With this point in mind, what differences of opinion might arise concerning the business cycle?
9. What explanations can you offer for the seesaw movement between budget surpluses and deficits before 1969 and the record of annual budget deficits afterward?
10. Important economic, social, and political developments have sometimes been linked to major economic woes. In the 1970s, the United States incurred high inflation rates relative to its economic past. Can you name any institutional changes that may have resulted from this bout with inflation?
11. "Economists disagree on macroeconomic policies; therefore, we may conclude that some economists are not as smart as other economists." Discuss.

12. To familiarize yourself with some of the macroeconomic topics that are discussed in the following chapters, read some recent back issues of the *Wall Street Journal.* Discuss some of the macroeconomic questions you would like to have answered that were not brought up in this chapter.

13. Make a list of the major macroeconomic problems of the day as conveyed to you through news magazines, newspapers, and television news programs. What are some of the economic policies that are currently being implemented to deal with the problems?

MEASURING GNP

WHAT THIS CHAPTER IS ABOUT

In a way, economists are like doctors. Just as the doctor wants to measure aspects of a patient's physiology to see how the patient is doing, the economist wants to measure the economy to see how it is doing. To find out, the economist must make use of macroeconomic measurements. A key macroeconomic measurement is gross national product (GNP), which is the major topic of this chapter.

FOUR ECONOMIC SECTORS AND FOUR TYPES OF EXPENDITURES

■

As stated in Chapter 5, economists divide the economy into four sectors: the *house-hold sector*, the *business sector*, the *government sector*, and the *foreign sector*. Each of these sectors makes expenditures. The expenditures of the household sector are called *consumption*; the expenditures of the business sector are called *gross private domestic investment*, or simply *investment*; the expenditures of the government sector are called *government expenditures* and the expenditures of the foreign sector are called *net exports*. We discuss each type of expenditure next.

Household Sector: Consumption

Consumption expenditures (*C*) include (1) spending on durable goods, (2) spending on nondurable goods, and (3) spending on services.

Durable goods are goods that are expected to last for more than a year, such as a refrigerator, oven, or car. *Nondurable goods* are goods that are not expected to last for more than a year, such as food. *Services* are intangible items such as lawn care, car repair, and entertainment. In 1990, consumption was $3,658 billion.

Business Sector: Gross Private Domestic Investment

Gross private domestic investment (usually denoted by *I*, for *investment*) is the sum of (1) the purchases of newly produced capital goods, sometimes referred to as **fixed investment**[1], and (2) changes in business inventories, sometimes referred to as **inventory investment.** For example, if business spent $500 billion on newly produced capital goods, and its inventories increased by $150 billion, then (gross private domestic) investment would equal $650 billion. In 1990, investment was $745 billion.

Government Sector: Government Expenditures

Government expenditures (*G*) consist of the total dollar amounts spent by federal, state, and local governments on final goods and services. Government **transfer payments,** which are payments to persons that are not made in return for goods and services currently supplied, are not included in government expenditures. Social Security benefits and welfare payments are two examples of transfer payments, since neither is a payment for current productive efforts.[2] In 1990, government expenditures were $1,098 billion.

Foreign Sector: Net Exports

Net exports is equal to exports (*X*) minus imports (*M*). Net exports can be positive or negative. If positive, then exports are greater than imports; if negative, then imports are greater than exports. In 1990, net exports were −$38 billion.

---

[1]Fixed investment also includes new residential housing. Government statisticians include consumer expenditures on new residential housing in gross private domestic investment because they believe that a new house is an investment good that will provide a stream of services far into the future.

[2]Specifically, Social Security and welfare payments are examples of *government transfer payments*. Beside government transfer payments, there are personal and business transfer payments. For now, we are only concerned with government transfer payments.

Economists divide the economy into four sectors: household, business, government, and foreign.

■

Fixed Investment
Business purchases of capital goods, such as machinery and factories, and consumer purchases of new residential housing.

Inventory Investment
Changes in the stock of unsold goods.

Transfer Payments
Payments that are not made in return for goods and services currently supplied.

The Spending Stream, Injections, and Leakages

In this section we discuss the spending stream, injections, and leakages.

The Spending Stream.   Consider an economy with only two sectors: a household sector and a business sector. Since there is no government sector, there are no taxes to be paid. And since there is no foreign sector, (U.S.) business firms do not sell export goods and (U.S.) households do not buy import goods.

In this two-sector economy, business firms do two things: They sell goods and services to households, and they purchase the factors of production (land, labor, capital, and entrepreneurship) from households. In short, business firms are *sellers* in the goods and services markets, and they are *buyers* in factor (resource) markets.

Similarly, households do two things: They buy goods and services from business firms, and they sell factors (resources) to firms. In short, they are *buyers* in the goods and services markets, and they are *sellers* in factor (resource) markets.

We start with two conditions: (1) Business firms sell everything they produce. (2) Households spend their entire income on goods and services as soon as they receive it. For example, suppose the entire output of business firms consists of 1,000 units of *X,* where each unit of *X* is sold for $4. Households spend $4,000 ($4 × 1,000 units) to purchase the 1,000 units of *X.* The $4,000 the business firms receive goes for the factors (resources) they buy. The payment to labor is called *wages;* the payment to land is called *rent;* the payment to capital is called *interest;* and the payment to entrepreneurship is called *profits.*

As you can see, the $4,000 is being passed around from one sector to the other. The household sector, in its role as buyer of goods and services, pays the $4,000 to business firms. Business firms, in their role as seller of goods and services, receive the $4,000 in payment for the goods and services they sell to households.

But then the business firms, in their role as buyers of factors (resources), pay out the $4,000 to households. Households, in their role as sellers of factors (such as labor) receive the $4,000 in payment for the factors they sell to business firms.

The process of passing the $4,000 from the household sector to the business sector and then from the business sector to the household sector, over and over again, describes a *spending stream.* For now, think of a spending stream as you would a real stream (of water). Water flows from one place to another in a real stream, and dollars flow from one sector to another in a spending stream.

Leakages and Injections.   As in a real stream, the water level can rise or fall. If there is a heavy rain, the water level in the stream will rise. If there is a drought, the water level in the stream will fall.

Similarly, in the spending stream, its level of spending can rise or fall. To illustrate, let's return to our spending stream of $4,000 at the point where business firms are paying the $4,000 to households for factors purchased. The household sector now has the $4,000 in its possession. Suppose that instead of spending the entire $4,000 on goods and services produced by the business sector, households decide to spend only $3,000 on consumer goods. They decide to save $1,000. What happens to the spending in the spending stream? It falls, much like the water level in a real stream might fall. The spending stream now only has $3,000 in it instead of $4,000. In our example, *saving* is considered a **leakage:** A leakage is an outflow or withdrawal of expenditures from the spending stream. Stated differently, any part of income that does not go to purchase (U.S.) goods and services is considered a leakage.

The households that saved the $1,000 placed it in the **credit market.** A credit market is a market that channels funds from savers (lenders) to borrowers. Suppose

---

Business firms are sellers in goods and services markets and buyers in factor (resource) markets.

■

Leakage
An outflow or withdrawal of expenditures from the spending stream. Any part of income that does not go to purchase (U.S.) goods and services is considered a leakage.

Credit Market
A market that channels funds from savers (lenders) to borrowers.

now that business firms borrow the $1,000 that households saved and use it to purchase a new capital good. Notice what business firms are doing: They are *buying* a capital good, which is an investment expenditure. Up until this time, all that business firms have done is (1) sell goods and services in the goods and services markets and (2) buy factors in factor markets. Now, to this list we add (3) buy a good in the goods and services markets.

How does this investment expenditure by business firms (in the goods and services markets) affect the spending stream? We left the spending stream when it was down to $3,000. The $1,000 purchase by business firms is an **injection,** or an inflow of expenditures, into the spending stream. Any expenditures on (U.S.) goods and services besides consumption expenditures is considered an injection. As a result of this $1,000 injection, the spending stream rises to $4,000.

Let us summarize a few key points.

1. The spending stream (initially) consists of the consumption expenditures of the household sector, wherein households spend their entire income on consumer goods.

2. The spending stream can rise or fall depending on whether there are injections into, or leakages out of, the spending stream.

3. Saving is a leakage; investment is an injection.

Types of Injections and Leakages. In our example earlier, saving was a leakage and investment was an injection. What are other injections and leakages?

We remind ourselves that any expenditure on (U.S.) goods and services besides consumption expenditures is considered an injection. For example, as we saw earlier, investment spending is an injection. But so are government spending and foreign spending on U.S. goods and services (exports).

We remind ourselves that any part of income that does not go to purchase (U.S.) goods and services is considered a leakage. For example, as we saw earlier, saving is a leakage. But so are taxes (when people pay taxes they can't use those funds to buy U.S. goods and services) and the spending that Americans do when they buy foreign goods (imports).

In summary, investment expenditures, government expenditures, and exports are injections. Saving, taxes, and imports are leakages.

Total Expenditures. The sum of the expenditures on goods and services made by the different sectors of the economy comprise *total expenditures.* For example, if the four sectors of the economy together spend $5 trillion on goods and services, then total expenditures equal $5 trillion.

Sum of the expenditures made by the
four sectors of the economy =
Total Expenditures

A Four-Sector Economy

Many of the key activities that take place in an economy can be seen with the help of a *circular-flow diagram,* such as the one in Exhibit 6–1. This is a circular-flow diagram of a four-sector economy. Consider what is happening in each sector.

Household Sector. First, households are making consumption expenditures on U.S. goods and services. As you can see in Exhibit 6–1, the "consumption expenditures arrow" flows into U.S. goods and services markets.

Households are buyers in goods and services markets and sellers in factor (resource) markets.

■

Injection
Any expenditure on (U.S.) goods and services besides consumption expenditures is considered an injection. In short, any nonconsumption expenditure.

EXHIBIT 6–1
The Circular-Flow Diagram of a Four-Sector Economy

The circular-flow diagram shows the economic activities of the four sectors of the economy. Households (1) make consumption expenditures, (2) save, (3) pay net taxes, and (4) buy imported goods. Businesses (1) borrow funds and (2) make investment expenditures. Government (1) borrows funds (2) collects net taxes and (3) makes expenditures. Foreigners (1) buy American goods. (In the exhibit, we have simplified things by assuming that only households buy imported goods. In the real world, households, businesses, and government buy imported goods. If we modified the diagram to take this into account, the investment expenditures and government expenditures arrows would flow into foreign economies as well as into the U.S. goods and services markets. Also, in the real world, foreigners are lenders in the U.S. credit market. We have not shown this in the exhibit.)

Second, households are saving. As we learned earlier, saving is a leakage—it does not go to buy goods and services. (Notice that the "saving arrow" *does not* flow into goods and services markets.) Saving finds its way into a credit market, which channels funds from savers (or lenders) to borrowers.

Third, households are paying **net taxes.** Net taxes is equal to taxes minus transfer payments. Earlier, we defined *transfer payments* as payments to persons that are not made in return for goods and services currently supplied, for example, a Social Security payment to a retired person. What happens is that taxes flow from households to government, and transfer payments flow from government to households. Net taxes is simply the difference between the two.

Fourth, households are buying imported goods. We discuss this later.

Net Taxes
Taxes minus transfer payments.

Business Sector. First, business firms borrow funds in the credit market (see the "business borrowing arrow" in Exhibit 6–1). Second, businesses use the borrowed funds, and perhaps some nonborrowed funds, too, to buy new capital goods. The purchase of new capital goods is investment. Notice that the "investment expenditures arrow" flows into U.S. goods and services markets.

Government Sector. The government is involved in three activities: First, it collects net taxes from the household sector; second, it borrows funds in the credit market; and third, it uses borrowed and perhaps nonborrowed funds to purchase goods and services. Notice that the "government expenditures arrow" flows into the U.S. goods and services markets.

Foreign Sector. In Exhibit 6–1, we see that two things are going on in the foreign sector. First, U.S. households are buying imported goods from foreigners. This is a leakage from the U.S. spending stream, since the money spent on imported goods is spent in foreign goods and services markets, not U.S. goods and services markets. (Notice that the "imports arrow" does not flow into the U.S. goods and services markets.)

Second, foreigners are buying U.S. exported goods. This is an injection into the U.S. spending stream, since the money spent on exported goods does go into U.S. goods and services markets. (Notice that the "exports arrow" does flow into the U.S. goods and services market.)[3]

Economists are keenly aware of the constraints that operate in different areas of human activity. They use their knowledge of these constraints to gain insights into the workings of the economy. Here is an illustration, in two steps.

Step 1: The Constraint. In Exhibit 6–1, we showed that the household sector places its savings in the credit market and that both the business and government sectors borrow funds in the credit market. It follows that the total amount of funds that business and government borrow *cannot be greater* than the total amount of funds that households save. Simply put, business and government borrowing is *constrained* by household saving.

Step 2: The Insight. With the knowledge of this constraint, we can see how government actions may affect the economy. For example, the principal reason government borrows funds is because it must finance budget deficits, and

[3]A third thing that is happening in the foreign sector is that foreign funds are coming into the credit market. We have ignored this fact to keep the analysis relatively simple at this stage.

the larger the deficits, the more funds that are borrowed. But funds the government borrows cannot be borrowed by business, too. And the less business borrows, the smaller investment spending will be. Insight: Deficits, originating in the government sector, *may reduce* the amount of investment spending in the economy.[4]

Where Do Total Expenditures Go?

Where do the dollars that flow into U.S. goods and services markets go? In Exhibit 6–1, we see that total expenditures end up in business firms (the "total expenditure arrow" flows out of goods and services markets and into business firms).

But what do the business firms do with the expenditures made by the four sectors of the economy? Recall that business firms do not produce goods and services out of thin air. It takes factors of production, or resources—*land, labor, capital,* and *entrepreneurship*—to produce goods and services. Each of these factors receives a payment for its use: *wages* (to labor), *rent,* (to land), *interest* (to capital), and *profits* (to entrepreneurship).

So, ultimately, the total expenditures received by business firms end up as factor payments. For example, let's say that total expenditures equal $40 billion. Some of the $40 billion will go to pay for labor, some will go to pay for land, some will go to pay for capital goods, and some will go to pay for entrepreneurship. The sum of the factor payments—that is, wages + rents + interest + profits—will equal total expenditures.

Total expenditures = Sum of factor payments

With this in mind, consider Exhibit 6–1 again. Notice that total expenditures flow into business firms (purple arrow) and factor payments flow out of business firms (dark blue arrow). Factor payments are made in factor (or resource) markets—such as the labor market, the capital goods market, and so on. The recipients of the factor payments are members of the household sector. The factor payments that households receive are considered *income.* Therefore, we conclude that the sum of the factor payments is equal to total income.

Sum of factor payments = Total income

Key Points Concerning a Four-Sector Economy

Let us review some key points.

1. In a four-sector economy, total expenditures is the sum of the expenditures made by the four sectors of the economy.

Sum of the expenditures made by the four sectors of the economy =
Total expenditures

2. Business firms receive total expenditures. This total dollar amount is used to make factor payments to labor (wages), land (rent), capital (interest), and entrepreneurship (profits). Therefore,

Total expenditures = Sum of factor payments

[4]We say "may reduce" the amount of investment spending in the economy because some economists argue that as the government finances the deficit, citizens perceive higher taxes in the future and thus save more today in order to pay the higher taxes tomorrow. If this happens, the pool of funds firms at their disposal to borrow from grows. Much more will be said about this in a later chapter.

3. The recipients of the factor payments consider the payments to be income. Therefore,

$$\text{Sum of factor payments} = \text{Total income}$$

4. Since *total expenditures* = sum of factor payments (point 2), and the sum of factor payments = *total income* (point 3), it follows that

$$\text{Total expenditures} = \text{Total income}$$

Later, we will see that economists measure the gross national product (GNP) in two ways: by the *expenditure approach* and by the *income approach*. For now, we simply note that the two ways to measure GNP will give us the same dollar figure, since, as we have just learned in point 4, *total expenditures* equal *total income*.

GROSS NATIONAL PRODUCT

In Chapter 5, we said that much of what economists discuss in macroeconomics has to do with the price level, (P), real GNP (Q), or both. Gross national product (GNP) has to do with both, since it is the product of P *times* Q. In Exhibit 6–2, you see GNP figures for selected nations.

GNP Is a Flow Variable

Gross national product is *the total market value of all final goods and services produced annually in an economy.* For example, suppose we deal with a one-good economy: Here, only 10 units of one good are produced and each unit sells for $4. The GNP of the one-good economy is $40—or the *price* of each unit of the good *times* the *quantity*. If we move to a large economy, where there are thousands of goods produced and thousands of different prices, GNP is the price level (P) *times* real GNP (Q).

GNP is a **flow variable** as opposed to a **stock variable.** A flow variable is a variable that can only be meaningfully measured over a period of time. For example, if someone were to ask you your income, it would be important to specify your income over *some time period*—a week, or a month, or a year. If you simply stated your income as, say, $4,000, it would not be clear if you were talking about $4,000 a year, $4,000 a month, or $4,000 a week, since some people fall into each of these three categories.

A stock variable is one that can be meaningfully measured at a moment in time. The U.S. money supply is a stock variable. If someone were to ask how much the money supply is, it would not be necessary to specify a time period. We would not say that the money supply is $800 billion a week, or a month, or a year. We would simply say that the money supply is $800 billion, period.

The Common Denominator in GNP

How can different goods, such as bicycles, radios, and carpets, be added together to form a meaningful measurement? After all, all goods are not measured in the same units. Some are measured in pounds, others in feet and inches, and so on. All goods, however, are sold for dollar price, which serves as a common denominator. In the definition of GNP, the words *total market value* refer to *total dollar value at current prices.* For this reason, economists sometimes refer to GNP more

Gross National Product (GNP)
The total market value of all final goods and services produced annually in an economy.

Flow Variable
A variable that can only be meaningfully measured over a period of time. GNP is a flow variable.

Stock Variable
A variable that can be meaningfully measured at a moment in time. For example, the nation's money supply is a stock variable.

EXHIBIT 6–2
GNP in Selected Nations, 1987 (in billions)

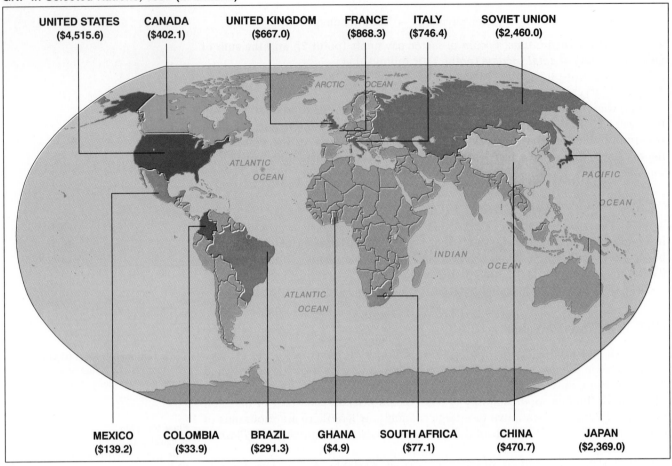

| UNITED STATES ($4,515.6) | CANADA ($402.1) | UNITED KINGDOM ($667.0) | FRANCE ($868.3) | ITALY ($746.4) | SOVIET UNION ($2,460.0) |

| MEXICO ($139.2) | COLOMBIA ($33.9) | BRAZIL ($291.3) | GHANA ($4.9) | SOUTH AFRICA ($77.1) | CHINA ($470.7) | JAPAN ($2,369.0) |

SOURCES: U.S. Bureau of the Census, *Statistical Abstract of the United States,* 1990 (Washington, D.C.: U.S. Government Printing Office, 1990), and Council of Economic Advisers, *Economic Report of the President, 1991* (Washington, D.C.: U.S. Government Printing Office, 1991).

Nominal GNP
The value of final goods and services produced in a given year in that year's prevailing market prices. The terms GNP, nominal GNP, and current-dollar GNP are used interchangeably.

specifically as *current-dollar GNP* or **nominal GNP.** In this text, GNP refers to current-dollar or nominal GNP.

Why calculate GNP? Is it so important to have a measurement of the total value of all final goods and services produced annually in a nation's economy? Many economists argue that measuring GNP gives economists and governmental policy makers a "fix" on the economy that they would not otherwise have and without which they could not formulate appropriate economic policies as easily or as precisely.

Why Measure Final Goods?

Final Good
A good in the hands of its final user.

Intermediate Good
A good that is an input in the production of a final good.

The words **final goods** in the definition of GNP mean a good in the hands of its final or ultimate user. In contrast, an **intermediate good** has not reached its final user. For example, the car that you buy is a final good. In producing the car, the car company had to purchase such things as steel, glass, rubber, plastic, and so

116

on. These goods are called intermediate goods: They are inputs in the production of the final good—the car.

Gross national product takes into account (measures the value of) only final goods (and services). The reason is that the national income accountants who calculate GNP do not want to count the same goods more than once. They do not want to commit the error of **double counting.**

Double Counting
Counting a good more than once when computing GNP.

To illustrate, suppose a book is a final good and that intermediate goods paper, ink, and glue go together to make it. Let us also suppose that the final good, the book, is sold for $20 and that intermediate goods paper, ink, and glue are sold for $10, $6, and $4, respectively.

If we were to count the market value of the book *and* the market value of each of the intermediate goods, we would be counting the intermediate goods twice.

Doing this (which is wrong, but not so easy to see as wrong)

(1)

Market value of book	$20
Market value of paper	10
Market value of ink	6
Market value of glue	4
	$40

is the same as doing this (which is obviously wrong):

(2)

Market value of paper	$10
Market value of ink	6
Market value of glue	4
Market value of paper	10
Market value of ink	6
Market value of glue	4
	$40

It is clear in (2) that we are counting the intermediate goods *twice.* It is not so clear that we are doing this in (1), *but we are.* Since the market value of the book is the sum of the market values of paper, ink, and glue, the total in (1) equals the total in (2). To avoid double counting, national income accountants compute GNP by counting the total market value of *only final goods and services* produced annually in an economy. In our example, this would be the market value of the book ($20).

What GNP Omits

Some exchanges that take place in an economy are omitted from the GNP measurement. As the following list indicates, these range from sales of used cars to illegal drug deals.

Certain Nonmarket Goods and Services. If a family hires a person through the classified section of the newspaper to cook and clean, the service is counted in GNP. If a family member performs the same tasks, however, their services will not be counted in GNP. The difference is that, in the first case, a service is actually bought and sold for a price in a market setting, and in the other, it is not.

There are, however, some nonmarket goods that GNP does not omit. For example, the market value of food produced on a farm but consumed by the farm family is estimated, and this *imputed value* is part of GNP.

Underground Economy
Unreported exchanges that take place outside the normal recorded market channels. Some underground activities deal with illegal goods; others deal with legal goods and tax evasion.

Underground Activities, Both Legal and Illegal.   The **underground economy** consists of unreported exchanges that take place outside the normal recorded market channels.[5] Some underground activities deal with illegal goods (such as cocaine), and others deal with legal goods and tax evasion.

Illegal goods and services are not counted in GNP because no record exists of such transactions. There are no written records of illegal drug sales, illegal gambling, and prostitution. Neither are there written records of some legal activities that individuals want to keep from government notice. For example, a gardener might agree to do some gardening work only on the condition that he is paid in cash. Obviously, it is not illegal for a person to buy or sell gardening services, but still the transaction might not be recorded if one or both of the parties does not want it to be. Why might the gardener want to be paid in cash? Perhaps he doesn't want to pay taxes on the income received—an objective more easily accomplished if there is no written record of the income being generated.

Sales of Used Goods.   GNP is a measurement of current production (that is, occurring during the current year). A used car sale, for example, does not enter into the current year statistics because the car was counted when it was originally produced.

Financial Transactions.   The trading of stocks and bonds is not counted in GNP because it does not represent the production of new assets, but simply the trading of assets (stocks or bonds for money).

Government Transfer Payments.   Government transfer payments—such as Social Security benefits and veterans' benefits—are not counted in GNP because they do not represent a payment to individuals for current production.

Leisure.   Leisure is a good, in much the same way that cars, houses, and shoes are goods. More new cars, houses, and shoes get counted in GNP, but more leisure does not because it is too difficult to quantify. In this century in the United States, the length of the work week has fallen—indicating to us that the leisure time individuals have to consume has increased—but GNP computations do not take this into account.

Bads Generated in the Production of Goods.   Economic growth often comes with certain *bads*. For example, producing more cars, furniture, and steel often generates more air and water pollution—considered bads by most people. (Remember from Chapter 1 that a bad is anything from which individuals receive disutility.) GNP counts the additional goods and services, but it does not net out the additional air and water pollution, thus overstating, some economists argue, our overall economic welfare.

---

[5]Other adjectives beside *underground* have been used to describe the type of economy we are discussing: subterranean, irregular, hidden, unrecorded, unofficial, concealed, parallel, informal, unobserved, submerged, shadow, cash, clandestine, moonlight, twilight, second, counter, the back door, and off the books.

The Underground Economy

Economists estimate that the underground economy in the United States is larger than the economies of many countries—within the range of 5 to 12 percent of GNP. If we settle on 8 percent as a reasonable estimate, then this amounts to $437 billion in 1990. This is larger than the GNP of Belgium, Denmark, Greece, Ireland, Luxembourg, Portugal, Spain, Austria, Finland, Norway, Sweden, Switzerland, Turkey, Australia, New Zealand, and many more countries.

In a study conducted by the U.S. Department of Commerce, the United States was estimated to have a larger underground economy (relative to its GNP) than Switzerland and Japan, but smaller than Sweden, Norway, Canada, and Italy. Some economists argue that the relative size of the underground economy grows when the tax burden becomes heavier, *ceteris paribus*.

How do economists judge the size of the underground economy, which, after all, is not visible? Their estimates are based on the assumption that there is a strong association between the amount of cash (relative to checks) individuals use in making their exchanges and the amount of underground economic activity. Since underground economic activity is based on cash, some economists argue that the more cash that is demanded relative to other forms of making monetary payment, the larger the relative size of the underground economy. For example, in recent years most banks in the Miami area have witnessed a huge increase in the use of cash, which likely indicates an increase in the underground illicit drug trade.

If the underground economy is between 5 and 12 percent of GNP, then official economic statistics both overstate and understate the economic truth. For example, growth rates in GNP understate the growth of the overall economy, and unemployment rates certainly overstate the true unemployment rate.

Question:

Suppose a radio is produced during this year but is not sold to any customer. Is the radio counted as part of GNP?

Answer:

Yes, it is. To illustrate, suppose a firm produces 10,000 radios this year, but only sells 9,000 radios. The remaining 1,000 radios become part of inventory, and are considered, by national income accountants, to have been "bought" by the firm that produced them.

Our definition of *investment* includes (1) the purchases of new capital goods *and* (2) changes in inventory. In other words, the radio that is produced but not sold is added to inventory and is considered to be a part of investment. If the radio is sold next year, it will not be counted again in GNP since it was produced the year before and thus no longer represents current production.

Follow-up Question:

Suppose someone reads in the newspaper that investment in the United States is up from last year. Is this good for the economy?

Answer:

The article in the newspaper does not specify if investment is up because business firms are buying more new capital goods or because consumers are buying fewer goods than expected and consequently inventories are rising (much to the dismay of business firms). To answer the question, we need to know not only that investment is up, buy *why* it is up.

GNP: Is It a Measurement of Happiness of Well-Being?

Are the persons in a country with a higher GNP, or higher per capita GNP, better off or happier than the persons in a country with a lower GNP, or lower per capita GNP? We cannot answer that question because well-being and happiness are subjective. A person with more goods may be happier than a person with fewer goods, but possibly not. For all we know, the person with fewer goods, but a lot of leisure, little air pollution, and a relaxed way of life, may be much happier than the person with many goods, little leisure, and a polluted, stressful environment.

We make this point to warn against reading too much into GNP figures. GNP figures are useful for obtaining an estimate of the productive capabilities of an economy, but they are not necessarily a measurement of happiness or well-being.

TWO WAYS OF MEASURING GNP

Gross national product is measured by the Bureau of Economic Analysis (BEA), which is a division of the U.S. Department of Commerce. The BEA uses two approaches to measure GNP: the *expenditure approach* and the *income approach.* Exhibit 6–3 provides an overview of each approach.

EXHIBIT 6–3
Two Approaches to Measuring GNP

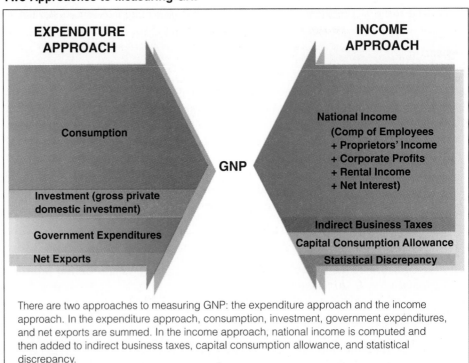

There are two approaches to measuring GNP: the expenditure approach and the income approach. In the expenditure approach, consumption, investment, government expenditures, and net exports are summed. In the income approach, national income is computed and then added to indirect business taxes, capital consumption allowance, and statistical discrepancy.

The Expenditure Approach

The expenditure approach to measuring GNP sums the expenditures made by the four sectors of the economy. This may give you reason to pause, since the definition of GNP on page 115 did not mention expenditures. Rather, GNP was defined as the total market value of all final goods and services *produced* annually in an economy.

The discrepancy is cleared up quickly once we remember that national income accountants assume that anything that is produced but not sold (to consumers) is "bought" by the firm that produced it. In other words, if something is produced but not sold it goes into business inventory and is considered investment. Thus, we can measure GNP by summing the expenditures made by the four sectors of the economy. GNP equals consumption (C) plus investment (I) plus government expenditures (G) plus net exports ($X - M$) (Exhibit 6–4).

$$GNP = C + I + G + (X - M)$$

Question:

In recent years, there has been added interest in international economic events. How do residents in foreign nations affect the U.S. GNP?

Answer:

One way is through the net exports component of GNP. Suppose foreigners increase their purchases of American exports. In the GNP equation—GNP = $C + I + G + (X - M)$—exports (X) rise, and this increases U.S. GNP, *ceteris paribus*. On the other hand, if foreigners decrease their purchases of American exports, U.S. GNP falls, *ceteris paribus*. In general, whether we are talking about the interna-

EXHIBIT 6–4
Components of GNP (Expenditure Approach)

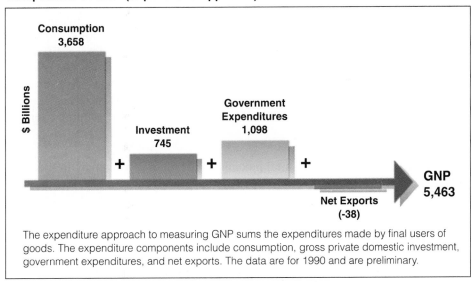

The expenditure approach to measuring GNP sums the expenditures made by final users of goods. The expenditure components include consumption, gross private domestic investment, government expenditures, and net exports. The data are for 1990 and are preliminary.

SOURCE: Council of Economic Advisers, *Economic Report of the President*, 1991 (Washington, D.C.: U.S. Government Printing Office, 1991).

tional economic arena or the domestic economic arena, anything that raises (lowers) *C, I, G,* or *X* will raise (lower) GNP; anything that raises (lowers) *M* will lower (raise) GNP.[6]

The Income Approach

National Income
The sum of the payments to suppliers of the factors of production. It is equal to the compensation of employees + proprietors' income + corporate profits + rental income of persons + net interest.

The second approach to measuring GNP is the income approach, which has two steps: First, we add up the payments to the factors of production, which gives us **national income (NI).** Second, we adjust national income for indirect business taxes, a capital consumption allowance (or depreciation), and a statistical discrepancy. (We define these terms in our discussion.)

Factor payments include wages, rents, interest, and profits. Note, though, that national income accountants have fancier terms for factor payments than wages, rent, interest, and profits. They are compensation to employees, proprietors' income, corporate profits, rental income of persons, and net interest.

Compensation of Employees.   Compensation of employees consists of wages and salaries paid to employees plus employers' contributions to Social Security and employee benefit plans, as well as the monetary value of fringe benefits, tips, and paid vacations. Compensation of employees is the largest component of national income. In 1990, it accounted for 73.4 percent of national income. Note that compensation of employees is not 73.4 percent of GNP because national income does not equal GNP.

Proprietors' Income.   Proprietors' income includes all forms of income earned by self-employed individuals and the owners of unincorporated businesses, including unincorporated farmers. Included in farm income is an estimate of the value of the food grown and consumed on farms. In 1990, proprietors' income accounted for 8 percent of national income.

Corporate Profits.   Corporate profits include all the income earned by the stockholders of corporations. Some of the profits are paid out to stockholders in the form of dividends, some are kept within the firm to finance investments (these are called undistributed profits or retained earnings), and some are used to pay corporate profits taxes. (The portion of corporate profits that goes to pay corporate profits taxes is counted as income "earned" by households even though households do not receive the income.) In 1990, corporate profits accounted for 6.9 percent of national income.

Rental Income (of Persons).   Rental income is the income received by individuals for the use of their nonmonetary assets (land, houses, offices). It also includes returns to individuals who hold copyrights and patents. Finally, it includes an imputed value to owner-occupied houses. For example, someone may own the house she lives in, and therefore not pay any rent, but for purposes of national income accounting a rental value is imputed. In short, homeownership is viewed as a business that produces a service that is sold to the owner of the business. In 1990, net rental income accounted for 1.1 percent of national income.

[6]For information on how exports and imports affect real GNP, see the Economics In Our Times in Chapter 8.

Net Interest. This is the interest income received by U.S. households and government minus the interest they paid out. In 1990, it was 10.6 percent of national income.

National Income and GNP: A Slight Modification

In the circular-flow diagram in Exhibit 6–1, total expenditures equalled total income. We would expect, then, that GNP, equal to the sum of the expenditures made by the four sectors of the economy, would equal national income. This is not the case, however. For example, GNP in 1990 was $5463 billion and national income was $4417.5 billion. This is because there are two nonincome expense items—indirect business taxes and the capital consumption allowance—that are not paid to factor owners, plus a relatively minor statistical discrepancy. If we add the two nonincome expense items and the statistical discrepancy to national income, the sum equals GNP.

Indirect Business Taxes. The main items that comprise indirect business taxes include excise taxes, sales taxes, and property taxes. These taxes are not part of national income because they are not considered a payment to any factor of production. (Recall that national income is the sum of factor payments.) They are, however, included in total expenditures, and therefore are picked up in the expenditure approach to measuring GNP. Therefore, we must add indirect business taxes to national income in order to move closer to comparable approaches to measuring GNP.

Question:

Earlier, it was noted that corporate profits taxes are considered a factor payment. Now, we learn sales taxes are not considered a factor payment. Why is one tax considered a factor payment whereas the other is not?

Answer:

National income accountants consider corporate profits taxes to be income "earned" by households, even though they are not directly received as income by households. Therefore, corporate profits taxes are included in national income. A sales tax, however, is not considered to be income earned by anyone. Therefore, it is not considered a factor payment and is not included in national income.

Capital Consumption Allowance. Some capital goods are used up in the production process through natural wear, obsolescence, or accidental destruction (for example, the machinery that breaks down and no longer works). The cost to replace these capital goods is called the **capital consumption allowance, or depreciation.** Replacing depreciated capital does not actually represent new production; therefore, we reduce the value of total production by this amount to show net production for the year (see the discussion of net national product in the next section). For our purposes here, however, capital consumption is added to national income in order to move us closer to GNP.

Statistical Discrepancy. GNP and national income are measured using different sets of data. Hence, statistical discrepancies or pure measurement errors often occur and must be accounted for in the national income accounts.

Capital Consumption Allowance or Depreciation
The estimated amount of capital goods used up in production through natural wear, obsolescence, and accidental destruction.

The Income and Expenditure Approaches Compared

Exhibit 6–5 illustrates the income approach to measuring GNP for 1990. GNP equals national income (the sum of compensation of employees, proprietors' income, corporate profits, rental income, and net interest) + indirect business taxes + capital consumption allowance + statistical discrepancy. Compare Exhibit 6–5 with Exhibit 6–4, which illustrates the expenditure approach to measuring GNP. You will see that we get the same dollar amount.

OTHER NATIONAL INCOME ACCOUNTING MEASUREMENTS

Besides gross national product (GNP) and national income(NI), three other national income accounting measurements are important. They are net national product, personal income, and disposable income. The five measurements—gross national product, national income, net national product, personal income, and disposable income—are often used interchangeably as measurements of the output produced and income earned in an economy.

Net National Product

If we use the expenditure approach to measuring GNP, we add consumption, investment, government expenditures, and net exports. Investment (or, more specifically, gross private domestic investment) includes fixed investment and inventory

EXHIBIT 6–5
Components of GNP (Income Approach)

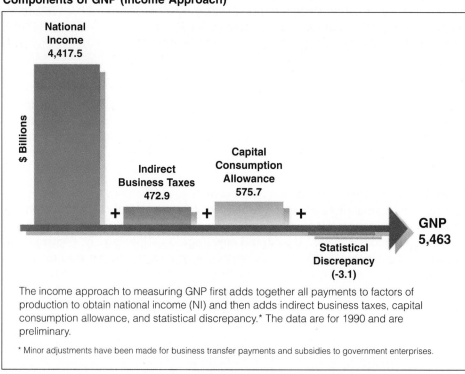

The income approach to measuring GNP first adds together all payments to factors of production to obtain national income (NI) and then adds indirect business taxes, capital consumption allowance, and statistical discrepancy.* The data are for 1990 and are preliminary.

* Minor adjustments have been made for business transfer payments and subsidies to government enterprises.

No Communication with the Outside World: The BEA at Work

When the economists at the Bureau of Economic Analysis sit down to measure GNP, they are beginning a lengthy—and secret—procedure. Two main teams of economists and statisticians do the job. One team measures GNP using the income approach; the other team measures GNP using the expenditure approach.

Initially, each team works independently of the other. Within both teams are subteams of economists and statisticians who compute the individual items. One subteam might be computing consumption, another subteam might be computing investment, and so on. On the morning before the

day the GNP figures are officially released to the public, both teams come together in a conference room in order to sum the figures and check each other's work. For example, the consumption figures are added to the investment figures and so on, and the income-approach team checks to see if its figure for GNP is equal to the figure computed by the expenditure-approach team. If they find discrepancies, they are worked through.

During this time, no one is allowed in or out of the room—except to go to the restroom, but then they must make their visits in pairs. Also, no phone calls—in or out—are allowed.

Absolute secrecy is the rule. Secrecy is important because a leak of the GNP figure could give some people an advantage over others in the bond market, futures markets, and so on.

When the work has been completed (usually late at night), each person in the room is sworn to secrecy. One person takes the GNP figure to the chairman of the Council of Economic Advisers. The chairman then gives the GNP figure to the president of the United States. The next morning, the secretary of the Commerce Department releases the GNP figure to the press.

---

investment. Some of the fixed investment, however, simply goes to replace worn-out or obsolete capital goods. It does not go for new goods. In short, gross private domestic investment contains within it the capital consumption allowance. If we subtract the capital consumption allowance from GNP, we are left with **net national product (NNP)**.[7] NNP measures the total value of new goods available in the economy in a given year, after worn-out capital goods have been replaced. According to Exhibit 6–5, in 1990 the capital consumption allowance was $575.7 billion and GNP was $5,463 billion. It follows that net national product was the difference between the two, or $4,887.3 billion.

Net National Product (NNP)
GNP minus the capital consumption allowance.

$$NNP = GNP - \text{capital consumption allowance}$$

Personal Income

Not all income earned is received, and not all income received is earned. An example of "income earned but not received" is undistributed profits. Undistributed profits are earned by stockholders but are not received by them. Instead, they are usually reinvested by the corporation. An example of "income received but not earned" is Social Security benefits.

Personal income (PI) is the amount of income that individuals actually receive. It is equal to national income minus such major earned-but-not-received items such as undistributed corporate profits, social insurance taxes (Social Security con-

Personal Income (PI)
The amount of income that individuals actually receive. It is equal to national income minus undistributed corporate profits, social insurance taxes, and corporate profits taxes, plus transfer payments.

[7]If we subtract the capital consumption allowance from gross private domestic investment, we are left with *net private domestic investment.* Instead of saying that net national product (NNP) = gross national product − capital consumption allowance, we could say that NNP = consumption + net private domestic investment + government expenditures + net exports.

tributions), and corporate profits taxes plus transfer payments (which are received but not earned).[8] In 1990, personal income was $4,645.6 billion.

$$PI = NI - \text{undistributed corporate profits} - \text{social insurance taxes} - \text{corporate profits taxes} + \text{transfer payments}$$

Disposable Income

Disposable Income (DI)
That portion of personal income that can be used for consumption or saving. It is equal to personal income minus personal taxes (especially income taxes).

The portion of personal income that can be used for consumption or saving is referred to as **disposable income (DI).** It is equal to personal income minus personal taxes (especially income taxes). Sometimes disposable income is referred to as spendable income or take-home pay. In 1990, disposable income was $3,945.8 billion.

$$DI = \text{personal income} - \text{personal taxes}$$

Per-Capita Macroeconomic Measurements

Often economists prefer to work with per-capita economic measurements rather than totals. Any of the five macroeconomic measurements we have discussed— GNP, NNP, NI, PI, or DI—can be converted to a per-capita measurement by dividing by population. For example, if we take the total disposable income in 1990, $3,945.8 billion, and divide it equally among the approximately 251 million people in the United States in 1990, per-capita disposable income would be approximately $15,717. Some economists suggest this is a better measure of the "well-being" of citizens than total disposable income because it adjusts for the number of people who will live on the $3,945.8 billion.

CHAPTER SUMMARY

Types of Expenditures

■ There are four sectors in the economy: household, business, government, and foreign. Each sector makes expenditures. The expenditures of the household sector are called *consumption;* the expenditures of the business sector are called *gross private domestic investment,* or simply, *investment;* the expenditures of the government sector are called *government expenditures;* the expenditures of the foreign sector are called *net exports.*

■ Consumption expenditures include spending on durable goods, nondurable goods, and services.

■ Investment is the sum of the purchases of newly produced capital goods and changes in business inventories. It also includes expenditures on new residential housing.

■ Government expenditures consist of the total dollar amount spent by federal, state, and local governments on final goods and services. Government expenditures do not include transfer payments.

[8]In footnote 2, we gave examples of government transfer payments (Social Security payments, welfare payments) and also noted that government transfer payments are not the only kind of transfer payment. In our definition of personal income, we use the term *transfer payments* to include all varieties.

- Net exports is the total foreign spending on domestic goods minus the total domestic spending on foreign goods, or exports minus imports.
- The sum of the expenditures on goods and services made by the different sectors of the economy equals *total expenditures.*

Total Expenditures, the Sum of Factor Payments, and Total Income

- Business firms *sell* final goods and services and *buy* factors of production (or resources). As sellers, business firms receive the total expenditures made in an economy. As buyers, they pay out the total expenditures in the form of factor payments (payments for land, labor, capital, and entrepreneurship). The recipients of the factor payments consider the payments income. We conclude that total expenditures = sum of factor payments = total income.

Gross National Product

- Gross national product (GNP) is the total market value of all final goods and services produced annually in an economy. The words *total market value* refer to total dollar value at current prices. Therefore, we can speak of current-dollar or nominal GNP.
- To avoid the problem of double counting, only final goods and services are counted in GNP.
- GNP omits certain nonmarket goods and services, both legal and illegal underground activities, the sale of used goods, financial transactions, and transfer payments. GNP is not adjusted for the amount of leisure people consume (even though leisure is a good) or for the bads (like pollution) that sometimes accompany production.

Measuring GNP

- GNP can be measured in two ways: by the expenditure approach and by the income approach. In the expenditure approach, expenditures of different sectors of the economy are summed. These expenditures are consumption, investment, government expenditures, and net exports.

$$GNP = C + I + G + (X - M)$$

- In the income approach, national income (NI) is calculated and then added to indirect business taxes, capital consumption allowance, and statistical discrepancy.

$$GNP = NI + \text{indirect business taxes} + \text{capital consumption allowance} + \\ \text{statistical discrepancy}$$

Measurements Other Than GNP

- Net national product (NNP) equals gross national product (GNP) minus capital consumption allowance.

$$NNP = GNP - \text{capital consumption allowance}$$

- National income (NI) equals the sum of factor payments.

$$NI = \text{compensation of employees} + \text{proprietors' income} + \text{corporate profits} \\ + \text{rental income} + \text{net interest}$$

- Personal income (PI) equals national income (NI) minus undistributed profits, social security insurance taxes, and corporate profits taxes plus transfer payments.

$$PI = NI - \text{undistributed profits} - \text{social insurance taxes} - \text{corporate profits}$$
$$\text{taxes} + \text{transfer payments}$$

- Disposable income (DI) equals personal income (PI) minus personal taxes.

$$DI = PI - \text{personal taxes}$$

Key Terms and Concepts

Fixed Investment	Gross National Product	Underground Economy
Inventory Investment	Flow Variable	National Income
Transfer Payments	Stock Variable	Capital Consumption
Leakage	Nominal GNP	Allowance
		(Depreciation)
Credit Market	Final Good	Net National Product
Injection	Intermediate Good	Personal Income
Net Taxes	Double Counting	Disposable Income

QUESTIONS AND PROBLEMS

1. "I just heard on the news that GNP is higher this year than it was last year. This means that we're better off this year than last year." Comment.

2. Which of the following are included in the calculation of this year's GNP? (a) Twelve-year-old Johnny mowing his family's lawn; (b) Dave Malone buying a used car; (c) Barbara Wilson buying a bond issued by General Motors; (d) Ed Ferguson's receipt of a Social Security payment; (e) the illegal drug transaction at the corner of Elm and Fifth.

3. Discuss the problems you see in comparing the GNP of one country, say, the United States, with the GNP of another country, say, the People's Republic of China.

4. The manuscript for this book was typed by the author. Had he hired someone to do the typing, GNP would have been higher than it was. What other activities would increase GNP if they were done differently? What activities would decrease GNP if they were done differently?

5. What do you think the growth in the underground economy is dependent on? Explain your answer.

6. Using the following data, calculate the following: (a) gross national product (GNP); (b) net national product (NNP); (c) national income (NI); (d) personal income (PI); (e) disposable income (DI); (f) saving (S). All numbers are in billions of dollars.

Consumption	1,732.0
Investment	445.3
Government expenditures	530.3
Net exports	32.1
Capital consumption allowance	303.8

Indirect business taxes	213.3
Statistical discrepancy	4.9
Social insurance taxes	216.5
Transfer payments	405.6
Undistributed profits	91.0
Corporate profits taxes	77.7
Personal taxes	340.0
Dividends	0.0

7. How would an increase in social insurance taxes (Social Security contributions) affect gross national product? How would an increase affect net national product? How would it affect personal income?

8. Is it possible for personal income to rise as disposable income falls?

9. A business firm produces a good this year that it doesn't sell. As a result, the good is added to its inventory. How does this inventory good find its way into GNP?

10. Identify each of the following as an *injection* or a *leakage:* (a) saving, (b) investment expenditures, (c) imports, (d) taxes, (e) government expenditures, (f) exports.

11. Suppose the household sector saves $100 billion this year and the business sector borrows $100 billion to spend on the purchase of new capital goods. This is an example of a leakage (saving) being equally offset by an injection (investment). Give two other examples of a leakage being equally offset by an injection.

12. In Exhibit 6–1, we showed both the business and government sectors borrowing funds in the credit markets. Government borrows largely to finance budget deficits, which exist if government spends more than its tax receipts. Business borrows largely to purchase new capital goods. Suppose government increases its borrowing because of bigger budget deficits. How might government's action affect business borrowing to purchase new capital goods?

THE TWIN DEFICITS: BUDGET AND TRADE

A federal budget deficit exists if government expenditures (G) are greater than tax receipts (T): $G > T$. A trade deficit exists if imports (M) are greater than exports (X): $M > X$. In this appendix, we examine the link between the two deficits.

We start with what we know about GNP. Roughly speaking, GNP equals disposable income (DI) plus taxes (T).[1]

$$\text{GNP} = DI + T \tag{1}$$

Now one can do two things with disposable income, consume (C) it or save (S) it. Thus:

$$\text{DI} = C + S \tag{2}$$

Combining equations (1) and (2), we have

$$\text{GNP} = C + S + T \tag{3}$$

In this chapter, one of the ways we defined GNP was

$$\text{GNP} = C + I + G + (X - M) \tag{4}$$

In short, equations (3) and (4) are two different ways of expressing GNP. Since they are equal,

$$C + I + G + (X - M) = C + S + T \tag{5}$$

If we subtract C from both sides, we have

$$I + G + (X - M) = S + T \tag{6}$$

Rearranging the terms in a way that is appropriate to macroeconomic and international economic analysis, we have

$$G - T = (S - I) - (X - M) \tag{7}$$

---

[1]We say "roughly speaking" because this is not exactly correct. For our purposes here, however, a simplified version is sufficient and does not lead to any loss in content. For the precise definitions of GNP, DI, and many other macroeconomic measurements, see this chapter.

If $G > T$, such that there is a budget deficit, and $M > X$, such that there is a trade deficit, then the equation says

$$\text{Budget deficit} = (S - I) + \text{trade deficit} \qquad (8)$$

You might wonder why we changed the minus $(-)$ sign in equation (7) to a plus sign $(+)$ in equation (8). This is because if $M > X$, then net exports, or the difference between X and M, is negative. On the right side of equation (7), we would have $(S - I) - (\text{negative net exports})$. But a negative times a negative is a plus. So this can be rewritten as $(S - I)$ + trade deficit.[2] In other words, then, equation (8) says that the *budget deficit equals the amount of saving over investment plus the trade deficit.*

For example, if the budget deficit is $200 billion, and saving is greater than investment by $40 billion, it follows that the trade deficit is $160 billion. Put this way, it is easy to see the link between the budget deficit and the trade deficit. For instance, if the budget deficit rises, say, from $200 billion to $210 billion, and the difference between S and I remains constant, then the trade deficit rises.[3] This tells us that one way to reduce the trade deficit is to reduce the budget deficit.

APPENDIX SUMMARY

- A budget deficit exists if government expenditures are greater than tax receipts.
- A trade deficit exists if imports are greater than exports.
- The link between the budget deficit and the trade deficit is: Budget deficit = $(S - I)$ + trade deficit, where S = saving and I = investment. For example, if the budget deficit is $200 billion, and saving is greater than investment by $40 billion, it follows that the trade deficit is $160 billion.
- Assuming that the difference between saving and investment remains constant, one way to reduce the trade deficit is to reduce the budget deficit.

QUESTIONS AND PROBLEMS

1. Explain why the budget deficit equals the difference between saving and investment plus the trade deficit.
2. Suppose the budget deficit is $200 billion, saving is $660 billion, and investment is $630 billion. How much money is the American public providing to finance the U.S. budget deficit? Where does the remainder come from? (As you think about this question, keep in mind that the budget deficit = $(S - I)$ + trade deficit.)
3. Explain why $C + I + G + (X - M) = C + S + T$.

[2]Try this numerical example. Let $G = \$100$, $T = \$50$, $S = \$40$, $I = \$20$, $X = \$10$, and $M = \$40$. Substituting into the equation $G - T = (S - I) - (X - M)$, we get $\$100 - \$50 = (\$40 - \$20) - (\$10 - \$40)$, or $\$50 = (\$20) - (-\$30)$. This $-\$30$ is negative net exports. Instead of *subtracting* a negative $30 from $20, we are simply *adding* a positive $30 to $20. As you can see, the results are the same; that is, $\$20 - (-\$30) = \$50 = \$20 + \$30$.
[3]This explanation of the link between budget and trade deficits is mechanical. The economics of *why* there is a link between the two deficits depends on such things as the balance of payments, the causes of currency appreciation, the link between budget deficits and real interest rates, and more.

MEASURING THE PRICE LEVEL, REAL GNP, AND UNEMPLOYMENT

WHAT THIS CHAPTER IS ABOUT

In the last chapter, we discussed how to measure gross national product (GNP), which, in our *P–Q* terminology, is *P times Q.* In this chapter, we discuss how to measure the price level, *P;* real GNP, *Q;* and the unemployment rate, which is related to changes in real GNP.

THE PRICE LEVEL

In Chapter 5, we defined the *price level* as the weighted average of the prices of all goods and services. Economists measure the price level by constructing a **price index.** There are two major price indices: the *consumer price index (CPI)* and the *GNP deflator.* We discuss both in this section.

Consumer Price Index

The most widely cited price index is the **consumer price index (CPI).** The CPI is calculated by the Bureau of Labor Statistics through its sampling of thousands of households and businesses. When a news report says that the "cost of living" increased by, say, 7 percent, it is usually referring to the CPI.[1]

The CPI is based on a representative group of goods and services purchased by a typical household.[2] This representative group of goods is called the *market basket.* To simplify, let's say that the market basket is made up of only three goods instead of the many goods it actually contains. Our market basket will consist of 10 pens, 5 shirts, and 3 pairs of shoes.

To calculate the CPI, we must first calculate the total dollar expenditure of the market basket in two years: the current year and the **base year.** The base year is a benchmark year that serves as a basis of comparison for prices in other years.

In Exhibit 7–1, by multiplying the quantity of each good in the market basket (column 2) by the current-year price of each good (column 3) the current-year expenditure on each good is computed (column 4). By adding the dollar amounts in column 4, the total dollar expenditure on the market basket in the current year is obtained. This amount is $167. To find the total expenditure on the market basket in the base year, we multiply the quantity of each good in the market basket (column 2) times base-year price (column 5) and then sum the figures in column 6. This gives us $67.

To find the CPI for the current year, we use the formula:

$$\text{CPI}_{\text{current year}} = \frac{\text{Total dollar expenditure on market basket in current year}}{\text{Total dollar expenditure on market basket in base year}} \times 100$$

Plugging in the numbers, we see that the CPI for the current year is 249.

$$\text{CPI}_{\text{current year}} = \$167/\$67 \times 100 = 249$$

Question:

What does the CPI in the base year equal?

Answer:

When the base year *is* the current year, the numerator—total dollar expenditure on market basket in current year—turns out to be the same as the denominator—total dollar expenditure on market basket in base year. Dividing the numerator ($67 in our example in Exhibit 7–1) by the denominator ($67) gives us 1. When we multiply 1 times 100, we get 100. The CPI in the base year is 100.

---

[1] While changes in the CPI are often used to compute the change in the "cost of living," one's cost of living usually takes into account more than is measured by the CPI. For example, the CPI does not include taxes, yet taxes are a part of most person's cost of living.

[2] Notice that when we discuss the CPI we are only talking about goods and services that the household sector buys. The purchases of other sectors of the economy are not taken into account.

Price Index
A measure of the price level.

Consumer Price Index
The most widely cited index number for the price level; the weighted average of prices of a specific set of goods and services purchased by a typical household.

Base Year
The year chosen as a point of reference or comparison for prices in other years; a benchmark year.

EXHIBIT 7–1
Computing the Consumer Price Index
This exhibit uses hypothetical data to show how the CPI is computed. To find the "total dollar expenditure on the market basket in the current year," we multiply the quantities of goods in the market basket times current-year prices and sum. This gives us $167. To find the "total dollar expenditure on the market basket in the base year," we multiply the quantities of goods in the market basket times base-year prices and sum. This gives us $67. We then divide $167 by $67 and multiply times 100.

(1) GOODS IN MARKET BASKET	(2) MARKET BASKET	(3) CURRENT-YEAR PRICES	(4) CURRENT-YEAR EXPENDITURES (2) x (3)	(5) BASE-YEAR PRICES	(6) BASE-YEAR EXPENDITURES (2) x (5)
Pens	10 pens	$ .70	$ 7.00	$ .20	$ 2.00
Shirts	5 shirts	14.00	70.00	7.00	35.00
Shoes	3 pairs of shoes	30.00	90.00	10.00	30.00
Totals			**$167.00**		**$67.00**
			Total dollar expenditure on market basket in current year		Total dollar expenditure on market basket in base year

$$CPI_{current\ year} = \frac{\text{Total dollar expenditure on market basket in current year}}{\text{Total dollar expenditure on market basket in base year}} \times 100$$

$$= \frac{\$167}{\$67} \times 100$$

$$= 249$$

The consumer price index in 1988 for selected nations is noted in Exhibit 7–3; also noted is the average annual inflation rate of the selected nations during the period 1980–88.

Percentage Change in the CPI and Your Cost of Living

Suppose we learn that prices, as measured by the CPI, have risen 10 percent over the last year. Does this mean that your cost of living has risen by 10 percent? Not necessarily. Your cost of living may have risen by 10 percent, less than 10 percent, or more than 10 percent. The reason is that you may or may not have bought the bundle of goods that is in the market basket that is used to compute the CPI.

For example, suppose that the market basket contains 4 units of good A (4A), 3B, and 17C. Your market basket might contain 3A, 3B, 15C, and 2D. In short, your bundle of goods—*your* market basket—is not the same bundle of goods that is in *the* market basket, so the change in the prices you pay for goods will be different from the change in the prices that people pay for goods in the typical market basket.

GNP Deflator

The CPI measures the price level of those goods and services households purchase for their consumption. Households, however, are not the only ones that purchase goods and services. Business firms, government, and foreigners purchase goods,

EXHIBIT 7–2
CPI, 1980–1990

Year	Consumer Price Index (1982–84 = 100)
1980	82.4
1981	90.9
1982	96.5
1983	99.6
1984	103.9
1985	107.6
1986	109.6
1987	113.6
1988	118.3
1989	124.0
1990	130.7

$$\frac{96.5+99.6+103.9}{3} = 100$$

SOURCE: Council of Economic Advisers, *Economic Report of the President*, 1991 (Washington, D.C.: U.S. Government Printing Office, 1991).

too. The **GNP deflator** is the weighted average of prices of all goods and services produced in an economy and purchased by households, firms, government, and foreigners.

The GNP deflator is calculated much the same way that the CPI is calculated, except that with the GNP deflator, we take into account all goods and services produced. To illustrate, consider Exhibit 7–4.

We have assumed that in a tiny economy in the current year, four goods are produced: pens, shirts, shoes, and bricks (column 1). Column 2 lists the quantity of each good produced in the current year, and column 3 lists the price of each good in the current year. In column 4, we multiply *current-year quantities* times *current-year prices*. When we sum column 4, we get $199, which represents the

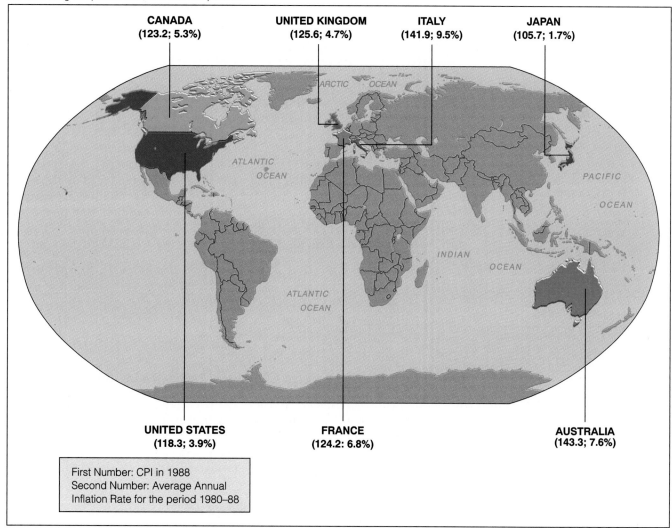

A 6 percent rise in the CPI is not necessarily a 6 percent rise in your cost of living.

GNP Deflator
The weighted average of prices of all goods and services produced in an economy.

EXHIBIT 7–3
Consumer Price Index for Selected Nations, 1988
In the exhibit, 1982–84 = 100. The first number in parentheses under the name of the nation is the CPI for 1988; the second number is the average annual inflation rate for the period 1980–88. For example, in the United States in 1988, CPI = 118.3. The average annual inflation rate in the United States during the period 1980–88 was 3.9 percent.

CANADA
(123.2; 5.3%)

UNITED KINGDOM
(125.6; 4.7%)

ITALY
(141.9; 9.5%)

JAPAN
(105.7; 1.7%)

ARCTIC OCEAN

ATLANTIC OCEAN

PACIFIC OCEAN

INDIAN OCEAN

ATLANTIC OCEAN

UNITED STATES
(118.3; 3.9%)

FRANCE
(124.2: 6.8%)

AUSTRALIA
(143.3; 7.6%)

First Number: CPI in 1988
Second Number: Average Annual
Inflation Rate for the period 1980–88

SOURCE: U.S. Bureau of the Census, *Statistical Abstract of the United States,* 1990 (Washington, D.C.: U.S. Government Printing Office, 1990).

EXHIBIT 7–4
Computing the GNP Deflator

This exhibit uses hypothetical data to show how the GNP deflator is computed. To find nominal GNP, we multiply current-year quantities times current-year prices and sum. To find real GNP, we multiply current-year quantities times base-year prices and sum. We find the GNP deflator by dividing nominal GNP by real GNP and multiplying times 100.

(1) GOODS	(2) CURRENT-YEAR QUANTITIES	(3) CURRENT-YEAR PRICES	(4) CURRENT-YEAR EXPENDITURES AT CURRENT PRICES (2) x (3)	(5) BASE-YEAR PRICES	(6) CURRENT-YEAR EXPENDITURES AT BASE-YEAR PRICES (2) x (5)
Pens	10	$ .70	$ 7.00	$ .20	$ 2.00
Shirts	5	14.00	70.00	7.00	35.00
Shoes	3	30.00	90.00	10.00	30.00
Bricks	8	4.00	32.00	2.00	16.00
Totals			**$199.00** Nominal $GNP_{current\ year}$		**$83.00** Real $GNP_{current\ year}$

$$\text{GNP deflator}_{current\ year} = \frac{\text{Nominal GNP}_{current\ year}}{\text{Real GNP}_{current\ year}} \times 100$$

$$= \frac{\$199}{\$83} \times 100$$

$$= 239.7$$

value of the total output produced by the economy in the current year at *current prices*. In other words, $199 is the nominal GNP of the economy.[3]

Next, we want to calculate the value of the total output produced by the economy in the current year at *base-year prices*. To do this, we multiply the *current quantities* (column 2) times *base-year prices* (column 5) and then sum the figures in column 6. When we sum column 6, we get $83. (This is called *real GNP*, about which more will be said shortly.) The formula we use to calculate the GNP deflator is:

$$\text{GNP deflator}_{current\ year} = \frac{\text{Nominal GNP}_{current\ year}}{\text{Real GNP}_{current\ year}} \times 100$$

Plugging in the numbers, we get:

$$\text{GNP deflator}_{current\ year} = 199/83 \times 100 = 239.7$$

How to Compute Percentage Change in Prices (Using the GNP Deflator)

Exhibit 7–5 shows the GNP deflator for 1980 through 1900. The base year is 1982; thus, the GNP deflator for the base year is 100.

Now, suppose we want to know how much prices have risen between, say, 1983 and 1986. We compute the percentage change in prices by using this general formula:

$$\text{Percentage change in prices} = \frac{\text{GNP deflator}_{later\ year} - \text{GNP}_{earlier\ year}}{\text{GNP deflator}_{earlier\ year}} \times 100$$

EXHIBIT 7–5
GNP Deflator, 1980–1990

Year	GNP Deflator (1982 = 100)
1980	85.7
1981	94.0
1982	100.0
1983	103.9
1984	107.7
1985	110.9
1986	113.8
1987	117.4
1988	121.3
1989	126.3
1990	131.5

SOURCE: Council of Economic Advisers, *Economic Report of the President,* 1991 (Washington, D.C.: U.S. Government Printing Office, 1991).

[3]Recall from Chapter 6 that the terms *GNP, nominal GNP,* and *current-dollar GNP* are interchangeable.

In our example, the GNP deflator for the later year (1986) is 113.8, and the GNP deflator in the earlier year (1983) is 103.9. Plugging the numbers into the formula we get:

$$\text{Percentage change in prices} = \frac{113.8 - 103.9}{103.9} \times 100 = 9.5$$

REAL GNP

∎

In the last section, we described how the price level (P) is measured. In this section, we look at real GNP (Q). *Real GNP*—how much is it, how much has it changed, is it headed up or down, and so on—is central to our discussion in later chapters. For example, later we will learn that changes in real GNP affect the unemployment rate and that the roller coaster ride real GNP sometimes finds itself on constitutes the business cycle.

Real GNP: A Simple Example

Suppose in year 1, in a tiny economy, only one unit of a good is produced and sold for $10. The GNP of the economy is $10, or price ($10) *times* quantity (1). In Year 2, the GNP rises to $40.

Year 1: GNP = $10
Year 2: GNP = $40

Would you know *why* GNP is higher in the second year? The answer should be "no." You wouldn't know if GNP was higher in the second year because price was higher ($40 instead of $10), or because quantity was higher (4 units instead of 1 unit), or because both price *and* quantity were higher ($20 and 2 units).

This is the same problem that economists have when they look at (nominal) GNP figures. For example, the GNP figures for 1985 and 1986 were $4,014.9 and $4,231.6, respectively. A simple look at the two figures does not tell us if the higher figure in 1986 is due to (1) more output having been produced in 1986 than 1985, (2) higher prices in 1986 than 1985, or (3) more output produced in 1986 than 1985 *and* higher prices in 1986 than in 1985, and so on.

A more meaningful measurement than GNP is *real GNP*. **Real GNP** is GNP valued in base year prices or GNP adjusted for price changes. For example, in 1985, real GNP was $3,618.7 billion, and in 1986 real GNP was $3,717.9 billion. Do we know why the 1986 real GNP is higher than the 1985 real GNP? The answer is "yes." Look at it this way: (1) Since real GNP is *GNP valued in base-year prices,* this means that (2) the output produced in 1985 and the output produced in 1986 are *both* valued in base-year prices; therefore, (3) the only way the dollar figure for 1986 could be higher than the dollar figure for 1985 is if more output was produced in 1986 than 1985.

We conclude that a comparison of GNP figures does not tell us why the GNP is higher or lower in one year than in another year. But a comparison of real GNP figures does. If the real GNP figure is lower in year 1 than in year 2, it is because less output was produced in year 1 than in year 2. If the real GNP figure is higher in year 1 than in year 2, it is because more output was produced in year 1 than in year 2.

Real GNP
GNP (output) valued in base year prices.

How Do You Know If You're Beating Inflation or If Inflation Is Beating You?

The **(annual) inflation rate** is defined as the annual percentage increase in some price index—such as the CPI or GNP deflator. For example, if we want to use the CPI to measure the annual inflation rate, we would use this formula:

(Annual) inflation rate

$$= \frac{CPI_{given\ year} - CPI_{previous\ year}}{CPI_{previous\ year}} \times 100$$

Suppose the CPI in year 1 is 100 and the CPI in year 2 is 110. Prices are 10 percent higher in year 2 than in year 1 (110 − 100/100 × 100 = 10 percent). The inflation rate in year 2 is 10 percent.

If prices, on average, are 10 percent higher in year 2 than in year 1, this means that each dollar a person has in his or her possession in year 2 has lost 10 percent of its value as compared with year 1. Look at this way. Dollars are used to *buy* goods and services for which people pay *prices*. Thus, if prices, on average, are 10 percent higher, each dollar buys 10 percent fewer goods and services than it did before prices increased. Or, stated differently, what $1,000 could buy in year 1 will take $1,100 to buy in year 2.

Whether a person is (1) keeping up with, (2) not keeping up with, or (3) more than keeping up with inflation depends on whether his or her income is (a) rising by the same per-

centage as, (b) a lesser percentage than, or (c) a greater percentage than the inflation rate, respectively. Another way to look at this is to compute and compare a person's **real income** in different years. Real income is a person's **(money) income** adjusted for any change in prices. Real income is computed the following way:

Real income$_{given\ year}$

$$= \frac{(Money)\ income_{given\ year}}{CPI_{given\ year}} \times 100$$

Let's consider three cases.

Case 1. Keeping Up with Inflation: Real Income Stays Constant. Jim earns $50,000 in year 1 and $55,000 in year 2. The CPI in year 1 is 100 and in year 2 it is 110. Jim's income has risen by 10 percent ($55,000 − $50,000/$50,000 × 100 = 10 percent), and the inflation rate is 10 percent (110 − 100/100 × 100 = 10 percent). Since Jim's income has risen by the *same percentage* as the inflation rate, he has kept up with inflation, or, in other words, his *real income* is the same in the two years. In year 1, it is $50,000 ($50,000/100 × 100 = $50,000), and in year 2 it is $50,000 ($55,000/110 × 100 = $50,000).

Case 2. Not Keeping Up with Inflation: Real Income Falls. Karen earns $50,000 in year 1 and $52,000 in year 2. The CPI in year 1 is 100 and in

year 2 it is 110. Karen's income has risen by 4 percent and the inflation rate is 10 percent. Since her income has risen by a *lesser percentage* than the inflation rate, she has not kept up with inflation. Karen's real income has fallen from $50,000 in year 1 to $47,272 in year 2.[4]

Case 3: More Than Keeping Up With Inflation: Real Income Rises. Carl earns $50,000 in year 1 and $60,000 in year 2. The CPI in year 1 is 100 and in year 2 it is 110. Carl's income has risen by 20 percent and the inflation rate is 10 percent. Since his income has risen by a *greater percentage* than the inflation rate, he has more than kept up with inflation. Carl's real income has risen from $50,000 in year 1 to $54,545 in year 2.[5]

[4]Real income$_{year\ 1}$ $= \dfrac{\$50,000}{100} \times 100$

$= \$50,000.$

Real income$_{year\ 2}$ $= \dfrac{\$52,000}{110} \times 100$

$= \$47,272.$

[5]Real income$_{year\ 1}$ $= \dfrac{\$50,000}{100} \times 100$

$= \$50,000.$

Real income$_{year\ 2}$ $= \dfrac{\$60,000}{110} \times 100$

$= \$54,545.$

THINKING LIKE AN ECONOMIST

Comparing one thing with something else can be extremely useful. For example, in each of the three cases noted in the Economics in Our Times above, we compared the percentage change in a person's (money) income with the *inflation rate*. Through this comparison, we learned something that we could not have learned had we looked at either factor alone: We learned how a person fared under inflation. Making comparisons is part of the economic way of thinking.

How To Measure Real GNP

Real GNP is measured by multiplying the current-year quantity of each final good and service produced times its *base-year price* and then summing. We did this in Exhibit 7–4 (page 136) for our four-good economy. The quantities of each good produced are listed in column 2. The base-year prices for these goods are noted in column 5. By multiplying the current-year quantity for each good by its base-year price, we get the current-year expenditure at base-year prices in column 6. Summing the figures in column 6 gives us real GNP.

Real GNP is also computed this way:

$$\text{Real GNP}_{\text{given year}} = \frac{\text{Nominal GNP}_{\text{given year}}}{\text{GNP deflator}_{\text{given year}}} \times 100$$

For example, if nominal GNP in year 1 is $4,000 billion, and the GNP deflator that year is 115, then real GNP is $3,478 billion, expressed in base year prices.

$$\text{Real GNP}_{\text{year 1}} = \frac{\$4{,}000 \text{ billion}}{115} \times 100 = \$3{,}478 \text{ billion}$$

MEASURING UNEMPLOYMENT

Every month, the Bureau of Census surveys 60,000 households to gather information on labor market activities. Later, the Bureau of Labor Statistics (BLS) processes this information and derives the number of Americans unemployed. We explain the details in the following sections.

Who Are the Unemployed?

The total population of the United States can be broken down into two broad groups (Exhibit 7–6). One group consists of persons who are (1) under 16 years of age, (2) in the armed forces, or (3) institutionalized—that is, they are in a prison, mental institution, or home for the aged. The second group, which consists of all others in the total population, is called the *noninstitutional adult civilian population.*

We can take the noninstitutional adult civilian population, in turn, and break it down into two groups: The first consists of those persons *not in the labor force;* the second consists of those persons in the *civilian labor force.*[6] Those persons *not in the labor force* are persons who are neither working nor looking for work. For example, persons who are retired, engaged in own-home housework, or who choose not to work fall into this category.

Persons in the civilian labor force fall into one of two categories: *employed* or *unemployed.* A person is employed if he or she

1. Did at least one hour of work as a paid employee during the survey week.
2. Worked in his or her own business or profession.
3. Worked at least 15 hours per week as an "unpaid" worker on a family-owned farm or business.
4. Was temporarily absent from work for reasons of illness, vacation, strike, or bad weather.

Real Income
Income that has been adjusted for price changes.

(Money) Income
The current-dollar amount of a person's income.

(Annual) Inflation Rate
The annual percentage change in some price index—such as the CPI or GNP deflator.

[6]Although our definition of the "civilian labor force" excludes persons in the armed forces, some recent measures of the labor force include them. If we add members of the armed forces residing in the United States, we then speak about the "labor force" instead of the civilian labor force.

EXHIBIT 7–6

Breakdown of the U.S. Population and the Labor Force

In 1990, the noninstitutional adult civilian population consisted of 188 million people; the civilian labor force was 124.7 million people, of whom 117.9 million were employed and 6.8 million were unemployed.

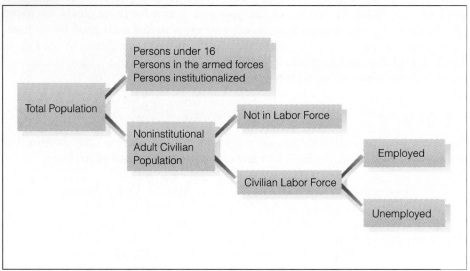

A person is unemployed if he or she

1. Did not work during the survey week, actively looked for work within the past four weeks, and is currently available for work.
2. Is waiting to be called back to a job from which he or she has been laid off.
3. Is waiting to report to a job within 30 days.

Question:

Suppose a person has been unsuccessfully searching for work for 15 months. He finally gives up his search. For the past 7 months he simply has been sitting at home. Is this person considered to be unemployed?

Answer:

No, this person is considered to be a *discouraged worker,* not an unemployed worker. To be unemployed, a person must meet three conditions: (1) not have worked during the survey week, (2) be available to work, and (3) actively have looked for work within the past four weeks. The person here definitely meets condition (1), probably meets condition (2), but he fails to meet condition (3).

Follow-up Question:

What category in Exhibit 7–6 does a discouraged worker fit into?

Answer:

He or she fits into the category of *not in the labor force.* In short, unemployed persons are in the *civilian labor force,* and discouraged workers are *not in the labor force.*

The Unemployment and Employment Rates

The unemployment and employment rates are both measures of the health of the economy. The **unemployment rate** is the percentage of the civilian labor force that is unemployed. It is equal to the number of persons unemployed divided by the number of persons in the civilian labor force. (Exhibit 7–7 gives the unemployment rate in the United States for the period 1980–1990.)

$$\text{Unemployment rate (U)} = \frac{\text{Number of persons unemployed}}{\text{Number of persons in the civilian labor force}}$$

The **employment rate** is the percentage of the noninstitutional adult civilian population that is employed. It is equal to the number of persons employed divided by the number of persons in the noninstitutional adult civilian population.

$$\text{Employment rate (E)} = \frac{\text{Number of persons employed}}{\substack{\text{Number of persons in the noninstitutional} \\ \text{adult civilian population}}}$$

It is important to notice that the denominator in the unemployment rate is different from the denominator in the employment rate. (See Exhibit 7–7 for the employment rate in the United States for the period 1980–1990.)

Economists usually point to three reasons why the commonly used unemployment rate may not be as accurate a measure of the health of the economy as the employment rate.

First, the unemployment rate can increase *even without a slowdown in the economy.* It increases simply if more individuals wish to become members of the civilian labor force. Suppose 1,000 persons currently not in the labor force decide to join the civilian labor force. Furthermore, suppose that 400 of them become employed, and 600 of them are unemployed.

What happens to the unemployment rate? The denominator increases by 1,000 and the numerator increases by 600. If the percentage change in the numerator is greater than the percentage change in the denominator, the unemployment rate increases.

What happens to the employment rate? The numerator increases by 400, but the denominator stays the same, and therefore the employment rate increases at the same time that the unemployment rate increases.

Unemployment Rate
The percentage of the civilian labor force that is unemployed: Unemployment rate = number of unemployed persons/number of persons in the civilian labor force.

Employment Rate
The percentage of the noninstitutional adult civilian population that is employed: Employment rate = number of persons employed/number of persons in the noninstitutional adult civilian population.

EXHIBIT 7–7
The Unemployment and Employment Rates, 1980–90*
*The sum of the unemployment and employment rates do not equal 100 percent.

Year	Unemployment Rate (percent)	Employment Rate (percent)
1980	7.1	59.2
1981	7.6	59.0
1982	9.7	57.8
1983	9.6	57.9
1984	7.5	59.5
1985	7.2	60.1
1986	7.0	60.7
1987	6.2	61.5
1988	5.5	62.3
1989	5.3	63.0
1990	5.5	62.7

SOURCE: Council of Economic Advisers, *Economic Report of the President, 1991* (Washington, D.C.: U.S. Government Printing Office, 1991).

Second, some economists argue that the unemployment rate is *higher* than it would be if the "welfare incentive" were taken into account. The welfare incentive exists because, to qualify for certain welfare programs, a person must be declared unemployed. In short, there is an incentive to become unemployed. The welfare incentive does not affect the employment rate because neither the number of persons employed (numerator) nor the noninstitutional adult civilian population (denominator) changes as a result of it.

Third, other economists argue that the unemployment rate is *lower* than it would be if the "discouraged worker effect" were taken into account. Earlier, we noted that discouraged workers are classified as "not in the labor force." Economists who think it more accurate to place discouraged workers in the category of the unemployed naturally argue that the unemployment rate is lower than it would be if they were. People who quit actively searching for work before finding work reduce the unemployment rate, even though nothing in the economy may have changed. They do not affect the employment rate, however.

Question:

If the unemployment rate is 10 percent, does it follow that the employment rate is 90 percent?

Answer:

No. Remember that the denominator in the employment rate (number of persons in the noninstitutional adult civilian population) is not the same as the denominator in the unemployment rate (number of persons in the civilian labor force). For this reason, it does not follow that if the unemployment rate is 10 percent, the employment rate is 90 percent. Also, a quick look at Exhibit 7–7 shows that the unemployment rate plus the employment rate does not equal 100 percent.

ECONOMIC STATISTICS IN POLITICS

■

Adding the inflation rate to the unemployment rate gives us what economists commonly call the *discomfort index.* In 1976, Jimmy Carter, running against Gerald Ford for the presidency of the United States, renamed the discomfort index the *misery index,* and then used the existing relatively high misery index in his campaign against Ford. Carter said that the misery index was higher under Ford than it had been under the preceding five presidents. Many political observers believe that Carter's effective use of the misery index helped him win the election.

Then in 1980, Ronald Reagan, running for the presidency against Jimmy Carter, used the same measure against him, with equal success. The misery index seems to be an easy way to focus voters' attention on a president's economic record.

Question:

If the state of the economy matters so much to the way people vote in a presidential election, why is it that in many presidential elections, the state of the economy is hardly discussed relative to such things as foreign policy, abortion, the crime rate, and so on. Aren't these the issues that matter to the American voter?

Can Economics Pick the Winner?

The political use that has been made of the discomfort, or misery, index shows that the state of the economy can have an impact on how people vote. In fact, many economists and political observers believe that the state of the economy is a *major factor* that voters take into account when they are deciding how they will cast their ballot in a presidential election.

Most studies indicate that the unemployment rate and the inflation rate (the two components of the misery index) do not predict the winners of presidential elections as well as (1) the recent change in real GNP (which is related to changes in the unemployment rate) and (2) the infla-

tion rate in the year preceding the election.

If the economy is growing, as evidenced in real GNP, and inflation is low, then voters tend to vote for the person representing the incumbent party. If the economy is slowing, or has turned down, and inflation is high, then voters tend to vote against the person representing the incumbent party. This means that *voters largely vote their pocketbooks.* If growth is rapid and inflation is low, then their pocketbooks are full and they are happy. A vote for the incumbent party is a vote to keep the good times rolling. If growth is weak or nonexistent and inflation is high,

then pocketbooks are sagging and people are unhappy. A vote against the incumbent party is a vote to throw out the rascals who did this to us.

One model that has impressive results in using economic data to predict elections is the DRI (Data Resources, Inc.) model, named after an economics forecasting firm. The model correctly predicted the winner of the last 11 presidential elections. Also, its forecast of the percentage of the vote received by the winner is close to the actual percentage of the vote received by the winner.

Answer:

They probably matter, but the real question is *how much* they matter. Also, simply because one issue (say, foreign policy) may get more media attention in a presidential race than the state of the economy, it does not necessarily follow that foreign policy is more important to voters than the state of the economy.

But the main point is this: Economic models have used "recent changes in real GNP" and "inflation rate" as factors to predict presidential elections. And so far, these models have consistently predicted presidential winners and (close to) the percentage of the vote they receive. There is no guarantee, though, that these models will continue to make accurate predictions, since it is possible that pocketbook issues may become less important in the future.

CHAPTER SUMMARY

Consumer Price Index

■ The CPI is the most widely cited index number for the price level; it is the weighted average of prices of a specific set of goods and services purchased by a typical household. To calculate the CPI for the current year, use this formula:

$$\text{CPI}_{\text{current year}} = \frac{\text{Total dollar expenditure on market basket in current year}}{\text{Total dollar expenditure on market basket in base year}} \times 100$$

GNP Deflator

■ The GNP deflator is a weighted average of prices of all goods and services produced in an economy and purchased by households, firms, government, and foreigners. To calculate the GNP deflator for the current year, use this formula:

$$\text{GNP deflator}_{\text{current year}} = \frac{\text{Nominal GNP}_{\text{current year}}}{\text{Real GNP}_{\text{current year}}} \times 100$$

Percentage Change in Prices

■ To find the percentage change in prices using the CPI, use this formula:

$$\text{Percentage change in prices} = \frac{\text{CPI}_{\text{later year}} - \text{CPI}_{\text{earlier year}}}{\text{CPI}_{\text{earlier year}}} \times 100$$

■ To find the percentage change in prices using the GNP deflator, use this formula:

$$\text{Percentage change in prices} =$$
$$\frac{\text{GNP deflator}_{\text{later year}} - \text{GNP deflator}_{\text{earlier year}}}{\text{GNP deflator}_{\text{earlier year}}} \times 100$$

Inflation Rate

■ To compute the (annual) inflation rate, use this formula:

$$\text{(Annual) inflation rate} = \frac{\text{CPI}_{\text{given year}} - \text{CPI}_{\text{previous year}}}{\text{CPI}_{\text{previous year}}} \times 100$$

Real Income

■ Real income is (money) income adjusted for any change in prices. To compute real income in a given year, use this formula:

$$\text{Real Income}_{\text{given year}} = \frac{\text{(Money) income}_{\text{given year}}}{\text{CPI}_{\text{given year}}} \times 100$$

Real GNP

■ Real GNP is GNP valued in base year prices and adjusted for price changes. To compute real GNP in a given year, use this formula:

$$\text{Real GNP}_{\text{given year}} = \frac{\text{Nominal GNP}_{\text{given year}}}{\text{GNP deflator}_{\text{given year}}} \times 100$$

The Unemployed, Unemployment, and Employment Rates

■ A person is unemployed if he or she (1) did not work during the survey week, actively looked for work during the past four weeks, and is currently available for work; (2) is waiting to be called back to a job from which he or she has been laid off; or (3) is waiting to report to a job within 30 days.

■ A discouraged worker is classified as "not in the labor force," not as "unemployed." A discouraged worker is a person who is available for work and who has looked for work, but is currently no longer looking.

■ The unemployment rate is equal to the number of unemployed persons divided by the civilian labor force. The employment rate is equal to the number of employed persons divided by the noninstitutional adult civilian population.

■ Some economists maintain that the employment rate is a better measure of the health of the economy than the unemployment rate. They argue that the unemployment rate may increase even if there is no slowdown in the economy. In addition, it is sometimes argued that the unemployment rate is higher than it would be otherwise because individuals cannot qualify for certain welfare benefits unless they are unemployed. At the same time, it can also be argued that the unemployment rate is lower than it would be if the "discouraged worker effect" were taken into account.

Key Terms and Concepts

Price Index	Base year	Real Income
Consumer Price Index (CPI)	GNP Deflator	(Money) Income
	Real GNP	Unemployment Rate
	(Annual) Inflation Rate	Employment Rate

QUESTIONS AND PROBLEMS

1. Assume the market basket contains 10X, 20Y, and 45Z. The current-year prices for goods X, Y, and Z are $1, $4, and $6, respectively. The base-year prices are $1, $3, and $5, respectively. What is the CPI in the current year?

2. If the total dollar expenditures on the market basket in the current year is $400, and the total dollar expenditures on the market basket in the base year is $360, what is the CPI in the current year? in the base year?

3. Using Exhibit 7–2, compute the percentage change in prices between (a) 1980 and 1981, (b) 1983 and 1987, and (c) 1984 and 1986.

4. What is the difference(s) between the CPI and the GNP deflator?

5. Using Exhibit 7–5, compute the percentage change in prices between (a) 1983 and 1984, (b) 1985 and 1987, and (c) 1983 and 1984.

6. In 1980 U.S. GNP was $2,732.0 billion and real GNP was $3,187.1 billion. How is it possible for real GNP to be greater than GNP?

7. Suppose Stephanie's (money) income in 1985, 1986, and 1987 is $30,000, $35,000, and $40,000, respectively. Using the data in Exhibit 7–2, compute Stephanie's real income in each of these years.

8. Using the hypothetical data in the following table, calculate real GNP for the years noted. (GNP and real GNP are in billions of dollars.)

Year	Nominal GNP	GNP defaltor	Real GNP
1	$4,989	121	?
2	4,886	122	?
3	5,221	143	?
4	5,333	155	?

9. Economists prefer to compare real GNP figures for different years instead of (nominal) GNP figures. Why?

10. John earned $45,000 in year 1 and $55,000 in year 2. It follows that John is better off in terms of the quantity of goods and services he can buy in year 2 than year 1. Comment.

11. Which of the following persons would be included in the civilian labor force: (a) a farmer working on his own farm, (b) a 14-year-old boy looking for a summer job, (c) a 57-year-old man who was laid off 18 months ago and has quit looking for work because he thinks he doesn't have the skills to fill any of the jobs he would want, (d) a full-time college student, (e) a person working 37 hours a week as a sales clerk in a department store at the local mall, (f) a person fired from work yesterday?

12. Is it possible for the unemployment rate to fall when the number of persons unemployed is rising? Explain your answer.

13. Some economists speak of the *underemployed*—persons who are working at jobs beneath their education and skills. For example, a person with a Ph.D. in English literature may drive a taxi in Washington, D.C. because he can't find other work. Do you think the problem of the underemployed is as serious as the problem of the unemployed? Why?

14. What is wrong with saying that an unemployed person is a person who is not working?

15. Here are some data: noninstitutional adult civilian population = 100 million persons; civilian labor force = 87 million persons; total population = 240 million persons; employed persons = 45 million persons. Calculate the following: (a) unemployment rate, (b) employment rate, (c) number of persons not in the labor force, and (d) number of discouraged workers.

16. Why is it that the sum of the unemployment and employment rates does not equal 100 percent?

17. "Models that use "recent changes in real GNP" and "inflation rate" to predict presidential election winners have high predictive power; therefore, nothing beyond these two factors matters when it comes down to how people vote in presidential elections." Discuss.

THE AGGREGATE DEMAND— AGGREGATE SUPPLY FRAMEWORK

WHAT THIS CHAPTER IS ABOUT

In order to see changes in GNP ($P \times Q$), the price level (P), and real GNP (Q), we need a new framework. This is the aggregate demand—aggregate supply (*AD–AS*) framework, which we develop in this chapter. We first discuss aggregate demand, next aggregate supply, and then the two sides of the economy together. In examining aggregate demand, we derive the aggregate demand curve and briefly discuss shifts in it. Then we apply the same procedure to aggregate supply, and look at short-run and long-run aggregate supply curves as well. The latter are particularly important to our discussions of macroeconomic theory and policy debates in later chapters.

AGGREGATE DEMAND

■

Aggregate Demand (*AD*) Curve
A curve that shows the quantity demanded of real GNP at different price levels, *ceteris paribus.*

Real balance effect
The change in the purchasing power of dollar-denominated assets that results from a change in the price level.

Monetary wealth
The value of a person's monetary assets. *Wealth,* as distinguished from *monetary wealth,* refers to the value of all assets owned, both monetary and nonmonetary. In short, a person's wealth equals his or her monetary wealth (such as $1,000 cash) plus nonmonetary wealth (a car or a house).

Purchasing power
The quantity of goods and services that can be purchased with a unit of money. Purchasing power and the price level are inversely related: As the price level goes up (down), purchasing power goes down (up).

EXHIBIT 8–1
The Aggregate Demand Curve

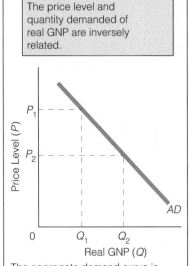

Aggregate Demand Curve
The price level and quantity demanded of real GNP are inversely related.

The aggregate demand curve is downward-sloping, specifying an inverse relationship between the price level and the quantity demanded of real GNP.

Just as there are two sides to a market, there are two sides to an economy—a demand side and a supply side. Aggregate demand relates to the demand side, and aggregate supply relates to the supply side. In this section, we discuss aggregate demand and develop an aggregate demand curve.

The Aggregate Demand Curve

Take a look at Exhibit 8–1. On the vertical axis is the *price level.* In the last chapter, we discussed two measures of the price level—the CPI and the GNP deflator. Think of the price level in the exhibit as the GNP deflator. As we move up the vertical axis, the price level rises; as we move down the vertical axis, the price level falls.

On the horizontal axis is *real GNP.* As we move to the right on the horizontal axis, real GNP rises; as we move to the left on the horizontal axis, real GNP falls.

Now take a look at the curve drawn in the space between the two axes. This is an **aggregate demand (*AD*) curve.** The *AD* curve shows the quantity demanded of real GNP at different price levels, *ceteris paribus.* Notice that the higher price level (P_1) corresponds to a lower quantity demanded of real GNP (Q_1), and the lower price level (P_2) corresponds to a higher quantity demanded of real GNP (Q_2). In short, the price level and the quantity demanded of real GNP are inversely related.

Why Does the Aggregate Demand Curve Slope Downward?

The downward-sloping *AD* curve is the graphical representation of the inverse relationship between the price level and the quantity demanded of real GNP. So when we ask, Why does the AD curve slope downward? we are essentially asking, Why is there an inverse relationship between the price level and the quantity demanded of real GNP? The answer leads us to the topics of (1) the real balance effect, (2) the interest rate effect, and (3) the international trade effect.

Real Balance Effect. The **real balance effect** states that the inverse relationship between the price level and the quantity demanded of real GNP is established through changes in the value of person's **monetary wealth,** or *money holdings.*

To illustrate, start with a person who has $50,000 in cash. Now suppose the price level rises. As this happens, the **purchasing power** of the $50,000 falls. That is, the $50,000 that once could buy, say, 100 television sets at $500 each, can now buy 80 sets at $625 each.

A decrease in the purchasing power of the person's $50,000 is identical to saying that his monetary wealth has decreased. (After all, isn't the $50,000 less valuable when it can buy less than when it can buy more?) And as he becomes less wealthy, he buys fewer goods.

In summary, a *rise in the price level* causes purchasing power to fall, which decreases a person's monetary wealth. As people become less wealthy, *the quantity demanded of real GNP falls.*

Now suppose the price level falls. As this happens, the purchasing power of the person's $50,000 rises. That is, the $50,000 that once could buy 100 television sets at $500 each, can now buy 125 sets at $400 each. An increase in the purchasing power of the person's $50,000 is identical to saying that his monetary wealth has increased. And as he becomes wealthier, he buys more goods.

In summary, *a fall in the price level* causes purchasing power to rise, which increases a person's monetary wealth. As people become wealthier, the *quantity demanded of real GNP rises.*

Interest Rate Effect. The **interest rate effect** states that the inverse relationship between the price level and the quantity demanded of real GNP is established through changes in household and business spending that is sensitive to changes in interest rates.

Let's consider a person who buys a fixed bundle of goods (food, clothing, and shelter) each week. Now suppose the price level rises. This reduces the purchasing power of the person's money. With less purchasing power (per dollar), she will have to acquire *more money* in order to buy her fixed bundle of goods. In her attempt to acquire more money, she goes to a bank and requests a loan. In terms of simple supply-and-demand analysis, the *demand for credit* increases. Subsequently, the price of credit, which is the *interest rate,* rises.[1] As the interest rate rises, households borrow less to finance, say, automobile purchases, and firms borrow less to finance new capital goods spending. Thus, the quantity demanded of real GNP falls.

If the price level falls, the purchasing power of a person's money increases. With more purchasing power (per dollar), she can purchase her fixed bundle of goods with *less money.* What does she do with (part of) this gain in her financial wealth? She saves it. In terms of simple supply-and-demand analysis, the *supply of credit* increases. Subsequently, the interest rate drops. As the interest rate drops, households and businesses borrow more and so they end up buying more goods. Thus, the quantity demanded of real GNP rises.

The International Trade Effect. The **international trade effect** states that the inverse relationship between the price level and the quantity demanded of real GNP is established through foreign sector spending, which includes U.S. spending on foreign goods (imports) and foreign spending on U.S. goods (exports).

Suppose the price level in the United States rises. As this happens, U.S. goods become relatively more expensive than foreign goods. As a result, both Americans and foreigners buy fewer U.S. goods. The quantity demanded of (U.S.) real GNP falls.

Now suppose the price level in the United States falls. As this happens, U.S. goods become relatively cheaper than foreign goods. As a result, both Americans and foreigners buy more U.S. goods. The quantity demanded of (U.S.) real GNP rises.

For a review of the three effects—real balance, interest rate, and international trade—see Exhibit 8–2.

A Change in the Quantity Demanded of Real GNP versus a Change in Aggregate Demand

In Chapter 3, we learned that there is a difference between a *change in quantity demanded* and a *change in demand.* Similarly, there is a difference between *a change in the quantity demanded of real GNP* and *a change in aggregate demand* (or what amounts to the same thing, a *change in the demand for real GNP).*

We know that a change in the quantity demanded of real GNP is brought about by a change in the price level. As the price level falls (rises), the quantity demanded of real GNP rises (falls), *ceteris paribus.* In Exhibit 8–3a, a change in the quantity demanded of real GNP is represented as a movement from one point (*A*) on AD_1 to another point (*B*) on AD_1.

Interest Rate Effect
The changes in household and business buying as the interest rate changes.

International Trade Effect
The change in foreign sector spending as the price level changes.

[1]In the credit market, there is a demand for, and a supply of, credit. The price of credit is the interest rate. As in other markets, when the demand for credit rises, the price of credit (interest rate) rises; when the supply of credit rises, the price of credit (interest rate) falls.

EXHIBIT 8–2
Why the Aggregate Demand Curve Is Downward Sloping

This exhibit outlines the three effects that explain why the *AD* curve is downward sloping. Each effect relates to a change in the price level leading to a change in the quantity demanded of real GNP.

Type of Effect	How It Works	Graphical Representation of What Happens
Real Balance Effect	***Price level rises*** → purchasing power falls → monetary wealth falls → **buy fewer goods.** ***Price level falls*** → purchasing power rises → monetary wealth rises → **buy more goods.**	
Interest Rate Effect	***Price level rises*** → purchasing power falls → borrow money in order to continue to buy fixed bundle of goods → demand for credit rises → interest rate rises → businesses and households borrow less at higher interest rate → **buy fewer goods.** ***Price level falls*** → purchasing power rises → less money needed to buy fixed bundle of goods → save more → supply of credit rises → interest rate falls → businesses and households borrow more at lower interest rate → **buy more goods.**	
International Trade Effect	**Price level in U.S. rises** relative to foreign price levels → U.S. goods relatively more expensive than foreign goods → both Americans and foreigners **buy fewer U.S. goods**. **Price level in U.S. falls** relative to foreign price levels → U.S. goods relatively less expensive than foreign goods → both Americans and foreigners **buy more U.S. goods**.	

EXHIBIT 8–3

A Change in the Quantity Demanded of Real GNP versus a Change in Aggregate Demand

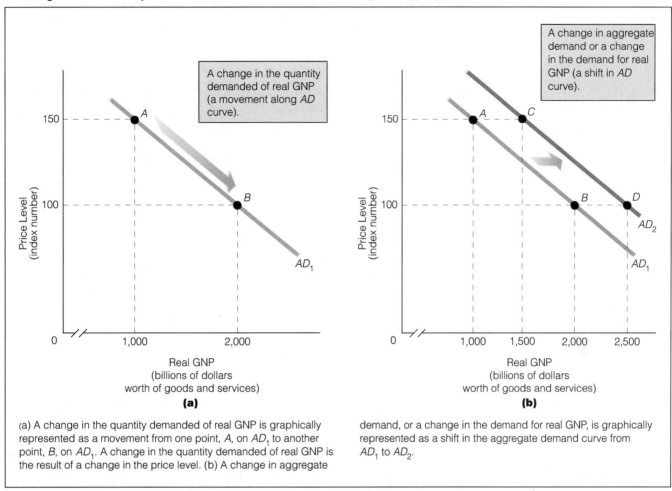

(a) A change in the quantity demanded of real GNP is graphically represented as a movement from one point, *A*, on AD_1 to another point, *B*, on AD_1. A change in the quantity demanded of real GNP is the result of a change in the price level. (b) A change in aggregate demand, or a change in the demand for real GNP, is graphically represented as a shift in the aggregate demand curve from AD_1 to AD_2.

A change in aggregate demand, or a change in the demand for real GNP, is represented in Exhibit 8–3b as a shift in the aggregate demand curve from AD_1 to AD_2. Notice that with a shift in the aggregate demand curve, the quantity demanded of real GNP changes even though the *price level remains constant*. For example, at a price level (index number) of 150, the quantity demanded of real GNP is $1,000 billion on AD_1 in Exhibit 8–3b. But at the same price level (150), the quantity demanded of real GNP is $1,500 billion on AD_2.

Changes in Aggregate Demand

Here are some facts established in earlier chapters:

Fact 1: There are four sectors in the economy: household, business, government, and foreign.

Fact 2: Each of these four sectors buys some of the real GNP produced in this country.

Fact 3: The expenditures (on real GNP) made by the household sector are called *consumption* (*C*); the expenditures made by the business sector are called *invest-ment* (*I*); the expenditures made by the government sector are called *government expenditures* (G); and the expenditures made by the foreign sector are called *net exports* (X−M).

Fact 4: Total spending, or total expenditures, is the sum of the expenditures made by the four sectors of the economy. For example, if C = $100 billion, I = $50 billion, G = $60 billion, and X−M = $20 billion, then total spending (total expenditures) is $230 billion.

To understand changes in aggregate demand, remember: *At a given price level,* anything that increases any of the four components of total spending (C, I, G, or X−M), increases aggregate demand and shifts the AD curve to the right. Also, *at a given price level,* anything that decreases any of the four components of total spending decreases aggregate demand and shifts the AD curve to the left.

Question:

In reminding the reader that total spending changed at a given price level, why is it important to specify at a given price level?

Answer:

We specify *at a given price level* because the expenditures of persons may change for more than one reason. Consider an individual's purchases of goods and services. Her spending, or *consumption,* will change for one of two reasons: (1) if the price level changes or (2) if the price level is constant and some nonprice factor changes.

Suppose the price level falls, *ceteris paribus.* From our discussion of the real balance effect, we learned that a lower price level increases the purchasing power of a person's money, so her monetary wealth increases and she ends up buying more goods and services.

Suppose now the price level remains constant and some nonprice factor changes; for example, the person's income taxes decrease, *ceteris paribus.* As this happens, her disposable (after-tax) income rises and she ends up buying more goods and services.

Here, then, are two cases where spending changes. The causal factor in the first case was a "change in the price level" and the causal factor in the second case was a "change in income taxes."

Economists distinguish between changes in spending according to whether the price level is constant or not. In general, a change in the price level changes the *quantity demanded of real GNP.* And a change in a nonprice factor—such as income taxes in our example—changes *aggregate demand* or the *demand for real GNP.*

Question:

What is the difference between total spending *or* total expenditures *and* aggregate demand? *Sometimes they sound as if they are the same thing?*

Answer:

Total expenditures refers to the sum of the expenditures made by the four sectors of the economy at a given price level—that is, the sum of consumption, investment, government expenditures, and net exports. This sum is a specific dollar amount, say, $4 trillion.

Aggregate demand is not a specific dollar amount; instead, it is a *schedule* consisting of the different amounts of real GNP that households, businesses, government, and foreigners are willing and able to buy at different price levels. For instance, a given aggregate demand may specify that the four sectors of the economy are willing and able to buy $3 trillion worth of goods and services at a price level (CPI) of 112, *and* $3.3 trillion worth of goods and services at a price level of 105, and so on. Simply put, think of aggregate demand as consisting of *different* dollar amounts of real GNP that the four sectors of the economy are willing and able to purchase at different price levels.[2]

Much of the controversy and debate that takes place in macroeconomics is focused on aggregate demand.

Shifts in the Aggregate Demand Curve: A Brief Comment

It is customary at this point to list and explain some of the (nonprice) factors that can change aggregate demand and thereby shift the AD curve. We have chosen not to follow custom. We owe you a reason as to why. The major reason is that much of the controversy and debate that takes place in macroeconomics is focused on aggregate demand. Our objective in this text is to convey the full specifics of this debate, and this requires us to discuss the factors that influence aggregate demand in their proper context, giving attention to arguments and counterarguments. For example, when we discuss government expenditures we begin by showing that an increase in government expenditures can shift the AD curve to the right and that a decrease in government expenditures can shift the AD curve to the left. But also related to increases in government expenditures are the questions of how the expenditures are financed (through taxes or borrowed funds?) and the degree of *crowding out*—that is, the degree to which, say, consumer expenditures fall as government expenditures rise. At this point, you perhaps do not know the important details of these issues, and that makes our point. We feel it better to wait until we have fully explained these issues before we discuss government expenditures and its effect on aggregate demand.

For now, we leave you with the general statement regarding aggregate demand that we made earlier:

At a given price level, anything that increases any of the four components of total spending (C, I, G, or net exports), increases aggregate demand and shifts the AD curve to the right. Also, *at a given price level,* anything that decreases any of the four components of total spending, decreases aggregate demand and shifts the AD curve to the left.

AGGREGATE SUPPLY

In this section, we first talk about what the aggregate supply curve is and what factors can shift it. Then we distinguish between the short-run and long-run aggregate supply curves.

The Short-Run Aggregate Supply Curve

A **short-run aggregate supply (SRAS) curve** is illustrated in Exhibit 8–4. It shows the real GNP producers will offer for sale at different price levels, *ceteris paribus.* Notice that the SRAS curve is upward sloping, indicating a direct relationship between the price level and the quantity supplied of real GNP. It is likely that the direct relationship between these two variables will hold *for a while.*

Short-Run Aggregate Supply (SRAS) Curve Shows the real GNP producers will offer for sale at different price levels, *ceteris paribus.*

[2]We see this when we look at the aggregate demand (*AD*) curve, which shows the quantity demanded of real GNP at different price levels: so much quantity demanded at P_1, so much quantity demanded at P_2, and so on.

EXHIBIT 8–4
The Short-Run Aggregate
Supply Curve

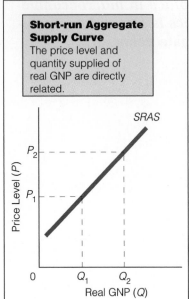

Short-run Aggregate Supply Curve
The price level and quantity supplied of real GNP are directly related.

The short-run aggregate supply curve is upward-sloping, specifying a direct relationship between the price level and the quantity supplied of real GNP.

To explain why, consider firms that produce goods. Each firm's profit per unit is equal to price per unit minus cost per unit (profit per unit = price per unit − cost per unit). If price rises while costs per unit stay constant, there will be greater profit in producing goods, and it is likely firms will produce more. If price falls while costs per unit stay constant, there will be less profit in producing goods, and it is likely firms will produce less. The response is summarized in the upward-sloping SRAS curve.

We offer one proviso. In the preceding example, *prices changed* and *unit production costs remained constant*. It is unlikely that this configuration between prices and costs would last for more than a few months. Initially, an increase in the price of goods might occur without any increase in unit production costs; for example, labor costs may remain constant owing to existing labor contracts. But eventually costs adjust upward. In other words, the aggregate supply curve in Exhibit 8–4, which represents a direct relationship between the price level and quantity supplied of real GNP, holds for a configuration of prices and costs (specifically, rising or falling prices and constant costs) that is only temporary. This is why economists refer to this curve as the *short-run* aggregate supply curve.

Shifts in the Short-Run Aggregate Supply Curve

The factors that can shift the short-run aggregate supply curve include the wage rate, prices of nonlabor inputs, productivity, and supply shocks. In a later chapter, we add inflation expectations to this list.

The Wage Rate. Changes in the wage rate have a major impact on the position of the SRAS curve, since wage costs are usually a firm's major cost item. The impact of a rise or fall in equilibrium wage rates can be understood in terms of the equation given earlier: profit per unit = price per unit − cost per unit. Higher wage rates mean higher costs and, at constant prices, translate into lower profits and a reduction in the number of goods managers of firms will want to produce. Lower wage rates mean lower costs and, at constant prices, translate into higher profits and an increase in the number of goods managers will decide to produce.

The impact of higher and lower equilibrium wages is shown in Exhibit 8–5. We start with $SRAS_1$. At the given price level, P, real GNP is Q_1. Next, we introduce higher wage rates. As we just mentioned, this reduces a firm's profits at a given price level; consequently, there is a reduction in production. In the diagram, we move from Q_1 to Q_2, which at the given price level corresponds to point B. Point B represents a point on a new aggregate supply curve ($SRAS_2$). We see that a rise in equilibrium wage rates leads to a leftward shift in the aggregate supply curve. The steps are simply reversed for a fall in equilibrium wage rates.

Prices of Nonlabor Inputs. There are other inputs in the production process besides labor. Changes in their prices affect the SRAS curve in the same way as wage-rate changes. An increase in the price of a nonlabor input (say, oil) shifts the SRAS curve leftward; a decrease in the price of a nonlabor input shifts the SRAS curve rightward.

Productivity. Productivity describes the output produced per unit of input employed over some period of time. For example, consider the input labor. Increases in labor productivity cause the SRAS curve to shift rightward; decreases in labor productivity cause the SRAS curve to shift leftward. A host of factors lead to increased labor productivity, including a more educated labor force, a larger stock of capital goods, technological changes, and improved management techniques.

EXHIBIT 8–5
Wage Rates and a Shift in the Short-Run Aggregate Supply Curve

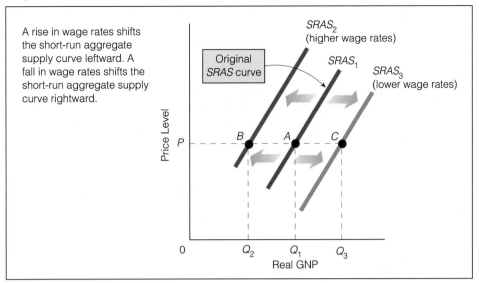

A rise in wage rates shifts the short-run aggregate supply curve leftward. A fall in wage rates shifts the short-run aggregate supply curve rightward.

Supply Shocks. Major natural or institutional changes on the supply side of the economy that affect aggregate supply are referred to as *supply shocks.* Bad weather that wipes out a large part of the midwestern wheat crop would be considered a supply shock. So would a major cutback in the supply of oil coming to the United States from the Middle East. Supply shocks are of two varieties. There are *adverse supply shocks* (examples just given), which shift the *SRAS* curve leftward, and *beneficial supply shocks,* which shift it rightward. Examples of the latter include a major oil discovery and unusually good weather leading to the increased production of a food staple. These supply shocks are reflected in resource or input prices.

Short-Run Equilibrium: Putting *AD* and *SRAS* Together

It is time to put the two sides of the economy together. Exhibit 8–6 shows an aggregate demand (*AD*) curve and a short-run aggregate supply (*SRAS*) curve. We consider the "quantity demanded of real GNP" and the "quantity supplied of real GNP" at three different price levels: P_1, P_2, and P_E.

At P_1, the quantity supplied of real GNP (Q_2) is greater than the quantity demanded (Q_1). There is surplus of goods. As a result, the price level drops and firms decrease output and consumers increase consumption. Why do consumers increase consumption as the price level drops? (Hint: Think of the real balance effect.)

At P_2, the quantity supplied of real GNP (Q_1) is less than the quantity demanded of real GNP (Q_2). There is a shortage of goods. As a result, the price level rises, firms increase output, and consumers decrease consumption. In instances of both surplus and shortage, economic forces are moving the economy toward P_E, where the quantity demanded of real GNP equals the (short-run) quantity supplied of real GNP. This is the point of **short-run equilibrium.** P_E is the short-run equilibrium price level; Q_E is the short-run equilibrium real GNP.

A change in either aggregate demand, short-run aggregate supply, or both will obviously affect the price level and/or real GNP. For example, an increase in aggregate demand raises the equilibrium price level and, in the short run, real GNP

Short-Run Equilibrium
In the economy, the condition that exists when the quantity demanded of real GNP equals the (short-run) quantity supplied of real GNP. This condition is met where the aggregate demand curve intersects the short-run aggregate supply curve.

155

EXHIBIT 8–6
Short-Run Equilibrium

At P_1, the quantity supplied of real GNP is greater than the quantity demanded. As a result, the price level falls and firms decrease output. At P_2, the quantity demanded of real GNP is greater than the quantity supplied. As a result, the price level rises and firms increase output. Short-run equilibrium occurs at point E, where the quantity demanded of real GNP equals the (short-run) quantity supplied. This is at the intersection of the aggregate demand (AD) curve and the short-run aggregate supply ($SRAS$) curve. (Note: Although real world AD and $SRAS$ curves can, and likely do, have some curvature to them, we have drawn both as straight lines. This does not affect the analysis. Whenever the analysis is not disturbed, we follow suit throughout the text.)

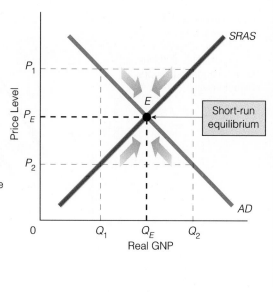

(Exhibit 8–7a). An increase in short-run aggregate supply lowers the equilibrium price level and raises real GNP (Exhibit 8–7b). A decrease in short-run aggregate supply raises the equilibrium price level and lowers real GNP (Exhibit 8–7c).

THE LONG-RUN AGGREGATE SUPPLY CURVE

In this section, we discuss the long-run aggregate supply ($LRAS$) curve and long-run equilibrium. To understand why the $LRAS$ curve looks the way it does, we need to take a short detour through some issues related to unemployment.

Frictional Unemployment

Every day, demand conditions change in some markets, causing qualified individuals with transferable skills to leave some jobs and move to others. To illustrate, suppose there are two computer firms, A and B. For some reason, the demand for firm A's computers falls, and the demand for firm B's computers rises. Consequently, firm A produces fewer computers. With fewer computers being produced, firm A doesn't need as many employees, so it fires some employees. Firm B ends up producing more computers. With more computers being produced, firm B hires additional employees.

The employees fired from firm A have skills that they can transfer to firm B—after all, both firms produce computers. However, it takes time for persons to transfer from one firm to another. During this time, they are said to be *frictionally unemployed;* and the unemployment owing to the natural "frictions" of the economy, caused by changing market conditions and represented by qualified individuals with transferable skills who change jobs, is called **frictional unemployment.** We use the symbol U_F to designate the frictional unemployment rate.

Frictional Unemployment
The unemployment due to the natural "frictions" of the economy, caused by changing market conditions and represented by qualified individuals with transferable skills who change jobs.

EXHIBIT 8–7
Changes in Short-Run Equilibrium

(a) An increase in aggregate demand increases the price level and real GNP. (b) An increase in short-run aggregate supply decreases the price level and increases real GNP.

(c) A decrease in short-run aggregate supply increases the price level and decreases real GNP.

In a dynamic, changing economy like ours, there will always be frictional unemployment. Many economists believe that the basic cause of frictional unemployment is imperfect or incomplete information, which prevents individuals from leaving one job and finding another instantly.

Consider the situation where there are 1,000 job vacancies and 1,000 persons with the qualifications to fill the jobs. Will there be some unemployment? It is likely that there will be, because not every one of the 1,000 job seekers will know where an available job is, nor will all employers give the job to the first applicant who knocks on the door (employers don't know if "better" applicants are around the corner). Matching qualified workers with jobs takes time.

Structural Unemployment

Structural unemployment is unemployment due to structural changes in the economy that eliminate some jobs and create others for which the unemployed are unqualified. Most economists argue that structural unemployment is largely the consequence of automation (labor-saving devices) and long-lasting shifts in demand. The major difference between the frictionally unemployed and the structurally unemployed is that the latter do not have transferable skills. Their choice is between prolonged unemployment and retraining. For example, suppose there is a pool of unemployed automobile workers and a rising demand for computer analysts. If the automobile workers do not currently have the skills necessary to become computer analysts, they are structurally unemployed. We shall use the symbol U_S to designate the structural unemployment rate.

Natural Unemployment

If we add the frictional unemployment rate to the structural unemployment rate we get the **natural unemployment rate** (or natural rate of unemployment). We shall

Structural Unemployment
Unemployment due to structural changes in the economy that eliminate some jobs and create others for which the unemployed are unqualified.

Natural Unemployment Rate
Unemployment caused by frictional and structural factors in the economy. Natural unemployment rate = frictional unemployment rate + structural unemployment rate. For some economists, this is the unemployment rate toward which the economy tends to return; it is the long-run average unemployment rate.

use the symbol U_N to designate the natural unemployment rate. Currently most economists' estimate of the natural unemployment rate is between 4.0 and 6.5 percent.

$$U_N = U_F + U_S$$

The (Actual) Unemployment Rate

Neither TV news reporters nor newspaper journalists cite the frictional, structural, or natural unemployment rates. You will not hear a newscaster say, "Today in Washington the frictional unemployment rate was reported to be 3 percent." Instead, she might say, "Today in Washington the unemployment rate was reported to be 6.9 percent." Notice there is no adjective before the word *unemployment.*

Recall that we measure the unemployment rate as follows:

$$\text{Unemployment rate } (U) = \frac{\text{Number of persons unemployed}}{\text{Number of persons in the civilian labor force}^3}$$

Suppose the unemployment rate (U) is computed to be 7 percent. This, then, is the unemployment rate that *actually* exists in the economy. Soon, we examine the (actual) unemployment rate in relation to the natural unemployment rate.

What Is Full Employment?

What do you think of when you hear the term *full employment?* Most people think full employment only exists if the (actual) unemployment rate is zero. But full employment of this type does not exist in a dynamic, changing economy, owing to *frictional* and *structural* changes that continually occur. In fact, it is *natural* for some unemployment to exist—some *natural* unemployment, that is. For this reason, economists do not equate **full employment** with a zero (0) unemployment rate. Instead, for economists, *full employment* exists when the economy is operating at its natural unemployment rate. For example, if the natural unemployment rate is 5 percent, then full employment exists when the unemployment rate (in the economy) is 5 percent.

Full Employment
The condition that exists when the unemployment rate is equal to the natural unemployment rate.

Question:

In other words, the economy can be operating at full employment and some people will be unemployed. Is this correct?

Answer:

Yes, that is correct.

Cyclical Unemployment

The unemployment rate that exists in the economy is not always at its natural rate. The difference between the existing unemployment rate and the natural unemployment rate is the **cyclical unemployment rate** (U_C).

$$U_C = U - U_N$$

Cyclical Unemployment Rate
The difference between the unemployment rate and the natural unemployment rate.

[3]The "number of persons in the civilian labor force" excludes persons in the armed forces. If we add members of the armed forces residing in the United States, we would then speak about the "number of persons in the *labor force.*"

When the unemployment rate (U) that exists in the economy is greater than the natural unemployment rate (U_N), the cyclical unemployment rate (U_C) is *positive*. For example, if $U = 8$ percent, and $U_N = 6$ percent, then $U_C = 2$ percent.

When the unemployment rate that exists in the economy is less than the natural unemployment rate, the cyclical unemployment rate is *negative*. For example, if $U = 4$ percent and $U_N = 6$ percent, then $U_C = -2$ percent.

Changes in Real GNP and Changes in the Unemployment Rate

There is always some unemployment rate (U) in the economy. And no matter what the unemployment rate is—5 percent, 6 percent, whatever—there is always some real GNP (Q) that is being produced at that unemployment rate.

All other things held constant, we expect a *higher real GNP* level to be associated with a *lower unemployment rate* and a *lower real GNP* level to be associated with a *higher unemployment rate.* In other words, real GNP and the unemployment rate are *inversely related*—as one goes up, the other goes down.

But why? The reason is that more workers are needed to produce more output and fewer workers are needed to produce less output, *ceteris paribus.* Since more workers are needed to produce more output (more real GNP), fewer persons remain unemployed and the unemployment rate drops, *ceteris paribus.* Since fewer workers are needed to produce less output, more persons are unemployed and the unemployment rate rises, *ceteris paribus.*

Ceteris Paribus Makes All the Difference

Here are some real-world data. In 1980, real GNP was $3,187.1 billion and the unemployment rate was 7.1 percent. In 1981, real GNP had risen to $3,248.8 billion and the unemployment rate had risen to 7.6 percent. The data show that real GNP and the unemployment rate are *directly* related, not *inversely* related as we just stated. What is wrong?

Recall that the inverse relationship between real GNP and the unemployment rate is conditioned by *ceteris paribus*—all other things held constant. To illustrate, let's first measure the unemployment rate, which is equal to the number of persons unemployed divided by the number of persons in the civilian labor force. For example, if there are 100,000 unemployed persons and the civilian labor force is 1 million persons, the unemployment rate is 10 percent. Let's say that at this 10 percent unemployment rate, real GNP is $500 billion.

Now suppose real GNP rises to $520 billion. *All other things held constant,* we would expect the unemployment rate to drop. But suppose all other things are not constant. Suppose that as the number of persons unemployed falls to 98,000, the civilian labor force does not stay constant at 1 million persons, but falls to 900,000 persons. When we divide the number of persons unemployed (98,000) by the civilian labor force (900,000) we get an unemployment rate of 10.9 percent. In other words, we witness a *rising* real GNP (from $500 to $520 billion) associated with a *rising* unemployment rate (from 10 to 10.9 percent).

Does this then mean that a *falling* real GNP will be associated with a *falling* unemployment rate? Not necessarily. For example, real GNP in 1981 was $3,248.8 billion and the unemployment rate was 7.6 percent. In 1982, real GNP had *fallen* to $3,166.0 billion and the unemployment rate had *risen* to 9.7 percent.

The *ceteris paribus* condition makes all the difference. So a higher real GNP is associated with a lower unemployment rate, and a lower real GNP is associated with a higher unemployment rate, as long as we add *ceteris paribus.*

The economy is always in **one** *of three states: (1) producing* Q_N, *(2) producing less than* Q_N, *or (3) producing more than* Q_N.

■

Natural Real GNP
The real GNP that is being produced at the natural unemployment rate.

Natural Real GNP and the Natural Unemployment Rate

Suppose the economy is currently operating at its natural unemployment rate (U_N). The real GNP that is produced when the economy is at the natural unemployment rate is called **natural real GNP.** We use the symbol Q_N to represent natural real GNP. At U_N, the economy is producing Q_N.

Three States of the Economy

The economy is always in one of three economic states. Before we outline them, we review four symbols: Q = real GNP being produced in the economy, Q_N = natural real GNP, U = unemployment rate that exists in the economy, and U_N = natural unemployment rate. The three economic environments include:

1. $Q = Q_N$. The real GNP being produced in the economy is equal to the natural real GNP. When this occurs, it follows that the unemployment rate in the economy (U) equals the natural unemployment rate (U_N). When the economy is in this situation, it is said to be in *long-run equilibrium:*

$$Q = Q_N$$
$$\text{and}$$
$$U = U_N$$

Recessionary Gap
The condition where the real GNP the economy is producing is less than the natural real GNP, and the unemployment rate that exists is greater than the natural unemployment rate.

2. $Q < Q_N$. The real GNP being produced in the economy is less than the natural real GNP. When this occurs, it follows that the unemployment rate in the economy is greater than the natural unemployment rate. When the economy is in this situation, it is said to be in a **recessionary gap:**

$$Q < Q_N$$
$$\text{and}$$
$$U > U_N$$

Why is it the case that if $Q < Q_N$, it follows that $U > U_N$? The reason is that fewer workers are needed to produce less output than more output, *ceteris paribus.* Since Q is less than Q_N in our example, fewer workers are needed to produce Q than Q_N; thus, more workers are unemployed at Q than at Q_N.

Inflationary Gap
The condition where the real GNP the economy is producing is greater than the natural real GNP, and the unemployment rate that exists is less than the natural unemployment rate.

3. $Q > Q_N$. The real GNP being produced in the economy is greater than the natural real GNP. When this occurs, it follows that the unemployment rate in the economy is less than the natural unemployment rate. When the economy is in this situation, it is said to be in an **inflationary gap:**

$$Q > Q_N$$
$$\text{and}$$
$$U < U_N$$

Why is it the case that if $Q > Q_N$, it follows that $U < U_N$? The reason is that more workers are needed to produce more output than less output, *ceteris paribus.* Since $Q > Q_N$ in our example, more workers are needed to produced Q than Q_N; thus, fewer workers are unemployed at Q than at Q_N. (See Exhibits 8–8 and columns 1–3 in Exhibit 8–9 for a quick review of these points.)

Let's take a close look at column 4 of Exhibit 8–9, a graphical representation of the three states of the economy. The large black dot in each diagram represents the current position of the economy.

The first diagram shows the economy in long-run equilibrium ($Q = Q_N$). The second diagram shows the economy in a recessionary gap ($Q < Q_N$). The third

EXHIBIT 8–8
The Unemployment Rate and the Natural Unemployment Rate

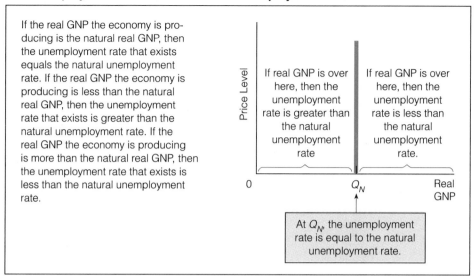

If the real GNP the economy is producing is the natural real GNP, then the unemployment rate that exists equals the natural unemployment rate. If the real GNP the economy is producing is less than the natural real GNP, then the unemployment rate that exists is greater than the natural unemployment rate. If the real GNP the economy is producing is more than the natural real GNP, then the unemployment rate that exists is less than the natural unemployment rate.

If real GNP is over here, then the unemployment rate is greater than the natural unemployment rate

If real GNP is over here, then the unemployment rate is less than the natural unemployment rate.

At Q_N, the unemployment rate is equal to the natural unemployment rate.

diagram shows the economy in an inflationary gap ($Q > Q_N$). We will use similar graphs representing the three states of an economy throughout the text.

Inverse Relationship between Real GNP and the Unemployment Rate

Remember, if the economy is producing a real GNP level greater than the natural real GNP, the unemployment rate is lower than the natural unemployment rate; and if the economy is producing a real GNP level less than the natural real GNP, the unemployment rate is greater than the natural unemployment rate. Exhibit 8–10 will help you keep this in mind.

In Exhibit 8–10, we have added an additional horizontal axis to the standard *AD–AS* diagram. The first horizontal axis is the "real GNP" axis; the second horizontal axis is the "unemployment rate" axis. What is important is to notice that the origin (0) for real GNP is on the *far left,* and the origin for the unemployment rate is on the *far right.* This means that as we move *rightward* along the real GNP axis, real GNP gets larger. And as we move *leftward* along the unemployment rate axis, the unemployment rate gets larger.[4]

The juxtaposition of the origins of the two axes is necessary in order that we maintain the inverse relationship between real GNP and the unemployment rate. That is, as real GNP grows, the unemployment rate falls; and as real GNP declines, the unemployment rate rises.

Now let us look at the three states of the economy in terms of Exhibit 8–10. First, suppose the economy is in long-run equilibrium producing Q_N. If we look directly below Q_N, we notice that the natural unemployment rate (U_N) corresponds to it.

[4]The way the two horizontal axes are drawn (one under the other) may suggest that a 1 percent change in real GNP (Q) will bring about a 1 percent change in the unemployment rate (U). We state emphatically that this need not be the case. Furthermore, according to Okun's law (named after Arthur Okun who was a member of President John Kennedy's Council of Economic Advisers) it *is not* the case. Okun's law holds that for every 3 percent that real GNP rises above (falls below) its natural level, the unemployment rate falls below (rises above) its natural level by 1 percent. That is, a 3 percent increase in real GNP above its natural level will decrease the unemployment rate by 1 percent below its natural level.

EXHIBIT 8–9
Three States of the Economy

The conditions that define the three stages of an economy are noted in the exhibit, along with a graphical representation of each.

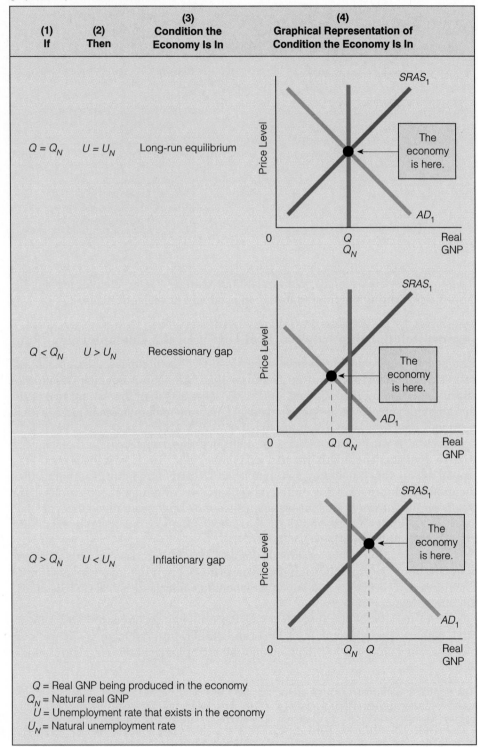

(1) If	(2) Then	(3) Condition the Economy Is In	(4) Graphical Representation of Condition the Economy Is In
$Q = Q_N$	$U = U_N$	Long-run equilibrium	
$Q < Q_N$	$U > U_N$	Recessionary gap	
$Q > Q_N$	$U < U_N$	Inflationary gap	

Q = Real GNP being produced in the economy
Q_N = Natural real GNP
U = Unemployment rate that exists in the economy
U_N = Natural unemployment rate

EXHIBIT 8–10
A Diagram With Two Horizontal Axes

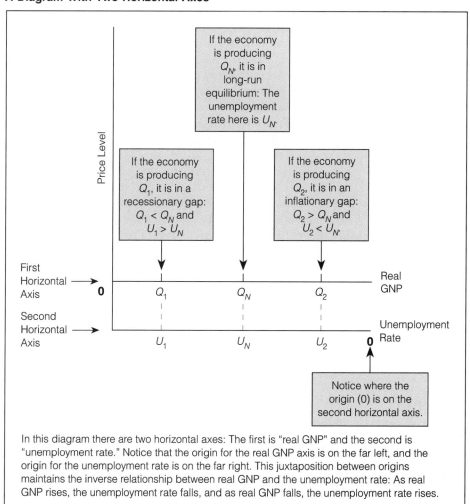

If the economy is producing Q_N, it is in long-run equilibrium: The unemployment rate here is U_N.

If the economy is producing Q_1, it is in a recessionary gap: $Q_1 < Q_N$ and $U_1 > U_N$.

If the economy is producing Q_2, it is in an inflationary gap: $Q_2 > Q_N$ and $U_2 < U_N$.

Price Level

First Horizontal Axis → 0 Q_1 Q_N Q_2 Real GNP

Second Horizontal Axis → U_1 U_N U_2 0   Unemployment Rate

Notice where the origin (0) is on the second horizontal axis.

In this diagram there are two horizontal axes: The first is "real GNP" and the second is "unemployment rate." Notice that the origin for the real GNP axis is on the far left, and the origin for the unemployment rate is on the far right. This juxtaposition between origins maintains the inverse relationship between real GNP and the unemployment rate: As real GNP rises, the unemployment rate falls, and as real GNP falls, the unemployment rate rises.

Now suppose the economy produces Q_1. Since Q_1 is less than Q_N, we know the economy is in a recessionary gap. The unemployment rate that corresponds to Q_1 is U_1. Is the natural unemployment rate higher or lower than U_1? A quick look at the second horizontal axis tells us that U_1 lies farther away from the origin than U_N, so U_1 is greater than U_N.

Next, suppose the economy produces Q_2. Since Q_2 is greater than Q_N, we know the economy is in an inflationary gap. The unemployment rate that corresponds to Q_2 is U_2. Is the natural unemployment rate higher or lower than U_2? A quick look at the second horizontal axis tells us that U_2 lies closer to the origin than U_N, so U_2 is less than U_N.

Although, throughout this text, we draw the standard *AD–AS* diagram with one horizontal axis (real GNP) and one vertical axis (price level), the two-horizontal-axes diagram in Exhibit 8–10 may clarify the relationship between different unemployment rates in the different states of the economy.

How Can the Unemployment Rate Be Less Than the Natural Unemployment Rate?

When the economy is in an inflationary gap, the unemployment rate that exists in the economy is less than the natural unemployment rate. For example, if the natural unemployment rate is 6 percent, the unemployment rate is, say, 4 percent.

But how can the economy do better than the natural unemployment rate, which, after all, is equated with full employment? To explain, we need to make use of two production possibilities frontiers.

In Exhibit 8–11, the two production possibilities frontiers are the *physical PPF* (purple curve) and the *institutional PPF* (blue curve). The physical PPF illustrates different combinations of goods the economy can produce given the physical constraints of (1) finite resources and (2) the current state of technology. The institutional PPF illustrates different combinations of goods the economy can produce given the physical constraints of (1) finite resources, (2) the current state of technology, and (3) any institutional constraints. Broadly defined, an institutional constraint is anything that prevents economic agents from producing the maximum real GNP physically possible. For example, the minimum wage law, which is an institutional constraint, specifies that workers must be paid a wage rate at least equal to the legislated minimum wage. One effect of this is that those unskilled persons whose value to employers falls below the legislated minimum wage will not be hired. Fewer workers means less output produced, *ceteris paribus.* (This is why the institutional *PPF* lies closer to the origin than the physical *PPF.)*

Within the confines of society's physical *and* institutional constraints, there is a natural unemployment rate. This state of affairs is represented by any point on the institutional *PPF.* In the exhibit, points *A, B,* and *C* are all such points.

EXHIBIT 8–11
The Physical and Institutional PPFs

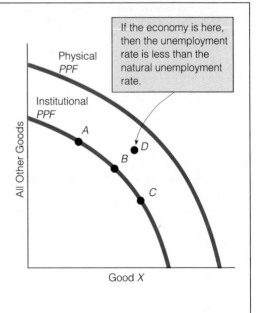

A society has both a physical *PPF* and an institutional *PPF*. The physical *PPF* illustrates different combinations of goods the economy can produce given the physical constraints of 1) finite resources and 2) the current state of technology. The institutional *PPF* illustrates different combinations of goods the economy can produce given the physical constraints of 1) finite resources, 2) the current state of technology, and 3) any institutional constraints. The economy is at the natural unemployment rate if it is located on its institutional *PPF,* such as at points *A, B,* or *C.* An economy can never operate beyond its physical PPF, but it is possible for it to operate beyond its institutional *PPF,* since institutional constraints are not always equally effective. If the economy does operate beyond its institutional *PPF,* such as at point *D,* then the unemployment rate that exists in the economy is lower than the natural unemployment rate.

If the economy is here, then the unemployment rate is less than the natural unemployment rate.

An economy can never operate beyond its physical *PPF,* but it is possible for it to operate beyond its institutional *PPF.* For example, suppose inflation reduces the purchasing power of the minimum wage, thus reducing or eliminating the constraining properties of the minimum wage law on the unskilled labor market.[5] This would make one of society's institutional constraints ineffective, allowing the economy to temporarily move beyond the institutional constraint.

Logic dictates that if the economy is operating at the natural unemployment rate when it is located *on* its institutional PPF, then it must be operating at an unemployment rate lower than the natural rate when it is located *beyond* its institutional PPF (but below its physical PPF). Because society's institutional constraints are not always equally effective, it is possible for an economy to be operating at an unemployment rate below the natural rate.

RECESSIONARY AND INFLATIONARY GAPS

In this section, we first discuss what happens when the economy is in a recessionary gap, then what happens when the economy is in an inflationary gap.

What Happens If the Economy Is in a Recessionary Gap?

Some economists contend that if the economy is in a recessionary gap, it can, under its own forces, eliminate that gap smoothly and quickly. In other words, the economy can heal itself. We explain the process.

In Exhibit 8–12a, the quantity supplied of real GNP in the short run (Q_1) is equal to the quantity demanded of real GNP (Q_1). The economy is in short-run equilibrium at point E. And since the real GNP the economy produces (Q_1) is *less than* natural real GNP (Q_N), the economy is in a recessionary gap. (Yes, it is possible for the economy to be in a recessionary gap *and* in short-run equilibrium, too.)

In a recessionary gap, the unemployment rate is *greater than* the natural unemployment rate. Consequently, as old wage bargains expire, firms end up paying workers lower wage rates. This is because unemployment is relatively high: The number of job seekers is high compared with the number of jobs to be filled.[6]

Exhibit 8–12b shows what happens. As wage rates fall (costs fall), the *SRAS* curve shifts rightward from $SRAS_1$ ultimately to $SRAS_2$. As a result of the increase in short-run aggregate supply, the price level falls. As the price level falls, the quantity demanded of real GNP rises owing to the real balance, interest rate, and international trade effects. As we learned earlier, when the price level falls, we move from one point on the aggregate demand curve to another point on the same curve. In Exhibit 8–12b, this is a movement down the AD_1 curve from point E to point E'.

As long as the economy's real GNP is less than Q_N, the price level will continue to fall.

Ultimately, the economy moves to long-run equilibrium at point E', corresponding to P_2 and Q_N.

[5]Inflation reduces the real (inflation-adjusted) minimum wage. If the minimum wage rate is $5 and the price level is 1, the real minimum wage rate is $5 (or $5 divided by the price level, 1). If the price level rises to 2, then the real minimum wage rate falls to $2.50 (which is $5 divided by the price level, 2). The lower the real minimum wage, the greater the number of unskilled workers that employers will hire, because the demand curve for unskilled labor is downward sloping.

[6]In this discussion of the economy eliminating a recessionary gap, we have emphasized wages adjusting. Besides wages, other input prices may adjust as well.

EXHIBIT 8–12
A Recessionary Gap and Its Automatic Removal

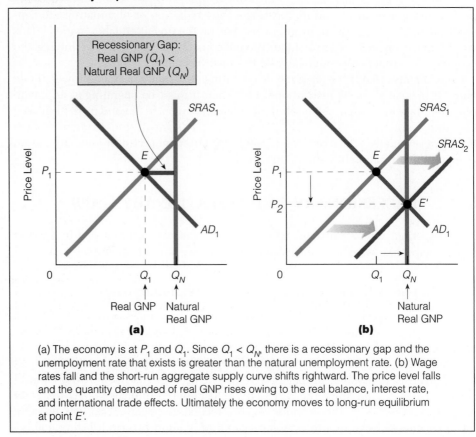

(a) The economy is at P_1 and Q_1. Since $Q_1 < Q_N$, there is a recessionary gap and the unemployment rate that exists is greater than the natural unemployment rate. (b) Wage rates fall and the short-run aggregate supply curve shifts rightward. The price level falls and the quantity demanded of real GNP rises owing to the real balance, interest rate, and international trade effects. Ultimately the economy moves to long-run equilibrium at point E'.

What Happens If the Economy Is in an Inflationary Gap?

Some economists contend that if the economy is in an inflationary gap, it can, under its own forces, eliminate that gap smoothly and quickly. In other words, the economy can heal itself. We explain the process.

In Exhibit 8–13a, the quantity supplied of real GNP in the short run (Q_1) is equal to the quantity demanded of real GNP (Q_1). The economy is in short-run equilibrium at point E. And since the real GNP the economy produces (Q_1) is *greater than* natural real GNP (Q_N), the economy is in an inflationary gap.

In an inflationary gap, the unemployment rate is *less than* the natural unemployment rate. Consequently, as old wage bargains expire, firms end up paying workers higher wage rates. This is because unemployment is relatively low: The number of job seekers is low compared with the number of jobs to be filled.[7]

Exhibit 8–13b shows what happens. As wages rates rise (costs rise), the SRAS curve shifts leftward from $SRAS_1$ ultimately to $SRAS_2$. As a result of the decrease in short-run aggregate supply, the price level rises. As the price level rises, the quantity demanded of real GNP falls owing to the real balance, interest rate, and international trade effects. As we learned earlier, when the price level rises, we

[7]In this discussion of the economy eliminating an inflationary gap, we have emphasized wages adjusting. Besides wages, other input prices may adjust as well.

EXHIBIT 8–13
An Inflationary Gap and Its Automatic Removal

(a) The economy is at P_1 and Q_1. Since $Q_1 > Q_N$, there is an inflationary gap and the unemployment rate that exists is less than the natural unemployment rate. (b) Wage rates rise and the short-run aggregate supply curve shifts leftward. The price level rises and the quantity demanded of real GNP falls owing to the real balance, interest rate, and international trade effects. Ultimately the economy moves to long-run equilibrium at point E'.

move from one point on the aggregate demand curve to another point on the same curve. In Exhibit 8–13b, this is a movement up the AD_1 curve from point E to point E'.

As long as the economy's real GNP is greater than Q_N, the price level will continue to rise.

Ultimately the economy moves to long-run equilibrium at point E', corresponding to P_2 and Q_N.

Economists, like other scientists, are often interested in knowing whether there is a natural resting place for the phenomena they are studying. For example, think of a natural resting place for a ball thrown high into the air. The natural resting place for it is the ground. Gravity pulls the ball downward. Think of a natural resting place for a competitive market. It is where the quantity demanded of a good equals the quantity supplied of the good. Markets are "at rest" when they are in equilibrium.

Macroeconomists want to know if there is a natural resting place for the economy. Some economists think there is. They think the natural resting place for the economy is where natural real GNP is being produced and the natural unemployment rate exists. Economists who believe that the economy can eliminate both recessionary and inflationary gaps smoothly and quickly

THINKING LIKE
AN ECONOMIST

CHAPTER 8
THE AGGREGATE DEMAND—
AGGREGATE SUPPLY FRAMEWORK
■

by itself, and thus return to its natural state, may use the analogy of a person's normal body temperature, which is 98.6 degrees.

If a person's body temperature rises above normal, he is said to have a fever. In most cases, the body itself eliminates the fever in time; that is, there is a return to normal. If the person's body temperature is below normal, in most cases this is an aberration and in time his temperature will edge its way back up to normal. In short, a temperature below normal and a temperature above normal are temporary states. Just as the body has a natural resting place—at 98.6 degrees—so does the economy. Thinking in terms of a "natural resting place," an "equilibrium," or a "benchmark" is part of the economic way of thinking. However, not all economists agree as to where the natural resting place of the economy is.

A Different Analysis of Recessionary and Inflationary Gaps

It may not be true that when either a recessionary or an inflationary gap exists, the economy will move *smoothly and quickly* to the natural real GNP level. Some economists argue that (1) there is no guarantee that the economy will in all cases automatically work itself out of a recessionary or inflationary gap; and (2) even in those instances when the economy does automatically work toward long-run equilibrium, it may take too long for the economy to reach its natural real GNP level.

Another point is this. In our discussion of a recessionary gap, we argued that because the unemployment rate is greater than the natural unemployment, when old wage bargains expire, employers will be able to pay workers lower wage rates because unemployment is relatively high. Because of the lower wage rates, the *SRAS* curve shifts rightward—thus moving the economy towards its natural real GNP level.

Now some economists would say that *wages are not likely to fall when the unemployment rate is greater than the natural unemployment rate.* They argue that wage rates are often sticky or inflexible in the downward direction. If this is correct, consider how it changes our analysis. If the economy is in a recessionary gap, and wage rates are inflexible in the downward direction, then even though the unemployment rate is greater than the natural unemployment rate, wage rates will not fall. But if wage rates do not fall, the *SRAS* curve will not shift rightward. And if the *SRAS* curve does not shift rightward, the economy will not automatically move toward its natural real GNP level. We conclude, then, that the economy may not always be able to automatically eliminate a recessionary gap by itself. Instead, the economy may get *stuck* in a recessionary gap.

These issues are explored in greater detail in the forthcoming theory chapters.

The Long-Run Aggregate Supply Curve

The possibility of automatic adjustments in the economy gives rise to the concept of the **long-run aggregate supply (*LRAS*) curve.** The *LRAS* curve shows the real GNP the economy is prepared to supply at different price levels, assuming wage rates and all other input prices have fully adjusted to eliminate a recessionary or inflationary gap.

As we described earlier, if wage rates and other prices are flexible, there is a tendency for an economy in either a recessionary or inflationary gap to settle down eventually at its natural real GNP level. It follows that the vertical (green) line locked in on natural real GNP, Q_N, in Exhibits 8–12 and 8–13 is the *LRAS* curve. It also follows that **long-run equilibrium** is at the intersection of the *AD* curve and

Long-Run Aggregate Supply Curve
The long-run aggregate supply curve shows the real GNP the economy is prepared to supply at different price levels, assuming wage rates and all other input prices have fully adjusted to eliminate a recessionary or inflationary gap.

Long-Run Equilibrium
The condition that exists in the economy when the real GNP being produced equals the natural real GNP and the unemployment rate that exists equals the natural unemployment rate. In long-run equilibrium, the quantity demanded of real GNP equals the (long-run) quantity supplied of real GNP. This condition is met at the intersection of the aggregate demand curve and the long-run aggregate supply curve.

How Does Foreign Buying of U.S. Goods Affect the U.S. Price Level, Real GNP, and Unemployment Rate?

"At a given price level, anything that increases any of the four components of total spending (*C, I, G,* or net exports—*X−M*), increases aggregate demand and shifts the *AD* curve to the right. Also, *at a given price level,* anything that decreases any of the four components of total spending decreases aggregate demand and shifts the *AD* curve to the left."

Also, "anything that shifts the *AD* curve also changes the price level and real GNP in the short run. For example, if the *AD* curve shifts rightward, the price level and real GNP rise."

Let us put these two pieces of knowledge together in two examples to show how the residents of foreign nations can affect the U.S. real GNP, price level, and unemployment rate in the short run.

Example 1: Suppose foreigners begin to buy more U.S. goods, so exports (*X*) increase, *ceteris paribus.*[8]

[8]In this text, we assume that if the physical quantity of U.S. goods purchased by foreigners rises (falls) that exports (*X*) rise (fall). Remember, exports do not refer to the physical goods themselves, but to the total foreign spending on domestic goods. Exports is a dollar amount.

This causes U.S. net exports (*X−M*) to increase. And if U.S. net exports increase, the *AD* curve shifts rightward. Essentially, people (consisting of Americans and foreigners, too) are collectively buying more U.S. real GNP at a given price level.

As a result of a rightward shift in the *AD* curve, the price level and real GNP in the United States rise in the short run. Finally, if real GNP rises, the U.S. unemployment rate falls (Exhibit 8–14).

Example 2: Suppose foreigners begin to buy fewer U.S. goods, so exports (*X*) decrease, *ceteris paribus.*

EXHIBIT 8–14
A Foreign–U.S. Economic Link

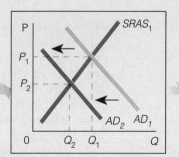

EXAMPLE 1

Foreigners buy more U.S. goods, so *X*↑ → If *X*↑, then (*X − M*)↑ → If (*X − M*)↑ then *AD*↑, so *AD* curve shifts rightward → [graph: P axis, P_2, P_1, $SRAS_1$, AD_1, AD_2, Q_1, Q_2, Q axis] → As a result, *P*↑, *Q*↑, and the unemployment rate ↓

EXAMPLE 2

Foreigners buy fewer U.S. goods, so *X*↓ → If *X*↓, then (*X − M*)↓ → If (*X − M*)↓ then *AD*↓, so *AD* curve shifts leftward → [graph: P axis, P_1, P_2, $SRAS_1$, AD_2, AD_1, Q_2, Q_1, Q axis] → As a result, *P*↓, *Q*↓, and the unemployment rate ↑

Foreign buying of U.S. goods can affect the U.S. price level, real GNP, and unemployment rate as we have outlined in the exhibit.

169

This causes U.S. net exports $(X-M)$ to decrease. And if U.S. net exports decrease, the *AD* curve shifts leftward. As a result, the price level and real GNP in the United States fall in the short run. Finally, if real GNP falls, the U.S. unemployment rate rises (Exhibit 8–14).

So far, then, we know this: Anything that affects foreign buying of U.S. goods affects (1) U.S. net exports, and thus (2) the *AD* curve in the United States, and consequently (3) the price level, real GNP, and unemployment rate in the United States.

In other words, there is an economic link between what happens in foreign nations and what happens in the United States.

the *LRAS* curve. Recall that short-run equilibrium is at the intersection of the *AD* curve and the *SRAS* curve. Both the long-run and short-run equilibrium positions, as well as the *LRAS* curve, are represented in Exhibit 8–15. (In Exhibit 8–15, does a recessionary or inflationary gap exist in the short run? The answer is an inflationary gap.)

CHAPTER SUMMARY

Aggregate Demand

EXHIBIT 8–15
The LRAS Curve and Short- and Long-Run Equilibrium

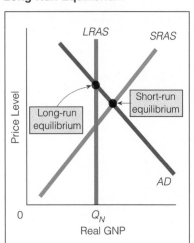

Short-run equilibrium exists at the point where the *AD* curve and the *SRAS* curve intersect. Long-run equilibrium exists at the point where the *AD* curve and the *LRAS* curve intersect. The *LRAS* curve is a vertical line at natural real GNP, Q_N.

■ The aggregate demand (*AD*) curve shows the quantity demanded of real GNP at different price levels, *ceteris paribus*.

■ The aggregate demand curve slopes downward, indicating an inverse relationship between the price level and the quantity demanded of real GNP.

■ The aggregate demand curve slopes downward because of the real balance, interest rate, and international trade effects.

■ The real balance effect states that the inverse relationship between the price level and the quantity demanded of real GNP is established through changes in the value of a person's monetary wealth or money holdings. Specifically, a fall in the price level causes purchasing power to rise, or increases a person's monetary wealth. As people become wealthier, the quantity demanded of real GNP rises. A rise in the price level causes purchasing power to fall, or reduces a person's monetary wealth. As people become less wealthy, the quantity demanded of real GNP falls.

■ The interest rate effect states that the inverse relationship between the price level and the quantity demanded of real GNP is established through changes in household and business spending that is sensitive to changes in interest rates. Specifically, as the interest rate rises, businesses and households borrow less and so they end up buying fewer goods. Thus, the quantity demanded of real GNP falls. As the interest rate falls, businesses and households borrow more and so they end up buying more goods. Thus, the quantity demanded of real GNP rises.

■ The international trade effect states that the inverse relationship between the price level and the quantity demanded of real GNP is established through foreign sector spending. Specifically, as the price level in the United States rises, U.S. goods become relatively more expensive than foreign goods and both Americans and foreigners buy fewer U.S. goods. The quantity demanded of (U.S.) real GNP falls. As the price level in the United States falls, U.S. goods become relatively less expensive than foreign goods and both Americans and foreigners buy more U.S. goods. The quantity demanded of (U.S.) real GNP rises.

■ At a give price level, anything that increases any of the four components of total spending (consumption, investment, government expenditures, or net exports) increases aggregate demand and shifts the *AD* curve to the right. At a given price level, anything that decreases any of the four components of total spending decreases aggregate demand and shifts the *AD* curve to the left.

Short-Run Aggregate Supply

■ The short-run aggregate supply (*SRAS*) curve shows the real GNP that producers will offer for sale at different price levels, *ceteris paribus*.

■ The *SRAS* curve is upward sloping, indicating a direct relationship between the price level and the quantity supplied of real GNP.

■ A decrease in wage rates, a decrease in the price of nonlabor inputs, an increase in productivity, and a beneficial supply shock all shift the *SRAS* curve to the right. An increase in wage rates, an increase in the price of nonlabor inputs, a decrease in productivity, and an adverse supply shock all shift the *SRAS* curve to the left.

Short-Run Analysis in the *AD–AS* Framework

■ Diagrammatically, short-run equilibrium exists at the intersection of the *AD* and *SRAS* curves. A shift in either or both of these curves can change the price level and real GNP.

Natural Unemployment Rate and Natural Real GNP

■ The natural unemployment rate equals the frictional unemployment rate plus the structural unemployment rate.

■ Natural real GNP is the level of real GNP that is produced when the economy is operating at the natural unemployment rate.

Three Economic States

■ The economy is always in one of three economic states: (1) long-run equilibrium, (2) a recessionary gap, or (3) an inflationary gap.

■ In long-run equilibrium, the real GNP that the economy is producing is equal to the natural real GNP. Also, the unemployment rate that exists in the economy is equal to the natural unemployment rate.

■ In a recessionary gap, the real GNP that the economy is producing is less than the natural real GNP. Also, the unemployment rate that exists in the economy is greater than the natural unemployment rate.

■ In an inflationary gap, the real GNP that the economy is producing is greater than the natural real GNP. Also, the unemployment rate that exists in the economy is less than the natural unemployment rate.

One View of the Economy

■ Some economists contend that the economy can eliminate both recessionary and inflationary gaps smoothly and quickly by itself. They say the economy works this way: First, assume the economy is in a recessionary gap. The unemployment rate is greater than the natural unemployment rate. As old wage bargains expire, wage rates fall. This shifts the *SRAS* curve to the right and brings down the price level. As the price level drops, the quantity demanded of real GNP rises. Ultimately, the economy moves to long-run equilibrium where the real GNP the economy produces equals the natural real GNP.

■ Now assume the economy is in an inflationary gap. The unemployment rate is less than the natural unemployment rate. As old wage bargains expire, wage rates rise. This shifts the *SRAS* curve to the left and increases the price level. As the price level rises, the quantity demanded of real GNP falls. Ultimately, the economy moves to long-run equilibrium where the real GNP the economy produces equals the natural real GNP.

Another View of the Economy

■ Some economists argue that (1) there is no guarantee that the economy will in all cases automatically work itself out of a recessionary or inflationary gap; and (2) even in those instances when the economy does automatically work toward long-run equilibrium, it may take too long for the economy to reach its natural real GNP level.

■ Some economists argue that when the economy is in a recessionary gap, and the unemployment rate is greater than the natural rate, wage rates may be inflexible downward and thus not adjust to eliminate the recessionary gap. According to these economists, the economy may get stuck in a recessionary gap.

Long-Run Analysis in the *AD–AS* Framework

■ The long-run aggregate supply (*LRAS*) curve shows the real GNP the economy is prepared to supply at different price levels, assuming wage rates and other input prices have fully adjusted to eliminate a recessionary or inflationary gap.

■ Diagrammatically, long-run equilibrium is at the intersection of the *AD* and *LRAS* curves.

Key Terms and Concepts

Aggregate Demand (AD) Curve	Short-Run Equilibrium	Cyclical Unemployment Rate
Real Balance Effect	Frictional Unemployment	Natural Real GNP
Monetary Wealth	Structural Unemployment	Recessionary Gap
Purchasing Power	Natural Unemployment Rate	Inflationary Gap
Interest Rate Effect	Full Employment	Long-Run Equilibrium
International Trade Effect		Long-Run Aggregate Supply (LRAS) Curve
Short-Run Aggregate Supply (SRAS) Curve		

1. Is aggregate demand a specific dollar amount? For example, is it correct to say that aggregate demand is, say, $1 trillion this year?

2. In the short run, what is the impact on the price level and real GNP of each of the following:

a. an increase in consumption brought about by something other than a change in the price level

b. a decrease in exports brought about by something other than a change in the price level

c. an increase in imports brought about by something other than a change in the price level

d. an increase in investment brought about by something other than a change in the price level

e. a fall in wage rates

f. an adverse supply shock

g. a decline in productivity

h. a beneficial supply shock

i. a fall in nonlabor input prices

j. a rise in nonlabor input prices

3. What does it mean to say that the economy can get "stuck" in a recessionary gap?

4. Why might the natural rate of unemployment be 5 percent in one country and 2 percent in another?

5. Within the *AD–AS* framework, note at least three areas where debates among economists may arise.

6. If real GNP is less than natural real GNP, it follows that the unemployment rate that exists in the economy is greater than the natural rate of unemployment. Explain why.

7. One of the assumptions in an economic theory we discuss in Chapter 14 (the strict quantity theory of money) is that real GNP is constant in the short run. Draw the short-run aggregate supply curve that corresponds to this assumption.

8. Why do you think some positive natural rate of unemployment is always likely to exist?

9. What might government do to shift the long-run aggregate supply curve leftward? What might it do to shift it rightward?

10. If the economy is operating at a point on its short-run aggregate supply curve that is below natural real GNP, where is the economy in terms of its production possibilities frontier? Explain your answer. (You may need to review the material on the production possibilities frontier in Chapter 2).

11. Diagrammatically represent an economy in a recessionary gap. Next, explain the process of how the economy eliminates the gap by itself.

12. Diagrammatically represent an economy in an inflationary gap. Next, explain the process of how the economy eliminates the gap by itself.

13. Are the real balance, interest rate, and international trade effects relevant to a change in quantity demanded of real GNP or to a change in aggregate demand? Explain your answer.

14. What effect do the economic actions of the Japanese, English, Germans, and French (to name the residents of a few foreign nations) have on the U.S. real GNP?

15. Can an economy be in long-run equilibrium and in an inflationary gap, too? Can an economy be in short-run equilibrium and in an inflationary gap, too? Explain your answers.

16. Consider the following data:

Price Level	Quantity Demanded of Real GNP	Quantity Supplied of Real GNP in the Short Run	Quantity Supplied of Real GNP in the Long Run
		(billions of 1982 dollars)	
100	4,800	3,700	4,400
105	4,600	3,900	4,400
110	4,500	4,200	4,400

a. At a price level of 110, is the economy in short-run equilibrium? Explain your answer.

b. At a price level of 105, is the economy in long-run equilibrium? Explain your answer.

c. Will the price level in long-run equilibrium be greater than, less than, or equal to 110? Explain your answer.

PART

III

MACROECONOMIC THEORY AND FISCAL POLICY

CHAPTER 9

KEYNESIAN THEORY: EMPHASIS ON UNEMPLOYMENT

WHAT THIS CHAPTER IS ABOUT

In the course of studying macroeconomics, you will learn about four theories, or schools of thought. In this chapter we first discuss classical theory and then Keynesian theory, which was born out of a major economic event—the Great Depression.

A REFRESHER ON THEORY AND A NOTE ON LABELS

The role of theory in economics can be summarized in the following three statements.

1. The purpose of a theory is to better understand the world. It is built on the critical variables that (the theorist believes) explain and predict the phenomenon under consideration.
2. The process of focusing on a limited number of variables to explain or predict an event is called abstraction.
3. A theory is better judged by its predictions than by its assumptions.

No doubt there will be times in your reading when you will say, "This theory is too abstract," or "This theory doesn't take enough into consideration," or "I don't understand why the theory assumes what it does." We urge you to resist the natural temptation to judge theories without a fair hearing. Remember, *all* theories are abstract and *all* theories make assumptions, and it is better to judge a theory by how well it predicts than by its assumptions, level of abstraction, or anything else.

Theories have names, or labels. Four macroeconomic theories or schools of thought are called *classical, Keynesian, monetarist,* and *new classical.* Once you know the names, there is the temptation to ask, Which theory is correct? You may even think, Why can't economists just tell us which theory is correct and ignore all the rest? Wouldn't this save time? Wouldn't it be less confusing?

Well, maybe, except that economists do not agree about which theory is correct. Also, *the objective at hand is to teach economics—not a particular view of the economy and not just one theory.* If economics seems a little messier than mathematics, engineering, or biology, that is not necessarily bad, and it doesn't necessarily mean that economics is any less of a science. It may simply suggest that the answers to economic questions are not as forthcoming as they are in some other disciplines.

There is plenty of time for you to decide which theory is correct, or which theory is wrong, or which theory is right or wrong under certain conditions. For now, we simply want to learn what each theory says.

Also, as you read, keep in mind that the economic labels *classical, Keynesian, monetarist,* and *new classical* are sometimes used differently from, say, religious or ethnic labels. For example, when a person says he is Asian, he not only tells you what he is, but what he is not (he is not African-American, Hispanic, and so on). Or when someone calls herself a Buddhist, she is not only telling you what she is, but she is also telling you what she is not. This kind of label is exclusive: Being one thing excludes a person from being something else.

Economic labels are not as rigid. It is possible for an economist to describe himself as "largely a monetarist," but "with Keynesian tendencies *at times,* or *under certain conditions.*" We offer a medical analogy.

Dr. Diane Newcombe is a physician. She believes that about 90 percent of the time the body has sufficient healing powers to cure itself. But 10 percent of the time, it does not. For example, it can cure a cold, but probably not some types of cancer. If someone were to label Dr. Newcombe as a believer in the healing properties of the body, this is largely true, but still it may be slightly misleading since she is not a believer in the healing properties of the body under all conditions or at all times.

Similarly, when we use the labels *classical, Keynesian, monetarist,* and *new classical,* we are talking about the essence of the particular macroeconomic theory.

We remind ourselves that economists and others may choose a small portion from one and much from another.

Also, each of the four theories is changing in small, but occasionally far-reaching, ways. For example, Keynesian theory today has more of a micro foundation, or incentive-based aspect to it, than it did 15 years ago.

Finally, as you read about the different macroeconomic theories, try to place these ideas in the three macroeconomic categories: the P–Q category, the inherently stable–inherently unstable category, and the effective–ineffective category. We are ready to show you how. We start with classical theory.

THE CLASSICAL THEORY

In this section, we present the classical theory as it relates to unemployment and production. This discussion is important for three reasons.

First, it gives us knowledge of an important school of economics, the classical school. This school includes among its members such famous economists of the past as Adam Smith, Jean Baptiste Say, Jeremy Bentham, David Ricardo, and John Stuart Mill.

Second, classical theory provides the backdrop for the development of Keynesian theory.

Third, classical theory makes up a large part of the intellectual heritage of monetarism and the new classical school of economics, which we discuss in later chapters. Neither development can be fully understood without knowing something about the classical theory on which they are based.

Classical Theory On Production, Unemployment, and Demand and Supply in the Macroeconomy

Here is what classical theory has to say on some topics.

1. On Production. The economy is always close to or on its production possibilities frontier. This means that the economy is always close to or at the point of producing natural real GNP (Q_N) or the full-employment real GNP (Q_F).[1] Another way to say this is that the economy is always on or near its *LRAS* curve.

2. On Unemployment. The economy is always close to or at full employment, or the natural unemployment rate. This follows from (1), since if the economy is producing natural real GNP, it does so at the natural unemployment rate.

3. On Demand and Supply in the Macroeconomy. Whatever real GNP is produced and supplied will be demanded.

Overall, the classical economists believed that the economy is a self-adjusting mechanism that stabilizes itself at full-employment output, or natural real GNP. This position is based on (1) Say's law, (2) interest rate flexibility, and (3) wage–price flexibility.

Say's Law

The nineteenth-century French economist Jean Baptiste Say is credited with expounding the principle that has come to be known as **Say's law**: Supply creates its own demand. Say's basic idea is most easily understood in terms of a barter

Say's Law
Supply creates its own demand. Production creates demand sufficient to purchase all goods produced.

[1]Recall from Chapter 8 that if the economy is operating on its (institutional) production possibilities frontier (PPF) it is at the natural unemployment rate producing natural real GNP.

179

economy. Consider a person baking bread to trade; he is a supplier of bread. Why does he do what he does? According to Say, the baker works at his trade because he plans to demand other goods. As he is baking his bread, the baker is thinking of the goods and services he will obtain in exchange for it. Thus, his act of supplying bread is linked to his demand for other goods. Supply creates its own demand.

If the supplying of some goods is simultaneously the demanding of other goods, then Say's law implies that there cannot be either (1) a general overproduction of goods (where total supply in the economy is greater than total demand) or (2) a general underproduction of goods (where total demand is greater than total supply).

Now suppose the baker is baking bread in a money economy. Does Say's law hold? Over a period of time, the baker earns an income as a result of his supplying bread. But what does he do with his income? For one thing, he buys goods and services. However, his demand for goods and services does not necessarily match the income that he generates through his actions as a supplier of bread. It is possible that the baker spends less than his full income because he engages in saving. Noting this, we might think that Say's law does not hold in a money economy since the act of supplying goods and services, and thus earning income, need not create an equal amount of demand. The classical economists disagreed. They argued that even in a money economy, where individuals sometimes spend less than their full incomes, Say's law still holds. Their argument was partly based on the assumption of interest rate flexibility.

Interest Rate Flexibility

As we noted in Chapter 6, saving is a leakage and investment is an injection. For Say's law to hold in a money economy, funds saved (leaked) must give rise to an equal amount of funds invested (injected); that is, what leaves the spending stream through one door must enter through another door. If not, then leakages may be greater than injections, and thus some of the income earned from supplying goods may not be used to demand goods (goodbye Say's law). As a result, there will be an overproduction of goods.

The classical economists argued that saving is matched by an equal amount of investment because of interest rate flexibility in the credit market. To understand their argument, take a look at Exhibit 9–1, where I represents investment and S represents saving. First, notice that I_1 is downward sloping, indicating an inverse relationship between the amount of funds firms invest and the interest rate (i). The reason for this is straightforward. The interest rate is the cost of borrowing funds, so therefore the higher the interest rate, the fewer funds firms borrow and invest; and the lower the interest rate, the more funds firms borrow and invest.

Notice that S_1 is upward sloping, indicating a direct relationship between the amount of funds households save and the interest rate. The reason is that the higher the interest rate, the higher the reward for saving (or the higher the opportunity cost of consuming), and therefore the fewer funds will be consumed and the more funds will be saved. Market-equilibrating forces move the credit market to interest rate i_1 and equilibrium point E_1, where the number of dollars households save ($100,000) equals the number of dollars firms invest ($100,000).

Suppose now that saving increases at each interest rate. We represent this by a rightward shift in our saving curve from S_1 to S_2. The classical economists believed that an increase in saving (leakages) will put downward pressure on the interest rate, moving it to i_2, thereby increasing the number of dollars firms invest. Ulti-

EXHIBIT 9–1
The Classical View of the Credit Market

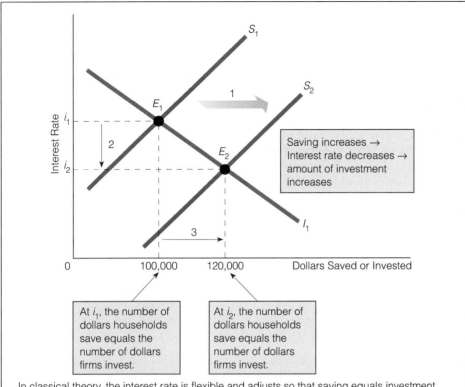

Saving increases →
Interest rate decreases →
amount of investment
increases

At i_1, the number of
dollars households
save equals the
number of dollars
firms invest.

At i_2, the number of
dollars households
save equals the
number of dollars
firms invest.

In classical theory, the interest rate is flexible and adjusts so that saving equals investment.
Thus, if saving increases and the saving curve shifts rightward from S_1 to S_2 (arrow 1), the
increase in saving eventually puts pressure on the interest rate and moves it downward from
i_1 to i_2 (arrow 2). A new equilibrium is established at E_2 (arrow 3), where once again the amount
households save equals the amount firms invest.

mately, the number of dollars households save ($120,000) will once again equal
the number of dollars firms invest ($120,000). Interest rate flexibility ensures that
saving equals investment, so that leakages equal injections. (What goes out one
door comes in the other door.) In short, changes in the interest rate uphold Say's
law in a money economy where there is saving.

Wage–Price Flexibility

According to the classical economists, *even if* interest rate adjustments do not
equate saving and investment in a reasonable time, other prices in other markets
will adjust in a way that ensures there will be no general overproduction of
goods—at least not for long.

Specifically, classical economists assumed that *prices in goods and services mar-*
kets and prices in labor markets (wages) will adjust in accordance with the laws
of supply and demand. For example, suppose households temporarily save more
than firms are willing to invest and, consequently, total spending in the economy
decreases. According to classical theory, real GNP will not fall and the unemployment rate will not rise *as long as* the prices of goods *quickly adjusted downward,*
which classical economists believed would occur.

Classical economists believed that as demand falls, competing producers of goods will lower their prices to rid themselves of surpluses. With lower demand and lower prices, it is still possible to sell as many units of a good as were sold at the original higher demand and higher prices. For example, $100 will buy 5 lamps at $20 each, and $50 will also buy 5 lamps if the price falls to $10.

But what happens to firms' profits? Although business firms can maintain their sales and production levels by lowering prices, won't this result in lower profits or even losses? The classical economists answered this question by arguing that because of falling demand and falling prices for goods and services, the demand for labor (and other resources) will fall, too. As a result, wage rates will fall, and eventually a new equilibrium wage rate will be established at the point at which the quantity of labor demanded equals the quantity of labor supplied. All those who want to work at the market-determined wage rate will have an opportunity to do so: There would be no **involuntary unemployment.**

Involuntary Unemployment
A condition where people who want to work at the market-determined wage rate cannot find work at this wage rate.

Classical Economic Policy: Laissez-Faire

The classical economists believed in the self-equilibrating, stabilizing properties of the market economy. For them, full-employment, or natural, real GNP was the norm. If the economy became "ill," it certainly was capable of healing itself through changes in prices, wages, and interest rates. This view led classical economists to advocate a macroeconomic policy of **laissez-faire,** or noninterference. As the classical economists viewed things, government did not have an economic management role to play.

Laissez-faire
A public policy of not interfering with market activities.

Major Tenets of Classical Theory

The P–Q Category. Classical economists believed that the economy is always close to or at the point of producing real GNP (Q_N). (In Chapter 14, we discuss classical theory with regard to the price level, P.)

The Inherently Stable–Inherently Unstable Category. Classical economists believed that the economy is inherently stable. The economy can smoothly and quickly equilibrate itself at full employment, or natural, real GNP.

The Effective–Ineffective Category. Classical economists believed in the principle of laissez-faire—that government should not interfere in the nation's economy. Such interference would be ineffective at solving economic problems; it would lead to more problems, not fewer.

KEYNESIAN THEORY: BACKGROUND

On the morning of October 10, 1932, John Maynard Keynes, age 49, walked into a lecture hall at Cambridge University in Cambridge, England. He began to speak: "Gentlemen, the change in the title of these lectures—from 'The Pure Theory of Money' to 'The Monetary Theory of Production' is significant." The impact of that lecture, and the 29 that followed over a period of four years, was felt far and wide. The discussions of economists, presidents, and prime ministers soon had to take into account the theories of John Maynard Keynes. The first shot of the Keynesian revolution had been fired.

Some economists argue that there would not have been a Keynesian revolution had there not been a Great Depression. (See the interview with Paul A. Samuelson in this chapter.) During these years, many economists and laypersons alike viewed the severe economic downturn as more than a temporary departure from classical theory equilibrium at natural real GNP. There was a general feeling that perhaps something more fundamental was wrong. Between 1929 and 1933, real GNP fell by approximately 30 percent; over the same period of time, the unemployment rate rose from 3.2 percent to 24.9 percent, real investment declined 75 percent, and real consumption dropped 20 percent. The macroeconomic policy of laissez-faire was being challenged. In such unusual and distressful economic circumstances, many persons wondered out loud why the government couldn't help. In this setting, Keynes wrote his *General Theory* (short for *The General Theory of Employment, Interest and Money*). We begin our discussion of Keynesian theory by pointing out a few of Keynes's criticisms of classical theory.

Keynes on Say's Law

Say's law maintained that there will always, or nearly always, be enough total demand or purchasing power in the economy to buy the full-employment, or natural, real GNP. Keynes disagreed, citing both empirical and theoretical reasons.

The Great Depression itself was enough of an empirical reason. Massive unemployment and a sharp decline in real GNP called Say's law into question.

On a theoretical level, Keynes argued that *it is possible to have saving (a leakage) greater than investment (an injection) such that total spending will be insufficient to buy the goods produced, resulting in a turndown in economic activity.* The classical view said interest rate flexibility would ensure a balance between saving and investment. Keynes emphasized that individuals save and invest for a host of reasons and that no single factor, such as the interest rate, links these activities. Furthermore, he believed that saving is more responsive to changes in income than to changes in the interest rate and that investment is more responsive to technological changes, business expectations, and innovations than to changes in the interest rate. In summary, whereas the classical economists believed that saving and investment depend on the interest rate, Keynes believed that both saving and investment depend on a number of factors that may be far more influential than the interest rate.

Consider the difference between Keynes and the classical economists on saving. As we noted earlier, the classical economists held that saving is directly related to the interest rate: As the interest rate goes up, saving rises; as the interest rate goes down, saving falls, *ceteris paribus.*

Keynes thought this might not always be true. If individuals are saving for a certain goal—say, a retirement fund of $100,000—then they might save less per period at an interest rate of 12 percent than at an interest rate of 5 percent, since a higher interest rate means that less saving is required per period to meet the goal within a set time. For example, if the interest rate is 5 percent, $50,000 saved earns $2,500 in interest income per year; if the interest rate is 10 percent, $25,000 saved earns $2,500.

As to investment, although Keynes believed that the interest rate is important in determining the level of investment, he did not think it is as important as other variables, such as the expected rate of profit on investment. Keynes argued that if business expectations are pessimistic, then it is unlikely there will be much investment, no matter how low the interest rate.

The difference between classical economists and Keynes on the degree of flexibility in wage rates has theoretical consequences.

■

Empirical Evidence: Saving and Interest Rates

The classical economists stated that a *strong direct relationship* exists between saving and the interest rate (in other words, changes in the interest rate greatly affect saving). Keynes argued that a *weak direct relationship* exists between the two (changes in the interest rate mildly affect saving). Who is right?

In a study published in 1978, economist Michael Boskin calculated that a 10 percent increase in the real after-tax interest rate caused U.S. saving to increase between 2 and 6 percent. So the Boskin study supports the idea of a strong direct relationship between saving and the interest rate—score one for the classical economists.

However, a study published in 1983 by economists Irwin Freund and Joel Hasbrouck found that U.S. saving is not affected by changes in the real after-tax interest rate—score one for Keynes. Additionally, in a 1984 study, economists Vito Tanzi and Eytan Sheshinski found a time period in which U.S. saving actually fell as real after-tax interest rates were rising. Given the difference in the empirical results, the relationship between saving and interest rates (strong direct: classical; weak direct: Keynes; or negative: Tanzi and Sheshinski) is still up in the air. Why is it so hard for economists to establish the true relationship between saving and interest rates? We can only list some possibilities: (1) The relationship may be different at different times. (2) Measuring the real after-tax interest rate may be difficult (for example, measuring the real interest rate requires knowing something about the expectations of individuals with respect to future prices, and this is not easy to calculate). (3) Not all other things can be held constant as economists try to find the relationship between the two variables.

Keynes on Wage–Price Flexibility

Recall that the classical economists believed that not only a change in the interest rate but also changes in prices and wages will obtain natural real GNP. Keynes also disagreed with the classical economists on the issue of wage–price flexibility, citing two points.

On Prices. Keynes noted that the internal structure of an economy is not always competitive enough to allow prices to fall. Recall from Chapter 3 how the forces of supply and demand operated when price was above equilibrium. In this case, a surplus was generated and price fell until the quantity supplied of the good equaled the quantity demanded. Keynes suggested that perhaps because of anticompetitive or monopolistic elements in the economy, price would not fall.

On Wages. Keynes believed that there was a natural resistance from employees to employer's proposed wage cuts. Also, labor unions would resist wage cuts. According to Keynes, the wage rate may be inflexible in the downward direction.

The difference between classical economists and Keynes on the degree of flexibility in wage rates has theoretical consequences. We illustrate with the aid of Exhibit 9–2. Suppose we start at point 1 in (a). The economy here is in a recessionary gap, since the real GNP the economy is producing, Q_1, is less than natural real GNP, Q_N. This means the unemployment rate that exists is greater than the natural unemployment rate. According to the classical view of how the economy works, wage rates will soon fall. As this happens, the short-run aggregate supply (*SRAS*) curve shifts rightward, ultimately intersecting the aggregate demand curve at point 2. The economy is now in long-run equilibrium producing the natural real GNP.

EXHIBIT 9–2
Classical and Keynesian Views Contrasted

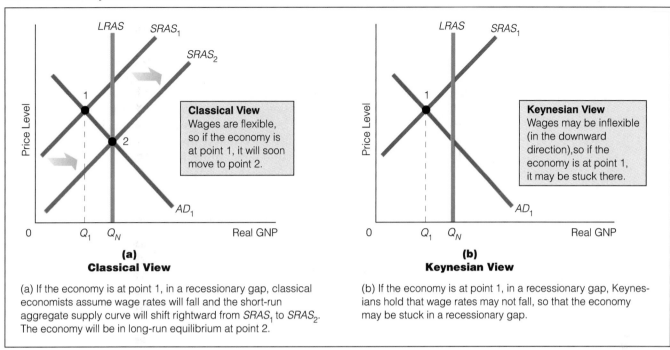

(a)
Classical View

(b)
Keynesian View

(a) If the economy is at point 1, in a recessionary gap, classical economists assume wage rates will fall and the short-run aggregate supply curve will shift rightward from $SRAS_1$ to $SRAS_2$. The economy will be in long-run equilibrium at point 2.

(b) If the economy is at point 1, in a recessionary gap, Keynesians hold that wage rates may not fall, so that the economy may be stuck in a recessionary gap.

Now let's look at how things turn out if wage rates do not fall. Suppose we start at point 1 in (b). Again, the economy is in a recessionary gap with the unemployment rate greater than the natural unemployment rate. According to the Keynesian view of how the economy works, wage rates may not fall. But if wage rates do not fall, then the *SRAS* curve will not shift to the right. And if the *SRAS* curve doesn't shift to the right, then the economy is stuck in a recessionary gap.

In summary, *the classical view that wages are flexible logically implies that the economy can eliminate a recessionary gap by itself. An economy doesn't get stuck in a recessionary gap. The Keynesian view that wages are inflexible (in the downward direction) implies that the economy may not be able to eliminate a recessionary gap by itself. An economy may get stuck in a recessionary gap.*

Keynes thus believed that the economy was inherently unstable—that is, it may not automatically cure itself of a recessionary gap: It may not easily and smoothly move toward full-employment, or natural, real GNP. In conclusion, equilibrium—or the balance of forces—in the economy may not be where the economy is producing natural real GNP, but in fact may be at some real GNP level below natural real GNP, for example, at Q_1 in Exhibit 9–2b.

This view is, of course, diametrically opposed to the classical view, which held that the economy is inherently stable and thus capable of moving itself to the position of producing natural real GNP.

On Prices and Wages.   Keynes also made the point that even if prices and wages were flexible in the downward direction, this would not ensure a move to full-employment, or natural, real GNP. Here Keynes criticized the classical economists for confusing the consequences of a (single) price decline with a decline in the price level. Simply because a decline in the price of a single good or resource causes the quantity demanded of the good or resource to rise, it does not follow that a decrease in the prices of *all* goods and resources will bring about the same result. In short, what is true for a single market may not be true for all markets together (the economy).[2] For example, Keynes argued that a widespread cut in wages will result in a widespread cut in incomes and that as incomes decline, so will demand. Thus, he concluded, far from helping matters, a widespread cut in wages will make an already bad situation worse. Instead of real GNP rising and the unemployment rate falling, it is likely that real GNP will fall and the unemployment rate will rise.

Contrary to the classical position on unemployment—that we are always at or near full employment—Keynes believed that high levels of unemployment could exist for extended periods of time. Accordingly, it follows that the economy is not always close to or on its production possibilities frontier.

The revolutionary aspect of Keynesianism has been captured by L. Tarshis:

> I was also a bit surprised by his [Keynes's] concern over too low a level of output [real GNP]. I had been assured by all I had read that the economy would bob to the surface, like a cork held under water—and output would rise, of its own accord, to an acceptable level. But Keynes proposed something far more shocking: that the economy could reach an *equilibrium* position, with output far below capacity [far below natural real GNP or full-employment real GNP].[3]

A Modification of Keynesian Theory

Many economists criticized earlier versions of the Keynesian theory because, they argued, it didn't offer a rigorous explanation for inflexible wages. Some of the later versions made up for this deficiency by focusing on, among other things, long-term contracts and efficiency reasons for firms paying higher than market wages.

For example, some economists argue that long-term labor contracts are often advantageous to both employers and workers. The benefits firms may perceive from long-term contracts include fewer labor negotiations (labor negotiations can be costly) and the decreased likelihood of worker strikes (the firms have a breathing spell during the time of the contract). The benefits workers may perceive from long-term contracts include fewer strikes (which can be costly for them, too) and the added sense of security long-term contracts provide.

Long-term contracts come with costs as well as benefits for both firms and workers, but some economists believe that in many instances the benefits outweigh the costs and that firms and workers enter into the long-term contracts for mutually advantageous reasons. When they do, (nominal) wage rates are "locked in" for the period of the contract, and therefore cannot adjust downward to market-clearing levels given a fall in aggregate demand. The result is that the economy may get stuck at point 1 in Exhibit 9–2b for a long time and there may be high levels of unemployment lasting for many years. Keynesian economists believe that the theory explains the long-run levels of unemployment characteristic of some business cycles.

In a similar vein, economists who work with efficiency wage models also believe that there are (other) solid microeconomic reasons for inflexible wages. Economist George Akerlof argues that firms sometimes find it in their best interest to pay wage rates above market-clearing levels. According to the **efficiency wage models,**

Efficiency Wage Models
These models hold that it is sometimes in the best interest of firms to pay their employees higher than equilibrium wage rates.

[2]The view that what is true for a part of the whole is true for the whole is the fallacy of composition (see Chapter 1).

[3]L. Tarshis, "Keynesian Revolution," in *The New Palgrave: A Dictionary of Economics,* vol. 3 (London: The Macmillan Press, 1987), p. 48.

ECONOMICS IN OUR TIMES

Interview: George Akerlof

George Akerlof has made major contributions to economic theory in the areas of asymmetric information, methodology, and labor market behavior. He is one of the major innovators of efficiency wage models. Akerlof is currently at the University of California, Berkeley.

Professor Akerlof, Keynesians have often argued that sticky wages, or wages that are inflexible in the downward direction, can prevent labor markets from clearing, thus causing the economy to get stuck at less than full-employment output. You, and others who have worked with efficiency wage models, have put forth reasons why it may be rational for firms to pay wages above market-clearing levels. What are a few of these reasons?

Firms sometimes pay wages above market-clearing levels because higher wages can lead to increased productivity. There are five basic reasons why this is the case. The most basic of these has to do with higher worker morale. Workers in firms with higher profits feel they deserve high wages, and firms with high profits pay higher wages than firms with low profits. If the firms do not pay these high wages, the workers invaria-

bly find a way of retaliating. Other reasons firms pay high wages are because they want to lower quit rates, stop unionization, give workers an incentive not to shirk, and attract a higher quality worker.

The efficiency wage model holds that in some labor markets, labor productivity is a function of the real wage paid by the firm. Specifically, as wages are cut, productivity falls, and as wages rise, productivity rises. Do you have a specific example where this is the case?

The most dramatic example of a rise in productivity following an increase in

wages came after Henry Ford's payment to his workers of the $5-a-day wage in 1914. Prior to his announcement, there was massive worker turnover at the Ford Motor Company. After the announcement, quits fell to an extremely low level.

One of the implicit messages of the efficiency wage model is that firms would rather stabilize wages than employment. That is, they'd rather lay off workers than cut wages. Wouldn't you think that layoffs might demoralize workers more than wage cuts, therefore prompting larger declines in productivity?

Certainly, both wage cuts and layoffs cause demoralization, but there is a big difference as to where the demoralized person ends up if he gets a wage cut than if he gets laid off. With wage cuts, the demoralized person stays at the firm. With layoffs, the demoralized person stays at home or looks for another job. As far as the firm goes, it is probably better to have the demoralized person at home than at the firm working. Also, when there are layoffs, the workers who stay with the firm are likely to be thankful they were not laid off, and in fact their morale may improve.

labor productivity depends on the wage rate the firm pays employees. Specifically, a cut in wages can cause labor productivity to decline, which, in turn, raises the firm's costs. By paying a wage higher than the market level, firms provide an incentive to workers to be productive and to minimize shirking, among other things. If shirking declines, so do the monitoring (management) costs of the firm.

The economist Robert Solow has argued that "the most interesting and important line of work in current macroeconomic theory is the attempt to reconstruct plausible microeconomic underpinnings for a recognizably Keynesian macroeconomics."[4] Many Keynesian economists believe the efficiency wage models can perform this task. They believe that although these models are fairly new, they have already provided a solid microeconomic explanation for inflexible wages, and

[4]Robert Solow, "Another Possible Source of Wage Stickiness," in *Efficiency Wage Models of the Labor Market*, edited by George Akerlof and Janet Yellen (Cambridge: Cambridge University Press, 1986), p. 41.

CHAPTER 9
KEYNESIAN THEORY: EMPHASIS ON
UNEMPLOYMENT

■

187

thus are capable of explaining the facts characteristic of continuing unemployment problems in some economies.

Keynes: The Classical Theory Is a Special Case

Keynes called his major work *The General Theory of Employment, Interest and Money*. Keynes did not believe that his theory was true only under special conditions. He did, however, view the classical theory as a theory that held only under special conditions: (1) when prices and wages are perfectly flexible (particularly in the downward direction); (2) perhaps in less severe economic downturns when it is possible to adjust back to full employment without massive and widespread wage cuts; and (3) in situations where investment and saving are somewhat responsive to changes in interest rates. Keynes stressed this point in the opening words of the *General Theory*.

> I shall argue that the postulates of the classical theory are applicable to a special case only and not to the general case, the situation which it assumes being a limiting point of the possible positions of equilibrium. Moreover, the characteristics of the special case assumed by the classical theory happen not to be those of the economic society in which we actually live, with the result that its teaching is misleading and disastrous if we attempt to apply it to the facts of experience.[5]

KEYNESIANISM:
THE COMPONENTS OF TOTAL EXPENDITURES

Keynesianism was a response to a real event and to a theory. The event was the Great Depression. The theory was classical theory, which some say did not predict and could not explain the high levels of unemployment that existed during the years of the Great Depression. So, for both empirical and theoretical reasons, the focus of Keynesian theory was unemployment. In terms of our P–Q category, unemployment relates to real GNP (Q).[6] That is, if the unemployment rate is too high, it could only mean that real GNP is too low (relative to natural real GNP).

We know from the *AD–AS* framework that aggregate demand and aggregate supply determine real GNP. For example, in Exhibit 9–3, AD_1 and $SRAS_1$ bring about real GNP. It follows that if real GNP is too low, it must mean one of three things.

1. Short-run aggregate supply is too low. Graphically, this means the *SRAS* curve intersects the *AD* curve to the left of natural real GNP. In Exhibit 9–3, this is where $SRAS_2$ intersects AD_1 at point A.
2. Aggregate demand is too low. Graphically, this means the *AD* curve intersects the *SRAS* curve to the left of natural real GNP. In Exhibit 9–3, this is where AD_2 intersects $SRAS_1$ at point B.
3. Both aggregate demand and short-run aggregate supply are too low. In Exhibit 9–3, this is where AD_2 intersects $SRAS_2$ at point C.

[5]John Maynard Keynes, *The General Theory of Employment, Interest and Money* (1936; reprint, London: Macmillan, 1970), p. 3.
[6]L. Tarshis, in *The New Palgrave: A Dictionary of Economics* (vol. 3, London: The Macmillan Press, 1987, p. 48) says that "after several years of plunging production, followed by a sluggish recovery, his [Keynes's] decision to examine the forces that determined output [real GNP] made sense, but after even more decades of regarding prices as the proper object of enquiry for economists the shift was not easy" (vol. 3, p. 48).

EXHIBIT 9–3
If Real GNP Is Too Low It Means . . .

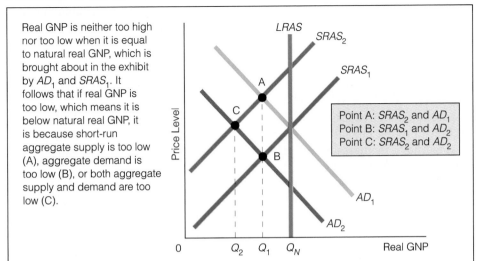

Real GNP is neither too high nor too low when it is equal to natural real GNP, which is brought about in the exhibit by AD_1 and $SRAS_1$. It follows that if real GNP is too low, which means it is below natural real GNP, it is because short-run aggregate supply is too low (A), aggregate demand is too low (B), or both aggregate supply and demand are too low (C).

Point A: $SRAS_2$ and AD_1
Point B: $SRAS_1$ and AD_2
Point C: $SRAS_2$ and AD_2

Keynesian economics, usually emphasizes (2), aggregate demand being too low, so we need to understand something about the components of aggregate demand.

In Chapter 8, we stated that "at a given price level, anything that decreases any of the four components of total expenditures decreases aggregate demand and shifts the AD curve to the left." We deduce that if aggregate demand is too low, it must mean that, at a given price level, total expenditures are too low. The components of total expenditures are (1) household spending, or consumption (C), (2) business spending, or investment (I), (3) government spending, or government expenditures (G), and (4) foreign sector spending, or net exports ($X - M$). We focus our attention, therefore, on each of the four components of total expenditures.

First, we discuss a private economy, where there is a household, business, and foreign sector but no government sector. This will give us an understanding of the Keynesian view on how the private economy works. In the next chapter, we introduce government into the picture to get an idea of how many Keynesians view the government's impact on the private economy.

THE PRIVATE ECONOMY
■

Our purpose is to study the components of total expenditures in a private economy so that we understand what affects aggregate demand, and indirectly, real GNP and unemployment. In a private economy without government, there are three types of spending: consumption, investment, and net exports. The theoretical framework in which we study these three types of expenditures makes the following assumptions:

1. Wages and prices are fixed. Throughout most of the analysis (there are a few exceptions), all magnitudes (such as consumption, investment, and net exports) are real, or inflation-adjusted, magnitudes (such as real consumption, and so on). Remember this point, not only as you read, but as you view the exhibits, too.

2. The monetary side of the economy is excluded. For the most part, we do not discuss how changes in the money supply might affect the economy.

3. There is no government sector. When there is no government, there are no taxes or government transfer payments. Because of this, national income is *nearly* equal to disposable income. It makes no difference to our analysis if we assume that they are equal. Y is the symbol used for national income and Y_d is the symbol used for disposable income. Throughout our analysis, $Y = Y_d$, and both are denominated in real terms.

The Consumption Function

Keynes made three basic points about consumption and disposable income: (1) Consumption depends on disposable income. (2) Consumption and disposable income move in the same direction. (3) When disposable income changes, consumption changes by less.

These three points make a specific statement about the relationship between consumption and disposable income. The statement specifying this relationship is called the **consumption function.** We represent the consumption function as

$$C = C_0 + MPC(Y_d)$$

We know that C is consumption and that Y_d is disposable income. Let us discuss the *MPC* and C_0.

MPC. This stands for **marginal propensity to consume,** which is the ratio of the change in consumption to the change in income.

$$MPC = \Delta C/\Delta Y$$

The symbol Δ stands for "change in." We would read it this way: "The *MPC* is equal to the *change in* consumption divided by the *change in* income." To illustrate, suppose consumption rises from $800 to $900 as income rises from $1,000 to $1,200. If we divide the change in consumption, which is $100, by the change in income, which is $200, we see that the *MPC* equals .50.

C_0. This is **autonomous consumption.** Autonomous consumption does not change as income changes; it changes due to factors *other* than income.

Think of consumption as being made up of two parts: one part that is independent of income—called *autonomous consumption*—and a second part that is dependent on income—called **induced consumption.**

Look again at the consumption function. Suppose C_0 = $800, *MPC* = .80 and Y_d = $1,500. If we were to plug the numbers into the consumption function—$C = C_0 + MPC(Y_d)$—we would see that C = $2,000 (since $2,000 = $800 + .80 ($1,500)). With an eye on the consumption function, here are three ways in which C can be increased:

1. Raise autonomous consumption. Say autonomous consumption goes from $800 to $1,000. This would raise consumption, C, to $2,200 (since $2,200 = $1,000 + .80 ($1,500)).

2. Raise disposable income. Say disposable income goes from $1,500 to $1,800. This would raise C to $2,240 (since $2,400 = $800 + .80 ($1,800)). The $400 increase in consumption from $2,000 to $2,400 is due to an increase of $400 in *induced consumption.* Specifically, the increased consumption was *induced* by an increase in disposable income.

3. Raise the *MPC*. Suppose the *MPC* rises to .90. This would raise C to $2,150 (since $2,150 = $800 + .90 ($1,500)).

Consumption Function
The relationship between consumption and disposable income; in the consumption function used here, consumption is directly related to disposable income and is positive even at zero disposable income: $C = C_0 + MPC(Y_d)$.

Marginal Propensity to Consume (*MPC*)
The ratio of the change in consumption to the change in income: $MPC = \Delta C/\Delta Y$

Autonomous Consumption
That part of consumption that is independent of income.

Induced Consumption
That part of consumption that changes as income changes.

In Exhibit 9–4, we have calculated different levels of consumption spending for different levels of income. We have set C_0 equal to $200 billion and MPC equal to .80; thus, we have $C = \$200$ billion $+ .8(Y_d)$. Additionally, we have calculated different saving levels at different income levels. How did we calculate this? Since we know that $C = C_0 + MPC(Y_d)$, and we also know that households can only consume or save, it follows that saving is the difference between disposable income and consumption: $S = Y_d - (C_0 + MPC(Y_d))$.

The MPC and the MPS

In Exhibit 9–4, for every $1 change in income, there is an $.80 change in consumption. For example, at an income of $1,200 billion, consumption is $1,160 billion; but at an income of $1,400 billion, consumption is $1,320 billion. This is a difference of $160 billion, or $.80 additional consumption for every $1 of extra income. This means the $MPC = .80$.

The **marginal propensity to save (MPS)** is the ratio of the change in saving to the change in income.

$$MPS = \frac{\Delta S}{\Delta Y}$$

Marginal Propensity to Save (MPS)
The ratio of the change in saving to the change in income: $MPS = \Delta S/\Delta Y$.

Since we know that additions to income can only be used for consumption or saving, that is, $\Delta C + \Delta S = \Delta Y$, it follows that the marginal propensity to consume (MPC) plus the marginal propensity to save (MPS) must equal 1.

$$MPC + MPS = 1$$

In Exhibit 9–4, since we set the marginal propensity to consume at .80, it follows that the marginal propensity to save is .20. Notice that for every $1 change in income, saving changes by $.20; or, for every $200 change in income (column 2), there is a $40 change in saving (column 6).

The APC and APS

Return to Exhibit 9–4. If we were to calculate the marginal propensity to consume (MPC) at an income level of $1,400, we would find it equal to $160/$200, or .80

EXHIBIT 9–4
Consumption and Saving at Different Levels of Real Disposable Income (Real National Income) (in billions)
Since there is no government sector, real national income (Y) = real disposable income (Y_d). Our consumption function is $C = C_0 + MPC(Y_d)$, where C_0 has been set at $200 billion and $MPC = .80$. Since we know that saving is the difference between Y_d and C, then $S = Y_d - (C_0 + MPC(Y_d))$.

(1) Real Disposable Income (Real National Income), $Y_d = Y$	(2) Change in Real Disposable Income, ΔY_d	(3) Consumption, $C = C_0 + MPC(Y_d)$	(4) Change in Consumption, $\Delta C = MPC(\Delta Y_d)$	(5) Saving, $S = Y_d - (C_0 + MPC(Y_d))$	(6) Change in Saving, $\Delta S = \Delta Y_d - \Delta C$
$ 800	$ ___	$ 840	$ ___	− $40	$__
1,000	200	1,000	160	0	40
1,200	200	1,160	160	40	40
1,400	200	1,320	160	80	40
1,600	200	1,480	160	120	40
1,800	200	1,640	160	160	40

191

$(MPC = \Delta C/\Delta Y)$. Now suppose we were to calculate C/Y at the same income level. This would give us $\$1,320/\$1,400$, or .94. This fraction (C/Y) is called **average propensity to consume** (APC). It is the proportion of income spent on consumption.

$$APC = \frac{C}{Y}$$

A similar concept, the **average propensity to save** (APS), is the proportion of income saved.

$$APS = \frac{S}{Y}$$

Once again, since saving and consumption are the only ways households can dispose of income, it follows that

$$APC + APS = 1$$

In summary, it is important to differentiate between "marginal" and "average" magnitudes. Although they may sound alike, the MPC and APC, and the MPS and APS, are not one and the same. The average magnitudes, APC and APS, refer to the *fractions of income* that are consumed and saved, respectively. On an individual basis, if a person has an income of $\$1,000$ and her consumption is $\$600$ and her saving is $\$400$, then $APC = .60$ and $APS = .40$. The marginal magnitudes, MPC and MPS, refer to the *fractions of any change in income* that are consumed and saved, respectively. On an individual basis, if a person's income rises by $\$100$, and her consumption rises by $\$70$, and her saving rises by $\$30$, then $MPC = .70$ and $MPS = .30$.

Shifts in the Consumption Function

Exhibit 9–5 diagrams a consumption function. Notice that we did not start the consumption function at the origin. This is because given our consumption function, $C = C_0 + MPC(Y_d)$, consumption (C) is greater than zero even when dispos-

EXHIBIT 9–5
The Consumption Function, $C = C_0 + MPC (Y_d)$

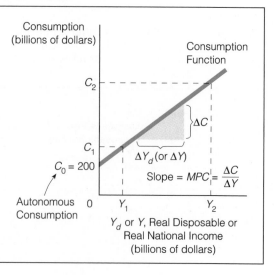

Even at a real national or real disposable income of 0 ($Y = Y_d = 0$), consumption is positive as long as $C_0 > 0$. A change in Y or Y_d will lead to a movement along the consumption function. A change in the following factors will lead to a shift in the consumption function: wealth, expectations about future prices and income, the price level, the interest rate, and taxes (assuming real national income, not real disposable income, is on the horizontal axis). Since we have assumed that prices are fixed, the consumption (C) on the vertical axis is "real cosumption."

able income is zero.[7] Previously, we specified that C_0 equals \$200 billion and that the *MPC* is .80. Therefore, consumption (*C*) equals \$200 billion when disposable income is zero [C = \$200 + .8(0) = \$200]. Also, in our exhibit, the slope of the consumption function represents the marginal propensity to consume.

At this point, we need to distinguish between a *shift* in the consumption function and a *movement* along the consumption function. The distinction between a shift in a curve and a movement along a curve was made in Chapter 3 when we discussed demand curves. We said there that a change in price *moved* us from one point on the demand curve to another point on the same curve, but that a change in preferences, a change in the price of substitutes, a change in the price of complements, and so on would *shift* the entire demand curve.

For the consumption function, a change in real national income will lead to a movement along the consumption function. This is easily seen by picking two points on the horizontal axis in Exhibit 9–5 and drawing a line upward (from each point) until it touches the consumption function. For example, at Y_1 consumption is C_1, and at Y_2 consumption is C_2. There is a different level of consumption spending at each income level.

A shift in the consumption function may be brought about by a host of factors. We refer to these factors as the nonincome determinants of consumption, which include wealth, expectations about future prices and income, the price level, the interest rate, and taxes. *The effects of the nonincome determinants of consumption are captured in the C_0 (autonomous consumption) term.* Exhibit 9–6 illustrates factors leading to a shift in the consumption function.

[7]For a consumption function that does begin at the origin, see the appendix to this chapter, where we discuss the permanent-income hypothesis.

EXHIBIT 9–6
Factors that Shift the Consumption Function

The following lead to a shift upward in the consumption function:	The following lead to a shift downward in the consumption function:
1. an increase in wealth	1. a decrease in wealth
2. expectation of higher future prices	2. expectation of lower future prices
3. expectation of higher future income	3. expectation of lower future income
4. a decrease in the price level	4. an increase in the price level
5. a decrease in the interest rate	5. an increase in the interest rate
6. a decrease in taxes	6. an increase in taxes

Wealth. Individuals consume, not only on the basis of their present income, but also on the basis of their wealth. Consider two individuals, each receiving an income of $30,000 a year. One has $75,000 in the bank, and the other has no assets at all. Which would you expect to spend more of her income on consumption goods this year? We would expect the person with the $75,000 in the bank to consume the greater amount. Greater wealth makes individuals feel financially more secure and thus more willing to spend. Increases in wealth shift the consumption function upward, and decreases in wealth shift the consumption function downward (see Exhibit 9–6).

Expectations about Future Prices and Income. If individuals expect higher future prices, they will tend to increase current consumption expenditures in order to buy goods at the lower current prices. If individuals expect lower future prices, they will do the opposite. An expectation of a higher future income will shift the consumption function upward; an expectation of a lower future income will shift the consumption function downward (see Exhibit 9–6).

The Price Level. (See the discussion of the real balance effect in Chapter 8.) As the price level rises, the purchasing power of money declines, and individuals are less wealthy. As a result, they consume less; thus, the consumption function shifts downward. As the price level falls, the purchasing power of money rises, and individuals are more wealthy. As a result, they consume more; thus, the consumption function shifts upward.

Note that the effect on the consumption function we are describing here works through changes in *wealth,* not *income.* We learned earlier that an increase in income moves us up along the consumption function, and a decrease in income moves us down along the consumption function.

In summary, a change in income moves us *along* the consumption function; a change in wealth *shifts* the consumption function (see Exhibit 9–6).

Interest Rate. Current empirical work shows that spending on consumer durables is sensitive to the interest rate. Since many of these items are financed by borrowing, an increase in the interest rate increases the monthly payments linked to their purchase and thereby reduces their consumption, shifting the consumption function downward. A decrease in the interest rate generally works in the opposite direction, shifting the consumption function upward (see Exhibit 9–6).

Taxes. We have been discussing the mechanics of a private economy with no government sector. Suppose for a minute we add government to the picture. With government comes taxation, and taxes can influence consumption. As taxes increase, we would expect less consumer spending for the same amount of received income; as taxes decrease, we would expect more consumer spending for the same amount of received income. Thus, an increase in taxes leads to a shift downward in the consumption function, and a decrease in taxes leads to a shift upward. (This assumes that real national income, and not real disposable income, is on the horizontal axis.)

Investment

Compared with consumption, investment is unstable and volatile. In Exhibit 9–7, we have plotted the percentage changes in (real) consumption and (real) investment from 1969 to 1990. Notice that the annual percentage change in consumption

EXHIBIT 9–7
Percentage Changes in Consumption and Investment, 1969–90.

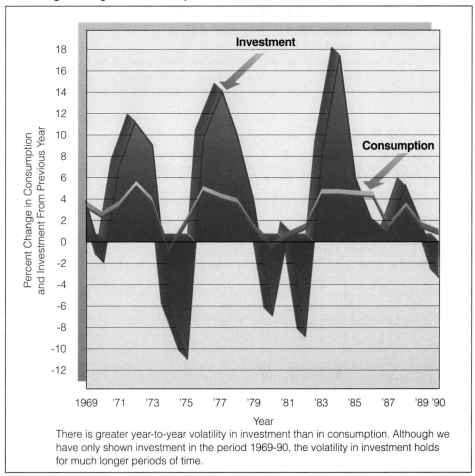

There is greater year-to-year volatility in investment than in consumption. Although we have only shown investment in the period 1969-90, the volatility in investment holds for much longer periods of time.

SOURCE: Council of Economic Advisers, *Economic Report of the President*, 1991 (Washington, D.C.: U.S. Government Printing Office, 1991).

is less volatile than the annual percentage change in investment. One reason that investment is more volatile than consumption is that expectations play a more important role in determining investment spending than consumption spending. We say more about this when we discuss the factors that can shift the investment function. First, however, we need to identify it.

The Investment Function

In our theory, investment is autonomous. Stated differently, investment does not depend on income. Our investment function specifies that

$$I = I_0$$

which says that (total) investment is autonomous investment; or (total) investment is equal to its autonomous component only (Exhibit 9–8).

The investment function we have specified ($I = I_0$) is consistent with Keynes's ideas about investment in the short run, mainly, that most current investment

EXHIBIT 9–8
The Investment Function

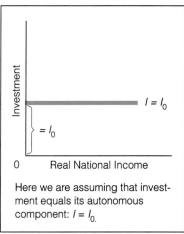

Here we are assuming that investment equals its autonomous component: $I = I_0$.

195

expenditures result from past investment expenditure decisions. For example, a business might have decided two years ago to build a new factory, but owing to the time needed for design and construction, the factory is only currently being built.

Notice that the investment function in Exhibit 9–8 is parallel to the horizontal axis on which (current) real national income has been placed, indicating that investment is independent of real national income: A change in income, from a lower level to a higher level or vice versa, does not lead to a change in investment.

Shifts in the Investment Function

A number of factors can shift the investment function (Exhibit 9–9). We explain each of them as follows.

Interest Rate. Whether a firm borrows the funds to invest or uses its own funds, it incurs an opportunity cost in the form of interest lost. As the interest rate rises, the cost of a given investment project rises, and there is less investment; as the interest rate falls, the cost of a given investment project falls, and there is more investment, *ceteris paribus*. A rise in the interest rate will shift the investment function downward; a fall in the interest rate will shift it upward.

Expectations about Future Sales. Businesses invest because they expect to sell the goods they produce. If businesses become optimistic about future sales, investment spending will grow; if they become pessimistic about future sales, investment spending will contract. Optimism of this kind leads to an upward shift in the investment function; pessimism leads to a downward shift in the investment function.

Business Taxes. Again, let us add the government sector to the discussion. In a model that includes government, business taxes are relevant to investment spend-

EXHIBIT 9–9
Factors that Shift the Investment Function

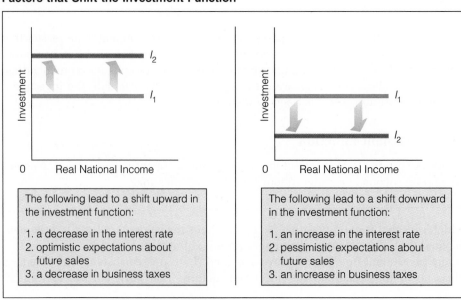

The following lead to a shift upward in the investment function:

1. a decrease in the interest rate
2. optimistic expectations about future sales
3. a decrease in business taxes

The following lead to a shift downward in the investment function:

1. an increase in the interest rate
2. pessimistic expectations about future sales
3. an increase in business taxes

ing decisions. Businesses naturally consider expected after-tax profits when making their investment decisions. An increase in business taxes will lower expected profitability and decrease investment spending; a decrease in business taxes will raise expected profitability and increase investment spending. An increase in business taxes shifts the investment function downward; a decrease in business taxes shifts the investment function upward.

The Net Exports Function

To round out our discussion of the private economy, we discuss net exports. We know that net exports = exports − imports. In our simple model, there is no change in exports as (U.S.) real national income changes; in other words, exports are autonomous. Imports, though, rise as (U.S.) real national income rises. This is based on the idea that as Americans have more income, they buy more goods, some of which are foreign goods.

In Exhibit 9–10a, notice that the exports function is drawn parallel to the real national income axis, indicating no change in exports as real national income changes. In Exhibit 9–10b, the imports function is drawn sloping upward, indicating that as U.S. real national income rises, imports rise.

In Exhibit 9–10c, we have drawn the net export function. Since net exports = exports − imports, we have simply (a) taken exports at three different income

EXHIBIT 9–10
The Net Exports Function

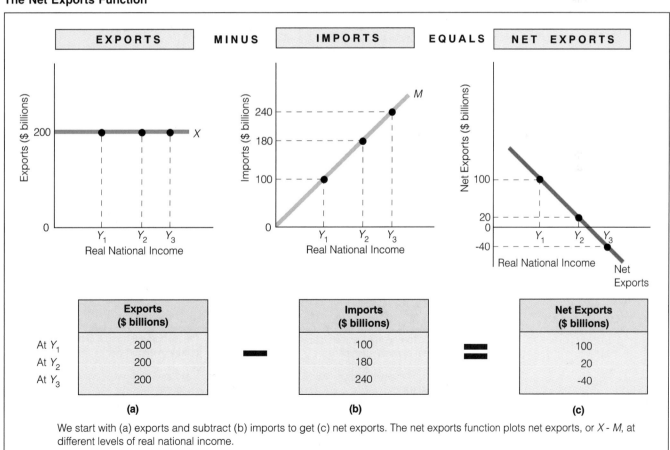

	Exports ($ billions)		Imports ($ billions)		Net Exports ($ billions)
At Y_1	200		100		100
At Y_2	200		180		20
At Y_3	200		240		-40
	(a)		(b)		(c)

We start with (a) exports and subtract (b) imports to get (c) net exports. The net exports function plots net exports, or X - M, at different levels of real national income.

levels, (b) subtracted imports at the same three income levels, and (c) plotted the respective net export dollar amounts at the three income levels. The downward-sloping curve that connects the three points is the net exports function.

Shifts in the Net Exports Function

A number of factors can shift the net exports function (Exhibit 9–11). We explain each of them as follows.

Foreign Real National Income.   As foreign real national income rises, foreigners buy more U.S. goods and services; thus, U.S. exports rise.[8] This shifts the export function upward (see Exhibit 9–10a). As a result, at every level of U.S. real national income (Y_1, Y_2, and Y_3 in Exhibit 9–10), net exports rises. The net export function shifts upward. Applying the same logic, if foreign real national income falls, the net export function shifts downward.

Price Levels in the U.S. and in Foreign Nations.   As the foreign price level rises relative to the U.S. price level, U.S. goods look more attractive to both foreigners and Americans. Consequently, exports rise and imports fall, and the net exports function shifts upward. As the foreign price level falls relative to the U.S. price level, foreign goods look more attractive to foreigners and Americans. Consequently, exports fall and imports rise, and the net exports function shifts downward.[9]

[8]As in Chapter 8, we assume that as the physical quantity of U.S. goods that foreigners buy rises, so does exports (X). Recall that exports refer to the total dollar spending on domestic goods, not to the physical goods themselves. In other words, exports is a dollar amount.

[9]Saying that the foreign price level rises (falls) relative to the U.S. price level is the same as saying that the U.S. price level falls (rises) relative to the foreign price level.

EXHIBIT 9–11
Factors that Shift the Net Exports Function

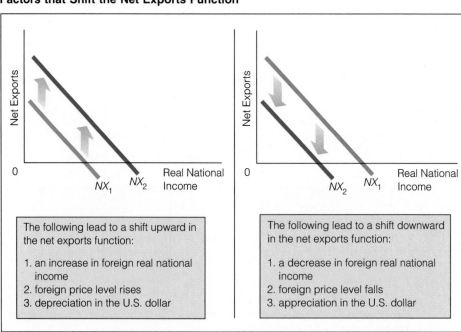

The Depreciation and Appreciation of the U.S. Dollar. The **exchange rate** is the price of one currency in terms of another currency; for example, $1.50 = £1. A currency has **appreciated** in value if it takes more of a foreign currency to buy it. A currency has **depreciated** in value if it takes more of it to buy a foreign currency. For example, a movement in the exchange rate from $1.50 = £1 to $1.80 = £1 means that more dollars are necessary to buy one pound, so the pound has appreciated. And since more dollars are necessary to buy one pound, the dollar has depreciated.

A depreciation in a nation's currency makes foreign goods more expensive. Consider an English coat that is priced at £200 when the exchange rate is $1 = £1. To buy the English coat for £200, an American has to pay $200, or $1 for every £1. Now suppose the dollar depreciates to $2 = £1. The American has to pay $400 for the coat. Things are symmetrical here, so an appreciation in a nation's currency makes foreign goods cheaper. For example, if the exchange rate goes from $1 = £1 to $.80 = £1, the American no longer has to pay $200 for the English coat, but only $160 ($.80 per pound *times* £200 = $160).

The depreciation and appreciation in the U.S. dollar affect the net exports function. As the dollar depreciates, foreign goods become more expensive, Americans cut back on imported goods, and foreigners (whose currency has appreciated) increase their purchases of U.S. exported goods. If exports rise and imports fall, net exports increase, shifting the net exports function upward.

As the dollar appreciates, foreign goods become cheaper, Americans increase their purchases of imported goods, and foreigners (whose currency has depreciated) cut back on their purchases of U.S. exported goods. If exports fall and imports rise, net imports decrease, shifting the net exports function downward.

Changes in Consumption, Investment, and Net Exports and Changes in Aggregate Demand

In Chapter 8, we stated that *at a given price level,* anything that increases total expenditures increases aggregate demand and shifts the *AD* curve to the right; and *at a given price level,* anything that decreases total expenditures decreases aggregate demand and shifts the *AD* curve to the left.

Since we know that total expenditures in an economy is composed of (1) consumption, (2) investment, (3) government expenditures, and (4) net exports, we can reword our statement to read, *At a given price level,* anything that increases consumption, investment, government expenditures, or net exports increases aggregate demand and shifts the *AD* curve to the right, and *at a given price level* anything that decreases consumption, investment, government expenditures, or net exports decreases aggregate demand and shifts the *AD* curve to the left.

In this section, we have discussed those factors that can increase and decrease (1) consumption, (2) investment, and (3) net exports. It follows that we indirectly have been discussing those factors that can increase and decrease aggregate demand and consequently can shift the *AD* curve rightward and leftward, respectively.[10]

[10]In discussing consumption, we stated that an increase in the price level shifts the consumption function downward and a decrease in the price level shifts the consumption function upward. It is perhaps easy to conclude that since a change in the price level changes consumption, a change in the price level changes aggregate demand, too. This is incorrect, however. Remember, in our discussion of changes in aggregate demand, we are holding the price level constant ("At a *given* price level . . .") We repeat: A change in the price level does not change aggregate demand; it changes the quantity demanded of real GNP or real national income.

Exchange Rate
The price of one currency in terms of another currency; for example, $1.50 = £1.

Appreciation
An increase in the value of one currency relative to other currencies. A currency has appreciated if it takes more of a foreign currency to buy it.

Depreciation
A decrease in the value of one currency relative to other currencies. A currency has depreciated if it takes more of it to buy a foreign currency.

Total Expenditures (TE)
and
Total Production (TP)

Here we focus on the three possible relationships between total expenditures (*TE*) and total production (*TP*). Our discussion is similar to that in Chapter 8 concerning the three possible relationships between real GNP (*Q*) and natural real GNP (Q_N). Whereas *Q* and Q_N are standard fare in the *AD–AS* framework, *TE* and *TP* are standard fare in the income–expenditure (*I–E*) framework, a framework of analysis that is Keynesian in its origins.

In this section, we allow prices and wages to change, but we exclude the monetary sector and government.

Three Possible States

We learned that the three possible states between real GNP (*Q*) and natural real GNP (Q_N) are (1) $Q = Q_N$; (2) $Q < Q_N$; and (3) $Q > Q_N$. These three states of the economy can also be discussed in terms of *total expenditures (TE)* and *total production (TP)*. Throughout our discussion, we assume that business firms collectively want to hold $300 billion worth of goods in inventory: no more, no less.

1. TE = TP. We start with firms holding their optimum inventory level, $300 billion worth of goods. Then firms produce $4,000 billion worth of goods, and members of the three sectors (household, business, and foreign) buy $4,000 billion worth of goods. In short, total expenditures (*TE*) equal total production (*TP*); the economy is in equilibrium.

2. TP > TE. We start with firms holding their optimum inventory level, $300 billion worth of goods. Then firms produce $4,000 billion worth of goods, and members of the three sectors buy $3,800 billion worth of goods and services. Since producers produce more than individuals buy, the difference adds to inventories. Inventory levels *unexpectedly* rise to $500 billion, which is $200 billion more than the $300 billion firms see as optimal.

This unexpected rise in inventories signals to firms that they have overproduced. Consequently, they cut back on the quantity of goods they produce, or cut prices, or both. The cutback in production causes real GNP to fall, bringing real GNP closer to the (lower) real GNP that members of the three sectors want to buy.

3. TE > TP. We start with firms holding their optimum inventory level, $300 billion worth of goods. Then firms produce $3,900 billion worth of goods, and members of the three sectors buy $4,100 billion worth of goods. But how can individuals buy more than firms produce? The answer is that firms make up the difference out of inventory. In our example, inventory levels fall from $300 billion to $100 billion, since individuals purchase $200 billion more of goods than firms produced (to be sold). In fact, this example points out the reason firms maintain inventories in the first place: to be ready to meet an unexpected increase in sales.

The unexpected fall in inventories signals to firms that they have underproduced. Consequently, they increase the quantity of goods they produce, or raise prices, or both. The rise in production causes real GNP to rise, in the process bringing real GNP closer to the (higher) real GNP that members of the three sectors want to buy.

The Graphical Representation of the Three States of the Economy

The three states of the economy can be represented by the *total expenditures (TE)* curve. We develop the curve by the following procedure.

1. In a private economy with no government, total expenditures consists of (a) consumption, (b) investment, and (c) net exports.

2. We know that there is an autonomous and induced component to consumption. Overall, consumption rises as real GNP rises (Exhibit 9–12a).[11]

3. Investment is assumed to be autonomous; it does not change as real GNP rises (Exhibit 9–12b).

4. Exports are assumed to be autonomous; exports do not change as real GNP rises (Exhibit 9–12c).

5. Imports are assumed to rise as real GNP rises (Exhibit 9–12d).

6. Total expenditures in a private economy without government equals $C + I + (X - M)$. In Exhibit 9–12, we have summed consumption, investment, and net export expenditures at two real GNP levels, Q_1 and Q_2. Plotting this in Exhibit 9–12e gives us two points, A and B. The curve that connects them is the total expenditures curve.

Now look at the income–expenditure diagram in Exhibit 9–13. On the horizontal axis you will find real GNP, and on the vertical axis you will find total production (*TP*). Midway between the two is a 45-degree line. Any point on the 45-degree line is equidistant from the two axes; that is, any point on the line has the characteristic that real GNP equals total production.

Also, in the exhibit, you will see the *TE* curve superimposed. We add *TE* to the vertical axis as a result.

Let's now view three real GNP levels, Q_E, Q_1, and Q_2. Q_E represents equilibrium real GNP, since at this real GNP level, $TE = TP$. (*TE* is obtained by running a line up from Q_E to the *TE* curve, and *TP* is obtained by running a line up from Q_E to the 45-degree line. We see that *TE* and *TP* are $3,450 billion.)

At Q_1, $TP > TE$, $4,800 billion > $4,000 billion. Here the members of the three sectors purchase less than is being produced. What happens? As we learned earlier, this results in inventories higher than planned, which signals firms that they have overproduced, which causes firms to cut back on production, which decreases real GNP. The economy tends to move from Q_1 to Q_E.

At Q_2, $TE > TP$, $3,000 billion > $2,000 billion. Here the members of the three sectors purchase more than is being produced. What happens? As we learned earlier, this results in inventories lower than planned, which signals firms that they have underproduced, which causes firms to increase their production, which increases real GNP. The economy tends to move from Q_2 to Q_E.

THE MULTIPLIER

According to Keynesian theory, a change in any autonomous spending component can cause a multiple change in real GNP or real national income. There are three

---

[11]We have made a subtle change here. Instead of speaking about *real national income,* we use the term *real GNP.* This is acceptable since in Chapter 6 we learned that GNP = national income + indirect business taxes + capital consumption allowance + statistical discrepancy. To simplify things, economists occasionally let GNP = NI. Of course, in our discussion so far, there is no government and thus no indirect business taxes, and therefore the difference between GNP and national income is smaller than it would be if government were in the picture. However, even if government were in the picture, we could permit GNP to serve as a proxy for national income since we are interested in the *directional* and *magnitudinal* changes in GNP and national income, and they tend to move up and down together. Now, if GNP = NI, we can let real GNP = real national income.

EXHIBIT 9–12
The Derivation of the Total Expenditures (TE) Curve

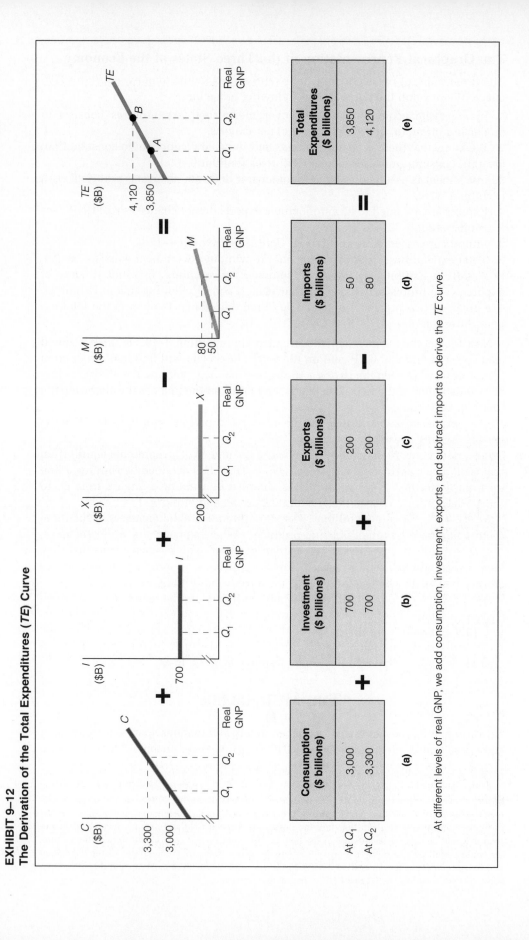

	Consumption ($ billions)		Investment ($ billions)		Exports ($ billions)		Imports ($ billions)		Total Expenditures ($ billions)
At Q_1	3,000	+	700	+	200	−	50	=	3,850
At Q_2	3,300		700		200		80		4,120
	(a)		**(b)**		**(c)**		**(d)**		**(e)**

At different levels of real GNP, we add consumption, investment, exports, and subtract imports to derive the TE curve.

EXHIBIT 9–13
The Income–Expenditure Diagram

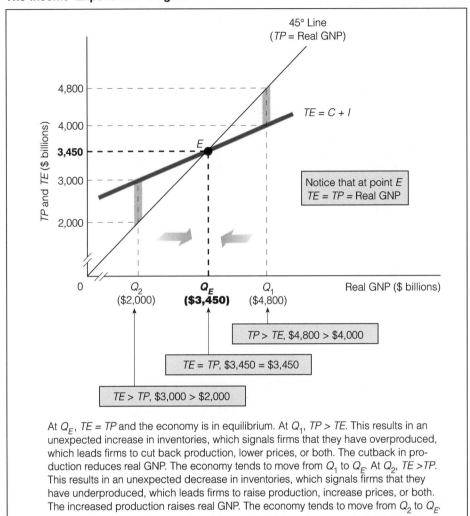

At Q_E, $TE = TP$ and the economy is in equilibrium. At Q_1, $TP > TE$. This results in an unexpected increase in inventories, which signals firms that they have overproduced, which leads firms to cut back production, lower prices, or both. The cutback in production reduces real GNP. The economy tends to move from Q_1 to Q_E. At Q_2, $TE > TP$. This results in an unexpected decrease in inventories, which signals firms that they have underproduced, which leads firms to raise production, increase prices, or both. The increased production raises real GNP. The economy tends to move from Q_2 to Q_E.

autonomous spending components we noted when we discussed total expenditures in a private economy without government: *autonomous consumption, autonomous investment,* and *autonomous exports.* We describe the multiplier process by introducing a change in autonomous investment.

Investment and the Multiplier

Suppose the relevant total expenditures curve is TE_1 and the economy is in equilibrium at E_1 (Exhibit 9–14). Suppose now that the interest rate falls, causing an increase in autonomous investment. An increase in investment will cause the total expenditures (TE) curve to shift upward from TE_1 to TE_2. (The vertical distance between the two TE curves is the amount by which autonomous investment has increased.) Now TE_2 is the relevant total expenditures curve and the economy is in equilibrium at E_2. It is important to notice that the change in real GNP from Q_1 to Q_2 is greater than the change in autonomous investment. We see that arrow 2, which indicates the change in real GNP, is longer than arrow 1, which indicates

EXHIBIT 9–14

A Change in Autonomous Investment Spending Relative to a Change in Real National Income

An increase in autonomous investment spending shifts the TE curve from TE_1 to TE_2 and brings about an increase in real GNP from Q_1 to Q_2. The increase in real GNP is greater than the increase in real autonomous investment spending—compare the length of arrow 2 with the length of arrow 1.

the change in autonomous investment. In other words, a change in autonomous investment of amount X brings about a change greater than X (say, $X+$) in real GNP; a change in autonomous investment changes real GNP by some multiple.

The multiple is called the **multiplier.** It is the number that is multiplied by the change in autonomous spending to obtain the change in real GNP. It is equal to

$$\text{Multiplier } (m) = \frac{1}{1 - MPC}$$

Multiplier (m)
The number that is multiplied by the change in autonomous spending to obtain the change in real GNP: $m = 1/(1 - MPC)$.

Let's work through an example (Exhibit 9–15).

1. We start with a $60 increase in autonomous investment spending (column 2).
2. This increase in autonomous investment spending generates income equal to itself: $60 spent on goods by one person is $60 received as income by some other person (column 3).
3. We assume that the $MPC = .80$. So if income increases by $60, then consumption changes by 80 percent of $60, or $48.
4. The $48 is spent, generating income equal to itself.
5. Again, if $MPC = .80$, then consumption changes by 80 percent of $48, or $38.40.
6. And so on.

The total change in real GNP or real national income is $300. Here is the formula we used:

$$\Delta \text{ Real GNP} = m \times \Delta \text{ Autonomous spending}$$

In our example, $MPC = .80$, so the multiplier equals 5 ($1/1 - MPC = 5$). The change in autonomous (investment) spending was $60; $60 times 5 equals $300.

EXHIBIT 9–15

Autonomous Investment and the Multiplier

A $60 change in autonomous investment ultimately changes real GNP or real national income by $300 ($MPC = .80$). The process begins with an increase in autonomous investment, which leads to a change in income, a change in consumption, another change in income, another change in consumption, and so on.

(1) EXPENDITURE ROUND	(2) CHANGE IN AUTONOMOUS INVESTMENT	(3) CHANGE IN REAL GNP OR REAL NATIONAL INCOME	(4) *MPC*	(5) CHANGE IN CONSUMPTION
Round 1	$60.00	$ 60.00	.80	$ 48.00
Round 2		48.00	.80	38.40
Round 3		38.40	.80	30.72
Round 4		30.72	.80	24.57
.		.	.	.
All other rounds		122.88	.80	98.88
TOTALS		$300.00		$240.00 (Approx.)

The Multiplier and Reality

We have discussed the multiplier in simple terms: A change in autonomous spending leads to an even larger change in real GNP.

We must note two points, however. First, the multiplier takes time to work itself out. In a textbook or on a blackboard, we go from an initial increase in autonomous investment spending to a multiple increase in real GNP in seconds. In the real world, it takes many months.

Second, for the multiplier to increase real GNP (the way we have described), idle resources must exist at each expenditure round.

Recall that one of the simplifying assumptions in our original theoretical framework (page 189) is that prices and wages are fixed or constant. It follows that if we experience an increase in real GNP (output is increasing) at each expenditure round, idle resources must be available to be brought into production. If this were not the case, then increased spending would simply result in higher prices and no increase in real GNP. Thus, there would be an increase in GNP ($P \times Q$), but not in real GNP (Q).

Question:

Does the multiplier analysis work in reverse? That is, if there had been a decrease in autonomous investment spending of $60, and the MPC equaled .80, would there have been a decrease in real GNP of $300?

Answer:

Yes.

KEYNESIAN THEORY IN THE *AD–AS* FRAMEWORK

In this section, we introduce the aggregate supply curve and discuss Keynesian theory within the *AD–AS* framework.

Three Other Aggregate Supply Curves

You are accustomed to seeing the (short-run) aggregate supply curve drawn as upward sloping. There are three other possible aggregate supply curves.

Horizontal *AS* Curve.   Suppose we draw the aggregate supply curve as horizontal, as in Exhibit 9–16a. Here we are assuming that the price level will remain fixed no matter how aggregate demand changes. (You can see this by noting the light *AD* curves superimposed on the aggregate supply curve.) If the aggregate demand curve shifts rightward from AD_1 to AD_2, the price level remains at P_1. If the aggregate demand curve shifts leftward from AD_1 to AD_3, the price level remains at P_1. The only effect of a change in aggregate demand (when the aggregate supply curve is horizontal) is a change in real GNP.

Some economists posit that the economy's aggregate supply curve would be horizontal when there are many idle resources in the economy, perhaps during a deep recession or depression. In such a setting, an increase in aggregate demand may not put any upward pressure on prices.

Kinked *AS* Curve.   Another aggregate supply curve has two distinct portions: It is horizontal up to the full-employment, or natural, real GNP level, and then it is vertical, as in Exhibit 9–16b. Changes in the horizontal section will affect real GNP only, as a shift from AD_1 to AD_2 illustrates. An increase in aggregate demand that shifts the aggregate demand curve out of the horizontal section into the vertical section increases the price level and real GNP, as the shift from AD_2 to AD_3 illustrates. Finally, any change in aggregate demand in the vertical section changes only the price level, as the shift from AD_3 to AD_4 illustrates.

EXHIBIT 9–16
Three Aggregate Supply Curves

(a) Changes in aggregate demand change real GNP only. (b) Changes in aggregate demand in the horizontal section change real GNP only, changes in aggregate demand in the vertical section change the price level only, and an increase in aggregate demand moving the *AD* curve from the horizontal to the vertical section changes both real GNP and the price level. (c) Changes in aggregate demand in the horizotal section (not shown) change real GNP only, and changes in aggregate demand in the vertical section (not shown) change the price level only. Changes in aggregate demand in the upward-sloping portion (shown) change both real GNP and the price level.

What Caused the Great Depression?
A Keynesian Answer

Many people believe that the stock market crash caused the Great Depression. To most economists, however, the stock market crash was primarily an effect, not a cause. They would say that deeper, more fundamental, problems in the economy caused the stock market crash. But what were these problems? The Keynesian explanation for the Great Depression emphasizes investment spending. To grasp the entire story, we need to see what was going on in the years before the Great Depression.

Keynesians point to the sharp increase in investment demand in the early 1920s. They argue that this increased demand arose for a number of reasons.

First, World War I had left much of Europe in ruins; Europeans therefore turned to the United States for many goods. Increased European demand for American goods (U.S. exports) led to greater production in U.S. factories and to increased U.S. investment spending (on factories and machinery) to meet the new higher demand.

Second, the end of the war unleashed American consumers' pent-up demand for goods. As a result, firms began to produce and invest more. Third, people after the war were optimistic about the future; they believed that the world was entering a period of peace and that the newest changes in technology would lead to a higher standard of living. Some economists argue that this heightened positive outlook encouraged business firms to invest beyond the level that reality indicated.

In the middle of the 1920s, the productive capacity of many industries caught up with the increased European and unleashed American demand for goods. In some industries, firms had excess productive capacity. As a result, investment demand began to fall. Then the multiplier, which brings about a greater fall in real GNP than in investment, came into play. In turn, the decline in real GNP led to a fall in consumption, suggesting even less need for productive capacity and therefore less investment spending. In this process, the economy folded in on itself: A decline in investment led to a decline in real GNP, which led to a decline in consumption, which led to a decline in real GNP, and so on.

Not all economists agree with this explanation of the Great Depression, which explicitly maintains that the cause of the Depression was a reduction in investment spending coming off an investment boom. Some economists argue that investment was not the destabilizing element that caused the Great Depression, but rather that investment was itself destabilized by other factors. Was any factor particularly destabilizing? As we see in Chapter 14, one group of economists—called monetarists—argue that the money supply can be singled out.

Three-Stage *AS* Curve. Another scenario is for the aggregate supply curve to begin to slope upward between the point at which there are many idle resources and full-employment, or natural, real GNP. For example, the *AS* curve in Exhibit 9–16c has three sections: a horizontal section, indicating many idle resources; a vertical section at natural real GNP; and a section that slopes upward between the other two sections where resources are becoming shorter in supply but full employment has not yet been reached. Changes in aggregate demand in the horizontal section affect real GNP only;[12] changes in aggregate demand in the vertical section affect the price level only; and changes in the upward-sloping portion affect both the price level and real GNP, as the shift from AD_1 to AD_2 illustrates.

[12]In the case where the aggregate supply curve is horizontal, an increase in aggregate demand will increase real GNP only and have no effect on the price level. Some economists have referred to this as the *passive supply hypothesis,* which posits that no matter how much demand increases, supply (output) rises to meet it. With this in mind, consider a major difference between classical theory and Keynesian theory (with a horizontal *AS* curve): Whereas the classical notion was that *supply creates its own demand,* the Keynesian notion has been characterized as *demand creates its own supply.*

*Here is a very Keyne-
sian notion: the econ-
omy can be in equilib-
rium, and stuck in a
recessionary gap, too.*

■

Keynesian Theory in the *AD–AS* Framework: Equilibrium and a Recessionary Gap

In Exhibit 9–17a, equilibrium in the income–expenditure framework is at point E where the *TE* curve crosses the 45-degree line. This equilibrium point, E, corresponds to *one point* on the aggregate demand curve, namely point E', in (b). In (c), we add the short-run aggregate supply curve and see that the economy is in equilibrium at point E'. Notice that the equilibrium real GNP, Q_E, is lower than natural real GNP, Q_N: The economy is in a recessionary gap. We remind ourselves of the words of L. Tarshsis: "Keynes proposed something far more shocking: that the economy could reach *equilibrium* position, with output far below capacity [far below natural real GNP, or full-employment real GNP]." Here, then, is a very Keynesian notion: The economy can be in equilibrium and stuck in a recessionary gap, too.

According to many Keynesian economists, the economy is stuck in a recessionary gap because aggregate demand is too low. For example, if aggregate demand were represented in (d) by AD_2 instead of AD_1, then the economy would not be stuck in a recessionary gap. But, of course, saying that aggregate demand is too low is the same as saying that total expenditures in (a) are too low. In short, private spending—composed of household spending (consumption), business spending (investment), and foreign spending (net exports)—is too low to stabilize the economy at its natural real GNP level.

So what should be done? Many Keynesians would argue that the federal government should enter the economic picture to implement actions and policies that would stimulate the economy toward natural real GNP. In short, government ought to pursue those macroeconomic policies that increase aggregate demand. The key policy Keynesians propose is fiscal policy, which we discuss in the next chapter.

An economist's *view of the economy* and his *policy suggestions* are often linked. For example, classical economists, who view the economy as inherently stable, believe in a policy of laissez-faire: Government should keep hands off the economy. Keynesians, however, who view the economy as inherently unstable, suggest an economic role for government to play. In short, policy suggestions are sometimes a consequence of how one views the internal or inherent workings of an economy.

Major Tenets of Keynesian Theory

The P–Q Category. Keynesian theory focuses on high unemployment and a too-low level of real GNP, Q. It is less concerned with the price level, P.

The Inherently Stable–Inherently Unstable Category. Keynesian economists believe that the economy is inherently unstable. The economy cannot always smoothly and quickly equilibrate itself at full-employment, or natural, real GNP.

The Effective–Ineffective Category. Keynesian economists believe that government has a role to play in managing the economy and that it can do so effectively. Keynesians do not advocate laissez-faire (see Chapter 10).

EXHIBIT 9–17

A Keynesian View of the Economy: In Equilibrium and Stuck in a Recessionary Gap, Too.

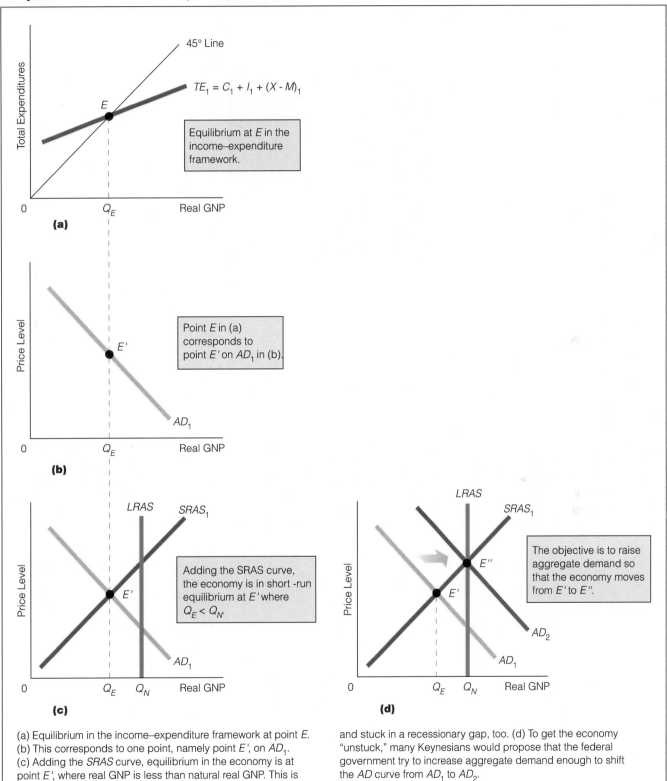

(a) Equilibrium in the income–expenditure framework at point *E*.
(b) This corresponds to one point, namely point *E'*, on AD_1.
(c) Adding the *SRAS* curve, equilibrium in the economy is at point *E'*, where real GNP is less than natural real GNP. This is a very Keynesian notion: The economy can be in equilibrium

and stuck in a recessionary gap, too. (d) To get the economy "unstuck," many Keynesians would propose that the federal government try to increase aggregate demand enough to shift the *AD* curve from AD_1 to AD_2.

Interview: Paul A. Samuelson

Paul A. Samuelson was the first American economist to win the Nobel Prize in Economics (1970). He has made fundamental contributions to economic theory and greatly raised the level of scientific analysis in all branches of economics. When academic Keynesianism first came to the United States, it entered the door through Harvard University, where Samuelson was a graduate student and research fellow. Samuelson is currently at the Massachusetts Institute of Technology.

Professor Samuelson, you were a graduate student and junior fellow at Harvard University during the time the Keynesian revolution was occurring. You've said of this time that "Harvard was precisely the right place to be." Would you tell us something about the excitement you felt learning and doing research in economics during this period?

First, let me emphasize that I had my undergraduate training at the University of Chicago, and that was a great period there for neoclassical, pre-Keynesian economics. I did not want to leave Chicago, I would have stayed there forever, but the Social Science Research Council gave me an unusual fellowship, the only requirement being that I had to go elsewhere. So choosing between Columbia and Harvard, I went to Harvard. And I've always been grateful for that decision because the three great revolutions that were to follow, and were taking place in the last part of the 1930s, were largely ignored by my teachers at the University of Chicago.

The Keynesian revolution, which you refer to, grew out of the Great Depression and gave economists their first handle on macroeconomic fluctuations from a theoretical point of view. I resisted the Keynesian revolution because of my firm neoclassical training, and

I've never regretted that because it made me fully aware of the insecure microeconomic foundations of Keynesianism. But the big moment came when I realized that I'd rather have an imperfect theory that could grapple with the facts than an elegant one that really had no room in it for the phenomenon of mass unemployment in 1933.

The economist Axel Leijonhufvud has stated that the "central issue in macroeconomic theory is . . . the extent to which the economy may be regarded as a self-regulating system. In short, the issue is how well or badly its 'automatic' mechanisms perform." Professor Samuelson, how well or badly do you think the economy's "automatic" mechanisms perform?

There are efficient markets at the micro level—the modern theory of finance is a triumph when it comes to the relative pricing of General Motors preferred stock and common stock and put and call options. But it provides no guarantees that the whole of the Standard and Poor's 500 Index will not be pulled upward to 150 percent of reproduction cost of all the earning assets of American capitalism.

I don't think it is a superhuman task to make the mixed economy more stable, using the free market to do most of the day's business, but with the government in there as the ultimate stabilizer. [See Chapter 10.] Today we have just as much material for mass bankruptcies and debtor default and great banks failing (leading small banks to have runs on them) as we ever did in 1929. Still, I'm quite confident that nothing like what I lived through in the Midwest is going to happen. Under populist democracy, the rather simple things that can be done will be done to prevent the whole financial system from creating a self-fulfilling downward movement, not unlike the self-fulfilling mania for tulips in seventeenth-century Holland on the upside.

Generally, what are your thoughts on laissez-faire capitalism and a mixed economy?

My generation of economists were taught, from textbooks written about 1929, that laissez-faire capitalism was pretty much optimal. Not until John Maynard Keynes did we have a handle to diagnose and prescribe for the Great Depression that was erupting around us and that was departing from the market-clearing utopia of neoclassical equilibrium.

Fortunately modern economists have been able to build upon, and improve upon, orthodox economics. We came to grips with departures from perfect competition, and devised theories of welfare economics that could analyze income inequality characteristic of market economies.

Pure capitalism gave way everywhere to the mixed economy. In the mixed economy most of production and resource allocation is done by the market mechanisms of prices and costs, of profits and losses, and of self-interest. Why? Because experience has taught societies

Interview: Paul A. Samuelson

the hard way that alternative modes of economic organization cannot match *market efficiency.*

Efficiency divorced from human equity and welfare is without point. Democracies have converged toward the mixed economy in which the extremes of inequality and instability are moderated—under a process of law—by fiscal taxes and transfers, by regulations, and by macroeconomic stabilization poli-

cies. Since none of us can know in advance which of us will be most hurt and most blessed by the vicissitudes of dynamic markets, the Welfare State is our form of mutual insurance, and we choose it out of the same long-run self-interest and limited altruism that motivates market behavior.

Long study of the evidence of history and experience has impressed on me that economics does need *both a cool*

head and a warm heart. One is pointless without the other; the other degenerates merely into wishful thinking.

Sophie Tucker, a famous nightclub singer at the period between the Great Wars, used to say: "I've been rich. I've been poor. Believe me, rich is better." Autobiographically, I've lived under pure and under modified capitalism. Believe me, the mixed economy is better.

CHAPTER SUMMARY

Classical Theory

■ Classical theory holds that the economy is always close to or on its production possibilities frontier, which means the economy is always close to or at the point of producing natural real GNP; it is always close to or at full employment; and whatever real GNP that is produced is demanded.

■ All economists believe that Say's law (supply creates its own demand) holds in a barter economy. Here, there can be no general overproduction or underproduction of goods and services. Classical economists believed that Say's law also holds in a money economy. In their view, even if there is a leakage (saving) from the spending stream, economic forces are at work producing an equal and offsetting injection (investment).

■ In classical theory, interest rates, wages, and prices are flexible.

Keynes on Classical Economics

■ Keynes believed that the classical case (where the economy settled into equilibrium at full employment) was a special case. Keynes called his theory the "general theory."

■ Contrary to Say's law, Keynes believed that it is possible to have saving (a leakage) greater than investment (an injection), such that total spending will be insufficient to buy the goods produced. Keynes challenged the classical notion of interest rate flexibility, which "guaranteed" that increases in saving would be offset by equal increases in investment. He argued that saving and investment are dependent on other factors besides the interest rate and that the interest rate is actually one of the less important factors when it comes to changes in saving and investment.

■ Keynes's view that wages and prices are inflexible in the downward direction implies that the economy may get stuck in a recessionary gap.

■ Some economists have argued that there are microeconomic reasons why wages are inflexible in the downward direction. First, there are contracts that may lock wages in for a few years. These contracts may benefit both firms and employees. Second, efficiency wage theorists argue that firms sometimes find it in their best interest to pay wage rates above market-clearing levels since labor productivity depends on the wage the firm pays employees. Specifically, a cut in wages can cause labor productivity to decline, which, in turn, raises the firm's costs.

The Consumption, Investment, and Net Export Functions

■ Keynes made three points about consumption and disposable income: (1) Consumption depends on disposable income. (2) Consumption and disposable income move in the same direction. (3) As disposable income changes, consumption changes by less. These three ideas are incorporated into the consumption function, $C = C_0 + MPC(Y_d)$, where C_0 is autonomous consumption, MPC is the marginal propensity to consume, and Y_d is disposable income.

■ The way the consumption function is specified, consumption is greater than zero even when disposable income is zero.

■ A change in income will lead to a movement along the consumption function. A change in any one of the following factors will shift the consumption function: wealth, expectations about future prices and income, the price level, the interest rate, and taxation.

■ The investment function in the basic theory, $I = I_0$, is consistent with Keynes's idea that investment in the short run is independent of real national income, mainly, that most investment expenditures in the current period are a result of investment spending decisions made in past periods.

■ A change in any one of the following factors will shift the investment function: the interest rate, expectations about future sales, and business taxes.

■ A change in any one of the following factors will shift the net exports function: foreign real national income, price levels in the United States and in foreign nations, and the appreciation and depreciation of the U.S. dollar.

Total Expenditures and Total Production

■ If total expenditures (*TE*) equal total production (*TP*), the economy is in equilibrium. If *TP* > *TE,* the economy is in disequilibrium and inventories unexpectedly rise, signaling firms to cut back production, lower prices, or both. If *TE* > *TP,* the economy is in disequilibrium and inventories unexpectedly fall, signaling firms to increase production, raise prices, or both.

The Multiplier

■ A change in autonomous spending will bring about a multiple change in real national income or real GNP. This multiple change will be equal to $1/(1 - MPC)$ (the multiplier) times the change in autonomous spending. For example, if the multiplier = 5, and the change in autonomous investment = $400, then the change in real national income or real GNP = $2,000.

A Keynesian Theme

■ Keynes proposed that the economy could reach its equilibrium position with real GNP below natural real GNP; that is, the economy can be in equilibrium and be stuck in a recessionary gap, too.

Key Terms and Concepts

Say's Law

Involuntary
Unemployment

Laissez-faire

Efficiency Wage Models

Consumption Function

Marginal Propensity to
Consume

Autonomous
Consumption

Induced Consumption

Marginal Propensity to
Save

Average Propensity to
Consume

Average Propensity to
Save

Exchange Rate

Appreciation

Depreciation

Multiplier

QUESTIONS AND PROBLEMS

1. Given that classical economists believe in Say's law and interest rate and wage–price flexibility, what would the classical aggregate supply curve look like and why?

2. The economist Axel Leijonhufvud said, "The central issue in macroeconomic theory is . . . the extent to which the economy, or at least its market sectors, may properly be regarded as a self-regulating system. . . . How well or badly, do its automatic mechanisms perform?" Is there any debate between classical and Keynesian economists on this point? What does each group say?

3. Answer the following questions:

a. Suppose the MPC = .80 and that it is the same at all real income levels. Suppose autonomous consumption decreases by $500. How much does real national income change?

b. Suppose the MPS = .10 and that it is the same at all real income levels. Suppose autonomous investment increases by $100. How much does real national income change?

c. Suppose the MPC = .70 and that it is the same at all real income levels. Suppose autonomous consumption increases by $500 and autonomous investment decreases by $80. How much does real national income change?

4. In this chapter, a distinction was made between a shift in a curve or function and a movement along a curve or function. With respect to consumption, we saw that a change in real disposable income (or real national income) would lead to a movement along the consumption function, whereas a change in wealth, the price level, and so on would shift it. To add some jargon here, real disposable income is considered to be a "movement parameter" (in that a change in real disposable income will bring about a movement along a given consumption function), and wealth and so on are referred to as "shift parameters" (in that a change in wealth will bring about a shift in the consumption function). In terms of Exhibit 9–5, how does one distinguish between a movement and shift parameter?

5. Economists are often asked to make predictions. Suppose, for simplicity's sake, that the economy could be accurately summarized in the following two equations: $C = C_0 + MPC(Y_d)$ and $I = I_0$. Furthermore, assume that you know I = $1,000 and C_0 = $750, currently. Someone asks you to predict what equilibrium real national income will be one year from today. What problems might you encounter in making this prediction? Do you think it is easier for economists to explain or to predict? Why?

6. Explain the difference between the classical and Keynesian theory applied to the following: (a) leakages and injections; (b) full-employment, or natural, real GNP; (c) wage–price flexibility; (d) laissez-faire.

7. Suppose the aggregate supply curve has three portions to it: One is flat, or horizontal; one is upward sloping; and one is vertical. Explain why the effect on the price level is not always unambiguous, given a change (increase or decrease) in aggregate demand.

8. What happens if total expenditures is greater than total production? What happens if total production is greater than total expenditures?

9. Give two reasons why wage rates may be inflexible in the downward direction?

10. According to Akerlof, why might firms want to stabilize wages instead of employment?

11. What did Keynes mean when he said that classical theory is "applicable to a special case only"?

12. Explain the effect on the total expenditures (*TE*) curve of each of the following: (a) an increase in foreign national income, (b) depreciation of the U.S. dollar, (c) a fall in business taxes, (d) appreciation of the U.S. dollar, (e) an increase in wealth.

13. What is the classical view of the economy? What is the Keynesian view of the economy?

14. What is the relationship between a school's (for example, classical or Keynesian) view of the economy and its position on laissez-faire?

THE MULTIPLIER–ACCELERATOR THEORY OF THE BUSINESS CYCLE

Many Keynesians often point to changes in business investment, residential construction, and/or government spending as the cause of the business cycle. For example, a business cycle contraction might result from a decrease in business investment or government spending that lowers aggregate demand and imposes a net loss of sales on business firms. Since in Keynesian theory (nominal) wages are assumed inflexible in the downward direction, the major consequence of a fall in aggregate demand will come in the form of reduced output or real GNP instead of lower prices. A decline in output gets translated into a fall in income, and since consumption is a function of income, consumption will fall, which leads to an even lower level of aggregate demand. The original decrease in business investment or government spending snowballs into lower levels of consumption that generate a multiple (remember the multiplier?) decrease in output.

THE ACCELERATOR PRINCIPLE AND THE MULTIPLIER– ACCELERATOR PROCESS

The multiplier process just described postulates a cause–effect relationship running from decreases in business investment to multiple decreases in output. Many business cycle theorists have stated that often the cause–effect relationship runs the other way: from decreases in output to decreases in investment. The idea that investment depends on output, in particular the *growth* of output—given the condition of a constant relationship between an economy's capital stock and output— is captured in what economists call the **accelerator principle.** We illustrate how the accelerator principle works in Exhibit 9C–1, where all dollar figures are in millions.

Exhibit 9C–1 displays data for two industries: the furniture industry and the furniture machine industry. We assume that $2 of furniture machines are needed for every $1 of furniture produced. For example, if the furniture industry wants to

Accelerator Principle
The idea that investment depends on the growth rate of output. The accelerator principle assumes a constant relationship between an economy's capital stock and output.

215

EXHIBIT 9C–1

The Accelerator Principle

All numbers are in millions. The accelerator principle here shows that (1) if the growth rates of annual furniture sales decrease, net investment, gross investment, and furniture machine sales decrease in absolute terms; (2) the furniture industry moves from boom to bust even though annual furniture sales by the furniture industry do not decrease at all.

		FURNITURE INDUSTRY					FURNITURE MACHINE INDUSTRY
	(1)	(2)	(3)	(4)	(5)	(6)	(7)
	Annual Furniture Sales	Furniture Machines Needed	Furniture Machines On Hand	Net Investment in Furniture Machines = (2) − (3)	Furniture Machines That Require Replacement	Gross Investment In Furniture Machines = (4) + (5)	Sales Of Furniture Machines = (6)
Year 1	$10	$20	$20	$ 0	$2	$ 2	$ 2
	↑40%						
Year 2	14	28	20	8	2	10	10
	↑42%						
Year 3	20	40	28	12	2	14	14
	↑10%						
Year 4	22	44	40	4	2	6	6
	0%						
Year 5	22	44	44	0	2	2	2
	0%						
Year 6	22	44	44	0	2	2	2

produce $10 million worth of furniture (see first entry in column 1), this requires $20 million worth of furniture machinery (see first entry in column 2). We also assume that each year the furniture industry needs to replace $2 million worth of machinery because of normal wear and tear (depreciation). Let us look at the situation for each of six years.

Year 1: Annual furniture sales are $10 million (column 1). This requires $20 million worth of furniture machinery (column 2). The industry currently has $20 million worth of machinery on hand (column 3). Column 4 notes the *net* investment the industry will need to make in furniture machinery this year. The dollar amount ($0) is found by subtracting the dollar worth of machines the industry has on hand from the dollar worth of machines the industry needs to satisfy its annual sales—that is, the dollar figure in column 2 minus the dollar figure in column 3. Column 5 notes the replacement investment in machinery the industry will need to make. Column 6 notes the industry's *gross* investment in machinery. This is equal to any net investment plus the replacement investment of $2 million—column 4 + column 5. Gross investment equals $2 million in year 1. Finally, in column 7, we note the dollar sales of furniture machines made by the furniture machine industry. This is equal to the gross investment of the furniture industry. In year 1, this is $2 million.

Year 2: Annual furniture sales increase 40 percent to $14 million. Since it takes $2 worth of furniture machines for every $1 worth of furniture produced, $28 million worth of furniture machines is required. Currently, the furniture industry has $20 million worth of furniture machines. This means it will need to make a net investment in furniture machines of $8 million. Adding its replacement investment this year ($2 million, column 5) to its net investment ($8 million, column 4), we obtain a total of $10 million gross investment (column 6). This is equal to furniture machines sales in year 2.

Year 3. In this year, furniture sales are $20 million, 42 percent higher than they were last year. This results in a gross investment of $14 million (column 6) and furniture machines sales of the same amount.

Year 4. In this year, furniture sales are $22 million, $2 million higher than in year 3, but the growth rate in sales (10 percent) is less than in the previous year (42 percent). What is the result? Gross investment in furniture machines falls from $14 million to $6 million. Furniture machine sales fall to $6 million.

Year 5. In this year, furniture sales are exactly what they were last year, $22 million. As a result, gross investment in furniture falls to $2 million, as do furniture machine sales.

Year 6: Once again, furniture sales are exactly what they were last year, $22 million. Gross investment and furniture machine sales are steady at $2 million. From this we can make the following conclusions:

1. If the *growth* rate of annual furniture sales increases, net investment, gross investment, and furniture machine sales increase in absolute terms.
2. If the *growth* rate of annual furniture sales decreases, net investment, gross investment, and furniture machine sales decrease in absolute terms. To put it differently, even if annual furniture sales increase or remain constant in absolute terms, as long as the *growth* rate in furniture sales decreases, net investment, gross investment, and furniture machine sales will also decrease.
3. The furniture machine industry moves from boom to bust (from sales of $2 million to $10 million to $14 million at the peak, down to $6 million and then to $2 million), even though annual furniture sales by the furniture industry do not decrease at all.

THE MULTIPLIER–ACCELERATOR EXPLANATION OF THE BUSINESS CYCLE

Combining the multiplier and the accelerator, we have an explanation of the business cycle. We describe the process by assuming that the economy is tending toward full employment, real GNP is rising, and business sales are rising at an *increasing* rate. Because of the accelerator, this results in increased investment. And because of the multiplier, the increased investment increases real GNP by a multiple of itself. In short, the accelerator and multiplier work together to expand the economy and move it faster toward full-employment output.

In time, however, the economy approaches full employment. At this point, the growth rate in business sales slows down. Because of the accelerator, investment falls. And because of the multiplier, there is a multiple decrease in real GNP. As real GNP falls, sales decrease further, leading to another round of cuts in investment. At some point, the economy will bottom out and the process is likely to repeat itself.

What we have here, then, is a story of boom and bust: a story of the business cycle. It is important to notice, too, that the multiplier–accelerator theory of the business cycle holds that the boom naturally leads into the bust, and the bust naturally leads into the boom. The theory implies that the private sector itself contains the seeds of the business cycle. As the believers in the multiplier–accelerator theory of the business cycle might say, the private economy is inherently unstable.

■ The accelerator principle holds that investment is dependent on output, or more specifically, the *growth rate of output.* In the accelerator analysis, there is a constant relationship between an economy's capital stock and output.

■ The multiplier-accelerator theory of the business cycle holds that if the economy is growing toward full employment, and sales are increasing at an increasing rate, then investment will increase, and via the multiplier, real GNP will increase by some multiple. Once the economy nears full employment, there is a slowdown in the growth rate of sales, investment falls, and via the multiplier, there is a multiple decrease in real GNP, which, in turn, leads to a further decrease in sales, investment, and real GNP. Once the economy bottoms out, the process reverses itself. A key implication of the multiplier-acceleratory theory of the business cycle is that the private economy is inherently unstable.

QUESTIONS AND PROBLEMS

1. Some economists criticize the multiplier-accelerator theory of the business cycle as being too mechanical and rigid. What do you think they mean by this? Is this a fair criticism? Would it be better to criticize the theory's predictions instead of its structure? Why?

2. Suppose the dollar amounts in column (1) of Exhibit 9C–1 are $12 million, $20 million, $24 million, $26 million, $26 million, and $26 million. Furthermore, suppose that $2 of furniture machines are needed for every $1 of furniture produced and that currently $20 million worth of furniture machines are on hand (first entry in column 3). Given this data, fill in the dollar amounts in columns (2)–(7).

APPENDIX

D

THE PERMANENT-INCOME HYPOTHESIS

Take another look at Exhibit 9–5 on page 192. You will notice that the consumption function does not go through the origin, but instead starts at a level of consumption spending of $200 billion. We specified an autonomous consumption component (C_0), which means that even if disposable income is 0 ($Y_d = 0$), consumption (C) will be greater than 0 because C_0 is positive; that is, $C = C_0 + MPC(Y_d)$.

Do real-world consumption functions take on the shape of the hypothetical consumption function in Exhibit 9–5? The answer is that some do and some do not. We explain by first discussing two types of statistical studies: cross-sectional studies and time-series studies.

In a cross-sectional study of the consumption function, the researcher does the following: (1) She divides the population into different income groups. (2) She then notes the consumption spending of the average family in the different income groups. Note that consumption spending is examined at one particular point in time. That is, in a cross-sectional study, the researcher picks one point in time, takes a cross section of families (which means that she categorizes or groups families according to some criterion), and records the consumption of the average family in each group.

When plotted, the data from cross-sectional studies of consumption take on the shape of the consumption function in Exhibit 9–5. That is, there is a direct relationship between consumption and disposable income; the consumption function does not start at the origin, but at some level of consumption spending above zero; and, following from the latter, the marginal propensity to consume is different from the average propensity to consume.

Finally, the data show that as disposable income increases, the average propensity to consume decreases; that is, high-income groups consume less and save more (in percentage terms) of their disposable incomes than do low-income groups. This finding is consistent with the way we have drawn our consumption function in Exhibit 9–5. Specifically, while the *MPC* is the slope of the consumption function, the *APC* is the slope of a ray extending from the origin to a point on the consumption function. You can visualize that the slope of this ray will become less as disposable income increases. (To see this, draw rays extending from the origin to different points on the consumption function.)

EXHIBIT 9D–1

A Cross-Sectional and a Time-Series Consumption Function: Does the Permanent-Income Hypothesis Explain Why There Are Two?

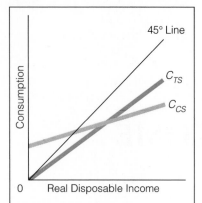

Plotting cross-sectional consumption data gives the consumption function C_{CS}. Plotting time-series consumption data gives the consumption function C_{TS}.

Thus, we can conclude that in cross-sectional consumption studies, the consumption function looks like the consumption function in Exhibit 9–5.

In time-series consumption studies, this is not the case. Here we find that the consumption function looks like the consumption function C_{TS} in Exhibit 9D–1.

Notice that this consumption function is different from the consumption function generated through cross-sectional studies (labeled C_{CS}). First, it extends outward from the origin; second, it always lies below the 45° line (this is not the case for C_{CS}); third, the *MPC* (measured by the slope of the consumption function) is equal to the *APC* (measured by the slope of the ray extending through the origin to a point on the consumption function).

In a time-series study of consumption, the researcher does the following: (1) He chooses his time period (for example, five years). (2) He decides how many periods within each year he will collect data on total consumption and total income (for example, in a quarterly time-series study, the researcher collects data on total consumption and total income in each of the four quarters of the year). The difference between a cross-sectional and time-series study is that in the former data are collected at one point in time, while in the latter, data are collected over time. Simply put, it is the difference between a snapshot, which gives us a picture of what is happening at an instant in time, and a movie, which gives us a picture of what is happening over time.

In summary, the empirical evidence suggests that there are two consumption functions: a cross-sectional consumption function and a time-series consumption function. Sometimes these are referred to as the short-run consumption function and the long-run consumption function, respectively. The two consumption functions are different. The short-run consumption function says the *APC* declines as disposable income increases, whereas the long-run consumption function says that it is constant over disposable income. Many economists believe that the existence of the two consumption functions and the inconsistency between them can be explained with the aid of the permanent-income hypothesis.

The permanent-income hypothesis, suggested by Nobel Prize–winner Milton Friedman, states that consumption is a function of permanent income, not current disposable income (as our consumption function in this chapter holds). A person's permanent income is her average, normal, or long-run income over some period of time. The time period over which she "calculates" her permanent income can be anywhere from a couple of years to many years. Suppose, for example, that Walters "calculates" her permanent income over a five-year time period. Walters expects the following disposable income for each year: year 1 = $50,000, year 2 = $55,000, year 3 = $120,000, year 4 = $60,000, year 5 = $20,000. Her average or permanent income is $61,000. The permanent-income hypothesis holds that consumption will be a function of this dollar figure, $61,000, in each of the five years, not the different dollar amounts in the different years.

A consumption function that specifies consumption as a function of current (disposable) income and one that specifies consumption as a function of permanent, or long-run, income often have quite different implications. For example, consider year 3 where Walters's current (disposable) income is $120,000, but her permanent income is $61,000—only $1,000 more than one-half of her current income. The permanent-income hypothesis holds that Walters's consumption in year 3 will be based on $61,000. The consumption function that specifies consumption as a function of current income holds that Walters's consumption in year 3 will be based on $120,000. The absolute difference in consumption spending between the two models is likely to be quite large.

In addition, the change in consumption spending between year 2 and year 3 will be different in the two hypotheses. The current-income hypothesis holds that there will be a rather large jump in consumption spending from year 2 to year 3 because there is a rather large jump in income during this period. The permanent-income hypothesis, however, holds that even though current income has taken a large jump between the two years, permanent income has not—and consumption spending is a function of the latter.

Now let us put this information together with our two consumption functions in Exhibit 9D–1. When a researcher is deriving a consumption function based on cross-sectional data, it is likely that (at that particular point in time) she will find many high-income persons are receiving current incomes that are above their permanent incomes and that their *APS*s are high (relative to others) and their *APC*s are low (relative to others) because they are spreading out their consumption over time: a little less consumption now, a little more consumption later. On the other hand, at the same point in time, many low-income persons are probably receiving current incomes that are below their permanent incomes, and therefore their *APS*s are low (relative to others) or negative, and their *APC*s are high (relative to others) because they, too, are spreading out their consumption over time: a little more consumption now, a little less consumption later. At low-income levels, then, we might expect to see dissaving: consumption expenditures greater than current income.[13] For both high-income and low-income groups, their *APC*s and *APS*s are likely to be different over time than they are at one particular point in time. And when we compare the *APC*s and *APS*s in the cross-sectional (short-run) studies with the *APC*s and *APS*s in the time-series (long-run) studies, this is what we find.

In short, the permanent-income hypothesis holds that we will (empirically) observe two consumption functions: one for the short run, or one based on cross-sectional data; and one for the long run, or one based on time-series data. The short-run consumption function is a picture of consumption spending while individuals are spreading out their consumption spending; the long-run consumption function is a picture of consumption spending after it has been spread out.

APPENDIX SUMMARY

■ In a cross-sectional study of consumption, the researcher divides the population into different income groups and notes the consumption spending of the average family in the different income groups. In a time-series study of consumption, the researcher chooses a time period and then decides how many periods within the time period she will collect data on consumption and income. The difference between a cross-sectional and time-series study is that in the former data are collected at one point in time, while in the latter, data are collected over time.

■ Milton Friedman hypothesized that consumption is a function of permanent income, not current income. A person's permanent income is her average, normal, or long-run income over some time period.

[13]Consider the case of a poor medical student who, because he believes his future income as a physician will be quite large, dissaves in the present.

■ The permanent income hypothesis holds that permanent changes in income have a major effect on consumption while transitory changes have a minor effect.

■ The permanent income hypothesis holds that we will (empirically) observe two consumption functions: one for the short run, or one based on cross-sectional data; and one for the long run, or one based on time series data. The short-run consumption function is a picture of consumption spending while individuals are spreading out their consumption spending; the long-run consumption function is a picture of consumption spending after it has been spread out.

QUESTIONS AND PROBLEMS

1. A person's average income is $37,000 a year for 10 years. In the eleventh year, his income unexpectedly jumps to $80,000, but there is little chance that this higher income level will continue into the future. According to the permanent income hypothesis, would we expect a large or small increase in consumption spending? Explain your answer.

2. Explain why the cross-sectional consumption function lies above the time-series consumption function at low levels of income but not at high levels of income.

3. Explain why poor medical students often dissave.

CHAPTER 10

FISCAL POLICY

WHAT THIS CHAPTER IS ABOUT

Can the federal government's spending and taxing powers be successfully used to stabilize the economy—that is, to eliminate both recessionary and inflationary gaps? This question underlies much of our discussion in this chapter. In other terms, it asks whether fiscal policy is effective or ineffective at meeting certain macroeconomic goals.

FISCAL POLICY

In this section, we define a budget deficit, a budget surplus, and a balanced budget, and describe the workings of fiscal policy.

The Federal Budget: Expenditures and Tax Receipts

The federal budget is composed of two, not necessarily equal, parts: expenditures (G) and tax receipts or revenues (T). If expenditures outstrip tax receipts, a **budget deficit** exists—which the federal government has had each year since 1970; if tax receipts outstrip expenditures, a **budget surplus** exists; and if expenditures equal tax receipts, a **balanced budget** exists.

What Is Fiscal Policy?

Fiscal policy refers to changes in government expenditures and taxation to achieve particular macroeconomic goals, such as low unemployment, stable prices, and economic growth. For example, fiscal policy might be used to move the economy out of a recessionary or inflationary gap. If it is used to increase either aggregate demand or aggregate supply, it is called **expansionary fiscal policy.** If it is used to decrease either aggregate demand or aggregate supply, it is called **contractionary fiscal policy.** A particular fiscal policy that is deliberately brought about through government action is referred to as **discretionary fiscal policy.** It follows that there can be either (1) discretionary expansionary fiscal policy or (2) discretionary contractionary fiscal policy.

In contrast, a policy measure that occurs automatically in response to economic events and is the result of past governmental decisions is referred to as **automatic fiscal policy** (or built-in fiscal policy). It follows that there can either be (1) automatic expansionary fiscal policy or (2) automatic contractionary fiscal policy.

As Exhibit 10–1 illustrates, discretionary expansionary fiscal policy includes deliberate actions by policy makers that increase government spending, decrease taxes, or both. Discretionary contractionary fiscal policy includes deliberate actions by government that decrease government spending, increase taxes, or both.

Notice that unemployment compensation and welfare payments are examples of both automatic expansionary and automatic contractionary fiscal policies. For example, if the economy turns down (real GNP declines), more people will become unemployed and eligible for unemployment benefits. We would also expect that some people would become eligible for welfare assistance. Unemployment compensation and welfare payments soften an economic downturn by preventing consumption spending (and therefore aggregate demand) from falling as much as it would if these two programs had not been in place. In short, during an economic downturn, unemployment compensation and welfare payments are automatic expansionary fiscal measures that reduce the intensity of the fall.

The two programs also moderate the intensity of an economic upturn. As individuals find jobs, many no longer receive welfare payments or unemployment compensation. Instead, increased deductions from payrolls for state and local programs and for union unemployment funds reduce the increase in disposable income going to employed workers.

Budget Deficit
Government expenditures outstrip tax receipts.

Budget Surplus
Tax receipts outstrip government expenditures.

Balanced Budget
Government expenditures equal tax receipts.

Fiscal Policy
Changes in government expenditures and taxation to achieve particular macroeconomic goals, such as low unemployment, stable prices, economic growth, and so on.

Expansionary Fiscal Policy
Fiscal policy designed to increase aggregate demand or aggregate supply.

Contractionary Fiscal Policy
Fiscal policy designed to decrease aggregate demand or aggregate supply.

Discretionary Fiscal Policy
Deliberate changes of government expenditures and taxes to achieve particular economic objectives.

Automatic Fiscal Policy
Changes in government expenditures or taxes that occur automatically without (additional) congressional action.

Question:

Does discretionary expansionary fiscal policy result in a budget deficit?

EXHIBIT 10–1
Four Types of Fiscal Policy

	Expansionary	Contractionary
Discretionary	Policymakers $\uparrow G$ or $\downarrow T$ or both **(1)**	Policymakers $\downarrow G$ or $\uparrow T$ or both **(2)**
Automatic	Unemployment Compensation Welfare Payments **(3)**	Unemployment Compensation Welfare Payments **(4)**

In this exhibit, G = government spending; T = taxes. The four types of fiscal policy include (1) discretionary expansionary, (2) discretionary contractionary, (3) automatic expansionary, and (4) automatic contractionary. Notice that unemployment compensation and welfare payments are examples of automatic expansionary fiscal policy and automatic contractionary fiscal policy.

Answer:

It can, but not necessarily. Whether it does depends on (1) the state of the budget before the expansionary fiscal policy is enacted and (2) the amount of expansionary fiscal stimulus. Suppose there is a budget surplus of $100 billion and government spending is increased by $20 billion. As a result, the surplus shrinks—but there is still a surplus. But if the budget was balanced before the increased spending, a deficit results. Finally, if the budget was in deficit before the increased spending, the expansionary fiscal action will increase the size of the deficit.

THE RISE OF DISCRETIONARY FISCAL POLICY

Discretionary fiscal policy did not always play as important a role as it did in the 1960s, and '70s. The story of the rise of discretionary fiscal policy—from the halls of academia to the hallways of Congress and the White House—is an interesting one, which we summarize briefly here.

The Old-Time Fiscal Religion

Before the Keynesian revolution in economics, laypersons and economists alike generally accepted the following standards:

1. The federal budget should be balanced. The Adam Smith notion that "what is prudence in the conduct of every private family, can scarce be folly in that of a great kingdom" was generally accepted. Since most persons believed that it was wrong for individuals to go into debt, particularly year after year, it was also widely accepted that a country should not pile up debt by running annual deficits. There was, however, one exception to the balanced budget rule. It was permissible for countries to run budget deficits during wartime. But after the war, a surplus was required to counteract the earlier deficits.

2. Increased federal spending should be tied to higher taxes so that individuals can clearly and correctly judge the true cost of government. The Swedish economist Knut Wicksell argued that individuals could only make an informed evaluation of various proposals for government expenditure if they were presented with a tax bill at the same time the proposal for additional spending was made. This was what we call the "menu approach to government spending." Next to each government program or activity would be its tax price. Citizen-taxpayers would review the menu, consider the prices (taxes) they would have to pay if they chose A over B, or B over C, and then make their choices—with their eyes wide open and with reality in full view.

3. Government spending and taxing powers should be directed to providing the citizenry with publicly demanded goods and services and should not be used to manipulate macroeconomic variables. People believed that it is beyond the proper role of government to manage the economy; the government's only proper role is to provide demanded goods and services that the economy cannot privately, through ordinary market forces, supply for itself. Related to this was the belief that the market economy is inherently stable. This is the classical notion that the economy naturally self-equilibrates at the full-employment, or natural, real GNP level.

Discretionary Fiscal Policy Moves to Center Stage

Beginning in the 1930s, many economists came to accept the Keynesian notion that the economy may be inherently unstable. The old-time fiscal religion was thrust aside by the new fiscal religion, which stated that expansionary fiscal policy should be implemented when aggregate demand is "too low," or when there is a recessionary gap—even if this meant budget deficits; and contractionary fiscal policy should be implemented when aggregate demand is "too high," or when there is an inflationary gap—even if this meant budget surpluses.

In the 1960s and '70s, the political implications of the new fiscal religion became explicit. To some economists, it seemed that expansionary fiscal policy—where government spending (G) was increased and/or taxes (T) reduced—was much easier to implement than contractionary fiscal policy—where government spending was decreased and/or taxes raised. Politicians, it was suggested, would readily increase G or lower T because these measures were popular with voters. But they would not so readily, if at all, call for decreases in G or increases in T because this usually met with voter resistance. Some economists began to ask if there was a political bias to the new fiscal religion. Would expansionary fiscal policy become the order of the day and contractionary fiscal policy be relegated to the dustbin? Would the political bias of the new fiscal religion result in a long string of annual budget deficits?

Question:

Do individuals who favor discretionary fiscal policy also favor big government?

Answer:

This is not necessarily the case. For example, consider two persons, Connors and Jordan. Connors favors "big government" and Jordan favors "small government." Is it possible for both of them also to favor discretionary fiscal policy? The answer is yes. Connors, who favors "big government," will advocate increases in government spending if he thinks the situation calls for expansionary fiscal policy. On the other hand, Jordan, who favors "small government," will advocate decreases in taxes.

Both measures—increased spending and decreased taxes—are expansionary fiscal measures. Similarly, if Connors thinks contractionary fiscal policy is required, he will advocate increases in taxes, while Jordan will advocate decreases in government spending. So one can be in favor of big government or small government and still advocate the use of discretionary fiscal policy.

DEMAND-SIDE FISCAL POLICY

Government spending and taxation can affect the demand or the supply side of the economy. We focus on the demand side in this section and discuss the supply side in the next section. First, we examine fiscal policy in the Keynesian theory; then we discuss the effectiveness of, and problems associated with, fiscal policy.

How Do Changes in G and T Affect Aggregate Demand?

Before discussing demand-side fiscal policy, we need to know the mechanics of how fiscal policy actually affects aggregate demand. Since fiscal policy deals with both increases and decreases in G and T, we need to know (1) how an increase in G affects aggregate demand; (2) how a decrease in G affects aggregate demand; (3) how an increase in T affects aggregate demand; and (4) how a decrease in T affects aggregate demand.

In Chapter 8, we said that *at a given price level*, anything that increases total expenditures—the components of which are consumption, investment, government expenditures, and net exports—increases aggregate demand and shifts the AD curve to the right; and *at a given price level*, anything that decreases total expenditures decreases aggregate demand and shifts the AD curve to the left. As we can see, an increase in government expenditures—which is a component of total expenditures—increases aggregate demand and shifts the AD curve to the right; a decrease in government expenditures decreases aggregate demand and shifts the AD curve to the left.[1]

A change in taxes can directly affect either or both consumption and investment, both of which are components of total expenditures. For example, a decrease in income taxes will increase disposable (after-tax) income, and households can, and perhaps will, consume more goods and services at a given price level—thus shifting the AD curve to the right. An increase in income taxes will decrease disposable (after-tax) income and lead to the opposite effect.

Fiscal Policy in Keynesian Theory

In Exhibit 10–2a, the economy is initially at point 1 and in a recessionary gap. Aggregate demand is too low to move the economy to equilibrium at the natural real GNP level. A familiar Keynesian prescription is to enact discretionary expansionary fiscal policy measures (an increase in government spending, a decrease in taxes, or both) to shift the aggregate demand curve rightward from AD_1 to AD_2 and move the economy to point 2 and to the natural real GNP level.

[1]We question this stated effect on aggregate demand of an increase or decrease in government expenditures later in the chapter when we discuss the issue of crowding out.

EXHIBIT 10–2

Fiscal Policy in Keynesian Theory: Ridding the Economy of Recessionary and Inflationary Gaps

(a)
Discretionary Expansionary Fiscal Policy for a Recessionary Gap

(b)
Discretionary Contractionary Fiscal Policy for an Inflationary Gap

(a) Discretionary expansionary fiscal policy is used within Keynesian theory to eliminate a recessionary gap. Increased government spending, decreased taxes, or both lead to a rightward shift in the aggregate demand curve from AD_1 to AD_2, restoring the economy to the natural level of real GNP, Q_N. (b) Discretionary contractionary

fiscal policy is used to eliminate an inflationary gap. Decreased government spending, increased taxes, or both lead to a leftward shift in the aggregate demand curve from AD_1 to AD_2, restoring the economy to the natural level of real GNP, Q_N.

Of course, at this point someone might ask, Why not simply wait for the short-run aggregate supply curve to shift rightward and intersect the aggregate demand curve at point 2'? The Keynesians have usually responded that (1) the economy is stuck at point 1 and won't move naturally to point 2'; or (2) it takes too long for the short-run aggregate supply curve to shift rightward, and in the interim we must deal with the high cost of unemployment and lower level of real GNP.

In Exhibit 10–2b, the economy is initially at point 1 and in an inflationary gap. In this situation, Keynesians are likely to propose a discretionary contractionary fiscal measure (a decrease in government spending, an increase in taxes, or both) to shift the aggregate demand curve leftward from AD_1 to AD_2 and move the economy to point 2.

The Calculations

According to Keynesian economists, a change in government spending will change real GNP by some multiple of itself. (This is the multiplier principle we discussed in Chapter 9.) Specifically, the change in real GNP is equal to the multiplier (m), which is $1/1 - MPC$, times the change in autonomous spending. In our example, the "change in autonomous spending" is equal to the "change in government spending."

$$(1) \quad \Delta Q = m \times \Delta G$$

For example, if the marginal propensity to consume is .80 (80 percent), then the multiplier is 5. So, if there is an increase in government spending of $4 billion, the increase in real GNP is five times this amount, or $20 billion.

Now instead of raising government spending by $4 billion, let's lower taxes by $4 billion. Assuming the same multiplier, will this raise real GNP by $20 billion? In other words, is a decrease in taxes of $4 billion equal in its expansionary fiscal effects to an increase in government spending of $4 billion?

The answer is no. Look at it this way. When government spending increases, 100 percent of every dollar of increased spending immediately goes to increase total expenditures. But when taxes are decreased, households experience an increase in disposable income. Some part of the tax cut is spent and some is saved. The amount that goes for saving depends on the marginal propensity to save. For example, if the marginal propensity to save is 20 percent, then 20 percent of each tax dollar reduction goes for saving, and the remainder (80 percent) goes for consumption, which in turn goes to increase aggregate demand.

What do we conclude? A dollar spent by government is a dollar spent; a dollar tax cut is a dollar partly saved and partly spent.

To calculate the change in real GNP given a change in taxes (T), we use the following formula:

$$(2) \quad \Delta Q = -MPC(m) \times \Delta T$$

In our example, a $4 billion cut in taxes increases real GNP by $16 billion. The arithmetic is simple: $-MPC(m) = -.80(5) = -4$, which we then multiply by the change in taxes ($-$$4 billion) to get $16 billion. We conclude that a $4 billion increase in government spending increases real GNP by more than a $4 billion tax cut does.

With this knowledge, now consider the net effect of an increase in government spending of $4 billion, which is an expansionary fiscal measure, and a simultaneous increase in taxes of $4 billion, which is an equal contractionary fiscal measure. Assuming we started from a position of a balanced budget, we are maintaining this state of affairs by raising taxes to the same degree we raise government expenditures.

What will be the change in real GNP? We obtain our answer by breaking down the problem into two parts. First we ask, What will be the increase in real GNP if government spending is increased by $4 billion? Then we ask, What will be the decrease in real GNP if taxes are increased by $4 billion? Finally, we note the difference, if any, between the two dollar amounts.

Assuming $MPC = .80$, the multiplier is 5, so that the increase in real GNP given an increase in government spending of $4 billion is $20 billion. (We have simply plugged the numbers into equation 1.) The change in real GNP given an increase of $4 billion in taxes is $-$$16 billion (equation 2). The difference between the two dollar amounts is a positive $4 billion.

We conclude: If government spending is increased $4 billion and taxes are increased $4 billion (to maintain the balance between expenditures and revenues), real GNP increases by $4 billion. In general terms: The change in real GNP is equal to the change in government spending when government spending and taxes change by the same dollar amount and in the same direction. This is what economists call the **balanced budget theorem.**

Question:

Simply, the balanced budget theorem seems to say that if government spending goes up by $X, and taxes go up by $X, real GNP will go up by $X. Is this correct?

Balanced Budget Theorem
A change in real GNP is equal to the change in government spending when government spending and taxes change by the same dollar amount and in the same direction.

229

Answer:

Yes. What the balanced budget theorem implies is that it is possible to increase government spending, maintain the budget in balance, and increase real GNP as well. For many persons, this is an ideal situation.

Crowding Out: Calling the Effectiveness of Fiscal Policy into Question

Many of the criticisms of the predicted effects of fiscal policy on aggregate demand and real GNP, as well as the multiplier analysis and the balanced budget theorem, come under the general heading of **crowding out**. This term refers to a decrease in private expenditures (consumption and so on) as a consequence of increased government spending or the financing needs of the deficit. The following are all possible examples of crowding out:

Crowding Out
The decrease in private expenditures that occurs as a consequence of increased government spending or of the financing needs of the deficit.

1. The government spends more on public libraries, and individuals buy fewer books at bookstores.[2]
2. The government spends more on public education, and individuals spend less on private education.
3. The government spends more on public transportation, and individuals spend less on private transportation.
4. The government spends more on social programs and defense without increasing taxes; the size of the deficit increases; the government is required to borrow more loanable funds to finance the larger deficit; real interest rates rise; as a result, investment decreases.

Believers in the existence of the crowding-out phenomenon argue that because of higher real interest rates (example 4) and the direct substitution of public services for consumer spending (examples 1–3), increases in government spending induce consumers and investors to spend less. Government spending crowds out private spending—either directly (examples 1–3) or indirectly (example 4).[3]

Furthermore, crowding out can be either complete or incomplete.[4] **Complete crowding out** occurs when the decrease in one or more components of private spending completely offsets the increase in government spending. For example, if government spending on public education increases by $100 million, and individual spending on private education drops $100 million as a result, we have complete crowding out.

Complete Crowding Out
The decrease in one or more components of private spending completely offsets the increase in government spending.

Incomplete Crowding Out
The decrease in one or more components of private spending only partially offsets the increase in government spending.

Incomplete crowding out occurs when the decrease in one or more components of private spending only partially offsets the increase in government spending. For example, government spending on public libraries increases by $25 million, and individuals spend $5 million less on books at bookstores.

Whether we are dealing with complete or incomplete crowding out, the crowding-out effect suggests that discretionary expansionary fiscal policy will have an impact on aggregate demand and real GNP less than the Keynesian theory predicts.

---

[2]We are not saying *if* government spends more on public libraries, individuals will *necessarily* buy fewer books at bookstores; rather, if they do, this would be an example of crowding out. The same holds for examples 2, 3, and 4.
[3]Some economists refer to the direct substitution of public services for private spending as *direct crowding out* and the decrease in investment caused by higher real interest rates as *indirect crowding out*.
[4]Alternatively, crowding out can be zero (no crowding out), complete (100 percent), or incomplete (somewhere between zero and complete).

In Exhibit 10–3, we illustrate the consequences of complete and incomplete crowding out. We also compare each with the case in Keynesian theory.

In 10–3, the economy is initially at point 1, Q_1. In Keynesian theory, expansionary fiscal policy increases the aggregate demand curve to AD_2 and moves the economy to point 2, Q_N. This implicitly assumes there is zero, or no, crowding out. With incomplete crowding out, the aggregate demand curve only increases (on net) to AD_2' because the initial stimulus in aggregate demand, due, say, to increased government spending, is partially offset by a fall in private expenditures. The economy moves to point 2', Q_2'. In the case of complete crowding out, the initial stimulus in aggregate demand, due to increased government spending, is completely offset by a fall in private expenditures such that the aggregate demand curve does not move (on net) at all. With complete crowding out, expansionary fiscal policy has no effect on the economy. The economy remains at point 1, Q_1.

Crowding Out, the Real Interest Rate, and Foreign Loanable Funds

Will there be less crowding out if, in response to higher real interest rates, loanable funds are attracted from abroad? Suppose the federal government either increases government spending or cuts taxes, and runs a larger budget deficit. The financing of the larger deficit increases the demand for loanable funds (demand for credit) and the real interest rate. Because of the higher real interest rate, investment declines. There is crowding out.

Now suppose we return to the point where real interest rates increased and ask ourselves if something might have been left out of the story. Many economists argue that the higher real interest rates will attract loanable funds from abroad. Foreigners, in search of the highest rates of return (actually, the highest after-tax real returns) will help finance the deficit by lending funds to the federal government through their purchases of U.S. Treasury securities. This action increases the supply of loanable funds (supply of credit) and keeps the real interest rate from rising, or rising as much.

How does the inflow of foreign funds affect crowding out? At first glance, it might appear to moderate it, since it dampens the increase in the real interest rate and thus the fall in investment. But a closer look is required. Before foreigners buy

Crowding out calls the effectiveness of fiscal policy into question.

EXHIBIT 10–3
Zero, Incomplete, and Complete Crowding Out

The effects of zero, incomplete, and complete crowding out in the *AD–AS* framework. Starting at point 1, expansionary fiscal policy shifts the aggregate demand curve to AD_2 and moves the economy to point 2 and Q_N. The Keynesian theory that predicts this outcome assumes zero, or no, crowding out; an increase in, say, government spending does not reduce private expenditures. With incomplete crowding out, an increase in government spending causes private expenditures to decrease by less than the increase in government expenditures. On net, the aggregate demand curve shifts to AD_2'. The economy moves to point 2' and Q_2'. With complete crowding out, an increase in government spending is completely offset by a decrease in private expenditures, and on net aggregate demand does not increase at all. The economy remains at point 1 and Q_1.

The increase (if any) in real GNP due to expansionary fiscal policy depends on the degree of crowding out.

Economic thinking views the world as essentially one country.

U.S. Treasury securities, they must exchange their domestic currency for U.S. dollars. This action increases the demand, and price, of U.S. dollars in the foreign exchange market. In short, the dollar will appreciate in value relative to other currencies: More of other currencies will be required to buy a dollar. In turn, this will make foreign goods cheaper for Americans, and American goods more expensive for foreigners. Economists predict that Americans will import more and export less. We conclude that some of the crowding out of private expenditures will come in the form of a decrease in net exports.

Question:

Does it follow that an increase in the size of the federal budget deficit can affect U.S. international trade?

Answer:

Trade Deficit
The situation where the value of exports is less than the value of imports.

Yes. To explain more fully, the United States is said to have a **trade deficit** if the value of its exports is less than the value of its imports. Let's suppose that the United States currently has a budget deficit of $100 billion and a trade deficit of $60 billion. The Congress increases government expenditures but does not raise taxes. As a result, the deficit becomes larger. Consequently, the U.S. Treasury demands more funds in the loanable funds market and the real interest rate rises. Then, as we said, the higher real interest rate causes foreign lenders to purchase interest-paying U.S. Treasury securities. In order to buy the securities, foreigners end up increasing their demand for U.S. dollars; thus, the dollar appreciates in value relative to foreign currencies. This makes foreign goods cheaper for Americans and American goods more expensive for foreigners. Americans import more and export less, thus widening the trade deficit beyond the original $60 billion. This is how a bigger budget deficit can lead to a bigger trade deficit.

THINKING LIKE AN ECONOMIST

Economic changes, like a stone thrown into a lake, often have a ripple effect. We have just seen how an increase in government spending can affect (1) the budget deficit, (2) interest rates, (3) the value of the dollar relative to other currencies, (4) the purchases of both foreigners and Americans, and (5) the U.S. trade deficit. These are quite a few ripples, and there are plenty more that we have not discussed. Economists have a mindset that takes the ripple effect into account: A change over here brings about a change way over there. Simply put, this means the laws of economics do not take notice of a nation's borders; economic effects do not ripple outward until they reach a national frontier and then stop, but may be worldwide in scope. This is where the political and economic way of thinking differ. Political thinking views the world as composed of hundreds of sovereign nations; economic thinking views the world as essentially one country.

The New Classical View of Fiscal Policy: Crowding Out with No Increase in Interest Rates

In our explanation of crowding out, we emphasized both direct substitution and real interest rate effects. In the first case, crowding out is a result of individuals thinking along this line: "Government has increased its expenditures on books in public libraries, so I shall decrease my private spending on books, which is a substitute for library books." In the second case, employers are thinking this way:

"The real interest rate has gone up (as a result of increased financing needs related to the deficit), so we shall reduce investment spending." Here, then, are two ways of understanding individuals' motives behind the crowding-out phenomenon.

According to the *new classical school of economics* there is yet another way of looking at what people may do. These economists believe that individuals, in response to expansionary fiscal policy measures, a larger deficit, and greater deficit-financing requirements, think the following: "A larger deficit implies more debt this year and higher future taxes. I'll simply save more in the present so I can pay the higher future taxes required to pay interest and to repay principal on the new debt."

Thus, the new classical macroeconomics theory offers a few predictions:

1. Current consumption will fall as a result of expansionary fiscal policy. An increase in government spending that increases the size of the deficit and the amount of debt financing will cause individuals to save more (consume less) to pay the higher future taxes.
2. Deficits do not bring higher real interest rates. The reason is simple: Deficits merely substitute future taxes for current taxes. Individuals save more to pay for their higher future taxes. The increased saving increases the supply of loanable funds and offsets the increased demand for loanable funds that is a consequence of the financing requirements of the deficit.

We illustrate these two new classical predictions in Exhibit 10–4. In (a), the economy is initially at point 1. If individuals do not anticipate higher future taxes as a result of expansionary fiscal policy, the aggregate demand curve will shift rightward from AD_1 to AD_2. However, new classical economists believe that individuals do anticipate higher future taxes, and therefore will reduce their consumption (and increase their saving) to pay the higher future taxes. In this case, the aggregate demand curve does not shift at all. What is the conclusion? Expansionary fiscal policy, given the condition of anticipated higher future taxes, leaves real GNP, unemployment, and the price level unchanged. Expansionary fiscal policy is not stimulative—it is not effective.

In (b), the loanable funds market is initially in equilibrium at point 1 and the real interest rate is i_1. As a result of the government implementing an expansionary fiscal policy measure, we have a deficit. The deficit requires financing, and so the demand for loanable funds shifts rightward from D_1 to D_2. At the same time, individuals perceive the deficit in terms of higher future taxes and increase their saving by enough to offset the higher future taxes. This action shifts the supply of loanable funds from S_1 to S_2. What is the conclusion? There is no change in the real interest rate.

The new classical position on expansionary fiscal policy might be summarized as follows: As long as expansionary fiscal policy is translated into higher future taxes (which new classical economists think is likely), there will be no change in real GNP, unemployment, the price level, or real interest rates. The analysis also holds for contractionary fiscal policy.

Question:

It doesn't seem that people will necessarily save enough to offset their higher future taxes completely, since many people won't live long enough to pay the higher future taxes. Won't some simply say, "I'd rather the government run a deficit today, and have lower taxes now, because when the higher future taxes roll around, I

EXHIBIT 10-4
The New Classical View of Expansionary Fiscal Policy

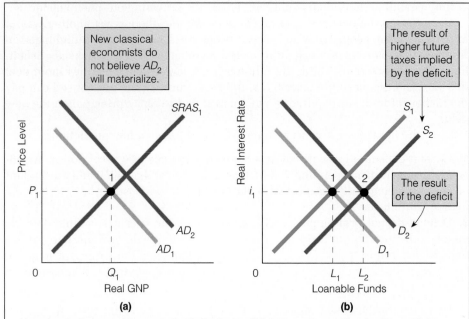

New classical economists argue that individuals will link expansionary fiscal policy to higher future taxes and decrease their current consumption and increase their saving as a result. (a) The decreased consumption prevents the aggregate demand curve from shifting rightward from AD_1 to AD_2. (b) The increased saving causes the supply of loanable funds to shift rightward from S_1 to S_2, thus offsetting the increased demand for loanable funds and maintaining the existing level of real interest rates. The new classical position on both (anticipated) expansionary and contractionary fiscal policy is that neither affects real GNP, unemployment, the price level, or real interest rates.

won't be here. Future taxpayers will have to pay for the increased government expenditures that I enjoyed."

If many of these assumed savers won't be paying the future taxes, there will be no reason to save more. Have the new classical economists thought of this?

Answer:

They have. One new classical economist, Robert Barro, points to the fact that individuals leave bequests to their children, implying that they care about their children's welfare and, indirectly, about the tax burden their children will one day face. He argues that today's taxpayers, reacting to an increased budget deficit, will increase their saving in order to leave more to their children, who will have to pay the higher future taxes.

On the topic of deficits and interest rates, there is some empirical evidence. In August 1981, the Congress passed a tax reduction bill that was to be phased in over the following three years. According to the new classical position, individuals would likely see this as resulting in a larger deficit, more debt financing, and higher future taxes. In reaction, they would increase their saving so that they, or their children, would be able to pay off the higher future taxes. Did they respond in kind? Most economists think not. The personal saving rate fell after 1981 from approximately 6.3 percent to an average of 4.8 percent in 1982–85.

Although this calls into question the new classical position on deficits, saving, and interest rates, there is some support for the position. For one thing, numerous empirical studies have found no statistically significant direct relationship between annual changes in the budget deficit and real interest rates. On the other hand, some economists have pointed out that although such a short-term relationship has not been found, the persistently high deficits of the early and mid-1980s were associated with high real interest rates. The question whether deficits cause higher real interest rates has not been definitely answered.

Lags and Discretionary Fiscal Policy

Suppose it were proved, beyond a shadow of a doubt, that discretionary fiscal policy is effective at changing real GNP. Would it hold that discretionary fiscal policy ought to be used to solve the problems of inflationary and recessionary gaps? Many economists would answer "not necessarily." The reason is because of lags. There are five types of lags.

1. The data lag. Policymakers are not aware of what is happening in the economy the day or week after it happens. For example, if the economy turns down in January, this may not be apparent for two to three months.

2. The wait-and-see lag. Once policymakers are aware of a downturn in economic activity, they are not likely to enact counteractive measures immediately. Instead, they probably will adopt a more cautious, wait-and-see attitude. They will want to be sure that the observed events are more than a very short-run phenomenon.

3. The legislative lag. Once policymakers decide that some type of fiscal policy measure is required, Congress or the president will have to propose the measure, build political support for it, and get it passed. This can take many months.

4. The transmission lag. Once a fiscal policy measure is enacted, it takes time to put the policy into effect. For example, a discretionary expansionary fiscal policy measure of increased spending for public works projects will require construction companies to submit bids for the work, prepare designs, negotiate contracts, and so on.

5. The effectiveness lag. Once a policy measure is actually implemented, it takes time for it to affect the economy. If government spending is increased on Monday, the aggregate demand curve does not shift rightward on Tuesday.

Taking these five lags together, some economists argue that discretionary fiscal policy is not likely to have the impact on the economy that policymakers will be hoping for. The problem is that, by the time the full impact of the policy is felt, the economic problem the policy was designed to solve may no longer exist, or may not exist to the degree it once did, or the problem may have changed altogether.

We illustrate this point in Exhibit 10–5. Suppose the economy is currently in a recessionary gap at point 1. The recession is under way before government officials recognize it. Once recognized, however, Congress and the president consider enacting expansionary fiscal policy in the hopes of shifting the *AD* curve from AD_1 to AD_2 and intersecting the *SRAS* curve at point 1', at natural real GNP. But in the interim, unknown to everybody, the economy is "healing" itself: The *SRAS* curve is shifting to the right. Government officials don't see this yet because it takes time to collect and analyze data on the economy.

Thinking that the economy is not healing itself, or not healing itself quickly enough, Congress begins the process of enacting expansionary fiscal policy. In

EXHIBIT 10–5
Fiscal Policy May Destabilize the Economy

In this scenario, the *SRAS* curve is shifting rightward (healing the economy of its recessionary gap), but this information is unknown by policy makers. Policy makers implement expansionary fiscal policy, and the *AD* curve ends up intersecting *SRAS₂* at point 2 instead of *SRAS₁* at point 1'. Policy makers thereby move the economy into an inflationary gap, thus destabilizing the economy.

This is the objective.

Starting point.

This is where the economy ends up.

Recessionary Gap

Inflationary Gap

time, the *AD* curve shifts rightward. But by the time the increased demand is felt in the goods and services markets, the *AD* curve intersects the *SRAS* curve at point 2. In short, the government has moved the economy from point 1 to point 2, and not, as it had hoped, from point 1 to point 1'. The government has moved the economy into an inflationary gap. Instead of stabilizing and moderating the business cycle, it has intensified it.

Crowding Out, Lags, and the Effective–Ineffective Category

The issue of crowding out and lags may be placed in the effective–ineffective category (see Chapter 5). Specifically, those economists who believe crowding out is zero and that the lags are insignificant conclude that fiscal policy is *effective* at moving the economy out of a recessionary gap. Those economists who believe crowding out is complete and/or that the lags are significant conclude that fiscal policy is *ineffective* at moving the economy out of a recessionary gap. Keynesians usually view fiscal policy as effective, and new classical economists usually view it as ineffective.

SUPPLY-SIDE FISCAL POLICY
■

Fiscal policy effects may be felt on the supply side as well as the demand side of the economy. For example, a reduction in tax rates may alter an individual's incentive to work and produce, thus altering aggregate supply. We discuss the relevant issues in this section.

Marginal Tax Rates and Aggregate Supply

When fiscal policy measures affect tax rates, they may affect the aggregate supply curve as well as the aggregate demand curve. Consider a reduction in an individ-

Interview: Alice Rivlin

Alice M. Rivlin was the director of the Congressional Budget Office (CBO) from its inception in 1973 until 1983. As such, she is an economist with extensive knowledge of the budget process. In 1985 Dr. Rivlin became the first woman to be elected president of the American Economic Association. She is currently at the Brookings Institution.

Dr. Rivlin, what is the role of the CBO in the budget process, and what is a typical workday like for the director?

The CBO is the informational and analytical arm of the congressional budget process. It provides information, analysis, and projections to the Congress as it considers budget alternatives. In a sense it is a counterpart to the Office of Management and Budget (OMB), which provides the president with the information, analysis, and projections that go into his budget proposals. It is different than the OMB in the sense that the CBO works for the Congress and therefore has to be a nonpartisan agency. It doesn't make recommendations to the Congress in the way that the OMB might make recommendations to the president. It always gives options and alternatives to the Congress to consider.

The director of the CBO spends part of the time directing the agency itself, considering what projections to make about the economic situation and the budget itself, reviewing reports the agency is going to put out, and interacting with the staff over the actual product. Part of the time the director spends explaining these things to the Congress and to the world at large. My time was spent in meetings with staff, in testimony before the Congress (when the Congress was in session I sometimes testified several times a week), and talking to other parts of the federal government, state and local governments, university groups, and others interested in the budget process.

What did you like best about being the director of the Congressional Budget Office?

I enjoyed having the chance to create an organization that makes high quality economic analyses available to political decision-makers. Policy decisions are always hard, but I believe the chances of good policy are improved by having the best analyses available of the consequences of alternative choices. That's what we tried to do at CBO.

From your discussions with members of Congress, which factor—politics or fiscal policy considerations—more sharply influences the size and composition of the budget?

I don't think most politicians make a sharp distinction in their minds between "politics" and "right fiscal policy" most of the time. Nor do I find it easy to make the distinction myself. Most politicians try to do what they think is in the national interest and especially in the interest of their constituents. They are very concerned with being perceived as "fair." In practice, most of them become persuaded that policies that especially benefit their areas are indeed good for the country, or are, at least, "fair." If they have defense industries in their district, they

become genuinely convinced of the need for a strong defense and the importance to that defense of the particular weapons produced in their district. If they have a large farming constituency, they become dedicated to the idea that the national interest involves strong support for farmers.

The fact that politicians tend to see the national interest in terms of what is good for their constituents does not strike me as a major problem. That is how representative democracy is supposed to work. The fact that political campaigns are heavily financed by private money, however, is a serious problem. It enhances the power of people and industries with strong economic interest and plenty of cash, often to the detriment of the rest of the population.

What is the major long-run consequence of running annual budget deficits?

If the government is using a large fraction of the nation's savings to finance the budget deficit, less is available to finance productive investment. It is possible to compensate by borrowing the savings of other countries, but this leaves us indebted to them. In the long run, persistent federal deficits cut domestic investment and reduce the future standard of living.

Occasionally you are on television answering economic questions for members of the press. Are you impressed or disappointed in the press's knowledge of economics?

Many reporters are knowledgeable about economics—and some are not—but television coverage of economic matters seems to be extremely poor. The networks apparently assume that most people find economics boring and can only tolerate a 30 second sound byte, not a full explanation of what is happening. The networks also like to feature economists with extreme views and tend to neglect the more sensible middle-of-the-road views of the bulk of the profession. In general, I believe the major newspapers do a much better job than the television networks of explaining economic issues.

What are the consequences of economic illiteracy on the individual's level? on society's level?

Individuals who fail to master the rudiments of economics increase the chances that they will make bad economic decisions themselves—about careers, purchases, investments, retirement plans, and so on. If a large part of

the public is illiterate about economic issues, it is much harder for the political system to make constructive decisions about economic policy. The federal deficit persists, for example, because most people do not understand why it is so important for the future of the country to get it down.

What got you interested in economics?

My interest in economics grew out of concern for improving public policy, both domestic and international. I was a teenager in the tremendously idealistic period after World War II when it seemed terribly important to get nations

working together to solve the world's problems peacefully. I was initially interested in foreign aid, economic development in poorer countries, and facilitating international trade generally.

My interest shifted later to the domestic economy, but never away from public policy issues. My interest in economics has always revolved around such issues as: how to make the tax system fairer; how to make the economy more productive; how to make the education and health systems work better, and so on.

Marginal Tax Rate
The change in a person's tax payment divided by a change in the person's taxable income: Δtax payment/Δtaxable income.

ual's marginal income tax rate. The **marginal tax rate** is equal to the change in a person's tax payment divided by a change in the person's taxable income: Δtax payment/Δtaxable income.

For example, if Smith's taxable income increases by $1, and her tax payment increases by $.40, her marginal tax rate is 40 percent; if her taxable income increases by $1, and her tax payment increases by $.28, then her marginal tax rate is 28 percent. All other things held constant, lower marginal tax rates increase the incentive to engage in productive activities (work) relative to leisure and tax-avoidance activities. As resources shift from the latter to the former, short-run aggregate supply increases. If the lower marginal tax rates are permanent, and not simply a one-shot affair, most economists predict that not only will the short-run aggregate supply curve shift rightward but the long-run aggregate supply curve will shift rightward, too. In Exhibit 10–6, we illustrate the predicted effect of a permanent marginal tax rate cut on aggregate supply.

Question:

Why would individuals want to work more and take less leisure if marginal tax rates were reduced? It seems that they would probably want to do the opposite. After all, with lower marginal tax rates, individuals will be left with higher disposable incomes and therefore will have less need to work.

Answer:

What we actually have here are two forces, pulling in opposite directions. Given a cut in marginal tax rates, two things will happen: (1) Individuals will have more disposable income. (2) The amount of money they can earn (and keep) by working increases. As a result of effect 2, individuals will choose to work more (would you want to work more or fewer hours if you could keep 90 cents out of every dollar earned as opposed to, say, 50 cents out of every dollar earned?). As a result of effect 1, individuals will choose to work less. Overall, what happens on net, whether an individual works more or less, depends on whether effect 1 or effect

EXHIBIT 10–6
The Predicted Effect of a Permanent Marginal Tax Rate Cut on Aggregate Supply Only

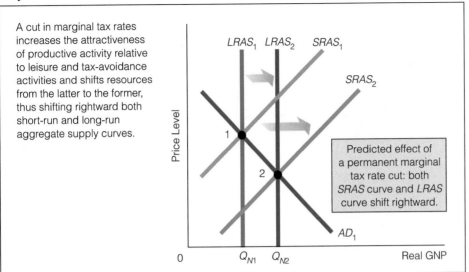

A cut in marginal tax rates increases the attractiveness of productive activity relative to leisure and tax-avoidance activities and shifts resources from the latter to the former, thus shifting rightward both short-run and long-run aggregate supply curves.

Predicted effect of a permanent marginal tax rate cut: both *SRAS* curve and *LRAS* curve shift rightward.

2 is stronger. If effect 2 is stronger than effect 1, the individual (on net) will work more; if effect 1 is stronger than effect 2, the individual will (on net) work less. In the analysis of marginal tax rates and aggregate supply, we implicitly assumed that in the aggregate, a marginal tax rate cut (on net) increases work activity.[5]

The Laffer Curve: Tax Rates and Tax Returns

If (marginal) income tax rates were reduced, would income tax revenues increase or decrease? Most people think the answer is obvious—lower tax rates mean lower tax revenues. The economist Arthur Laffer explained why this may not be the case.

As the story is told, Arthur Laffer, while dining with a journalist at a restaurant in Washington, D.C., drew the curve in Exhibit 10–7 on a napkin. The curve came to be known as the **Laffer curve.** Laffer's objective was to explain the different possible relationships between tax rates and tax revenues.

In the exhibit, tax revenues are on the horizontal axis and tax rates are on the vertical axis. Laffer made three major points using the curve:

1. There are two (marginal) tax rates at which zero tax revenues are collected—0 and 100 percent. Obviously, no tax revenues will be raised if the tax rate is zero, and if the tax rate is 100 percent, no one would work and earn income if the entire amount was to be taxed away.

2. An increase in tax rates could cause an increase in tax revenues. For example, an increase in tax rates from X percent to Y percent will increase tax revenues from T_X to T_Y.

3. A decrease in tax rates could cause an increase in tax revenues. For example, a decrease in tax rates from Z percent to Y percent will increase tax revenues from T_Z to T_Y. This was the point that brought public attention to the Laffer curve.

[5]Students of microeconomics will recognize "effect 1" as the *income effect* and "effect 2" as the *substitution effect.*

Laffer Curve
The curve, named after Arthur Laffer, that shows the relationship between tax rates and tax revenues. According to the Laffer curve, as tax rates rise from zero, tax revenues rise, reach a maximum at some point, and then fall with further increases in tax rates.

EXHIBIT 10–7
The Laffer Curve

When the tax rate is either 0 or 100 percent, tax revenues are zero. Starting from a zero tax rate, increases in tax rates first increase (region A to B) and then decrease (region B to C) tax revenues. Starting from a 100 percent tax rate, decreases in tax rates first increase (region C to B) and then decrease (region B to A) tax revenues. This suggests there is some tax rate that maximizes tax revenues.

B to C: Tax rate and tax revenues inversely related.

Laffer Curve

A to B: Tax rate and tax revenues directly related.

How is it that at different times both an increase in tax rates and a decrease in tax rates can increase tax revenues? This can happen because of the interrelationship of tax rates, the **tax base,** and tax revenues.

Tax revenues equal the tax base times the (average) tax rate.[6]

$$\text{Tax revenues} = \text{tax base} \times \text{(average) tax rate}$$

For example, a tax rate of 20 percent multiplied by a tax base of $100 billion generates $20 billion tax revenues.

Now, obviously, tax revenues are a function of two variables: the tax rate and the tax base. Whether tax revenues increase or decrease as the average tax rate is lowered depends on whether the tax base expands by a greater or lesser percentage than the percentage reduction in the tax rate. Exhibit 10–8 illustrates the point.

We start with a tax rate of 20 percent, a tax base of $100 billion, and tax revenues of $20 billion. We assume that as the tax rate is reduced, the tax base expands:

Tax Base
When referring to income taxes, the total amount of taxable income. The (average) tax rate × tax base = tax revenues.

[6]First, the average tax rate is equal to an individual's tax payment divided by his or her taxable income (tax payment/taxable income). Second, a lower average tax rate requires a lower marginal tax rate. This follows from the average–marginal rule, which says that if the marginal magnitude is below the average magnitude, then the average is pulled down; and if the marginal is above the average, the average is pulled up. Simply put, if an individual pays less tax on an additional taxable dollar (which is evidence of a marginal tax rate reduction), then his or her average tax rate naturally falls.

EXHIBIT 10–8
Tax Rates, the Tax Base, and Tax Revenues
Tax revenues equal the tax base times the (average) tax rate. If the percentage reduction in the tax rate is greater than the percentage increase in the tax base, tax revenues decrease (Case 1); if the percentage reduction in the tax rate is less than the percentage increase in the tax base, tax revenues will increase (Case 2). All numbers are in billions of dollars unless otherwise noted.

	(1) TAX RATE	(2) TAX BASE	(3) TAX REVENUES (1) × (2)	SUMMARY	
Start with:	20%	$100	$20	—	
Case 1:	15	120	18	↓ Tax rate	↓ Tax revenues
Case 2:	15	150	22.5	↓ Tax rate	↑ Tax revenues

The rationale is that individuals work more, invest more, enter into more exchanges, and shelter less income from taxes at lower tax rates.

However, the real question is, How much does the tax base expand following the tax rate reduction? Suppose the tax rate in Exhibit 10–8 is reduced to 15 percent. In Case 1, this increases the tax base to $120 billion: A 25 percent decrease in the tax rate (from 20 to 15 percent) brings on a 20 percent increase in the tax base (from $100 billion to $120 billion). Tax revenues drop to $18 billion.

In Case 2, the tax base expands by 50 percent to $150 billion. Since the tax base increases by a greater percentage than the percentage decrease in the tax rate, tax revenues increase (to $22.5 billion).

Of course, either case is possible. In the Laffer curve, tax revenues increase if a tax rate reduction is made in the downward-sloping portion of the curve (between points *C* and *B*); tax revenues decrease following a tax rate reduction in the upward-sloping portion of the curve (between points *A* and *B*).

Question:

Suppose a country's income tax rate is 30 percent. Would it follow that a reduction in the tax rate to 25 percent would increase tax revenues?

Answer:

It would depend on whether the 30 percent tax rate was in the downward-sloping portion of the Laffer curve (between points *C* and *B* in Exhibit 10–7) or in the upward-sloping portion (between points *A* and *B*). If the former, then tax revenues would increase; if the latter, then tax revenues would decrease. This is largely an empirical issue. We say "largely" because most economists believe it is obvious that a tax rate reduction from an extreme 100 percent to some lower rate will increase tax revenues.

Contrast the way economist Laffer thinks about a tax cut with the way the layperson thinks about it. As we said earlier, the layperson probably believes that a reduction in tax rates brings a reduction in tax revenues. The layperson is focused on the "arithmetic" of the situation. Laffer, however, is focused on the economic incentives. He asks, What does a lower tax rate imply in terms of a person's incentive to engage in productive activity? How does a lower tax rate affect one's tradeoff between work and leisure?

The layperson likely sees only the "arithmetic" effect of a tax cut; the economist sees the incentive effect.

Fiscal Policy: General Remarks

■ Fiscal policy refers to changes in government expenditures and taxation to achieve particular macroeconomic goals. Fiscal policy falls into one of four categories: discretionary expansionary, discretionary contractionary, automatic expansionary, and automatic contractionary.

■ The old-time fiscal religion emphasized balanced budgets except during wartime. The new fiscal religion advised the use of budget deficits and budget surpluses to help smooth out the business cycle.

■ Discretionary fiscal policy may be favored by those who favor big government, as well as by those who favor small government. An advocate of small government will favor reductions in taxes and in government spending as expansionary and contractionary fiscal policy measures, respectively. An advocate of big government will favor increases in government spending and in taxes as expansionary and contractionary fiscal policy measures, respectively.

Fiscal Policy in Keynesian Theory

■ In Keynesian theory, a change in government spending will change real GNP by more than an equal change in taxes. The relevant formulas are (1) $\Delta Q = m \times \Delta G$, where m = multiplier; and (2) $\Delta Q = -MPC(m) \times \Delta T$.

■ The balanced budget theorem holds that a change in real GNP is equal to the change in government spending when government spending and taxes change by the same dollar amount and in the same direction. For example, if government spending increases by $5 billion, and taxes are raised $5 billion, real GNP is predicted to increase by $5 billion.

Crowding Out

■ Crowding out refers to the decrease in private expenditures that occurs as a consequence of increased government spending and/or the greater financing needs of the budget deficit. The crowding-out effect suggests that discretionary expansionary fiscal policy does not work to the degree that Keynesian theory predicts.

■ Complete (incomplete) crowding out occurs when the decrease in one or more components of spending completely (partially) offsets the increase in government spending.

■ New classical economists argue that crowding out occurs when individuals decrease consumption spending in order to increase saving to pay the higher future taxes brought on by debt financing of the deficit.

Supply-Side Fiscal Policy

■ When fiscal policy measures affect tax rates, they may affect the aggregate supply curve as well as the aggregate demand curve. It is generally accepted that a marginal tax rate reduction increases the attractiveness of work relative to leisure and tax-avoidance activities, and thus leads to an increase in aggregate supply.

■ Tax revenues equal the tax base multiplied by the (average) tax rate. Whether tax revenues decrease or increase as a result of a tax rate reduction depends on whether the percentage increase in the tax base is greater or lesser than the percentage reduction in the tax rate. If the percentage increase in the tax base is greater than the percentage reduction in the tax rate, then tax revenues will increase. If the percentage increase in the tax base is less than the percentage reduction in the tax rate, then tax revenues will decrease.

Key Terms and Concepts

Budget Deficit

Budget Surplus

Balanced Budget

Fiscal Policy

Expansionary Fiscal
    Policy

Contractionary Fiscal
    Policy

Discretionary Fiscal
    Policy

Automatic Fiscal Policy

Balanced Budget
    Theorem

Crowding Out

Complete Crowding Out

Incomplete Crowding
    Out

Trade Deficit

Marginal Tax Rate

Tax Base

Laffer Curve

QUESTIONS AND PROBLEMS

1. Explain three ways crowding out may occur.

2. Why is crowding out an important issue in the debate over the use of discretionary fiscal policy?

 3. Some economists argue for the use of discretionary fiscal policy to solve economic problems; some argue against its use. What are some of the arguments on both sides?

 4. Assume $MPC = .80$ and that taxes are cut by \$4 billion and government spending is increased by \$7 billion. By what dollar amount will Keynesian economists predict real GNP will increase?

5. The debate over using government spending and taxing powers to stabilize the economy involves more than technical economic issues. Do you agree or disagree? Explain your answer.

6. The Laffer curve, which shows (among other things) that a tax rate reduction can increase tax revenues, became very popular and was widely cited a couple of years before, during, and for a few years after the presidential election of 1980. Why do you think this happened?

7. Is crowding out equally likely under all economic conditions? Explain your answer.

8. Tax cuts will likely affect aggregate demand and aggregate supply. Does it matter which is affected more? Explain in terms of the *AD–AS* framework.

9. Explain how a growing federal budget deficit may lead to a growing trade deficit.

10. What does complete crowding out imply about the value of the multiplier? Explain your answer.

11. Assume $MPC = .75$ and that taxes are raised by \$5 billion and government spending is decreased by \$12 billion. By what dollar amount will Keynesian economists predict real GNP will decrease?

FISCAL POLICY IN AN OPEN ECONOMY: INTERNATIONAL EFFECTS AND DOMESTIC FEEDBACKS

A budget deficit may have both (1) domestic effects and (2) international effects that feed back into the domestic economy. Consider each alone:

Domestic Effects

The domestic effects were outlined in this chapter in our discussion of Keynesian theory and expansionary fiscal policy. Here we saw that Keynesians (assuming zero crowding out) believed expansionary fiscal policy increased aggregate demand (see Exhibit 10–2a).

International Feedback Effects on the Domestic Economy

Here is an example. Start with a budget deficit. Suppose the Congress then adds an additional spending program and maintains everything else at status quo. As a result—one more spending program, no fewer spending programs, and no more taxes—the budget deficit grows. To finance the growing budget deficit, the U.S. Treasury borrows more funds in the credit or loanable funds market than it would have had to borrow if the latest spending program had not been passed. The increased demand for loanable funds raises the real interest rate. The higher U.S. interest rate attracts foreign capital. The demand for dollars in the foreign exchange market rises, and the dollar appreciates. Dollar appreciation has two effects: one relates to aggregate demand, the other to aggregate supply.

1. Aggregate Demand. As the dollar appreciates, foreign goods become cheaper; thus, Americans increase their purchases of imported goods and foreigners (whose currency has depreciated) cut back on their purchases of U.S. exported goods.[7] If exports fall and imports rise, net imports decrease and so do total expenditures. As we learned in Chapter 8, at a given price level, a decline in total expenditures causes the AD curve to shift leftward.

2. Aggregate Supply. American producers not only buy resources or inputs from other Americans but they buy resources from foreigners, too. When the price of foreign resources falls, this leads to a rightward shift in the SRAS curve. Dollar appreciation causes foreign resource prices to drop (just as when the dollar appreciates, foreign goods become cheaper). So, dollar appreciation causes the SRAS curve to shift rightward.

Now, suppose the U.S. AD curve shifts leftward by more than the SRAS curve shifts rightward, which most economists believe happens as a result of dollar appreciation. The result is said to be a decline in real GNP.

Domestic Effects and International Feedback Effects Together

So we have this situation: (1) The rising budget deficit affects the domestic economy directly and pushes real GNP upward; but (2) increased deficit financing raises U.S. real interest rates and prompts increased foreign capital inflows, an increased demand for dollars, and dollar appreciation; and, under typical conditions, an appreciated dollar feeds back into the domestic economy and pushes real GNP downward. Obviously, what happens on net depends on how strong the international feedback effects are on the domestic economy. Are they strong enough to offset the initial expansionary push in real GNP?

Even if the international feedback effects on the domestic economy do not outweigh the initial expansionary push in real GNP, and real GNP rises on net, still

[7]This was discussed in Chapter 9.

EXHIBIT 10E–1
Expansionary Fiscal Policy in Open and Closed Economies

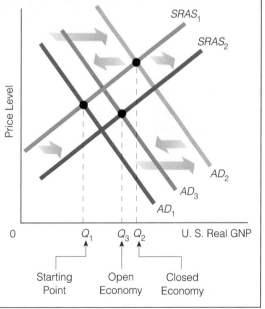

Expansionary fiscal policy raises real GNP more in a closed economy than in an open economy. For example, expansionary fiscal policy (in Keynesian theory) shifts the AD curve from AD_1 to AD_2. Because of the higher real interest rates, increased foreign capital inflows, and dollar appreciation, the AD curve shifts leftward from AD_2 to AD_3, and the SRAS curve shifts rightward from $SRAS_1$ to $SRAS_2$. In a closed economy, real GNP ends up at a lower level, Q_3.

Closed Economy
An economy that does not trade goods and services with other nations.

Open Economy
An economy that trades goods and services with other nations.

we can conclude that expansionary fiscal policy raises real GNP more in a **closed economy** than in an **open economy.** This is because in a closed economy the international feedback effects that reduce real GNP (see point 2) are absent.

Exhibit 10E–1 illustrates our point. In the Keynesian theory, expansionary fiscal policy shifts the aggregate demand curve from AD_1 to AD_2. But because of the higher real interest rates, increased foreign capital inflows, and dollar appreciation, the AD curve shifts leftward from AD_2 to AD_3, and the $SRAS$ curve shifts rightward from $SRAS_1$ to $SRAS_2$. In a closed economy, real GNP rises from Q_1 to Q_2. In an open economy, where international feedback effects play a role, real GNP ends up at a lower level, Q_3.

APPENDIX SUMMARY

The rising budget deficit affects the domestic economy directly and pushes real GNP upward; but increased deficit financing raises U.S. real interest rates and prompts increased foreign capital inflows, an increased demand for dollars, and dollar appreciation; and, under typical conditions, an appreciated dollar feeds back into the domestic economy and pushes real GNP downward. What happens on net depends on how strong the international feedback effects are on the domestic economy. If the international feedback effects outweigh the domestic effects, real GNP declines. If the domestic effects outweigh the international feedback effects, real GNP rises. Even if the domestic effects outweigh the international feedback effects, still real GNP will rise by a smaller amount in an open economy than in a closed economy.

QUESTIONS AND PROBLEMS

1. Explain how a rising budget deficit can cause the dollar to appreciate.
2. Explain how an appreciated dollar affects the AD curve.
3. Explain how an appreciated dollar affects the $SRAS$ curve.
4. Explain why fiscal policy is more expansionary in a closed economy than in an open economy.
5. Diagrammatically represent an economy where the international feedback effects of fiscal policy outweigh the domestic effects of fiscal policy.

MONEY, MACROECONOMIC THEORY, AND MONETARY POLICY

MONEY AND BANKING

WHAT THIS CHAPTER IS ABOUT

In our study of macroeconomics so far, we have focused on three variables: the price level (*P*), real GNP (*Q*), and the unemployment rate. Many economists believe that in order to understand why these variables change, it is important to understand money. We begin our discussion of money in this chapter, and continue to examine the topic in Chapters 12–15.

MONEY: WHAT IS IT, AND HOW DID IT COME TO BE?

Money is any good that is widely accepted for purposes of exchange.

The story of money starts with a definition and a history lesson. In this section, we discuss what money is and isn't (the definition) and how money came to be (the history lesson).

Money: A Definition

To the layperson, the words *income, credit,* and *wealth* are synonyms for *money.* In each of the next three sentences, the word *money* is used incorrectly; the word in parentheses is the word an economist would use.

1. "How much money (income) did you earn last year?"
2. "Most of her money (wealth) is tied up in real estate."
3. "It sure is difficult to get much money (credit) in today's tight mortgage market."

In economics, the words *money, income, credit,* and *wealth* are not synonyms. The most general definition of **money** is any good that is widely accepted for purposes of exchange (payment for goods and services).

Three Functions of Money

Money has three major functions. It functions as a medium of exchange, unit of account, and store of value.

Money As a Medium of Exchange. If there were no money, goods would have to be exchanged by **barter.** Suppose you wanted a shirt. You would have to trade some good in your possession, say, a jackknife, for the shirt. This would require you to locate a person who has a shirt *and* wants to trade it for a knife. In a money economy, this is not necessary. You can simply (1) exchange money for a shirt or (2) exchange the knife for money and then the money for the shirt. The buyer of the knife and the seller of the shirt do not have to be the same person. Money is the medium through which exchange occurs; hence, it is a **medium of exchange.** As such, money reduces the **transaction costs** of making exchanges. Exchange is easier and less time consuming in a money economy than in a barter economy.

Money As a Unit of Account. A **unit of account** is a common measurement in which values are expressed. Consider a barter economy. The value of *every* good is expressed in terms of *all other* goods. For example, one horse might equal 100 bushels of wheat, or 200 bushels of apples, or 20 pairs of shoes, or 10 suits, or 55 loaves of bread, and so on. This is not the case in a money economy. Here a person doesn't have to know what an apple's price is in terms of oranges, pizzas, chickens, or potato chips, as would be the case in a barter economy. He or she only needs to know the price in terms of money. And since all goods are denominated in money, determining relative prices is easy and quick. For example, if 1 apple is $1 and 1 orange is 50 cents, then 1 apple = 2 oranges.

Money As a Store of Value. The **store of value** function refers to a good's ability to maintain its value over time. This is the least exclusive function of money, since other goods—such as paintings, houses, and stamps—can do this, too. There have been times when money has not maintained its value well—for example, during high inflationary periods. For the most part, though, money has served as a satisfactory store of value. This allows us to accept payment in money for our pro-

Money
Any good that is widely accepted for purposes of exchange.

Barter
Exchanging goods and services for other goods and services without the use of money.

Medium of Exchange
Anything that is generally acceptable in exchange for goods and services. A function of money.

Transaction Costs
The costs associated with the time and effort needed to search out, negotiate, and consummate an exchange.

Unit of Account
A common measurement in which relative values are expressed. A function of money.

Store of Value
The ability of an item to hold value over time. A function of money.

250

ductive efforts and to hold on to that money until we decide how we want to spend it.

From a Barter to a Money Economy: The Origins of Money

At one time, there was trade but no money. Instead, there was barter. An apple would trade for two eggs, a banana for a peach.

Today we live in a money economy. How did we move from a barter to a money economy? Did some king or queen issue the edict "Let there be money"? Not likely. Money evolved in a much more natural, market-oriented manner.

Making exchanges takes longer (on average) in a barter economy than in a money economy. Suppose Smith wants to trade apples for oranges. He locates Jones who has oranges. Smith offers to trade apples for oranges, but Jones tells Smith that she does not like apples, she would rather have peaches.

In this situation Smith must either (1) find someone who has oranges and wants to trade oranges for apples or (2) find someone who has peaches and wants to trade peaches for apples, after which he must return to Jones and trade peaches for oranges.

Suppose Smith continues to search and finds Brown, who has oranges and wants to trade oranges for (Smith's) apples. In economics terminology, Smith and Brown are said to have a **double coincidence of wants.** Two people have a double coincidence of wants if what the first person wants is what the second person has and what the second person wants is what the first person has. A double coincidence of wants is a necessary condition for trade to take place.

Double Coincidence of Wants
In a barter economy, a requirement that must be met before a trade can be made. It specifies that a trader must find another trader who is willing to trade what the first trader wants and at the same time wants what the first trader has.

Now in a barter economy some goods are more readily accepted in exchange than other goods. This may originally have been the result of chance, but after traders notice the difference, their behavior tends to reinforce the effect. Suppose there are ten goods, A–J, and that good G is the most marketable of the ten. On average, good G is accepted 5 out of every 10 times it is offered in an exchange, while the remaining goods are accepted, on average, only 2 out of every 10 times. Given this difference, some individuals accept good G *simply because of its relatively greater marketability,* even if they have no plans to consume it. They accept good G because they know that it can be easily traded for most other goods at a later time (unlike the item originally in their possession).

The effect snowballs. The more people who come to accept good G for its relatively greater marketability, the greater its relative marketability becomes, which in turn causes more people to agree to accept it. This is how money evolved. Once the process of accepting good G evolves to the point where good G is *widely accepted for purposes of exchange,* good G is *money.* Historically, goods that have evolved into money include gold, silver, copper, cattle, rocks, and shells.

Question:

Isn't money an invention of government? After all, didn't the kings and emperors of long ago stamp their likenesses on money?

Answer:

Kings and emperors might have stamped their likenesses on a certain form of money—coins—but neither kings nor emperors, nor any government, invented money. Money predates government. Money largely evolved out of the self-interested actions of individuals who were trying to reduce the time and effort it took to make exchanges in a barter economy.

What Gives Money Its Value?

In the days when the dollar was backed by gold, people would say that gold gave paper money its value. Very few ever asked, But what gives gold *its* value?

Today there is no gold backing for our money. Our money has value because of its *general acceptability*. For example, you accept the dollar bill in payment for your goods and services because you know others will accept the dollar bill in payment for their goods and services. It sounds odd, but think about it.

Suppose one day the grocery store clerk doesn't accept the paper dollars you have in your wallet as payment for the groceries you want to buy. Also, neither the plumber nor the gas station attendant accepts your paper dollars for fixing your kitchen drain or for gas. If this were to happen, would you be as likely to accept paper dollars in exchange for what you sell? We think not. You accept paper dollars because you know that other people will accept paper dollars later when you try to spend them. Money is valued by you, and by others, because it is widely accepted in exchange for other goods that are valuable.

DEFINING THE MONEY SUPPLY
■

Money is any good that is widely accepted for purposes of exchange. We now ask ourselves: Is a ten-dollar bill money? Is a dime money? Is a checking account or a savings account money? What is included in the term *money,* that is, in the money supply? We turn next to a discussion of two of the more frequently used definitions of the money supply, M1 and M2.

M1

M1
Includes currency held outside banks + demand deposits + other checkable deposits + traveler's checks.

Currency
Includes coins and paper money.

Federal Reserve Notes
Paper money issued by the Fed.

Demand Deposits
A deposit of funds that can be withdrawn without restrictions and is transferable by check.

Commercial Banks
Privately owned, profit-seeking institutions that offer a wide range of services (checking accounts, savings accounts, loans) to customers.

M1 is sometimes referred to as the narrow definition of the money supply. M1 consists of currency held outside banks, demand deposits, other checkable deposits, and traveler's checks.[1] **Currency** includes coins minted by the U.S. Treasury and paper money. About 99 percent of the paper money in circulation is **Federal Reserve Notes** issued by the Federal Reserve District Banks. (Look at the paper money you have in your possession. At the top it reads "Federal Reserve Note.")

Demand deposits are funds that we place or have in our *checking accounts.* They are deposits that can be withdrawn *on demand,* or made payable to a third party by writing a check. In essence, they are "checkbook money." **Commercial banks** are the sole issuers of demand deposits. Other checkable deposits besides demand deposits include NOW (negotiable order of withdrawal) accounts at banks, savings banks, and savings and loan associations, and CUSD (credit union share draft) accounts.[2] M1 also includes traveler's checks.

M1 = currency outside banks + demand deposits + other checkable deposits + traveler's checks

Of the four major components of M1, the other checkable deposits component is the largest. For example, in 1990, demand deposits equaled $277.5 billion, other

[1]"Currency held outside banks" may sound awkward, but think of it this way: Say there is a total of $200 billion worth of currency. Some of this currency is in bank vaults ("currency inside banks") and some of this currency is in the wallets of people ("currency outside banks"). In short, currency has to be in one of two places: inside or outside a bank. M1 only takes into account that currency which is outside banks. We explain the reason for this distinction later.

[2]NOW accounts are interest-earning accounts on which checks can be written; CUSD accounts are similar to NOW accounts but are held by credit union members.

checkable deposits equaled $293.8 billion, and currency held outside banks equaled $245.9 billion. Traveler's checks were $8.3 billion. M1, the sum of these figures, was $825.5 billion (Exhibit 11–1). Exhibit 11–2 gives M1 figures between 1980 and 1990.

Question:

Listening to the news, one may hear that the money supply has increased by, say, 4 percent on an annual basis. Is the news broadcast referring to the growth in M1 when it refers to the money supply?

Answer:

Most of the time it is. Sometimes the news commentator will even use the term *M1*. There are, however, other major money supply figures that are sometimes mentioned. The most common of these is M2. This alternative measure of the money supply is introduced next.

EXHIBIT 11–1
The Components of M1

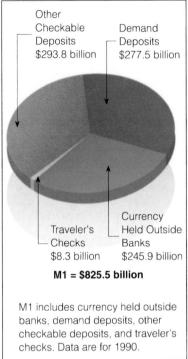

M1 = $825.5 billion

M1 includes currency held outside banks, demand deposits, other checkable deposits, and traveler's checks. Data are for 1990.

Source: Board of Governors of the Federal Reserve System.

EXHIBIT 11–2
M1 and M2, 1980–90

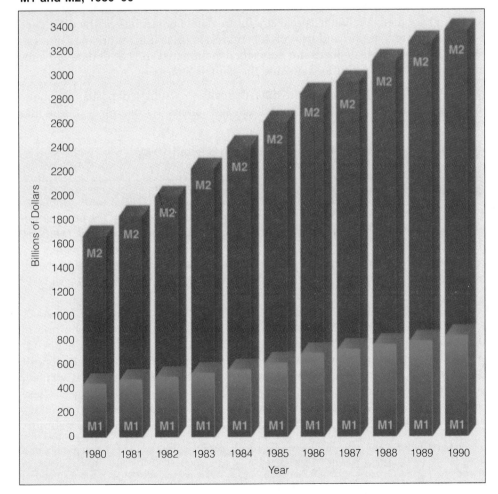

M2

M2 is sometimes referred to as the (most common) broad definition of the money supply. M2 is made up of M1 plus small-denomination time deposits, savings deposits, money market accounts, overnight repurchase agreements, and overnight Eurodollar deposits held by U.S. residents. **Time deposits** are interest-earning deposits with a specified maturity date that are subject to penalties for early withdrawal. "Small-denomination" time deposits are deposits of less than $100,000. Small-denomination time deposits are ordinarily the largest component of M2.

A **savings deposit** is a type of time deposit because in principle, although not always in practice, the depositor can be required to give advance written notice prior to withdrawal. Other than such notice, a savings deposit has no stipulated date of maturity.

Money market accounts with banks (called money market deposit accounts, MMDA) or with mutual fund companies (called money market mutual fund accounts, MMMF) are accounts that pay interest and offer limited check-writing privileges (privileges may be limited by restricting the number of checks or setting a minimum check denomination that may be written). Money market mutual funds invest in short-term, highly **liquid assets.**

Overnight repurchase agreements consist of an agreement by a financial institution to sell short-term securities to its customers, combined with an agreement to repurchase them at a higher price at a future date. For customers, the difference between the purchase price (lower price) and resale price (higher price) is interest. **Overnight Eurodollar deposits** are deposits denominated in U.S. dollars at banks and other financial institutions outside the United States.

M2 = M1 + small-denomination time deposits + savings deposits + money market accounts + overnight repurchase agreements + overnight Eurodollar deposits

Refer to Exhibit 11–2 for M2 figures between 1980 and 1990.[3]

Question:

Earlier it was said that money is any good that is widely accepted for purposes of exchange. It is easy to see how currency, a check written on a local bank (demand deposit), and a traveler's check would fit this definition, since all are widely accepted for purposes of exchange. But a person cannot go into a store and buy what he wants with a savings deposit. Why, then, count it as part of the money supply?

Answer:

First, a savings deposit is *not* counted in the most basic, or narrow, definition of the money supply, M1. Instead it is counted in M2. Many economists believe it should be part of the money supply, broadly defined, because a savings deposit can be turned into currency without incurring appreciable costs. If you wanted, you could turn your savings account into currency in just a short time. These economists thus see a difference in *degree,* but not in *substance,* between a savings deposit and currency. They think it should be counted as part of the money supply,

---

[3]Besides M1 and M2, there are two other money supply definitions, M3 and L. M3 includes M2 plus larger time deposits ($100,000 or more), term repurchase agreements, and Eurodollar deposits (these are longer-term repurchase agreements and Eurodollar deposits than are included in M2), and institutional money market mutual funds. L consists of short-term Treasury securities, commercial paper, savings bonds, and bankers' acceptances. In 1989, figures for M3 and L were $4,044.3 billion and $4,881.2 billion, respectively.

if only in M2 and not in M1. By the way, some economists speak of M1 as money and some components of M2 and other broader measures of the money supply as *near monies*. The language of "money" and "near money" addresses the point raised in the question.

Where Do Credit Cards Fit In?

Credit cards are commonly referred to as money—plastic money. But they are not money. A credit card is an instrument or document that makes it easier for the holder to obtain a loan. When Tina Ridges hands the department store clerk her MasterCard or Visa, she is, in effect, spending someone else's money (that already existed). The department store submits the claim to the bank, the bank pays the department store, and then the bank bills the holder of its credit card. By using her credit card, Tina has spent someone else's money and she ultimately must repay her credit card debt with money. These transactions shift around the existing quantity of money between various individuals and firms but do not change the total.

HOW BANKING DEVELOPED

■

Just as money evolved, so did banking. This section discusses the origins of banking. The discussion will shed some light on, and aid in our understanding of, modern banking.

The Early Bankers

Our money today is easy to carry and transport. But it was not always this way. For example, when money was principally gold coins, carrying it about was neither easy nor safe. First, gold is heavy. Second, transporting thousands of gold coins is an activity that can easily draw the attention of thieves. Individuals wanted to store their gold in a safe place. The person most individuals turned to was the goldsmith because he was already equipped with safe storage facilities. Goldsmiths were the first bankers. They took in other people's gold and stored it for them. To acknowledge that they held deposited gold, goldsmiths issued receipts called *warehouse receipts* to their customers.

Once people's confidence in the receipts had been established, they used the receipts to make payments in place of the gold itself (gold was not only inconvenient for customers to carry, it was also inconvenient for merchants to accept). In short, the paper warehouse receipts circulated as money. For instance, if Franklin wanted to buy something from Mason that was priced at 10 gold pieces, he might give his warehouse receipt to Mason instead of going to the goldsmith, obtaining the gold, and then delivering it to Mason. Using the receipts was easier than dealing with gold itself, for both Franklin and Mason.

At this stage of banking, warehouse receipts were fully backed by gold; they simply represented gold in storage. Goldsmiths later began to recognize that on an average day few people came to redeem their receipts for gold. Many individuals were simply trading the receipts for goods and seldom requested the gold that the receipts represented. In short, the receipts had become money, widely accepted for purposes of exchange.

Sensing opportunity, some goldsmiths began to lend out some of their customers' gold, thinking they could earn interest on the loans without defaulting on their pledge to redeem the warehouse receipts when presented. In most cases, the borrowers of the gold preferred warehouse receipts to the actual gold, and so the goldsmiths ended up writing out warehouse receipts beyond gold on deposit. The consequence of this lending activity was an increase in the money supply—measured in terms of gold and the paper warehouse receipts issued by the goldsmith-bankers. This was the beginning of **fractional reserve banking.** Under a fractional reserve system, banks create money by holding on reserve only a fraction of the money deposited with them and lending the remainder. Our modern-day banking system operates under a fractional reserve banking arrangement.

The Federal Reserve System

In the next chapter, we discuss the structure of **the Fed** (the popular name for the **Federal Reserve System**) and the tools it uses to change the money supply. Here we need only note that the Federal Reserve System is the central bank, which essentially is a bank's bank and has as its chief function to control the nation's money supply.

THE MONEY CREATION PROCESS
■

This section describes the important money supply process, specifically, how the banking system, working under a fractional reserve requirement, creates money.

The Bank's Reserves and More

Many banks have an account with the Fed, in much the same way that an individual has a checking account with a commercial bank. Economists refer to this account with the Fed as either a "reserve account" or "bank deposits at the Fed." Banks also have currency or cash in their vaults—simply called "vault cash"—on the bank premises.[4] If we add (1) bank deposits at the Fed and (2) the bank's vault cash, we get (total bank) **reserves.**

$$\text{Reserves} = \text{bank deposits at the Fed} + \text{vault cash}$$

For example, suppose someone walks into a bank and deposits $100,000 in cash. This $100,000 is added to the bank's vault cash; thus, it becomes part of the bank's *reserves*. Furthermore, if the bank previously had $2.4 million in its account with the Fed and zero dollars in vault cash, the $100,000 in vault cash brings the bank's total reserves to $2.5 million.

The Fed mandates that member commercial banks must hold a certain fraction of their deposits in reserve form (that is, in the form of a bank deposit at the Fed or as vault cash). This fraction, say, 1/10 or 10 percent, is called the **required reserve ratio (r).** The actual dollar amount of deposits held in reserve form is called **required reserves.**

$$\text{Required reserves} = r \times \text{demand deposits}$$

For example, assume that customers have deposited $10 million in a neighborhood bank. If the Fed mandates that a 10 percent reserve be maintained against total deposits, required reserves for the bank equal $1 million—.10 × $10 million = $1 million.

[4]Earlier we said that there is "currency outside banks" and "currency inside banks." Vault cash is "currency inside banks."

Fractional Reserve Banking
A banking arrangement that allows banks to hold reserves equal to only a fraction of their deposit liabilities.

The Federal Reserve System (the Fed)
The central bank of the United States.

Reserves
The sum of bank deposits at the Fed and vault cash.

Required-Reserve Ratio (r)
A percentage of each dollar deposited that must be held on reserve (at the Fed or in the bank's vault).

Required Reserves
The minimum amount of reserves a bank must hold against its deposits as mandated by the Fed.

The difference between a bank's (total) reserves and its required reserves is its **excess reserves.**

$$\text{Excess reserves} = \text{Reserves} - \text{Required reserves}$$

For example, if the bank's (total) reserves are $2.5 million, but its required reserves are $1 million, then it holds excess reserves of $1.5 million.

Banks make loans with excess reserves. If the bank uses the $1.5 million excess reserves to make loans, it earns interest income. If it does not make any loans, it does not earn interest income. Hence banks have an incentive to make loans.

The Banking System Creates Demand Deposits: The Money Expansion Process

The banks in the banking system are prohibited from printing their own currency. Nevertheless, *the banking system can create money by creating demand deposits,* which, as we learned earlier, are part of the money supply.[5] Here is how this happens.

We start the process with Fred (his name rhymes with Fed), who has the ability to snap his fingers and create, out of thin air, $1,000. One day he snaps his fingers and does just this. He instantly deposits the newly created $1,000 into an account at Bank A. We can see this transaction in the following **T-account.** A T-account is a simplified balance sheet that records the *changes* in the bank's assets and liabilities.

BANK A

Assets		Liabilities	
Reserves	+ $1,000	Demand deposits	+ $1,000

Because the deposit initially is added to vault cash, the bank's reserves have increased by $1,000. The bank's demand deposit liabilities also have increased by $1,000.

Next, the banker divides the $1,000 reserves into two categories: required reserves and excess reserves. As previously stated, the amount of required reserves depends on the required-reserve ratio specified by the Fed. We'll set the required-reserve ratio at 10 percent. This means the bank is required to hold $100 in reserves against the deposit, and is holding an additional $900 in excess reserves. The previous T-account can be modified to show this:

BANK A

Assets		Liabilities	
Required reserves	+ $100	Demand deposits	+ $1,000
Excess reserves	+ $900		

On the left-hand side of the T-account, we have a total of $1,000, and on the right-hand side we also have a total of $1,000. By dividing total reserves into "required" and "excess," we can see how many dollars the bank is holding over and above the Fed requirements. These excess reserves can be used to make new loans.

Suppose that Bank A makes a loan of $900 to Jenny Johnson. The left-hand side (assets side) of the bank's T-account looks like this:

[5]When we use the term *money supply,* we are referring to M1.

Excess Reserves
Any reserves held beyond the required amount. The difference between total reserves and required reserves.

T-Account
A simplified balance sheet that shows the changes in a bank's assets and liabilities.

BANK A

Assets		Liabilities
Required reserves	+$100	See the next T-account.
Excess reserves	+$900	
Loans	+$900	

The dollars Jenny borrowed are placed in a (checking) account, shown in the bank's T-account by an increase in demand deposit liabilities of $900, as shown here:

BANK A

Assets	Liabilities	
See the previous T-account.	Demand deposits	+$1,000
	Demand deposits (Jenny Johnson)	+$ 900

Before we continue, notice that the money supply has increased. When Jenny Johnson borrowed $900 and the bank put that amount into her account, no one else in the economy had any less money and Jenny Johnson had more than before. Her new demand deposit is money. (Again, demand deposits are a part of M1.) Consequently, the money supply has increased.

Now suppose that Jenny spends the $900 on a new stereo. She writes a $900 check to the stereo retailer, who deposits the full amount of the check into Bank B. First, what happens to Bank A? It uses its excess reserves to honor Jenny Johnson's check when it is presented by Bank B, and simultaneously reduces her account balance by $900 to zero. Bank A's situation is shown here:

BANK A

Assets		Liabilities	
Required reserves	+$100	Demand deposits	+$1,000
Excess reserves	−$900	Demand deposits (Jenny Johnson)	−$900
Loans	+$900		

The situation for Bank B is different. Because of the stereo retailer's deposit, it now has $900 that it didn't have previously. This increases Bank B's reserves and demand deposit liabilities by $900:

BANK B

Assets		Liabilities	
Reserves	+$900	Demand deposits (stereo retailer)	+$900

Note that as a result of the stereo purchase there has been no change in the overall money supply. Dollars have moved from Jenny Johnson's checking account to the stereo seller's checking account.

The process continues in much the same way for Bank B as it did earlier for Bank A. Only a fraction (10 percent) of the retailer's $900 has to be kept on reserve (required reserves on $900 = $90), and the remainder constitutes excess reserves ($810), which can be lent to still another borrower. That loan will create $810 in new demand deposits and thus expand the money supply by that amount. The process continues with Banks C, D, E, and so on until the dollar figures become so small that things come to a halt. Exhibit 11–3 summarizes what happens as the $1,000 originally created by a snap of Fred's fingers works its way through the banking system.

Looking back over the entire process, this is what has happened.

■ Fred created $1,000 worth of money out of thin air and instantly deposited it into an account at Bank A.
■ The reserves of Bank A (a member of the banking system) increased. The reserves of no other bank decreased.
■ The banking system, with Fred's new $1,000 in hand, created demand deposits (created money).

We started with $1,000 in *new* funds deposited in Bank A, and that was the basis of several thousand dollars worth of new bank loans and demand deposits. In this instance, the $1,000 initially injected into the economy ultimately caused bankers to create $9,000 in demand deposits. When this amount is added to Fred's $1,000, we can see that the money supply has expanded by $10,000. A formula that shows how we arrive at this result is

$$\text{Maximum } \Delta DD = 1/r \times \Delta R$$

where ΔDD = the change in demand deposits; r = the required-reserve ratio; and

EXHIBIT 11–3
The Banking System Creates Demand Deposits (Money)
In this exhibit, the required-reserve ratio is 10 percent, and the simple deposit multiplier is 10 ($1/r$ = 1/.10 = 10). We have assumed that there is no cash leakage and that excess reserves are fully lent out; that is, banks hold zero excess reserves.

(1) BANK	(2) NEW DEPOSITS (new reserves)	(3) NEW REQUIRED RESERVES	(4) DEMAND DEPOSITS CREATED BY EXTENDING NEW LOANS (equal to new excess reserves)
A	$1,000.00	$100.00	$900.00
B	900.00	90.00	810.00
C	810.00	81.00	729.00
D	729.00	72.90	656.10
E	656.10	65.61	590.49
⋮	⋮	⋮	⋮
TOTALS (rounded)	$10,000	$1,000	$9,000

ΔR = the change in reserves resulting from the original injection of funds.[6] The arithmetic for this example is

$$\text{Maximum } \Delta DD = 1/.10 \times \$1,000$$
$$= 10 \times \$1,000$$
$$= \$10,000$$

Simple Deposit Multiplier
The reciprocal of the required-reserve ratio, $1/r$.

In the formula, $1/r$ is known as the **simple deposit multiplier.** It is the reciprocal of the required-reserve ratio (r).

$$\text{Simple deposit multiplier} = 1/r$$

Why Maximum? Answer: No Cash Leakages and Zero Excess Reserves

There are a few things to notice about the money expansion process. First, we implicitly assumed that all monies were deposited into bank checking accounts. For example, when Jenny Johnson wrote a check to the stereo retailer, the retailer endorsed the check and deposited the *full amount* into Bank B. In reality, the retailer might have deposited less than the full amount and kept a few dollars in cash balances. This is referred to as a **cash leakage.** If there had been a cash leakage of $300, then Bank B would not have received $900, but only $600. This would change the second number in column 2 in Exhibit 11–3 to $600 and the second number in column 4 to $540. Therefore, the totals in column 2 of Exhibit 11–3 would be much smaller. Reducing the flow of dollars into banks by a cash leakage means that banks have fewer dollars to lend. Fewer loans mean banks put less into borrowers' accounts, so less money is created than in the earlier case (when cash leakages = 0).

Cash Leakage
Occurs when funds are held as currency instead of being deposited into a checking account.

Second, it was also implicitly assumed that every bank lent out *all* its excess reserves, leaving every bank with zero excess reserves. Following Fred's $1,000 deposit, for example, Bank A had excess reserves of $900, and it made a new loan for the full amount. Banks generally want to loan out all of their excess reserves to earn additional interest income, but there is no law, natural or legislated, that says every bank has to lend out every penny of excess reserves. If banks do not lend all their excess reserves, then demand deposits and the money supply will increase by less than in the original situation (where banks did lend all their excess reserves).

Who Created What?

There were two major players in the demand deposit expansion process we described: (1) Fred and (2) the banking system. *Together* they created or expanded the money supply by $10,000. Fred *directly* created $1,000 and thus made it possible for banks to create $9,000 in demand deposits as a by-product of extending new loans. In short, Fred created money *out of thin air,* and the banking system created money *out of money.*

An easy formula for finding the maximum change in demand deposits (money

---

[6]Since only demand deposits, and no other component of the money supply, change in this example, we can rewrite "Maximum $\Delta DD = 1/r \times \Delta R$" as "Maximum $\Delta M = 1/r \times \Delta R$" where ΔM = the change in the money supply. In this chapter, the only component of the money supply that we allow to change is demand deposits. For this reason, we can talk about changes in demand deposits and the money supply as if they are the same—which they are, given our specification.

supply) *brought about by the banking system,* or the maximum change in demand deposits *after* the initial deposit of Fred's $1,000, is

$$\text{Maximum } \Delta DD \text{ (brought about by the banking system)} = 1/r \times \Delta ER$$

where ΔDD = the change in demand deposits; r = the required-reserve ratio; ΔER = the change in excess reserves of the first bank to receive the new injection of funds.[7]

The arithmetic here is

$$\text{Maximum } \Delta DD \text{ (brought about by the banking system)} = 1/.10 \times \$900 = 10 \times \$900 = \$9,000$$

Question:

What would have happened if Fred had decided to keep the original $1,000 in his pocket rather than depositing it in Bank A?

Answer:

If Fred had kept the money rather than depositing it, the process (of money expansion) would not have gone as described in Exhibit 11–3. For the money expansion process to continue as described, dollars must be deposited in checking accounts, and banks must extend loans. This process began once Fred had placed the $1,000 into his checking account.

It Works In Reverse: The "Money Destruction" Process

In the preceding example, Fred created $1,000 out of thin air and instantly deposited it into a demand deposit account at Bank A. This simple act created a multiple increase in demand deposits and the money supply. The process also works in reverse. Suppose Fred withdraws the $1,000 and destroys it with a snap of his fingers. As a result, bank reserves decline. The multiple deposit contraction process is symmetrical to the multiple deposit expansion process. This is what happens.

Again, we set the required-reserve ratio at 10 percent. The situation for Bank A looks like this:

BANK A

Assets		Liabilities	
Reserves	−$1,000	Demand deposits	−$1,000

Losing $1,000 in reserves places Bank A in a reserve deficiency position. Specifically, it is $900 short. Remember, Bank A held $100 reserves against the initial $1,000 deposit, so it loses $900 in reserves that backed other deposits ($1,000 − $100 = $900). The bank must take immediate action to correct this reserve deficiency. What can it do? One of the things it can do is to reduce its outstanding loans. Funds from loan repayments can be applied to the reserve deficiency *rather than being used to extend new loans.* As borrowers repay $900 worth of loans,

---

[7]Once again, since only demand deposits, and no other component of the money supply, change in this example, we can rewrite "Maximum ΔDD (brought about by the banking system)" as "Maximum ΔM (brought about by the banking system)."

they draw down their checking balances by that amount, causing the money supply to decline by $900.

Let's assume that the $900 loan repayment to Bank A is written on a check issued by Bank B. Once the check has cleared, reserves and customer deposits at Bank B fall by $900. This situation is reflected in Bank B's T-account.

BANK B

Assets		Liabilities	
Reserves	− $900	Demand deposits	− $900

Bank B now faces a situation similar to Bank A's earlier situation. Losing $900 in reserves places Bank B in reserve deficiency. It is $810 short. Remember, Bank B held $90 against the $900 deposit, so it loses $810 that backed other deposits ($900 − $90 = $810). Bank B seeks to recoup $810 by reducing its outstanding loans by an equal amount.

If a customer is asked to pay off an $810 loan and does so by writing a check on his account at Bank C, that bank's reserves and deposits both decline by $810. As a result, Bank C is now in reserve deficiency; it is $729 short. Remember, Bank C held $81 against the $810 deposit, so it is short $729 that backed other deposits ($810 − $81 = $729).

As you can see, the figures are exactly the same ones given in Exhibit 11–3, with the exception that each change is negative rather than positive. When Fred withdrew and destroyed the $1,000 (that he had earlier created and deposited), the money supply ended up declining by $10,000.

In Exhibit 11–4, we show the money supply expansion and contraction process in brief.

We Change Our Example: No More Fred

Let's change our example somewhat. This time there is no Fred. No such person exists; no one can snap his fingers and create $1,000, or any other amount, out of thin air. This time we speak about Jack, a mere mortal who does not possess the unusual talents of Fred. Jack cannot create money out of thin air.

EXHIBIT 11–4
The Money Supply Expansion and Contraction Processes

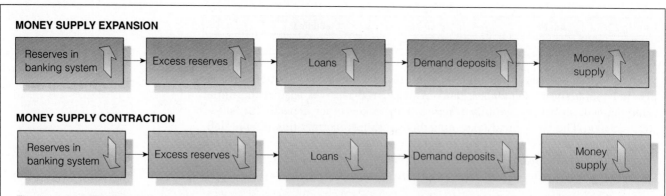

The money supply expands if reserves enter the banking system; the money supply contracts if reserves exit the banking system. In expansion, reserves rise, thus excess reserves rise, more loans are given out, and demand deposits rise. Since demand deposits are part of the money supply, the money supply rises. In contraction, reserves fall, thus excess reserves fall, fewer loans are given out, and demand deposits fall. Since demand deposits are part of the money supply, the money supply falls.

Suppose that Jack currently has $1,000 in cash in a shoebox in his bedroom. He decides that he doesn't want to keep this much cash around the house, so he takes it to Bank A and opens up a checking account. This act, as far as it has gone, does not change the money supply. Initially, the $1,000 in the shoebox was currency outside a bank, and thus part of the money supply. When Jack took the $1,000 from his shoebox and placed it in a bank, there was $1,000 *less* currency outside a bank and $1,000 *more* demand deposits. *So far,* this act has changed the *composition* of the money supply, not its *size.*

The $1,000 could not create a multiple of itself when it was in a shoebox in Jack's bedroom. However, once that $1,000 is placed in a checking account, the banking system has $1,000 more reserves than before, and thus has excess reserves that can be used to extend new loans. This means the money supply can expand in much the same way as we saw earlier. Recall that new demand deposits are created with each new loan. At maximum, the banking system can create $9,000 worth of new loans and demand deposits, just as in the Fred example. (We have assumed again that $r = .10$.) The primary difference between the two examples is where they began. Fred created $1,000 in new money, whereas banks created $9,000 by making new loans. Together they created $10,000. Jack deposited previously existing dollars—a transaction that does not directly affect the money supply—whereas banks used the new reserves to make $9,000 in new loans. In this case, the money supply increased by $9,000. Except for Fred's ability to create money, the two cases are identical.

Although we seldom notice, the money supply expands (as new loans are made) and contracts (as existing loans are paid off) every day. The "multiplier effect" is the result of a fractional reserve system of banking. Under fractional reserve banking, those who deposit cash in checking accounts maintain the same amount of money (both cash and demand deposits are money) and the bank where the cash is deposited has excess reserves that it can lend. Whatever funds the borrower receives is money also, so the money supply has increased. Further rounds of money expansion result when the loan is spent and funds are deposited in other banks.

Transferring Funds with a Push of a Button

Checks are useful instruments for transferring funds, but processing them generates a lot of paperwork that can be costly. It costs an estimated several billion dollars a year to process all the checks written in the United States (including losses due to bad checks). In recent years, check-processing costs have been going up relative to the costs of computer services, so many banks have begun to use the *electronic funds transfer system (EFTS)*—a system in which payments are made by electronic telecommunications.

Here's how the system works for a consumer. Suppose Jean goes into a store and decides to buy a pair of shoes priced at $50. Instead of paying cash or writing a check, Jean hands the shoe clerk her *debit card.* The debit card allows funds to be transferred out of Jean's bank account into the shoe store's account. The clerk runs the debit card through a desktop device much like the devices stores currently use to verify MasterCard and Visa purchases. The clerk enters the amount of Jean's purchase, and Jean enters her (secret) personal identification number (PIN). This permits Jean to access her checking account by remote terminal. She then commands a $50 fund transfer from her account to the store's account, probably at another bank. The operation takes a matter of seconds. As soon as the store has verified that the funds transfer has been completed, Jean leaves the store with her shoes.

The Savings and Loan Crisis

The story of the savings and loan crisis, which has made headlines in the past few years, can be told in two ways: in general terms of what happened and why and in terms of a specific person and institution. We'll tell it both ways. First, this is what happened and why.

A savings and loan, like a bank, accepts deposits from some people and lends the funds to others. For most of its history, the savings and loan industry, unlike the banking industry, has principally lent funds to home-buyers at a fixed interest rate. Also, for most of its history, it has lived under *Regulation Q,* which made it illegal for savings and loans to pay their depositers an interest rate higher than the stipulated interest rate ceiling mandated by government.

All went well for awhile. Then, in the 1970s, the inflation rate began to rise and savings and loans began to get squeezed. Money market mutual fund (MMMF) institutions, which were not under the jurisdiction of Regulation Q, began to proliferate and offer depositers higher rates of interest. Even though savings and loan depositers' deposits were insured by the federal government (up to $40,000 per account at the time), and MMMF deposits were not, still, for many people, the higher interest rates paid by the MMMFs made up for the difference (especially since MMMF money was largely "invested" in low-risk Treasury securities). Savings and loans began to lose deposits. Consequently, they had to borrow funds from other sources to avoid selling off their loans and other assets to repay depositers. Since these deposits cost savings and loans more interest than the interest they earned on mortgages and other assets, their profits were negative for the year. After a few years, the investments of savings and loan owners would be completely

dissipated and the savings and loan would be bankrupt.

Before that could happen, in 1982 Congress passed the Garn—St. Germain Act. Among the law's many provisions, savings and loans were given the right to invest in high risk ventures—quite unlike the home loans they were accustomed to making. To increase their earnings above interest expenses, many savings and loans became involved in speculative ventures about which their managers knew little. Faced with the prospect of failure, savings and loan owners were willing to bet their future on the possibility of large payoffs. Since depositors were insured—by this time up to $100,000 per account—they had little to lose from bad investments, and, as noted, savings and loan managers and owners had little chance of surviving without making radical changes in their way of doing business.

Against this background, many savings and loans began making loans to high risk oil exploration companies, commercial real estate, and other businesses. This was a kind of one-sided bet. Any profits they might earn would be theirs to keep; any loss would fall on taxpayers, who would have to repay depositors at failed savings and loans.

In any event, many of the high-risk, high-payoff ventures did not come through, and by the late 1980s, one-third of all the savings and loan institutions in the country were in financial trouble. The federal government had to offer a bailout that would end up costing American taxpayers between $200 to $400 billion.

Now consider the case of one individual and one savings and loan.[8] In

[8]Much of this story is from Martin Mayer's *The Greatest-Ever Bank Robbery: The Collapse of the Savings and Loan Industry* (New York: Charles Scribner's Sons, 1990).

June 1983, Ranbir Sahni, a former Air India pilot, acquired Tokay Savings and Loan Association, which was renamed American Diversified Savings Bank of Lodi, California. With capital requirements of only 3 percent of total assets, Sahni's American Diversified could own $100 million in assets. All Sahni had to do to get $100 million in assets was put up $3 million himself and then promise people that he would pay them a high interest rate if they would place their savings in his institution. At the time, American Diversified paid the highest return in the country, and the average account was $80,807, which was 10 times the average account in the average savings and loan. Between June 1983 and December 1985, American Diversified's assets increased from $11.7 million to $1.1 billion.

The money at American Diversified was "invested" in financial futures, options, stocks, shopping centers, condominiums, junk bonds, windmill farms, and a chicken farm (with which it was hoped chicken excrement could be processed into methane to power a new type of automobile).

In 1988, American Diversified was declared insolvent. Its losses totaled $800 million.

The Emerging Crisis in the Banking Industry

Between 1942 and 1980, 198 banks failed. In two years, 1989 and 1990, 362 banks failed. In the late-1980s and early-1990s, commercial banks began to fail in record numbers, causing some people to wonder if the banks would go the way of the savings and loans. What caused so many banks to fail at this time? Many economists argued that the problems in the banking industry were similar to the problems in the savings and loan industry: inflation in the 1970s led savers to leave the banks and move toward money market mutual funds and the like. Bank managers for the first time in a long time had to scramble to offer their depositers a higher return. They turned to higher-risk loans, first in agriculture and oil and gas, then to Third World nations, and finally to junk bonds and real estate. Many of those loans ended up turning bad.

A Last Word

Some say the savings and loan crisis was created by greedy S&L owners who didn't operate according to sound and conservative banking practices. In short, the banker was a gambler. Economists would disagree. Economists don't place as much emphasis on *individuals* as the cause of economic events as on *institutions* and *policies*. The economist would ask, Under what conditions, institutions, or policies is the banker likely to act like a gambler? For example, would the S&L owner be more careful with other peoples' money if he had to invest more of his own funds and could pass less of the risk on to taxpayers? Would depositers be more watchful of the S&Ls if there were less or no deposit insurance? Institutions and policies matter. Economists do not believe that S&L owners are careless, and depositers are asleep, under *all* institutions and policies—only under some. To economists, economic crises are not caused by "bad" people, but rather by "wrong" policies.

No cash was used, no checks were written, only a card was put through a machine and a few buttons were punched. Some people predict that this type of fund transfer will become so commonplace that soon the United States will become a cashless, checkless society.

We are not at that point yet. And some say we never will be as long as people are afraid that computer thieves can gain access to their accounts. As you read this, companies that provide EFT services are working to improve computer security so that potential debit card users will feel more comfortable with the new technology.

CHAPTER SUMMARY

What Money Is

■ Money is any good that is widely accepted for purposes of exchange.

■ Money serves as a medium of exchange, a unit of account, and a store of value.

■ Money evolved out of a barter economy as traders attempted to make exchange easier. A few goods that have been used as money include gold, silver, copper, cattle, rocks, and shells.

■ Money existed before formal governments existed.

■ Our money today has value because of its general acceptability.

The Money Supply

■ M1 includes currency held outside banks, demand deposits, other checkable deposits, and traveler's checks. M2 includes M1, small-denomination time deposits, savings deposits, money market accounts, overnight repurchase agreements, and overnight Eurodollar deposits. Credit cards are not money. When a credit card is used to make a purchase, a liability is incurred. This is not the case when money is used to make a purchase.

The Money Creation Process

■ Banks in the United States operate under a fractional reserve system in which they maintain only a fraction of their deposits in the form of reserves (that is, in the form of deposits at the Fed and vault cash). Excess reserves are typically used to extend loans to customers. When banks make these loans, they credit borrowers' checking accounts and thereby increase the money supply. When banks reduce the volume of loans outstanding, they reduce demand deposits and decrease the money supply.

■ A change in the *composition* of the money supply can change the *size* of the money supply. For example, suppose M1 = $400, where the breakdown is $150 in currency outside banks and $250 in demand deposits. Suppose now the $150 is placed into a demand deposit account. Initially, this changes the composition of the money supply but not its size. M1 is still $400 with $0 in currency outside banks and $400 in demand deposits. Later, when the banks have had time to create new loans (demand deposits) with the new reserves provided by the $150 deposit, the money supply expands.

Key Terms and Concepts

Money	Demand Deposits	Fractional Reserve Banking
Barter	Commercial Banks	
Medium of Exchange	M2	Federal Reserve System (the Fed)
Transaction Costs	Time Deposit	
Unit of Account	Savings Deposit	Reserves
Store of Value	Money Market Account	Required Reserve Ratio
Double Coincidence of Wants	Liquid Asset	Required Reserves
	Overnight Repurchase Agreement	Excess Reserves
M1		T-Account
Currency	Overnight Eurodollar Deposits	Simple Deposit Multiplier
Federal Reserve Notes		Cash Leakage

QUESTIONS AND PROBLEMS

1. Suppose, magically, 10,000 new dollars (never seen before) fall from the sky into the hands of Joanna Ferris. What are the minimum increase and the maximum increase in the money supply that may result? Assume the required-reserve ratio is 10 percent.

2. In question 1, suppose the $10,000 Joanna Ferris deposited into her demand deposit account had come from a friend, Ethel, instead of out of the sky. Additionally, Ethel gave Joanna the money by writing a check on her checking account.

Would the maximum increase in the money supply still be what you found it to be in question 1? Explain your answer.

3. Suppose that instead of Joanna getting $10,000 from the sky, or a check from a friend, she gets it from her mother who had it buried in a can in her back yard. In this case, would the maximum increase in the money supply be what you found it to be in question 1? Explain your answer.

4. What is the important point to be learned from the answers to questions 1, 2, and 3?

5. During the Civil War, both gold dollars and U.S. paper dollars (or greenbacks) existed. The North printed a tremendous number of greenbacks to finance the war with the South. There was no fixed exchange rate between the gold dollars and the greenbacks. Would you predict that the paper dollars would or would not drive the gold dollars out of circulation?

6. Does inflation, which is an increase in the price level, affect the three functions of money? If so, how?

7. Some economists have proposed that the Fed move to a 100 percent required-reserve ratio. This would make the simple deposit multiplier 1 ($1/r = 1/1.00 = 1$). Do you think banks would argue for or against the move? Explain your answer.

8. Money makes exchange easier. Would twice the money supply make exchange twice as easy? Would half the money supply make exchange one-half as easy?

9. Explain why gold backing is not necessary to give paper money value.

10. Describe the money supply contraction process.

12

THE FEDERAL RESERVE SYSTEM

WHAT THIS CHAPTER IS ABOUT

We stated in the last chapter, but have not yet showed, that changes in the money supply are important to understanding changes in the price level (P), real GNP (Q), and the unemployment rate. If this is true, then the institution that actually changes the money supply is important, too. This institution is the Federal Reserve System, which we discuss in this chapter.

THE FEDERAL RESERVE SYSTEM

■

Economists of almost all persuasions agree that the money supply plays an important role in the economy. In the previous chapter, we defined the money supply and showed how the banking system could expand or contract it. An important part of the money expansion and contraction process is the total amount of bank reserves. We see in this chapter that the Fed is able to influence the money supply by controlling bank reserves. Before explaining how the Fed does that, we talk about the structure of the institution itself.

The Structure of the Federal Reserve System

The Federal Reserve System is the central bank of the United States. Other nations' central banks include the Bank of Sweden, the Bank of England, the Banque de France, the Bank of Japan, the Deutsche Bundesbank, and so on. The Federal Reserve System came into existence with the Federal Reserve Act of 1913 and began operations in November 1914. Its principal components are the Board of Governors, the 12 Federal Reserve District Banks, and the approximately 6,000 member commercial banks (Exhibit 12–1). A map showing the 12 Federal Reserve Districts appears in Exhibit 12–2.

EXHIBIT 12–1
The Federal Reserve System

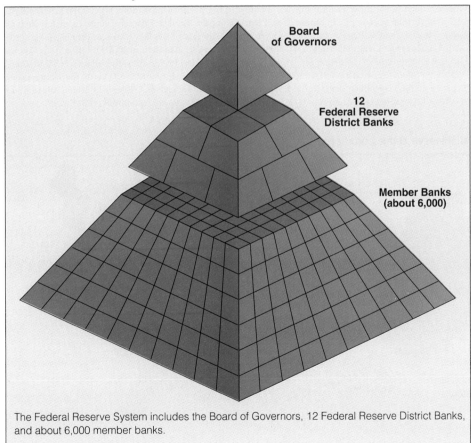

Board of Governors

12 Federal Reserve District Banks

Member Banks (about 6,000)

The Federal Reserve System includes the Board of Governors, 12 Federal Reserve District Banks, and about 6,000 member banks.

The most important responsibility of the Fed is to control the nation's money supply.

Board of Governors
The governing body of the Federal Reserve System.

Federal Open Market Committee (FOMC)
The 12-member policy-making group within the Fed. This committee has the authority to conduct open market operations.

Open Market Operations
The buying and selling of government securities by the Fed.

The **Board of Governors** controls and coordinates the activities of the Federal Reserve System. The Board is made up of seven members, each appointed to 14-year terms by the president with Senate approval. To reduce political influence on Fed policy, the terms of the governors are staggered—with one new appointment every other year—so a president cannot "pack" the Board. The president also designates one member as chairman of the Board for a four-year term.[1]

The major policy-making group within the Fed is the **Federal Open Market Committee (FOMC).** Authority to conduct **open market operations**—or the buying and selling of government securities—rests with the FOMC (more on open market operations later). The FOMC has 12 members, including the seven-member Board of Governors and five Federal Reserve District Bank presidents (four of the five positions are rotated among the Federal Reserve District Bank presidents). The president of the Federal Reserve Bank of New York holds a permanent seat on the FOMC, owing to the large amount of financial activity that takes place in New York City and the New York Fed's responsibility for executing open market operations.

The most important responsibility of the Fed is to control the nation's money supply. In meeting its responsibility, it is theoretically independent of politics, the Congress, and the president of the United States. It is not obligated to seek the advice of Congress or the president on monetary matters; it must only inform both of its plans. Many economists argue, however, that although the Fed is theoretically independent, there have been times when that independence has not been asserted. In general, it may be accurate to say that the Fed is independent of pol-

[1]The chairman plays an important role as a member of the Board of Governors. Economist Edward Kane tells a story that amusingly illustrates this: "During one of his last days as Chairman of the Federal Reserve Board, Paul Volcker is reputed to have treated the rest of the Governors to lunch. So as not to waste the Governors' valuable time, a waiter arrived quickly to take their orders. Ordering first, Volcker said that he would have the prime rib, which happened to be the restaurant's blue-plate special that day. Presuming that a trained economist such as Volcker would not want to order a la carte, the waiter asked, 'What about the vegetables?' Paul replied, '*They* can order for themselves.'" Edward J. Kane, "The Impact of a New Federal Reserve Chairman," *Contemporary Policy Issues,* vol. 6 (January 1988), p. 89.

EXHIBIT 12–2
Federal Reserve Districts and Federal Reserve Bank Locations

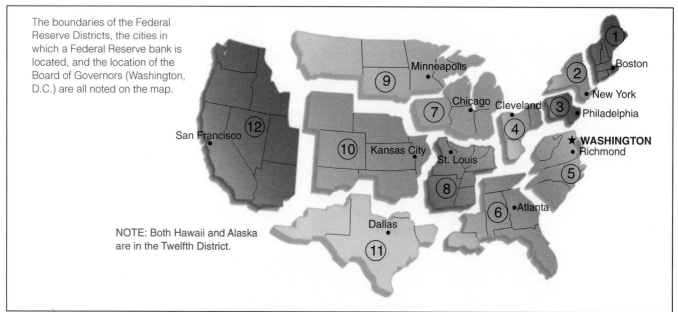

The boundaries of the Federal Reserve Districts, the cities in which a Federal Reserve bank is located, and the location of the Board of Governors (Washington, D.C.) are all noted on the map.

NOTE: Both Hawaii and Alaska are in the Twelfth District.

itics on a day-to-day basis, but probably subject to political influence (to what degree is a point of debate) over longer periods when general policy directions are set.

Functions of the Federal Reserve System

The Fed has eight major responsibilities or functions, the first of which we have noted.

1. Control the money supply. A full explanation of how the Fed does this comes later in this chapter.

2. Supply the economy with paper money (Federal Reserve Notes). The Federal Reserve banks have Federal Reserve Notes on hand to meet the demands of the banks and the public. Suppose it is the Christmas season and more people are going to their banks and withdrawing larger-than-usual amounts of $1, $5, $20, $50, and $100 notes. Commercial banks will need to replenish their vault cash, and so they will turn to their Federal Reserve banks. The Federal Reserve banks will meet this cash need by issuing more paper money (they act as passive suppliers of paper money). The actual printing of the paper money takes place at the Bureau of Engraving and Printing in Washington, D.C., but it is issued to commercial banks by the 12 Federal Reserve banks. On each Federal Reserve Note, an emblem on the left front side indicates which Federal Reserve District Bank issued the note. Check one and see. (In the trivia department, we note that today's Federal Reserve Notes are 6.14 × 2.61 inches and .0043 inches thick, which means a stack of 233 notes measure an inch high.)

3. Provide check-clearing services. When someone in New York writes a check to a person in Los Angeles, the Fed plays a role in moving money from the New Yorker's account to the Californian's account. It happens this way. Harriet Dodson writes a check on her New York bank and sends the check to George Adams in Los Angeles. George takes the check to his local bank, endorses it, and deposits it into his checking account. George's Los Angeles bank sends the check to the Federal Reserve Bank of San Francisco, which serves as the clearinghouse for checks in that particular district. The Federal Reserve Bank of San Francisco then sends the check to the Federal Reserve Bank of New York, which sends the check to Harriet's local New York bank, which sends the check back to Harriet with her monthly statement. There is a corresponding movement of funds in the opposite direction: Harriet's account is reduced, and dollars are forwarded by her bank to the New York Fed, to the San Francisco Fed, to George's Los Angeles bank, to George's account.

4. Hold depository institutions' reserves. As noted in our last chapter, banks are required to keep reserves against customer deposits either in the vault or in reserve accounts at the Fed. These accounts are maintained by the 12 Federal Reserve banks for member banks in their respective districts.

5. Supervise member banks. Without warning, the Fed can examine the books of member commercial banks to see the nature of the loans they have made, monitor compliance with bank regulations, check the accuracy of bank records, and so on. If the Fed finds that a bank has not been maintaining established banking standards, it can pressure it to do so.

6. Serve as the government's banker. The federal government collects and spends large sums of money. As a result, it needs a checking account for many of the same reasons an individual does. Its primary checking account is with the Fed. The Fed is the government's banker.

7. Serve as the lender of last resort. A traditional function of a central bank is to

Everything You Wanted to Know About Federal Reserve Notes but Were Too Busy Spending Them to Ask

Did you know the following facts about Federal Reserve Notes?

1. The average life of a typical $1 bill is 18 months. After 18 months, the typical note has been handled so often that it is worn out or badly torn.

2. Old money is sent to Federal Reserve District Banks to be exchanged for new.

3. Old used money is destroyed by machines that shred it to one-sixteenth of an inch.

4. If you have more than one-half of a Federal Reserve Note (say, one-third has been torn off), you can redeem it at a Federal Reserve bank. If you have less than one-half of a note, it will not be redeemed unless the treasurer of the United States is satisfied that the remainder of the note was totally destroyed.

5. Federal Reserve banks pay about 3 cents for each note produced by the Bureau of Engraving and Printing.

6. If you find a star at the end of the serial number on a Federal Reserve Note, this means the note is (a) a replacement for a note damaged in the printing process, (b) a replacement for a note found to be damaged on inspection at the Bureau of Engraving and Printing, or (c) the last note in a 100,000,000-note series.

7. On the back of the $1 note is the Great Seal of the United States. The Latin inscription, *E Pluribus Unum,* means "Out of Many, One." On the seal's reverse (located on the left side of the back of the note) are two inscriptions: *Annuit Coeptis,* meaning "He Has Favored Our Undertakings," and *Novus Ordo Seclorum,* meaning "A New Order of the Ages." Also on the reverse of the seal in Roman numerals, at the base of an unfinished pyramid, is the year the Declaration of Independence was signed, 1776.

---

serve as the lender of last resort for banks suffering cash management, or liquidity, problems.

8. Serve as a fiscal agent for the Treasury. The U.S. Treasury often issues (auctions) Treasury bills, notes, and bonds. These **U.S. Treasury securities** are sold to raise funds to pay the government's bills. The Federal Reserve District Banks receive the bids for these securities and process them in time for weekly auctions.

U.S. Treasury Securities
Bonds and bondlike securities issued by the U.S. Treasury when it borrows.

Question:

What is the difference between the Treasury and the Fed?

Answer:

The U.S. Treasury is a budgetary agency, the Fed a monetary agency. When the federal government spends funds, it is the Treasury's job to collect the taxes and borrow the funds needed to pay suppliers and others.[2] In short, the Treasury has an obligation to manage the financial affairs of the federal government. Except for coins, the Treasury does not issue money. It cannot create money "out of thin air" as the Fed can. The Fed is principally concerned with the availability of money and credit for the entire economy. It does not issue Treasury securities. It does not have an obligation to meet the financial needs of the federal government. Its responsibility is to provide a stable monetary framework for the economy.

---

[2]The Internal Revenue Service (IRS) is within the Treasury.

THE MONETARY BASE AND MONEY MULTIPLIER

In this section, we discuss the monetary base and the money multiplier—what the monetary base is and the relationship between it and the money supply.

The Monetary Base

The **monetary base** (sometimes called *high-powered money* or *base money)* is composed of reserves plus currency held by the nonbanking public.

$$\text{Monetary base } (B) = \text{reserves } (R) + \text{currency outside banks } (C)$$

In abbreviated form, $B = R + C$. If we openly identify what reserves equal, we can rewrite the equation as

$$\text{Monetary base} =$$
$$\text{bank deposits at the Fed} + \text{vault cash} + \text{currency outside banks}$$

Every time the Fed buys or sells something, the monetary base changes.[3] For example, suppose the Fed hires an economic consultant and pays her with a $50,000 check written on its own account. Where did the $50,000 that the Fed pays the economic consultant come from? The answer, odd as it sounds, is "out of thin air."[4]

That's correct: *The Fed can create money out of thin air.* This simply means that the Fed has the legal authority to create money. The difference between you and the Fed is as follows: You have a checking account and the Fed has a checking account. There is a balance in each account. The Fed can take a pencil and increase the balance in its account at will—legally. If you do this, however, and then write a check for a dollar amount you don't have in your account, your check bounces. Fed checks don't bounce.

To return to our example, once the $50,000 check is in the hands of the economic consultant, it is part of the monetary base. Specifically, the $50,000 will end up in one of three places: as a deposit at the Fed, as vault cash, or as currency outside a bank. Decisions made by the economic consultant and her bank influence to a great degree which of these destinations is most likely.

First, suppose the consultant deposits the check into her checking account at her local bank. The bank in turn sends the check to the Fed for collection. The Fed then increases the bank's balance in its reserve account (at the Fed) by $50,000. In this case, the $50,000 adds to bank reserves.

Second, the bank could have asked the Fed for the $50,000 in cash and then put the cash in its own vault. This too would have added to reserves.

Third, instead of depositing the $50,000 into her checking account, the economic consultant could have simply asked her local bank to cash the check. The Fed's check then would have been turned into currency outside a bank.

Regardless of the route taken—as a bank's deposit at the Fed, as vault cash, or as currency outside a bank—the Fed's check has contributed $50,000 to the monetary base. (Remember, monetary base = reserves [which equal bank deposits at the Fed + vault cash] + currency outside banks.) And in each instance the money supply will also increase. As we learned in Chapter 11, if the $50,000 is added to bank reserves, the money supply will expand by a multiple of that amount. If the

Every time the Fed buys or sells something, the monetary base changes. As the monetary base changes, so does the money supply—often by a multiple of the change in the base.

Monetary Base
The sum of reserves and currency outside banks.

---

[3]What the Fed usually buys and sells are government securities. For now, though, it is buying the services of an economic consultant.

[4]Recall the Fred example in the last chapter. The Fed and Fred are a lot alike: Both can create money out of thin air.

$50,000 is converted to currency, the money supply will increase by an equal amount.

The process can work in reverse. The Fed can decrease the monetary base and the money supply by selling something. Suppose the Fed sells a $10,000 government security from its asset portfolio to a private investor. Hannah Ferris writes a check to the Fed on her local account in order to buy the security. (Alternatively, Hannah might have paid for the security with currency, although that is unlikely.) The Fed first collects the funds the check represents (which reduces either the bank's deposit at the Fed or its vault cash) which *removes the funds from the economy altogether*. Since either vault cash or deposits at the Fed fall, bank reserves decline and, following a contraction of loans and deposits, the money supply falls.

Question:

It is difficult to understand how the Fed "removes funds from the economy altogether." For example, if Natalie sells something to Teresa, money moves from Teresa to Natalie, and then Natalie spends the money. It doesn't leave the economy. Does something different happen when the Fed is doing the selling?

Answer:

Yes, it is different when the Fed is doing the selling. When the Fed makes a sale, it collects the money, and it is as if the money has disappeared. Dollars held by the Fed are not considered part of the money supply or bank reserves.

Follow-up Question:

The text states that if either vault cash or deposits at the Fed increase, the monetary base increases, and so does the money supply. Also, if either vault cash or deposits at the Fed decrease, the monetary base decreases, and so does the money supply. In short, the monetary base and money supply move up and down together. But does the money supply move up or down by the same amount as the monetary base? For example, if the monetary base goes up by $1 million, does the money supply go up by $1 million, too?

Answer:

No, it usually doesn't. The monetary base includes bank reserves, and since we operate under a *fractional* reserve banking system, another $1 million in reserves can be used by banks to create a *multiple* expansion in the total volume of demand deposits. The exception occurs when the monetary base grows as a result of the public acquiring more currency. If individuals or businesses prefer to hold the new base money as currency—permanently—then the money supply does rise dollar for dollar with the monetary base. However, this is unlikely in practice. In the general case, the money supply will increase by a multiple of the monetary base growth.

From the Simple Deposit Multiplier to the Money Multiplier

We saw in Chapter 11 that the simple deposit multiplier is equal to $1/r$ (where r is the required-reserve ratio). If we multiply the simple deposit multiplier by any incremental excess reserves injected into the banking system, we obtain the *max-*

imum possible change in demand deposits (money supply) that the banking system can generate. The simple deposit multiplier *does not* adjust for cash leakages or positive excess reserves. Since such things as cash leakages and positive excess reserves really do exist, the simple deposit multiplier *overstates* the *actual* change in the money supply that follows a change in reserves. A more complete multiplier, such as the **money multiplier,** does not. The money multiplier measures the *actual change* in the money supply for a dollar change in the monetary base. For example, if the money multiplier is 3.4, then a $1 million increase in the monetary base leads to a $3.4 million increase in the money supply. For a $1 rise in the monetary base, there is a $3.40 rise in the money supply. We compute the multiplier this way:

Money multiplier = money supply/monetary base

In December 1990, the M1 money supply was $825 billion, whereas the monetary base was $309 billion. Dividing the money supply by the monetary base suggests that the money multiplier was 2.67. Consequently, each $1 worth of monetary base resulted in $2.67 worth of money supply.

Rearranging terms in equation 1, we see that

Money supply = money multiplier × monetary base

Now if we are told that the monetary base increases to $315 billion, we can multiply that figure by the money multiplier to find that M1 equals $841 billion (2.67 × $315 billion = $841 billion, rounded off).

Question:

If the Fed knows the money multiplier, and the Fed controls the monetary base, then can't the Fed control the money supply precisely? It seems as if it should be able to hit any money supply target it wants. For example, if it wants to increase the money supply by $10 million, and the money multiplier is 2.67, the monetary base should be increased by $3.74 billion, since 2.67 times 3.74 billion equals $10 million. All the Fed has to do is buy $3.74 billion worth of government securities to bring this about. Isn't this so?

Answer:

That is not exactly the case. The Fed is aware of past values for the money multiplier, but can't be certain what it will be next week or next month. Fluctuations in currency holdings by the public and in excess reserves held by banks affect the money multiplier's value, yet remain outside the Fed's control. Although such factors do not change by much, they are not constant and often prove difficult to predict in advance. For that reason, the degree of precision implied in the question is not possible. (Exhibit 12–3 shows money multipliers from 1970 to 1990.)

FED TOOLS FOR CONTROLLING THE MONEY SUPPLY

The three major tools the Fed has at its disposal to influence the money supply are (1) open market operations, (2) the required-reserve ratio, and (3) the discount rate.

Money Multiplier
Measures actual change in the money supply for a dollar change in the monetary base.

EXHIBIT 12–3
The Money Multiplier, 1970–90
The money multiplier is defined as the ratio of M1 to the monetary base. Specifically, it is the M1 money multiplier.

YEAR	MONEY MULTIPLIER
1970	3.02
1971	3.01
1972	3.02
1973	2.95
1974	2.85
1975	2.80
1976	2.78
1977	2.77
1978	2.75
1979	2.71
1980	2.68
1981	2.71
1982	2.74
1983	2.76
1984	2.73
1985	2.83
1986	3.00
1987	2.90
1988	2.86
1989	2.88
1990	2.67

SOURCE: Board of Governors of the Federal Reserve System.

Open Market Operations

Recall that any time the Fed buys or sells anything, it affects the monetary base and thus the money supply. The main "thing" it buys and sells is U.S. government securities, which are bonds the government originally sold to investors when it needed to borrow funds.[5] When the Fed buys and sells such securities in the financial markets, it is said to be engaged in *open market operations.*

Open Market Purchases. Consider an open market purchase of government securities by the Fed. If the Fed buys $5 million worth of government securities from Bank ABC in Minneapolis, the securities leave the possession of the bank and go to the Fed. The Fed pays for the securities by increasing Bank ABC's reserves on deposit at the Fed by $5 million. As we learned in Chapter 11, this increases (total bank) reserves in the banking system by $5 million (remember that reserves = bank deposits at the Fed + vault cash). The transaction shows up in the Fed's T-account as follows:

THE FED

Assets	Liabilities
Government securities + $5 million	Reserves on deposit in Bank ABC's account + $5 million

As we can see, the Fed has assets of $5 million more in government securities, and it is holding (as liabilities) $5 million more for Bank ABC.

The situation for Bank ABC looks like this:

BANK ABC

Assets	Liabilities
Government securities − $5 million Reserves on deposit at the Fed + $5 million	No change

Bank ABC has $5 million less in securities and $5 million more in *reserves.*[6] We saw in Chapter 11 that as the reserves of one bank increase with no offsetting decline in reserves for other banks, the money supply expands through a process of increased loans and demand deposits. In summary, an open market purchase by the Fed increases the money supply.

This example illustrates an earlier point. When the Fed purchases government securities, it is creating money out of thin air by issuing currency or by issuing checks that banks and the general public accept. By reversing the process, the Fed can reduce the money supply.

Question:

If the Fed buys a government security from a bank, from whom did the bank get the security in the first place?

[5]Actually, what the Fed buys and sells when it conducts an open market operation are U.S. Treasury bills, notes, and bonds and government agency bonds. Government securities is a broad term that includes all of these financial instruments.

[6]Economists will sometimes say that an open market purchase changes the monetary base and at other times that an open market purchase changes reserves. These are equivalent statements. If currency outside banks is unchanged, a change in reserves equals a change in the monetary base.

Answer:

The bank probably gets the security from the U.S. Treasury. Suppose the federal government wants to spend $1 trillion and tax revenues are $850 billion. This means there is a budget deficit of $150 billion. This deficit has to be financed: The federal government has to find some way of raising the $150 billion. It is the U.S. Treasury's task to raise the $150 billion by offering (for sale) *Treasury securities*—which include Treasury bills, notes, and bonds. These Treasury securities are promises to pay the holder of them. For example, if Taylor buys a Treasury security (for, say, $9,500) and the face value of it is $10,000, then the U.S. Treasury is making a promise to Taylor that it will redeem the security at maturity for $10,000.

Suppose a bank has purchased some Treasury securities a few months ago. Later, the Fed comes along and offers to buy those Treasury securities from the bank. The bank agrees. This, then, is an open market purchase of government (Treasury) securities.

Open Market Sales.   Open market sales refer to Fed sales of government securities to banks and others. Suppose the Fed sells $5 million worth of government securities to Bank XYZ in Atlanta. The Fed surrenders securities to Bank XYZ and is paid with $5 million previously deposited in Bank XYZ's account at the Fed. Reserves in the banking system and the monetary base both decline by $5 million.

The transaction shows up in the Fed's T-account as follows:

THE FED

Assets	Liabilities
Government securities − $5 million	Reserves on deposit in Bank XYZ's account − $5 million

The situation for Bank XYZ looks like this:

BANK XYZ

Assets	Liabilities
Government securities + $5 million Reserves on deposit at the Fed − $5 million	No Change

Now that Bank XYZ's reserves have declined by $5 million, it is reserve deficient. As Bank XYZ (and other banks) adjust to the lower level of reserves, they reduce their total loans outstanding, which reduces the total volume of demand deposits and money in the economy. Exhibit 12–4 gives a summary of how open market operations affect the money supply.

The Required-Reserve Ratio

The Fed can also influence the money supply by changing the required-reserve ratio. Recall the Fred example from the previous chapter. When Fred snaps his fingers, $1,000 appears out of thin air. Fred deposits the $1,000 in Bank A, so if the required-reserve ratio (r) is 10 percent, then Bank A must hold $100 worth of reserves. That leaves $900 for Bank A to loan out, at which time an equal amount of new deposits is created. If we assume no cash leakage and if banks hold none of the newly deposited funds as excess reserves, then the banking system as a whole can create $9,000 in new demand deposits (money). Adding this to the

EXHIBIT 12–4
Open Market Operations
An open market purchase increases reserves (and the monetary base), which leads to an increase in the money supply. An open market sale decreases reserves (and the monetary base), which leads to a decrease in the money supply. (Note: We have assumed here that the Fed purchases government securities from, and sells government securities to, commercial banks.)

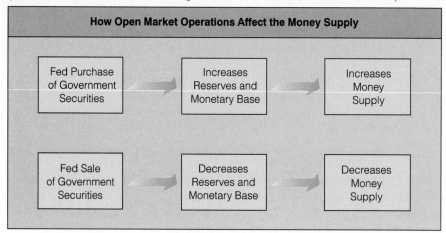

$1,000 created by Fred, the money supply is $10,000 higher than originally. The relevant formula is

$$\text{Maximum } \Delta DD = 1/r \times \Delta R$$
$$= 1/.10 \times \$1,000$$
$$= 10 \times \$1,000$$
$$= \$10,000$$

But suppose Fed officials decide to increase the required-reserve ratio from 10 percent to 20 percent. Now when Fred deposits the original $1,000, Bank A is required to hold $200 on reserve and can only create $800 worth of new loans and demand deposits. The money supply will be less when $r = 20$ percent than it was when r was 10 percent. Here are the calculations:

$$\text{Maximum } \Delta DD = 1/.20 \times \$1,000$$
$$= 5 \times \$1,000$$
$$= \$5,000$$

If the Fed were to lower the required-reserve ratio to 5 percent, Bank A could make a $950 loan and create $950 worth of new demand deposits. Other banks could also create new demand deposits. The money supply would be larger as a result (relative to when $r = 10$ percent). When $r = 5$ percent,

$$\text{Maximum } \Delta DD = 1/.05 \times \$1,000$$
$$= 20 \times \$1,000$$
$$= \$20,000$$

So we conclude that an increase in the required-reserve ratio leads to a decrease in the money supply, and a decrease in the required-reserve ratio leads to an increase in the money supply. In other words, there is an inverse, or opposite, relationship between the required-reserve ratio and the money supply. As r goes up, the money supply goes down; as r goes down, the money supply goes up.

The Discount Rate

Banks not only provide loans to their customers but they also borrow funds when they need them. Consider Bank ABC. Currently, it has zero excess reserves: It is fully loaned up. Then one of two things happens:

- **Case 1:** Brenda Tappen walks into the bank and applies for a loan to buy new equipment for her horse ranch. The bank loan officer believes she is a good credit risk and that the bank could profit by granting her the loan. But the bank has no funds to lend.
- **Case 2:** Andrew Ferguson walks into the bank and closes down his checking account. As a result, the bank loses reserves and now is reserve deficient.

In Case 1, the bank *wants* funds so that it can make a loan to Brenda Tappen and increase its profits. In Case 2, the bank *needs* funds to meet its **reserve requirements.** In either case, there are two major places the bank can go to acquire a loan: to the **federal funds market,** which basically means the bank goes to another commercial bank for the loan, or to the Fed (to its Federal Reserve District Bank). At both places, the bank will pay an interest rate. The rate it pays for the loan in the federal funds market is called the **federal funds rate.** The rate it pays for the loan from the Fed is called the **discount rate.** Bank ABC will try to minimize its costs by borrowing where the interest rate is lower, *ceteris paribus.* Suppose the discount rate is much lower than the federal funds rate; thus Bank ABC goes to the Fed for funds. If we assume the Fed grants the bank a loan, the Fed's T-account looks like this:

Reserve Requirement
The rule that specifies the amount of reserves a bank must hold to back up deposits.

Federal Funds Market
A market where banks lend reserves to one another, usually for short periods.

Federal Funds Rate
The interest rate in the federal funds market; the interest rate banks charge one another to borrow reserves.

Discount Rate
The interest rate the Fed charges depository institutions that borrow reserves from it.

THE FED

Assets		Liabilities	
Loan to Bank ABC	+ $1 million	Reserves on deposit in Bank ABC's account	+ $1 million

Bank ABC's T-account reflects the same transaction from its perspective.

BANK ABC

Assets		Liabilities	
Reserves on deposit at the Fed	+ $1 million	Loan from the Fed	+ $1 million

Notice that when Bank ABC borrows from the Fed, its reserves increase while the reserves of no other bank decrease. The result is increased reserves for the banking system as a whole, so the money supply increases. We can summarize by saying that when a bank borrows at the Fed's *discount window,* the money supply increases.

Question:

Do banks borrow from other banks when the discount rate is greater than the federal funds rate and borrow from the Fed when the discount rate is less than the federal funds rate?

Answer:

That is not always the case. Banks do not particularly care to borrow from the Fed for a number of reasons, which we discuss shortly. If the federal funds rate and the discount rate were equal (say, both were 7 percent), most banks would prefer to borrow funds from other banks than to borrow from the Fed. But, of course, as the discount rate falls relative to the federal funds rate (say, the discount rate falls to 5 percent, and the federal funds rate stays at 7 percent), this preference on the part of banks becomes more expensive to satisfy; and banks will be less likely to satisfy it. It comes down to this: As the discount rate falls relative to the federal funds rate, banks are more likely to borrow from the Fed. As the discount rate rises relative to the federal funds rate, banks are more likely to borrow from other banks. In effect, it is the spread (or difference) between the two rates that often matters. We discuss this next.

The Spread Between Discount Rate and Federal Funds Rate

The discount rate may be lower than the federal funds rate, and a bank may still go to the federal funds market for a loan. Here are the reasons why:

1. The bank may know that the Fed is hesitant to extend loans to banks that want to take advantage of profit-making opportunities such as the loan to Brenda Tappen (Case 1).

2. The bank doesn't want to have to deal with the Fed bureaucracy that regulates it, particularly if Fed officials interpret a request for a loan as mismanagement.

3. The bank realizes that acquiring a loan from the Fed is a privilege and not a right, and the bank doesn't want to wear this privilege too thin too quickly; it never knows when it may need the borrowing privilege the Fed has extended to it more than it currently needs it.

Banks basically look at the spread (the difference) between the federal funds rate and the discount rate in deciding where to borrow funds. If the discount rate is only slightly lower (1/4–1/2 percent lower) than the federal funds rate, most banks will pay the extra charge and borrow from other commercial banks. If the discount rate is significantly lower than the federal funds rate (2–3 percent lower), most banks will borrow from the Fed.

It follows that an increase in the discount rate relative to the federal funds rate reduces bank borrowings from the Fed. As banks borrow less from the Fed and *pay back* Fed loans previously taken out, reserves fall, and ultimately the money supply declines.

A decrease in the discount rate relative to the federal funds rate increases bank borrowings from the Fed. As banks borrow more from the Fed, reserves rise, and ultimately the money supply increases.

A summary of the effects of the different monetary tools of the Fed can be found in Exhibit 12–5.

Question:

Does the Fed use one monetary tool more than the others when it wants to change the money supply? If so, which one and why?

Answer:

The Fed today uses open market operations much more than the other two tools. It feels that open market operations have certain advantages over the other two tools. These advantages include the following:

EXHIBIT 12–5
Fed Monetary Tools and Their Effects on the Money Supply
The following Fed actions increase the money supply: purchasing government securities on the open market, lowering the required-reserve ratio, and lowering the discount rate relative to the federal funds rate. The following Fed actions decrease the money supply: selling government securities on the open market, raising the required-reserve ratio, and raising the discount rate relative to the federal funds rate.

FED MONETARY TOOL	MONEY SUPPLY
OPEN MARKET OPERATION	
Buys government securities	Increases
Sells government securities	Decreases
REQUIRED-RESERVE RATIO (*r*)	
Raises *r*	Decreases
Lowers *r*	Increases
DISCOUNT RATE	
Raises rate (relative to the federal funds rate)	Decreases
Lowers rate (relative to the federal funds rate)	Increases

1. Open market operations are flexible. The Fed can buy or sell small, medium, or large amounts of government securities and can control the size of the transaction.

2. Open market operations can easily be reversed. If yesterday the Fed purchased $50 million worth of government securities, but now realizes that $40 million would have been a more appropriate figure, it can sell $10 million worth of securities today to correct the situation.

3. Open market operations can be implemented quickly. If the Fed decides it wants to change the monetary base and therefore the money supply, it places an order with a government securities dealer, and the trade is executed immediately.

The Best Is Yet to Come

This chapter is as important for the questions it raises as for the questions it answers:

- Why would the Fed want to increase the money supply?
- Why would the Fed want to decrease the money supply?
- Can the Fed create too much money? What happens if it does?
- Can the Fed create too little money? What happens if it does?

These questions are answered in chapters to come. This chapter has only scratched the surface of what there is to know about money matters. The most interesting part of the story has yet to be told.

CHAPTER SUMMARY

The Federal Reserve System

- The Federal Reserve System is made up of a seven-member Board of Governors, 12 Federal Reserve District Banks, and about 6,000 member banks. The major policy-making group within the Fed is the Federal Open Market Committee. It is a 12-member group, made up of the seven members of the Board of Governors and five Federal Reserve District Bank presidents.

■ The major responsibilities of the Fed are to (1) control the money supply, (2) supply the economy with paper money (Federal Reserve Notes), (3) provide check-clearing services, (4) hold depository institutions' reserves, (5) supervise member banks, (6) serve as the government's banker, (7) serve as a lender of last resort, and (8) serve as a fiscal agent for the Treasury.

Monetary Base

■ The monetary base equals reserves plus currency outside banks.
■ Every time the Fed buys or sells anything, it automatically changes the monetary base.

Money Multiplier

■ The money multiplier measures the actual change in the money supply for a dollar change in the monetary base. It is the ratio of the money supply to the monetary base. Stated differently, the money supply is the product of the money multiplier times the monetary base (money supply = money multiplier × monetary base).

Controlling the Money Supply

■ The following Fed actions increase the money supply: lowering the required-reserve ratio, purchasing government securities on the open market, and lowering the discount rate relative to the federal funds rate. The following Fed actions decrease the money supply: raising the required-reserve ratio, selling government securities on the open market, and raising the discount rate relative to the federal funds rate.

Open Market Operations

■ An open market purchase by the Fed increases the money supply. An open market sale by the Fed decreases the money supply.

Changes in the Required-Reserve Ratio

■ An increase in the required reserve ratio leads to a decrease in the money supply. A decrease in the required-reserve ratio leads to an increase in the money supply.

Changes in the Discount Rate

■ An increase in the discount rate relative to the federal funds rate leads to a decrease in the money supply. A decrease in the discount rate relative to the federal funds rate leads to an increase in the money supply.

Key Terms and Concepts

Board of Governors

Federal Open Market
   Committee (FOMC)

Open Market
   Operations

Monetary Base

Money Multiplier

Reserve Requirement

Federal Funds Market

Federal Funds Rate

Discount Rate

QUESTIONS AND PROBLEMS

1. Is it possible for the monetary base to increase without an increase in reserves? If so, explain how.

2. Money supply = money multiplier × monetary base. This means that if the money supply is to rise, either the money multiplier or the monetary base must rise. Between 1980 and 1990, the M1 money supply doubled. After taking a look at the money multiplier during this period (see Exhibit 12–4), answer the following question: What was largely responsible for this increase?

3. Explain how an open market purchase increases the money supply.

4. Suppose the Fed raises the required-reserve ratio. This is normally thought to reduce the money supply. However, commercial banks find themselves with a reserve deficiency after the required-reserve ratio is increased and are likely to react by requesting a loan from the Fed. Does this action prevent the money supply from contracting as predicted by the theory?

5. Suppose Bank A borrows reserves from Bank B. Now that Bank A has more reserves than previously, will the money supply increase?

6. If the simple deposit multiplier turned out to be equal to the money multiplier (which isn't likely), what would this imply?

7. There are two towns in two different Federal Reserve Districts. One is a tourist town, the other is not. In which town would you expect to find more Federal Reserve Notes issued by Federal Reserve District Banks *other than* the one in the district in which the town is located? Explain why.

8. Suppose you read in the newspaper that all last week the Fed conducted open market purchases and that on Tuesday of last week it lowered the discount rate. What would you say the Fed was up to?

9. Suppose the Fed increases the monetary base by $350 million. Does it matter whether the $350 million is all in reserves, or all in currency, to how much the money supply will expand? Explain your answer.

10. Some people have referred to the Fed as a "legal counterfeiter." Explain why you think such terminology either is or is not a misrepresentation of the Fed's role.

11. Fill in the blank.

Money Supply ($ billions)	Monetary Base ($ billions)	Money Multiplier
715	A	4.2
B	209	3.1
802	241	C
692	D	2.5
E	321	2.6
796	255	F

INFLATION

WHAT THIS CHAPTER IS ABOUT

In *P–Q* terms, this chapter
relates to the price level, or
P. Specifically, it relates to
a *rising price level,* which is
what inflation is. In this
chapter, we discuss both
the causes and effects of
inflation.

WHAT IS INFLATION, AND HOW DO WE MEASURE IT?

In everyday usage, the word **inflation** refers to *any* increase in the price level.[1] Economists, though, like to differentiate between *two types* of increases in the price level: a *one-shot* increase and a *continued* increase. This gives us two types of inflation, which we discuss in this section.

Inflation
An increase in the price level.

One-Shot Inflation

One-shot inflation is exactly what it sounds like: it is a one-shot, or one-time, increase in the price level. Suppose the CPI for years 1–5 is as follows:

One-Shot Inflation
A one-time increase in the price level. An increase in the price level that does not continue.

Year	CPI
1	100
2	110
3	110
4	110
5	110

Notice that the price level is higher in year 2 than in year 1, but that after year 2 it does not change. In other words, it takes a "one-shot" jump in year 2 and then stabilizes. This is an example of *one-shot inflation.*

Continued Inflation

Now suppose the CPI for years 1–5 is as follows:

Year	CPI
1	100
2	110
3	120
4	130
5	140

Notice that the CPI goes from 100 to 110, then from 110 to 120, and so on. Each year the CPI is higher than in the year before. We have a *continued* increase in the price level. This is an example of **continued inflation.**

Continued Inflation
A continued increase in the price level.

Measuring the Inflation Rate

The nightly news reporter usually speaks of a percentage change in the price level—that is, of an *inflation rate.* Calculating an inflation rate is a simple matter. We can use either of the two commonly used price indices, the consumer price index (CPI) or the GNP deflator. Suppose we choose the consumer price index. We learn that the CPI this year is 121 and that the CPI last year was 110. To find the annual inflation rate, we use this formula:

$$\text{Annual inflation rate} = \frac{\text{CPI this year} - \text{CPI last year}}{\text{CPI last year}} \times 100$$

In this case, the annual inflation rate is 10% [(121 − 110)/110 × 100 = 10%].

[1]Remember from Chapter 7 that the price level can be measured using the CPI or the GNP deflator.

*One-shot inflation can
originate on the demand
side or on the supply
side of the economy.*

■

Question:

*Suppose there is an increase in a particular price, say, the price of television sets,
but not in the price level. Is this inflation?*

Answer:

No, it isn't. The reason is that a rise in the price of one good may be offset by a
decline in the price of another good, leaving the price level unchanged. A rise in
a *single price* is not inflation. A rise in the *price level* is inflation.

THEORIES OF ONE-SHOT INFLATION
■

In Chapter 8, we learned that a shift rightward in the AD curve, or a shift leftward
in the $SRAS$ curve, would raise the price level. We conclude that one-shot inflation
can originate on either the demand-side, or the supply-side, of the economy.

One-Shot Inflation: Demand-Side Induced

In Exhibit 13–1a, the economy is initially in long-run equilibrium at point 1. The
real GNP the economy is producing (Q_1) is the same as the natural real GNP (Q_N).
Suppose now the aggregate demand curve shifts rightward from AD_1 to AD_2. As
this happens, the economy moves to point 2, where the price level is P_2 and real
GNP is Q_2.

EXHIBIT 13–1
One-Shot Inflation: Demand-Side Induced

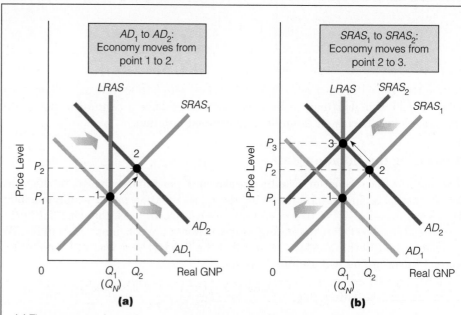

(a) The aggregate demand curve shifts rightward from AD_1 to AD_2. As a result, the price level
increases from P_1 to P_2; the economy moves from point 1 to point 2. (b) Since the real GNP
the economy produces (Q_2) is greater than the natural real GNP, the unemployment rate that
exists is less than the natural unemployment rate. Wage rates rise and the short-run aggregate
supply curve shifts leftward from $SRAS_1$ to $SRAS_2$. Long-run equilibrium is at point 3.

Starting in panel (b) at point 2, we notice that the real GNP the economy is producing (Q_2) is greater than natural real GNP. This means that the unemployment rate that exists in the economy is lower than the natural unemployment rate (see Chapter 8). Consequently, as old wage contracts expire, workers are paid higher wage rates because unemployment is relatively low. As wage rates rise, the *SRAS* curve shifts leftward from $SRAS_1$ to $SRAS_2$. The long-run equilibrium position is at point 3. The price level and real GNP at each of our three points are as follows:

Point	Price Level	Real GNP
1 (start)	P_1	$Q_1 = Q_N$
2	P_2	Q_2
3 (end)	P_3	$Q_1 = Q_N$

Notice that at point 3 the economy is at a *higher* price level, but at the *same* real GNP level, as at point 1.

Question:

In the example, the price level goes from P₁ to P₂ to P₃. Is this a one-shot increase in the price level (one-shot inflation) or a continued increase in the price level (continued inflation)?

Answer:

In the example, the price level rises (from P_1 to P_2 to P_3) and then stabilizes at P_3. Since the price level *stabilizes,* we cannot characterize it as *continually rising,* and so the change in the price level in our example is *not* representative of continued inflation. We have here one-shot inflation.

One-Shot Inflation: Supply-Side Induced

In Exhibit 13–2a, the economy is initially in long-run equilibrium at point 1. The real GNP the economy is producing (Q_1) is the same as the natural real GNP (Q_N). Suppose now the short-run aggregate supply curve shifts leftward from $SRAS_1$ to $SRAS_2$. As this happens, the economy moves to point 2 where the price level is P_2 and real GNP is Q_2.

Starting in panel (b) at point 2, we notice that the real GNP the economy is producing (Q_2) is less than natural real GNP. This means that the unemployment rate that exists in the economy is greater than the natural unemployment rate. Consequently, as old wage contracts expire, workers are paid lower wage rates because unemployment is relatively high. As wage rates fall, the short-run aggregate supply curve shifts rightward from $SRAS_2$ to $SRAS_1$. The long-run equilibrium position is at point 1 again. (If wage rates are somewhat inflexible, it may take a long while to move from point 2 to point 1.) The price level and real GNP at each of our three points are as follows:

Point	Price Level	Real GNP
1 (start)	P_1	$Q_1 = Q_N$
2	P_2	Q_2
1 (end)	P_1	$Q_1 = Q_N$

Notice that at point 3 the economy is at the *same* price level, and at the *same* real GNP level, as at point 1.

EXHIBIT 13–2
One-Shot Inflation: Supply-Side Induced

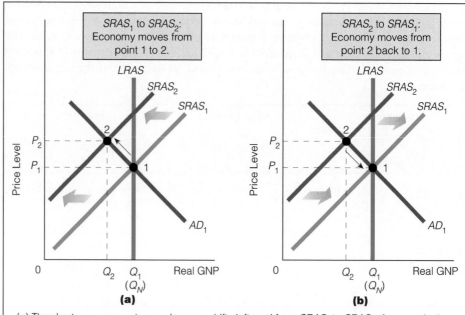

(a) The short-run aggregate supply curve shifts leftward from $SRAS_1$ to $SRAS_2$. As a result, the price level increases from P_1 to P_2; the economy moves from point 1 to point 2. (b) Since the real GNP the economy produces (Q_2) is less than the natural real GNP, the unemployment rate that exists is greater than the natural unemployment rate. Some economists argue that wage rates fall and the short-run aggregate supply curve shifts rightward from $SRAS_2$ (back) to $SRAS_1$. Long-run equilibrium is at point 1.

Confusing Demand-Induced and Supply-Induced One-Shot Inflation

Demand-induced and supply-induced one-shot inflation can be easily confused.[2] To illustrate, suppose the Federal Reserve System increases the money supply. Because there is more money in the economy, there can be greater total spending at any given price level. Consequently, the AD curve shifts rightward.

Next, prices begin to rise. Soon after, wage rates begin to rise. Many employers, perhaps unaware that the money supply has increased, certainly are aware that they are paying their employees higher wages. Thus, it is possible that they will think the higher price level is due to higher wage rates and not to the increased money supply that preceded the higher wage rates. In conclusion, what may look like a supply-induced rise in the price level is really a demand-induced rise in the price level.

Now let's explain this same story in terms of our diagrams in Exhibit 13–1. In (a), the AD curve shifts rightward because, as we said, the money supply increases. Employers, however, are unaware of what is happening in panel (a). What they see is panel (b). They end up paying higher wage rates to their employees and the $SRAS$ curve shifts leftward. Unaware that the AD curve shifted rightward in (a), but aware that the $SRAS$ curve shifted leftward in (b), they mistakenly conclude that the rise in the price level originated with a supply-side factor (higher wage rates) and not with a demand-side factor (an increase in the money supply).

[2]Sometimes the terms "demand-side inflation" and "supply-side inflation" are used.

It is a common phenomenon to believe that what we see with our eyes, or experience in our daily lives, *causes* the effects we notice. Witness, in our last example, employers' mistaken belief that the stimulus for the rise in the price level was a rise in wage rates (which they had first-hand experience of) and not an increase in the money supply (which they probably did not know had occurred). But the economist knows that the *cause* of something may be far removed from our personal orbit. This awareness is part of the way an economist thinks.

THINKING LIKE AN ECONOMIST

THEORY OF CONTINUED INFLATION
■

The CPI and GNP deflator figures for the United States for 1960–1990 are noted in Exhibit 13–3. Both price indices have *continually* increased, indicating *continued inflation* in the United States. For this reason, our discussion of continued inflation in this section is extremely relevant.

EXHIBIT 13–3
Consumer Price Index and GNP Deflator, 1960–90
Notice that both the CPI and the GNP deflator have continually increased during the period 1960–90. The U.S. inflation of the past three decades has been *continued inflation.*

YEAR	CONSUMER PRICE INDEX (1982–84=100)	GNP DEFLATOR (1982=100)
1960	29.6	30.9
1961	29.9	31.2
1962	30.2	31.9
1963	30.6	32.4
1964	31.0	32.9
1965	31.5	33.8
1966	32.4	35.0
1967	33.4	35.9
1968	34.8	37.7
1969	36.7	39.8
1970	38.8	42.0
1971	40.5	44.4
1972	41.8	46.5
1973	44.4	49.5
1974	49.3	54.0
1975	53.8	59.3
1976	56.9	63.1
1977	60.6	67.3
1978	65.2	72.2
1979	72.6	78.6
1980	82.4	85.7
1981	90.9	94.0
1982	96.5	100.0
1983	99.6	103.9
1984	103.9	107.7
1985	107.6	110.9
1986	109.6	113.8
1987	113.6	117.4
1988	118.3	121.3
1989	124.0	126.3
1990	130.7	131.5

SOURCE: Council of Economic Advisers, *Economic Report of the President, 1991* (Washington, D.C.: U.S. Government Printing Office, 1991).

From One-Shot Inflation to Continued Inflation

What can turn one-shot inflation into continued inflation? The answer is *continued increases in aggregate demand.* This process is illustrated in Exhibit 13–4.

Beginning at point 1 in Exhibit 13–4a, the aggregate demand curve shifts rightward from AD_1 to AD_2. The economy moves from point 1 to point 2. We know from our previous discussion that this is not the end of the story. At point 2, the unemployment rate that exists in the economy is less than the natural unemployment rate. As a result, wage rates rise and cause the short-run aggregate supply curve to shift leftward from $SRAS_1$ to $SRAS_2$. The economy moves from point 2 to point 3. At point 3, the economy is in long-run equilibrium.

Suppose that starting at point 3, the economy experiences another rightward shift in the aggregate demand curve (to AD_3). The process repeats itself, and the economy moves from point 3 to point 4 to point 5. Still another rightward shift in the aggregate demand curve moves the economy from point 5 to point 6 to point 7. We have stopped at point 7, but we could have continued. We notice that the result of this process is a continually rising price level—from P_1 to P_7 and beyond. We conclude that *continued increases in aggregate demand cause continued inflation.*

Suppose now we look at things from the supply-side of the economy. Beginning at point 1 in Exhibit 13–4b, the short-run aggregate supply curve shifts leftward

EXHIBIT 13–4
Changing One-Shot Inflation into Continued Inflation

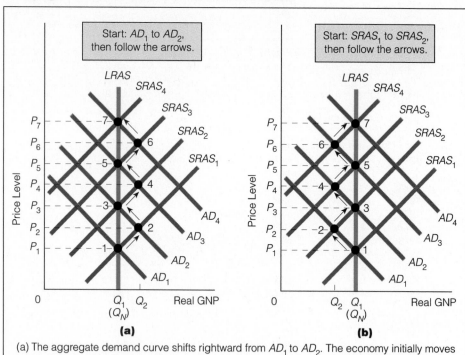

(a) The aggregate demand curve shifts rightward from AD_1 to AD_2. The economy initially moves from point 1 to point 2 and finally to point 3. Continued increases in the price level are brought about through continued increases in aggregate demand. (b) The short-run aggregate supply curve shifts leftward from $SRAS_1$ to $SRAS_2$. The economy initially moves from point 1 to point 2. The economy will return to point 1 unless there is an increase in aggregate demand. We see here, as in (a), that continued increases in the price level are brought about through continued increases in aggregate demand.

from $SRAS_1$ to $SRAS_2$. The economy moves from point 1 to point 2. At point 2, the unemployment rate that exists in the economy is greater than the natural unemployment rate. According to some economists, there is a natural tendency for wage rates to fall and the $SRAS$ curve to shift rightward, moving the economy back to point 1.

This natural tendency of the economy to return to point 1 will be offset, however, if the aggregate demand curve shifts rightward. Then, instead of moving from point 2 back to point 1, the economy moves from point 2 to point 3. At point 3, the economy is in long-run equilibrium, and a higher price level exists than existed at point 2.

Suppose the economy experiences another leftward shift in the aggregate supply curve ($SRAS_3$). The economy moves from point 3 to point 4, and would naturally return to point 3 unless aggregate demand shifted rightward. If the latter occurs, the economy moves to point 5. The same process moves the economy from point 5 to 6 to 7, where we have decided to stop. We notice that the result of this process results in a continually rising price level—from P_1 to P_7 and beyond. Again, we conclude that *continued increases in aggregate demand cause continued inflation.*

Question:

Can't continued declines in short-run aggregate supply (SRAS) also propel the price level continually higher? For example, suppose a labor union continually bargains for and receives higher wage rates for its members. Each time the union receives higher wage rates, the SRAS curve shifts leftward. And each time the SRAS curve shifts leftward, wouldn't the economy experience a higher price level?

Answer:

Theoretically, continued declines in $SRAS$ can lead to continued rises in the price level, *ceteris paribus.* It is possible, but not likely, that $SRAS$ continually declines. For it to do so, however, workers would have to continually increase their wage demands as unemployment rises above its natural level. This is not consistent with our supply-and-demand model outlined in Chapter 3, where we learned that a surplus leads to downward pressure on price (wages).

(See Economics in Our Times, "A Lot of Finger Pointing Goes on During a Rapid Inflation.")

What Causes Continued Increases in Aggregate Demand?

So far, we know that continued increases in aggregate demand cause continued inflation. But what causes continued increases in aggregate demand?

To answer this question, think back to Chapter 8. There we stated that *at a given price level, anything that increases total spending increases aggregate demand and shifts the AD curve to the right.* With this in mind, consider an increase in the money supply. If there is more money in the economy, there can be greater total spending at a given price level. Consequently, aggregate demand increases and the *AD* curve shifts rightward.

Economists are widely agreed that the *only factor* that can change continually in such a way as to bring about continued increases in aggregate demand is the *money supply.* Specifically, *continued increases in the money supply lead to continued increases in aggregate demand, which generate continued inflation.*

| Continued increases in the money supply | → | Continued increases in aggregate demand | → | Continued inflation |

A Lot of Finger Pointing Goes on During a Rapid Inflation

During a rapid and continued rise in the price level, individuals usually point fingers at the persons or group they feel are responsible for the inflation. Labor unions are often the target of finger pointing. Some individuals will make the following argument (see if you can pick out the analytical error).

Labor unions bargain for and receive higher wage rates, and the higher wage rates get translated into higher prices. Because of the higher prices, labor unions again bargain for and receive higher wage rates (their members can't make ends meet on the old wages), and again higher wage rates get translated into higher prices, and on and on. Here we have a *wage–price spiral*, prompted by the labor unions.

Do unions cause continued inflation? The answer is no, at least not directly. To illustrate, when a labor union bargains for and receives higher wage rates, the short-run aggregate supply curve shifts leftward, as in Exhibit 13–5. A shift in the short-run aggregate supply curve from

$SRAS_1$ to $SRAS_2$ raises the price level from P_1 to P_2 and lowers real GNP from Q_1 to Q_2. As real GNP falls, the unemployment rate rises. If labor unions respond to the higher price level by again bargaining for and receiving higher wages, the $SRAS$ curve will shift leftward again, with the same results—a higher price level, a

lower real GNP, and a higher unemployment rate.

Are labor unions likely to push the $SRAS$ curve leftward *continually*? It is unlikely, since such a policy only leads to higher unemployment. Labor unions are not likely to go against their long-run employment objectives.

EXHIBIT 13–5
Do Unions Cause Continued Inflation?

Suppose a labor union bargains for and receives higher wage rates for its members, pushing the short-run aggregate supply curve leftward. The price level rises and real GNP falls. At the lower real GNP level, the unemployment rate is higher. Will the union continue such actions? It is unlikely it will. Continued (successful) attempts at pushing the $SRAS$ curve leftward will put increasingly more union members out of work.

It is important to realize that the money supply can continually increase without reducing one of the four components of total spending—that is, consumption, investment, government expenditures, or net exports.

We note this because someone might ask, Can't government expenditures increase continually, too? First, there are both real and political limits beyond which government expenditures cannot go. The real upper limit is 100 percent of GNP. We do not know what the political upper limit is, but it is likely that it is less than 100 percent of GNP. In either case, once the limit is reached, government expenditures can no longer increase.

Second, some economists argue that government expenditures that are not financed with new money may crowd out one of the other components of total spending (see the discussion of crowding out in Chapter 10). Thus, increases in government expenditures are not guaranteed to raise total spending, because if government expenditures rise, consumption, say, may fall to the degree that government expenditures have increased. For example, for every additional dollar government spends on public education, households may spend one less dollar on private education.

The emphasis on the money supply as the only factor that can continue to increase and thus cause continued inflation has led most economists to agree with Nobel Laureate Milton Friedman that "inflation is always and everywhere a monetary phenomenon." (The "inflation" that Friedman is referring to is "continued inflation.")

Question:

Suppose the following scenario occurs: (1) The federal government runs continual budget deficits, that is, government expenditures are greater than tax revenues year after year. (2) The U.S. Treasury finances the budget deficit by selling Treasury securities to the public. (3) In response to step 2, the Fed conducts open market operations and purchases a large percentage of the Treasury securities. As long as steps 1 through 3 are repeated continually, would continued inflation result?

Answer:

This question is based on a condition, and the answer is "Yes, given the condition specified, and holding all other things constant." If there are *continued* deficits, and if the Fed *continues* to conduct open market purchases in response to Treasury financing of the deficits, continued increases in aggregate demand and continued inflation will occur. Notice, though, that the *money supply* is continuing to increase; thus, inflation has a monetary origin.

THE EFFECTS OF INFLATION

In this section, we discuss a few of the many effects of inflation. It is important to keep in mind that inflation may be *anticipated* or *unanticipated*. Unanticipated inflation catches people off guard. With anticipated inflation, people expect it and try to adjust for it. But simply because people anticipate inflation doesn't mean they necessarily anticipate the proper *rate* of inflation. They may either *correctly* anticipate inflation ("I said there would be a 5 percent inflation rate this year, and there is") or they may *incorrectly* anticipate inflation ("I said there would be a 5 percent inflation rate this year and it turned out to be 8 percent instead"). Here and throughout the remaining macroeconomic chapters, we develop the idea that the effects of inflation may be different depending on whether inflation is unanticipated, correctly anticipated, or incorrectly anticipated.

In this section, we discuss the effects mainly of unanticipated inflation. From time to time, you will see how things might be different if inflation is either correctly or incorrectly anticipated.

Who Does Inflation Hit and What Does It Do?

Savers, borrowers, and people who hold money are some of the people who feel the effects of inflation. How does inflation affect these people, and what are some of its other effects?

Inflation and People Who Hold Money. With inflation, the purchasing power of money declines. For example, if the inflation rate is 10 percent this year, then it

Does Dog Racing Cause Continued Inflation?

Look at the data in Exhibit 13–6. There you will see 1980–88 data for the CPI, M1, consumption, government expenditures, and dog races. Dog races?

The theory of continued inflation states that continued increases in the money supply cause continued inflation. Is this confirmed by the small set of data presented in the exhibit? Yes, since a quick look at columns (2) and (3) shows that both the CPI and the money supply have continually increased during the period 1980–88.

But, of course, a look at column (2) and any column (4)–(6) shows the same thing. In column (4) consumption has continually increased; in col-

umn (5) government expenditures have continually increased; and in column (6) the number of dog races has continually increased.

Let's conduct a simple experiment. Suppose you lose the knowledge that you have gained in this chapter. Answer the following questions the way you would have answered them before you learned the cause of continued inflation.

1. If shown the data in columns (2) and (4) and then told that continued increases in consumption *cause* continued inflation, would you have believed us? ☐ Yes ☐ No

2. If shown the data in columns (2) and (5) and then told that continued increases in government expenditures *cause* continued inflation, would you have believed us? ☐ Yes ☐ No
3. If shown the data in columns (2) and (6) and then told that continued increases in dog races *cause* continued inflation, would you have believed us? ☐ Yes ☐ No

Most readers will answer "yes" to questions 1–2 and "no" to question 3. Perhaps you did, too. Why? The answer is probably that the data in columns 4–5 are economic data, and it seems plausible that continued changes in economic data could

EXHIBIT 13–6
Continued Increases in Several Factors
Here we show data for the CPI, money supply, consumption, investment, government expenditures, and (number of) dog races for the period 1980–88. Notice that there is a continued increase in all factors.

(1) Year	(2) Consumer Price Index (1982–84 = 100)	(3) M1 Money Supply ($ billions)	(4) Consumption ($ billions)	(5) Government Expenditures ($ billions)	(6) Dog Races
1980	82.4	408.9	1,732.6	530.3	5,855
1981	90.9	436.5	1,915.1	588.1	6,379
1982	96.5	474.5	2,050.7	641.7	6,499
1983	99.6	521.2	2,234.5	675.0	8,257
1984	103.9	552.1	2,430.5	735.9	8,661
1985	107.6	620.1	2,629.4	820.8	9,590
1986	109.6	724.7	2,797.4	872.2	10,654
1987	113.6	750.4	3,009.4	921.4	11,156
1988	118.6	787.5	3,238.2	962.5	12,904
	↑ Continued increases in CPI	↑ Continued increases in money supply	↑ Continued increases in consumption	↑ Continued increases in government expenditures	↑ Continued increases in number of dog races

SOURCES: Council of Economic Advisers, *Economic Report of the President*, 1991 (Washington, D.C.: U.S. Government Printing Office, 1991) and U.S. Bureau of the Census, *Statistical Abstract of the United States, 1990* (Washington, D.C.: U.S. Government Printing Office, 1990).

cause continued inflation. But the data in column 6 are not economic data and therefore the link between changes in it and continued inflation is less certain. Also, to most persons it seems unbelievable that the number of dog races has anything to do with continued inflation.

Consider this: You may have accepted the consumption or government expenditures theory of inflation over the "dog races" theory simply because either one of the first two theories *seems plausible* and the third does not. But, in truth, all three theories are incorrect.

In addition, what may seem like a *cause* of continued inflation may in fact be an *effect* of some other factor. For example, couldn't it be the case that continued increases in consumption is the *effect* of continued increases in the money supply?

The lesson is one that was stated in Chapter 1: Association is not causation. Simply because two events are associated it does not necessarily follow that one is the cause and the other is the effect. But in the flurry of economic facts and theories, this is a lesson that is easily forgotten.

takes $110 this year to buy what $100 bought the year before. Economists often refer to inflation as a "tax" on peoples' money holdings, because like a real tax it reduces their ability to buy as many goods and services.

Inflation and Savers. Suppose Michael and Melissa Pearson put $6,000 into a savings account that pays interest at a fixed annual rate of 5.25 percent. Furthermore, suppose the annual inflation rate turns out to be 10 percent. What has inflation done to the real (inflation-adjusted) return on Michael and Melissa's savings? It has caused it to be negative. Michael and Melissa will end up with $6,315 at the end of the year, but because of the 10 percent inflation rate they will need $6,600 to purchase what they could have purchased with $6,000 the year before. The real return on their savings is *minus* 4.75 percent (+5.25% − 10% = −4.75%).

Today most savings accounts pay an interest rate that has been (upwardly) adjusted for an *expected inflation rate.* The rate they pay is the **nominal interest rate,** which is equal to the **real interest rate** plus the expected inflation rate.[3]

Nominal interest rate = real interest rate + expected inflation rate

Simply because most savings accounts offer an interest rate to savers that has been adjusted upward for the expected inflation rate, it doesn't necessarily follow that savers are guaranteed a positive real return on their savings. After all, the expected inflation rate may turn out to be much less than the actual inflation rate.

To illustrate, we need to distinguish between the **ex ante real interest rate** and the **ex post real interest rate.** *Ex ante* means "before" and *ex post* means "after." Here, *ex ante* refers to *before* the actual inflation rate has been realized, and *ex post* refers to *after* the actual inflation rate has been realized.

Ex ante real interest rate = nominal interest rate − expected inflation rate

Ex post real interest rate = nominal interest rate − actual inflation rate

Suppose the nominal interest rate is 8 percent and the expected inflation rate is 4 percent. It follows that the ex ante real interest rate is 4 percent. Now suppose

Nominal Interest Rate
The interest rate actually charged (or paid); the market interest rate. Nominal interest rate = real interest rate + expected inflation rate.

Real Interest Rate
In general, the inflation-adjusted interest rate. However, sometimes it is better to refer to either the *ex ante real interest rate* or the *ex post real interest rate* (see below).

Ex ante real interest rate
The nominal interest rate minus the expected inflation rate.

Ex post real interest rate
The nominal interest rate minus the actual inflation rate.

[3]A broader definition is nominal interest rate = real interest rate + expected rate of change in the price level, because we will not always be dealing with an expected inflation rate; we could be dealing with an expected deflation rate. (Deflation is a fall in the price level.) Saying "the expected rate of change in the price level" allows for either inflation or deflation.

the actual inflation rate turns out to be 9 percent. This means the ex post real interest rate is −1 percent.

Inflation and Lenders and Borrowers. Suppose Susan, a borrower, borrows $1,000 from Joann, a lender. Furthermore, suppose Susan agrees to pay Joann back in one year at a 7 percent rate of interest. If there is unanticipated inflation, Susan will be paying back the loan with dollars worth less in terms of their purchasing power than the dollars Joann lent her. We conclude that unanticipated inflation redistributes buying power from lenders to borrowers.

Inflation and Social Tension. Does inflation cause social tension? Some of the effects of inflation on savers, creditors, and homebuyers are likely to lead to a degree of social tension. It is not uncommon for affected individuals to blame certain persons or groups (sometimes mistakenly) for the inflation. Scapegoats abound. For example, corporations or labor unions are easy targets.

Inflation and Past Decisions. Inflation often turns past decisions into mistakes. Consider the contractor who last year contracted to build a shopping mall for $50 million. He agreed to this dollar figure based on his estimates of the prices of the resources he would need to build the mall. All of a sudden, inflation hits. Prices of labor, concrete, trucks, nails, tile, roofing, and so forth rise. Now the contractor may look back on his decision to build the mall for only $50 million as a mistake, a costly mistake for him.

Inflation and Uncertainty. Staying with our contractor, suppose he takes a loss on the shopping mall. Time passes, and he is offered the opportunity to bid on the construction of another mall. He notes a few important facts: (1) He took a loss on the last shopping mall because unanticipated inflation hit. (2) At present, there is a specific inflation rate, say, 4 percent, but the contractor doesn't know if the inflation rate next year will be 4 percent, less than 4 percent (if so, how much less?), or more than 4 percent (if so, how much more?). (3) The contractor realizes that he doesn't know what the future will bring on the inflation front, and because of this, his bid on the shopping mall, if accepted, may result in another financial disaster for him. Our point is simply that with inflation comes uncertainty, and this added uncertainty is likely to cause some individuals to decide not to enter into long-term contracts. It follows that many mutually advantageous exchanges will go unrealized.

Inflation and Hedging against Inflation. What do individuals in an inflation-prone economy do that individuals in a stable price economy do not do? They try to hedge against inflation. They try to figure out what investments offer the best protection against inflation. Would gold, real estate, or fine art be the best hedge? They travel to distant cities to hear "experts" talk on inflation. They subscribe to newsletters that claim to predict future inflation rates accurately. All this, obviously, requires an expenditure of resources—resources, we remind ourselves, that once expended in the effort to protect against inflation can no longer be used to build factories or produce shoes, houses, or cars. An effect of inflation is that it causes individuals to try to hedge against it, thereby diverting resources away from strictly productive activities.

Inflation and International Competitiveness

We live in a world economy where the U.S. inflation rate relative to other nations' inflation rates matters. To illustrate, suppose the U.S. CPI is 110 and the French CPI is 110, too. In relative terms, the U.S. and France are on equal footing. Now suppose the U.S. CPI rises to 120 and the French CPI rises to 112. The U.S. inflation rate is 9 percent and the French inflation rate is 1.8 percent. In relative terms, U.S. goods have become more expensive and French goods have become cheaper. Both Americans and the French end up buying more French goods and fewer American goods, *ceteris paribus*. The United States has become less competitive relative to France. In Exhibit 13–7 we note the inflation rate for selected nations during the period 1983–88.

Expectations, Nominal Interest Rates, and Inflation

In the preceding discussion, we mentioned that individuals form an expected inflation rate, which is included in the nominal interest rate (the nominal interest rate equals the real interest rate *plus* the expected inflation rate). Here we focus on the expected inflation rate and the nominal interest rate, specifically, on two major questions: (1) How is the expected inflation rate formed? (2) Since a change in the money supply can affect the two components of the nominal interest rate—that is, the real interest rate and the expected inflation rate—what is the directional pattern and time path traveled by the nominal interest rate in response to a change in the money supply?

The Expected Inflation Rate: How Is It Formed?

Two theories of expectations seek to explain how individuals form the expected inflation rate. One is **adaptive expectations;** the other is **rational expectations.** Adaptive expectations theory holds that individuals form the expected inflation rate based on past inflation rate experience and that they only gradually modify their expectations as the present and future unfold. For example, suppose the inflation rate has been 5 percent for the past seven years. Adaptive expectations theory would predict that the expected inflation rate in year 8 would be 5 percent. This would be the case *even if* the chairman of the Fed's Board of Governors said

Adaptive Expectations
Expectations that individuals form from past experience and modify slowly as the present and the future become the past (as time passes).

Rational Expectations
Expectations that individuals form based on past experience and also on their predictions about the effects of present and future policy actions and events.

EXHIBIT 13–7
Inflation Rates, Selected Nations and Selected Years

NATION	1983–84	1984–85	1985–86	1986–87	1987–88
United States	4.3	3.6	1.9	3.7	4.0
Argentina	626.7	672.1	90.1	98.2	(NA)
Brazil	197.0	226.9	145.2	229.7	682.3
Canada	4.3	4.0	4.2	4.4	4.0
France	7.4	5.8	2.5	3.3	2.7
Israel	373.8	304.6	48.1	19.9	16.2
Japan	2.3	2.0	.6	—	.7
Switzerland	2.9	3.4	.8	1.4	1.9
United Kingdom	5.1	6.1	3.4	4.2	4.9

SOURCE: U.S. Bureau of the Census, *Statistical Abstract of the United States,* 1990 (Washington, D.C.: U.S. Government Printing Office, 1990).

that the Fed expected to immediately and sharply increase the money supply growth rate. Since this piece of information does not relate to *past* inflation rate experience (but rather to *future* inflation), adaptive expectations theory assumes it is not taken into consideration.

Rational expectations theory holds that individuals form the expected inflation rate, not only on the basis of their past experience with inflation, but also on their predictions about the effects of present and future policy actions and events. In short, the expected inflation rate is formed by looking at the past, present, and future. Again, suppose the inflation rate has been 5 percent for the past seven years. All of a sudden, individuals hear the chairman of the Fed's Board of Governors talking about sharply "stimulating the economy." Rational expectationists would argue that the expected inflation rate might automatically jump upward, based on the current words of the chairman.

A major difference between adaptive and rational expectations is the speed at which the expected inflation rate changes. If the expected inflation rate is formed adaptively, then it is slower to change (since it is based only on the past, and individuals will wait until the present and the future become the past before they change their expectations) than if it is formed rationally (where it is based on the past, present, and future).

As we see in later chapters, whether the expected inflation rate is formed adaptively or rationally will have important consequences on the effects of monetary and fiscal policy. In this chapter, however, we are concerned about its effects on the nominal interest rate. The slower the expected rate of inflation changes, the slower the nominal interest rate adjusts to its long-run position, given a change in the money supply; the faster the expected rate of inflation changes, the faster the nominal interest rate adjusts to its long-run position, given a change in the money supply. We illustrate this in the next section.

Increases in the Money Supply and Changes in the Nominal Interest Rate

As we said earlier, the money supply can affect the two components of the nominal interest rate—the real interest rate and the expected inflation rate. Here we first review how the money supply affects the real interest rate and then how it affects the expected inflation rate.

How the Money Supply Affects the Real Interest Rate.   Suppose the Federal Reserve buys government securities from the public. As we learned in Chapter 12, this open market purchase increases the reserves of the banking system and ultimately leads to more bank lending. In short, it leads to an increase in the supply of loanable funds. An increase in the supply of loanable funds leads to a decrease in the price of loanable funds, or a decrease in the real interest rate. Because the real interest rate falls, so does the nominal interest rate, since the nominal rate is equal to the real rate plus the expected inflation rate. This decrease in the real and nominal interest rates due to an increase in the supply of loanable funds is referred to as the **liquidity effect.**

We also know from Chapter 11 that an increase in bank lending activity increases the money supply. The increase in the money supply leads to an increase in aggregate demand and to an increase in GNP. (In terms of our *AD–AS* diagram, an increase in the money supply shifts the *AD* curve rightward, which causes both the price level, *P*, and real GNP, *Q*, to rise in the short run. Since both *P* and *Q* rise, so does GNP, which is *P times Q.*) Most economists hold that an increase in

Liquidity Effect
The decrease in the real and nominal interest rates due to an increase in the supply of loanable funds.

GNP will bring about an increase in the demand for loanable funds (greater than the increase in supply). The notion here is that with rising GNP, many individuals who ordinarily would not have tried to borrow will demand credit. This increased demand for loanable funds puts upward pressure on the real interest rate and therefore the nominal interest rate, too. This increase in the real and nominal interest rates brought on by the increase in GNP is referred to as the **income effect.**

Income Effect
The increase in the real and nominal interest rates brought on by an increase in GNP.

How the Money Supply Affects the Expected Inflation Rate. Earlier, we established that continued increases in the money supply cause continued inflation. We also established that the expected inflation rate, using either adaptive or rational expectations, is a function of past inflation rates (although using rational expectations, it is a function of more than simply this).

It follows that there is an indirect link between the expected inflation rate and increases in the money supply. We would expect that the greater the increases in the money supply, the greater the inflation rate and the higher the expected inflation rate, *ceteris paribus*. From this we can conclude that the higher the expected inflation rate, the higher the nominal interest rate. The increase in the nominal interest rate due to a higher expected inflation rate is referred to as the **expectations effect.**[4]

Expectations Effect
The increase in the nominal interest rate due to a higher expected inflation rate.

In summary, the money supply affects the real interest rate and therefore the nominal interest rate via the liquidity and income effects. In addition, the money supply affects the expected inflation rate, and therefore the nominal interest rate, via the expectations effect. We conclude that the money supply affects the nominal interest rate via three effects: liquidity, income, and expectations. Exhibit 13–8 illustrates these three effects.

Question:

A look at Exhibit 13–8 might lead one to conclude that given an increase in the money supply, the liquidity effect kicks in first, the income effect occurs next, and lastly the expectations effect occurs. Is this the ordering of occurrence: liquidity effect, income effect, and then expectations effect?

Answer:

No. Exhibit 13–8 does not illustrate the sequence of effects; it simply illustrates the effects. For one, we learn that given an increase in the money supply the liquidity effect pushes the nominal interest rate downward, and the income and expectations effects push it upward. The exhibit also illustrates that the income effect is approximately the same size as the liquidity effect and more or less offsets it. (To see this, notice in the exhibit that the income effect moves i_1 up by about the same amount that the liquidity effect moves i_2 down.) Thus, the net effect on the nominal interest rate is derived from the expectations effect.

Timing of the Adjustment

Exhibit 13–8 raises an important question, mainly, how much time passes between point 1 and point 4? Or, to put it differently, how long is the period between the increase in the money supply (point 1) and the full impact of the liquidity, income, and expectations effects (points 1–4) on the nominal interest rate? Early research,

---

[4]Sometimes the expectations effect is called the *Fisher effect* after economist Irving Fisher who described it in detail.

EXHIBIT 13–8
The Liquidity, Income, and Expectations Effects

using data from 1945 through the 1960s, estimated that the liquidity effect lasted between 4 to 9 months, the income effect lasted about 6 months, and the time period between points 1 and 4 was several years. Some recent studies, however, based on more recent data, show that the liquidity effect is dominant for only about one month. From this we conclude that (1) the expectations effect is kicking in more quickly, and (2) the time period between points 1 and 4 has been reduced.

What accounts for this? Most economists explain it by saying that over time individuals appear to have formed their expectations of the future inflation rate based on present monetary growth and past inflation rates, instead of only past inflation rates. As a consequence, the expectations effect starts to occur earlier than in the past. This experience lends support to the rational expectations view of inflation expectations.

The Definition of Measurement of Inflation

■ Inflation is an increase in the price level. One-shot inflation is a one-time increase in the price level. Continued inflation is a continued increase in the price level.

■ The consumer price index (CPI) and the GNP deflator are both used to measure inflation.

One-Shot Inflation

■ One-shot inflation can result from an increase in aggregate demand or a decrease in short-run aggregate supply.

■ Both an increase in aggregate demand and a decrease in short-run aggregate supply have short- and long-run effects on real GNP and the price level (see Exhibits 13–1 and 13–2). Starting from long-run equilibrium, the short-run effects of an increase in aggregate demand are that real GNP and the price level increase. The long-run effects of an increase in aggregate demand are that real GNP returns to its original level and the price level increases. Starting from long-run equilibrium, the short-run effects of a decrease in short-run aggregate supply are that real GNP decreases and the price level increases. The long-run effects of a decrease in short-run aggregate supply are that real GNP and the price level return to their original levels.

Continued Inflation

■ To change temporary inflation into continued inflation, it is necessary and sufficient to have a continued increase in aggregate demand.

■ Continued increases in the money supply cause continued increases in aggregate demand and continued inflation.

The Effects of Inflation

■ The effects of inflation are often different depending on whether inflation is unanticipated, correctly anticipated, or incorrectly anticipated. In this chapter, we discussed mainly the effects of unanticipated inflation.

■ Inflation is a "tax" on peoples' money holdings.

■ Inflation either lowers the real rate of return on savings or turns it negative.

■ Inflation redistributes purchasing power from lenders to borrowers.

■ Inflation can lead to social tension, particularly if individuals do not understand the cause of inflation.

■ Inflation may turn past decisions into mistakes.

■ Inflation causes increased uncertainty and may cause some individuals to choose not to enter into long-term contracts.

■ Inflation causes individuals to try to hedge against it; in the process they divert resources away from strictly productive activities.

■ An increase in the U.S. inflation rate relative to its trading partners' inflation rates leads to a decline in U.S. competitiveness in the international marketplace.

Expectations, Nominal Interest Rates, and Inflation

■ The nominal interest rate = real interest rate + expected inflation rate.

■ Both the adaptive expectations and rational expectations theories explain how individuals form the expected inflation rate. Adaptive expectations holds that individuals form the expected inflation rate based on past inflation rates. Rational expectations holds that individuals form the expected inflation rate based on past inflation rates and on their predictions of the effects of present and future policy actions and events.

■ A major difference between adaptive and rational expectations is the speed at which the expected inflation rate changes. If the expected inflation rate is formed adaptively, it changes more slowly (since it is based only on the past and individuals must wait until the present and the future become the past before they change their expectations) than if it is formed rationally (where it is based on the past, present, and future).

The Money Supply and Nominal Interest Rates

■ The money supply affects both the real interest rate and the expected inflation rate; hence it follows that the money supply also affects the nominal interest rate since the nominal interest rate = real interest rate + expected inflation rate.

■ The money supply affects the nominal interest rate via three effects: liquidity, income, and expectations. The decrease in the real and nominal interest rates due to an increase in the supply of loanable funds is referred to as the liquidity effect. The increase in the real and nominal interest rates brought on by an increase in GNP is referred to as the income effect. The increase in the nominal interest rate due to a higher expected inflation rate is referred to as the expectations effect.

Key Terms and Concepts

Inflation

One-Shot Inflation

Continued Inflation

Nominal Interest Rate

Real Interest Rate

Ex Ante Real Interest Rate

Ex Post Real Interest Rate

Adaptive Expectations

Rational Expectations

Liquidity Effect

Income Effect

Expectations Effect

QUESTIONS AND PROBLEMS

1. "A loaf of bread, a computer, and automobile tires have gone up in price; therefore, we are experiencing inflation." Do you agree or disagree with this statement? Explain your answer.

2. What is the difference in the long run between a one-shot increase in aggregate demand and a one-shot decrease in short-run aggregate supply?

3. In recent years, economists have argued over what the true value of the real interest rate is at any one time and over time. Given that the nominal interest rate = real interest rate + expected inflation rate, it follows that the real interest rate = nominal interest rate − expected inflation rate. Why do you think there is so much disagreement over the true value of the real interest rate?

4. Suppose there has been an increase in the price level in each of the last three years. Does this mean the money supply must have increased during this three-year period?

5. Here is the CPI for a few years. Calculate the inflation rate for 1981–89.

Year	CPI
1980	82.4
1981	90.9
1982	96.5
1983	99.6
1984	103.9
1985	107.6
1986	109.6
1987	113.6
1988	118.3
1989	124.0
1990	130.7

6. "One-shot inflation may be a demand-side (of the economy) or supply-side phenomenon, but continued inflation is likely to be a demand-side phenomenon." Do you agree or disagree with this statement? Explain your answer.

7. How might the Fed influence the international competitiveness of the United States?

8. "An increase in the money supply causes continued inflation." Explain why this statement is false.

9. Explain how demand-induced one-shot inflation may appear as supply-induced one-shot inflation.

10. What would we have to observe before we could conclude that continued inflation was a supply-side phenomenon?

CLASSICAL AND MONETARIST THEORY: EMPHASIS ON THE PRICE LEVEL AND GNP

WHAT THIS CHAPTER IS ABOUT

In Chapter 9, we learned that the main focus of Keynesian theory is on high unemployment and therefore on "real GNP that is below natural real GNP." In *P–Q* terms, Keynesians are interested in *Q.* In this chapter, we discuss classical economics and monetarism. Classical economics looks at the price level, or *P,* and monetarism emphasizes GNP, or *P times Q.* Both classical economists and monetarists regard the money supply as the major explanatory variable of changes in *P* and GNP.

CLASSICAL MONETARY THEORY

Classical monetary theory revolves around the equation of exchange and the simple quantity theory of money.

The Equation of Exchange

The equation of exchange is an identity that states that the money supply (M) multiplied by velocity (V) must be equal to the price level (P) times real GNP (Q).

$$MV = PQ$$

What is **velocity?** It is the average number of times a dollar is spent to buy final goods and services in a year. Think of an economy with only 10 one-dollar bills. In January, the first of the 10 one-dollar bills moves from Smith's hands to Jones's hands to buy good X. Then in June it goes from Jones's hands to Brown's hands to buy good Y. And in December it goes from Brown's hands to Peterson's hands to buy good Z. Over the course of the year, this dollar bill has changed hands 3 times.

The other dollar bills also change hands during the year. The second dollar bill changes hands 5 times, the third 6 times, the fourth 2 times, the fifth 7 times, the sixth 1 time, the seventh 2 times, the eighth 2 times, the ninth 3 times, and the tenth 4 times. Given this information, we calculate the number of times the average dollar changes hands in making a purchase. In this case the number is 3.5. This number (3.5) is velocity.

In a large economy such as ours, it is impossible to figure out how many times each dollar changes hands, and therefore it is impossible to calculate velocity the way we have done here. Instead a different way is used.

First, we calculate GNP; next, we calculate the average money supply; finally, we divide GNP by the average money supply to obtain velocity. For example, if $4,800 billion worth of transactions occur in a year, and the average money supply during the year is $800 billion, a dollar must have been used on average 6 times during the year to purchase goods and services. In symbols, we have

$$V \equiv \text{GNP}/M$$

(The sign $\equiv$ means "must be equal to"; this is an identity.) Since we know that GNP is equal to $P \times Q$, we can rewrite this as

$$V \equiv P \times Q/M$$

If we multiply both sides by M, we get

$$M \times V \equiv P \times Q$$

which is the **equation of exchange.** Exactly what the equation of exchange tells us can be interpreted in different ways. Here are a few of them:

1. The money supply multiplied by velocity must equal the price level times real GNP: $M \times V \equiv P \times Q$.
2. The money supply multiplied by velocity must equal GNP: $M \times V \equiv \text{GNP}$ (since $P \times Q \equiv \text{GNP}$). (Recall that when we use the letters "GNP" alone, we are referring to nominal GNP.)
3. Total spending (measured by MV) must equal the total sales revenues of business firms (measured by PQ): $MV \equiv PQ$.

In fact, the third way of explaining the equation of exchange is perhaps the most intuitively simple to understand. It simply says that the total expenditures (of

Velocity
The average number of times a dollar is spent to buy final goods and services in a year.

Equation of Exchange
An identity stating that the money supply times velocity must be equal to the price level times real GNP.

Simple Quantity Theory of Money
The theory that assumes that V and Q are constant and predicts that changes in M lead to strictly proportional changes in P.

buyers) must equal the total sales (of sellers). Consider a simple economy where there is only one buyer and one seller. If the buyer buys a book for $20, then the seller receives $20. Stated differently, the money supply in the example, or $20, times velocity, 1, is equal to the price of the book, $20, times the quantity of the book, 1.

From the Equation of Exchange to the Simple Quantity Theory of Money

Saying that the money supply times velocity must equal GNP is not a theory of the macroeconomy. For example, if M increases, it does not necessarily follow that GNP increases. Why? Because as M increases, V may decrease, and therefore MV may not increase at all. And if MV does not increase, neither will GNP.

To turn the equation of exchange into a theory, we need to make some assumptions about the variables in the equation. Many eighteenth-century classical economists, as well as the American economist Irving Fisher (1867–1947) and the English economist Alfred Marshall (1842–1924), assumed that changes in velocity are so small that for all practical purposes velocity can be assumed constant (especially over short periods of time) and that real GNP, or Q, is fixed in the short run. Hence, they turned the equation of exchange, which is simply true by definition, into a theory by assuming that both V and Q are fixed, or constant. With these two assumptions, we have the **simple quantity theory of money.** If V and Q are constant, we would predict that changes in M will bring about *strictly proportional* changes in P. This point is illustrated in Exhibit 14–1.

On the left side of the exhibit, the key assumptions of the simple quantity theory are noted: V and Q are constant. Also, $M \times V = P \times Q$ is noted. We use the equal sign (=) instead of the identity sign ($\equiv$) because we are speaking about the simple quantity theory and not the equation of exchange. (The = sign here represents "is predicted to be equal"; that is, given our assumptions, $M \times V$, or MV, is predicted to be equal to $P \times Q$, or PQ.)

Starting with the first row, the money supply is $500, velocity is 4, real GNP (Q) is 1,000 units, and the price level, or price index, $2.[1] GNP therefore equals $2,000. In the second row, the money supply increases by 100 percent—from $500 to $1,000—and both V and Q are constant, at 4 and 1,000, respectively. The price level moves from $2 to $4. On the right-hand side of the exhibit, we see that a 100 percent increase in M predicts a 100 percent increase in P. Changes in P are predicted to be strictly proportional to changes in M.

---

[1] You are perhaps used to seeing real GNP written as a dollar figure and a price index as a number without a dollar sign in front of it. We have switched things for purposes of this example, as it is easier to think of Q as "so many units of goods" and P as the average price paid per unit of these goods.

EXHIBIT 14–1

Assumptions and Predictions of the Simple Quantity Theory of Money
The simple quantity theory of money assumes that both V and Q are constant. (A bar over each indicates this in the exhibit.) The prediction is that changes in M lead to strictly proportional changes in P. (Note: For purposes of this example, think of Q as "so many units of a good" and of P as the "average price paid per unit of these goods.")

ASSUMPTIONS OF SIMPLE QUANTITY THEORY							PREDICTIONS OF SIMPLE QUANTITY THEORY	
M	× $\overline{V}$	= P	× $\overline{Q}$	= GNP			% Change in M	= % Change in P
$ 500	4	$2	1,000	$2,000				
1,000	4	4	1,000	4,000			+ 100%	+ 100%
1,500	4	6	1,000	6,000			+ 50	+ 50
1,200	4	4.80	1,000	4,800			− 20	− 20

Does the Fed Think in Terms of *MV = PQ*?

There is some evidence that the Fed looks at the economy in terms of *MV = PQ*. A few research economists at the Fed have proceeded this way:

First, they set *M* equal to the actual money supply (they use *M*2, so let's set *M*2 equal to $3,600 billion). Then they set *V* equal to the long-run average velocity of the money supply (they use *M*2 velocity, which is relatively stable with a mean value of 1.59). Next, they set *Q* in the equation equal to Q_N, or natural real GNP. The implicit assumption here is that the economy moves toward its natural real GNP level.

By checking whether the current unemployment rate is near the natural unemployment rate, economists know whether the current real GNP (*Q*) is or is not approximately equal to natural real GNP (Q_N). For now, let's say the economy is currently operating at natural unemployment, so that the current real GNP and the natural real GNP are the same at $4,200 billion. Placing the numbers (dollars in billions) into our equation, we get:

$$M \times V = P \times Q$$

$$\$3,600 \times 1.59 = ? \times \$4,200$$

On the left side of the equation, we get $5,724 (which is *M* × *V*). On the right side of the equation, we get $4,200*P* (which is *P* times *Q*). Solving for *P*, we get 1.36 ($5,724/$4,200 = *P* = 1.36). Multiplying by 100, we get 136.

What does the number "136" tell us? It tells us simply that if (1) the economy is moving toward its natural real GNP level, (2) velocity is stable at 1.59, and (3) the money supply is $3,600 billion, then the price level that will be established by the economy in the long run is 136.

Fed economists could then compare the predicted long-run price level (136) with the current price level—say, as measured by the GNP deflator. Suppose the current GNP deflator (124) is lower than the predicted long-run price level (136). Fed economists may conclude that current monetary policy (recall that the current money supply in our example is $3,600) will tend to raise the price level in the long run. In short, current monetary policy is inflationary. This gives Fed officials information about where the economy is headed if they simply hold fast. Of course, if price stability is currently a major goal, they may want to reverse course.

In the third row, *M* increases by 50 percent, and *P* is predicted to increase by 50 percent. In the fourth row, *M* decreases by 20 percent, and *P* is predicted to decrease by 20 percent.

In summary, the simple quantity theory assumes that both *V* and *Q* are constant in the short run, and therefore predicts that changes in *M* lead to strictly proportional changes in *P*.

Question:

A key question would seem to be: Are V and Q constant in the short run as the classical economists assumed? If they are not, then shouldn't the simple quantity theory of money, which assumes that they are, be disregarded?

Answer:

To a degree, the answer depends on how we define the short run. If we consider the short run as 24 hours, it is unlikely that either *V* or *Q* is going to change. If the time frame is a period of months, it is likely that *V* and *Q* would only register tiny changes, so small, in fact, that we might want to overlook them. Over a longer period, though, both *V* and *Q* can and do change. For example, the average annual change in velocity during the period 1987–1990 was approximately 3.0 percent, and the average annual change in real GNP during this period was approximately 2.8 percent.

Suppose we found that both velocity and real GNP were not constant, even for reasonably short periods of time. In short, suppose the assumptions of the theory are not 100 percent accurate. Is this a good enough reason to discard the theory? Many economists answer no. They argue that a theory should be evaluated in terms of the accuracy of its predictions instead of the degree of realism of its assumptions (see Chapter 1).

Follow-up Question:

Well, then, perhaps the question should be: Does the simple quantity theory of money predict well? Does it make predictions that are consistently substantiated by the facts?

Answer:

The simple quantity theory of money says that changes in the money supply bring about strictly proportional changes in prices. We do not always observe this strict proportionality. But what we do observe is that countries with higher money supply growth rates tend to have higher price level growth rates than those countries with lower money supply growth rates. And this definitely is a theme of the simple quantity theory of money. To illustrate briefly, during the period 1969–84, Argentina's annual money supply growth rate was 79.3 percent, and its annual growth rate in prices was 80.6 percent. During the period 1950–83, the annual growth rate in the U.S. money supply was 5.3 percent, and its annual growth rate in prices was 4.3 percent. As Exhibit 14–1 makes clear, the simple quantity theory of money predicts that larger percentage increases in the money supply will bring about greater percentage increases in the price level.

MONETARISM

∎

Economists who call themselves *monetarists* have not been content to rely on the simple quantity theory of money. For one, they do not hold that velocity is constant; instead, they believe that velocity moves in a predictable way. They conclude that changes in the money supply and/or money demand change GNP.

The Demand for Money

Before pursuing monetarist theory, we need to discuss the demand for money (or money demand). Following are several statements that explain this phenomenon.

1. Money is a good and thus there is a demand for it. In Chapter 11, we defined money as a good—specifically, a good that is widely accepted for purposes of exchange. There is a demand for money, just as there is a demand for apples, telephones, socks, music keyboards, and other goods.

2. Individuals demand money in order to hold it, not to consume it. If a person demands an orange, most likely she buys it in order to consume it. The demand for money is not the same. People demand money, not to consume it, but to *hold* it. One of many reasons people hold money is to be ready to take advantage of opportunities that may arise in the future. In short, gains can be made from demanding, or holding, the most liquid asset of all—money.

3. Money is not the same as income, or anything else that might be incorrectly equated with money. Money is a *stock,* income is a *flow.* A stock is measured at one point in time; a flow is measured over time. For example, Alice may say that she has $25,000. This is a given amount of money at one instant in time. The

$25,000 is a stock; specifically, Alice's *money stock.* Alternatively, Alice may say that she earns $1,000 per month. In this case, we have a time period, one month. The $1,000 is Alice's income.

Suppose George, an employee at a furniture company, tells us that he is going to demand more money from his boss. Do you think George is demanding more *money* or more *income?* He said money, which is a stock, but it is likely that he means income. He probably doesn't want more money at one instant in time—a lump-sum payment right now—but rather a greater money flow *over time;* that is, a higher income every month.

When we talk about the demand for money, we are talking about the demand for a stock.

4. The quantity supplied of money must necessarily equal the quantity (or amount) of money that people actually hold. We shall let the symbol M^S stand for "quantity supplied of money" and the symbol M^{AH} stand for the "quantity of money actually held." So we are saying that $M^S = M^{AH}$.

Suppose M1 is $800 billion. It follows that the quantity of money that people actually hold must *also* be $800 billion. The reason is simple: Someone must be holding the money, the money must belong to someone.[2]

5. The quantity supplied of money (or the quantity of money people actually hold) does not necessarily equal the quantity demanded of money. We shall let the symbol M^d stand for "quantity demanded of money." So we are saying that M^S (and therefore M^{AH}, too) does not necessarily equal M^d.

To see this, suppose, once again, that M^S (and M^{AH}) is $800 billion. It does not necessarily follow that the quantity demanded of money (M^d) is also $800 billion. The quantity demanded of money may be more or less than $800 billion. For example, suppose that at the current level of GNP, the quantity demanded of money is $750 billion. This means that individuals are actually holding more money than they desire to hold given the present economic environment. As we shall soon see, this will bring about a particular behavioral response.

The Money Market Equilibrium Condition

In our discussion of supply and demand in Chapter 3, we noted that market equilibrium exists at the point at which the quantity supplied of a good equals the quantity demanded of the good ($Q_s = Q_d$). Money is a good, and therefore the same condition describes money market equilibrium. Money market equilibrium occurs when the quantity supplied of money equals the quantity demanded of money.

The money market equilibrium condition is

$$M^S = M^d$$

Since $M^S = M^{AH}$, the money market equilibrium condition can be rewritten as

$$M^S = M^{AH} = M^d$$

It follows that there is disequilibrium in the money market when M^S (or M^{AH}) is greater than, or less than, M^d.

[2]If you come across any money that does not belong to you, nor to anyone else, please write the author a letter telling him where it can be found. Many thanks.

The Demand for Money in the *MV–PQ* Framework

Again, consider the equation of exchange, $MV \equiv PQ$. The M in the exchange stands for the quantity supplied of money; thus $M = M^S$. Additionally, PQ is the same as GNP. We can rewrite the equation of exchange as

$$M^S \times V \equiv PQ$$

or

$$M^S \times V \equiv \text{GNP}$$

Now we add a piece of information we have recently acquired: When the money market is in equilibrium, $M^S = M^d$. Knowing that $M^S = M^d$ in equilibrium, we can substitute M^d in the equation of exchange for M^S. We get

$$M^d \times V = PQ$$

We then divide both sides of the modified equation of exchange by V. This gives us

$$M^d = 1/V \times PQ$$

If we let the fraction, $1/V$, equal k (that is, $k = 1/V$), we have

$$M^d = kPQ$$

This says that the quantity demanded of money equals k (a fraction, or the reciprocal of velocity, $1/V$) times PQ, or GNP.

With this simple equation in front of us, it is immediately clear that M^d increases if either k, P, or Q increases and that M^d decreases if either k, P, or Q decreases.

Of course, the net effect on M^d depends on the percentage change in one variable measured against the percentage change in another variable. For example, an *increase* in k accompanied by a proportionally greater *decrease* in P would *decrease* M^d. What are the economic reasons (as opposed to the arithmetical reasons) why M^d increases as P and Q increase?

First, consider P, the price level. As the price level increases, more money is needed to buy a specific bundle of goods—for example, a week's worth of groceries. Next, consider that as Q (real GNP) increases, the number and magnitude of transactions are usually assumed to increase, so individuals will hold larger money balances.[3]

In Exhibit 14–2, PQ, or GNP, is plotted against M^d. We see that as PQ increases, M^d increases; as PQ decreases, M^d decreases. Connecting different levels of PQ, or GNP, with different levels of M^d, we obtain a **money demand line.** Our money demand line represents the direct relationship between the quantity demanded of money and GNP. Changes in PQ, or GNP, will move us from one point on the money demand line to another point on the same line.

Money Demand Line
The graphical representation of the direct relationship between the quantity demanded of money and GNP.

k and *V:* What Variables Affect Them?

Given the equation $M^d = kPQ$, we know that a change in k will bring about a change in the quantity demanded of money: If k increases, so will M^d; if k decreases, so will M^d. But what factors will change k? We discuss three. Note, also, that any variable that changes k also changes velocity (V) since $k = 1/V$. Thus, the following variables can change both k and V.

---

[3]It follows that as the price level decreases, less money is needed to buy any specific bundle of goods. As real GNP decreases, the number and magnitude of transactions are usually assumed to decrease, so that individuals will hold smaller money balances.

Interest Rate. Holding money comes with certain benefits and costs. The cost of holding money is approximated by the interest rate (return) on close substitutes for money, such as bonds, stocks, and savings accounts. If the interest rate on these close substitutes increases (relative to the net return on holding money), individuals desire to hold a smaller fraction of their incomes in money balances, causing a decrease in k.

A similar point can be made of velocity. If the interest rate on the close substitutes for money increases, individuals desire to hold lower money balances and turn over more quickly those money balances they do hold. In short, velocity increases.

Alternatively, if the interest rate on close substitutes for money decreases (relative to the net return on holding money), individuals desire to hold a larger fraction of their incomes in money balances, causing an increase in k. This is the same as saying that velocity decreases.

We summarize: As the interest rate increases, k decreases, and V increases; as the interest rate decreases, k increases, and V decreases.[4]

Expected Rate of Inflation. When individuals expect an increase in the inflation rate, they desire to hold a smaller fraction of their incomes in money balances. The reason is that as the inflation rate rises, the purchasing power of money falls. (In Chapter 13, we said that inflation acts as a tax on peoples' money holdings.) We conclude, then, that an expected increase in the inflation rate will decrease k and increase V. On the other hand, when individuals expect a decrease in the inflation rate, they desire to hold a larger fraction of their incomes in money balances; therefore k increases and V decreases.

The Frequency with Which Employees Receive Paychecks. Economists argue that the more frequently an employee receives a paycheck, the less money (on average) that employee will hold—which implies that the smaller k is. For example, an employee who receives a paycheck twice a month will hold less money (on average) than if he or she receives a paycheck once a month, even if the annual salary is the same in both cases. To illustrate, consider two cases for an employee, Liz.

■ *Case 1:* Here Liz earns $24,000 a year and is paid on the first of each month ($2,000 a month). We assume that she always maintains a $1,000 minimum balance in her checking account. On the first day of the month, when Liz deposits her $2,000 monthly check into her checking account, the balance rises to $3,000. We shall assume that her checking account decreases a little each day as she makes purchases and that by the end of each month she has spent her entire monthly income. This means that on the last day of the month—the day before payday—her checking account balance is $1,000. Therefore, her average checking account balance—or her average money balance holding—is $2,000 (which is halfway between $3,000 and $1,000). If we divide her $24,000 annual income by her average money balance holding of $2,000, we obtain her personal velocity. This is 12.

■ *Case 2:* Now suppose Liz's workplace decides to pay its employees twice a month. Every two weeks, Liz receives a $1,000 paycheck instead of a $2,000 pay-

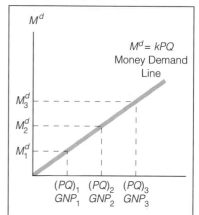

EXHIBIT 14–2
Plotting M^d against PQ, or GNP

M^d

$M^d = kPQ$
Money Demand Line

M_3^d
M_2^d
M_1^d

$(PQ)_1$ $(PQ)_2$ $(PQ)_3$
GNP_1 GNP_2 GNP_3

As PQ, or GNP, increases, the quantity demanded of money, M^d, increases; as PQ, or GNP, decreases, the quantity demanded of money decreases. The money demand line represents this direct relationship.

---

[4]Economists tend to speak about "the" interest rate when, in fact, they are referring to one specific rate among several. We follow this practice in this text. As our present discussion has shown, there is an interest rate (return) on savings, an interest rate (return) on bonds, and an interest rate (return) on stocks. In reality, an individual compares the interest rate (return) on each of these close substitutes for money with the net return on money in order to decide how much money to hold. Speaking about "the" interest rate may incorrectly suggest that only one asset is being compared with money.

check every month. On the first of the month, Liz deposits $1,000 into her checking account and her checking balance rises to $2,000 (remember, she always has a $1,000 minimum balance). Again, we shall assume that Liz draws down the account until on the day before payday she has only the $1,000 minimum balance in her account. Her average money balance holding is now $1,500 (halfway between $1,000 and $2,000). Her personal velocity this time is 16 ($24,000/$1,500 = 16).

Comparing cases 1 and 2, we conclude that the more frequently Liz gets paid, the smaller the money balance that she holds. When she got paid *once* a month, her average money holding was *$2,000;* when she got paid *twice* a month, her average money holding was *$1,500*. This means that the more frequently Liz gets paid, the less money she needs to hold to cover a given number of transactions.

In more technical terms, we can say that the more frequently Liz gets paid, the larger V is and the smaller k is.

For a quick review of the factors that can affect k and V, see Exhibit 14–3.

As *k* Changes, the Money Demand Line Rotates

Anything that causes k or V to change causes the money demand line to rotate. To illustrate, as k decreases—meaning individuals desire to hold a smaller fraction of their income in money balances—the money demand line rotates downward from M_1^d to M_2^d (Exhibit 14–4). This is because as k decreases, M^d falls at a given level of GNP. In the exhibit, M^d falls from $200 billion to $100 billion at a GNP level of $1,000.

As k increases—meaning individuals desire to hold a larger fraction of their income in money balances—the money demand line rotates upward from M_1^d to M_3^d. This is because as k increases, M^d rises at a given level of GNP. In the exhibit, M^d rises from $200 billion to $333 billion at a GNP level of $1,000 billion.

An Increase in the Money Supply

We previously stated that the money market is in equilibrium when $M^s = M^{AH} = M^d$. It is important to remember this as we proceed.

First, consider Exhibit 14–5. At point 1, the money market equilibrium condition is satisfied: $M^s = M^{AH} = M^d$. Now suppose the Fed increases the money supply from M_1^s to M_2^s, or from $600 billion to $700 billion.

EXHIBIT 14–3
Changes in *k* and *V*
An increase in the interest rate, an expected increase in the inflation rate, and an increase in the frequency with which employees receive paychecks all decrease *k* and increase *V*. A decrease in the interest rate, an expected decrease in the inflation rate, and a decrease in the frequency with which employees receive paychecks all increase *k* and decrease *V*.

CONDITIONS	*k*	*V*
Increase in interest rate	Decreases	Increases
Decrease in interest rate	Increases	Decreases
Expected increase in the inflation rate	Decreases	Increases
Expected decrease in the inflation rate	Increases	Decreases
Increase in the frequency with which employees receive paychecks	Decreases	Increases
Decrease in the frequency with which employees receive paychecks	Increases	Decreases

EXHIBIT 14–4
As *k* Changes, the Money Demand Line Rotates

As *k* decreases, individuals desire to hold a smaller fraction of their incomes in money balances, and the money demand line rotates downward. As *k* increases, individuals desire to hold a larger fraction of their incomes in money balances, and the money demand line rotates upward.

Initially, GNP does not change: it remains at $4,000 billion. However, now M^s and M^{AH} are greater than M^d: $700 billion is greater than $600 billion. This can be seen at point 2.

When $M^s = M^{AH} > M^d$, we say that individuals are *holding too much money* (holding excess money balances) at the current level of GNP.

But can individuals really ever be holding too much money? The answer is yes: Individuals can hold too much money *relative* to other goods they desire—such as bonds, stocks, cars, houses, paintings, television sets, and so on. In fact, when individuals are holding too much money, they trade money for other goods; that is, they increase their spending. As a consequence, prices and/or output (P and/or Q) increase. This leads to an increase in PQ, or GNP.

But what happens as PQ, or GNP, rises? As we stated earlier, M^d rises since $M^d = kPQ$. The economy moves up the money demand line from point 1 in Exhibit 14–5 to point 3. At point 3, the money market is in equilibrium, since $M^s = M^{AH} = M^d$.

We conclude that an increase in the money supply increases GNP, *ceteris paribus*.

A Decrease in the Money Supply

Consider Exhibit 14–6. At point 1, the money market equilibrium condition is satisfied: $M^s = M^{AH} = M^d$. Now suppose the Fed decreases the money supply from M_1^s to M_2^s, or from $700 billion to 600 billion.

Initially, GNP does not change: it remains at $4,666 billion. However, now the M^s and M^{AH} are less than M^d: $600 billion is less than $700 billion. This can be seen at point 2.

EXHIBIT 14–5
An Increase in M^s

Starting at point 1, $M^S = M^{AH} = M^d$. Then the money supply increases from M^S_1 to M^S_2. This results in individuals holding too much money (excess money balances); consequently, individuals trade money for other goods, and prices and/or output increase. In either case, GNP increases. As this occurs, the economy moves up the demand line. Equilibrium is at point 3, where once again $M^S = M^{AH} = M^d$.

When $M^s = M^{AH} < M^d$, we say that individuals are *holding too little money* (holding deficient money balances) at the current level of GNP. In fact, when individuals are holding too little money, they cut back on their spending in order to accumulate more money. As a consequence, prices and/or output (P and/or Q) decrease. This leads to a decrease in PQ, or GNP.

But what happens as PQ, or GNP, falls? As we stated earlier, M^d falls since $M^d = kPQ$. The economy moves down the money demand line from point 1 in Exhibit 14–6 to point 3. At point 3, the money market is in equilibrium, since $M^s = M^{AH} = M^d$. We conclude that a decrease in the money supply decreases GNP, *ceteris paribus*.

Three States of the Economy in Monetarism

In earlier chapters, we noted that the economy had to be in one of three states: recessionary gap ($Q < Q_N$), inflationary gap ($Q > Q_N$), or long-run equilibrium ($Q = Q_N$). Two of these states—recessionary and inflationary gaps—are disequilibrium states of the economy and one is not.

This threefold classification of the economy can also be used to categorize monetarism. Using our terms M^s, M^{AH}, and M^d, the economy is always in one of the following states:

1. $M^s = M^{AH} > M^d$

2. $M^s = M^{AH} < M^d$

3. $M^s = M^{AH} = M^d$

EXHIBIT 14–6
A Decrease in M^s

Starting at point 1, $M^S = M^{AH} = M^d$. Then the money supply decreases from M_1^S to M_2^S. This results in individuals holding too little money (deficient money balances); consequently, individuals cut back on their spending. As a result GNP decreases. As this occurs, the economy moves down the money demand line. Equilibrium is at point 3, where once again $M^S = M^{AH} = M^d$.

In short, individuals can hold (1) too much, (2) too little, or (3) the right amount of money. The first two are disequilibrium states and the third is not. In Exhibit 14–7 we show these three states and note what happens to spending and GNP in each case.

"Equilibrium" and "disequilibrium" are important categories for the economist: A market is either in equilibrium or disequilibrium; an economy is either in equilibrium or disequilibrium. When a market or an economy is in equilibrium, the economist knows that economic forces are in balance. When a market or an economy is in disequilibrium, the economist knows that there

EXHIBIT 14–7
The Monetarist Position
If $M^s = M^{AH} > M^d$, individuals are holding too much money, they increase their spending, and GNP rises. If $M^s = M^{AH} < M^d$, individuals are holding too little money, they then decrease their spending, and GNP falls. If $M^s = M^{AH} = M^d$, individuals are holding the right amount of money and do not change their spending.

CONDITION	INDIVIDUALS ARE HOLDING . . .	SPENDING . . .	GNP . . .
$M^s = M^{AH} > M^d$ (Disequilibrium)	Too Much Money	Increases	Rises
$M^s = M^{AH} < M^d$ (Disequilibrium)	Too Little Money	Decreases	Falls
$M^s = M^{AH} = M^d$ (Equilibrium)	The Right Amount of Money	Does Not Change	Does Not Change

are changes to be made. The economist then tries to figure out what those changes will be and why.

In a way, "equilibrium" is "home," and "disequilibrium" is "away from home." And for the economist, economic forces are usually trying to move things home—to equilibrium. Much of economics is simply the story of what goes on during the trip.

The Big Question: How Stable Are *k* and *V*?

We know that $M^d = kPQ$. If we divide both sides by PQ, we are left with $M^d/PQ = k$.

With this in mind, let us return to Exhibit 14–5. At the first equilibrium position, point 1, $M^d = \$600$ billion and $(PQ)_1 = \$4,000$. Calculating k at point 1, we get .15. Now let us move to the second equilibrium position, point 2, where $M^d = \$700$ billion and $(PQ)_2 = \$4,666$. Calculating k at point 2, we get .15. It is noticeable that k equals .15 at both equilibrium positions. In short, where we increased M^s, and found that this led to an increase in PQ, or GNP, k did not change.

What does it mean if k does not change? It means that the money demand line does not rotate downward or upward since only a change in k will do this. Stated differently, if k does not change, it means that the demand for money (how much money individuals want to hold as a percentage of their incomes) is completely stable. Again, we need to remind ourselves that saying the demand for money is stable does not imply that the quantity demanded of money is stable. The demand for money refers to either the money demand line or the percentage of income held as money, whereas the quantity demanded of money refers to the absolute number of dollars held. As we said, it is possible for individuals to maintain money balances at 15 percent (of their incomes) no matter what their incomes, while at the same time holding more money (in absolute terms) at a GNP of $4,666 billion than at $4,000 billion.

Most monetarists do not maintain that k and V are completely stable (that is, never changing), but do hold that both are highly stable. They allow for small changes in k and V; furthermore, they hold that these changes are predictable.

Whether k and V are highly stable and predictable is an empirical issue. Here we simply ask what the implications would be if the monetarist position on k and V is correct.

First, and most important, the monetarist position implies that changes in the money supply strongly affect GNP in a predictable manner (Exhibit 14–8).

Consider two extreme cases: case 1, where k and V are completely stable; and case 2, where k and V are largely unstable. Suppose the money supply increases from M_1^s to M_2^s. In case 1, k is completely stable, so the economy moves from point A to point B and GNP rises from GNP$_1$ to GNP$_2$.

In case 2, as the money supply increases, k increases, and because k increases, the money demand line rotates upward from M_1^d to M_2^d.[4] We have greatly accentuated this upward rotation in the money demand line, so much that our new equilibrium is at point C, giving us the same GNP level we had at point A before the money supply increased. Because of this large change in k, and consequent large change in the money demand line, the initial impact of an increased money supply on GNP is *completely offset*.

We conclude that the degree to which an increase in the money supply leads to

[5]We are implicitly assuming that as the money supply increases, the interest rate decreases. As we have learned, when the interest rate decreases, k increases, rotating the money demand line upward.

EXHIBIT 14–8
The Demand for Money and GNP

M^d changes and completely offsets increase in money supply. No change in PQ or GNP. Economy ends up here.

M^d is stable as money supply increases. Increase in PQ or GNP. Economy ends up here.

Economy starts here.

Two extreme cases are illustrated here. Starting at point A, the money supply increases from M^S_1 to M^S_2. If the demand for money is stable—that is, k, or V, is stable—then the economy moves to point B. GNP increases from GNP_1 to GNP_2. If, however, k increases as the money supply increases, then the money demand line rotates upward. We have accentuated the rotation in the demand line so that we end up at point C. We conclude that the degree to which an increase in the money supply increases GNP depends on the degree to which k rises in response to an increase in the money supply.

an increase in GNP depends on the degree to which k rises in response to an increase in the money supply. The less k rises, the greater the increase in GNP given an increase in the money supply; the more k rises, the smaller the increase in GNP given an increase in the money supply.

In summary, the monetarist position specifies that the demand for money is highly stable. To put it differently, monetarists maintain that V and k are highly stable and predictable. This means that both change, but only slightly, and not in an erratic or random way. The monetarist conclusion–prediction is that changes in the money supply will strongly affect GNP.

Stating Monetarism *MV–PQ* Terms

We have presented monetarism in terms of the money demand equation, $M^d = kPQ$, and M^s. Since in equilibrium $M^s = M^d$, it is easy to replace M^d with M^s, and we see that in equilibrium $M^s = kPQ$. What does this tell us? It tells us that a change on the left-hand side of the equation—in M^s—will bring about a strictly proportional change on the right-hand side of the equation, in PQ, if k is constant. For example, suppose $M^s = \$600$ billion, $PQ = \$4,000$ billion, and $k = .15$. Now let M^s rise to $\$700$ billion, which is a 16.6 percent increase. If k is constant, then PQ rises to $\$4,666$ billion—or by a 16.6 percent increase. In more general terms, monetarism states that the smaller the change in k, the closer the percentage change in PQ will come to equaling the percentage change in M^s.

What we have just said about monetarism can be translated into MV–PQ terms. This is because the two equations, $M^d = kPQ$ and $M^s = kPQ$, are no more than a rewritten version of $MV = PQ$ since $k = 1/V$. Speaking in $MV = PQ$ terms, monetarism states that the smaller the change in V, the closer the percentage change in PQ will come to equaling the percentage change in the money supply.

Keynesian and Monetarist Theory Contrasted

In Chapter 9, we learned that Keynesians focus on the spending components of total expenditures—C, I, G, and net exports. Monetarists take a broader-brush approach by focusing on the money supply and money demand. This is indicated by their use of the equation of exchange, $MV = PQ$, and the money demand equation, $M^d = kPQ$.

In Keynesian theory, a change in any of the autonomous spending components of C, I, G, or net exports affects GNP through the *multiplier*. Since Keynesians want to know *how much* GNP will change given a change in an autonomous spending component, they are naturally interested in the value of the multiplier. Much of the work in Keynesian theory has been on the value of the multiplier and whether it is stable. (What is it equal to today? Will it be the same next month or next year?)

In monetarist theory, a change in the money supply affects GNP through velocity. For example, if $V = 5$, a \$1 change in the money supply affects PQ, or GNP, by \$5, whereas if $V = 2$, a \$1 change in the money supply affects PQ, or GNP, by \$10. Since monetarists want to know how much PQ, or GNP, will change given a change in the money supply, they are naturally interested in the value of velocity. Much of the work in monetarism has been on the value of velocity and whether it is stable.

For Keynesians, a change in the money supply has to affect one of the three spending components of the private sector—consumption, investment, or net exports—before it affects GNP. In short, the link between changes in the money supply and changes in GNP is an indirect one. Monetarists believe there is a direct link between changes in the money supply and GNP. As we have discussed in this chapter, an increase in money supply causes individuals to find they are holding *too much money* at the given GNP level; consequently, they increase their spending, driving GNP up.

Association Is Not Causation: That Lesson Again

Monetarists hold that changes in the money supply bring about changes in GNP. Their theoretical explanation of this cause–effect relationship has been outlined in this chapter. Empirically, they have showed that, true enough, there is a strong association between changes in the money supply and changes in GNP. But association is not causation. It is possible that X and Y move up and down together, but knowing this doesn't indicate if (1) X is the cause and Y is the effect; or (2) Y is the cause and X is the effect; or (3) both X and Y are the effects of some, yet undetermined, cause.

What holds for X and Y might hold for the money supply and GNP. Monetarists state that money supply changes are the cause of GNP changes. But might it be the other way around? Keynesians sometimes argue that a decrease in autonomous

What Caused the Great Depression? A Monetarist Answer

In Chapter 9, we presented the Keynesian explanation of the Great Depression: A major drop in investment spending led to a multiple change in real GNP, which, in turn, prompted reductions in consumption and investment. In the background, the Keynesian theme—"the economy does not necessarily equilibrate at full-employment output"—could be heard.

The monetarist explanation of the Great Depression, mainly why the Great Depression was as long and severe as it was, focuses on the money supply and on government programs that worked against the natural full-employment tendencies of the economy.

For example, the monetarists point to the sharp drop in the money supply between 1929 and 1933 during which M1 fell by slightly more than one-fourth. Their theoretical framework indicates that such a drop is sure to depress GNP. (Think of what a decrease in the money supply does to the aggregate demand curve: The *AD* curve shifts leftward.)

Most monetarists argue that the economy could have recovered from its depressed state in a shorter period of time (the Depression lasted about ten years), even after the sharp drop in the money supply, if wages and prices had been allowed to fall to free-market levels. Instead, monetarists argue, government pursued policies that propped up prices and wages. (Think of what this does to the *SRAS* curve; it shifts leftward.) For example, monetarists point to

President Franklin D. Roosevelt's National Recovery Act, which was designed to allow price-fixing agreements among firms. In addition, they point to the many farm programs that were established to boost crop prices and to new regulations in the communications industry that stifled price cutting. Finally, on the wage front, the monetarists maintain that major labor legislation passed at the time strengthened the hand of labor unions in bargaining for wage increases. Monetarists claim that together these policies and programs made the Depression more severe and longer lasting.

consumption and/or autonomous investment will lower GNP and lead to a drop in the money supply. The drop in the money supply is due to individuals borrowing less as a result of the decreased economic activity. In short, Keynesians have argued that the line of cause and effect may run from total spending to GNP to the money supply, while monetarists have argued that it runs from the money supply to GNP.

If we observe that changes in the money supply and GNP are positively associated, which line of causation—Keynesian or monetarist—should be given greater credence? The answer is neither or both. A Keynesian can rightfully argue that a strong positive association between money supply and GNP is as consistent with the "GNP–money supply" line of causation as it is with the monetarist "money supply–GNP" line of causation.

Monetarists build support for their explanation of the money supply–GNP link by pointing to monetary episodes where money supply changes have not been prompted by economic conditions. One of the best examples of such an episode occurred in 1936–37 when the Federal Reserve increased reserve requirements to improve its control of monetary policy. As a result, the money supply declined. Monetarists contend that this drop in the money supply was not the result of the Fed responding to economic conditions (the Great Depression was in full force), and therefore comes close to being a "controlled experiment," wherein one variable is changed independently of others. What were the consequences? Soon after the money supply fell, GNP fell. Monetarists point to this monetary episode, and

CHAPTER 14
CLASSICAL AND MONETARIST
THEORY: EMPHASIS ON THE PRICE
LEVEL AND GNP

■

to a few characteristically similar ones, as evidence that their explanation of the cause–effect relationship between money supply and GNP is correct. Not all economists have accepted the monetarist explanation, however.

A Change in GNP Without a Change in the Money Supply

Within the (general) monetarist framework, it is possible to get a change in GNP even if the money supply does not change. Suppose the economy is currently at point 1 in Exhibit 14–9. At point 1, the money market equilibrium condition is satisfied: $M^s = M^{AH} = M^d$. Now suppose k decreases (demand for money falls), causing the money demand line to rotate downward from M_1^d to M_2^d, or from $700 billion to $600 billion at the original GNP level.

Initially, GNP does not change: It remains at $4,200 billion. However, now M^s and M^{AH} are greater than M^d: $700 billion is greater than $600 billion. This can be seen at point 2.

When $M^s = M^{AH} > M^d$, we say that individuals are *holding too much money* at the current level of GNP. They increase their spending, and prices and/or output rise. This leads to an increase in PQ, or GNP.

But what happens as PQ, or GNP, rises? As we stated earlier, M^d rises since $M^d = kPQ$. The economy moves up M_1^d from point 2 in Exhibit 14–9 to point 3. At point 3, the money market is in equilibrium, since $M^s = M^{AH} = M^d$. We conclude that a fall in k, or a decrease in the demand for money, will increase GNP, *ceteris paribus*. It follows that a rise in k, or an increase in the demand for money, will decrease GNP, *ceteris paribus*.

EXHIBIT 14–9
A Decrease in M^d

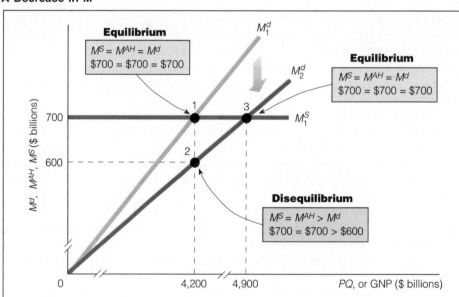

Starting at point 1, $M^S = M^{AH} = M^d$. Then money demand decreases from M_1^d to M_2^d. This results in individuals holding too much money (excess money balances); consequently, individuals trade money for other goods, and prices and/or output increase. In either case, GNP increases. As this occurs, the economy moves up the money demand line. Equilibrium is at point 3, where once again $M^S = M^{AH} = M^d$.

Interview: Allan Meltzer

Allan Meltzer, a leading proponent of monetarism, has made significant contributions to the modern quantity theory of money. He is well known for his proposed monetary rule, which many monetarists believe, if implemented, would stabilize the price level. Meltzer is currently at Carnegie-Mellon University.

What in your mind are the main propositions of monetarism?

I think there are three main propositions. The first is the importance of the rate of money growth for short-run determination of output and for long-run inflation. The second is that steady, reliable monetary growth is a condition for stable long-term growth of economic activity, and stable, long-term growth in the money stock (in relation to real output growth) is the necessary condition for avoiding inflation. The third is the importance of rules vs. discretionary policy actions to reduce risk, uncertainty, and variability.

What do you predict will be a major economic problem the United States will have to face in the mid-1990s and how do you think it should solve that problem?

My ability to forecast the future is limited, but I expect the United States will have difficulty adjusting to a world in which several other countries are as wealthy and productive as the United States. U.S. policies—political and social as well as economic—will have to reflect this continuing change in relative wealth. We could accept our position and continue to accept our high stan-

dard of living. We may want to increase our efficiency or our growth rate. If so, we must improve the quality of our educational system and devote more resources to investment. We should remove the bias in favor of current consumption in our tax and government spending policies and give more choice of schools and curricula.

What do you think has been the most promising research development in economics in the past decade?

Two areas have developed—finance and political economy or public choice. Finance theory has developed a much improved understanding of how markets work. Political economy has replaced the assumption that the government acts to achieve the public's interest with an analysis of how collective decisions are made when individuals act in their own (enlightened) interest.

What got you interested in economics?

Economics is a social science. At its best it is concerned with ways (1) to improve well being by allowing individuals the freedom to achieve their personal aims or goals and (2) to harmonize their individual interests. I find working on such issues challenging, and progress is personally rewarding.

You are actively involved in economics research. What questions are you currently trying to answer?

For the past decade, I have been trying to learn more about why people willingly choose the tax, spending, and monetary policies that they do, how they decide on the amount of income redistribution and the form the redistribution takes. I took some time out, however, to read most of the collected papers of John Maynard Keynes and to write a book about them.

Would you give an example to illustrate how economists think about problems?

Two of the most important ideas in economics are the law of demand and the law of supply. These laws tell us that as price falls, quantity demanded increases and quantity supplied falls. These laws are very general. People respond to price and cost changes even if markets are not organized. Many people either do not believe these laws work, or they do not understand them. They favor policies that try to prevent adjustment to price changes or to prevent prices from changing.

Question:

Earlier, it was stated that monetarists believe the demand for money, or k or V, is highly stable. This implies that monetarists would predict that changes in GNP are (for the most part) brought about by changes in the money supply instead of changes in the demand for money. Is this true?

Answer:

Yes, it is true.

Changes in Money Supply and Money Demand and Consequent Changes in Aggregate Demand

In Chapter 13, when we discussed inflation, we learned that an increase in the money supply would shift the AD curve rightward and a decrease in the money supply would shift the AD leftward.

Besides changes in the money supply, changes in money demand also change aggregate demand. To illustrate, suppose we start in equilibrium where $M^s = M^{AH} = M^d$. Now suppose money demand falls, giving us $M^s = M^{AH} > M^d$. In this setting, individuals are holding *too much money* and therefore increase their spending. As a result of increased spending, the AD curve shifts rightward (Exhibit 14–10).

Next, suppose that starting from equilibrium, money demand rises. Thus, we have $M^s = M^{AH} < M^d$. In this setting, individuals are holding *too little money* and therefore they decrease their spending. As a result of decreased spending, the AD curve shifts leftward.

Monetarism in the *AD–AS* Framework

Monetarist theory is easy to view in terms of the AD–AS framework. Let's start in long-run equilibrium in our AD–AS framework ($Q = Q_N$) and where $M^s = M^{AH} = M^d$ in our monetarist framework. Now suppose the Federal Reserve decreases the money supply. As we know, this brings about $M^s = M^{AH} < M^d$. In this setting,

EXHIBIT 14–10
Money Supply, Money Demand, and the *AD* Curve

An increase in money supply and a decrease in money demand shift the AD curve rightward. A decrease in money supply and an increase in money demand shift the AD curve leftward.

people are holding too little money, and thus they decrease their spending. A decrease in spending shifts the aggregate demand (AD) curve leftward from AD_1 to AD_2 in Exhibit 14–11. Real GNP decreases from Q_1 to Q_2, and the economy is now in a recessionary gap at point 2. Whereas Keynesians might say that the economy would get stuck at point 2 (because of inflexible wages in the downward direction), monetarists argue that wages are flexible enough to rid the economy of a recessionary gap. For monetarists, wages will fall in a recessionary gap, the short-run aggregate supply (SRAS) curve will shift rightward from $SRAS_1$ to $SRAS_2$, and the economy will again be in long-run equilibrium. Since real GNP has moved back to its original level, monetarists say that monetary policy has no lasting (long-run) effect on the real side of the economy. They believe the main effect is on the price level (P). And because monetarists believe that the economy is inherently stable and that it equilibrates itself at natural real GNP, they, like classical economists, believe the government has only a minimal role to play in the economy.

Major Tenets of Monetarism

Using our three macroeconomic categories, here is what monetarism has to say.

The P–Q Category. Monetarism states that changes in money supply and money demand are the major determinants of changes in P times Q, or GNP.

The Inherently Stable–Inherently Unstable Category. Unlike Keynesians, monetarists believe that the economy is inherently stable and that it equilibrates at natural real GNP. The economy may find itself in either a recessionary or inflationary gap, but this is only a temporary state of affairs.

The Effective–Ineffective Category. Similar to the classical economists, monetarists believe that the government should not interfere in the nation's economy, that such interference often leads to more problems, not fewer. In the next chapter, we learn that monetarists advocate certain rules (in particular, a monetary rule) for

EXHIBIT 14–11
Monetarist Theory in the *AD–AS* Framework

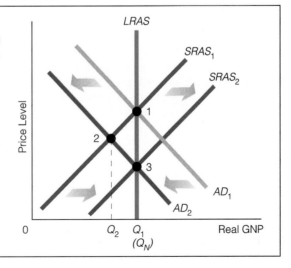

The economy is initially at point 1 in long-run equilibrium. Then the Federal Reserve decreases the money supply. As a result, people end up holding too little money and they cut back on their spending. A decrease in spending shifts the aggregate demand curve from AD_1 to AD_2. The economy is now in a recessionary gap at point 2. Monetarists believe that wages are flexible and that they will fall in a recessionary gap, shifting the short-run aggregate supply curve leftward from $SRAS_1$ to $SRAS_2$. In time, the economy is back again in long-run equilibrium.

Interview: Milton Friedman

Milton Friedman has made significant and lasting contributions in the areas of economic methodology, monetary theory, consumption theory, political economy and more. Friedman won the Nobel Prize in Economics in 1976. He is currently at the Hoover Institution.

What is the monetarist view of how the economy works?

There is no monetarist view of how the economy works. Monetarism is concerned with one aspect of the economy and one aspect only. That aspect is the effect of changes in monetary institutions and in the quantity of money on the price level in the long run and on fluctuations in output and prices in the short run. Communist China, laissez-faire Hong Kong, the quasi-socialist United States are economies that work very differently. However, all of them have monetary institutions and all of them have a medium of circulation called money. Hence, the general principles of monetary theory apply to all three economies.

What do you think is the main contribution of each of the following macroeconomic schools of thought: classical, Keynesian, monetarist, and new classical?

In a comment at an American Economic Association session some years back entitled "What Have We Learned about Money in the Past Twenty-five Years?" I said that it was easier to say what we had learned in the past 25 years than to say what we had learned in the past 200 years. Classical views about money are often oversimplified by limiting them to the long-period relationship between the nominal quantity of money and the price level. That was one aspect of classical teaching that has survived the test of experience, but the classical writers on money from David Hume to

Henry Thornton to Irving Fisher presented a much more sophisticated and subtle analysis which covered the short run as well as the long run. They provided us with our fundamental understanding of monetary phenomena. The Keynesian school changed the problems on which scholars put major emphasis but, in my opinion, contributed no substantive and lasting results about the relations between money and other magnitudes. The major impact was on the language that we use. The contribution of the monetarist school was essentially to revive, refurbish, restate, and test the analysis of the classical school. Its major contribution, as I see it, was its emphasis on testing the propositions of monetary theory, whether Keynesian or classical, by empirical evidence. The new classical school has fostered greater attention to the price theoretical foundations of monetary relations and has expanded our understanding of the role of expectations.

Why do the best and the brightest of the economics profession sometimes view the economy so differently?

For two reasons. First, time perspective. Many differences arise out of the relative importance attached to the short

period and over the long period. Second, differences in values, in particular the values attached to equality on the one hand and freedom on the other.

Would you give an example to illustrate how economists think about problems?

Consider the argument so often made that the U.S. cannot compete against foreign countries, say specifically Japan, because U.S. wages are higher than Japanese wages. The economist will reply, "Wages? The Japanese worker is paid in yen; the American worker is paid in dollars. How are you comparing the Japanese wage and the American wage? What determines the exchange rate between dollars and yen?" Suppose at the existing exchange rate, Japanese producers could price every product lower than United States producers could. The Japanese would sell, but what would the Japanese do with the dollars they received? By assumption, they don't want to buy American goods since they are all more expensive; they want to buy Japanese goods. But they can only buy Japanese goods with yen. To get yen, they must induce someone to sell them yen for dollars. The only way they can do that is by offering a higher dollar price for yen. But as the dollar price of yen goes up, Japanese goods become more expensive in the United States, U.S. goods become cheaper in Japan, and pretty soon there are some items, those for which in economists' jargon the U.S. has a comparative advantage, that the Japanese will start buying from the United States. The exchange rate will not settle down until the Japanese find a use for all the dollars they acquire by selling goods to the United States either by buying American goods, investing the dollars in the United States, or buying goods made in other countries that want to use the dollars to spend or invest in the U.S.

What got you interested in economics?

When I started college in 1928, I intended to be an actuary and I planned to major in mathematics. For reasons I no longer recall, I started taking some economics courses. The Great Depression hit about that time and economics clearly became a vital subject. When I graduated, I was offered a scholarship in applied mathematics at Brown and a scholarship in economics at Chicago. The choice was easy in 1932.

What do you think has been the most promising research development in economics in the past decade?

It takes more than a decade to recognize a promising development. In the past several decades I believe that the most promising research developments have been public choice and rational expectations.

What persons have had the greatest influence on your thinking and how would you summarize what you learned from each of them?

The persons who had the greatest influence on my thinking were Arthur R. Burns, Jacob Viner, Frank Knight, Wesley Mitchell, Friedrich Hayek. From Arthur Burns, I learned the importance of carefulness, thoroughness, and attention to detail in statistical and economic research. From Jacob Viner, I received my first exposure to the beauty of economic theory. Frank Knight made me realize the broader aspects of economics and the ramifications of economics in many other directions. Wesley Mitchell impressed on me the importance of clear, accurate, concise exposition of scientific findings. Friedrich Hayek made clear the dynamic role of the price system as a mode of transmitting information.

What do you consider your best piece of work and why?

I regard *The Theory of the Consumption Function* as my best piece of work. It presents an original hypothesis, deduces its implications, and tests those implications with a wide range of evidence. It comes closer than anything else I have done to corresponding to the ideal of positive economics that I stated in my essay on "The Methodology of Positive Economics." I trust that the rest of my work has many of the same characteristics, even though it may not exemplify them so comprehensively.

You have expressed a strong admiration for Adam Smith and Thomas Jefferson. Are there individuals in other disciplines—such as literature and philosophy—for whom you have a strong admiration, or who have had a strong influence on your life?

A. V. Dicey through his book, *Lectures on the Relation between Law and Public Opinion in the Nineteenth Century;* the authors of the Federalist Papers—Alexander Hamilton, James Madison, and John Jay; Karl Popper, the philosopher, both through his work on methodology and through his writings on an open society; and George Orwell through his extensive writings. I find it hard to single out any one or two persons in literature who had a special influence on me.

---

government to follow, which would seem to suggest that monetarists want government to act in some way in the economy. However, since these rules restrict government, they are best viewed as part of an overall laissez-faire approach. What many monetarists are proposing that government do is to limit or restrict itself so that it cannot play an active role in managing the economy.

We started with a simple diagram of money demand and supply (such as Exhibit 14–5). Looking at this diagram, it was easy to see that a change in either would change GNP. But this leads us to ask: Who or what can change the money supply? Who or what can change money demand?

We know that the Fed, the banks, and the public can change the money supply (Chapters 11, 12). The Fed can affect the money supply by changing bank reserves, the banks by changing the percentage of excess reserves they choose to lend out, and members of the public by changing the percentage of their funds they choose to deposit into a bank. Knowing this makes the analysis richer.

We have seen in this chapter that a change in k (or V) will change money demand. But what factors can change k? We have noted three: the interest

THINKING LIKE AN ECONOMIST

CHAPTER 14
CLASSICAL AND MONETARIST
THEORY: EMPHASIS ON THE PRICE
LEVEL AND GNP

■

rate, the expected rate of inflation, and the frequency with which employees receive paychecks.

Notice the process of analysis here. We started with the two main variables that can change GNP—money supply and money demand—and proceeded to examine them in depth. In doing so, we learned specifically what can change GNP. We learn more about the "economic puzzle" by taking the bigger pieces and breaking them down into smaller ones.

$MV \equiv PQ$

■ The equation of exchange is an identity: $M \times V \equiv P \times Q$. Exactly what the equation tells us can be interpreted in different ways. Here are a few: (1) The money supply multiplied by velocity must equal the price level times real GNP: $M \times V \equiv P \times Q$. (2) The money supply multiplied by velocity must equal GNP: $M \times V \equiv$ GNP. (3) Total expenditures (measured by MV) must equal the total sales revenues of business firms (measured by PQ): $MV \equiv PQ$

■ The equation of exchange is not a theory of the macroeconomy. However, the equation of exchange can be turned into a theory if assumptions are made about some of the variables in the equation. For example, if we assume that both V and Q are constant, then we have the simple quantity theory of money, which predicts that changes in the money supply cause strictly proportional changes in the price level.

M^s, $M^{AH,}$ and M^d

■ The quantity supplied of money (M^s) necessarily equals the quantity of money that people actually hold (M^{AH}). The quantity demanded of money (M^d) may be equal to, greater than, or less than M^s and M^{AH}.

■ In equilibrium, $M^s = M^{AH} = M^d$.

■ When $M^s = M^{AH} > M^d$, individuals are holding too much money; consequently, spending increases and GNP rises.

■ When $M^s = M^{AH} < M^d$, individuals are holding too little money; consequently, spending decreases and GNP falls.

Money Demand

■ $M^d = kPQ$. This says that the quantity of money demanded is a function of k, P, and Q. Anything that causes k, P, and Q to rise (fall) will increase (decrease) the quantity demanded of money.

■ The following decrease k: (1) an increase in the interest rate; (2) an expected increase in the inflation rate; and (3) an increase in the frequency with which employees receive paychecks. The following increase k: (1) a decrease in the interest rate; (2) an expected decrease in the inflation rate; and (3) a decrease in the frequency with which employees receive paychecks.

Changes in the Money Supply, Money Demand, and Aggregate Demand

■ An increase in the money supply will lead to a rightward shift in the *AD* curve. A decrease in the money supply will lead to a leftward shift in the *AD* curve. A decrease in money demand will lead to a rightward shift in the *AD* curve. An increase in money demand will lead to a leftward shift in the *AD* curve.

Monetarism, *k*, and velocity

■ Monetarists believe that *k*, or *V*, is stable and predictable. They conclude that changes in GNP are largely brought about by changes in money supply.

How Monetarists View the Economy

■ Monetarists view the economy as stable and as equilibrating at natural real GNP.

Key Terms and Concepts

Velocity
Equation of Exchange

Simple Quantity Theory
  of Money

Money Demand Line

QUESTIONS AND PROBLEMS

1. If the money supply increases by 10 percent, velocity increases by 1 percent, and real GNP (*Q*) decreases by 2 percent, what would monetarists predict that the percentage increase in the price level will be? Explain your answer.

2. What are different ways of saying that the demand for money is stable?

3. If credit cards become more widely used in the economy, what, if anything, will happen to velocity and why?

4. Using the *MV–PQ* framework of analysis, assume that *M*, *V*, and *Q* can all change and therefore can affect *P*. List the different configurations of *M*, *V*, and *Q* that are predicted to lead to a rise in *P*.

5. What is the difference between the equation of exchange and the simple quantity theory of money?

6. Calculate M^d at each of the following different levels of *k* and *PQ*: (a) $k = 1/4$; $PQ = \$350$ billion; (b) $k = 1/5$; $PQ = \$700$ billion; (c) $k = 1/10$; $PQ = \$1,000$ billion; (d) $k = 1/3$; $PQ = \$1,250$ billion; (e) $k = 1/8$; $PQ = \$2,000$ billion.

7. Suppose M^d is $300 billion at a GNP level of $900 billion in year 1 and $400 billion at a GNP level $1,000 billion in year 2. Is the demand for money the same in both years? Explain your answer.

8. If individuals collectively are holding too much money, how can they ever hold the optimum or right amount of money, since no one is ever going to burn money or throw it away?

9. In this chapter, we listed three factors that can change *k*: the interest rate, the expected rate of inflation, and the frequency with which employees receive paychecks. What other factors do you think might change *k*?

10. Suppose $M^{AH} = \$300$, $M^d = \$250$, and $PQ = \$1,200$ (all numbers in billions). From this, we know that $M^{AH}/PQ > M^d/PQ$. We also know that we are in monetary disequilibrium. If k in $M^d = kPQ$ is the same at the new monetary equilibrium point as it is at present, by how much must PQ increase?

11. What would be the directional change in GNP, given the following changes: (a) a decrease in the interest rate; (b) an increase in the expected rate of inflation; (c) an increase in money supply; (d) a decrease in money demand.

12. Suppose you are explaining to a friend who has had no training in economics that there are times when individuals find themselves holding too much money. Your friend says that that would never happen to her. She says that she has never held too much money, but rather that she has always held too little money. As she says this, she hands a ten-dollar bill to the cashier in the grocery store. What could you say that would help your friend understand that individuals can and do sometimes find that they are holding too much money?

13. In this chapter, we learned that PQ does not change unless either M or V changes (recall that $MV = PQ$). This implies that before a fiscal policy measure can affect GNP, or PQ, it must affect V. Do you think a change in government spending or taxes would affect V directly or indirectly through a change in some variable that directly affects V? If indirectly, what variable do you suggest?

15

MONETARY POLICY

WHAT THIS CHAPTER IS ABOUT

The goals of **monetary policy** are to stabilize the price level (P), achieve low unemployment (which is related to changes in real GNP, or Q), and promote economic growth (which is also related to Q), among other things. Economists generally agree that monetary policy affects the economy. However, they disagree over the degree to which, and under what conditions, it does this. This chapter focuses more on the disagreements than the agreements economists have over monetary policy.

THE MONEY MARKET

■

Like all markets, the money market has two sides: a demand side and a supply side.[1] We discuss both in this section.

The Demand Curve for Money

To illustrate a demand curve for a good, we place the price of the good on the vertical axis and the quantity of the good on the horizontal axis (see Chapter 3). To illustrate the **demand curve for money balances** (and money is a *good)*, we place the *price of holding money balances* on the vertical axis and the quantity of money on the horizontal axis. But before we do this, we must ask: What is the price of holding money balances?

The price of holding money balances—specifically, the opportunity cost of holding money—is the *interest rate*. In previous chapters, we learned that money is one of many forms in which individuals may hold their wealth and that by holding money they forfeit the opportunity to hold as much of their wealth in other forms. For example, the person who holds $1,000 in cash gives up the opportunity to purchase a $1,000 asset (for example, a bond) that yields interest. Thus, the interest rate is the opportunity cost of holding money. One pays the price of forfeited interest by holding money.

Exhibit 15–1a illustrates the demand curve for money (balances). As the interest rate increases, the opportunity cost of holding money increases, and individuals choose to hold less money. As the interest rate decreases, the opportunity cost of holding money decreases, and individuals choose to hold more money.

[1]In everyday langauge, the term *money market* is often used to refer to the market for short-term securities, where there is a demand for, and supply of, short-term securities. This is not the money market we are discussing. In our money market, there is a demand for, and supply of, money.

EXHIBIT 15–1
The Demand Curve For, and Supply Curve of, Money

(a) The demand curve for money is downward sloping. (b) The supply curve of money is a vertical line at the quantity of money, which is largely, but not exclusively, determined by the Fed.

The Supply Curve of Money

In Exhibit 15–1b, we have drawn the supply curve of money as a vertical line at the quantity of money largely determined by the Fed. The money supply is not exclusively determined by the Fed because, as we learned in Chapters 11 and 12, both the banks and the public are important players in the money supply process. For example, if banks do not lend out their entire excess reserves, the money supply will not be as large as it will be if they do.

Equilibrium in the Money Market

Equilibrium in the money market exists when the quantity demanded of money equals the quantity supplied. In Exhibit 15–2, equilibrium exists at the interest rate i_1. At a higher interest rate, i_2, the quantity supplied of money is greater than the quantity demanded, and there is an excess supply of money. At a lower interest rate, i_3, the quantity demanded of money is greater than the quantity supplied of money, and there is an excess demand for money. Only at i_1 are the quantity demanded and the quantity supplied of money equal. Here there are no "shortages" or "surpluses" of money, no excess demands or excess supplies. Individuals are holding the amount of money they want to hold.

TRANSMISSION MECHANISMS

Consider two markets: the money market and the goods and services market. Economists have different ideas about the *degree of impact* that changes in the money market have on the goods and services market and whether that impact is *direct* or *indirect*. The routes or channels that ripple effects created in the money market travel to affect the goods and services market are known as the **transmission mechanism.** We discuss two major transmission mechanisms: the Keynesian and the monetarist.

Transmission Mechanism
The routes or channels that ripple effects created in the money market travel to affect the goods and services market (represented by the aggregate demand and aggregate supply curves in the *AD–AS* framework).

EXHIBIT 15–2
Equilibrium in the Money Market

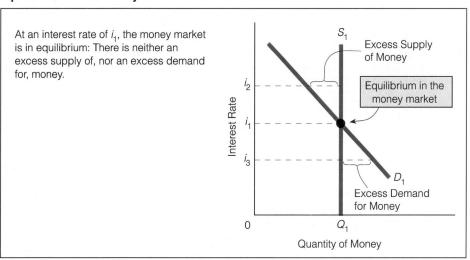

At an interest rate of i_1, the money market is in equilibrium: There is neither an excess supply of, nor an excess demand for, money.

The Keynesian Transmission Mechanism: Indirect

The Keynesian link between the money market and the goods and services market is an indirect one. With the aid of Exhibit 15–3, we describe the Keynesian transmission mechanism market by market.

The Money Market. Suppose the money market is in equilibrium at the interest rate i_1 in (a). Suddenly, the Fed increases the reserves of the banking system through an open market purchase. This results in an increase in the money supply. (See Exhibit 15–3a where the money supply shifts rightward from S_1 to S_2.) The process, we recall, is that increasing the reserves of the banking system in turn increases the excess reserves of the system and results in more loans being made. A greater supply of loans puts downward pressure on the price of a loan (the interest rate), as reflected in the movement from i_1 to i_2 in (a).

The Investment Goods Market. A fall in the interest rate stimulates investment spending. In the investment goods market in (b), investment spending rises from I_1 to I_2.

The Goods and Services Market (*AD–AS* Framework). An increase in investment spending increases total expenditures, and anything that increases total expenditures at a given price level shifts the aggregate demand curve to the right, as shown in (c). If we assume the economy is in the horizontal section of the aggregate supply curve, which is relevant to the basic Keynesian theory, real GNP rises from Q_1 to Q_2 and there is no change in the price level. As a result of the increase in real GNP, the unemployment rate drops.

In summary, when the money supply increases, the Keynesian transmission mechanism works as follows: An increase in the money supply lowers the interest rate, which causes investment spending to rise and the *AD* curve to shift rightward. As a result, real GNP increases and the unemployment rate drops. The process works in reverse for a decrease in the money supply.

EXHIBIT 15–3
The Keynesian Transmission Mechanism

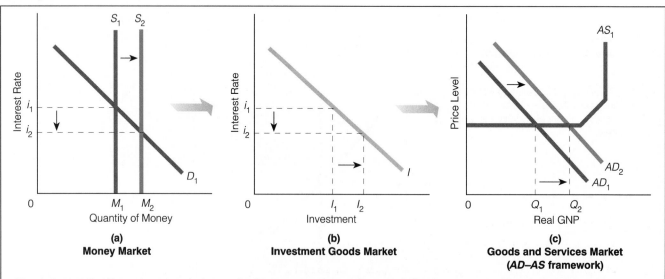

(a)
Money Market

(b)
Investment Goods Market

(c)
Goods and Services Market
(*AD–AS* framework)

Here is the way the Keynesian transmission mechanism operates given an increase in the money supply. (a) An increase in the money supply brings on a lower interest rate. (b) As a result, investment spending increases. (c) As investment spending increases, total expenditures rise and the aggregate demand curve shifts rightward. Real GNP rises from Q_1 to Q_2.

The Keynesian Mechanism May Get Blocked

As we said earlier, the Keynesian transmission mechanism is indirect. Changes in the money market do not directly affect the goods and services market (and thus real GNP) since the investment goods market stands between the two markets. This means that it is possible (although not likely) that the link between the money market and the goods and services market could be broken in the investment goods market. We explain.

Interest-Insensitive Investment. In Chapter 9, we learned that, in contrast to the classical economists, Keynes believed that investment is not always responsive to interest rates. For example, when business firms are pessimistic about future economic activity, a decrease in interest rates will do little, if anything, to increase investment spending. When investment is completely insensitive to changes in interest rates, the investment demand curve is vertical, as in Exhibit 15–4a.

Consider what this means in terms of Exhibit 15–3. If the investment demand curve is vertical, a fall in interest rates will not increase investment spending, and if investment spending does not increase, neither will aggregate demand or real GNP. In addition, unemployment won't fall. Thus, the Keynesian transmission mechanism would be short-circuited in the investment goods market, and the link between the money market in (a) of Exhibit 15–3 and the goods and services market in (c) would be broken.

The Liquidity Trap. Keynesians have sometimes argued that the demand curve for money could become horizontal at some low interest rate. Before we discuss why this might be, we need to understand the consequences of it. First, notice that in Exhibit 15–4b, the demand curve for money becomes horizontal at i_1. This horizontal section of the demand curve for money is referred to as the **liquidity trap.**

Liquidity Trap
The horizontal portion of the demand curve for money.

EXHIBIT 15–4
Breaking the Link between the Money Market and the Goods and Services Market: Interest-Insensitive Investment and the Liquidity Trap

The Keynesian transmission mechanism allows the link between the money market and the goods and services market to be broken in two places. (a) If investment spending is totally interest insensitive, a change in the interest rate will not change investment spending; therefore, aggregate demand, real GNP, and unemployment will not change. (b) If the money market is in the liquidity trap, an increase in the money supply will not lower the interest rate. It follows that there will be no change in aggregate demand, real GNP, and unemployment.

What happens if the money supply is increased when the money market is in the liquidity trap, for example, from S_1 to S_2? The money market moves from point 1 to 2, and individuals are *willing to hold all the additional money supply* at the given interest rate.

What does this mean in terms of the Keynesian transmission mechanism illustrated in Exhibit 15–3? Obviously, if an increase in the money supply does not lower the interest rate, then there will be no change in investment spending, aggregate demand, or real GNP. The liquidity trap can break the link between the money market and the goods and services market.

The Keynesian transmission mechanism, being indirect, allows for both interest-insensitive investment demand and the liquidity trap; therefore, Keynesians conclude, there may be times when monetary policy will be unable to increase real GNP and decrease unemployment. Viewing the money supply as a string, some economists have argued that "you can't push on a string." In other words, you can't always force real GNP up by increasing (pushing upward) the money supply.

Question:

The liquidity trap, or the horizontal section of the demand curve for money, seems to come out of the clear blue sky. Why might the demand curve for money become horizontal at some low interest rate?

Answer:

To understand the explanation of the liquidity trap, one must first understand the relationship between bond prices and interest rates, which is the topic of the next section.

Bond Prices and Interest Rates

Consider Jessica Howard who buys good X for $100 today and sells it one year later for $110. What is her actual rate of return? It is 10 percent, since the difference in the selling price and buying price (or $10) divided by the buying price ($100) is 10 percent.

Now suppose good X is a bond: Jessica buys the bond for $100 and sells it one year later for $110. This time we phrase our question this way: What is her actual *interest rate return,* or what interest rate did the buyer earn? The answer is the same: 10 percent.

Staying with the example, suppose Jessica buys the bond for $90 instead of $100, but still sells it for $110. What is her interest rate return? It is 22 percent ($20 is 22 percent of $90). Our point is simple: As the price of a bond decreases, the actual interest rate return, or simply the interest rate, increases.

Let's look at a slightly more complicated example that illustrates the inverse relationship between bond prices and interest rates in another way. Suppose last year Rob Zelicki bought a bond for $1,000 that promises to pay him $100 a year indefinitely. The annual interest rate return is 10 percent. Suppose today, however, that because market or nominal interest rates are higher than they were last year, bond suppliers have to promise to pay $120 a year to any bondholder who buys a $1,000 bond today.

What will this do to the price Rob can get in the market for his $1,000 bond bought last year, assuming he wants to sell it? Will anyone pay Rob $1,000 for an (old) bond that pays $100 a year when a new $1,000 bond that pays $120 a year can be purchased? The answer is a definite no. This means that Rob will have to lower the price of his bond below $1,000. How far below $1,000 will he have to lower it? The price will have to be far enough below $1,000 so that the interest rate return on his old bond will be competitive with (equal to) the interest rate return on *new* bonds. Rob's bond will sell for $833. At a price of $833 for the old bond, a buyer of the bond will receive $100 a year and an interest rate of 12 percent, which is the same interest rate he or she would receive by buying a new bond for $1,000 and receiving $120 a year. Thus, $100 is the same percentage of $833 as $120 is of $1,000—12 percent. Looking back, we conclude that an increase in the market interest rate is inversely related to the price of old or existing bonds.

Keeping this in mind, consider the liquidity trap again. The reason an increase in the money supply does not result in an excess supply of money at a low interest rate is because individuals believe bond prices are so high (since low interest rates mean high bond prices) that an investment in bonds is likely to turn out to be a bad deal. Individuals would rather hold all the additional money supply than use it to buy bonds, which, they believe, are priced so high that they have no place to go but down. As an aside, we might mention that empirical evidence has not supported the existence of the liquidity trap.

Question:

If interest rates and bond prices move in opposite directions, shouldn't people buy bonds when they expect interest rates to fall and sell bonds when they expect interest rates to rise?

Answer:

That's correct. The objective is to buy low and sell high. Bond prices are at their lowest when interest rates are at their highest, so when interest rates appear to be at their highest, buy bonds. The flip side says that bond prices are at their highest when interest rates are at their lowest, so when interest rates appear to be at their lowest, sell bonds. By the way, all this is easier said than done. Predicting interest rates is a tough business, and economic forecasters often miss the mark. However, they still do better than noneconomists (which, depending on how one looks at these things, might not be saying much).

The Monetarist Transmission Mechanism: Direct

In monetarist theory, there is a direct link between the money market and the goods and services market. The monetarist transmission mechanism is short. Changes in the money market have a direct impact on aggregate demand, as illustrated in Exhibit 15–5. An increase in the money supply from S_1 to S_2 in (a) leaves individuals with an excess supply of money. They increase their spending on a wide variety of goods. Households buy more refrigerators, personal computers, television sets, clothes, and vacations. Businesses purchase additional machinery. The aggregate demand curve in (b) is directly affected. In the short run, real GNP rises from Q_1 to Q_2 and unemployment falls.

MONETARY POLICY AND THE PROBLEM OF INFLATIONARY AND RECESSIONARY GAPS

In Chapter 10, we discussed how discretionary expansionary and contractionary fiscal policies might be used to rid the economy of recessionary and inflationary gaps, respectively. Later, we questioned the effectiveness of discretionary fiscal

The Keynesian transmission mechanism is indirect from the money market to the goods and services market; the monetarist transmission mechanism is direct.

EXHIBIT 15–5
The Monetarist Transmission Mechanism

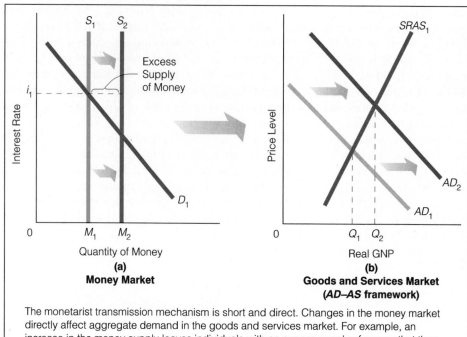

The monetarist transmission mechanism is short and direct. Changes in the money market directly affect aggregate demand in the goods and services market. For example, an increase in the money supply leaves individuals with an excess supply of money that they spend on a wide variety of goods.

policy. In this section, we discuss how monetary policy might be used to eliminate both recessionary and inflationary gaps.

In Exhibit 15–6, the economy is in a recessionary gap at point 1; aggregate demand is too low to bring the economy into equilibrium at its natural level of real GNP. Economist A argues that in time the short-run aggregate supply curve will shift rightward and pass through point 2', so it is best to leave things alone. Economist B states that it takes too long for the economy to get to point 2' on its own, and in the interim the economy suffers the high cost of unemployment and a lower level of output. Economist C maintains that the economy is *stuck* in the recessionary gap. Economists B and C propose expansionary monetary policy to move the economy along to its natural real GNP level. An appropriate increase in the money supply will shift the aggregate demand curve rightward to AD_2, and the economy will be in long-run equilibrium at point 2. The recessionary gap is eliminated through the use of expansionary monetary policy.[2]

In (b), the economy is experiencing an inflationary gap at point 1. Economist A argues that in time the economy will move to point 2', so it is best to leave things alone. Economist B argues that it would be better to decrease the money supply so that aggregate demand shifts leftward to AD_2, and the economy moves to point 2. Economist C agrees with B and says that the price level is lower at point 2 than at 2', although real GNP is the same at both points.

[2]In a static framework, expansionary monetary policy refers to an increase in the money supply, and contractionary monetary policy refers to a decrease in the money supply. In a dynamic framework, expansionary monetary policy refers to an increase in the *growth rate* of the money supply, while contractionary monetary policy refers to a decrease in the *growth rate* of the money supply. In the real world, where things are constantly changing, the growth rate of the money supply is more indicative of the direction of monetary policy.

EXHIBIT 15–6
Monetary Policy: Ridding the Economy of Recessionary and Inflationary Gaps

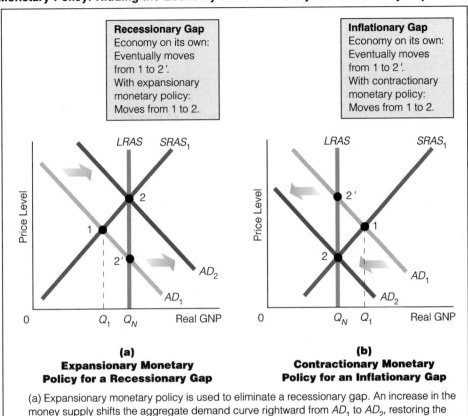

Recessionary Gap
Economy on its own:
Eventually moves
from 1 to 2'.
With expansionary
monetary policy:
Moves from 1 to 2.

Inflationary Gap
Economy on its own:
Eventually moves
from 1 to 2'.
With contractionary
monetary policy:
Moves from 1 to 2.

(a)
Expansionary Monetary
Policy for a Recessionary Gap

(b)
Contractionary Monetary
Policy for an Inflationary Gap

(a) Expansionary monetary policy is used to eliminate a recessionary gap. An increase in the money supply shifts the aggregate demand curve rightward from AD_1 to AD_2, restoring the economy to the natural level of GNP, Q_N. (b) Contractionary monetary policy is used to eliminate an inflationary gap. A decrease in the money supply shifts the aggregate demand curve leftward from AD_1 to AD_2, restoring the economy to Q_N.

Most Keynesians believe that the natural forces of the market economy work much more quickly and assuredly at eliminating an inflationary gap than a recessionary gap. In terms of Exhibit 15–6, they argue that it is much more likely that the short-run aggregate supply curve in (b) will shift leftward and pass through point 2', eliminating the inflationary gap, than that the short-run aggregate supply curve in (a) will shift rightward and pass through point 2', eliminating the recessionary gap. The reason is that wages and prices rise more quickly than they fall. (Recall that many Keynesians believe wages are inflexible *in the downward direction.*) Consequently, Keynesians are more likely to advocate expansionary monetary policy to eliminate a stubborn recessionary gap than contractionary monetary policy to eliminate a not-so-stubborn inflationary gap. As a result, it has been argued that Keynesian monetary policy has an inflationary bias to it. Keynesians often retort that this is not necessarily bad if, indeed, wages and prices are less flexible downward than upward.

Question:

Would Keynesians advocate expansionary monetary policy to eliminate a recessionary gap if they believed that the money market was in the liquidity trap or that investment spending was interest insensitive?

Answer:

No, they would not. In these two cases, Keynesians would say that expansionary monetary policy is *ineffective* at eliminating a recessionary gap. They would be likely to propose discretionary expansionary fiscal policy instead. Because Keynesians view monetary policy as sometimes ineffective and fiscal policy as always effective, they are sometimes called *fiscalists*.

MONETARY POLICY AND THE ACTIVIST–NONACTIVIST DEBATE

In Chapter 10, we noted that some economists argue against the use of discretionary fiscal policy because it is ineffective (owing to crowding out) or works in unintended and undesirable ways (owing to lags). Other economists, notably Keynesians, believe that neither is the case and that discretionary fiscal policy not only can, but also should, be used to smooth out the business cycle. This argument is part of the activist–nonactivist debate, which encompasses both fiscal and monetary policy. In this chapter, we address only monetary policy, although much of what we say here is relevant to fiscal policy as well.

Activists state that monetary and fiscal policies should be deliberately used to smooth out the business cycle. They are in favor of economic **fine tuning,** which is the (usually frequent) use of discretionary monetary and fiscal policies to counteract even small undesirable movements in economic activity. **Nonactivists** argue against the use of deliberate discretionary fiscal and monetary policies. They believe that discretionary policies should be replaced by a stable and permanent monetary and fiscal framework and that rules should be established in place of activist discretionary policies. For example, nonactivists advocate a balanced budget rule on the fiscal side and a **monetary rule**—a monetary policy based on a predetermined steady growth rate in the money supply—on the monetary side. The activist ranks are mostly made up of Keynesians; the nonactivist ranks are mostly made up of monetarists and new classical economists.[3]

The Case for Activist Monetary Policy

The case for activist monetary policy rests on three major claims:

1. The economy does not always equilibrate quickly enough at the natural real GNP or full-employment output. Consider the economy at point 1 in Exhibit 15–6a. If left to its own workings, some economists maintain, the economy will eventually move to point 2'. Activists often argue that it takes too long for the economy to move from point 1 to 2' and that too much lost output and too high an unemployment rate must be tolerated in the interim. They believe that an activist monetary policy speeds things along so that higher output and a lower unemployment rate can be achieved more quickly.

2. Activist monetary policy works; it is effective at smoothing out the business cycle. Activists are quick to point to the undesirable consequences of the constant (nonactivist) monetary policy of the mid-1970s. In 1973, 1974, and 1975, the

---

[3]Because an economist is a Keynesian, it does not follow that he or she *always* advocates activist monetary and fiscal policies. Nor does it follow that a monetarist or new classical economist *always* advocates nonactivist monetary and fiscal policies. We are speaking of the general policy inclinations of Keynesians, monetarists, and new classical economists.

Activists
Persons who argue that monetary and fiscal policies should be deliberately used to smooth out the business cycle.

Fine-tuning
The (usually frequent) use of discretionary monetary and fiscal policies to counteract even small undesirable movements in economic activity.

Nonactivists
Persons who argue against the deliberate use of discretionary fiscal and monetary policies. They believe in a permanent, stable, rule-oriented monetary and fiscal framework.

Monetary Rule
Describes monetary policy that is based on a predetermined steady growth rate in the money supply.

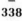

money supply growth rates were 5.5 percent, 4.3 percent, and 4.8 percent, respectively. These percentages represent a near constant growth rate in the money supply. The economy, however, went through a recession during this time (real GNP fell between 1973 and 1974 and between 1974 and 1975). Activists argue that an activist and flexible monetary policy would have reduced the high cost the economy had to pay in terms of lost output and higher unemployment.

3. Activist monetary policy is flexible; nonactivist monetary policy, which is rule oriented, is not. Flexibility is a desirable quality in monetary policy; inflexibility is not. The implicit judgment of activists is that the more closely monetary policy can be designed to meet the *particulars* of a given economic environment, the better. For example, at certain times the economy requires a sharp increase in the money supply; at other times, a sharp decrease; at still other times, only a slight increase or decrease. They argue that activist monetary policy can change as the monetary needs of the economy change; nonactivist, rule-oriented, "the-same-for-all-seasons" monetary policy cannot.

The Case for Nonactivist Monetary Policy

The case for nonactivist monetary policy rests on three major claims:

1. There is sufficient flexibility in wages and prices in modern economies to allow the economy to equilibrate at reasonable speed at the natural level of real GNP. For example, nonactivists point to the sharp drop in union wages in 1982 in response to high unemployment. In addition, they argue that government policies largely determine how flexible wages and prices turn out to be. For example, when government decides to cushion people's unemployment (such as through unemployment compensation), wages will not fall as quickly as when government does nothing. Nonactivists believe that a laissez-faire, hands-off approach by government would promote speedy wage and price adjustments and therefore a quick return to natural real GNP.

2. Activist monetary policies may not work. Economists who believe individuals form their expectations rationally (rational expectations) argue that there are really two types of monetary policy—monetary policy that is anticipated by the public and monetary policy that is unanticipated. Anticipated monetary policy *may not* be effective at changing real GNP or the unemployment rate. This is a subject we discuss in detail in the next chapter, but here is a brief explanation.

Suppose the public correctly anticipates that the Fed will soon increase the money supply by 10 percent. Consequently, the public reasons that aggregate demand will increase and prices will rise. (Recall that an increase in the money supply shifts the *AD* curve rightward; Exhibit 15–7.) Workers are particularly concerned about the expected higher price level because they know higher prices decrease the buying power of their wages. In an attempt to maintain their *real wages,* workers bargain for and receive higher money wage rates—which shifts the *SRAS* curve to the left. Now if the *SRAS* curve shifts leftward (owing to higher wage rates) *to the same degree* as the *AD* curve shifts rightward (owing to the increased money supply), then there is no change in real GNP. Real GNP stays constant at Q_1. We conclude that an *anticipated* increase in the money supply will be ineffective at raising real GNP.

3. Activist monetary policies are likely to be destabilizing rather than stabilizing; they are likely to make matters worse rather than better. Nonactivists point to lags as the main reason that activist monetary policies are likely to be destabilizing. For example, economist Robert Gordon has estimated that the total lag in monetary

EXHIBIT 15–7
Expansionary Monetary Policy and No Change in Real GNP

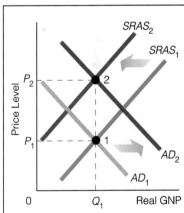

If expansionary monetary policy is anticipated (thus a higher price level is anticipated), workers may bargain for and receive higher wage rates. It is possible that the *SRAS* curve will shift leftward to the degree that expansionary monetary policy shifts the *AD* curve rightward. Result: no change in real GNP.

339

policy (consisting of the data, recognition, legislative, transmission, and effectiveness lags discussed in Chapter 10) is 13.3 months.[4] To nonactivists, such a long lag makes it almost impossible to conduct effective activist monetary policy. They maintain that by the time the Fed's monetary stimulus arrives on the scene, the economy may not need any stimulus, and thus it will likely destabilize the economy.[5] The stimulus in this instance makes things worse rather than better.

We illustrate this last point in Exhibit 15–8. Suppose the economy is currently in a recessionary gap at point 1. The recession is underway before Fed officials recognize it. Once recognized, however, Fed officials consider expanding the money supply in the hopes of shifting the *AD* curve from AD_1 to AD_2 and intersecting the *SRAS* curve at point 1′, at natural real GNP. In the interim, however, unknown to everybody, the economy is healing itself: The *SRAS* curve is shifting to the right. Fed officials don't see this yet because it takes time to collect and analyze data on the economy.

Thinking that the economy is not healing itself, or not healing itself quickly enough, Fed officials go ahead and implement expansionary monetary policy. The *AD* curve shifts rightward. By the time the increased money supply is felt in the goods and services markets, the *AD* curve intersects the *SRAS* curve at point 2. In short, the Fed has moved the economy from point 1 to point 2, and not as it had hoped, from point 1 to point 1′. The Fed has moved the economy into an inflationary gap. Instead of stabilizing and moderating the business cycle, it has intensified it.

[4]Robert Gordon, *Macroeconomics,* 4th ed. (Boston: Little, Brown & Co., 1987), p. 423.
[5]Some nonactivists have recently argued that the 1990–91 U.S. recession was as moderate as it was because neither activist fiscal nor monetary policy was enacted.

EXHIBIT 15–8
Monetary Policy May Destabilize the Economy

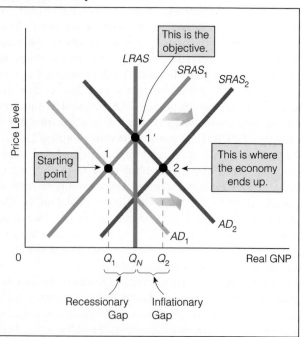

In this scenario, the *SRAS* curve is shifting rightward (healing the economy of its recessionary gap), but this information is unknown by Fed officials. Fed officials implement expansionary monetary policy and the *AD* curve ends up intersecting $SRAS_2$ at point 2 instead of $SRAS_1$ at point 1′. Fed officials end up moving the economy into an inflationary gap and thus destabilizing the economy.

Ask an economist a question and you are likely to get a conditional answer. For example, if you ask an economist whether monetary policy stabilizes or destabilizes the economy, she may answer that it can do either—depending on conditions. For instance, starting in a recessionary gap, *if* expansionary monetary policy shifts the *AD* curve rightward by just the right amount to intersect the *SRAS* curve and the *LRAS* curve at natural real GNP, *then* monetary policy stabilizes the economy. But *if* it shifts the *AD* curve rightward by more than this amount, it may move the economy into an inflationary gap, and *then* monetary policy destabilizes the economy. If–then thinking is common in economics, as are if–then statements.

NONACTIVIST MONETARY PROPOSALS

■

Activists are largely content to have monetary policy implemented by a discretionary Fed. Nonactivists are of the opposite mind. Here we outline two nonactivist monetary proposals: a monetary rule and a gold standard.

A Monetary Rule

As we noted earlier, a *monetary rule* describes monetary policy that is based on a predetermined steady growth rate in the money supply. The most direct and obvious, but not the only, objective of a monetary rule is to stabilize the price level. Some economists would like the monetary rule (monetary policy) to read as follows: *The annual money supply growth rate will be constant at the average annual growth rate of real GNP.* For example, if the average annual real GNP growth rate is approximately 3.3 percent, the money supply will be put on automatic pilot and will be permitted to grow at an annual rate of 3.3 percent. This will be the case no matter what the state of the economy. Some economists predict that such a policy will bring about a stable price level over time.

The prediction is based on the equation of exchange ($MV = PQ$). If the average annual growth rate in real GNP (Q) is 3.3 percent, and the money supply (M) grows at 3.3 percent, the price level should remain stable over time. (If Q is below 3.3 percent and M remains constant at 3.3 percent, P must increase so that PQ will still be equal to MV.) Monetary rule advocates argue that there will be some years when the growth rate in real GNP is below its average rate, bringing on an increase in the price level, and some years when the growth rate in real GNP is above its average rate, bringing on a fall in the price level, but over time the price level will be stable.

Critics point out that this monetary rule makes two assumptions: (1) Velocity is constant (there have been periods when it has not been constant). (2) The money supply is defined correctly. Critics argue that it is not clear yet which definition of the money supply (M1, M2, or some broader monetary measurement) is the proper one and therefore which money supply growth rate ought to be fixed.

Largely in response to the charge that velocity is not always constant, some monetary rule advocates would prefer that the monetary rule (monetary policy) read this way: *The annual growth rate in the money supply will be equal to the average annual growth rate in real GNP minus the growth rate in velocity.* With this monetary rule, the growth rate of the money supply is *not fixed.* It can vary from year to year, yet it is predetermined in that it is dependent on the growth rate in real GNP and on velocity.[6] To illustrate the workings of the rule, consider the following extended version of the equation of exchange.

$$\%\Delta M + \%\Delta V = \%\Delta P + \%\Delta Q$$

Suppose the percentage change in Q is $+3$ percent and the percentage change in V is $+1$ percent. The monetary rule here would specify that the growth rate in the money supply would be 2 percent ($3\% - 1\% = 2\%$). This would keep the price level stable; there would be a zero percent change in P:

$$\%\Delta M + \%\Delta V = \%\Delta P + \%\Delta Q$$
$$2\% + 1\% = 0\% + 3\%$$

Finally, some monetary rule proponents claim that even if a monetary rule does not adjust for changes in velocity, there is little cause for concern. Velocity instability is largely the result of unpredictable and volatile monetary policy. Once monetary policy is predictable and fixed, changes in velocity will be small and will occur within a narrow range.

Question:

If a monetary rule would bring about price level stability, why don't governments implement a monetary rule?

Answer:

First, not everyone is convinced that a monetary rule would bring about price level stability, owing to the problems of velocity and the correct definition of the money supply. Second, some people are strongly convinced that discretionary monetary policy is still much more effective at smoothing out the business cycle than non-activist monetary policy.

A Gold Standard

Gold Standard
The monetary arrangement whereby a nation backs its paper money totally or partially with gold.

If a nation backs its paper money totally or partially with gold, the nation is said to be on a **gold standard.** Most proponents of a gold standard maintain that it would stabilize the price level over time and restrain the money-creating activities of politicians, bureaucrats, and activist policy makers. Under a gold standard, the money supply would be tied to the stock of gold. As we can see, proponents of a monetary rule and proponents of a gold standard share the same objectives: to stabilize the price level over time and to reduce the amount of political and economic tinkering that can be applied to the money supply process.

The mechanics of a gold standard are as follows:

1. The government pegs the price of gold at some dollar amount. Most proponents of the gold standard claim that the dollar amount should be the market price of gold. Let's pick a price of $400. This, then, becomes the official price of gold. Initially, the free market price and the official price of gold are one and the same.

2. The government promises to buy and sell gold at the official price. Thus, if Schultz wants to buy gold from (or sell gold to) the government, the government will sell (or buy) gold at the price of $400. It is this government action that maintains the official price of gold equal to the market price and, according to the gold standard proponents, keeps the price level constant.

[6]This rule is based on the monetary rule put forth by Allan Meltzer, a long-standing monetarist. We omit some of the more technical points that are relevant to the Meltzer rule.

We explain the second point with the aid of Exhibit 15–9. In (a), the demand and supply curves represent the demand for and supply of gold in the private market, where gold is used as a commodity (jewelry, etc.). Because of inflation, the market price for gold rises to, say, $425, which is above the official price of $400, the price at which the government has agreed to buy and sell gold. This price discrepancy presents a profit opportunity to individuals. It is now possible for individuals to *buy* gold from the government at the $400 official price and *sell* gold in the market at the $425 market price, realizing a $25 profit (not taking into account exchange and transportation costs).

This transaction has an impact on the money supply, the market price of gold, and ultimately the price level. As individuals buy gold from the government, they exchange their cash or demand deposits (which are part of the money supply) for gold. The money supply in privately held hands is reduced, thus reducing aggregate demand and inflationary forces that originally pushed up gold prices. In the private gold market the policy increases the supply of gold; the supply curve shifts rightward from S_1 to S_2 until it intersects the demand curve at point 2, and thus the market price of gold falls until it hits the official price.

Proponents of the gold standard argue that by keeping the market price of gold constant over time—by selling gold to the market when the market price of gold is above the official price, as we have illustrated—the price level will be kept constant over time, too.

Consider the gold standard at work when the economy is in a recessionary gap and the price level is declining. In (b) the forces of supply and demand equilibrate at a $380 market price for gold. The official gold price, $400, is above the market

EXHIBIT 15–9
The Market for Gold and the Workings of a Gold Standard

(a)
Market Price > Official Price

(b)
Market Price < Official Price

(a) The market price for gold is greater than the official price. This will cause individuals to buy gold from the government and sell it in the private market for $425. This action will result in an increase in the supply of gold in the private market (from S_1 to S_2), a fall in the price of gold to the official level, a contraction in the money supply, and a lower price level.

(b) The market price for gold is below the official price. This will cause individuals to buy gold in the private market for $380 and sell it to the government for $400. This action will result in a decrease in the supply of gold in the private market (from S_1 to S_2), a rise in the price of gold to the official level, an expansion in the money supply, and a higher price level.

price, $380, so individuals have a monetary incentive to *buy* gold in the market at the lower price and *sell* it to the government at the higher price. Dollars received from government increase the privately held money supply. This increases aggregate demand and offsets deflationary tendencies in the economy. In the private gold market, the policy reduces the supply of gold and the supply curve shifts leftward from S_1 to S_2 until it intersects the demand curve at point 2. The market price of gold increases. The impact on the money supply, market price of gold, and price level has been to increase all three. A "too low" price level, represented by a market price for gold lower than the official price, has been pushed upward. The objective is to maintain the price level that is consistent with a $400 market price for gold. Neither price levels below nor above are acceptable.

Critics charge that a gold standard is no guarantee against inflation. For example, if a cheap source of gold is discovered, the supply of gold on the market will increase, driving the market price down below the official price, which in turn will place upward pressure on the money supply and price level. This is what happened soon after the California gold rush of 1849.

Critics also charge that a reduction in national output and an increase in unemployment will result if prices do not fall in the same proportion when the gold-backed money supply is reduced. For example, if money wages do not fall as quickly as the prices of other goods and services, *real wages* will rise, reducing the quantity demanded of labor services and output production.

CHAPTER SUMMARY

The Keynesian Transmission Mechanism

■ The Keynesian link between the money market and the goods and services market is indirect. Changes in the money market must affect the investment goods market before the goods and services market is affected. Assuming no liquidity trap and that investment is not interest insensitive, the transmission mechanism works as follows for an increase in the money supply: An increase in the money supply lowers the interest rate and increases investment spending. This increases aggregate demand and thus shifts the *AD* curve rightward. Consequently, real GNP rises and the unemployment rate falls. Under the same assumptions, the transmission mechanism works as follows for a decrease in the money supply: A decrease in the money supply raises the interest rate and decreases investment spending. This decreases aggregate demand and thus shifts the *AD* curve leftward. As a result, real GNP falls and the unemployment rate rises.

■ The Keynesian transmission mechanism may be short-circuited either by the liquidity trap or by interest-insensitive investment. Both are Keynesian notions. If either is present, Keynesians predict that expansionary monetary policy will be unable to change real GNP or unemployment.

The Monetarist Transmission Mechanism

■ The monetarist link between the money market and the goods and services market is direct. Changes in the money supply affect aggregate demand, period. An increase in the money supply causes individuals to increase their spending on a wide variety of goods.

Bond Prices and Interest Rates

■ Interest rates and the price of old or existing bonds are inversely related.

The Activist–Nonactivist Debate

■ Activists argue that monetary and fiscal policies should be deliberately used to smooth out the business cycle; they are in favor of economic fine-tuning. Nonactivists argue against the use of deliberate and discretionary fiscal and monetary policies; they propose a stable and permanent monetary and fiscal framework guided by rules.

■ The case for activist monetary policy rests on three major claims: (1) The economy does not always equilibrate quickly enough at the natural level of real GNP. (2) Activist monetary policy works. (3) Activist monetary policy is flexible, and flexibility is a desirable quality in monetary policy.

■ The case for nonactivist monetary policy rests on three major claims: (1) There is sufficient flexibility in wages and prices in modern economies to allow the economy to equilibrate in reasonable speed at the natural level of real GNP. (2) Activist monetary policies may not work. (3) Activist monetary policies are likely to make matters worse rather than better.

Nonactivist Monetary Proposals

■ A monetary rule describes monetary policy that is based on a predetermined steady growth rate in the money supply. In this chapter, we discussed two similar monetary rules. One proposes that the annual money supply growth rate remain constant at the average annual growth rate of real GNP. The second proposes that the annual money supply growth rate equal the average annual growth rate in real GNP minus the growth rate in velocity.

■ Critics of monetary rules state that flexible monetary policy, as in activist-discretionary monetary policy, is more effective at smoothing out the business cycle. Also, they argue that (1) velocity changes, and therefore a fixed money supply growth rule that doesn't take velocity changes into account will be destabilizing; (2) it is unclear what monetary aggregate the rule ought to apply to. Proponents of a monetary rule retort that (1) a monetary rule that takes velocity changes into account can be devised; (2) velocity would be more stable once a monetary rule was implemented, since the velocity instability that exists is due to unpredictable and volatile monetary policy.

■ A nation operates on a gold standard if it backs its paper money totally or partially with gold. The gold standard operates in the following way: If the market price of gold falls below the official price, individuals buy gold in the market and sell it to the government. In the process, the money supply expands; the predicted effect is a rise in the price level. If the market price of gold is above the official price, individuals buy gold from the government and sell it in the market. In the process, the money supply contracts; the predicted effect is a fall in the price level.

Key Terms and Concepts

Monetary Policy	Activists	Monetary Rule
Transmission Mechanism	Fine Tuning	Gold Standard
Liquidity Trap	Nonactivists	

1. Consider the following: Two researchers, A and B, are trying to determine whether eating fatty foods leads to heart attacks. Researchers A and B proceed differently. Researcher A builds a model where fatty foods *may* first affect X in one's body, and if X is affected, then Y may be affected, and if Y is affected, then Z may be affected. Finally, if Z is affected, the heart is affected, and the individual has an increased probability of suffering a heart attack. Researcher B doesn't proceed in this step-by-step fashion. She conducts an experiment to see if people who eat many fatty foods have a higher, lower, or equal incidence of heart attacks as people who eat few fatty foods. Which researcher's methods have more in common with the research methodology implicit in the Keynesian transmission mechanism? Which researcher's methods have more in common with the research methodology implicit in the monetarist transmission mechanism? Explain your answer.

2. If bond prices fall, will individuals want to hold more or less money? Explain your answer.

3. It has been suggested that nonactivists are not concerned with the level of real GNP and unemployment, since most (if not all) nonactivist monetary proposals set as their immediate objective the stabilization of the price level. Discuss.

4. Suppose the combination of more accurate data and better forecasting techniques made it easy for the Fed to predict a recession 10 to 16 months in advance. Would this strengthen the case for activism or nonactivism? Explain your answer.

5. Suppose it were proved that there is no liquidity trap and that investment is not interest insensitive. Would this be enough to disprove the Keynesian claim that expansionary monetary policy is not always effective at changing real GNP? Why or why not?

6. Both activists and nonactivists make good points for their respective positions. Do you think there is anything an activist could say to a nonactivist to convince him or her to accept the activist position, and vice versa? If so, what is it? If not, why not?

7. In the discussion of supply and demand in Chapter 3, we noted that if two goods are substitutes, the price of one and the demand for the other are directly related. For example, if Pepsi-Cola and Coca-Cola are substitutes, an increase in the price of Pepsi-Cola will increase the demand for Coca-Cola. Suppose that bonds and stocks are substitutes. We know that interest rates and bond prices are inversely related. What do you predict is the relationship between stock prices and interest rates? Explain your answer.

8. Argue the case for and against a gold standard.

9. Conduct the following exercise. Pick any week of the year. Quickly read through all the issues of the *Wall Street Journal* for that week, and write down the number of articles in which the word *Fed* is used, along with a brief summary of each article. Usually, the article will have to do with monetary policy. Many articles will also relate opinions as to what the Fed has done, is doing, and will do. The chief economist at a major firm may say that he thinks the Fed is positioning itself to ease up on money supply growth in the upcoming months. An economic forecaster at a major bank may say she thinks the newest member of the Board of Governors will be persuasive in arguing for a slight tightening of the money supply because of his reputation as a fierce opponent of inflation.

What is the point of this exercise? First, the large number of articles in which the Fed is mentioned will show you how important the Fed and monetary policy are to the economics, political, banking, and business communities. Second, the quotations from people (supposedly) in the know will show you how much guessing and difference of opinion surrounds Fed monetary policy. Third, the factors cited as influencing Fed actions will give you a rough idea of how individuals think the Fed determines monetary policy.

After you conduct this exercise, sit down and reflect on the following questions:

a. Is the Fed implementing an activist monetary policy?

b. How does the Fed go about deciding whether it should increase or decrease the rate of growth of the money supply?

c. Would there be as many articles in the *Wall Street Journal* on monetary policy if there were a monetary rule or gold standard? If not, why not?

d. Would I be better off or worse off if I could accurately predict monetary policy? What monetary institutions are necessary for the accurate prediction of monetary policy?

e. Is the secrecy and guessing that surrounds Fed monetary policy a small price to pay for what the Fed has done to stabilize the economy, or is it a high price to pay for what the Fed has done to destabilize the economy?

If answers to these questions are not easily forthcoming, do not be concerned. As long as you can either ask or recognize questions relevant to monetary policy, and possess some knowledge of what the answers may be, you are ready to join the interesting and continuing debate on monetary policy. That is an important accomplishment.

MONETARY POLICY IN AN OPEN ECONOMY

Monetary policy, like fiscal policy, can be discussed in a closed economy (where there is no international trade) and in an open economy (where there is international trade). In this chapter, we have discussed the effect of monetary policy in a closed economy. In this appendix, we enlarge the picture and look at both expansionary and contractionary monetary policy in an open economy.

Expansionary Monetary Policy

We have learned that expansionary monetary policy causes the *AD* curve to shift rightward according to Keynesian theory (without a liquidity trap and without interest-insensitive investment) and according to monetarist theory. In Exhibit 15F-1a, the *AD* curve shifts rightward from AD_1 to AD_2. It also affects the exchange value of the dollar and net exports. Here's how.

The Exchange Value of the Dollar. One consequence of expansionary monetary policy is an initial decline in interest rates. If U.S. interest rates decline relative to foreign nations' interest rates, then this will lead to an outflow of capital from the United States (in search of higher interest rate returns). Americans will supply more dollars in the foreign exchange market and demand more foreign currencies. As the supply of dollars increases, and the demand for foreign currencies increases, the U.S. dollar depreciates and foreign currencies appreciate. This affects both the *AD* and *SRAS* curves.

AD Curve (Affected by Net Exports). As the dollar depreciates and foreign currencies appreciate, U.S. goods become cheaper for foreigners, and foreign goods become more expensive for Americans. In turn, U.S. exports rise, U.S. imports fall, and U.S. net exports rise. An increase in net exports shifts the *AD* curve rightward. In Exhibit 15F-1a, the *AD* curve shifts from AD_2 to AD_3.

EXHIBIT 15F-1
Expansionary and Contractionary Monetary Policy in Open and Closed Economies

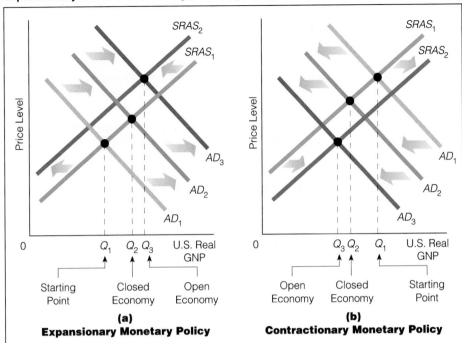

(a)
Expansionary Monetary Policy

(b)
Contractionary Monetary Policy

The consequences of expansionary monetary policy for both open and closed economies.
(a) The Fed increases the money supply and the AD curve shifts from AD_1 to AD_2. Real GNP rises from Q_1 to Q_2. The increased money supply leads to lower interest rates in the short run, promoting U.S. capital outflow and a depreciated dollar, which raises U.S. exports, lowers U.S. imports, and raises U.S. net exports. Higher net exports shift the AD curve rightward from AD_2 to AD_3. The depreciated dollar shifts the $SRAS$ curve leftward from $SRAS_1$ to $SRAS_2$. In the end, real GNP rises from Q_2 to Q_3. (Here we have drawn the AD curve shifting rightward by more than the $SRAS$ curve shifts leftward, which is typical given the initial event.) Expansionary monetary policy raises real GNP more in an open economy than in a closed economy.
(b) Contractionary monetary policy lowers real GNP more in an open economy than in a closed economy.

SRAS **Curve (Affected by Dollar Depreciation).** As the dollar depreciates, foreign inputs become more expensive for Americans. As a result, the *SRAS* curve shifts leftward from $SRAS_1$ to $SRAS_2$ in Exhibit 15F-1a.

A quick look at Exhibit 15F-1a, after both domestic and international feedback effects have been noted, shows us that monetary policy is more expansionary in an open economy than in a closed economy. In a closed economy, expansionary monetary policy increases real GNP from Q_1 to Q_2. In an open economy, expansionary monetary policy increases real GNP from Q_1 to Q_3.

This is in contrast to fiscal policy in an open economy, which we examined in Appendix E in Chapter 10. There we found that expansionary fiscal policy was less expansionary in an open economy than in a closed economy.

Contractionary Monetary Policy

As we have learned, contractionary monetary policy causes the AD curve to shift leftward. In Exhibit 15F-1b, the AD curve shifts rightward from AD_1 to AD_2. It also affects the exchange value of the dollar and net exports. Here's how.

The Exchange Value of the Dollar. One consequence of contractionary monetary policy is an initial rise in interest rates. If U.S. interest rates rise relative to foreign nations' interest rates, then this will lead to an inflow of capital into the United States (in search of higher interest rate returns). Foreigners will supply more of their currencies in the foreign exchange market and demand more dollars. As the supply of foreign currencies increases, and the demand for dollars increases, the U.S. dollar appreciates and foreign currencies depreciate. This affects both the *AD* and *SRAS* curves.

_AD_ Curve (Affected by Net Exports). As the dollar appreciates and foreign currencies depreciate, U.S. goods become more expensive for foreigners and foreign goods become cheaper for Americans. In turn, U.S. exports fall, U.S. imports rise, and U.S. net exports fall. A decrease in net exports shifts the *AD* curve leftward. In Exhibit 15F-1a, the *AD* curve shifts from AD_2 to AD_3.

SRAS Curve (Affected by Dollar Appreciation). As the dollar appreciates, foreign inputs become cheaper for Americans. As a result, the *SRAS* curve shifts rightward from $SRAS_1$ to $SRAS_2$ in Exhibit 15F-1b.

A quick look at Exhibit 15F-1b, after both domestic and international feedback effects have been noted, shows us that monetary policy is more contractionary in an open economy than in a closed economy. In a closed economy, contractionary monetary policy decreases real GNP from Q_1 to Q_2. In an open economy, contractionary monetary policy decreases real GNP from Q_1 to Q_3.

APPENDIX SUMMARY

■ Expansionary monetary policy affects the exchange rate of the dollar, which in turn affects net exports. The process works this way: (1) Expansionary monetary policy initially causes interest rates to decline; (2) If U.S. interest rates decline relative to foreign nations' interest rates, then there is an outflow of capital from the United States; (3) Americans supply more dollars and demand more foreign currencies; (4) As the supply of dollars increases, the dollar depreciates and foreign currencies appreciate; (5) Dollar depreciation makes U.S. goods cheaper for foreigners and foreign goods more expensive for Americans; (6) U.S. exports rise, U.S. imports fall, and U.S. net exports rise.

■ Contractionary monetary policy affects the exchange rate of the dollar, which in turn affects net exports. The process works this way: (1) Contractionary monetary policy initially causes interest rates to rise; (2) If U.S. interest rates rise relative to foreign nations' interest rates, then there is an inflow of capital into the United States; (3) Foreigners demand more dollars and supply more of their currencies; (4) As the demand for dollars increases, the dollar appreciates and foreign currencies depreciate; (5) Dollar appreciation makes U.S. goods more expensive for foreigners and foreign goods cheaper for Americans; (6) U.S. exports fall, U.S. imports rise, and U.S. net exports fall.

■ Monetary policy is more expansionary in an open economy than in a closed economy.

■ Monetary policy is more contractionary in an open economy than in a closed economy.

1. Explain why monetary policy is more expansionary in an open economy than in a closed economy.

2. Explain why monetary policy is more contractionary in an open economy than in a closed economy.

PART

V

EXPECTATIONS, MACROECONOMIC THEORY, AND POLICY ISSUES

JOB SEARCH THEORY, PHILLIPS CURVE ANALYSIS, AND NEW CLASSICAL THEORY: ENTER EXPECTATIONS

WHAT THIS CHAPTER IS ABOUT

In this chapter we discuss three related topics: job search theory, Phillips curve analysis, and new classical theory. Job search theory addresses unemployment and inflation expectations; Phillips curve analysis addresses inflation, unemployment, and inflation expectations; new classical theory addresses inflation, unemployment, inflation expectations, and economic policy.

THE ECONOMIC THEORY OF JOB SEARCH

How long does an unemployed person search for a job? The quick, and sometimes wrong, answer is until he or she finds a job. Consider Shirley Babbins, who voluntarily left her job as a secretary at a medical office three months ago. Since quitting her job, she has been offered work as a secretary in three other medical offices, as a secretary in two law offices, and as a part-time news reporter on a local radio station. She has turned down all six job offers and continues to search. In our example and in real life, a person doesn't necessarily search for a job only for as long as it takes to find a job. In this section, we discuss the economic theory of job search and relate it to the unemployment rate.

The Rational Search for Jobs

The economic theory of job search maintains that individuals are rational in their job searches: They consider both the costs and the benefits of searching for a job, and they search until the additional costs and additional benefits are equal. In practice, this translates into job searchers comparing *wages offered* with *reservation wages.*

The Wage Offer Curve. Most job searchers do not accept the first job they are offered because they cannot be sure that a better job is not waiting around the corner. In economic terms, job searchers do not possess complete information about job opportunities.

Consider 1,000 individuals searching for jobs. To simplify the analysis, let's assume that each individual compares the jobs he or she is offered only in terms of wages offered. If we were to plot the wage offers of each of the 1,000 individuals, we would no doubt find that some individuals received their highest wage offer with their first job offer, some received their highest wage offer with their tenth job offer, and many fell between the two extremes. On average, we would expect wage offers to increase (up to a point) as the job search period is extended. The wage offer curve in Exhibit 16–1a illustrates this pattern.

EXHIBIT 16-1
The Wage Offer and Reservation Wage Curves

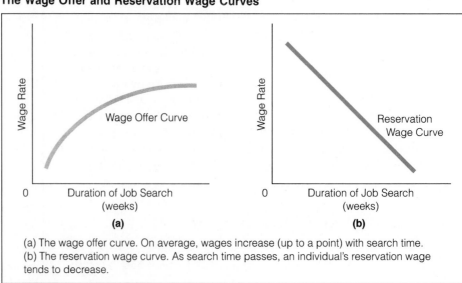

(a) The wage offer curve. On average, wages increase (up to a point) with search time.
(b) The reservation wage curve. As search time passes, an individual's reservation wage tends to decrease.

The Reservation Wage Curve. Individuals searching for jobs realize that the search is costly to them. Most of the cost consists of the wages they could have been earning had they accepted the last offer and not extended the search. For this reason, each job searcher has some notion of a wage offer that is good enough to accept without extending the search. The lowest wage a person will accept at any time in the job search process is called that person's **reservation wage.**

As search time passes, an individual's reservation wage tends to decrease for several reasons. First, individuals searching for jobs usually start out optimistic and often overestimate their market worth to employers. As time passes, they gain information about themselves and the labor market, and thus become more realistic. Second, long periods of unemployment draw down savings accounts and put pressure on the job searchers to return to work. Third, unemployment benefits do not extend indefinitely. The relationship between the reservation wage and time is illustrated by the *reservation wage curve* in Exhibit 16–1b.

The Optimal Search Time. When does a job searcher stop searching? The answer is when he or she receives a wage offer that equals his or her reservation wage. To put it differently, if the wage offer (W) is less than the reservation wage (R), the individual continues to search. The job searcher stops searching when $W = R$. Exhibit 16–2 represents the process. The optimal search time is X weeks, which is the length of time it takes until W equals R. Before X weeks have passed, $R > W$, and the job searcher continues to search because he has not received a wage offer high enough to stop him from searching further. In short, he evaluates his wage offers as being too low. As time passes, however, wage offers rise (on average), and the reservation wage falls. Eventually, the two are equal. At this point, the job search ends.

EXHIBIT 16-2
Optimal Search Time

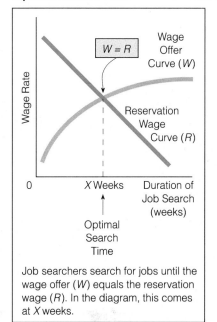

Job searchers search for jobs until the wage offer (W) equals the reservation wage (R). In the diagram, this comes at X weeks.

Reservation Wage
The lowest wage a person will accept at any time in the job search process.

When economists explain and predict behavior, they are usually *comparing* things. For example, in job search theory, *wages offered* are compared with *reservation wages* to explain and predict how long a person searches for a job. In the theory of supply and demand, the quantity demanded of a good is compared with the quantity supplied of a good to see if the market is in equilibrium. In the theory of opportunity cost, what one *is* doing is compared with what one *could be* doing to determine cost. Last, when discussing wages, economists assume that people are more interested in their real wages—their money wages compared with the price level—than in their money wages alone.

Comparing things illustrates that to know where we are, or how we are doing, it is important to have a reference point. Jones doesn't know whether a wage offer of $2,000 a month is good or not until she knows her opportunity costs. Smith doesn't know whether his salary increase makes him better off or not until he measures the percentage increase in his salary against the percentage increase in the price level. So, when economists compare things, they are acting on the knowledge that a reference point is often necessary to tell us how we stand.

Optimal Search Time and the Unemployment Rate

An increase in optimal search time is followed by an increase in the unemployment rate, *ceteris paribus*. Here is a simple numerical example to illustrate the point.

CHAPTER 16
JOB SEARCH THEORY, PHILLIPS
CURVE ANALYSIS, AND NEW
CLASSICAL THEORY: ENTER
EXPECTATIONS

■

357

A worker's inflation expectations affect how long he or she searches for a job.

Suppose the civilian labor force is composed of 100 individuals and there are 10 unemployed persons. It follows that the unemployment rate is 10 percent. Now consider two cases. In Case 1, the optimal search time is one week, and each week 10 persons become unemployed. In Case 2, the optimal search time is two weeks, and each week 10 persons become unemployed. As we can see, the only difference between Case 1 and Case 2 is that the optimal search time is longer in Case 2. Does an increase in the optimal search time increase the unemployment rate?

To help us answer this question, we turn to Exhibit 16–3. Consider Case 1. In week 1, there are 10 persons unemployed, so the unemployment rate is 10 percent. In week 2, 10 persons accept job offers (recall that the optimal search time is one week), and 10 persons become unemployed. We subtract 10 persons from, and add 10 persons to, the number of unemployed at the end of week 1. This gives us a total of 10 persons unemployed in week 2 and an unemployment rate of 10 percent. In week 3, 10 persons accept job offers, and 10 persons become unemployed. We subtract 10 persons from, and add 10 persons to, the number of unemployed persons at the end of week 3. This gives us a total of 10 persons unemployed in week 3 and an unemployment rate of 10 percent.

We turn now to Case 2, where the optimal search time is two weeks. Beginning in week 1, there are 10 persons unemployed, so the unemployment rate is 10 percent. In week 2, 10 persons are added to the ranks of the unemployed, but none of the previously unemployed accepts a job offer (recall that the optimal search time is two weeks). It follows that there are 20 persons unemployed in week 2 and that the unemployment rate is 20 percent. In week 3, 10 persons accept job offers (the two weeks optimal search time has passed), and 10 persons become unemployed. We therefore subtract 10 persons from, and add 10 persons to, the number of unemployed at the end of week 2. The total number of persons unemployed in week 3 is 20, and the unemployment rate is 20 percent. Our conclusion is that *as the optimal search time increases, the unemployment rate increases.*

Inflation Expectations and Optimal Search Time

A worker's inflation expectations affect how long he or she searches for a job. Consider Helen Rodriguez's job search. She has some idea of what she can buy

EXHIBIT 16-3
Optimal Search Time and the Unemployment Rate
Starting with a civilian labor force of 100 persons and 10 unemployed persons, we consider two cases: Case 1, where the optimal search time is one week, and each week 10 persons become unemployed; and Case 2, where the optimal search time is two weeks, and each week 10 persons become unemployed. As optimal search time increases, so does the unemployment rate—from 10 percent in Case 1 to 20 percent in Case 2.

CASE 1: OPTIMAL SEARCH TIME = 1 WEEK			
	Week 1	Week 2	Week 3
Unemployed persons	10	$10 - 10 + 10 = 10$	$10 - 10 + 10 = 10$
Unemployment rate	$\frac{10}{100} = 10\%$	$\frac{10}{100} = 10\%$	$\frac{10}{100} = 10\%$

CASE 2: OPTIMAL SEARCH TIME = 2 WEEKS			
	Week 1	Week 2	Week 3
Unemployed persons	10	$10 + 10 = 20$	$20 - 10 + 10 = 20$
Unemployment rate	$\frac{10}{100} = 10\%$	$\frac{20}{100} = 20\%$	$\frac{20}{100} = 20\%$

with the pay she is being offered. For example, if she is offered a salary of $40,000 per year, she has an idea of what $40,000 will buy over the period of time she receives it. Suppose, though, that her idea of what the $40,000 will buy is based on an expected inflation rate of 15 percent. The actual inflation rate, however, turns out to be 5 percent. Does her "too high" expected inflation rate, relative to the actual inflation rate, influence the time she spends searching for a job? Most likely it does. She believes that any salary offered to her has less purchasing power than it actually has, and therefore she is likely to search longer for a job (stay voluntarily unemployed longer) than she would if her expected inflation rate were accurate (equal to the actual inflation rate).

Unemployment Benefits and the Unemployment Rate

Can higher unemployment benefits raise the unemployment rate? Yes, if there is a relationship between unemployment benefits and optimal search time. But for this relationship to exist, a change in unemployment benefits must shift either the wage offer curve or the reservation wage curve. Does it?

Suppose the government announces that the amount of unemployment benefits paid per week will increase and that benefits will be available for more weeks. Instead of the average unemployment benefit being, say, $100 per week for 20 weeks, it will be $150 per week for 30 weeks. As a result, we predict that individuals' reservation wages will increase. One reason for this is that the job search pressure on savings isn't as great. As reservation wages increase, the reservation wage curve shifts rightward from R_1 to R_2 (Exhibit 16–4). As a result, the optimal search time increases from X_1 weeks to X_2 weeks, and the unemployment rate increases from U_1 to U_2.

The existence of unemployment benefits may explain why many jobs go unfilled, even in the midst of a high-unemployment period. For example, in 1982, when

EXHIBIT 16-4
Unemployment Benefits and the Unemployment Rate

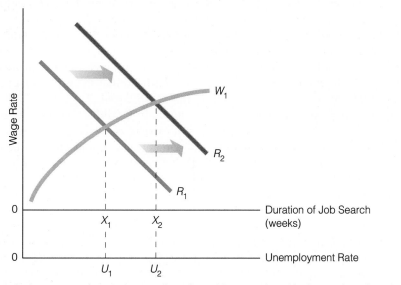

An increase in the amount of unemployment benefits paid per week and in the number of weeks benefits are available shifts the reservation wage curve (*R*) to the right; this increases the number of weeks a person searches for a job and, thus, the unemployment rate.

CHAPTER 16
JOB SEARCH THEORY, PHILLIPS
CURVE ANALYSIS, AND NEW
CLASSICAL THEORY: ENTER
EXPECTATIONS
■
359

the unemployment rate was at a relatively high 9.7 percent, there were slightly more than 6 million job openings. If unemployment benefits are high enough so that the monetary difference between being employed and being unemployed is small, we would expect that more persons will stay unemployed than if the difference between being employed and being unemployed is large.

This is not an argument against unemployment benefits or increases in unemployment benefits. We are simply pointing out that because unemployment benefits exist, the unemployment rate is higher than it would be otherwise. For other reasons, a society may prefer higher unemployment benefits and higher unemployment rates to lower unemployment benefits and lower unemployment rates. For example, some economists argue that there are benefits from individuals spending more time searching for a better job match.

THINKING LIKE
AN ECONOMIST

When an economist argues that higher unemployment benefits raise the unemployment rate, the layperson may conclude that the economist is against a system of unemployment benefits. But this misrepresents what the economist is saying. Economists who do positive economics ("what is" as opposed to "what should be") are not necessarily for or against a particular system or policy. Their world is the world of cause and effect. The economist who argues that higher unemployment benefits will increase the unemployment rate is not necessarily against raising unemployment benefits. He is simply showing us that there are no free lunches: There is a cost to higher unemployment benefits. Science advances when researchers tell us the truth as they see it—regardless of whether they like the particular truth or not.

The *LRAS* Curve Is Not Carved in Stone

Up to this point, we have said little about a shift in the *LRAS* curve. When we talked about a supply-side shift, it has been a shift in the short-run aggregate supply (*SRAS*) curve. What about the *LRAS* curve? Can it shift?

The answer is yes. The logic is easy to follow: Since the *LRAS* curve is set at the natural real GNP level (Q_N)—which corresponds to the natural unemployment rate (U_N)—anything that either increases or decreases the natural unemployment rate will automatically shift the *LRAS* curve leftward or rightward, respectively. More specifically, anything that changes either of the two components of the natural unemployment rate—that is, either the frictional unemployment rate or the structural unemployment rate—shifts the *LRAS* curve.

Here is an example. Suppose the economy in Exhibit 16–5 is at the natural real GNP level of Q_{N1} and the natural unemployment rate of U_{N1}, or 6 percent (where the frictional unemployment rate is 2 percent and the structural unemployment rate is 4 percent). The relevant long-run aggregate supply curve is $LRAS_1$.

Now suppose government permanently increases the length and amount of unemployment benefits. As we saw earlier, this shifts the reservation wage curve to the right (see Exhibit 16–4). As this happens, the optimal search time rises; consequently, the unemployment rate rises.

The natural unemployment rate is affected, too. As unemployment benefits increase and extend over more weeks, the pressure on the unemployed to find jobs decreases. Consider a person who is frictionally unemployed. With greater unemployment benefits, she doesn't have to find another job as quickly, and so she stretches out the job search. All other things held constant, this increases the frictional unemployment rate. But if the frictional unemployment rate rises, so does

EXHIBIT 16-5
A Shift in the *LRAS* Curve

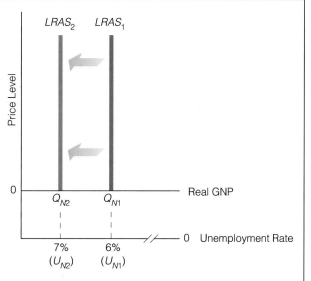

Anything that changes the natural unemployment rate causes a shift in the *LRAS* curve. For example, a permanent increase in unemployment benefits causes the frictional unemployment rate to rise. As a result, the natural unemployment rate increases (say, from 6% to 7%) and the *LRAS* curve shifts leftward from *LRAS*$_1$ to *LRAS*$_2$.

the natural unemployment rate. In our example, if the frictional unemployment rate goes up from 2 to 3 percent, and the structural unemployment rate is constant at 4 percent, then the natural unemployment rises to 7 percent.

In Exhibit 16–5, the economy moves leftward along the unemployment rate axis from U_{N1} (6 percent) to U_{N2} (7 percent) and leftward along the real GNP axis from Q_{N1} to Q_{N2}.

Given these changes, is $LRAS_1$ still the relevant long-run aggregate supply curve? The answer is no. The relevant long-run supply curve is now $LRAS_2$. In other words, since the natural unemployment rate has increased, the *LRAS* curve has shifted to the left. If the natural unemployment rate had decreased, the *LRAS* curve would have shifted to the right.

In summary, anything that raises the natural unemployment rate shifts the *LRAS* curve to the left; anything that lowers the natural unemployment rate shifts the *LRAS* curve to the right.

PHILLIPS CURVE ANALYSIS

In this section, we begin our discussion of the Phillips curve by focusing on the work of three economists, A. W. Phillips, Paul Samuelson, and Robert Solow.

1958: The Phillips Curve

In 1958, A. W. Phillips of the London School of Economics published a paper entitled "The Relation between Unemployment and the Rate of Change of Money Wages in the United Kingdom, 1861–1957," in the economics journal *Economica*. As the title suggests, Phillips collected data on the rate of change in money wages, sometimes referred to as *wage inflation,* and unemployment rates in the United Kingdom over a period of time. He then plotted the rate of change in money wages against the unemployment rate for each year. Finally, he fit a curve to the data points (Exhibit 16–6).

EXHIBIT 16-6
The Original Phillips Curve

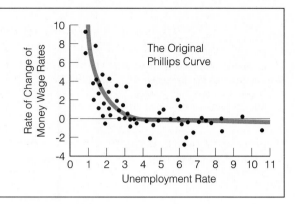

This curve was constructed by A. W. Phillips, using data for the United Kingdom from 1861 to 1913. (The relationship here is also representative of the experience of the United Kingdom through 1957). The original Phillips curve suggests an inverse relationship between wage inflation and unemployment; it represents a wage inflation–unemployment trade-off. (Note: Each dot represents a single year.)

Phillips Curve
A curve that originally showed the relationship between wage inflation and unemployment. Now it more often shows the relationship between price inflation and unemployment.

An Inverse Relationship. The curve came to be known as the **Phillips curve.** Notice that the curve is downward sloping, suggesting that the rate of change of money wage rates (wage inflation) and unemployment rates are inversely related. This inverse relationship suggests a trade-off between wage inflation and unemployment. Higher wage inflation means lower unemployment; lower wage inflation means higher unemployment. Policy makers concluded from the Phillips curve that it was impossible to lower both wage inflation *and* unemployment; one could do one or the other. So, the combination of low wage inflation *and* low unemployment was not likely. This was the bad news. The good news was that rising unemployment and rising wage inflation did not go together either. Thus, the combination of high unemployment *and* high wage inflation was also not likely.

The Theoretical Explanation for the Phillips Curve. What is the reason for the inverse relationship between wage inflation and unemployment? Early explanations centered on the state of the labor market given changes in aggregate demand. When aggregate demand is increasing, businesses expand production and hire more employees. As the unemployment rate falls, the labor market becomes tighter, and it becomes increasingly difficult to hire workers at old wages. Businesses end up offering higher wages to obtain additional workers. Unemployment and money wage rates move in opposite directions.

1960: Samuelson and Solow: The Phillips Curve Is Americanized

In 1960, two American economists, Paul Samuelson and Robert Solow, published an article in the *American Economic Review* in which they fit a Phillips curve to the U.S. economy from 1935 to 1959. Besides using American data instead of British data, they measured price inflation rates (instead of wage inflation rates) against unemployment rates. They found an inverse relationship between (price) inflation and unemployment (see Exhibit 16–7).[1]

From viewing the Phillips curve (such as the one in 16–7), economists concluded that **stagflation,** or high inflation together with high unemployment, was

Stagflation
The simultaneous occurrence of high rates of inflation and unemployment.

[1]Today, when economists speak of the Phillips curve, they are usually referring to the relationship between price inflation rates and unemployment rates, instead of wage inflation rates and unemployment rates.

extremely unlikely. The economy could register high unemployment and low inflation *or* low unemployment and high inflation.

Also, economists noticed that the Phillips curve presented policy makers with a *menu of choices.* For example, policy makers could choose to move the economy to any of the points on the Phillips curve in Exhibit 16–7. If they decided that a point like *A*, with high unemployment and low inflation, was preferable to a point like *D*, with low unemployment and high inflation, then so be it. It was simply a matter of reaching the right level of aggregate demand. To Keynesian economists, who were gaining a reputation for advocating *fine-tuning* the economy, that is, using small-scale measures to counterbalance undesirable economic trends, this conclusion seemed to be consistent with their theories and policy proposals.

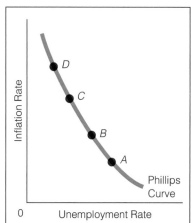

EXHIBIT 16-7
The Phillips Curve and a Menu of Choices

Samuelson and Solow's early work using American data showed that the Phillips curve was downward sloping. Economists reasoned that stagflation was extremely unlikely and that the Phillips curve presented policy makers with a menu of choices—point *A*, *B*, *C*, or *D*.

Question:

If the Phillips curve presents policy makers with a menu of choices (such as 5 percent inflation and 3 percent unemployment or 2 percent inflation and 4.5 percent unemployment, and so on), this implicitly assumes that the menu of choices does not change over time. The same combinations of inflation and unemployment rates exist year after year. Is it really this way in the real world?

Answer:

As we soon explain, the real world is not like this.

THE CONTROVERSY BEGINS

Next we discuss the work of Milton Friedman and the hypothesis that there are two, not one, Phillips curves.

The 1970s and 1980s: Things Aren't Always As We Thought

In the 1970s and early 1980s, economists began to question many of the conclusions about the Phillips curve. Their questions were largely prompted by events in the period after 1969. Consider Exhibit 16–8, which shows U.S. inflation and unemployment rates for the years 1961–90. The 1961–69 period, which is shaded, depicts the original Phillips curve trade-off between inflation and unemployment. The remaining period, 1970–90, as a whole does not, although some subperiods, such as 1976–79, do.

Focusing on the period 1970–90, we note two things: (1) Stagflation—high unemployment and high inflation—is possible. For example, 1975, 1981, and 1982 are definitely years of stagflation. Furthermore, the existence of stagflation implies that a trade-off between inflation and unemployment may not always exist. (2) Cycles of unemployment and inflation rates appear to have gravitated around a 6 percent unemployment rate—identified by the vertical line in Exhibit 16–8. This suggests that the unemployment rate tends to move toward some natural level in the long run.

Flashback to 1967: Friedman and the Natural Rate Hypothesis

Milton Friedman, in his presidential address to the American Economic Association in 1967 (published in the *American Economic Review*), attacked the idea of a permanent downward-sloping Phillips curve. Friedman's key point was that

CHAPTER 16
JOB SEARCH THEORY, PHILLIPS
CURVE ANALYSIS, AND NEW
CLASSICAL THEORY: ENTER
EXPECTATIONS

363

The period 1961–69 clearly depicts the original Phillips curve trade-off between inflation and unemployment. The later period, 1970–90, as a whole, does not. However, some subperiods do, such as 1976–79. The diagram presents empirical evidence that stagflation may exist; an inflation–unemployment trade-off may not always hold.

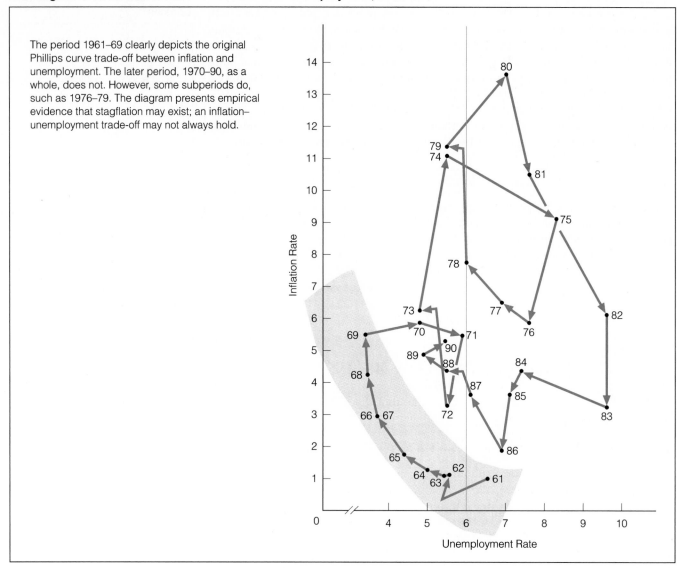

there are two, not one, Phillips curves: a short-run Phillips curve and a long-run Phillips curve. Friedman said, "There is always a temporary trade-off between inflation and unemployment; there is no permanent trade-off." In other words, there is a trade-off in the short run, but not in the long run. Friedman's discussion not only introduced two types of Phillips curves—short run and long run—to the analysis but also opened the macroeconomics door wide, once and for all, to expectations theory, that is, to the idea that peoples' expectations about economic events affect economic outcomes.

It is easy to illustrate both the short-run and long-run Phillips curves with the aid of Exhibit 16–9. We start with the economy in long-run equilibrium, operating at Q_1, which is equal to Q_N. This is shown in Window 1. In the main diagram, the economy is at point 1 at the natural rate of unemployment. Further, and most

EXHIBIT 16-9
Short-Run and Long-Run Phillips Curve

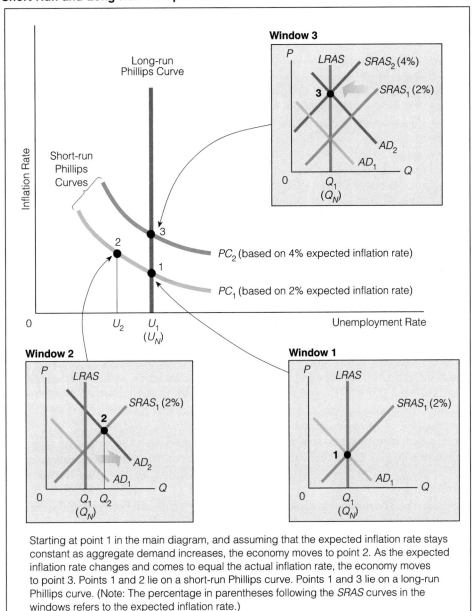

Starting at point 1 in the main diagram, and assuming that the expected inflation rate stays constant as aggregate demand increases, the economy moves to point 2. As the expected inflation rate changes and comes to equal the actual inflation rate, the economy moves to point 3. Points 1 and 2 lie on a short-run Phillips curve. Points 1 and 3 lie on a long-run Phillips curve. (Note: The percentage in parentheses following the *SRAS* curves in the windows refers to the expected inflation rate.)

important, we assume that the expected inflation rate and the actual inflation rate are the same, at 2 percent.

Now suppose government *unexpectedly* increases aggregate demand from AD_1 to AD_2, as shown in Window 2. As a result, the actual inflation rate increases (say, to 4 percent), but in the short run (immediately after the increase in aggregate demand), individual decision makers do not know this. Consequently, the expected inflation rate remains at 2 percent. In short, we have aggregate demand increasing at the same time that people's expected inflation rate remains constant. Because of this combination of events, certain things happen.

CHAPTER 16
JOB SEARCH THEORY, PHILLIPS
CURVE ANALYSIS, AND NEW
CLASSICAL THEORY: ENTER
EXPECTATIONS

■

365

Friedman argued that as long as the expected in-flation rate is not equal to the actual inflation rate, the economy is not in long-run equilibrium.

■

First, the higher aggregate demand causes temporary shortages and higher prices. Businesses respond to higher prices and higher profits by increasing output. Higher output requires more employees, so businesses start hiring more workers. Job vacancies increase and many currently unemployed individuals find work. Furthermore, many of the newly employed persons accept the prevailing wage rate; after all, they think the wages will have greater purchasing power than, in fact, they will turn out to have.

So far, the results of an increase in aggregate demand with no change in the expected inflation rate are (1) an increase in real GNP from Q_1 to Q_2 (see Window 2) and (2) a corresponding decrease in the unemployment rate from U_1 to U_2 (see the main diagram). Thus, the economy has moved from point 1 to point 2 in the main diagram.

This raises the question: Is point 2 a stable equilibrium? Friedman answered that it was not. He argued that as long as the *expected* inflation rate is not equal to the *actual* inflation rate, the economy is not in long-run equilibrium. For Friedman, as for most economists today, the movement from point 1 to point 2 on PC_1 is a short-run movement. Economists refer to PC_1, along which short-run movements occur, as a *short-run Phillips curve.*

In time, inflation expectations begin to change. As prices continue their climb, wage earners realize that their real (inflation-adjusted) wages have fallen. In hindsight, they realize that they accepted money wages based on an expected inflation rate (of 2 percent) that was too low. They revise their inflation expectations upward. At the same time, some wage earners quit their jobs because they do not choose to continue working at such low real wages. Eventually, the combination of some workers quitting their jobs and most (if not all) workers revising their inflation expectations upward causes wage rates to move upward. Higher wage rates shift the short-run aggregate supply curve from $SRAS_1$ to $SRAS_2$ (see Window 3), ultimately moving the economy back to the natural level of real GNP and the natural rate of unemployment (at point 3 in the main diagram). The movement from point 2 to point 3 was prompted by a discrepancy between the expected inflation rate and the actual inflation rate. The curve that connects point 1, where the economy started out, and point 3, where it ended up, is called the *long-run Phillips curve.*

Thus, the short-run Phillips curve exhibits a trade-off between inflation and unemployment, whereas the long-run Phillips curve does not. This is the idea implicit in what has come to be called the **natural rate hypothesis.** According to this hypothesis, in the long run, the economy returns to its natural rate of unemployment; lower unemployment cannot permanently be bought by higher inflation.

Natural Rate Hypothesis
The idea that in the long run, unemployment is at its natural rate. Within the Phillips curve framework, the natural rate hypothesis specifies that there is a long-run Phillips curve, which is vertical at the natural rate of unemployment.

RATIONAL EXPECTATIONS AND NEW CLASSICAL THEORY

■

Rational expectations has played a major role in the developing discussion of the Phillips curve controversy. The work of economists Robert Lucas, Robert Barro, Thomas Sargent, and Neil Wallace is relevant here. We turn to a discussion of rational expectations next.

1973: Rational Expectations and the New Classical Ratex Theory

In the early 1970s, a few economists, including Robert Lucas of the University of Chicago, began to question if there was even a short-run trade-off between inflation and unemployment. Essentially, what Lucas did was combine the natural rate hypothesis with rational expectations (sometimes simply referred to as **"ratex"**).[2]

Lucas and other *new classical economists,* as they came to be called, pointed out that the traditional natural rate hypothesis was based on adaptive expectations. As stated in Chapter 13, adaptive expectations theory holds that individuals form their inflation expectations based on past inflation rate experience. Stated differently, if people form the expected inflation rate *adaptively,* they are always looking over their shoulders to see what *has happened* (in the *past)*—as opposed to what *is* happening (in the *present),* or what they think *will* happen (in the *future).*

The new classical economists thought individuals formed their inflation expectations rationally; that is, taking into account not only what *has happened* but also what *is happening* and what *will happen*—in short, on all available and relevant information. But, of course, to say that individuals base their inflation expectations on, among other things, the effects of what will happen—for example, future policy actions—implies that individuals *anticipate* policy actions. Before we examine the details of the natural rate hypothesis with the rational expectations twist, let us discuss whether people do anticipate policy.

As long as some people anticipate policy, the consequences may be the same as if all persons do.

■

Ratex
Short for rational expectations.

Do People Anticipate Policy?

Suppose you picked a person at random on the street and asked him or her this question: What do you think the Fed will do in the next few months? Do you think you would be more likely to receive (1) an intelligent answer or (2) the response, "What's the Fed"? Most readers of this text will probably choose answer (2). There is a general feeling that the person on the street knows little about economics or economic institutions. The answer to our question—Do people anticipate policy?—seems to be no.

But suppose you were to ask the same question of a person picked at random on Wall Street. This time you would likely receive an informed answer. In this case, the answer to our larger question—Do people anticipate policy?—is likely to be yes.

We suggest that not all persons need to anticipate policy; as long as some do, the consequences may be the same *as if* all persons do. For example, Juanita Estevez is anticipating policy if she decides to buy 100 shares of SKA, because her best friend, Tammy Higgins, heard from her boyfriend, Kenny Urich, that his broker, Roberta Gunter, had told him that SKA's stock was going to go up. Juanita is anticipating policy because it is likely that Roberta Gunter obtained her information from a researcher in the brokerage firm who makes it his business to "watch the Fed" and to anticipate its next move. (In fact, many New York investment firms pay their professional "Fed watchers" a quarter of a million dollars per year or more. There is a life in economics beyond taking tests.)

Of course, anticipating policy is not done just for the purpose of buying and selling stocks. Labor unions hire professional forecasters to predict future inflation rates, which is important information to have during contract wage negotiations. Banks hire professional forecasters to predict inflation rates, which they incorporate into the interest rate they charge. Export businesses hire professional forecasters to predict the future exchange value of the dollar. The average investor may

[2]Rational expectations came on the economic scene in 1961 with the publication of the article "Rational Expectations and the Theory of Price Movements" by John Muth in the journal *Econometrica.* For about ten years, the article received little attention from the economics profession. Then, in the early 1970s, with the work of Robert Lucas, Thomas Sargent, Neil Wallace, Robert Barro, and other economists, the article began to be noticed.

subscribe to a business or investment newsletter in order to predict interest rates, the price of gold, or next year's inflation rate more accurately. The person thinking of refinancing his mortgage watches "Wall Street Week" on television to hear what this week's guest has to say about the Congress's most recent move and how it will affect interest rates in the next three months.

New Classical Theory: The Effects of Unanticipated and Anticipated Policy

There are two major assumptions of new classical theory: (1) Expectations are formed rationally. (2) Wages and prices are flexible. With these in mind, we discuss new classical theory in two settings: one where policy is unanticipated and the other where policy is anticipated.

Unanticipated Policy. Consider Exhibit 16–10a. The economy starts off at point 1, where $Q_1 = Q_N$. *Unexpectedly,* the Fed begins to buy government securities, and the money supply and aggregate demand increase. The aggregate demand curve shifts rightward from AD_1 to AD_2. Since the policy action was unanticipated, individuals are caught off guard, so the anticipated price level (P_1), on which the short-run aggregate supply curve is based, is not likely to change immediately.[4] In

[4]This is similar to saying, as we did in the discussion of the Friedman natural rate hypothesis, that individuals' expected inflation rate is less than the actual inflation rate.

EXHIBIT 16-10
Rational Expectations in an *AD–AS* Framework

(a)

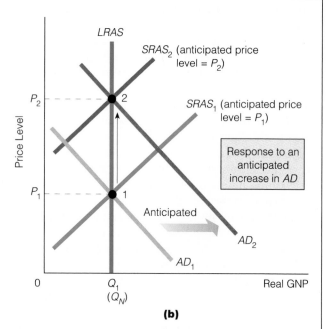

(b)

The economy is in long-run equilibrium at point 1 in both (a) and (b). In (a), there is an unanticipated increase in aggregate demand. In the short run, the economy moves to point 2. In the long run, it moves to point 3. In (b), there is an anticipated increase in aggregate demand. Because the increase is anticipated, the short-run aggre-

gate supply curve shifts from $SRAS_1$ to $SRAS_2$ at the same time the aggregate demand curve shifts from AD_1 to AD_2. The economy moves directly to point 2, which is comparable to point 3 in (a).

the short run, the economy moves from point 1 to point 2, from Q_1 to Q_2. (In Phillips-curve terms, the economy has moved up the short-run Phillips curve to a higher inflation rate and lower unemployment rate.) In the long run, workers correctly anticipate the higher price level and increase their wage demands accordingly. The short-run aggregate supply curve shifts leftward from $SRAS_1$ to $SRAS_2$ and the economy moves to point 3.

Anticipated Policy. Now consider the difference if policy is anticipated, in particular if it is *correctly* anticipated. When individuals anticipate that the Fed will buy government securities and that the money supply, aggregate demand, and prices will increase, they will adjust their present actions accordingly. For example, workers will bargain for higher wages so that their real wages will not fall when the price level rises. As a result, the short-run aggregate supply curve will shift leftward from $SRAS_1$ to $SRAS_2$ at the same time that the aggregate demand curve shifts rightward from AD_1 to AD_2 (see Exhibit 16–10b). The economy moves directly from point 1 to point 2. Real GNP does not change; throughout the adjustment period, it remains at its natural level. It follows that the unemployment rate does not change either. Simply put, there is no short-run trade-off between inflation and unemployment. The short-run Phillips curve and the long-run Phillips curve are one and the same; and the curve is vertical.

Question:

What is a simple, everyday (preferably noneconomic) example that illustrates the operation and effects of rational expectations in a setting where "policy" is unanticipated and one where it is anticipated?

Answer:

Suppose Jim's psychology class starts at 9 A.M. and it is "natural" for him to arrive one minute before class starts. In other words, his "natural waiting time" is one minute.

The first day of class, Jim arrives at 8:59, his instructor arrives at 8:59:30, and she starts class promptly at 9 A.M.

The second day of class, Jim arrives at 8:59, his instructor arrives at 9:01:30, and she starts class at 9:02. On this day, Jim has waited three minutes, which is above his natural waiting time of one minute.

The third, fourth, and fifth days of class are the same as the second. So, for the second through fifth days of class, Jim is operating at above his natural waiting time.

Finally, Jim adjusts. Instead of arriving at 8:59, he arrives at class at 9:01. This day the instructor again arrives at 9:01:30 and begins class at 9:02. Jim is back at his natural waiting time of one minute.

In this case, Jim did not initially anticipate that his instructor would be late: A change in the instructor's policy from the first day of class (when she arrived at 8:59:30) to the second through fifth days of class (when she arrived at 9:01:30) was unanticipated. As a result, Jim was moved away from his natural waiting of time for a few days. Finally, he adjusted back to it.

Now suppose that a change in the instructor's policy is anticipated. For example, the instructor announces on the first day of class that she will begin class two minutes late from now on. Knowing this, Jim no longer plans to arrive to class at

CHAPTER 16
JOB SEARCH THEORY, PHILLIPS
CURVE ANALYSIS, AND NEW
CLASSICAL THEORY: ENTER
EXPECTATIONS
■
369

8:59, but instead at 9:01; thus, he maintains his natural waiting time at one minute; never does he rise above or fall below it.

Policy Ineffectiveness Proposition (PIP)

Using rational expectations, we showed (see Exhibit 16–10) that if the rise in aggregate demand is *unanticipated,* there is a short-run increase in real GNP, but if the rise in aggregate demand is *correctly anticipated,* there is no change in real GNP.

We have studied two types of macroeconomic policies—fiscal and monetary—both of which theoretically can increase aggregate demand. For example, assuming there is no crowding out or incomplete crowding out, expansionary fiscal policy shifts the *AD* curve rightward. Expansionary monetary policy does the same. In both cases, expansionary policy is *effective* at increasing real GNP and lowering the unemployment rate in the short run. But what new classical economists call into question is just this. They argue that (1) if the expansionary policy change is *correctly anticipated,* (2) individuals form their expectations rationally, and (3) wages and prices are flexible, neither expansionary fiscal policy nor expansionary monetary policy will be able to increase real GNP and lower the unemployment rate in the short run. This is called the **policy ineffectiveness proposition (PIP).**

Think what this means. If, under certain conditions, expansionary monetary and fiscal policy are not effective at increasing real GNP and lowering the unemployment rate, the case for government fine-tuning the economy is called into question.

Policy Ineffectiveness Proposition (PIP)

If (1) a policy change is correctly *anticipated,* (2) individuals form their expectations rationally, and (3) wages and prices are flexible, then neither fiscal policy nor monetary policy is effective at meeting macroeconomic goals.

Question:

Are new classical economists saying that monetary and fiscal policies are never effective?

Answer:

No, they are saying that monetary and fiscal policies are not effective under a certain condition: When policy is correctly anticipated, people form their expectations rationally, and wages and prices are flexible.

Follow-up Question:

I know a number of people who do not anticipate policy and who do not seem to form their expectations by looking to the past, present, and future. Isn't this evidence that new classical theory is assuming things that are wrong and therefore is of little value?

Answer:

Remember, we do not judge a theory by its assumptions, but instead by the accuracy of its predictions. Certainly, all of us can find people who do not anticipate policy and who do not form their expectations rationally. But the point is whether these people are great enough in numbers to upset the prediction of the theory. It may be that enough people form their expectations rationally, and enough people anticipate policy, so that it is *as if* everyone does. New classical theory does not purport to describe reality perfectly. All theories—whether classical, Keynesian, monetarist, or new classical—are abstractions from reality.

Rational Expectations and Incorrectly Anticipated Policy

Suppose that wages and prices are flexible and people form their expectations rationally and anticipate policy—but this time they anticipate policy incorrectly. What happens?

To illustrate, consider Exhibit 16–11. The economy is in long-run equilibrium at point 1 where $Q_1 = Q_N$. The public believes the Fed will increase aggregate demand by increasing the money supply, but it incorrectly anticipates the *degree* to which aggregate demand will be increased. The public, thinking aggregate demand will increase from AD_1 to AD_2, immediately revises its anticipated price level to P_2 (the long-run equilibrium position of the AD_2 curve and the *LRAS* curve), and as a result the short-run aggregate supply curve shifts leftward from $SRAS_1$ to $SRAS_2$.

A problem arises, however, when the aggregate demand curve only shifts rightward from AD_1 to AD'_2. In short, the actual increase in aggregate demand is less than anticipated. As a result, the economy moves to point 2'; to a lower real GNP and a higher unemployment rate. From this we conclude that a policy designed to increase real GNP and lower unemployment can do just the opposite if the policy is less expansionary *than anticipated.*

EXHIBIT 16-11
The Short-Run Response to an Aggregate Demand-Increasing Policy That Is Less Expansionary Than Anticipated (in the New Classical Ratex Theory)

Starting at point 1, the public anticipates an increase in aggregate demand from AD_1 to AD_2. Based on this, the short-run aggregate supply curve shifts leftward from $SRAS_1$ to $SRAS_2$. It turns out, however, that the aggregate demand curve only shifts rightward to AD'_2 (less than anticipated). As a result, the economy moves to point 2', to a lower real GNP and a higher unemployment rate.

CHAPTER 16
JOB SEARCH THEORY, PHILLIPS
CURVE ANALYSIS, AND NEW
CLASSICAL THEORY: ENTER
EXPECTATIONS
■
371

ECONOMICS IN OUR TIMES

One Implication of Rational Expectations: If You Say You're Going to Do It, You Had Better Do It, Because If You Don't, Next Time No One Will Believe You, and That Could Cause Problems

Suppose the public sees the following scenario played out three times in three years. The federal government runs a deficit. It finances the deficit by borrowing from the public (issuing Treasury bills, notes, and bonds). The Fed conducts open market operations and buys many of the government securities. Aggregate demand increases and the price level rises. At the same time all this is going on, every elected representative says he or she will do what needs to be done to bring inflation under control. The chairman of the Fed says the Fed will soon move against inflation.

Three times elected representatives and the Fed chairman say they will move against inflation; three times they don't. This can create a situation like the one illustrated in Exhibit

16–11. Indeed, some economists believe such events go a long way toward explaining the 1981–82 recession. They maintain that the following scenario occurred: (1) President Reagan proposed, and the Congress approved, tax cuts in 1981. (2) Notwithstanding what some economists (namely, some supply-siders) were saying at the time—that the tax cuts would stimulate so much economic activity that tax revenues would increase—the public believed that tax cuts would decrease tax revenues and increase the size of the budget deficit. (3) People translated larger deficits into more government borrowing. (4) They anticipated greater money supply growth connected with larger deficits (they had experienced this before). (5) Greater

money supply growth would mean an increase in aggregate demand and the price level. (6) The Fed said it wouldn't finance the deficits (buy government bonds), but it had said this before and acted contrarily, so few people believed it this time. (7) The Fed actually did not increase the money supply as much as individuals thought it would. (8) This meant that monetary policy was not as expansionary as individuals had anticipated. (9) As a result, the economy moved to a point like 2' in Exhibit 16–11. Real GNP fell and unemployment increased; a recession ensued. Some economists contend that the 1981–82 scenario would have been different if in the past the Fed had done what it said it was going to do.

Major Tenets of New Classical Theory

In terms of our three macroeconomic organizational categories, here is what new classical theory has to say.

The P–Q Category. In new classical theory, there is a strong tendency for the economy to always return to its natural real GNP level (Q_N). Also, when policy is (correctly) anticipated, expectations are formed rationally, and wages and prices are flexible, policy changes affect only the price level (P) and not real GNP (Q), too. For example, see Exhibit 16–10b.

The Inherently Stable–Inherently Unstable Category. Unlike Keynesians, new classical economists believe that the economy is inherently stable and that it equilibrates at natural real GNP. The economy may find itself in either a recessionary or inflationary gap, but this is only a temporary state of affairs.

The Effective–Ineffective Category. New classical economists believe that under certain conditions—namely, policy is (correctly) anticipated and people form their expectations rationally, and wages and prices are flexible—neither fiscal nor monetary policy is effective. Like classical economists and monetarists, new classical economists largely advocate laissez-faire.

Interview: Thomas Sargent

As a graduate student at Harvard, Thomas Sargent developed a discomfort with macroeconomic models that assumed individual agents respond passively to economic policy. Today, he is considered one of the pioneers of rational expectations theory. Sargent is currently at Stanford University's Hoover Institution.

Professor Sargent, what is the basic property of the rational expectations model?

The rational expectations model basically has the property that all the agents in the model are doing the best that they can do whatever their situation is. They may be in very complicated situations, where they face a lot of uncertainty and have very imperfect information, but they are basically doing the best that they can do.

Some of the critics of rational expectations theory argue against its policy implications, a major one being that short-run government stabilization policies are ineffective. Are there others, however, who criticize the essence of the theory itself, that is, the idea that expectations are formed rationally? If so, what is their major criticism and how do you respond to it?

The first thing is that the so-called "policy ineffectiveness proposition" occurred only within a very special class of models that a lot of us don't think are very interesting. The main interest in rational expectations is to figure out how various policies are effective and to take into account dynamic effects that involve some element of imperfect foresight on the part of individuals. The really tough problems, and the scientifically challenging ones, are those that get us to study exactly how government policy matters and how you can optimally plan intervention in contexts in which it does matter.

Basically, the policy ineffectiveness proposition got started like this: Robert Lucas, Neil Wallace, and I worked with some models that embodied the transmission mechanism that was in the Keynesian models of the late-1960s. That mechanism had the property that the main effects (and in some models, all the effects) of monetary and fiscal policy were intermediated through policy surprises. For example, if you take a model in which all effects of policy are intermediated through surprises, and then take away the ability of the government to manipulate surprises— which is what you automatically do when you impose rational expectations—you get policy ineffectiveness. But that was a very special class of models, and much more interesting are the models where government policy has effects because it introduces distortions of various kinds—both good ones and bad ones: models in which there are externalities, models in which taxes distort effort, models in which monetary policy distorts effort, and this is the general case. When you do that, you get the result that policy matters.

As to the second part of the question, if you look at economic theory in general, rational expectations is now the dominant equilibrium concept. Nobody uses anything else. It is used in game theory. It was somewhat controversial in the 1970s, but I don't see it as controversial now.

It has been said that in the world of rational expectations, decision makers are like chess players: They anticipate the next move. Or is it better to say that they anticipate the next two moves? In fact, is it reasonable to ask how many moves ahead rational expectations theorists assume individuals anticipate? Or does this question miss the mark as to what rational expectations is about?

No, it doesn't miss the mark at all. It is exactly right. In a rational expectations equilibrium, you're in effect assuming that agents (to the best of their abilities) go an infinite number of moves ahead.

In the *Journal of Economic Literature* in March 1982, Maddock and Carter wrote a dialogue between two imaginary graduate students discussing rational expectations. One graduate student, Bernie, says that rational expectations "suggests that people anticipate the *effects* of policy." The other graduate student, Ernie, asks, "How on earth are people supposed to anticipate the effects of policy? I just can't see it. Have they all got econometric models under the sink?" How would you answer Ernie's question?

Well, they certainly don't have econometric models under the sink. I guess the way you can think of it is that people are trying to forecast what the policies are. If you're a person who is going to get affected by the corporate tax rate, or some kind of windfall profits tax, or a change in monetary regulation, it is in your interest to follow what is going on. And if you talk to people who are greatly affected by tax law, not only do they try to forecast it, they try to influence it, and they probably have a lot more information than you could get from an econometric model. For example, they know which congressman is voting for what.

Some people say that rational expectations is revolutionary. Is it?

It is revolutionary in two ways. One is in terms of a whole host of technical issues, in terms of the way people construct and estimate macroeconomic

models. There are essentially huge changes in econometric practices and huge changes in the way you set up models. It's a revolution in the sense that it requires tooling up with a different set of tools. One of the ways to think about it is to realize that Keynes talked about expectations, but he didn't have any tools to work with it. And the Keynesian models up to the late-1960s were always fudged. Theorists basically

fit distributed lags and left them uninterpreted. The way rational expectations got started is that persons within that tradition were trying to figure out what those distributed lags meant.

The second way in which rational expectations is revolutionary is in the sense that the disparity between micro and macro tends to vanish when you do rational expectations. You start to build models the exact same way.

EXHIBIT 16-12

The Short-Run Response to Aggregate Demand-Increasing Policy (in the New Keynesian Ratex Theory)

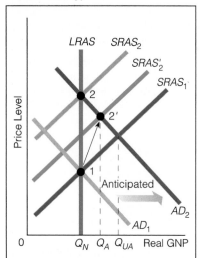

Starting at point 1, an increase in aggregate demand is anticipated. As a result, the short-run aggregate supply curve shifts leftward, but not all the way to $SRAS_2$ (as would be the case in the new classical ratex model). Instead it shifts only to $SRAS_2'$ because of some wage and price rigidities; the economy moves to point 2' (in the short run), and real GNP increases from Q_N to Q_A. If the policy had been unanticipated, real GNP would have increased from Q_N to Q_{UA}.

THE NONCLASSICAL OR NEW KEYNESIAN RATEX THEORY

We have seen that new classical theory assumes complete flexibility of wages and prices, since in the theory, an increase in the anticipated price level results in an immediate and equal rise in wages and prices, and the aggregate supply curve immediately shifts to the long-run equilibrium position.

In response to the assumption of flexible wages and prices, a few economists began to develop what has come to be known as the "nonclassical ratex theory," or the "New Keynesian ratex theory." This theory assumes that rational expectations is a reasonable characterization of how expectations are formed, but drops the assumption of complete wage and price flexibility. Economists who work with this theory argue that long-term labor contracts often prevent wages and prices from fully adjusting to changes in the anticipated price level. (Prices and wages are somewhat sticky, rigid, or inflexible.)

Consider the possible situation at the end of the first year of a three-year wage contract. Workers may realize that the anticipated price level is higher than they expected when they negotiated the contract, but will be unable to do much about it because their wages are locked in for the next two years. Price stickiness might also arise because firms often engage in fixed-price contracts with their suppliers. As we learned in Chapter 9, Keynesian economists today put forth microeconomic-based reasons why long-term labor contracts and above-market wages (efficiency wage theory) are sometimes in the best interest of both employers and employees.

To see what the theory predicts, look at Exhibit 16–12. The economy is initially in long-run equilibrium at point 1. The public anticipates an increase in aggregate demand from AD_1 to AD_2. As a result, the anticipated price level changes; because of some wage and price rigidities, however, the short-run aggregate supply curve does not shift all the way from $SRAS_1$ to $SRAS_2$, and the economy does not move from point 1 to point 2 (as in new classical theory). The short-run aggregate supply curve shifts instead to $SRAS_2'$ because some rigidities prevent complete wage and price adjustments. In the short run, the economy moves from point 1 to point 2', from Q_N to Q_A. It is interesting to note that had the policy been unanticipated, real GNP would have increased from Q_N to Q_{UA} in the short run.

Interview: Robert Solow

Robert Solow is the 1987 winner of the Nobel Prize in Economics. His major contributions have been in the field of economic growth theory. Solow is currently at the Massachusetts Institute of Technology.

In 1960, you and Paul Samuelson published a paper on the U.S. Phillips curve. What did you want your fellow economists to learn from this paper?

First, we wanted to suggest how hard it is to make inferences about causality from observed data on wage inflation and changes in unemployment. We knew that one shouldn't easily leap from a statistical relationship between the two variables to a causal relationship. We also wanted to get across that there was a price to pay in terms of inflation if there was an attempt to stimulate or expand the economy through the use of expansionary policy.

The question I often ask myself, and that other people ask me, is did we think there was a permanent trade-off between inflation and unemployment. Whereas the article contains the qualifications that work against a permanent trade-off, there is no doubt in my mind that we were very likely too optimistic about the stability of even the short-run trade-off. So, although in a court of law, so to speak, a jury would say "Yes, you said all the things you needed to say so you cannot be convicted of error," still we perhaps left a more optimistic impression of things than now seems to be justified.

What caused you to revise your degree of optimism—events or someone else's theoretical work?

It was a bit of both. In my case, it had to do more with events than the later work of Phelps and Friedman—to this day, I am not a believer in a meaningfully stable natural rate of unemployment. I think both the theory and the econometric evidence that underlie the

standard notions are flimsy. This doesn't mean that the picture we presented in 1960 is the right one. I would do it quite differently now. But I think what turned me into somewhat of a pessimist is the experience of the 1970s.

What do you think of the work of the rational expectation theorists?

I think that the notion of rational expectations is worth studying. There are places in economic and social life that are its natural habitat—like securities markets. One certainly wouldn't want to approach a study of stock or bond pricing with a mechanical theory of expectations. On the other hand, it does not seem to me that the labor market is a natural place for rational expectations to be functioning.

It is also important to keep in mind the distinction between the strong and weak versions of rational expectations. By the strong version, I mean either that expectations held by market participants are consistent with the true model of the economy, or that they are consistent with any detailed model of the economy. By the weak version, I mean that obvious hints from events will be picked up by participants. It seems to me that the weak version is much more closely related with reality than the strong version.

Why do you think rational expectationists persist in holding on to the extreme version of rational expectations in places like the labor market?

I think it is primarily because the strong version of rational expectations makes it possible to write down neat, complete theories, and weak versions are sloppy and indeterminate and less easy to deal with. And I also think that the rational expectations school prefers to sacrifice consistency with common observation in order to have a neat theory.

Is the world, to your way of thinking, a lot sloppier than these theories would suggest?

Yes, and I think any rational expectationist would agree that the world is sloppier than theories of this kind would suggest. But I would go further and say the world is sloppy enough that it would lead to outcomes that are quite different from those that a strict rational expectationist would find plausible.

Isn't this a major distinction between Keynesians and monetarists and between Keynesian and new classical economists? Keynesians always did seem to feel intuitively that the world is a lot messier than the others thought.

Well, yes, I think your description is right, and it may be for historical reasons. If you look at Keynes's own writings or his letters of the time, he placed a lot of importance on the fact that investment is a shot in the dark. The state of what he called long-term expectations was hardly probabilistic at all. It was affected by a whole host of things. So there was that historical connection.

Have you considered that economists of different schools might have different psychological inclinations? Some people I meet seem to see the world as pretty much black and white, whereas others see it as so many different shades of gray. I wonder if there is

something from one's childhood that inclines a person to believe that things are shaded or black and white when it comes to the economy.

In thinking about the people one knows—economists and others—the dichotomy you mention is visible. We all know people who can't stand ambiguity, and then there are others that don't mind it at all. And I think you could describe this as part of someone's psychological makeup. But I don't know any reason to suppose that its origins are in childhood. This could be something you learn in the course of your life.

Do you think economists' psychological makeup matters to the macroeconomics debate?

It matters in the sense that the schools people join have something to do with this. But I don't think it matters to the outcome of the debate. I am enough of an optimist to believe that no matter what my psychological reasons for believing something, if it doesn't stand up to logical analysis and fact, then I am going to lose.

What do you think has been the most promising Keynesian research development in the past decade?

I think the most promising theoretical research in macroeconomics is the line that leads to models of the economy that have more than one equilibrium. There are now several examples of this.

The usual background is that if you model the economy as having imperfect competition, then that gets you to the fact that business firms have to form expectations about what demand curves they will face in the future. And in order to do that, they normally have to form some expectations about aggregate demand in the economy. This leads to both high-level and low-level equilibria. In high-level equilibria, business firms think aggregate demand will be pretty good, and so they invest a lot and produce a lot and, consequently, aggregate demand *is* pretty good. On the other hand, if they were all pessimists, they would lay off workers and cut back investment, and they might bring on a type of low-level equilibria. It is that type of theorizing that strikes me as most promising. I hardly know whether to call it Keynesian or not, because he shared it with many others, but it is the most promising line of research for those who believe the economy is not quickly and immediately self-equilibrating.

What do you predict will be a major economic problem the United States will have to face in the mid-1990s, and how should it solve that problem?

I will guess that a main problem will be a continued slow erosion relative (not absolute) to other industrial countries—Germany, Japan, and so on. I don't think we will find this easy to deal with in terms of our own attitudes or in

terms of economic policy. What we ought to do to solve this problem is provide incentives for research and development, for a better workplace, and to save and invest.

What got you interested in economics?

I grew up in the 1930s and it was very hard not to be interested in economics. If you were a high school student in the 1930s, you were conscious of the fact that our economy was in deep trouble and no one knew what to do about it.

How would you describe how economists think?

I won't try to give you a deep answer to that question, but I believe there are two major ways of thinking economists use to approach problems. Let me describe it this way. The first thought many economists have about any question is to ask themselves how it fits into the notion of supply and demand. The first thought other economists have is to ask themselves how it fits into the notion of optimization. They observe something peculiar and ask themselves under what circumstances would it turn out to be the absolutely rational thing to do.

I am a supply-and-demand economist. When I come across something, I ask myself what is being transferred here and where does the supply come from and where does the demand come from.

CHAPTER SUMMARY

The Job Search Process

■ The economic theory of job search maintains that individuals are rational in their job search; they consider both the costs and benefits of searching for a job, and they search until the additional costs and additional benefits of the job search are equal. In practice, this means they search until they receive a wage offer that is equal to their reservation wage.

■ The optimal search time is the time it takes until the wage offer (W) equals the reservation wage (R). If the optimal search time increases, the unemployment rate increases; if the optimal search time decreases, the unemployment rate decreases.

The Phillips Curve

■ A. W. Phillips plotted a curve to a set of data points that exhibited an inverse relationship between wage inflation and unemployment. This curve came to be known as the Phillips curve. From the Phillips curve relationship, economists concluded that neither the combination of low inflation and low unemployment *nor* the combination of high inflation and high unemployment (stagflation) was likely.

■ Economists Samuelson and Solow fit a Phillips curve to the U.S. economy. Instead of measuring wage inflation against unemployment rates (as Phillips did), they measured price inflation against unemployment rates. They found an inverse relationship between inflation and unemployment rates.

■ Based on the findings of Phillips and Samuelson and Solow, economists concluded the following: (1) Stagflation, or high inflation and high unemployment, is extremely unlikely. (2) The Phillips curve presents policy makers with a menu of choices between different combinations of inflation and unemployment rates.

The Natural Rate Hypothesis

■ Milton Friedman pointed out that there are two types of Phillips curves: a short-run Phillips curve and a long-run Phillips curve. The short-run Phillips curve exhibits the inflation–unemployment trade-off; the long-run Phillips curve does not. Consideration of both short-run and long-run Phillips curves opened macroeconomics to expectations theory.

■ The natural rate hypothesis holds that *in the short run,* a decrease (increase) in inflation is linked to an increase (decrease) in unemployment, but that *in the long run,* the economy returns to its natural rate of unemployment. In other words, there is a trade-off between inflation and unemployment in the short run, but not in the long run.

■ Originally, the natural rate hypothesis was expressed in terms of adaptive expectations. Individuals formed their inflation expectations by considering past inflation rates. Later, the natural rate hypothesis came to be expressed in terms of rational expectations, too. Rational expectations theory holds that individuals form their expected inflation rate by considering present and past inflation rates, as well as all other available and relevant information—in particular, the effects of present and future policy actions.

New Classical Theory

■ Implicit in the new classical theory are two assumptions: (1) Individuals form their expectations rationally. (2) Wages and prices are completely flexible.

■ In new classical theory, policy has different effects (1) when it is unanticipated and (2) when it is anticipated. For example, if the public anticipates an increase in aggregate demand, the short-run aggregate supply curve will likely shift leftward at the same time the aggregate demand curve shifts rightward. If the public does not anticipate an increase in aggregate demand (but one occurs), then the short-run aggregate supply curve will not shift leftward at the same time the aggregate

CHAPTER 16
JOB SEARCH THEORY, PHILLIPS
CURVE ANALYSIS, AND NEW
CLASSICAL THEORY: ENTER
EXPECTATIONS
■
377

demand curve shifts rightward; it will shift leftward sometime later. If policy is anticipated, expectations are formed rationally, and wages and prices are completely flexible, then an increase or decrease in aggregate demand will change only the price level but not real GNP or the unemployment rate. The new classical theory casts doubt on the belief that the short-run Phillips curve is always downward sloping. Under certain conditions, it may be vertical (as is the long-run Phillips curve).

■ If policies are anticipated, but not credible, and rational expectations is a reasonable characterization of how individuals form their expectations, then certain policies may have unintended effects. For example, if the public believes that aggregate demand will increase by more than it (actually) increases (because policy makers have not done in the past what they said they would do), then anticipated inflation will be higher than it would have been, the short-run aggregate supply curve will shift leftward by more than it would have, and the (short-run) outcome of a policy that increases aggregate demand will be lower real GNP and higher unemployment (see Exhibit 16–11).

Nonclassical or New Keynesian Ratex Theory

■ Implicit in the nonclassical or New Keynesian ratex theory are two assumptions: (1) Individuals form their expectations rationally. (2) Wages and prices are not completely flexible (in the short run).

■ If policy is anticipated, the economic effects predicted by the new classical theory and nonclassical or New Keynesian theory are not the same (in the short run). Since the nonclassical or New Keynesian ratex theory assumes that wages and prices are not completely flexible in the short run, it follows that given an anticipated change in aggregate demand, the short-run aggregate supply curve cannot immediately shift to its long-run equilibrium position. The nonclassical or New Keynesian ratex theory predicts that there is a short-run trade-off between inflation and unemployment (in the Phillips curve framework) (see Exhibit 16–12).

Key Terms and Concepts

Reservation Wage	Natural Rate Hypothesis	Policy Ineffectiveness Proposition (PIP)
Phillips Curve	Ratex	

QUESTIONS AND PROBLEMS

1. Optimal search time will change if the wage offer curve shifts, the reservation wage curve shifts, or both curves shift. Name three factors that can change each curve. In each case, specify the directional change in the curve and the effect on optimal search time. Give reasons for the factors you choose and the directional changes you specify.

2. What is a major difference between adaptive and rational expectations? Give an example.

3. It has been said that the policy ineffectiveness proposition (connected with new classical theory) does not eliminate policy makers' ability to reduce unemployment through aggregate demand-increasing policies, since they can always increase aggregate demand by more than the public expects. What might be the weak point in this argument?

4. Why does the new classical theory have the word "classical" associated with it? Also, why has it been said that the classical theory failed where the new classical theory succeeds, as the former could not explain the business cycle ("the ups and downs of the economy"), but the latter can?

5. Suppose there were a permanent downward-sloping Phillips curve that offered a menu of choices of different combinations of inflation and unemployment rates to policy makers. How do you think society would go about deciding which point on the Phillips curve it wanted to occupy?

6. Suppose a short-run trade-off between inflation and unemployment currently exists. How would you expect this trade-off to be affected by a change in technology that permits the wider dispersion of economic policy news? Explain your answer.

7. Nonclassical or New Keynesian ratex theory holds that because of such things as long-term labor contracts, wages are not completely flexible. New classical economists often respond that experience teaches labor leaders to develop and bargain for contracts that allow for wage adjustments. Do you think the new classical economists have a good point? Why?

8. What evidence can you point to that suggests individuals form their expectations adaptively? What evidence can you point to that suggests individuals form their expectations rationally?

9. Explain both the short-run and long-run movements of the natural rate hypothesis if expectations are formed adaptively.

10. Explain both the short-run and long-run movements of the natural rate hypothesis if expectations are formed rationally and policy is unanticipated.

11. "Even if some people do not form their expectations rationally, this does not necessarily mean that new classical theory is of no value." Discuss.

12. Illustrate graphically what would happen if (1) individuals form their expectations rationally, (2) prices and wages are flexible, and (3) individuals underestimate the decrease in aggregate demand.

CHAPTER 16
JOB SEARCH THEORY, PHILLIPS
CURVE ANALYSIS, AND NEW
CLASSICAL THEORY: ENTER
EXPECTATIONS
■
379

BUSINESS CYCLES: THEORIES OF ECONOMIC EXPANSION AND CONTRACTION

WHAT THIS CHAPTER IS ABOUT

This chapter is about the business cycle—recurrent swings (up and down) in real GNP, or Q. Essentially, we bring together much of the material that we have discussed in previous chapters, such as Keynesian, monetarist, and new classical theories; different views of the economy; expectations theory; and more.

PRELIMINARIES

In this section, we define some terms and introduce several issues that will shape our discussion of **business cycles.** These can be summarized in four points:

1. There are four stages of the business cycle: expansion, peak, contraction, and trough. These four stages are often summarized by the words "boom and bust." In fact, the business cycle is sometimes called the *boom-and-bust cycle.* The contractionary, or bust, part of the business cycle is formally known as **recession.**

2. To many persons, the word *cycle* connotes both a certain period of time and inevitability. For example, a person might think that business cycles are always five years long and that they naturally occur every ten years. Neither idea is correct. First, business cycles can be long and they can be short. Business cycles have ranged in length from 1 to 12 years. Second, not all economists believe that business cycles are inevitable. Although some (perhaps many) economists argue that business cycles are extremely likely to occur, they are reluctant to state that business cycles will necessarily occur. For these reasons, many economists prefer to speak, more neutrally, of business *fluctuations* rather than business *cycles.*

3. Two important issues are relevant to a discussion of business cycles. One concerns the *cause* of the business cycle. Obviously, if there is a period of boom and bust, we are prompted to ask what caused it. The other concerns the economy's *adjustment path.* For example, if real GNP drops below the natural level, we are interested in knowing (a) whether it will adjust in the direction of the natural level and (b) how long the adjustment period will last.

4. What a person views as the cause of the business cycle, and what information he holds relevant to the economy's adjustment path, will influence the types of policies he proposes as a means of smoothing out the business cycle. For example, if a person believes the business cycle is a consequence of political factors, he will most likely propose particular political reforms to solve the problem. If someone thinks that the business cycle is caused by the inherent instabilities of the private sector, he is likely to propose that government stabilization policies be implemented.

BUSINESS CYCLE ORIGINS: DEMAND SIDE OR SUPPLY SIDE

Within the *AD–AS* framework of analysis, picture the economy at its long-run equilibrium position. This is where the three curves—*AD, SRAS,* and *LRAS*—intersect at the natural real GNP level. Within this framework, think of (1) what has to change to bring about a contraction in real GNP, and (2) what has to change to bring about an expansion in real GNP.

A Contraction in Real GNP (the Bust of the Business Cycle). A contraction in real GNP can be brought about by a change on the demand side of the economy or by a change on the supply side of the economy. On the demand side, a contraction in real GNP can be brought about by a decline in aggregate demand (Exhibit 17–1a). On the supply side, a contraction in real GNP can be brought about by a reduction in short-run aggregate supply (c) or a reduction in long-run aggregate supply (e).

An Expansion in Real GNP (the Boom of the Business Cycle). An expansion in real GNP can be brought about by a change on the demand side of the economy

Business Cycle
Recurrent swings (up and down) in real GNP.

Recession
A decline in real GNP that lasts for two consecutive quarters (six months) or more.

EXHIBIT 17–1

Business Contractions and Expansions

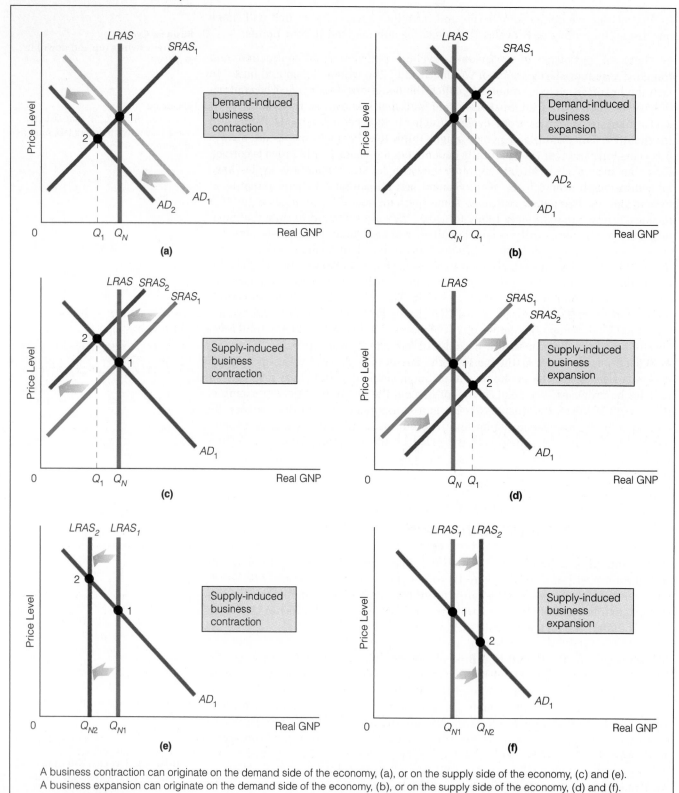

A business contraction can originate on the demand side of the economy, (a), or on the supply side of the economy, (c) and (e).
A business expansion can originate on the demand side of the economy, (b), or on the supply side of the economy, (d) and (f).

382

or by a change on the supply side of the economy. On the demand side, an expansion in real GNP can be brought about by an increase in aggregate demand (Exhibit 17–1b). On the supply side, an expansion in real GNP can be brought about by an increase in short-run aggregate supply (d) or an increase in long-run aggregate supply (f).

Keep Exhibit 17–1 in mind as we discuss the different business cycle theories in this chapter. Obviously, every business cycle contraction has to fit into panels (a), (c), or (e) in Exhibit 17–1, and every business cycle expansion has to fit into panels (b), (d), or (f). An entire business cycle—incorporating both the contraction and the expansion—must fit into any *two* panels in Exhibit 17–1, one chosen from the left side of the exhibit (the contraction) and the other chosen from the right side of the exhibit (the expansion). For example, a given business cycle may be explained using (a) to describe the contraction and (b) to describe the expansion. If so, this business cycle would have been totally demand induced—since both the contraction and the expansion originate on the demand side of the economy.

THREE DEMAND-INDUCED BUSINESS CYCLE THEORIES

■

Here we discuss three demand-induced business cycle theories: (1) the Friedman natural rate theory, (2) the new classical theory under the conditions of unanticipated and incorrectly anticipated policy, and (3) the Keynesian theory (old and new). We summarize these three theories, which have been discussed more fully in earlier chapters.

The Friedman Natural Rate Theory

In the Friedman natural rate theory, the business cycle occurs because there is a difference between individuals' expected inflation rate and the actual inflation rate. To put it differently, the business cycle is a consequence of imperfect information. Obviously, if there were perfect information, there would be no difference in the expected and actual inflation rates; people would know exactly what to expect.

A business cycle expansion in the Friedman natural rate theory is illustrated in Exhibit 17–2. Starting at point 1, the aggregate demand curve shifts rightward from AD_1 to AD_2. At first, the expected inflation rate does not increase even though the actual inflation rate is increasing. Why? Because in this theory, expectations are formed adaptively. In practical terms, workers are accepting jobs at lower real wages than they think they are accepting. The economy moves from point 1 to point 2, from Q_1 to Q_2—largely because workers are being "fooled" into accepting the lower real wages (this has prompted some economists to refer to the theory as the Friedman "fooling" theory). Later, workers learn that the inflation rate has increased, and they revise their expected inflation rate upward. The (short-run) aggregate supply curve shifts leftward and the economy moves to point 3.

Question:

If an increase in aggregate demand can cause the business cycle expansion, can a decrease in aggregate demand cause the business cycle contraction? If so, then what causes these increases and decreases in aggregate demand, and therefore the business cycle, in the Friedman natural rate theory?

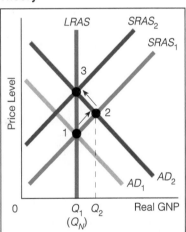

In the Friedman natural rate theory, the business cycle occurs because there is a difference between individuals' expected inflation rate and the actual inflation rate. Starting at point 1, the aggregate demand curve shifts rightward from AD_1 to AD_2. At first, the expected inflation rate does not rise to the new (higher) inflation rate. As a result, the economy moves from point 1 to point 2, from Q_1 to Q_2. Later, the expected inflation rate is revised upward and the economy moves to point 3.

Answer:

First, it is correct that an increase in aggregate demand can cause the business cycle expansion and that a decrease in aggregate demand can cause the business cycle contraction. As to what can cause these changes in aggregate demand in the Friedman natural rate theory, the answer involves the *causes* of the business cycle, which we discuss in an upcoming section. But since Friedman is a monetarist, an educated guess would be that changes in the money supply change aggregate demand.

The New Classical Theory (under the Conditions of Unanticipated Policy and Incorrectly Anticipated Policy)

When policy is unanticipated, the new classical theory generates the same results, and offers the same explanations, as the Friedman natural rate theory. In the short run, there is a change in real GNP, but in the long run, the economy returns to its natural real GNP level when the actual expected inflation rate is the same as the expected inflation rate.

In the case of incorrectly anticipated policy, the new classical theory generates a business cycle in the following way. Starting at point 1 in Exhibit 17–3, the

EXHIBIT 17–3
A Business Cycle Contraction in the New Classical Theory

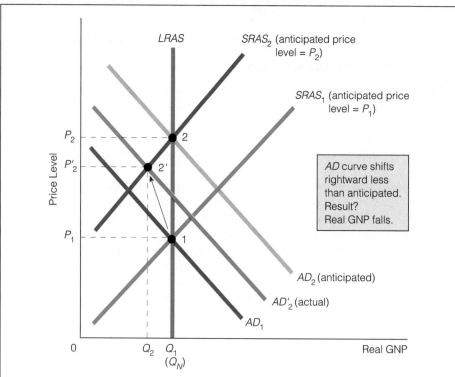

Starting at point 1, the public anticipates an increase in aggregate demand from AD_1 to AD_2. Based on this, the short-run aggregate supply curve shifts leftward from $SRAS_1$ to $SRAS_2$. It turns out, however, that the aggregate demand curve only shifts rightward to AD'_2 (less than anticipated). As a result, the economy moves to point 2', to a lower real GNP and a higher unemployment rate.

public anticipates an increase in aggregate demand from AD_1 to AD_2. Based on this, the short-run aggregate supply curve shifts leftward from $SRAS_1$ to $SRAS_2$, which is consistent with the expected long-run equilibrium price level of P_2. Later, it turns out that the aggregate demand curve only shifts rightward from AD_1 to AD'_2, which is less than the public anticipated (the public anticipated incorrectly). As a result, the economy moves to point 2', to a lower real GNP level.

The Keynesian Theory: Old and New

In Exhibit 17–4, the economy is initially at point 1. The aggregate demand curve shifts leftward from AD_1 to AD_2. As a result, the economy moves from Q_1 to Q_2, from point 1 to point 2. At point 2, the Keynesian theory holds, the economy may get *stuck*. This is based on the key assumption of inflexible wage rates in the downward direction. Earlier (old) versions of Keynesian theory were criticized for arbitrarily assuming that wage rates were inflexible downward or not thoroughly explaining why wage rates were inflexible. Some of the later (new) versions of Keynesian theory made up for this deficiency by focusing on, among other things, long-term contracts and efficiency reasons for firms paying higher than market wages.

The argument (see Chapter 9) is as follows. Long-term labor contracts are often advantageous to both employers and workers. The benefits firms may perceive from long-term contracts include fewer labor negotiations and the decreased likelihood of worker strikes. The benefits workers may perceive from long-term contracts include fewer strikes and an added sense of security.

So, in many instances, the benefits of long-term contracts outweigh the costs, and firms and workers enter into long-term contracts for mutually advantageous

EXHIBIT 17–4
A Business Cycle Contraction in the Keynesian Theory

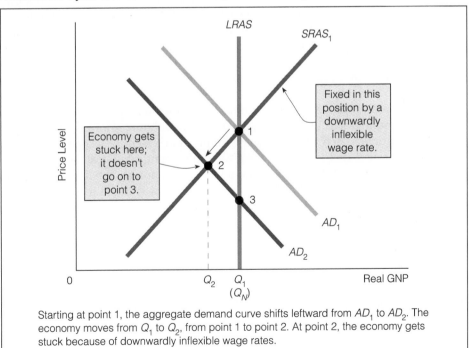

Starting at point 1, the aggregate demand curve shifts leftward from AD_1 to AD_2. The economy moves from Q_1 to Q_2, from point 1 to point 2. At point 2, the economy gets stuck because of downwardly inflexible wage rates.

reasons. When they do, (nominal) wage rates are locked in for the period of the contract, and therefore cannot adjust downward to market-clearing levels with a fall in aggregate demand. The result is that the economy may get stuck at point 2 in Exhibit 17–4 for a long time, and there may be high levels of unemployment lasting for many years. The theory, according to Keynesians, explains the long-run levels of unemployment characteristic of some business cycles.

Similarly, economists who work with efficiency wage models also believe that there are (other) solid microeconomic reasons for inflexible wages. Economist George Akerlof argues that firms sometimes find it in their best interest to pay wage rates above market-clearing levels. According to the *efficiency wage models,* labor productivity depends on the wage rate the firm pays employees. A cut in wages can cause labor productivity to decline, which, in turn, raises the firm's costs. By paying a wage higher than the market level, firms provide an incentive to workers to be productive and to minimize **shirking,** among other things. If shirking declines, so do the monitoring (management) costs of the firm.

Many Keynesian economists today believe that although the long-term contract and efficiency wage theories are fairly new, they have already provided a solid microeconomic explanation for inflexible wages and thus the characteristics of continuing unemployment problems in some economies.

Efficiency Wage Models
These models hold that it is sometimes in the best interest of firms to pay their employees higher than equilibrium wage rates.

Shirking
Behavior descriptive of a person who is putting forth less than the agreed-to effort when doing a job.

Question:

Assuming that every theory has its critics, how have economists criticized the Friedman natural rate theory, the new classical theory (under the conditions of unanticipated and incorrectly anticipated policy), and the Keynesian theory?

Answer:

The Friedman natural rate theory is criticized on the ground that it assumes workers will continually be fooled into accepting lower real wages than they think they are accepting. New classical economists charge that the Friedman natural rate theory does not allow for expectations to be formed rationally. They argue that if workers often see aggregate demand increase, and later notice the price level rise, they will soon connect the two events and begin to anticipate the latter when the former occurs. In short, new classical economists say it is not rational for workers to continue to be fooled.

The new classical theory is criticized for being unable to explain *long-term* high levels of unemployment in the presence of easily available information on prices and a key variable such as the money supply. For example, economist George Akerlof has argued that to say the high unemployment rate Great Britain experienced during the 10-year period in the late 1970s and early 1980s "is due to an unanticipated shock is simply unreasonable. Ten years is much too long a period of time for something to be unanticipated."[1]

Earlier versions of the Keynesian theory were criticized for arbitrarily assuming downwardly inflexible wage rates. This criticism cannot be made of later versions, since these versions try to explain why wages are inflexible. Still, the new Keynesian theory is criticized for its heavy emphasis on long-term contracts as the basis of the business cycle; it does not explain business cycles before the rise of labor unions and long-term contracts in the 1930s and 1940s and in the nonunion sector of today's economy.

[1]Telephone conversation with author, July 12, 1988.

Wages, Prices, and Business Cycles

In the Friedman natural rate theory and in the new classical theory, wages and prices are implicitly assumed to be flexible—the economy does not get stuck in a recessionary gap, and it always returns to the natural real GNP level. In the Keynesian theory, wages and prices are assumed to be inflexible.

Why not settle at least part of the debate among the three demand-induced theories of the business cycle by finding out whether wages and prices are flexible or not? There is a problem. To illustrate, clearly, some wages and prices are not instantly flexible: They do not rise immediately after an increase in demand, and they do not fall immediately after a decrease in demand. First, a decrease in aggregate demand is not instantly noticed by firms in the economy. Second, there may be some solid economic reasons why firms would want to keep prices constant over some period of time.

Consider a restaurant owner who has just finished printing new menus and posting new prices. If demand rises the week after the new menu is on the tables, it is unlikely the restaurant owner will immediately throw the new menus out and put newer ones in their place. There is a certain cost to having new menus printed. Also, the restaurant owner might reason that her customers will get angry at seeing new, higher prices posted in just one week's time. So, there is little doubt that some prices are somewhat inflexible in the real world. (The prices of financial securities are not; they can change by the minute.)

The real questions economists want answers to are (1) how many prices are inflexible, (2) how long are they inflexible, and (3) even if there are inflexible prices in the economy, is there any loss in predictive power from assuming that the economy works *as if* all prices are flexible.

Once again, we see theory at odds with reality. For example, new classical theory, which assumes flexible wages and prices, is at odds with a world in which some wages and prices are inflexible. But the real question we have to continue to ask is, Does it matter? Does the real world perform *as if* the simplified and abstract theory accurately describes its workings?

Our discussion here should not be read as an endorsement of any one business cycle theory. We simply want to bring out a key consideration in the theories—that is, the degree of flexibility in wages and prices, which in turn reflects on the inherent stability properties of an economy—and to once again remind us that a theory, however abstract, may still capture the essence of the way an economy works.

Forecasting Business Cycles

Think of yourself when you have the flu. There are usually three periods in the illness: (1) when you are coming down with the flu; (2) when you have the flu; and (3) when you are getting over the flu (but do not yet feel your old self). In each period, there is an indicator of what is happening.

In the first period, when you are coming down with the flu, you feel a little sluggish and tired. We might call this a *leading indicator* of the flu, in that it precedes the flu; it lets you know what's coming. In the period when you have the flu, you feel achy and you might have a slight fever. We shall call this a *coincident indicator* of the flu, in that it coincides with having the flu. Finally, in the period when you are getting over the flu, your temperature returns to normal and you are slightly more alert but you don't have all your energy back. We shall call this a *lagging indicator* of the flu. Thus, we have established a few indicators of your health and sickness.

Similarly, economists have devised a few indicators of the health and sickness of the economy. These indicators—called *leading, coincident,* and *lagging* indicators—are purported to do what their names suggest: *lead* economic upturns or downturns, *coincide* with economic upturns or downturns, and *lag* economic upturns or downturns. We would expect a leading indicator to rise before a boom and fall before a bust; we would expect a coincident indicator to reach its high (low) point coincident with a boom (bust); and finally, we would expect a lagging indicator to reach its high (low) point sometime after a boom (bust). The leading economic indicators are of particular interest to economists and business managers, since individuals often want to know what's coming.

An often-cited statistic is the *index of leading economic indicators*—composed of such factors as new orders for consumer goods, contracts for orders and new plant and equipment, and so on. No matter what it does—go up, go down, or stay the same—it is announced in the news media much the same way as the Dow Jones Industrial Average (DJIA) of stock prices. A decrease in the index portends a rocky economic road ahead; an increase, smoother sailing and generally good times.

How reliable is the index when it comes to predicting economic upturns and downturns? It is fairly reliable, but far from perfect. Many times it has dropped a few months before an economic downturn (pretty good), a few times it has dropped a whole year before an economic downturn (not so good), and a few times it has dropped and no economic downturn has materialized (bad). Despite the mixed bag of results, the index is still widely used.

Question:

Would it be correct to conclude from economists' less-than-perfect record of predicting and forecasting major economic movements that economics is not a science?

Answer:

We need to make two points. First, it would be incorrect to conclude from economists' prediction record that economics is not a science. Is physics, chemistry, or biology any less a science because the record of physicists, chemists, or biologists is not perfect when it comes to prediction?

Second, prediction and forecasting is not the be-all and end-all of a science. Sometimes, what we learn by scientifically approaching economic problems or issues is that we cannot predict perfectly.

In other words, there is a difference between approaching the study of the world in a scientific manner and being able to predict perfectly. *Sometimes, no matter how scientific one is, perfect prediction still remains beyond one's reach.*

CAUSES OF THE BUSINESS CYCLE

In the three theories discussed previously, a business cycle contraction or expansion is caused by a shift leftward or rightward, respectively, in the aggregate demand curve. But this leaves unanswered the question, What causes the aggregate demand curve to shift? In this section, we present a few of the answers economists have given to this question.

Money Supply Changes: Accelerators and Brakes

Many of the economists who endorse the Friedman natural rate theory are monetarists. We might guess from this that they would focus on the money supply when explaining the business cycle.

Monetarist empirical work on business cycles illustrates that, typically, money supply growth drops before economic contractions and rises before economic expansions. For most monetarists, severe contractions are caused by a large drop in either the absolute money supply or money supply growth rates. In everyday language, they say the Fed "slammed the monetary brakes on too hard."

On the other hand, major economic upturns or booms are caused by a large rise in the absolute money supply or money supply growth rates. In everyday terms, monetarists say the Fed "put the monetary accelerator to the floor." It is the movement from "hard on the monetary accelerator" to "hard on the monetary brakes" that most monetarists see as the direct cause of business cycles.

Question:

What is the monetarist solution to the business cycle?

Answer:

Monetarists are nonactivists when it comes to discretionary monetary policy (see Chapter 15). They advocate a monetary rule. In short, they argue that the money supply should grow by a fixed annual rate that is consistent with the average annual growth rate in real GNP and (in some versions of the monetary rule) adjusted for changes in velocity.

Business Investment, Residential Construction, and Government Spending

Many Keynesians often point to changes in business investment, residential construction, or government spending as the cause of the business cycle. For example, a business cycle contraction might result from a decrease in business investment or government spending that lowers aggregate demand and imposes a net loss of sales on business firms. The major consequence of a fall in aggregate demand will come in the form of reduced output and increased unemployment. A decline in output is translated into a fall in income, and since consumption is a function of income, consumption will fall, which leads to an even lower level of aggregate demand. The original decrease in business investment or government spending snowballs into lower levels of consumption that generate a multiple (remember the multiplier from Chapter 9) decrease in total output.

The Political Business Cycle

Some economists theorize that the underlying motivation of the business cycle is political. The theory of the "political business cycle" has different hypotheses, each of which focuses on different political factors.

One hypothesis is that the political business cycle is largely prompted at the congressional level, where elected representatives are motivated to enact economic expansionary fiscal measures, such as tax cuts or spending hikes, shortly before they go up for reelection. Another is that the Fed is a political–monetary institution that responds to political pressures exerted on it, as well as to bureaucratic and self-preserving proclivities internal to itself, and this goes a long way to explain the ups and downs of the economy. A third hypothesis is that the business cycle is largely prompted by presidential action. To illustrate, we sketch a possible scenario in terms of the Phillips curve framework developed in the last chapter.

The Phillips Curve as Political Toy. Some economists have argued that if there is a short-run trade-off between inflation and unemployment, it can be exploited for political gain. Of course, saying that a short-run inflation–unemployment trade-off *can be* exploited for political gain does not mean it *will be* exploited. We say more about this later. For now, consider Exhibit 17–5.

Suppose Edward Sumner is elected president of the United States in the year 2000. A few months after the election, the economy is at point 1 experiencing a (relatively) high inflation rate. No one blames President Sumner for the high inflation rate since he only recently took office. However, the president wants to get the inflation rate down because he is already thinking about his reelection. He proposes higher taxes and a cut in government spending (contractionary fiscal policy). His economic advisers tell him this will reduce aggregate demand and lower the inflation rate. The great majority of his proposals are accepted by the Congress since he is still in the "honeymoon" period (almost all presidents enjoy a "honeymoon" at the beginning of their terms when Congress passes their programs without much opposition). In addition, President Sumner starts putting both

EXHIBIT 17–5
Can Politicians Use the Inflation–Unemployment Trade-Off to Get Votes?

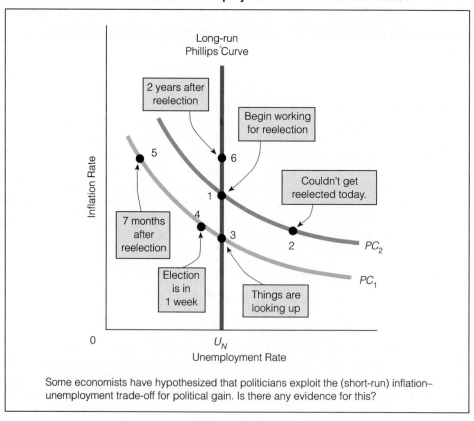

Some economists have hypothesized that politicians exploit the (short-run) inflation–unemployment trade-off for political gain. Is there any evidence for this?

public and private pressure on the Fed to reduce the money supply. To a large degree, the Fed complies.

As a result of these policies to reduce aggregate demand, the economy moves to point 2. The inflation rate falls, but at the (short-run) price of a huge increase in the unemployment rate. Newspaper editors all over the country begin saying that President Sumner's economic policies put people out of work. The public opinion polls show that President Sumner couldn't win reelection today if his life depended on it. For the most part, the president stays in the White House and says very little. He isn't too worried because the election is still a long time off, and his economic advisers assure him that things will soon be getting better. Sure enough, the economy begins to move toward its natural rate of unemployment as people revise their inflation expectations downward; that is, eventually, the economy moves to point 3. Inflation has been lowered considerably (relative to what it was at point 1), and in recent months the unemployment rate has fallen. President Sumner's standing rises in the polls. The same newspaper editors who were criticizing the president a few months ago are now praising him. The president and his advisers remind themselves that the public has a short memory.

Time passes, and it looks as if President Sumner will have to run against an extremely popular candidate from the other political party. The president decides to use the economy to help his reelection efforts. Starting at point 3, he proposes a cut in taxes (politically popular) and an increase in government spending (politically popular with groups receiving government benefits); he also urges the Fed to increase the money supply. The Congress doesn't cut taxes, but it does increase government spending, and the Fed does increase the money supply. As election day approaches, the economy moves toward point 4. One week before the election, unemployment is lower than it was at point 3, the inflation rate is slightly higher (but still not so much higher as to cause too much concern), and the economy appears to be strong and growing. President Sumner's campaign stresses that he has brought down both inflation and unemployment from the levels they were at when he took office (compare points 1 and 4). He moves up in the polls. On election day, President Sumner carries 42 of the 50 states and receives 61 percent of the popular vote.

The expansionary economic policies are still bubbling through the economy after the reelection; after seven months, the economy is at point 5. Two years after the reelection, the economy is at point 6—with a higher inflation rate and the same unemployment rate as when President Sumner first moved into the White House.

Is there a *political business cycle?* Might the ups and downs in the economy be largely the consequence of politicians trying to arrange the inflation and unemployment rates in a politically popular configuration before election day?[2] There are a number of points to consider. First, even if a president, or other elected representatives, wanted to exploit the short-run Phillips curve trade-off, there is no guarantee that it could be done. The economy can be pushed and shoved in different directions, but it doesn't always move exactly where elected representatives want it to move. In our story of President Sumner, the economy might have been at point 5 (with high inflation) instead of at point 4 (with low inflation) one week before the election if the *lags* in the economy had been shorter. What would that have done to the president's reelection prospects?

[2]On January 14, 1990, President Bush appointed two new members of the Board of Governors of the Federal Reserve System. Both members were said to be in favor of lower interest rates (brought about through expansionary monetary policy). Some speculated that Bush appointed these two members because of their views on lowering interest rates: With an impending economic recession and Bush facing reelection at the end of 1991, an expansionary monetary policy was the political medicine that Bush needed to increase the probability of a successful presidential campaign.

Second, there is no guarantee that the Congress and the Fed will do what the president wants them to do.

Third, although we have seen instances of presidents pushing for expansionary economic policies shortly before an election (a notable example is Richard Nixon in 1971–72),[3] there are also instances where presidents have not—even when high levels of unemployment existed and, one would think, their political careers were on the line.

Finally, new classical economists argue that under certain conditions there is no short-run trade-off between inflation and unemployment to exploit. Politicians can't exploit a trade-off between inflation and unemployment that largely doesn't exist.

Question:

Many people believe that government is trying its best to smooth out the business cycle and to achieve stable prices and low unemployment. This is, after all, what our elected representatives say they are trying to do. However, the economists who believe in the political business cycle theory imply that elected representatives are not trying to do what they say they are trying to do. The implication is that the economy is largely a toy to be pulled this way and that for political purposes. This is a serious charge. Is the economics profession agreed that this is happening?

Answer:

No, the economics profession is not agreed on this, although there are economists who believe the business cycle is largely politically induced. The research in this area continues.

We can say that whereas the political business cycle theory, like any other business cycle theory, may not explain all business cycles, it may explain some. For example, some presidents may be more likely than others to try to use the economy for political ends and thus prompt a politically induced business cycle.

A SUPPLY-INDUCED BUSINESS CYCLE THEORY

■

Business cycles may originate on the supply side as well as the demand side of the economy. One particular supply-induced business cycle theory that has generated research and controversy in recent years is the **real business cycle theory.**

The Real Business Cycle

Real Business Cycle Theory
The theory that business cycle contractions are generally brought about by aggregate supply changes that reduce the economy's capacity to produce.

Real business cycle theorists argue that a business cycle contraction can be brought about by a major supply-side change that reduces the capacity of the economy to produce. The illustration of one variant of the real business cycle in Exhibit 17–6 helps explain the argument that business cycles that *appear* to originate in aggregate demand changes may, in fact, be prompted by aggregate supply changes.

We start with an adverse supply shock that reduces the capacity of the economy to produce. (We give an example in the next section.) This is represented by a shift inward in the production possibilities frontier of the economy, or a leftward

---

[3]Richard Nixon was quite aware that the state of the economy can affect a candidate's bid for the presidency. In his memoirs, Nixon blamed his loss to John Kennedy in 1960 on the fact that President Eisenhower didn't push to reduce unemployment at the end of his term (when Nixon was his vice president).

EXHIBIT 17–6
Real Business Cycle Theory

We start with a supply side change capable of reducing the capacity of the economy to produce. This is manifested by a leftward shift of the long-run aggregate supply curve from $LRAS_1$ to $LRAS_2$, and a fall in the natural real GNP level from Q_{N1} to Q_{N2}. A reduction in the productive capacity of the economy filters to the demand side of the economy and, in our example, reduces consumption, investment, and the money supply. The aggregate demand curve shifts leftward from AD_1 to AD_2.

Real business cycle: $LRAS$ curve shifts before AD curve

shift in the long-run aggregate supply curve from $LRAS_1$ to $LRAS_2$, which moves the economy from point 1 to 2. As we showed in Chapter 16, a leftward shift in the long-run aggregate supply curve means that the natural real GNP level has fallen.

As a result of the leftward shift in the $LRAS$ curve, real GNP declines, which in this example is coincident with firms reducing their demand for labor and scaling back employment. Due to the lower demand for labor (which puts downward pressure on money wages) and the higher price level, real wages fall.

As real wages fall, workers choose to work less, and unemployed persons choose to extend the length of their job search. Due to less work and lower real wages, workers have less income. Lower incomes soon lead workers to reduce consumption.

Because consumption has fallen, or because businesses have become pessimistic (prompted by the decline in the productive potential of the economy), or both, businesses have less reason to invest. As a result, firms borrow less from banks, the volume of outstanding loans falls, and therefore the money supply falls. A decrease in the money supply causes the aggregate demand curve to shift leftward, from AD_1 to AD_2 in Exhibit 17–6, and the economy moves to point 3.

Real business cycle theorists sometimes point out how easy it is to confuse a demand-induced business cycle with a supply-induced business cycle. In our example, both the aggregate supply *and* the aggregate demand side of the economy change, although the aggregate supply side changes first. However, if the change in aggregate supply is overlooked, and only the changes in aggregate demand are observed (or, specifically, a change in one of the variables that can change aggregate demand, such as the money supply), then the business cycle will appear to be demand induced. In terms of Exhibit 17–6, the leftward shift in the $LRAS$ curve would be overlooked, but the leftward shift in the AD curve would be observed, giving the impression that the contraction is demand induced.

If real business cycle theorists are correct, the cause–effect analysis of the business cycle would be turned upside down. To take but one example, monetary changes may be a *result* of the business cycle, not its *cause*.

Question:

Why can't it be argued that the fall in the money supply caused the business cycle contraction illustrated in Exhibit 17–6? After all, didn't the fall in the money supply cause the aggregate demand curve to shift leftward?

Answer:

For the fall in the money supply to have caused the business cycle, it must have caused real GNP to decline. In Exhibit 17–6, this is not the case. In the exhibit, the business cycle contraction—evidenced by the fall in real GNP from Q_{N1} to Q_{N2}—is the result of a shift leftward in the long-run aggregate supply curve from $LRAS_1$ to $LRAS_2$. In short, because of this change in the $LRAS$ curve, the economy moved from point 1 to 2. Afterward, the aggregate demand curve shifted leftward from AD_1 to AD_2, but this shift did not decrease real GNP (it had already decreased). Instead, the shift in the AD curve only lowered the price level. This is why real business cycle theorists say that the money supply change is a *result* of the business cycle. In their view, the money supply responds to the real (supply-side) forces at work in the economy.

The Middle East, the *LRAS* Curve, College Graduates, and You

On August 2, 1990, Saddam Hussein's Iraqi forces moved into Kuwait and, some say, threatened the free flow of oil to the western world. Some western authorities argued that if Hussein, a despot, got hold of Kuwait's oil, he would then turn his attention to Saudi Arabia's oil fields. If Hussein were successful in his move against Saudi Arabia, he would control a sizable percentage of the world's oil and be able to raise the price of it by reducing its supply on the world market. Perhaps for this reason, among others, the United Nations ordered Hussein to withdraw his troops from Kuwait. President Bush did the same. January 15, 1990, at midnight, was set as the deadline date. The message to Hussein was, Get out of Kuwait or else!

Let's put the politics and national defense issues aside for a minute, and consider the economics of the situation. If western authorities were right about Hussein's intent, what effect would this have on the U.S. economy if Hussein's intent were realized? Business cycle theory gives us the answer.

Reducing the world's supply of oil is an adverse supply shock. With less oil, an important resource in the production process, the productive capability of the U.S. economy would decline (perhaps because the high price of oil would make it too costly to use certain types of machinery). The *LRAS* curve in the United States would shift leftward, as in Exhibit 17–6. Consequently, real GNP would fall and the unemployment rate would rise—the U.S. economy would have contracted.

What might this mean to current college graduates? With an economic recession underway, their chances of locating suitable employment would be diminished. In short, a despot, thousands of miles away, could affect their standard of living. The lesson? Political intrigue, military adventures, and ambitious designs for territorial and economic expansion on the opposite side of the globe can flow through economic channels—to you.

Interview: Charles Plosser

Charles Plosser is one of the major developers, and proponents, of real business cycle theory. Plosser is currently at the University of Rochester.

What is the essence of the real business cycle theory?

Modern real business cycle theory is comprised of two key elements. First, the models are equilibrium models. Second, and perhaps more distinctive, is that the models stress the importance of real rather than nominal shocks to the economic system as the primary source of impulses to the business cycle.

Would you give a few examples of how a real business cycle could get started? Is there evidence that real business cycles exist?

A real business cycle can be initiated in any number of ways. The formal models sometimes talk in terms of productivity or technological shocks which could include natural disasters. More generally, we can think of any sort of real disturbance or collection of disturbances that set off a business cycle. Some of these may be natural or unavoidable, others may be the result of specific policies. For example, the Arab oil embargo and associated rapid rise in oil prices in the mid-70s is an excellent example. More recently, the Gulf War and the resulting fall in consumer confidence combined with a brief spurt in oil prices could also be called an impulse to a real business cycle. Policy shocks can also be important. For example, a large temporary increase in income taxes and the elimination of the

investment tax credit in 1968 could be important real impulses to the mild recession of 1969–70.

What are the policy implications of real business cycle theory?

A key feature of most real business cycle models is that they are equilibrium models and do not stress the role of market failures or externalities in generating or propagating the business cycle. As a result, the role for stabilization policy is nil. Nevertheless, changes in policy (e.g. tax and regulatory policy) can be a source of real disturbances and therefore contribute to the variability of the economy.

What do you predict will be a major economic problem the United States will have to face in the mid-1990s and how should it solve that problem?

That's a tough question and I'm not sure I have a comparative advantage in answering it. Nevertheless, I will speculate that world trade will continue to be

a major economic issue through the 1990s. In some ways, this is surprising because most economists agree that free trade is superior to managed trade or protectionist policies. Yet, most public discussions perpetuate the idea that trade is a zero sum game. Economists must continue to explain why this is a false premise that runs counter to the very essence of what makes market economies so successful.

What do you think has been the most promising research development in economics in the past decade?

In the area of macroeconomics, I think that research on real business cycles has been a very important development. It has stimulated useful discussion both pro and con and challenged the conventional wisdom. As a result, it has changed the terms of debate and dramatically influenced the way economists think about economic fluctuations.

What got you interested in economics?

I was an engineer as an undergraduate with little knowledge of economics. I went to the University of Chicago Graduate School of Business to get an MBA and there became fascinated with economics. I was impressed with the seriousness with which economics was viewed as a way of organizing one's thoughts about the world to address interesting questions and problems. After working for a couple of years, I returned to the university to get my Ph.D.

Supply-and-demand theorizing is a major part of the way economists think—both on the micro- and macroeconomic level. Economists are quick to take events like the Iraqi invasion of Kuwait and see if and how they fit into a supply and demand framework.

THINKING LIKE AN ECONOMIST

The Friedman Natural Rate Theory, the New Classical Theory under Specific Conditions, and the Keynesian Theory

■ In the Friedman natural rate theory, the business cycle is a consequence of the difference between individuals' expected inflation rate and the actual inflation rate. To put it differently, the business cycle is a consequence of imperfect information. Sometimes, the Friedman natural rate theory is called the "fooling" theory, because it views the business cycle expansion (contraction) as the result of workers being fooled into thinking their real wages are higher (lower) than, in fact, they are.

■ The new classical theory explains the business cycle under conditions of unanticipated policy (in the same way the Friedman natural rate theory does) and incorrectly anticipated policy.

■ In the Keynesian theory, a decrease in aggregate demand can bring on a business cycle contraction. In both the earlier (old) and later (new) versions of the theory, wage rates are assumed to be downwardly inflexible. Critics charge that this assumption was arbitrarily made in the earlier version. In later versions, inflexible wage rates are said to be a consequence of voluntary long-term contracts and efficiency considerations.

Causes of the Business Cycle

■ Many causes of the business cycle have been suggested. Changes in aggregate demand can generate the business cycle, but this raises another question: What causes aggregate demand to change? Many monetarists hold that sharp changes in the money supply lead to sharp changes in aggregate demand and to the business cycle. Keynesians tend to stress changes in factors such as business investment, residential construction, and government spending. Some economists hold that the business cycle is largely the consequence of political factors, usually those directed at reelection. Real business cycle theorists generally emphasize aggregate supply changes as the cause of business cycles.

Real Business Cycle Theory

■ Real business cycles originate on the supply side of the economy. A real business contraction might follow this pattern: (1) An adverse supply shock reduces the economy's ability to produce. (2) The *LRAS* curve shifts leftward. (3) As a result, real GNP declines and the price level rises. (4) The number of persons employed falls, as do real wages, owing to a decrease in the demand for labor, which lowers money wages, and a higher price level. (5) Incomes decline. (6) Consumption and investment decline. (7) The volume of outstanding loans declines. (8) The money supply falls. (9) The *AD* curve shifts leftward.

Key Terms and Concepts

Business Cycle	Efficiency Wage Model	Real Business Cycle Theory
Recession		

1. Each of the following pertains to a theory or cause of the business cycle discussed in this chapter. Identify the cause or theory: (a) slamming on the monetary brakes too hard; (b) a change in real GNP when policy is incorrectly anticipated; (c) votes; (d) changes in natural real GNP; (e) investment spending sharply declines; (f) adverse supply shock; (g) individuals' expected inflation rate does not equal the actual inflation rate.

2. Which theory of the business cycle might justifiably be called a disequilibrium theory? Why?

3. How might the explanations of the business cycle of a monetarist and a real business cycle theorist differ?

4. How does the issue of wages and prices figure into business cycle theories?

5. Explain why wage rates may be inflexible.

6. Is the political business cycle theory a demand-induced or supply-induced theory? Explain your answer.

7. What is the difference in both the short run and the long run between the Friedman natural rate theory and the new classical theory under the condition of unanticipated policy?

8. Since some wages and prices in the economy are inflexible, the Keynesian theory, which assumes inflexible wages and prices, must be correct. Discuss.

9. When might adaptive expectations and rational expectations yield the same results?

10. Since it seems unreasonable to assume that workers are consistently fooled, the Friedman natural rate theory must be incorrect. Discuss.

CHAPTER

18

BUDGET DEFICITS AND THE NATIONAL DEBT

WHAT THIS CHAPTER IS ABOUT

Both the federal budget deficit and the national debt have received much public attention in the past decade, and it is likely this will continue in the immediate years to come. We discuss both the deficit and the debt in this chapter.

DEFICITS AND DEBT

A **budget deficit** occurs when government expenditures outstrip tax receipts during any single year; the **national debt,** which is sometimes called the federal or public debt, is the total sum of what the federal government owes its creditors. The debt at a given time is the sum of all past budget deficits minus repayments. The debt is a **stock** variable, the deficit is a **flow** variable. Think of the debt as the water in a bathtub, and the deficit as the water that flows out of the faucet into the tub. The more water that flows out of the faucet (the larger the deficits), the more water in the tub (the larger the debt). Exhibit 18–1 shows the deficit, deficit/GNP ratio, the debt, and debt/GNP ratio for the period 1980–90.

Who Bears the Burden of the Debt?

Who bears the burden of the debt? Or, to put it differently, who bears the burden of public spending financed by borrowing from the public? There are two main schools of thought here. One argues that the current generation bears the burden of the debt. The other argues that the future generation bears the burden of the debt.

One Answer: The Current Generation Bears the Burden of the Debt

According to this view, public borrowing only imposes a burden on the current generation. To illustrate, suppose government increases its spending on national defense, and finances the spending by borrowing the funds. Because more resources are devoted to building planes, ships, and tanks, fewer resources are available to produce television sets, radios, and cars. Some economists argue that the current generation must give up private goods (television sets and the like) to pay for the increased national defense.

But what happens when the bonds issued in the current year come due, say, 30 years later? Don't future taxpayers have to pay them off? The economist Abba Lerner answered yes, but added that as long as the debt is domestically held (only

Budget Deficit
Occurs when government expenditures outstrip tax receipts.

National Debt
The total sum of what the federal government owes its creditors.

Stock
A variable that is measured at one point in time.

Flow
A variable that is measured over a period of time. Flow variables are measured in terms of units per time period.

EXHIBIT 18-1
Deficits and Debt
Here we show the deficit, deficit/GNP ratio, the debt, and debt/GNP ratio for the period 1980–90.

Year	Budget Deficit ($ billions)	Deficit as a Percentage of GNP	National Debt ($ billions)	Debt as a Percentage of GNP
1980	61.3	2.24	709.3	25.96
1981	63.8	2.09	784.8	25.68
1982	145.9	4.60	919.2	29.03
1983	176.0	5.16	1,131.0	33.20
1984	169.6	4.49	1,300.0	34.46
1985	196.9	4.90	1,499.4	37.34
1986	206.9	4.88	1,736.2	41.02
1987	158.2	3.50	1,888.1	41.81
1988	141.7	2.90	2,050.3	42.06
1989	134.3	2.58	2,190.3	42.11
1990	161.3	2.96	2,410.4	44.12

SOURCE: Council of Economic Advisers, *Economic Report of the President, 1991* (Washington, D.C.: U.S. Government Printing Office, 1991).

Americans hold the debt), American taxpayers will be making payments to American bondholders. And if we lump both taxpayers and bondholders together, and realize that together they make up the future generation, then we can say that the future generation doesn't pay the debt. There is simply a *transfer* of funds from one part of the future generation, taxpayers, to another part of the future generation, bondholders. This is the *we owe it to ourselves* argument. According to this view, the future generation, as a whole, sacrifices nothing for the increased government expenditures in an earlier period.[1]

Question:

Is the entire national debt held by Americans?

Answer:

No, it isn't. In the past 10 years, foreigners have held approximately 15–20 percent of the national debt.

Follow-up Question:

If the entire debt is not held exclusively by Americans, then won't future taxpaying Americans have to pay off some of the debt to foreigners? If so, what would be the response of the economists who believe that only the current generation bears the burden of the debt?

Answer:

They'd say that to the degree that the national debt is held by foreigners, the future American generation (specifically, future American taxpayers) does not completely escape the burden of the debt.

Another Answer: The Future Generation Bears the Burden of the Debt

Economist James Buchanan has argued that although resources are drawn from the private sector when debt-financed public expenditures are made, the people who give up these resources do not pay for, or bear the burden of, the public expenditures secured. To illustrate, suppose again that the government issues debt to pay for more national defense. Some people buy the government bonds—these are current bondholders. As a result of this voluntary exchange, resources shift from the private to the public sector. Society ends up with more planes, ships, and tanks and fewer television sets and the like. So far, the debt situation is the same as described earlier.

Have the bondholders paid for the weapons systems? Buchanan would say no. What the bondholders have done, he argues, is entered into a voluntary trade; they have voluntarily decided to consume a little less today (by buying bonds they have less income to devote to consumption) and to consume a little more when their

[1]In our discussion, we assumed that the current generation gives up consumer goods (television sets and the like) and not capital goods. If it gives up capital goods, some economists within this general school of thought would argue that the capital stock passed on to future generations is smaller because of the debt-financed public expenditures, and therefore the future generation bears the burden of the debt in the form of a reduced capital stock.

bonds are paid off (since they will receive the principal plus interest, they can consume more over their lifetimes than if they had not purchased the bonds). What bondholders have paid for by sacrificing current private consumption is more future private consumption; they have not paid for more weapons systems. Buchanan argues that the persons who pay for the weapons systems are the future taxpayers, who must retire the debt when it comes due.

In summary, Buchanan's argument works like this: The government in year 1 says, "Who among you want to buy our government bonds?" Some people voluntarily raise their hands. What they are buying and "paying for" is the opportunity to increase their private consumption in the future over and above what it would have been had they not purchased the bonds. When the future comes, say, year 30, and the bonds need to be paid off, the government doesn't say, "Who among you want to pay your taxes so that the debt can be paid off?" Instead, it simply takes the funds from taxpayers—persons who back in year 1 were *future taxpayers*. These taxpayers are not paying for the opportunity of greater future private consumption, as were the bondholders in year 1; they are paying for debt-financed expenditures in year 1.

How does Buchanan deal with the fact that in year 30 there are both taxpayers *and* bondholders, both of whom made up the future generation from the perspective of year 1? Once again, since the taxpayers in year 30 pay the bondholders in year 30, and what the taxpayers lose, the bondholders gain, wouldn't it follow that *on net* the burden of the debt for this generation is zero?

As we learned earlier, some economists would answer yes. But Buchanan states that the argument is misleading. The bondholders in year 30 don't really gain anything; all they do is trade one asset (bonds) for another asset (money) of equal value. This generation of bondholders gains no more from this transaction than if it had exchanged a $20 bill for four $5 bills. The taxpayers in year 30 do, however, lose something—taxes. In conclusion, bondholders do not gain anything, and taxpayers lose something, so *on net* the next generation loses.

Real Deficits and Debt

Some economists believe that much of the talk about deficits and debt is misdirected. Economist Robert Eisner argues that deficits and debt should be viewed in real terms, not nominal terms. If this is done, the picture does *look* different (whether it *is* different, however, is what economists debate).

Eisner says that to obtain the real deficit, the national debt should be adjusted each year for inflation and subtracted from the actual or nominal deficit. Suppose, in 1994, the national debt is $3,000 billion. During the year, the federal government runs a $200 billion deficit. The $200 billion adds to the national debt, so that at the end of the year the debt has increased to $3,200 billion (the increase in the national debt from one year to the next equals the deficit over the year).

Now suppose the price level rises by 5 percent during 1994. This means the real value of the original $3,000 billion debt declines by 5 percent. In short, the nominal national debt rises from $3,000 to $3,200 billion during the year, but inflation reduces the real value of the debt by $150 billion ($3,000 billion × .05 = $150 billion). In effect, this $150 billion is as much a receipt for government as if it were a tax. If we take this "inflation tax" into account, the conventionally measured deficit is reduced to $50 billion ($200 billion − $150 billion = $50 billion). Currently, government accounting procedures do not adjust the debt for inflation.

Question:

To reduce the deficit, it seems necessary either to cut government expenditures or to raise tax receipts. In the preceding example, neither was done. How, then, did the deficit go from $200 billion to $50 billion?

Answer:

When the real value of the debt is reduced, the result is the same *as if* inflation had raised tax receipts. Consider a simple example. Suppose the federal government spends $200 billion and has tax receipts of $80 billion. In this case, the deficit is $120 billion. We'll assume that the national debt was zero before the deficit is run, so that the debt equals $120 billion after the deficit is run. Thus, in our simple model, the national debt = the deficit.

Now let the price level increase by 10 percent. If we adjust the national debt for the rise in prices, the real value of the debt falls by 10 percent—or $12 billion. But if the *real value* of the debt falls by $12 billion because of the rise in prices, the result is the same *as if* government had raised $12 billion more in taxes. One can think of it this way: A person borrows $100 and promises to pay back the $100 in a year, but during the year the price level rises 10 percent. She ends up paying back the loan with dollars that have 10 percent less purchasing power than the dollars she borrowed. For the lender, it is *as if* he received 10 percent fewer dollars than he thought he would receive at the time the loan was made. Increases in the price level redistribute buying power from creditors to debtors. With regard to the national debt, the federal government is a debtor.

How Is Some Legislation Like a Bond?

When the government issues debt in the form of a bond, it promises to make a monetary payment to the bondholder in the future. The federal government also has other ways of promising to make a monetary payment in the future: It can make a promise through legislation. The best example of this is Social Security. Under Social Security legislation, the federal government promises benefits to future retirees that must be paid out of future tax revenues. Some economists believe that Social Security promises and the like should be viewed as the *implicit national debt*. Arthur Andersen & Co., an accounting firm, in 1986 estimated that if the implicit obligations of the federal government (implicit national debt) were added to the explicit obligations of the federal debt (explicit national debt), the national debt would be approximately three times as large as the official estimate.

The Deficit: International Considerations

Is there a link between the budget deficit $(G > T)$ and the trade deficit $(M > X)$? In the appendix to Chapter 6, we demonstrated such a link. The substance of the argument is as follows: (1) If the deficit grows larger, the Treasury has to borrow more credit. This increases the demand for credit, and drives the interest rate up. (2) A higher U.S. interest rate will bring about an increase in foreign capital inflows (to receive the relatively higher rate of return). (3) This will result in a greater demand for the U.S. dollar and thus the appreciation of the dollar. (4) The appreciation of the dollar makes U.S. goods more expensive and foreign goods cheaper.

(5) As a result, we would expect people to buy more foreign goods and fewer U.S. goods—thus U.S. exports decline and imports rise. (6) A fall in exports and a rise in imports simply increases the size of the trade deficit. In theory, then, the budget deficit can affect the trade deficit.

An Example: When it Comes to Economics, Do National Borders Really Mean Much Any More?   Suppose there are two persons, Jones and Smith, both of whom live in the same small town in the Midwest. Jones is a farmer and Smith owns a small business in which he makes unique clocks, many of which he sells in Europe.

One day Jones and other farmers from across the country go to Washington to lobby for more generous federal benefits. They tell their elected representatives that times are hard and that the American farmer needs help—immediately. Soon afterward, the Congress increases federal spending on agricultural programs. We will assume that no other program in the budget is cut, taxes are not raised, and there is a budget deficit at the time the farm spending program is put into effect. As a result, the budget deficit widens.

The process we described earlier begins: (1) To finance the additional spending, the Treasury increases the demand for credit. (2) Interest rates rise. (3) There is an increased inflow of foreign capital. (4) There is greater demand for the U.S. dollar. (5) The dollar appreciates in value. (6) U.S. exports fall and imports rise. One of the persons initially hurt by the higher (international) value of the dollar is Smith, our clockmaker.

One day, farmer Jones is in Smith's store looking for a clock to buy for his wife on their 30th anniversary. Smith is showing him around. The two start talking about this and that. Smith mentions to Jones that his business has been slow recently because his customers in Europe are not buying as many of his clocks as they used to buy. Jones asks Smith what he thinks is the problem. Smith tells him that the rise in the value of the dollar has hurt him greatly. Jones sympathizes with him and says that the rise in the value of the dollar has even started to hurt his wheat sales to foreigners. "Do you have any idea how the dollar got to be so much higher?" Jones asks Smith. Smith says, "No idea at all." Then he adds, "I don't know who to blame for this." Jones says, "I don't either." Then Jones apologizes to Smith for having to buy one of the cheaper clocks in the store. "Because," he says, "things just aren't looking too good right now." Smith just sighs. He knows.

Our example is fictional, but not unrealistic. It shows that it is possible for our actions as Americans to help us in the short run, but hurt us in the long-run. Jones, who lobbies for and receives additional federal benefits today, undertakes an action the long-run effects of which harm him and other farmers who sell their produce abroad. Also, sometimes the actions of one American (Jones) can adversely affect another American (Smith). It is likely that Jones and Smith, talking together in Smith's clock shop, had very little idea of where their problems originated. Jones probably didn't think that a small part of his current problems originated with himself. He might have blamed anyone from his elected representatives, to major corporations, to the oil-producing nations, to the president of the United States for the fact that an appreciated dollar is making it harder for him to sell his produce abroad. Similarly, it is unlikely that Smith, standing in his shop talking to Jones, would have accused him, a neighbor, as part of the source of his current economic woes. After all, what does an American farmer have to do with the international value of the U.S. dollar?

Economic actions have ripple effects—often far dispersed from the source.

We sometimes see news reports on television of the rise and fall of the U.S. dollar on international exchange markets, often accompanied by film of men and women sitting packed together in a room in London, Zurich, New York, or Tokyo, each in front of a green-screened computer monitor with a telephone in both hands. The atmosphere is hectic, if not frantic. The sounds are of currency prices: so many German marks or French francs for the U.S. dollar. To the average viewer, there is no connection between such sights and sounds and the activities of a Midwestern farmer, perhaps plowing the fields, many thousands of miles away. To the economist, however, the connection is immediately apparent. The price of the dollar affects the farmer's sales abroad, for example. He knows that economic actions have ripple effects—often far dispersed from the source.

THE BALANCED BUDGET AMENDMENT

■

Deficits do not occur in a political vacuum. Neither do proposals to reduce deficits. In this section, we discuss a few deficit-reduction proposals. One proposal, in particular, has been widely discussed throughout the 1980s. It is the balanced budget amendment The balanced budget amendment seeks to solve the deficit problem at the constitutional level. Other proposals include the presidential-line veto, a national consumption tax, a value-added tax, and privatization.

The Balanced Budget Amendment

The balanced budget amendment contains the following provisions:

1. Congress must legislate annual budgets "in which total outlays are no greater than total receipts."
2. Total receipts may not rise "by a rate greater than the rate of increase in national income."
3. "The Congress and the President shall . . . ensure that actual outlays do not exceed the outlays set forth in the budget statement."
4. These provisions may be overridden in time of war or other emergencies.

Critics of the balanced budget amendment have raised a number of points:

1. To adopt a budget statement "in which total outlays are no greater than total receipts," the Congress must rely on economic forecasts of how the economy will perform. Different forecasters come up with different forecasts, raising the question, Whose forecasts should the Congress accept? In addition, if the chosen forecast turns out to be wrong, then the Congress will have failed to abide by the amendment and thus will be in violation of the law.
2. What happens if the Congress doesn't abide by the amendment? Will all members of Congress be put in jail?
3. Congress can evade the amendment by moving expenditures "off-budget."[2]
4. Abiding by the discipline of a balanced budget may cause the government to enact the wrong kind of fiscal policy. For example, suppose the economy experiences a recession, real GNP declines, and tax revenues fall. If the budget were previously in balance, either an expenditure cut or a tax increase would be nec-

---

[2]Currently, the federal government does not include all its expenditures in its official budget; some expenditures are moved "off-budget."

Proposals to Deal with the Deficit

The balanced budget amendment is not the only proposal that has been put forth to deal with large budget deficits. Some of the other proposals include the presidential line-item veto, a consumption tax, a value-added tax, and privatizing certain government functions.

The Presidential Line-Item Veto

The president submits a budget to the Congress in January or February of each year. Between then and October 1, the first day of the fiscal year, different subcommittees and full appropriations committees in both houses of Congress meet and put together appropriations bills to be voted on by the full Congress. Once passed by Congress, these appropriations bills are sent to the president for approval or veto. In recent years, the Congress has been sending the president *fewer* but *larger* appropriations bills. Large bills contain some things the president wants and some things the president does not want. But under existing law, the president can either sign the entire bill or veto the entire bill. The president cannot go through the large appropriations bill and veto certain lines of expenditure. Critics have pointed out that Congress can throw "pork-barrel" spending projects into a large appropriations bill, knowing full well that the president isn't likely to veto a bill that contains a number of vital appropriations. Currently, many spending projects that couldn't pass on their own—if examined one by one—are tossed into a large appropriations bill that the president must accept fully or not at all.

The presidential line-item veto would allow the president to go through a large appropriations bill and draw a line through (veto) specific appropriations. No longer would it be a matter of all or nothing. Proponents of the line-item veto say this will permit the president to hold the line on federal spending, and thus have an impact on the deficit in the right direction—down. Opponents sometimes argue that it will shift spending authority from the Congress to the president, contrary to the design of the Constitution. Others note that the line-item veto is a good idea when you agree with the president's choice of items to veto, but a bad idea when you do not. A conservative president is likely to veto different appropriations than a liberal president. Some line-item-veto advocates retort that no matter what type of president occupies the White House, a line-item veto will still restrain runaway federal spending (even though people won't always agree with the particular items vetoed). Restraining federal spending, they maintain, is of greater importance than the composition of federal spending.

National Consumption Tax

When considering proposals for a new tax, one must ask, Is this tax to be added to the current tax system, or is it a substitute for a current tax?

A national consumption tax is similar to a state sales tax, but it would be applied to all Americans. Is the proposed consumption tax an additional tax or is it to be a substitute for the income tax? Those who want the consumption tax as an additional tax often argue that it will add to total tax revenues and thereby lower the deficit. Those who want it as a substitute for the income tax rarely discuss the deficit at all; instead, they maintain that the consumption tax is preferable to the income tax; that is, consumption is a better base to tax than income.

The actual operation of a consumption tax would be simple. Suppose Liz Warner's income is $20,000 this year and that she saves 10 percent of this amount, or $2,000. The $18,000 difference between saving and income, or consumption, is taxed, say, at 5 percent. One of the arguments in favor of a consumption tax, which is unrelated to the deficit, is that it would encourage more saving, thus permitting more investment.

Value-Added Tax

Like the consumption tax, the value-added tax (VAT) is proposed by some as a supplementary revenue source and by others as a substitute for a current tax or taxes. Those who propose it as an additional tax often say that it is needed to reduce the deficit.

A value-added tax is essentially a multistage sales tax that is collected from firms (not from individuals like an income or consumption tax) at each stage in the production and distribution process. The base of a VAT is the *value added* to a good at each stage of its production. The value added is equal to the price a firm receives for a good minus its purchases of material inputs from other firms. Consider three firms: Firm A, a manufacturer; Firm B, a wholesaler; and Firm C, a retailer. Suppose Firm A hires workers and manufacturers a good that it sells to Firm B for $700. In this case, the value added by Firm A is $700, since Firm A sells a good to Firm B for $700, and it does not purchase any materials from other firms ($700 − $0 = $700). Firm B distributes the good to a retailing firm, Firm C, for $900. What is the value added by Firm B? The answer is $200, because Firm B had purchased the good from Firm A for $700 ($900 − $700 = $200). Finally, Firm C sells the good to a consumer for $1,000. What is the value added by Firm C? The answer is $100 because Firm C had purchased the good for $900 from Firm B ($1,000 − $900 = $100).

A VAT would tax the value added by each firm. The value added by Firm A ($700) would be taxed, as would the value added by Firm B ($200), and the value added by Firm C ($100). Notice that the total value added $700 + $200 + $100 = $1,000 is equal to the sales price of the good. In short, the tax base of a value-added tax is the same as a retail sales tax.

If firms are allowed to deduct purchases of capital goods, then the tax base essentially becomes total consumption in the economy. This makes the VAT and the consumption

tax sound similar, and in this regard they are. They are different, though, in that the consumption tax is assessed against individuals (it is a direct tax), and the VAT is assessed against firms. Even though individuals are the only ones that can ultimately pay taxes, critics of a VAT argue that its taxes are "hidden" from individuals. If a hidden tax is easier to raise than a visible tax, as some economists believe, then a value-added tax is more likely to lead to an overall greater tax burden in the long run than a consumption or income tax.

Privatization

Some economists maintain that the federal government currently per-

forms some functions that could be done better and less expensively by the private sector and that such functions should be turned over to the private sector, or *privatized*. This would lower the deficit in three ways. First, through reduced spending. Second, through increased revenues due to the sale of government assets. And in some cases, third, by eliminating government promises to provide future benefits. So far, such proposals have not been widely discussed or accepted. Privatization proposals have included Social Security (by expanding Individual Retirement Accounts as a private alternative to Social Security), the postal service, the wastewater grant program, and public housing, among other things.

essary to maintain the balance. However, both of these actions would worsen the recession in the Keynesian model.

The proponents of the balanced budget amendment also make several points:

1. Budget institutions should convey to the public the costs of government expenditures as clearly and directly as possible. Taxes are a clearer, more direct, more understandable way to do this than deficit financing is.
2. Continued deficits have harmful effects on the economy (maybe just as much or more than the "wrong" fiscal policy). Some economists have hypothesized that deficits lead to higher interest rates, crowding out (less private investment), lower long-run real GNP, and inflation.
3. The burden of the debt is paid for by future generations, and running up deficits and placing such a burden on future generations is wrong.

CHAPTER SUMMARY

Ownership and Burden of the Debt

■ Americans have to pay off the national debt, and it is mostly Americans to whom the debt will be paid off. The percentage of the debt owned by foreigners has been between 15 and 20 percent in the past decade.
■ There is a continuing debate in economics on who bears the burden of the national debt. Economists who hold that the burden of the debt falls on the current

generation argue that resources are used up only in the periods when spending programs take place. Thus, if government debt finances an expenditure on, say, weapons, the resources that go into producing the weapons must be given up by some persons during that current period, not later.

■ Economists who hold that the burden of the debt falls on future generations state that when government debt finances an expenditure, it issues debt that is purchased by bondholders. These bondholders voluntarily trade one asset (money) for another (bonds). What they purchase is greater future consumption, not the government expenditure. The people who pay for the government expenditure are those who pay higher taxes to retire the previously issued debt.

Real Deficits and Debt

■ Economist Robert Eisner maintains that deficits and debt ought to be discussed in real, not nominal, terms. The national debt should be adjusted each year for inflation and subtracted from the actual deficit to obtain the real deficit. For example, suppose the national debt rises from $1,000 billion to $1,100 billion in one year, but at the same time the price level rises by 10 percent. The nominal deficit for the year is $100 billion, but the real deficit is zero because the value of the national debt falls by $100 billion ($1,000 billion × .10 = $100 billion). If we subtract $100 billion from the nominal deficit, we have zero.

The Implicit National Debt

■ Some economists state that the national debt should take into account not only the explicit national debt but also the implicit national debt. (The official measurement of the national debt only includes the explicit debt.) They argue that legislation can be like a bond. A bond is a promise to make a monetary payment in the future, and some legislation (for example, Social Security) is similar, if not for all practical purposes the same.

Proposals to Reduce the Deficit

■ One major proposal to reduce budget deficits is the balanced budget amendment.
■ Critics of the balanced budget amendment make several points: (1) Balancing the budget depends on accurate forecasts of expenditures and revenues. Which forecasts should the Congress use? If the chosen forecast turns out to be wrong, then the Congress has failed to abide by the amendment and is in violation of the law. (2) What happens if the Congress does not abide by the amendment? Will all members of Congress be put in jail? (3) Congress can evade the amendment by moving expenditures "off-budget." (4) A balanced budget amendment makes it difficult to enact stabilizing fiscal policy.
■ Proponents of the balanced budget amendment also make several points: (1) Budget institutions should convey to the public the costs of government expenditures as clearly and directly as possible. The balanced budget amendment is such a budget institution. (2) Continued deficits have harmful effects on the economy (maybe just as much or even more than the "wrong" fiscal policy). (3) It is wrong to debt finance current government expenditures and have future generations pay for them.
■ Besides the balanced budget amendment, other measures such as the presidential line-item veto, a consumption tax, a value-added tax, and privatization have been proposed to deal with large deficits.

Key Terms and Concepts

Budget Deficit   Stock   Flow
National Debt

1. The national debt in year 1 is $1,500 billion, the national debt in year 2 is $1,575 billion. The price level in year 2 is 20 percent higher than it was in year 1. What is the nominal deficit and the real deficit?

2. Suppose the U.S. economy is in recession and the deficit is $146 billion. Using the Keynesian model, what are the predicted effects on the economy if the balanced budget amendment is in force?

3. "The national debt is a fraction of the GNP. The Jensens private debt is equal to their family income. It follows that the national debt is less of a problem than the Jensens private debt. Since you rarely hear anyone getting upset about the Jensens private debt, there is even less reason to get upset about the national debt. All this discussion about the seriousness of the national debt is simply empty talk." Discuss.

4. Economists are quick to point out that economics and politics are often at war with each other over deficits and debt. What do you think this means?

5. "A liberal president would not use the presidential line-item veto to restrain government spending, but a conservative president would." Discuss.

6. Are you in favor of the balanced budget amendment? Why? To what degree does your answer depend on your view of the stabilizing effects of fiscal policy?

7. In the 48 years between 1944 and 1991, the United States has witnessed a budget deficit in 36 years and a budget surplus in 12 years. Some people have concluded that recent U.S. fiscal history shows a bias toward running budget deficits. Offer some explanations for this deficit bias.

THE WORLD ECONOMY

PART

VI

INTERNATIONAL ECONOMICS: THEORY AND POLICY

INTERNATIONAL TRADE

WHAT THIS CHAPTER IS ABOUT

Economics is about trade, and trade crosses boundaries. People do not trade exclusively with people who live in their city, state, or nation. They trade with people in other countries, too (a person in Denver, Colorado, may step into a department store and purchase a Sony television set made in Japan). This chapter examines international trade and the prohibitions that are sometimes placed on it.

The reasons why we have international trade are the same as why we have any trade: individuals trade to make themselves better off.

INTERNATIONAL TRADE THEORY

In this section, we discuss some of the facts and figures of international trade, especially as they relate to the United States. We also introduce the important *law of comparative advantage.*

What Does the United States Export and Import?

In 1990, major U.S. exports included automobiles, computers, aircraft, corn, wheat, soybeans, scientific instruments, coal, and plastic materials. Its major imports included petroleum, automobiles, clothing, iron and steel, office machines, footwear, fish, coffee, and diamonds. Exhibit 19–1 shows the percentage breakdowns for broad categories of U.S. exports and imports for 1990.

Why Do People in Different Countries Trade with One Another?

The reasons why we have international trade are the same as why we have any trade, at any level. Individuals trade to make themselves better off. Pat and Zach, both of whom live in St. Paul, Minnesota, trade because they both value something the other has more than they value some of their own possessions. On an international scale, Elaine in the United States trades with Cho in China because Cho has something that Elaine wants.

Obviously, different countries have different terrain, climate, resources, skills, and so on. It follows that some countries will be able to produce some goods that other countries cannot produce or can produce only at extremely high costs.

EXHIBIT 19–1
U.S. Exports and Imports, 1990
SOURCE: Council of Economic Advisers, *Economic Report of the President, 1991* (Washington, D.C.: U.S. Government Printing Office, 1991).

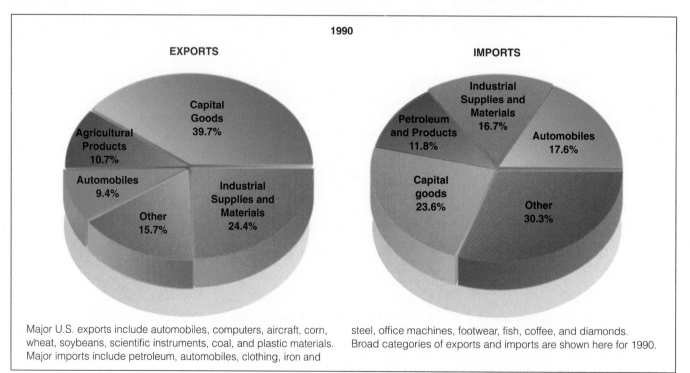

Major U.S. exports include automobiles, computers, aircraft, corn, wheat, soybeans, scientific instruments, coal, and plastic materials. Major imports include petroleum, automobiles, clothing, iron and steel, office machines, footwear, fish, coffee, and diamonds. Broad categories of exports and imports are shown here for 1990.

For example, Hong Kong has no oil, Saudia Arabia has a large supply. Bananas do not grow easily in the United States, but they flourish in Honduras. Americans could grow bananas, if they used hothouses, but it is cheaper for Americans to buy bananas from Hondurans than to produce bananas themselves.

How Do Countries Know What to Trade?

To explain how countries know what to trade, we need to discuss the concepts of *absolute advantage* and *comparative advantage*. Here is a simple model.

Absolute Advantage. Assume a two country–two good world. The countries are the United States and Japan, and the goods are food and clothing. Both countries can produce the two goods in the four different combinations listed in Exhibit 19–2. For example, with a given amount of resources, the United States can produce 90 units of food and 0 units of clothing, or 60 units of food and 10 units of clothing, and so on. With the same amount of resources used in the United States, Japan can produce 60 units of food and 0 units of clothing, and so on. Plotting the different combinations of the two goods each country can produce gives us the production possibilities frontiers in Exhibit 19–2.[1]

Notice that using the same amount of resources, the United States can produce more of one good (food) than Japan can, but Japan can produce more of another good (clothing) than the United States can. For example, using the same quantity of resources, the United States can produce 90 units of food whereas Japan can produce only 60 units, but Japan can produce 60 units of clothing whereas the United States can produce only 30 units. Economists would say that the United States has an **absolute advantage** in the production of food and Japan has an absolute advantage in the production of clothing.

A country has an absolute advantage in the production of a good if, using the same amount of resources as another country, it can produce more of a particular good. To put it differently, a country has an absolute advantage in the production of a good if, with fewer resources, it can produce the same amount of a good as another country.

Absolute Advantage
The situation where a country can produce more of a good than another country can produce with the same quantity of resources.

Suppose now that the United States is producing and consuming the two goods in the combination represented by point *B* on its production possibilities frontier, and Japan is producing and consuming the two goods in the combination represented by point *C'* on its production possibilities frontier. The United States is producing and consuming 60 units of food and 10 units of clothing, and Japan is producing and consuming 20 units of food and 40 units of clothing. We refer to this as the *no specialization–no trade (NS–NT)* case (column 1 in Exhibit 19–3).

Now suppose the two countries decide to specialize and trade. We call this the *specialization–trade (S–T)* case. The United States specializes in the production of food, producing 90 units, and Japan specializes in the production of clothing, producing 60 units. In short, the United States moves to point *A* on its production possibilities frontier, and Japan moves to point *D'* on its production possibilities frontier (column 2 in Exhibit 19–3).

After they have specialized in production, the two countries must settle on the terms of trade; that is, how much food will trade for how much clothing. The United States faces the following situation: For every 30 units of food it does not

[1]Notice that these are straight-line production possibilities frontiers, not curved ones. A straight-line production possibilities frontier indicates that resources can be transferred from the production of one good into another at *constant* opportunity cost. For a review, see Chapter 2.

EXHIBIT 19–2
Production Possibilities in Two Countries

UNITED STATES			JAPAN		
Points on Production Possibilities Frontier	Food	Clothing	Points on Production Possibilities Frontier	Food	Clothing
A	90	0	A'	60	0
B	60	10	B'	40	20
C	30	20	C'	20	40
D	0	30	D'	0	60

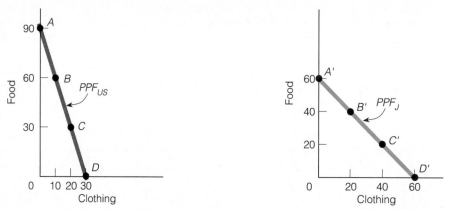

The United States has an absolute advantage in the production of food; Japan has an absolute advantage in the production of clothing. Initially, the United States produces at point B on its production possibilities frontier, and Japan produces at point C' on its production possibilities frontier. If the United States specializes in food production, and Japan in clothing production, and the United States trades 20 units of food to Japan for 10 units of clothing, both countries will be made better off.

produce, it can produce 10 units of clothing (see Exhibit 19–2). Thus, 3 units of food come at an opportunity cost of 1 unit of clothing (3F = 1C), or 1 unit of food comes at a cost of 1/3 unit of clothing (1F = 1/3C). Meanwhile, Japan faces the following situation: For every 20 units of food it does not produce, it can produce 20 units of clothing. Thus, 1 unit of food comes at an opportunity cost of 1 unit of clothing (1F = 1C). Recapping, for the United States 3F = 1C, and for Japan 1F = 1C.

With these cost ratios, it would seem likely that both countries could agree on terms of trade that specify 2F for 1C. The United States would prefer to give up 2 units of food instead of 3 units for 1 unit of clothing, whereas Japan would prefer to give up 1 unit of clothing and get 2 units of food instead of only 1. Suppose the two countries agree to the terms of trade of 2F = 1C and trade, in absolute amounts, 20 units of food for 10 units of clothing (column 3 in Exhibit 19–3).

Now the United States produces 90 units of food and trades (exports) 20 units to Japan, for which it receives in exchange (imports) 10 units of clothing. Thus, the United States consumes 10 units of clothing (received in trade from Japan)

EXHIBIT 19-3

Comparing the No Specialization–To Trade Case with the Specialization–Trade Case

NO SPECIALIZATION–NO TRADE CASE (NS–NT)			SPECIALIZATION–TRADE CASE (S–T)				
Country	(1) Production and Consumption in the NS–NT Case		(2) Production in the S–T Case		(3) Exports (−) Imports (+) Terms of Trade are 2F = 1C	(4) Consumption in the S–T Case (2) + (3)	(5) Gains from Specialization and Trade (4) − (1)
UNITED STATES							
Food	60	Point B in	90	Point A in	− 20	70	10
Clothing	10	Exhibit 19–2	0	Exhibit 19–2	+ 10	10	0
JAPAN							
Food	20	Point C' in	0	Point D' in	+ 20	20	0
Clothing	40	Exhibit 19–2	60	Exhibit 19–2	− 10	50	10

Column 1: Both the United States and Japan operate independently of each other. The United States produces and consumes 60 units of food and 10 units of clothing. Japan produces and consumes 20 units of food and 40 units of clothing.

Column 2: The United States specializes in the production of food; Japan specializes in the production of clothing.

Column 3: The United States and Japan agree to the terms of trade of 2 units of food for 1 unit of clothing. They actually trade 20 units of food for 10 units of clothing.

Column 4: Overall, the United States consumes 70 units of food and 10 units of clothing. Japan consumes 20 units of food and 50 units of clothing.

Column 5: Consumption levels are higher for both the United States and Japan in the S–T case than in the NS–NT case.

plus 70 units of food it has left over (recall that it produced 90 units and only traded away 20 units). (Column 4 in Exhibit 19–3 shows the situation for the United States.)

Now Japan produces 60 units of clothing and trades (exports) 10 units to the United States, and receives in exchange (imports) 20 units of food. Thus, Japan consumes 20 units of food (received in trade from the United States) plus 50 units of clothing it has left over (it only traded away 10 of the 60 units of clothing it produced). (Column 4 in Exhibit 19–3 shows the situation for Japan.)

Comparing the consumption levels of both countries in the no specialization–no trade case with the specialization–trade case, we find that both countries consume more in the specialization–trade case. The United States consumes 10 more units of food and no less clothing; Japan consumes 10 more units of clothing and no less food. Both countries have made themselves better off through specialization and trade.

Question:

In the example, both countries had an absolute advantage in the production of one good. Isn't this why they both benefited from specialization and trade? Would both have benefited if one country, say, the United States, had had an absolute advantage in the production of both goods?

Answer:

Yes, they would. Even if the United States had had an absolute advantage in the production of both goods, it could still have gained through specialization and trade. The classical economist David Ricardo pointed this out in the early nineteenth century. The discussion of *comparative advantage* in the next section explains this point further.

Comparative Advantage. Notice in Exhibit 19–4 that the United States is better than Japan at producing both food and clothing; it has an absolute advantage in the production of both goods. Now look at Exhibit 19–5, which shows that even under such conditions, both countries can gain from specialization and trade. Suppose, first, the two countries are not specializing or trading. The United States is producing and consuming the combination of the two goods represented by point *B* on its production possibilities frontier, and Japan is producing and consuming the combination of the two goods represented by point *B'* on its production possibilities frontier (column 1).

Now suppose the two countries decide to specialize and trade. Since the United States is better than Japan in the production of both goods, which good does the United States specialize in? Similarly, which good does Japan specialize in since it is not as efficient as the United States in the production of either good? The general answer to both questions is the same: *Countries specialize in the production of the good in which they have a* **comparative advantage.** A country has a comparative advantage in the production of a good when it can produce the good at lower opportunity cost than another country.

Comparative Advantage
The situation where a country can produce a good at lower opportunity cost than another country.

EXHIBIT 19–4
Production Possibilities in Two Countries

UNITED STATES			JAPAN		
Points on Production Possibilities Frontier	Food	Clothing	Points on Production Possibilities Frontier	Food	Clothing
A	90	0	A'	15	0
B	60	10	B'	10	5
C	30	20	C'	5	10
D	0	30	D'	0	15

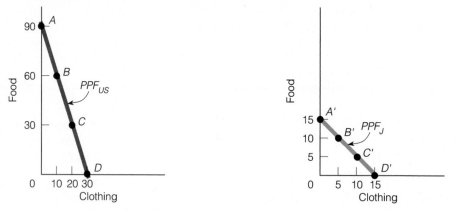

Even though the United States has an absolute advantage in the production of both goods, both countries can be made better off by specializing in and trading the good in which each has a comparative advantage. Gains from specialization and trade depend on comparative advantage, not absolute advantage.

EXHIBIT 19–5

Even If One Country Has an Absolute Advantage in Both Goods, Both Countries Can Gain from Specialization and Trade

Country	NO SPECIALIZATION–NO TRADE CASE (NS–NT) (1) Production and Consumption in the NS–NT Case		SPECIALIZATION–TRADE CASE (S–T) (2) Production in the S–T Case		(3) Exports (−) Imports (+) Terms of Trade are 2F = 1C	(4) Consumption in the S–T Case (2) + (3)	(5) Gains from Specialization and Trade (4) − (1)
UNITED STATES							
Food	60	Point B in	90	Point A in	− 20	70	10
Clothing	10	Exhibit 19–4	0	Exhibit 19–4	+ 10	10	0
JAPAN							
Food	10	Point B′ in	0	Point D′ in	+ 20	20	10
Clothing	5	Exhibit 19–4	15	Exhibit 19–4	− 10	5	0

Column 1: Both the United States and Japan operate independently of each other. The United States produces and consumes 60 units of food and 10 units of clothing. Japan produces and consumes 10 units of food and 5 units of clothing.
Column 2: The United States specializes in the production of food; Japan specializes in the production of clothing.
Column 3: The United States and Japan agree to the terms of trade of 2 units of food for 1 unit of clothing. They actually trade 20 units of food for 10 units of clothing.
Column 4: Overall, the United States consumes 70 units of food and 10 units of clothing. Japan consumes 20 units of food and 5 units of clothing.
Column 5: Consumption levels are higher for both the United States and Japan in the S–T case than in the NS–NT case.

For example, in the United States, the opportunity cost of producing 1 unit of clothing is 3 units of food (since for every 10 units of clothing it produces, it forfeits 30 units of food), whereas the opportunity cost of producing 1 unit of food is 1/3 unit of clothing. In Japan, the opportunity cost of producing 1 unit of clothing is 1 unit of food (since for every 5 units of clothing it produces, it forfeits 5 units of food). To recap, in the United States the situation is $1C = 3F$ and $1F = 1/3C$; in Japan the situation is $1C = 1F$ or, turning it around, $1F = 1C$.

We see that the United States can produce food at a lower opportunity cost ($1/3C$ as opposed to $1C$ in Japan), whereas Japan can produce clothing at a lower opportunity cost ($1F$ as opposed to $3F$ in the United States). Thus, the United States has a comparative advantage in food, and Japan has a comparative advantage in clothing.

Suppose the two countries specialize in the production of the good in which they have a comparative advantage (column 2), agree to the terms of trade $2F = 1C$, and trade in absolute amounts 20 units of food for 10 units of clothing (column 3).

Now the United States produces 90 units of food and trades 20 units to Japan, receiving 10 units of clothing in exchange. It consumes 70 units of food and 10 units of clothing (column 4, U.S. entry).

Now Japan produces 15 units of clothing and trades 10 to the United States, receiving 20 units of food in exchange. It consumes 5 units of clothing and 20 units of food (column 4, Japan entry).

Comparing the consumption levels in both countries in the two cases, the United States and Japan each consume 10 more units of food and no less clothing in the specialization–trade case than in the no specialization–no trade case (column 5).

We conclude that even when a country has an *absolute advantage* in the production of both goods (or when a country has an absolute disadvantage in the production of both goods), it stands to gain by specializing in producing and trading the good in which it has a *comparative advantage.*

Question:

Specialization and trade appear to allow a country's inhabitants to consume at a level beyond its production possibilities frontier. Is this correct?

Answer:

Yes, that is correct. To see this, turn back to Exhibit 19–4 and look at the *PPF* for the United States. In the *NS–NT* case, the United States consumes 60 units of food and 10 units of clothing—that is, the United States consumes at point *B* on its *PPF.* In the *S–T* case, however, it consumes 70 units of food and 10 units of clothing. A point that represents this combination of the two goods is outside the country's *PPF.*

How Do Countries Know When They Have a Comparative Advantage?

Government officials of a country do not sit down with piles of cost data before them and determine what their country should specialize in producing and then trade. Countries do not plot production possibilities frontiers on graph paper or calculate opportunity costs. Instead, it is individuals' desire to make a dollar, a franc, or a pound that determines the pattern of international trade; it is the desire to earn a profit that determines what a country specializes in and trades.

Take the case of Geoffrey, an enterprising Englishman who visits the United States. Geoffrey observes that beef is relatively cheap in the United States (compared with the price in England) and tea is relatively expensive. Noticing the price differences for beef and tea between his country and the United States, he decides to buy some tea in England, bring it to the United States, and sell it for the relatively higher U.S. price. With his profits on the tea transaction, he buys beef in the United States, ships it to England, and sells it for the relatively higher English price. It is obvious that what Geoffrey is doing is buying low and selling high; he is buying in the country where the good is cheap and selling it in the country where the good is expensive.

What are the consequences of Geoffrey's activities? First, he is earning a profit. The larger the price differences in the two goods between the two countries, and the more he reshuffles goods between countries, the more profit Geoffrey earns.

Second, Geoffrey's activities are moving each country toward its comparative advantage. The United States ends up exporting beef to England, and England ends up exporting tea to the United States. Just as the pure theory predicts, individuals in the two countries specialize in and trade the good in which they have a comparative advantage. The outcome is brought about spontaneously through the actions of individuals trying to make themselves better off; they are simply trying to gain through trade.

TRADE RESTRICTIONS

■

International trade theory shows that countries gain from free international trade; that is, from specializing in the production of the goods in which they have a comparative advantage and trading these goods for other goods. In the real world, however, there are numerous types of trade restrictions, which raises the question: If countries gain from international trade, why are there trade restrictions? We answer this and related questions in this section.

Why Are There Trade Restrictions in the Real World?

In the previous section, we learned that specialization and international trade benefit individuals in different countries. This occurs *on net.* Every person may not gain. Suppose Pam Dickson lives and works in the United States making clock radios. She produces and sells 12,000 clock radios per year for a price of $40 each. As the situation stands, there is no international trade. Individuals in other countries who make clock radios do not sell their clock radios in the United States.

Then one day things change. The U.S. market is opened up to clock radios from Japan. It appears that the Japanese manufacturers have a comparative advantage in the production of clock radios. They sell their clock radios in the United States for $25 each. Pam realizes that she cannot compete with this price. Her sales fall off to such a degree that she goes out of business. For Pam, personally, the introduction of international trade, *in this one instance,* has harmed her.

This raises the issue of the distributional effects of trade. Using the tools of supply and demand, we concentrate on two groups: U.S. consumers and U.S. producers. But first let's consider consumers' and producers' surplus.

Consumers' and Producers' Surplus

Consumers' surplus is the difference between the price buyers pay for a good and the maximum or highest price they would have paid for the good. It is a dollar measure of the benefit gained by being able to purchase a unit of a good for less than one is willing to pay for it. For example, if Yakov would have paid $10 to see the movie at the Cinemax, but only paid $4, his consumer surplus is $6.

Producers' surplus is the difference between the price sellers receive for a good and the minimum or lowest price for which they would have sold the good. It is a dollar measure of the benefit gained by being able to sell a unit of output for more than one is willing to sell it. For example, if Joan sold her knit sweaters for $14 each, but would have sold them for as low (but no lower) than $4 each, her producer surplus is $10 per sweater. Consumers' surplus is the consumers' net gain from trade, and producers' surplus is the producers' net gain from trade.

Both consumers' and producers' surplus are represented in Exhibit 19–6. In (a), consumers' surplus is the shaded triangle. This triangle is the area under the demand curve and above the equilibrium price out to the equilibrium quantity. Recall that the definition of consumers' surplus is highest price minus price paid. For example, notice in the window in (a) that consumers would have been willing to pay $7 for the 50th unit, but instead paid $5. Thus, the consumers' surplus on the 50th unit of the good is $2. If we add the consumers' surplus on each unit of the good between and including the first and the 100th (100 units being the equilibrium quantity), we obtain the shaded (consumers' surplus) triangle.

In (b), producers' surplus is represented by the shaded triangle. This triangle is the area above the supply curve and under the equilibrium price out to the equilibrium quantity. Keep in mind the definition of producers' surplus—price paid minus lowest price. For example, notice in the window in (b) that suppliers would have sold the 50th unit for as low as $3 but actually sold it for $5. Thus, the producers' surplus on the 50th unit of the good is $2. If we add the producers' surplus on each unit of the good between and including the first and the 100th, we obtain the shaded (producers' surplus) triangle.

Consumers' Surplus
The difference between the price buyers pay for a good and the maximum or highest price they would have paid for the good. It is a dollar measure of the benefit gained by being able to purchase a unit of a good for less than one is willing to pay for it.

Producers' Surplus
The difference between the price sellers receive for a good and the minimum or lowest price for which they would have sold the good. It is a dollar measure of the benefit gained by being able to sell a unit of output for more than one is willing to sell it.

EXHIBIT 19–6
Consumers' and Producers' Surplus

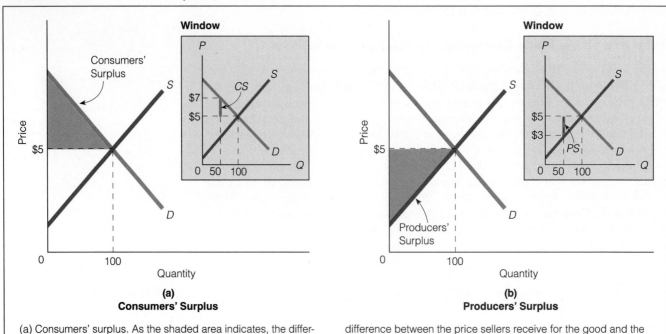

(a)
Consumers' Surplus

(b)
Producers' Surplus

(a) Consumers' surplus. As the shaded area indicates, the difference between the maximum or highest amount consumers would be willing to pay and the price they actually pay is consumers' surplus. (b) Producers' surplus. As the shaded area indicates, the difference between the price sellers receive for the good and the minimum or lowest price they would be willing to sell the good for is producers' surplus.

Exports Permitted and Prohibited

We now consider two cases: one where the U.S. government permits U.S. producers to export goods and one where it does not. Exhibit 19–7a illustrates the world market for wheat. The equilibrium world market price is P_W. At this price, U.S. consumers buy Q_1 amount of wheat in (b), and U.S. producers produce Q_2 amount of wheat. The difference between the two quantities ($Q_2 - Q_1$) is the amount of wheat U.S. producers export to the rest of the world.

Now suppose exports are prohibited; U.S. producers are no longer allowed to export wheat to the rest of the world. Price is now determined by domestic demand and supply. In the short term, this results in a surplus of wheat in the United States and drives price down. As a result, the price that is relevant to American wheat buyers is P_N in (b). In equilibrium, U.S. consumers buy Q_3 amount of wheat, U.S. producers produce and sell Q_3 amount of wheat, and no U.S. wheat is exported. Now compare the situation for U.S. consumers and producers when exports are permitted and when they are prohibited.

The Effects on U.S. Consumers. If exports are *permitted,* consumers' surplus is represented by the area $P_W AB$. This is the area under the demand curve and above the world equilibrium price P_W (which is the relevant equilibrium price if exports are permitted).

If exports are *prohibited,* U.S. consumers receive consumers' surplus equal to the area $P_N AD$. This is the area under the demand curve and above the equilibrium price P_N (which is the relevant equilibrium price if exports are prohibited).

EXHIBIT 19–7
Exports Permitted and Prohibited: The Effects on U.S. Consumers and Producers

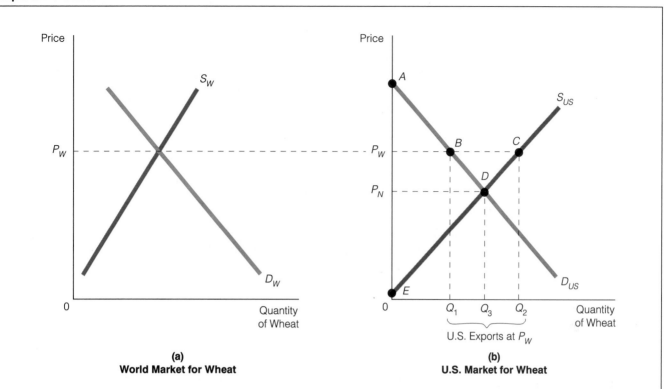

(a)
World Market for Wheat

(b)
U.S. Market for Wheat

U.S. CONSUMERS			U.S. PRODUCERS		
	Consumers' Surplus	Net Gain from Prohibiting Exports		Producers' Surplus	Net Gain from Permitting Exports
EXPORTS PERMITTED	$P_W AB$	$P_W BDP_N$	EXPORTS PERMITTED	$P_W CE$	$P_W CDP_N$
	Since $P_N AD > P_W AB$, U.S. consumers are better off if exports are prohibited.			Since $P_W CE > P_N DE$, U.S. producers are better off if exports are permitted.	
EXPORTS PROHIBITED	$P_N AD$		EXPORTS PROHIBITED	$P_N DE$	

$P_W CDP_N$ is greater than $P_W BDP_N$ by the area BCD. This area represents the net gain of a
policy of permitting exports over a policy of prohibiting exports. In short, there are net gains to free trade.

(c)

If exports are permitted, consumers' surplus is $P_W AB$ and producers' surplus is $P_W CE$. If exports are prohibited, consumers' surplus is $P_N AD$ and producers' surplus is $P_N DE$. The net gain to consumers of a policy that prohibits exports over a policy that permits exports is $P_W BDP_N$. The net gain to producers of a policy that permits exports over a policy that prohibits exports is $P_W CDP_N$. Since $P_W CDP_N > P_W BDP_N$, there is a net gain to free trade represented by the area BCD.

Consumers' surplus is greater when exports are prohibited than when they are permitted: $P_N AD > P_W AB$. U.S. consumers are helped by a policy that prohibits exports; they are hurt by a policy that permits exports.

The Effects on U.S. Producers. If exports are permitted, producers' surplus is $P_W CE$. This is the area above the supply curve and under the world equilibrium price P_W (which is the relevant equilibrium price if exports are permitted).

If exports are prohibited, U.S. producers receive producers' surplus equal to $P_N DE$. This is the area above the supply curve and under the equilibrium price P_N (which is the relevant equilibrium price if exports are prohibited). Producers' surplus is greater if exports are permitted than if they are prohibited: $P_W CE > P_N DE$. U.S. producers are helped by a policy that permits exports; they are hurt by a policy that prohibits exports.

How much better off, on net, are U.S. consumers if exports are prohibited than if they are permitted? The answer is represented by the area $P_W BDP_N$ in (b). Since consumers' surplus is larger when exports are prohibited ($P_N AD$) than when exports are permitted ($P_W AB$), the net gain to consumers of having exports prohibited is the difference between the two consumers' surplus areas, which is $P_W BDP_N$.

How much better off, on net, are U.S. producers if exports are permitted than if they are prohibited? Since producers' surplus is larger when exports are permitted ($P_W CE$) than when they are prohibited ($P_N DE$), the net gain to producers of having exports permitted is the difference between the two producers' surplus areas, which is $P_W CDP_N$. Looking at this area in (b), you will notice that it *includes* the net benefit to consumers of having exports prohibited—that is, area $P_W BDP_N$. This means that the net gain to producers of having exports permitted is greater than the net gain to consumers of having exports prohibited. The former is greater than the latter by the area *BCD*. *The area BCD represents the net gain of a policy of permitting exports over a policy of prohibiting exports.* In other words, there are net gains to free trade. Exhibit 19–7c summarizes this analysis.

Imports Permitted and Prohibited: The Effects on U.S. Consumers and Producers

The analysis of permitting and prohibiting imports follows the same steps as in the previous section. We begin, as we did before, at the world equilibrium price of P_W (Exhibit 19–8a). At this price for cars, U.S. consumers wish to buy Q_2 cars in (b); Q_1 of these cars will be bought from the U.S. producers of cars, and the difference between Q_2 and Q_1 ($Q_2 - Q_1$) will be bought from the foreign producers of cars. In short, U.S. consumers import $Q_2 - Q_1$ cars. In this case, where imports are permitted, consumers' surplus is represented by the area $P_W AC$, and U.S. producers receive producers' surplus equal to the area $P_W DE$.

Now suppose government passes legislation prohibiting foreign car imports. As a result, price rises to P_N. At this equilibrium price, U.S. consumers buy Q_3 cars and American producers sell Q_3 cars. U.S. consumers receive consumers' surplus equal to the area $P_N AB$, and U.S. producers receive producers' surplus equal to the area $P_N BE$.

Comparing the two situations, we notice that U.S. consumers receive higher consumers' surplus when imports are permitted ($P_W AC > P_N AB$), and U.S. producers receive higher producers' surplus when imports are prohibited ($P_N BE > P_W DE$).

The net gain to U.S. consumers of a policy that permits imports over one that

EXHIBIT 19–8
Imports Permitted and Prohibited: The Effects on U.S. Consumers and Producers

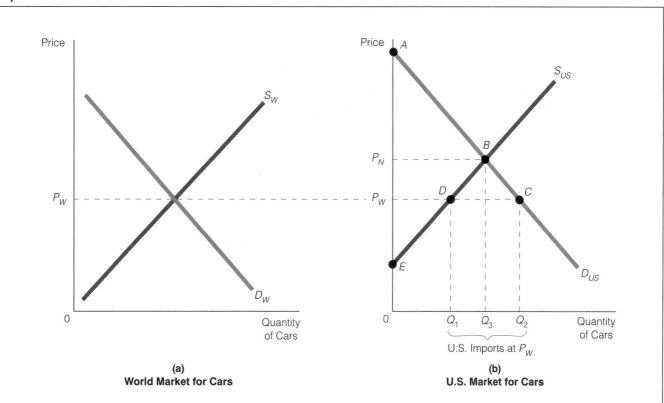

(a)
World Market for Cars

(b)
U.S. Market for Cars

U.S. CONSUMERS			U.S. PRODUCERS		
	Consumers' Surplus	Net Gain from Permitting Imports		Producers' Surplus	Net Gain from Prohibiting Imports
IMPORTS PERMITTED	P_WAC	P_NBCP_W	IMPORTS PERMITTED	P_WDE	P_NBDP_W
	Since $P_WAC > P_NAB$, U.S. consumers are better off when imports are permitted			Since $P_NBE > P_WDE$, U.S. producers are better off when imports are prohibited.	
IMPORTS PROHIBITED	P_NAB		IMPORTS PROHIBITED	P_NBE	

P_NBCP_W is greater than P_NBDP_W by the area BCD. This area represents the net gain of a policy of permitting imports over a policy of prohibiting imports. In short, there are net gains to free trade.

(c)

If imports are permitted, consumers' surplus is P_WAC and producers' surplus is P_WDE. If imports are prohibited, consumers' surplus is P_NAB and producers' surplus is P_NBE. The net gain to consumers of a policy that permits imports over a policy that prohibits imports is P_NBCP_W. The net gain to producers of a policy that prohibits imports over a policy that permits imports is P_NBDP_W. Since $P_NBCP_W > P_NBDP_W$, there is a net gain to free trade represented by the area BCD.

prohibits them is represented by the area P_NBCP_W. The net gain to U.S. producers of a policy that prohibits imports over one that permits them is represented by the area P_NBDP_W. Since the net gain to consumers of a policy that permits imports is greater than the net gain to producers of a policy that prohibits imports ($P_NBCP_W > P_NBDP_W$), we conclude that there is a net gain, represented by the area BCD, to the former policy (permits imports) over the latter (prohibits imports). Once again, the area BCD may be viewed as the net gain from free trade. See Exhibit 19–8c for a summary of the analysis.

If Free Trade Results in Net Gain, Why Do Nations Sometimes Restrict Trade?

Based on the preceding analysis, the case for free trade (no prohibitions on exports or imports) appears to be a strong one. The case for free trade has not gone unchallenged, however. Some persons maintain that at certain times, free trade should be restricted or suspended. In almost all cases, they argue that it is in the best interest of the public or country as a whole to do so. In short, they advance a public-interest argument. Other persons contend that the public-interest argument is only superficial; down deep, they say, it is a special-interest argument clothed in pretty words. As you might guess, the debate between the two groups is often heated.

Arguments for Trade Restrictions

Here are some arguments that have been advanced for trade restrictions.

The National-Defense Argument. It is often stated that certain industries—such as aircraft, petroleum, chemicals, and weapons—are necessary to the national defense. Suppose the United States has a comparative advantage in the production of wheat and the Soviet Union has a comparative advantage in the production of weapons. Should the United States specialize in the production of wheat, and then trade wheat to the Soviet Union in exchange for weapons? Many Americans would answer no. It is too dangerous, they maintain, to leave weapons productions to another country—whether that country is the Soviet Union, or England, or Canada.

The national-defense argument may have some validity. But even valid arguments may be abused. Industries that are not really necessary to the national defense may maintain otherwise. In the past, the national-defense argument has been used by some firms in the following industries: pens, pottery, peanuts, papers, candles, thumbtacks, tuna fishing, and pencils.

The Infant-Industry Argument. Alexander Hamilton, the first U.S. secretary of the treasury, argued that "infant" or new industries often need to be protected from older, established foreign competitors until they are mature enough to compete on an equal basis. Today, some persons voice the same argument. The infant-industry argument is clearly an argument for temporary protection. Critics charge, however, that once an industry is protected from foreign competition, removing the protection is almost impossible; the once infant industry will continue to maintain that it isn't old enough to go it alone. Critics of the infant-industry argument say that political realities make it unlikely that a benefit once bestowed will be removed.

Finally, the infant-industry argument, like the national-defense argument, may be abused. It may well be that all new industries, whether they could currently compete successfully with foreign producers or not, would argue for protection on infant-industry grounds.

The Antidumping Argument. **Dumping** is the sale of goods abroad at a price below their cost and below the price charged in the domestic market. If a French firm sells wine in the United States for a price below the cost of producing the wine and below the price charged in France, it is said to be *dumping* wine in the United States. Critics of dumping maintain that it is an unfair trade practice that puts domestic producers of substitute goods at a disadvantage. In addition, they charge that dumpers seek only to penetrate a market, drive out domestic competitors, and then raise prices. However, some economists point to the infeasibility of this strategy. Once the dumpers have driven out their competition and raised prices, their competition is likely to return. The dumpers, in turn, would have obtained only a string of losses (owing to their selling below cost) for their efforts. Second, opponents of the antidumping argument point out that domestic consumers benefit from dumping. They end up paying lower prices.

Dumping
The sale of goods abroad at a price below their cost and below the price charged in the domestic markets.

The Foreign-Export-Subsidies Argument. Some governments subsidize the firms that export goods. If a country offers a below-market (interest rate) loan to a company, it is often argued that the government subsidizes the production of the good the firm produces. If, in turn, that firm exports the good to a foreign country, domestic producers of substitute goods call foul. They complain that the foreign firm has been given an unfair advantage that they should be protected against.[2] Others say that one should not turn one's back on a gift (in the form of lower prices). If foreign governments want to subsidize their exports, and thus give a gift to foreign consumers at the expense of their own taxpayers, then the recipients should not complain. Of course, the recipients are usually not the ones who are complaining. Usually, the ones complaining are the domestic producers who can't sell their goods at as high a price because of the gift domestic consumers are receiving from foreign governments.

The Low-Foreign-Wages Argument. It is sometimes argued that American producers can't compete with foreign producers because American producers pay high wages to their workers, and foreign producers pay low wages to their workers. The American producers insist that free trade must be restricted or they will be ruined. What the argument overlooks is the reason American wages are high and foreign wages are low in the first place. In a word, the reason is productivity. High productivity and high wages are usually linked, as are low productivity and low wages. If an American worker, who receives $20 per hour, can produce (on average) 100 units of X per hour, working with numerous capital goods, the cost per unit may be lower than in the case of a foreign worker, who receives $2 per hour, but produces (on average) 5 units of X per hour, working by hand. In short, a country's high-wage disadvantage may be offset by its productivity advantage; a country's low-wage advantage may be offset by its productivity disadvantage. High wages do not necessarily mean high costs once productivity (and the costs of non-labor resources) are factored in.

[2]Words are important in this debate. For example, domestic producers who claim that foreign governments have subsidized foreign firms say that they are not asking for economic *protectionism,* but only for *retaliation,* or *reciprocity,* or simply *tit-for-tat*—words that have less negative connotation than the words their opponents use.

The Saving-Domestic-Jobs Argument. Sometimes the argument against completely free trade is made in terms of saving domestic jobs. Actually, we have already discussed this argument in its different guises. For example, the low-foreign-wages argument is one form of it. That argument continues along this line: If domestic producers cannot compete with foreign producers because foreign producers pay low wages and domestic producers pay high wages, domestic producers will go out of business and domestic jobs will be lost. The foreign-export-subsidies argument is another. Its proponents generally state that if foreign-government subsidies give a competitive edge to foreign producers, not only will domestic producers fail but as a result of their failure, domestic jobs will also be lost. The low-foreign-wages and foreign-export-subsidies arguments are also applied to the saving-domestic-jobs argument (so we will not repeat them here). In addition, critics of the saving-domestic-jobs argument (in all its guises) often argue that if a domestic producer is being outcompeted by foreign producers, and domestic jobs in a particular industry are being lost as a result, the world market is signaling that those labor resources could be put to better use in an industry in which the country holds a comparative advantage.

How Is Trade Restricted?

There are numerous ways to restrict free trade. Tariffs and quotas are two of the more commonly used methods.

Tariff
A tax on imports.

Tariffs. A **tariff** is a tax on imports. The primary effect of a tariff is to raise the price of the imported good to the domestic consumer. Exhibit 19–9 illustrates the effects of a tariff.

EXHIBIT 19–9
The Effects of a Tariff

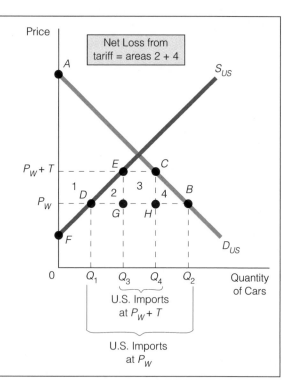

A tariff raises the price of cars from P_W to $P_W + T$, decreases consumers' surplus by areas 1 + 2 + 3 + 4, increases producers' surplus by area 1, and generates tariff revenues collected by government equal to area 3. Since consumers lose more than producers and government gain, a net loss results from a tariff.

The world price for cars is P_W. At this price, U.S. consumers are buying Q_2 cars: Q_1 from U.S. producers and the difference between Q_2 and Q_1 ($Q_2 - Q_1$) from foreign producers. In other words, U.S. imports at P_W are $Q_2 - Q_1$. In this situation, consumers' surplus is $P_W AB$ and producers' surplus is $P_W DF$.

Now suppose a tariff is imposed. The new price for imported cars in the U.S. car market rises to $P_W + T$ (the world price plus the tariff). At this price, U.S. consumers buy Q_4 number of cars: Q_3 from U.S. producers of cars and $Q_4 - Q_3$ from foreign producers. U.S. imports are $Q_4 - Q_3$, which is a smaller number of imports than at the pretariff price. An effect of tariffs, then, is to reduce imports. At the price $P_W + T$, consumers' surplus is $(P_W + T)AC$, and producers' surplus is $(P_W + T)EF$.

Because of the tariff, consumers' surplus is reduced by an amount equal to the areas $1 + 2 + 3 + 4$, and producers' surplus is increased by an amount equal to area 1. The government collects tariff revenues equal to area 3. This area is obtained by multiplying the number of imports ($Q_4 - Q_3$) times the tariff itself, which is the difference between $P_W + T$ and P_W ($P_W + T - P_W = T$).

In conclusion, the effects of the tariff are a decrease in consumers' surplus, an increase in producers' surplus, and tariff revenues for government. Since the loss to consumers (areas $1 + 2 + 3 + 4$) is greater than the gain to producers (area 1) plus the gain to government (area 3), it follows that a net loss results from a tariff. This is the other side of the coin that reads "There is a net gain to free trade."

Quotas. A **quota** is a legal limit on the amount of a good that may be imported. For example, the government may decide to allow no more than 100,000 foreign cars to be imported, or 10 million barrels of OPEC oil, or 30,000 Japanese television sets. A quota, reduces the supply of a good and raises the price of imported goods to domestic consumers (Exhibit 19–10).

Quota
A legal limit on the amount of a good that may be imported.

EXHIBIT 19–10
The Effects Of a Quota

A quota that sets the legal limit of imports at $Q_4 - Q_3$ causes the price of cars to increase from P_W to P_Q. As a result, consumers' surplus decreases by the areas $1 + 2 + 3 + 4$, producers' surplus increases by area 1, and importers receive higher total revenues on imports $Q_4 - Q_3$, or area 3. Since consumers lose more than producers and importers gain, a net loss results from a quota.

With a quota this area does not go to government (as it does with a tariff); however, see footnote 3.

Quota Only Allows
This Number
of Imports

U.S. Imports in
Absence of Quota

Once again, consider the situation in the U.S. car market. At a price of P_W U.S. consumers buy Q_1 cars from U.S. car producers and import $Q_2 - Q_1$ from foreign car producers. Consumers' surplus is $P_W AB$ (as it was in the tariff example) and producers' surplus is $P_W DF$. Suppose now that the U.S. government sets a quota equal to $Q_4 - Q_3$. Since this is the number of foreign cars U.S. consumers imported when the tariff was imposed (see Exhibit 19–9), the new price of cars rises to P_Q in Exhibit 19–10 (which is equal to $P_W + T$ in Exhibit 19–9). At P_Q, consumers' surplus is $P_Q AC$ and producers' surplus is $P_Q EF$. The decrease in consumers' surplus due to the quota is equal to the areas $1 + 2 + 3 + 4$; the increase in producers' surplus is equal to area 1.

But what about area 3? Is this area transferred to government, as was the case when a tariff was imposed? No, it isn't. This area represents the additional revenue earned by the importers (and sellers) of $Q_4 - Q_3$. Without the quota, those importers and sellers of $Q_4 - Q_3$ sold their imported cars for P_W. Their total revenue was therefore $P_W \times (Q_4 - Q_3)$, or the area $Q_3 GHQ_4$. Because of the quota, the price rises to P_Q and their total revenue is $P_Q \times (Q_4 - Q_3)$, or the area $Q_3 ECQ_4$. The difference between total revenues on $Q_4 - Q_3$ imports without a quota and with a quota is the area 3.

In conclusion, the effects of a quota are a decrease in consumers' surplus (areas $1 + 2 + 3 + 4$), an increase in producers' surplus (area 1), and an increase in total revenue for the importers who sell the allowed number of imported units (area 3). Since consumers lose more than domestic producers and importers gain, a net loss results from a quota.[3]

Question:

It appears that the following statements are true:

1. Tariffs and quotas generate a net loss (consumers lose more than producers, importers, and governments gain).
2. Tariffs and quotas exist in the real world.
3. Neither tariffs nor quotas would or could exist without government sanction.

Given these facts, would it be reasonable to conclude that governments, at least on the issue of international trade, do not try to promote the general welfare?

Answer:

Many persons have come to this conclusion. However, others argue that things aren't as black and white as the diagrams may make them appear. They say that the reasons for limiting trade (see the earlier section) have to be considered alongside the diagrams that clearly show a net loss from limiting free trade.

The Effects of Voluntary Export Restraints

The U.S. auto companies did not have a good year in 1980. The Big Three U.S. auto companies, General Motors, Ford, and Chrysler, sold over 1 million fewer

---

[3]It is perhaps incorrect to imply that government receives *nothing* from a quota. Although it receives nothing directly, it may gain indirectly. Economists generally argue that since government officials are likely to be the persons who will decide which importers will get to satisfy the quota, they will naturally be lobbied by importers; thus government officials will likely receive *something*, if only dinner at an expensive restaurant, while the lobbyist makes his or her pitch. In short, in the course of the lobbying, resources will be spent by lobbyists as they curry favor with those government officials or politicians who have the power to make the decision as to who gets to sell the limited number of imported goods. In economics, lobbyists' activities, geared toward obtaining a special privilege, are referred to as *rent seeking*.

cars in 1980 than in 1979. The Big Three blamed Japanese car imports for their problems and lobbied for protectionism. They said they needed a little time to catch their breath, retool for smaller cars, change their production processes, and cut costs. In a way, they were voicing the infant-industry argument. Given the age of the industries, some have preferred to call it the senile-industry argument.

In 1981, some members of Congress argued strongly for severe protectionist measures to be slapped on Japanese car imports. To prevent this, the Reagan administration proposed, and the Japanese agreed to, a **"voluntary" export restraint (VER)**. A voluntary export restraint is an agreement between two countries in which the exporting country voluntarily agrees to limit its exports to the importing country. (The effects of a voluntary export restraint can be analyzed the same way as a quota.) In this case, the export restraint was not really voluntary in the way the word is usually understood. The Japanese accepted the VER because, some say, they feared much worse measures if they didn't.

What happened as a result of the VER? In a *Wall Street Journal* article, Robert Crandall of the Brookings Institution reported that the effects of VER were:

"Voluntary" Export Restraint (VER)
An agreement between two countries in which the exporting country "voluntarily" agrees to limit its exports to the importing country.

1. In 1983, Japanese car imports were selling for about $1,500 more than they would have without the restraints.
2. In 1984, Japanese car imports were selling for about $2,500 more than they would have without the restraints.
3. In the period 1984–85, U.S. consumers paid about $10 billion more for Japanese cars than they would have in the absence of the restraints.
4. The restraints on imports allowed U.S. car companies to raise their prices by about $1,000 per car.
5. American consumers paid about $16.6 billion more for U.S-produced cars in 1984–85 because of the restraints.[4]

At What Price Jobs?

Suppose the U.S. government imposes a tariff on imported good X. As a result, the domestic producers of good X sell their goods for higher prices, receive higher producers' surplus, and are generally better off. Some of the domestic workers who produce good X are better off, too. Perhaps without the tariff on imports of good X, some of them would have lost their jobs.

Such scenarios raise two important questions: How many domestic jobs in the firms that produce good X are saved because of the tariff? How much do consumers have to pay in higher prices to save these jobs? Economists are interested in answering such questions. Here are a few answers for different industries at different times.

In 1977, tariffs and quotas were imposed on imports of foreign footwear. An estimated 21,000 domestic jobs were protected in the domestic footwear industry as a result. The average worker in the industry earned $8,340 (in 1980 dollars). Domestic consumers paid $77,714 for *each* $8,340 domestic footwear job protected.

As we stated earlier, in 1981, voluntary export restraints were placed on Japanese car imports. The U.S. International Trade Commission estimated that 44,000 domestic jobs were protected—at a cost of $193,000 per job.

In 1988, the consumer cost of voluntary export restraints on machine tools was $48 million, while the gain to U.S. machine tool manufacturers was $11 million. The consumer cost per job saved turned out to be $120,000.

[4]Robert W. Crandall, "Detroit Rode Quotas to Prosperity," *Wall Street Journal*, January 29, 1986, p. 30.

THINKING LIKE AN ECONOMIST

Free-Trade Agreements

Several recent agreements have given worldwide impetus to free trade. We describe them here.

The United States of Europe. At the end of 1992, the 12 nations that make up the European Community (EC) will essentially form a United States of Europe for trading purposes. In 1993, the seven nation European Free Trade Association will join the EC unification efforts to form the world's largest trading bloc, embracing 380 million consumers and accounting for 43 percent of world trade. A few of the European nations' objectives are to (1) abolish all tariffs and quotas on products traded by the nations, (2) establish a common system of tariffs for products imported into the nations, and (3) establish the free movement of capital and labor among the nations.

Economists are certain that the abolition of trade barriers among European nations will economically benefit those nations, although they note that if the United States of Europe raises trade barriers against the rest of the world, many of the benefits of the economic union will be dissipated.

The U.S.–Canadian Free-Trade Agreement. Canada is the largest trading partner of the United States. In 1988, President Reagan and Canadian Prime Minister Mulroney signed the U.S.–Canadian Free-Trade Agreement. According to the agreement, tariffs and quotas between the two countries will be eliminated over a 10-year period. It has been estimated that the free-trade agreement will bring gains of between $1 billion and $3 billion a year to each nation.

The U.S.–Mexico Free-Trade Area. Mexico is the third largest trading partner of the United States (Japan is the second). In 1990, President Bush and the president of Mexico endorsed the goal of a free-trade agreement between the two countries. In 1991, President Bush began negotiating with Mexico to achieve this free-trade agreement. This free-trade agreement, like the one that the United States has with Canada, will, if accepted by Congress, eventually eliminate completely the tariffs between the two nations, as well as other trade barriers.

International trade is a place where economics and politics often do battle. The simple tools of supply and demand and consumers' and producers' surplus tell us that there are net gains from free trade; limiting exports or imports serves only to make living standards, on the whole, lower than they would be if free trade were permitted.

But, on the other hand, are the harsh realities of life. Domestic producers may advocate quotas and tariffs to make themselves better off, but give little thought to the negative effects felt by foreign producers or domestic consumers. And domestic consumers may advocate policies that prohibit exports to make themselves better off, but give little thought to the negative effects felt by foreign consumers or domestic producers.

Perhaps the battle over international trade comes down to this: Policies are largely advocated, argued, and lobbied for based more on their *distributional effects* than on their aggregate or overall effects. On an aggregate level, free trade produces a net gain for society, whereas restricted trade produces a net loss. But economists understand that just because free trade *in the aggregate* produces a net gain, it does not necessarily follow that every single person benefits more from free trade than restricted trade. This chapter has presented numerous examples where a subset of the population gains more, in a par-

Interview: Lester Thurow

Lester Thurow is one of the more articulate, well-respected, and sometimes controversial economists on the public scene today. In recent years, he has appeared on numerous news programs to discuss such topics as international trade, industrial policy, productivity, and the trade deficit. He is currently at the Massachusetts Institute of Technology.

Professor Thurow, in your essay on declining industries in *The New Palgrave: A Dictionary of Economics*, you say, "Almost all countries protect their declining industries to some extent." They do this despite the fact that economists can show that protectionism comes with net costs to society. Why is there so much protectionism in the world?

I think the simple reason is that if you look at the pluses and the minuses from free international trade, the pluses may be bigger than the minuses but the pluses are spread over a very large number of people who all get a small addition to their incomes, and the minuses are spread over a relatively small number of people who take a huge cut in their incomes. For example, if we give $1 to all Americans, and take away $1,000 from each of 100 Americans, then the 100 Americans who are losing are going to put up a tremendous economic fight, and the millions of Americans who are winning are not, because what they are winning is a small amount of money ($1). And this would be the case even if the total winnings are greater than the total losses.

Which is one of the most protectionist nations in the world? Which is one of the least protectionist?

Hong Kong is clearly the least protectionist. Among industrial countries, Korea is one of the most protectionist.

Most Americans appear to believe that Japan is much more protectionist than the United States. Do you think this is true?

The two countries have about equal amounts of protection. At the end of the 1980s, about 25 percent of the products entering the United States were in some way restricted. Japan is no worse. The difference is that Japan has strategic protection while American's protection is "loser driven." Japan protects the strategic industries of the future such as amorphous metals. America protects those old dying industries that have political clout.

What do you predict will be a major economic problem in the United States in the mid-1990s, and how should it solve that problem?

In 1990, the weekly wages of what the Department of Labor calls nonsupervisory workers were 17 percent below where they were in 1973 after correcting for inflation. Low rates of productivity growth and what economists know as "factor price equalization" (in a world economy, unskilled American workers can be paid no more than unskilled workers in competing countries

such as Korea) will continue these trends in the 1990s. In the 1970s and 1980s, increasing female work effort meant that the average family could experience slowly rising real standards of living despite the fact that the wages of both husband and wife were falling. But the work potential of women has been almost fully utilized, and in the 1990s, falling wages will lead to falling family incomes as well.

You have had more opportunities than most economists to deal with the press, since in recent years you have been interviewed on a number of news programs. How would you rate the understanding of economics of most of the journalists who have interviewed you?

Somewhere between average and good. The real problem with the press, and especially the electronic press like television, is that they try to compress things into (at the most) 75 seconds, and there are many economic subjects that just cannot intelligently be discussed in that short time. So the problem is not ignorance, it is time.

Do you find this frustrating?

Well, you don't get frustrated when they interview you, because what they do is come to your office and take 45 minutes of tape and then they edit it down to 75 seconds. It is not so much the interview that is frustrating, it is what actually shows up on the air.

What got you interested in economics?

The belief, some would see it as naive belief, that economics was a profession where it would be possible to help make the world better.

ticular instance, from restricted trade than from free trade. In short, economists realize that real-world policies are often determined more by the answer to the question, How does it affect *me?* than by How does it affect *us?*

CHAPTER SUMMARY

Specialization and Trade

■ A country has an absolute advantage in the production of a good if, using the same amount of resources as another country, it can produce more of a particular good. A country has a comparative advantage in the production of a good it produces at lower opportunity cost than another country.

■ Individuals in countries that specialize and trade have a higher standard of living than would be the case if they did not specialize and trade.

■ Government officials do not sit down with cost data and determine what their country should specialize in and trade. Instead, the desire to earn a dollar, franc, or pound guides individuals' actions and produces the unintended consequence that countries specialize in and trade the good(s) in which they have a comparative advantage. However, trade restrictions can change this outcome.

International Trade: Distributional Effects

■ Consumers' surplus is greater if exports are prohibited than if they are permitted.

■ Producers' surplus is greater if exports are permitted than if they are prohibited.

■ Consumers' surplus is greater if imports are permitted than if they are prohibited.

■ Producers' surplus is greater if imports are prohibited than if they are permitted.

■ Producers lose more than consumers gain from a policy that prohibits exports. Thus, prohibiting exports results in a net loss.

■ Consumers lose more than producers gain from a policy that prohibits imports. Thus, prohibiting imports results in a net loss.

■ Producers gain more than consumers lose from a policy that permits exports. Thus, permitting exports results in a net gain.

■ Consumers gain more than producers lose from a policy that permits imports. Thus, permitting imports results in a net gain.

Arguments for Trade Restrictions

■ The national-defense argument states that certain goods—such as aircraft, petroleum, chemicals, and weapons—are necessary to the national defense and should be produced domestically whether the country has a comparative advantage in their production or not.

■ The infant-industry argument states that "infant" or new industries should be protected from free (foreign) trade so that they may have time to develop and compete on an equal basis with older, more established foreign industries.

■ The antidumping argument states that domestic producers should not have to compete (on an unequal basis) with foreign producers that sell products below cost and below the prices they charge in their domestic markets.

■ The foreign-export-subsidies argument states that domestic producers should not have to compete (on an unequal basis) with foreign producers that have been subsidized by their governments.

■ The low-foreign-wages argument states that domestic producers cannot compete with foreign producers that pay low wages to their employees when domestic producers pay high wages to their employees. In order that high-paying domestic firms may survive, limits on free trade are proposed.

■ The saving-domestic-jobs argument states that through low foreign wages or government subsidies (or dumping, and so forth), foreign producers will be able to outcompete domestic producers, and therefore domestic jobs will be lost. In order that domestic firms may survive, and domestic jobs not be lost, limits on free trade are proposed.

■ The arguments for trade restrictions are not accepted as valid by all persons. Critics often maintain that the arguments can be and are abused and, in most cases, are motivated by self-interest.

Tariffs and Quotas

■ A tariff is a tax on imports. A quota is a legal limit on the amount of a good that may be imported.

■ Both tariffs and quotas raise the price of imports.

■ Tariffs lead to a decrease in consumers' surplus, an increase in producers' surplus, and tariff revenues for the government. Consumers lose more through tariffs than producers and government (together) gain.

■ Quotas lead to a decrease in consumers' surplus, an increase in producers' surplus, and additional revenues for the importers that sell the quota. Consumers lose more through quotas than producers and importers (together) gain.

Key Terms and Concepts

Absolute Advantage	Producers' Surplus	Quota
Comparative Advantage	Dumping	"Voluntary" Export Restraint
Consumers' Surplus	Tariff	

QUESTIONS AND PROBLEMS

1. A production possibilities frontier is usually drawn for a country. One could, however, be drawn for the world. Picture the world's production possibilities frontier. Is the world positioned at a point on the curve or below the frontier? Give a reason for your answer.

2. Using the data in the table, answer the questions that follow: (a) In which good does Canada have a comparative advantage? (b) In which good does Italy have a comparative advantage? (c) What might be a set of favorable terms of trade for the two countries? (d) Prove that both countries would be better off in the specialization–trade case than in the no specialization–no trade case.

Points on Production Possibilities Frontier	CANADA		ITALY	
	Good X	Good Y	Good X	Good Y
A	150	0	90	0
B	100	25	60	60
C	50	50	30	120
D	0	75	0	180

3. "Whatever can be done by a tariff can be done by a quota." Discuss.

4. Consider two groups of domestic producers: those that compete with imports and those that export goods. Suppose the domestic producers that compete with imports convince the legislature to impose a high tariff on imports, so high, in fact, that almost all imports are eliminated. Does this policy in any way adversely affect domestic producers that export goods? How?

5. Suppose the U.S. government wants to curtail imports, would it be likely to favor a tariff or a quota to accomplish its objective? Why?

6. Suppose the land mass known to you as the United States of America had been composed, since the nation's founding, of separate countries instead of separate states. Would you expect the standard of living of the people who inhabit this land mass to be higher, lower, or equal to what it is today? Why?

7. Even though Jeremy is a better gardener and novelist than Bill is, he (Jeremy) still hires Bill as his gardener. Why?

8. Suppose that tomorrow a constitutional convention were called and you were chosen as one of the delegates from your state. You and the other delegates must decide whether it will be constitutional or unconstitutional for the federal government to impose tariffs and quotas or restrict international trade in any way. What would be your position?

9. Some economists have argued that since domestic consumers gain more from free trade than domestic producers gain from (import) tariffs and quotas, consumers should buy out domestic producers and rid themselves of costly tariffs and quotas. For example, if consumers save $400 million from free trade (through paying lower prices) and producers gain $100 million from tariffs and quotas, consumers can pay producers something more than $100 million but less than $400 million and get producers to favor free trade, too. Assuming this scheme were feasible, what do you think of it?

INTERNATIONAL FINANCE

WHAT THIS CHAPTER IS ABOUT

Chapter 19 presented the *real* side of international transactions—primarily, the goods being produced in one country and traded in others. Money did not figure prominently in the picture.

Chapter 20 presents the *monetary* side of international transactions. Here money does figure prominently in the picture. All types of monies are involved: U.S. dollars, Japanese yen, English pounds, French francs, Indian rupees, and more.

The two main topics of international finance are the balance of payments and exchange rates. We discuss both in this chapter.

THE BALANCE OF PAYMENTS

■

Countries keep track of their domestic level of production by calculating their gross national product; similarly, they keep track of the flow of their international trade (receipts and expenditures) by calculating their balance of payments. The **balance of payments** is a periodic statement (usually annual) of the money value of all transactions between residents of one country and residents of all other countries. The balance of payments provides information about a nation's imports and exports, domestic residents' earnings on assets located abroad, foreign earnings on domestic assets, gifts to and from foreign countries (including foreign aid), and official transactions by governments and central banks.

Balance of payments accounts record both debits and credits. A debit is indicated by a minus (−) sign, and a credit is indicated by a plus (+) sign. *Any transaction that supplies the nation's currency in the foreign exchange market is recorded as a* **debit.**

For example, if Americans buy Japanese television sets, they must first buy Japanese yen by selling (supplying) U.S. dollars. This import transaction is listed as a debit in the U.S. balance of payments.

Similarly, *any transaction that supplies a foreign currency in the foreign exchange market is recorded as a* **credit.** If the Japanese buy American computers, they must first buy U.S. dollars by selling (supplying) Japanese yen. This export transaction is listed as a credit in the U.S. balance of payments.

The international transactions that occur, and are summarized in the balance of payments, can be grouped into three categories, or three accounts: the current account, the capital account, and the official reserve account—and a statistical discrepancy. We have illustrated a U.S. balance of payments account for year Z in Exhibit 20–1. The data in the exhibit are hypothetical (to make our calculations simpler), but not unrealistic.

Question:

When Americans buy Japanese goods, they supply dollars and demand yen. When the Japanese buy American goods, they supply yen and demand dollars. Thus the first transaction is recorded as a debit (since it supplies the nation's currency) and the second as a credit (since it supplies a foreign currency) in the U.S. balance of payments. Is this correct?

Answer:

Yes, that is correct.

The Current Account

The **current account** includes all payments related to the purchase and sale of goods and services. There are three major components of the current account: exports of goods and services, imports of goods and services, and net unilateral transfers abroad.

Exports of Goods and Services.   Americans export goods (say, cars), they export services (such as insurance, banking, transportation, and tourism), and they receive investment income on assets they own abroad. All three activities increase the

---

Balance of Payments
A periodic statement (usually annual) of the money value of all transactions between residents of one country and residents of all other countries.

Debit
In the balance of payments, any transaction that either supplies the nation's currency or creates a demand for foreign currency in the foreign exchange market.

Credit
In the balance of payments, any transaction that either supplies a foreign currency or creates a demand for the nation's currency in the foreign exchange market.

Current Account
Includes all payments related to the purchase and sale of goods and services. Components of the account include exports, imports, and net unilateral transfers abroad.

EXHIBIT 20–1
U.S. Balance of Payments, Year Z

The data in this exhibit are hypothetical, but not unrealistic. All numbers are in billions of dollars. The plus and minus signs in the exhibit should be viewed as operational signs.

CURRENT ACCOUNT

1. EXPORTS OF GOODS AND SERVICES   `+340`
   a. Merchandise exports (including military sales)   +220
   b. Services   +30
   c. Income from U.S. assets abroad   +90

2. IMPORTS OF GOODS AND SERVICES   `–390`
   a. Merchandise imports (including military purchases)   –300
   b. Services   –40
   c. Income from foreign assets in U.S.   –50

Merchandise Trade Balance
Difference between value of merchandise exports (item 1a)
and value of merchandise imports (item 2a): +220 – 300 = –80

3. NET UNILATERAL TRANSFERS ABROAD   `–11`

Current Account Balance
Items 1, 2, 3: +340 – 390 – 11 = ⟶   `–61`

CAPITAL ACCOUNT   `–16`
4. OUTFLOW OF U.S. CAPITAL
5. INFLOW OF FOREIGN CAPITAL   `+60`

Capital Account Balance
Items 4 and 5: –16 + 60 = ⟶   `+44`

OFFICIAL RESERVE ACCOUNT   `–4`
6. INCREASE (–) IN U.S. OFFICIAL RESERVE ASSETS
7. INCREASE (+) IN FOREIGN OFFICIAL ASSETS IN U.S.   `+3`

Official Reserve Balance
Items 6 and 7: –4 + 3 = ⟶   `–1`

STATISTICAL DISCREPANCY   `+18`

TOTAL $0 $0
(always zero)

Balance of Payments =

Summary statistic of all ⟨⟩ items (items 1 - 7 and the statistical discrpancy)

+$340 – 390 – 11 – 16 + 60 – 4 + 3 + 18 = $0

or

Summary statistic of all ▢ items (current account balance, capital account balance, official reserve balance, and the statistical discrepancy)

–$61 + 44 – 1 + 18 = $0

Note: The pluses (+) and the minuses (–) in the exhibit serve two purposes. First, they distinguish between credits and debits. A plus is always placed before a credit, and a minus is always placed before a debit. Second, in terms of our calculations, we view the pluses and minuses as operational signs. In other words, if a number has a plus in front of it, we simply add it to our total. If a number has a minus in front of it, we simply subtract it from our total.

demand for U.S. dollars at the same time as they increase the supply of foreign currencies; thus, they are recorded as credits (+). For example, if a foreigner buys a U.S. computer, payment must ultimately be made in U.S. dollars. Thus, she is required to supply her nation's currency when she demands U.S. dollars. (We use *foreigner* in this chapter to refer to a resident of a foreign country.)

Imports of Goods and Services.   Americans import goods and services, and foreigners receive income on assets they own in the United States. These activities increase the demand for foreign currencies at the same time as they increase the supply of U.S. dollars to the **foreign exchange market**; thus, they are recorded as debits (−). For example, if an American buys a Japanese car, payment must ultimately be made in Japanese yen. Thus, he is required to supply U.S. dollars when he demands Japanese yen. Exhibit 20–1 shows that exports of goods and services totaled +$340 billion in year Z, and imports of goods and services totaled −$390 billion.[1]

If we look at the difference between the value of merchandise exports (1a in Exhibit 20–1) and the value of merchandise imports (2a in the exhibit), ignoring for now export and import services as well as income from U.S. assets abroad and income from foreign assets in the United States, we have the merchandise trade balance (or balance of trade). Specifically, the **merchandise trade balance** is the difference between the value of merchandise exports and the value of merchandise imports. In year Z, this was −$80 billion. If the value of a country's merchandise exports is less than the value of its merchandise imports, it is said to have a **merchandise trade deficit.** If the value of a country's merchandise exports is greater than the value of its merchandise imports, it is said to have a **merchandise trade surplus.** Exhibit 20–2 shows the U.S. merchandise trade balance from 1960 through 1989.

Foreign Exchange Market
The market in which currencies of different countries are exchanged.

Merchandise Trade Balance
The difference between the value of merchandise exports and the value of merchandise imports.

Merchandise Trade Deficit
The situation where the value of merchandise exports is less than the value of merchandise imports.

Merchandise Trade Surplus
The situation where the value of merchandise exports is greater than the value of merchandise imports.

Question:

In Exhibit 20–1, merchandise exports are +$220 billion (item 1a) and merchandise imports are −$300 billion (item 2a). Can't the merchandise trade balance be calculated simply by subtracting the merchandise imports from merchandise exports?

Answer:

Yes, it can be calculated by subtracting merchandise imports from merchandise exports. But we must be careful not to make the mistake of *subtracting a minus $300 billion from a positive $220 billion.* In other words, we don't say, Merchandise trade balance = $220 billion − (−$300 billion). This equals $520 billion. Instead, we simply subtract the *value of the merchandise imports,* which is $300 billion, from the value of the merchandise exports, which is $220 billion. In other words, Balance of trade = $220 billion − $300 billion. This equals −$80 billion.

In terms of calculations, the positive and minus signs in Exhibit 20–1 are operational signs. When a minus sign (−) appears in front of a number, we simply subtract that number from the total. When a positive sign (+) appears in front of a number, we add that number to the total.

---

[1]We realize that in everyday language, people do not say, "Exports were a *positive* $X billion, and imports were a *negative* $Y." Placing a plus sign (+) in front of exports and a minus sign (−) in front of imports simply reinforces the essential point that exports are credits and imports are debits. This is useful later when we calculate certain account balances.

Net Unilateral Transfers Abroad. *Unilateral transfers* are one-way money payments. They can go from Americans or the U.S. government to foreigners or to foreign governments. If an American sends money to a relative in a foreign country, or the U.S. government gives money to a foreign country as a gift or grant, or an American decides to retire in a foreign country and receives a Social Security check there, all these transactions are referred to as unilateral transfers.

Unilateral transfers can also go from foreigners or foreign governments to Americans or to the U.S. government. If a foreign citizen sends money to a relative living in the United States, this is a unilateral transfer.

If an American makes a unilateral transfer abroad, this gives rise to a demand for foreign currency and a supply of U.S. dollars; thus, it is entered as a debit item

EXHIBIT 20–2
U.S. Merchandise Trade Balance, 1960–89

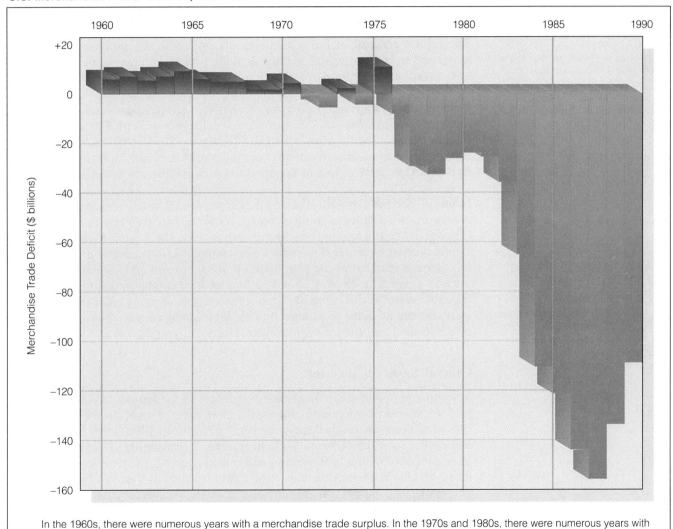

In the 1960s, there were numerous years with a merchandise trade surplus. In the 1970s and 1980s, there were numerous years with a merchandise trade deficit. The minus sign (–) in front of deficit figures signifies that merchandise exports were less than merchandise imports.

Source: Council of Economic Advisers, *Economic Report of the President, 1991* (Washington, D.C.: U.S. Government Printing Office, 1991), U.S. Commerce Department.

in the U.S. balance of payments accounts. If a foreigner makes a unilateral transfer to an American, this gives rise to a supply of foreign currency (and demand for U.S. dollars) and thus is entered as a credit item in the U.S. balance of payments accounts. For year Z, we have assumed that unilateral transfers made by Americans to foreign citizens were greater than unilateral transfers made by foreign citizens to Americans; thus, we get a negative *net* dollar amount, − $11 billion in this case. This is referred to as *net unilateral transfers abroad.*

Items 1, 2, and 3 in Exhibit 20–1—exports of goods and services, imports of goods and services, and net unilateral transfers abroad—are known as the current account. The **current account balance** is the summary statistic for these three items. In year Z, it is − $61 billion. The news media sometimes call the current account balance the *balance of payments.* To an economist, this is incorrect. As we shall soon see, the balance of payments includes several more items.

Capital Account

The **capital account** includes all payments related to the purchase and sale of assets and to borrowing and lending activities. Its major components are outflow of U.S. capital and inflow of foreign capital.

Outflow of U.S. Capital.   American purchases of foreign assets and U.S. loans to foreigners are outflows of U.S. capital. As such, they give rise to a demand for foreign currency and a supply of U.S. dollars on the foreign exchange market. Hence, they are considered a debit. For example, if an American wants to buy land in Brazil, U.S. dollars must be supplied to purchase (demand) Brazilian cruzados.

Inflow of Foreign Capital.   Foreign purchases of U.S. assets and foreign loans to Americans are inflows of foreign capital. As such, they give rise to a demand for U.S. dollars and to a supply of foreign currency on the foreign exchange market. Hence, they are considered a credit. For example, if a German buys a U.S. Treasury bill, German marks must be supplied to purchase (demand) U.S. dollars.

Items 4 and 5 in Exhibit 20–1—outflow of U.S. capital and inflow of foreign capital—comprise the capital account. The **capital account balance** is the summary statistic for these two items. It is equal to the difference between the outflow of U.S. capital and the inflow of foreign capital. In year Z, it is $44 billion.

Official Reserve Account

A government possesses official reserve balances in the form of foreign currencies, gold, its reserve position in the International Monetary Fund (discussed later), and *special drawing rights* (also discussed later). Countries with a deficit in the current and capital accounts can draw on their reserves. For example, if the United States has a combined deficit in its current and capital accounts of $5 billion, it can draw down its official reserves to meet this combined deficit. Viewing item 6, we see that the United States increased its reserve assets by $4 billion in year Z. This is a debit item since, if the United States acquires official reserves (say, through the purchase of a foreign currency), it has increased the demand for the foreign currency and supplied dollars. Thus, an increase in official reserves is like an outflow of capital in the capital account and appears as a payment with a negative sign. It follows that an increase in foreign official assets in the United States is a credit item. (Note: In recent years governments have not actively managed their reserve accounts.)

Current Account Balance
The summary statistic for exports of goods and services, imports of goods and services, and net unilateral transfers.

Capital Account
Includes all payments related to the purchase and sale of assets and to borrowing and lending activities. Components include outflow of U.S. capital and inflow of foreign capital.

Capital Account Balance
The summary statistic for the outflow of U.S. capital and the inflow of foreign capital. It is equal to the difference between the outflow of U.S. capital and the inflow of foreign capital.

Statistical Discrepancy

If someone buys a U.S. dollar with, say, Swiss francs, someone must sell a U.S. dollar. Thus, *dollars purchased = dollars sold.* In all the transactions discussed earlier—exporting goods, importing goods, sending money to relatives in foreign countries, buying land in foreign countries—dollars were bought and sold. The total number of dollars sold must always equal the total number of dollars purchased. However, balance of payments accountants do not have complete information; they can only record credits and debits that they observe. This means there may be more debits or credits than those observed in a given year. Suppose, in year Z, *all* debits are observed and recorded, but *not all* credits are observed and recorded—perhaps because of smuggling activities, secret bank accounts, people living in more than one country, and so on. To adjust for this, balance of payments accountants make use of the *statistical discrepancy,* which is that part of the balance of payments that adjusts for missing information. In Exhibit 20–1, the statistical discrepancy is +$18 billion. This means that $18 billion worth of credits (+) went unobserved in year Z. There may have been some hidden exports and unrecorded capital inflows that year.

What the Balance of Payments Equals

The balance of payments is the summary statistic for the following: exports of goods and services (item 1), imports of goods and services (item 2), net unilateral transfers abroad (item 3), the outflow of U.S. capital (item 4), the inflow of foreign capital (item 5), the increase in U.S. official reserve assets (item 6), the increase in foreign official assets in the United States (item 7), and the statistical discrepancy. Calculating the balance of payments, we have (in billions of dollars) $+340 - 390 - 11 - 16 + 60 - 4 + 3 + 18 = 0$.

Alternatively, the balance of payments is the summary statistic for the following: the current account balance, capital account balance, official reserve balance, and statistical discrepancy. Calculating the balance of payments we have (in billions of dollars) $-61 + 44 - 1 + 18 = 0$. The balance of payments for the United States in year Z equals *zero.* The fact is, the balance of payments *always* equals zero.

Question:

Why does the balance of payments always equal zero?

Answer:

The reason the balance of payments always equals zero is that the three accounts that comprise the balance of payments, when taken together, plus the statistical discrepancy, include all of the *sources* and all of the *uses* of dollars in international transactions. And since every dollar used must have a source, adding the sources (+) to the uses (−) necessarily gives us zero.

FLEXIBLE EXCHANGE RATES
■

If a U.S. buyer wants to purchase a good from a U.S. seller, the buyer simply turns over to the seller the required number of U.S. dollars. If, however, a U.S. buyer wants to purchase a good from a seller in France, it is a slightly different matter.

The American demand for British goods leads to a demand for British pounds and to a supply of U.S. dollars on the foreign exchange market.

Exchange rate
The price of one currency in terms of another currency; for example, 1 dollar = 2 marks.

Flexible Exchange Rate System
The system whereby exchange rates are determined by the forces of supply and demand for a currency.

First, the U.S. buyer must exchange her U.S. dollars for French francs, and then with the French francs she buys the good from the French seller. The market in which currencies of different countries are exchanged, as we mentioned earlier, is the foreign exchange market.

In the foreign exchange market, currencies are bought and sold for a price; **exchange rate** exists. For instance, it might take $1.50 to buy a British pound, 17 cents to buy a French franc, 58 cents to buy a German mark, or seven-tenths of 1 cent to buy a Japanese yen. In this section, we discuss how exchange rates are determined in the foreign exchange market when the forces of supply and demand are allowed to rule. Economists refer to this as a **flexible exchange rate system.** In the next section, we discuss how exchange rates are determined under a fixed exchange rate system.

The Demand and Supply of Currencies

To simplify our analysis, we assume that there are only two countries in the world, the United States and Great Britain. This, then, means there are only two currencies in the world, the dollar ($) and the pound (£). In this two-country–two-currency world, what constitutes the demand for dollars or the supply of dollars on the foreign exchange market? What constitutes the demand for pounds or the supply of pounds?

Odd as it may appear at first sight, the demand for dollars and the supply of pounds are linked, as are the demand for pounds and the supply of dollars. Suppose an American wants to buy a British Rolls Royce. Before he can purchase the Rolls Royce, the American must buy British pounds—hence, British pounds are demanded. But the American buys British pounds with dollars; that is, he supplies dollars to the foreign exchange market in order to demand British pounds. We conclude that the American demand for British goods leads to a demand for British pounds and to a supply of U.S. dollars on the foreign exchange market.

The story is similar if a British buyer wants to buy an American Cadillac. Before she can purchase the Cadillac, the British buyer must buy dollars—hence, U.S. dollars are demanded. The British buyer buys the dollars with pounds. We conclude that the British demand for American goods leads to a demand for U.S. dollars and to a supply of British pounds on the foreign exchange market. This process is illustrated in Exhibit 20–3.

In (a), we see the market for British pounds. (Exhibit 20–3b shows the market for U.S. dollars, which mirrors what is happening in the market for British pounds.) On the horizontal axis is the "quantity of pounds," and on the vertical axis, the exchange rate—the dollar price per pound. Notice that the demand curve for British pounds is downward sloping, indicating that as the dollar price per pound increases, Americans buy fewer pounds, and as the dollar price per pound decreases, Americans buy more pounds. For example, if it takes $1.90 to buy one pound, Americans will buy fewer pounds than they would if it takes $1.50 to buy one pound. Simply put, the higher the dollar price per pound, the more expensive British goods are for Americans and the fewer British goods Americans will buy; thus, a smaller quantity demanded of pounds.

The supply of pounds is upward sloping. It is easy to understand why if we recall that the supply of British pounds is linked to the British demand for American goods and U.S. dollars. Consider a $1.90 price for a pound compared with a price of $1.50 a pound. At $1.50 = £1, a British buyer gives up one pound for which he receives $1.50 in return. But at $1.90 = £1, a British buyer gives up one pound and receives $1.90 in return. At which exchange rate are American goods *cheaper* for the British? The answer is at the exchange rate of $1.90 = £1.

Here is an illustration. Think of an American computer with a price tag of $1,000. At an exchange rate of $1.90 = £1, the British will have to pay approximately £526 to buy the American computer ($1,000/$1.90 = £526). But at an exchange rate of $1.50 = £1, the British will have to pay approximately £667 pounds ($1,000/$1.50 = £667). To the British, the American computer is cheaper at the exchange rate of $1.90 per pound than at $1.50 per pound. It follows, then, that the higher the dollar price per pound, the greater the quantity demanded of dollars by the British (because American goods will be cheaper), and therefore the greater the quantity supplied of pounds to the foreign exchange market. The upward-sloping supply curve for pounds illustrates this.[2]

The British demand for American goods leads to a demand for U.S. dollars and to a supply of British pounds on the foreign exchange market.

THINKING LIKE AN ECONOMIST

We learned that the demand for dollars is linked to the supply of pounds and that the demand for pounds is linked to the supply of dollars. Economists often think in terms of one activity being linked to another because economics, after all, is about exchange. In an exchange, one gives (supply) and gets (demand): John "supplies" $25 in order to demand the new book from the shopkeeper; the shopkeeper supplies the new book in order that he may "demand" the $25. In such a transaction, we usually diagrammatically represent the demand for, and supply of, the new book—but we could also dia-

[2]Actually, the supply curve here is upward sloping because we have assumed that the British demand for American goods is price elastic. This assumption will hold for most of this chapter. We bring price elasticity of demand into the discussion explicitly when we discuss the J-curve later in the chapter.

EXHIBIT 20–3
Translating U.S. Demand for Pounds into U.S. Supply of Dollars and British Demand for Dollars into British Supply of Pounds

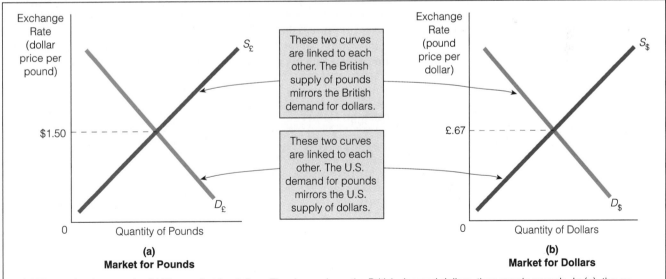

(a) The market for pounds. (b) The market for dollars. The demand for pounds in (a) is linked to the supply of dollars in (b): When Americans demand pounds, they supply dollars. The supply of pounds in (a) is linked to the demand for dollars in (b): When the British demand dollars, they supply pounds. In (a), the exchange rate is $1.50 = £1, which is equal to £.67 = $1 in (b). Exchange rates are the reciprocals of each other.

grammatically represent the demand for, and supply of, money. Of course, in international exchange, where monies are bought and sold *before* goods are bought and sold, this is exactly what we do.

The Equilibrium Exchange Rate

In a completely flexible exchange rate system, where the forces of supply and demand are allowed to rule, the equilibrium exchange rate (dollar price per pound) will be \$1.50 = £1 in Exhibit 20–4. At this dollar price per pound, the quantity demanded of pounds equals the quantity supplied of pounds. There are no shortages or surpluses of pounds. At any other exchange rate, however, either an excess demand for pounds or an excess supply of pounds exists.

Let's look at the exchange rate of \$1.90 = £1. At this exchange rate, a surplus of pounds exists. As a result, downward pressure will be placed on the dollar price of a pound (just as downward pressure would be placed on the dollar price of an apple if there were a surplus of apples). If, however, the exchange rate were \$1.10 = £1, there would be a shortage of pounds, and upward pressure would be placed on the dollar price of a pound.

It is also important to note that exchange rates are reciprocals of each other. To take a simple example, if 1 pound = 2 dollars, then 1 dollar = ½ pound.

Question:

Are the demand and supply curves in Exhibit 20–4 related in any way to the U.S. balance of payments in Exhibit 20–1?

Answer:

Yes, they are. For example, U.S. exports represent a demand for U.S. dollars by foreigners (and therefore constitute the supply of foreign currencies), while U.S. imports represent the U.S. demand for foreign currencies (and therefore constitute the supply of U.S. dollars). In fact, any dollar amount with a plus sign (+) in front of it in Exhibit 20–1 represents a demand for U.S. dollars and a supply of foreign currencies, and any dollar amount with a minus sign (−) in front of it represents a demand for foreign currencies and a supply of dollars.

EXHIBIT 20–4
The Foreign Exchange Market

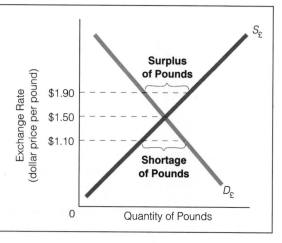

The demand for pounds is downward sloping: The higher the dollar price for pounds, the fewer pounds will be demanded; the lower the dollar price of pounds, the more pounds will be demanded. At \$1.90 = £1, there is a surplus of pounds, placing downward pressure on the exchange rate. At \$1.10 = £1, there is a shortage of pounds, placing upward pressure on the exchange rate. At the equilibrium exchange rate, \$1.50 = £1, the quantity demanded of pounds equals the quantity supplied of pounds.

Changes in the Equilibrium Exchange Rate

In Chapter 3, we learned that a change in the demand for a good, or the supply of a good, or both would change the equilibrium price of the good. The same holds true for the price of currencies. A change in the demand for pounds, or the supply of pounds, or both will change the equilibrium dollar price per pound. If the dollar price per pound rises—say, from $1.50 = £1 to $1.80 = £1—the pound is said to have **appreciated** and the dollar to have **depreciated.**

A currency has appreciated in value if it takes more of a foreign currency to buy it. A currency has depreciated in value if it takes more of it to buy a foreign currency. For example, a movement in the exchange rate from $1.50 = £1 to $1.80 = £1 means that more dollars are necessary to buy one pound, so the pound has appreciated (the other side of the coin is that fewer pounds are necessary to buy one dollar). And since more dollars are necessary to buy one pound, the dollar has depreciated.

If the equilibrium exchange rate can change owing to a change in the demand for, and supply of, a currency, then it is important to understand what factors can change the demand for, and supply of, a currency. Three are presented here.

A Difference in Income Growth Rates. An increase in a nation's income will usually cause the nation's residents to buy more of both domestic and foreign goods. The increased demand for imports will result in an increased demand for foreign exchange.

Suppose U.S. residents experience an increase in income, but British residents do not. As a result, the demand curve for pounds shifts rightward, as illustrated in Exhibit 20–5. This causes the equilibrium exchange rate to rise from $1.50 = £1 to $1.80 = £1. *Ceteris paribus,* if one nation's income grows, and another's lags behind, the currency of the higher-growth-rate country *depreciates,* and the currency of the lower-growth-rate country *appreciates.* To many persons this is paradoxical; nevertheless, it is true.

Differences in Relative Inflation Rates. Suppose the U.S. price level rises 25 percent at a time when Great Britain experiences stable prices. An increase in the U.S. price level will make British goods relatively less expensive for Americans

Appreciation
An increase in the value of one currency relative to other currencies.

Depreciation
A decrease in the value of one currency relative to other currencies.

EXHIBIT 20–5
The Growth Rate of Income and the Exchange Rate

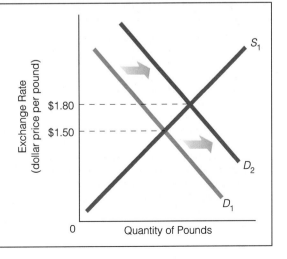

If U.S. residents experience a growth in income, but British residents do not, U.S. demand for British goods will increase, and with it, the demand for pounds. As a result, the dollar exchange rate will change; the dollar price of pounds will rise. The dollar depreciates, the pound appreciates.

and American goods relatively more expensive for the British. As a result, the American demand for British goods will increase, and the British demand for American goods will decrease.

How will this affect the demand for, and supply of, British pounds in Exhibit 20–6? The demand for British pounds will increase (British goods are relatively cheaper than they were before the U.S. price level rose), and the supply of British pounds will decrease (since American goods are relatively more expensive, the British buy fewer American goods; thus, they demand fewer U.S. dollars and supply fewer British pounds).

As Exhibit 20–6 shows, the result of an increase in the demand for British pounds and a decrease in the supply of British pounds is an appreciation in the pound and a depreciation in the dollar. It now takes more dollars and cents to buy one pound than it did before the U.S. price level increased 25 percent.

An important question is, How much will the U.S. dollar depreciate as a result of the rise in the U.S. price level vis-à-vis the British price level? (Recall that there is no change in the British price level.) The **purchasing power parity (PPP) theory** predicts that the U.S. dollar will depreciate by 25 percent.[3] This requires the dollar price of a pound to rise to $1.88 (since $1.88 − $1.50 = 38 cents, and 38 cents is approximately 25 percent of $1.50). A 25 percent depreciation in the dollar restores the original relative prices of American goods to British customers.

Consider a U.S. car with a price tag of $10,000. If the exchange rate is $1.50 = £1, a British buyer of the car will pay approximately £6,667. If the car price in-

Purchasing Power Parity (PPP) Theory
States that exchange rates between any two currencies will adjust to reflect changes in the relative price levels of the two countries.

---

[3]The PPP theory is sometimes referred to as the "inflation theory of exchange rates."

EXHIBIT 20–6
Inflation, Exchange Rates, and Purchasing Power Parity (PPP)

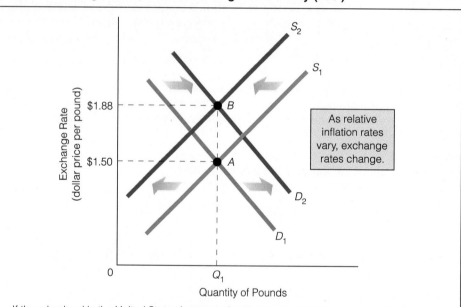

If the price level in the United States increases by 25 percent while the price level in Great Britain remains constant, the U.S. demand for British goods (and therefore pounds) will increase, and the supply of pounds will decrease. As a result, the exchange rate will change; the dollar price of pounds will rise. The dollar depreciates, and the pound appreciates. PPP theory predicts that the dollar will depreciate in the foreign exchange market until the original price (in pounds) of American goods to British customers is restored. In this example, this requires the dollar to depreciate 25 percent.

creases by 25 percent to $12,500, and the dollar depreciates 25 percent (to $1.88 = £1), the British buyer of the car will still only have to pay approximately £6,667 pounds.

In short, the purchasing power parity theory predicts that changes in the relative price levels of two countries will affect the exchange rate in such a way that one unit of a nation's currency will continue to buy the same amount of foreign goods as it did before the change in the relative price levels. In our example, because the higher U.S. inflation rate causes a change in the equilibrium exchange rate and leads to a depreciated dollar, one pound continues to have the same purchasing power it previously did.

On some occasions, the PPP theory of exchange rates has predicted accurately, whereas on others it has not. For the period 1973–86, it accurately predicted the exchange rate between the U.S. dollar and the Canadian dollar. It did not accurately predict the exchange rate between the U.S. dollar and the Japanese yen for the period 1973–79. In the period 1972–86, the theory accurately predicted the *trend* of the exchange rate between the U.S. dollar and British pound, but still the *actual exchange rate* between the two currencies diverged widely at times from the predicted exchange rate.

Many economists suggest that the theory does not always predict accurately because the demand for, and supply of, a currency are affected by more than the difference in inflation rates between countries. We have already noted that different income growth rates affect the demand for a currency and therefore the exchange rate. Shortly, we shall discuss other factors that affect the exchange rate. In the *long run,* however, and in particular when there is a *large difference* in inflation rates across countries, the PPP theory does predict exchange rates accurately.

Changes in Real Interest Rates. As was evident from the U.S. balance of payments, illustrated in Exhibit 20-1, more than goods flow between countries. There is financial capital, too, the flow of which is dependent on different countries' **real interest rates**—interest rates adjusted for inflation. Suppose we start at a position where the real interest rate is 3 percent in both the United States and in Great Britain. Then the real interest rate in the United States increases to 4.5 percent. What will happen? The British will increase the demand for dollars, and therefore supply more pounds to purchase financial assets in the United States that pay a higher real interest rate than financial assets in Great Britain. As the supply of pounds increases on the foreign exchange market, the exchange rate (dollar price per pound) will change; fewer dollars will be needed to buy pounds. In short, the dollar will appreciate and the pound will depreciate.

Real Interest Rate
The inflation-adjusted interest rate.

Combined Current and Capital Account Balances with Flexible Exchange Rates

In the following discussion, the current and capital accounts are lumped together into one account: the combined current and capital account.

Once again, consider the exchange rate of $1.90 = £1 in Exhibit 20-4. As we noted, at this exchange rate there is a surplus of pounds; more pounds are supplied than are demanded. But what does this mean in terms of the flow of goods, services, and funds between the two countries? Simply put, since the British are supplying more pounds than Americans are demanding, it implies that the British are demanding more dollars (since the demand for dollars is a reflection of the supply of pounds) than Americans are demanding pounds.

How does this affect the U.S. combined current and capital account and Great Britain's combined current and capital account? In the United States, the effect is that the sum total of the numbers that have a plus (+) in front of them in this combined account is greater than the sum total of the numbers that have a minus (−) in front of them.[4] In Great Britain, the effect is that the sum total of numbers that have a minus (−) in front of them in this combined account is greater than the sum total of the numbers that have a plus (+) in front of them.[5] This is a roundabout way of saying that at the exchange rate $1.90 = £1, there is a surplus in the U.S. combined current and capital account (pluses outweigh minuses) and a deficit in the British combined capital and current account (minuses outweigh pluses).

This is a temporary state of affairs, though, because the combined current and capital account deficit in Great Britain and the corresponding surplus in the United States are both the result of the above-equilibrium exchange rate, which is temporary. As soon as the exchange rate reaches its equilibrium level, the quantity demanded and supplied of pounds will be equal, as well as the quantity demanded and supplied of dollars (if the pound market is in equilibrium, so is the dollar market). In short, both the U.S. and British combined current and capital account will be balanced.[6]

FIXED EXCHANGE RATES
■

Fixed Exchange Rate System
The system where a nation's currency is set at a fixed rate relative to all other currencies, and central banks intervene in the foreign exchange market to maintain the fixed rate.

The major alternative to the flexible exchange rate system is the **fixed exchange rate system.** This system works the way it sounds: Exchange rates are fixed or pegged, they are not allowed to fluctuate freely in response to the forces of supply and demand. The workings of the fixed exchange rate system are described in the next sections.

Fixed Exchange Rates and the Central Bank (the Fed)

Once again, we deal with a two-country–two-currency world. Suppose this time the United States and Great Britain agree to fix or peg their currencies; that is, instead of letting the dollar depreciate or appreciate relative to the pound, the two countries agree to set the price of one pound at $1.90. They agree to the exchange rate $1.90 = £1. Generally, we call this the fixed exchange rate or the *official price*

---

[4]Recall that a plus (+) indicates a credit for the United States; it represents the demand for U.S. dollars. A minus (−), on the other hand, represents a debit for the United States; it represents the supply of dollars to the foreign exchange market, or the demand for a foreign currency. Since we have already said that the demand for dollars is greater than the demand for pounds, it follows that in the U.S. combined current and capital account, the sum total of the numbers that have a plus before them must be greater than the sum total of numbers that have a minus before them.

[5]In the British balance of payments a plus (+) represents a credit or the demand for pounds. A minus (−) represents a debit or the demand for foreign currency, which is the same as the supply of pounds. Once again, since we have already noted that the demand for dollars is greater than the demand for pounds, it follows that in the British combined capital and current account, the sum total of the numbers that have a minus in front of them is greater than the sum total of numbers that have a plus in front of them.

[6]This assumes there is no government intervention in the foreign exchange market.

of a pound.[7] Since we deal with more than one official price in our discussion, we refer to $1.90 = £1 as *official price 1* (Exhibit 20–7).

If the dollar price of pounds is above its equilibrium level (which is the case at official price 1), the pound is said to be **overvalued.** It follows that if the pound is overvalued, the dollar is **undervalued.** Similarly, if the dollar price of pounds is below its equilibrium level (which is the case at official price 2 in Exhibit 20–7), the pound is undervalued. It follows that if the pound is undervalued, the dollar must be overvalued.

Notice that at the fixed exchange rate, or official price 1, a surplus of pounds exists. As we previously pointed out, this means the quantity supplied of pounds is greater than the quantity demanded of pounds. Great Britain's combined current and capital account is in deficit.

But what about the U.S. combined current and capital account? Is it in deficit or surplus? Since the quantity supplied of pounds is greater than the quantity

Overvaluation
A currency is overvalued if its price in terms of other currencies is above the equilibrium price.

Undervaluation
A currency is undervalued if its price in terms of other currencies is below the equilibrium price.

---

[7]If the price of one pound is $1.90, it follows that the price of one dollar is approximately 52 pence. Thus, setting the official price of a pound in terms of dollars and cents automatically sets the official price of a dollar in terms of pounds and pence.

EXHIBIT 20–7
A Fixed Exchange Rate System

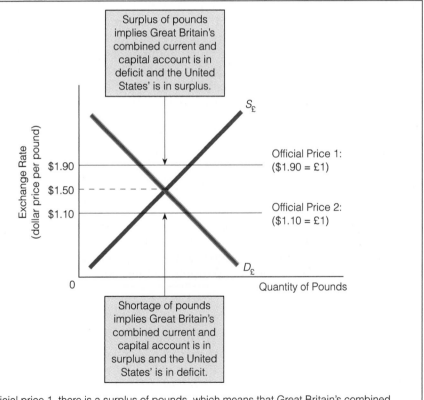

At official price 1, there is a surplus of pounds, which means that Great Britain's combined current and capital account is in deficit and the U.S. combined current and capital account is in surplus. To maintain the official price, the U.S. central bank, the Fed, could buy pounds. At official price 2, there is a shortage of pounds, which means Great Britain's combined current and capital account is in surplus and the U.S. combined current and capital account is in deficit. To maintain the official price, the Fed could sell pounds.

demanded of pounds, it follows that the quantity demanded of dollars is greater than the quantity supplied of dollars. (For a review of the link between the pound market and the dollar market, see Exhibit 20–3.)

If the United States and Great Britain were operating under a flexible exchange rate system, the exchange rate would soon fall to $1.50 = £1, and the disequilibrium condition in each nation's combined current and capital account would disappear. But the two nations are operating under a fixed exchange rate system. So what happens now?

To maintain the fixed exchange rate, the U.S. central bank, the Federal Reserve System (the Fed), could buy the surplus of pounds. This would show up in the official reserve account of the U.S. balance of payments as an increase in U.S. official reserve assets (see item 6 in Exhibit 20–1).

Alternatively, instead of the Fed buying pounds (to mop up the excess supply of pounds), the Bank of England could sell dollars (to eliminate the shortage of dollars, which is the other side of the coin of a surplus of pounds). Finally, there could be some combination of the two actions.

Suppose now that the exchange rate had been fixed at $1.10 = £1. This is *official price 2* in Exhibit 20–7. At this exchange rate, there is a shortage of pounds; the quantity demanded of pounds is greater than the quantity supplied. This implies a surplus in Great Britain's combined current and capital account and a consequent deficit in the U.S. combined current and capital account.

What happens? If the exchange rate is to be maintained, the Fed must now sell pounds to eliminate the shortage of pounds (alternatively, the Bank of England could buy dollars, or there could be some combination of the two actions). The United States will have to draw down the holdings of pounds that it might have acquired when the dollar price per pound was above the equilibrium level. Once again, this action will be recorded in the official reserve account of the U.S. balance of payments.

Question:

Why does the central bank, or the Fed, play a much larger role under a fixed exchange rate system than under a flexible exchange rate system?

Answer:

To support or maintain a fixed exchange rate, someone or something has to do the supporting or the maintaining. Central banks play this role. Under a flexible exchange rate system, there is no exchange rate to support or maintain; exchange rates simply respond to the forces of supply and demand.

Follow-up Question:

Suppose Great Britain and the United States agree to a fixed exchange rate, say, $1.90 = £1, and that at this exchange rate the U.S. combined current and capital account is in surplus and Great Britain's combined current and capital account is in deficit. Furthermore, suppose this condition continues indefinitely. Does the United States continue buying pounds indefinitely?

Answer:

A persistent deficit or surplus in a nation's combined current and capital account is usually dealt with in a way other than the nation continuing indefinitely to buy or sell the other nation's currency. We discuss this in the next section.

Options under a Fixed Exchange Rate System

A nation that persistently has a deficit or a surplus in its combined current and capital account has several options under a fixed exchange rate system. These include devaluation and revaluation, protectionist trade policies, and changes in macroeconomic policies.

Devaluation and revaluation. Suppose the United States and Great Britain have agreed to fix or peg the exchange rate at $1.90 = £1, which results in a *persistent* surplus in the U.S. combined current and capital account and a *persistent* deficit in Great Britain's combined current and capital account. At some point, the U.S. authorities tire of supporting the exchange rate by buying pounds, and/or the British authorities tire of supporting the exchange rate by selling dollars. The countries agree to reset the official price of the pound and the dollar. Suppose they reset it at its equilibrium level of $1.50 = £1. Afterward, economists say there has been a devaluation of the pound and a revaluation of the dollar. A **devaluation** occurs when the official price of a currency is lowered. A **revaluation** occurs when the official price of a currency is raised. If the official price of a pound is moved from $1.90 = £1 (or $1 = 52 pence) to $1.50 = £1 ($1 = 67 pence), it now takes fewer dollars and cents to buy a pound—so the pound has been devalued. It also takes more pence to buy a dollar—so the dollar has been revalued. The devaluation of the pound and revaluation of the dollar have the effect of eliminating the persistent disequilibrium situations in the two nation's combined current and capital accounts—at least for now.

> **Devaluation**
> An official governmental act that changes the exchange rate by lowering the official price of a currency.
>
> **Revaluation**
> An official governmental act that changes the exchange rate by raising the official price of a currency.

The situation could arise where one nation would want to reset the official price of the currencies and another nation would not. Suppose the United States is experiencing a surplus in its merchandise trade balance (exports of goods > imports of goods) at the official price of $1.90 = £1 and doesn't want to give this up. It may be that U.S. export businesses are lobbying U.S. authorities not to revalue the dollar. In short, U.S. export interests feel they are benefiting from the undervalued dollar (and overvalued pound) and want to keep things this way.

Protectionist trade policy (quotas and tariffs). A nation that has a merchandise trade deficit can erect quotas and tariffs to stem the tide of imports into the country. We saw in our last chapter how both tariffs and quotas meet this objective. Economists are quick to point out that merchandise trade problems are sometimes used as an excuse to promote trade restrictions—many of which simply benefit special interests.

Changes in monetary policy. Sometimes monetary policy can be used by a nation to support the exchange rate or the official price of its currency. Suppose the United States is continually running a merchandise trade deficit; year after year, imports are outstripping exports. To remedy this, the United States might enact a tight monetary policy to retard inflation and drive up interest rates (at least in the short run). The tight monetary policy will reduce the U.S. rate of inflation and thereby lower U.S. prices relative to prices in other nations. This will make U.S. goods relatively cheaper than they were before (assuming other nations didn't also enact a tight monetary policy) and promote U.S. exports and discourage foreign imports, as well as generate a flow of investment funds into the United States in search of higher real interest rates.

Some economists argue against fixed exchange rates because they think it unwise for a nation to adopt a particular monetary policy simply to maintain an international exchange rate. Instead, they believe domestic monetary policies should be used to meet domestic economic goals—such as price stability, low unemployment, low and stable interest rates, and so forth. This naturally leads us into a discussion of the case for and against fixed exchange rates for promoting international trade.

Promoting International Trade

Which are better, fixed or flexible exchange rates? Following is the case for each.

The Case for Fixed Exchange Rates. Proponents of a fixed exchange rate system often argue that fixed exchange rates promote international trade, whereas flexible exchange rates stifle it. A major advantage of fixed exchange rates is certainty: Individuals in different countries know from day to day what their nation's currency will trade for. With flexible exchange rates, individuals will not be as likely to enter into international trade because of the added risk of not knowing from one day to the next how many dollars or francs or pounds they will have to give up to get, say, 100 yen. Certainty is a necessary ingredient in international trade; flexible exchange rates promote uncertainty, which hampers international trade. Economist Charles Kindleberger, a proponent of fixed exchange rates, believes that having fixed exchange rates is analogous to having one currency in the entire United States instead of having one currency for each of 50 states: One currency in the United States promotes trade and 50 different currencies would hamper it. In Kindleberger's view:

> The main case against flexible exchange rates is that they break up the world market. . . . Imagine trying to conduct interstate trade in the USA if there were fifty different state monies, none of which was dominant. This is akin to barter, the inefficiency of which is explained time and again by textbooks.[8]

The Case for Flexible Exchange Rates. Advocates of flexible exchange rates, as we have noted, maintain that it is better for a nation to adopt the policies it wants to meet domestic economic goals than to sacrifice domestic economic goals to maintain an exchange rate. They also state that there is too great a chance that the fixed exchange rate will diverge greatly from the equilibrium exchange rate, creating persistent balance of trade problems. This leads deficit nations to impose trade restrictions (tariffs and quotas) that hinder international trade.

The Value of the Dollar and American Real Estate

When the dollar depreciates relative to the Japanese yen, dollar-denominated assets become cheaper for the Japanese to buy. During the last 20 years or so, the Japanese have begun to buy American hotels, businesses, land, apartment buildings, and so on. Some Americans have complained that the Japanese are buying out Americans and taking over the United States. A debate over the seriousness of the issue ensued.

Some people said the following:

1. Foreign investment in the United States unfairly drives up real estate prices for the American buyer. The idea here is that when the Japanese bid for real estate along with Americans, the price of real estate rises. Americans end up paying more

[8]Charles Kindleberger, *International Money* (London: Allen and Unwin, 1981), p. 174.

The Future Sometimes Looks Brighter with Futures: Or How to Lock in the Price of the Yen without Really Trying

Meet (the fictional) Bill Whatley, the owner of a Toyota dealership in San Diego. It is currently May, and Bill is thinking about buying a shipment of Toyotas in August. He knows that he must buy the Toyotas from Japan with yen, but he has a problem. At the present time, in May, the dollar price of yen is $.005. Bill wonders what will happen if the dollar price of yen rises in August when he plans to make his purchase. Suppose the dollar price of yen rises to $.006. If this happens, then instead of paying $15,000 for a Toyota priced at 3 million yen, he would have to pay $18,000.* This $3,000 difference may be enough to wipe out any profit on the sale of Toyotas.

*If a yen equals $.005, then a Toyota with a price tag of 3 million yen actually costs $15,000 ($.005 × 3,000,000 = $15,000). If a yen equals $.006, then a Toyota with a price tag of 3 million yen actually costs $18,000 (.006 × 3,000,000 = $18,000).

What is Bill to do? He could purchase a *futures contract* today for the needed quantity of yen in August. A futures contract is a contract in which the seller agrees to provide a particular good (in our example, a particular currency) to the buyer on a specified future date at an agreed-on price. In short, Bill can buy yen today at a specified dollar price and take delivery of the yen at a later date (in August).

But suppose the dollar price of yen falls to $.004 in August? If this happens, Bill would only have to pay $12,000 (instead of $15,000) for a Toyota priced at 3 million yen. Although this is true, Bill, like other car dealers, might not be interested in assuming the risk associated with changes in exchange rates. He may prefer to lock in a sure thing.

Who would sell yen to Bill? The answer is someone who is willing to assume the risk of changes in the value of currencies that Bill obviously is not—for example, Julie Jackson. Ju-

lie thinks to herself, "I think the dollar price of yen will go down between now and August. Therefore, I will enter into a contract with Bill stating that I will hand over to him 3 million yen in August for $15,000—the exchange rate specified in the contract being 1 yen = $.005. If I am right, and the *actual* exchange rate at the time is 1 yen = $.004, then I can purchase the 3 million yen for $12,000, and turn around and fulfill my contract with Bill by turning the yen over to him for $15,000. I walk away with $3,000 profit."

Many economists argue that futures contracts offer people a way of dealing with the risk associated with a flexible exchange rate system. If a person doesn't know what next month's exchange rate will be, and doesn't want to take the risk of waiting to see, then he or she can enter into a futures contract and effectively shift the risk to someone who voluntarily assumes it.

to buy real estate than if the demand was less. This is true enough; but the argument ignores the benefits to the sellers (perhaps American?) of American real estate. They benefit from the increased demand for real estate—whether it comes from other Americans, the Japanese, or someone else.

2. Foreign investment will result in foreign control of American businesses. The argument here is that if the Japanese, or other foreigners, buy American businesses, there will be a fundamental change in the nature of these businesses and ultimately Americans will be hurt. Looking at the opposite side of the coin, one may question whether foreigners will run American businesses differently from the way Americans run American businesses. Presumably, the Japanese buy American businesses to earn profits, which is the same reason Americans buy American businesses. The desire to earn profits limits one's behavior in a certain way, so that there will be little difference (if any) between a business in the United States owned by a foreigner and the same business owned by an American.

What Does the International Value of the Dollar Have to Do with Life on the Farm?

Peter Sutton, 36, is a farmer. His father is a farmer, as were his grandfather and great-grandfather. Peter hopes that his son, Ryan, will one day grow up to be a farmer.

In 1978, Peter bought a wheat farm in Kansas. At the time, farmland was selling at a premium, so Peter had to agree to meet stiff mortgage payments. Still, times were prosperous, and Peter could make the payments. He and his wife were working hard, but it was good, honest work, and they both enjoyed it.

In the meantime, the nation's elected representatives in Washington were discussing tax and spending cuts. In the end, however, not many of the spending cuts were passed, but the tax cuts were. The editor of the newspaper in the town near Peter's farm wrote a few editorials on expansionary fiscal policy. (She was proud that she had minored in economics in college.)

In late 1980s, Peter began to notice news stories about the increasingly strong dollar (that is, appreciating dollar). He didn't think much about it at first. But then in 1982, the dollar appreciated more, and in 1983, it appreciated even more, and so on into 1984 and 1985. In 1983, Peter's profits began to decline. The appreciated dollar made it more difficult for him to sell his wheat abroad. Also, as the German mark went from 2 to 3 marks per dollar, a bushel of wheat that sold for 12 marks in Germany earned only $4 instead of $6 for the American farmer who produced the wheat. Peter began to feel the pinch. Less income was coming in, but he still had his mortgage payments to meet. He fell six months behind and the bank threatened to foreclose on his farm.

Peter tried to work harder; he sold one of his cars and even sold some of his furniture, but each month he fell farther behind in his mortgage payments. Finally, in mid-1984, Peter lost his farm.

Many of Peter's farmer neighbors were in the same predicament. Some of them argued that the Congress should impose protectionist measures in order to decrease imports. The major television networks broadcast special features on the economic problems of farmers and their discontent with the government's policies.

Last week, Peter was visiting his brother in Oregon. His nephew, Jack, was home from college where he is a freshman. Jack, who is studious, was telling his Uncle Peter about what he had recently learned in his economics course. He also complained mildly that economics is too theoretical and doesn't relate to the real world. Unaware of his uncle's experiences, Jack mentioned the exchange rate value of the dollar as an example of economics that didn't really affect ordinary people.

Uncle Peter had a few things to say on the subject.

The Gold Standard

Once nations have decided to adopt the gold standard, they automatically fix their exchange rates. Suppose the United States defines a dollar as equal to $1/20$ of an ounce of gold and Great Britain defines a pound as equal to $1/5$ of an ounce of gold. This means that one ounce of gold could be bought with either $20 or £5. What, then, is the exchange rate between dollars and pounds? It is 4 dollars = 1 pound, or 1 dollar = $1/4$ pound. This is the *fixed* exchange rate between dollars and pounds.

To have an international gold standard, countries must do the following: (1) Define their currencies in terms of gold (for example, $1 = $1/20$ oz. of gold, £1 = $1/5$ oz. of gold, and so on). (2) Stand ready and willing to convert gold into paper money and paper money into gold at the rate specified (for example, the United States would buy and sell gold at $20 an ounce). (3) Link their money supplies to their holdings of gold. With this in mind, consider how a gold standard would work.

Let's again look at the two countries Great Britain and the United States, and assume that the exchange rate 1 dollar = $1/4$ pound is the equilibrium exchange rate. Then, a change occurs: Inflation raises British prices by 100 percent. A British tea set that was priced at £20 before the inflation is now priced as £40. At the fixed exchange rate, Americans find that they now have to give up $160 to buy the tea set, whereas before the British inflation they only had to give up $80. Consequently, Americans buy fewer tea sets; Americans import less.

At the same time, however, the British import more. The reason is that American prices are now relatively lower than before the British inflation. Suppose an American pair of shoes was $80 before the inflation. In relative terms, the cost was 1 British tea set, since the tea set cost £20 before the inflation and 1 dollar = ¼ pound. After the inflation, the American shoes are still $80 but the tea set is £40. This means the relative cost of American shoes has gone down to ½ British tea set (since 1 dollar = ¼ pound). To the British, the inflation in their country has made American goods relatively cheaper. The British end up buying more American goods; they import more.

We see, then, that the British inflation has decreased American imports and increased American exports; at the same time, it has decreased British exports and increased British imports. The U.S. merchandise trade balance moves into surplus; the British trade balance moves into deficit.

The British have to pay for the difference between their imports and exports with gold. Gold is therefore shipped to the United States. An increase in the supply of gold in the United States expands the U.S. money supply. A decrease in the supply of gold in Great Britain contracts the British money supply. Prices are affected in both countries. In the United States, prices begin to rise; in Great Britain, prices begin to fall. As U.S. prices go up and British prices go down, the earlier situation begins to reverse itself. American goods look more expensive to the British, and they begin to buy less, whereas British goods look cheaper to Americans, and they begin to buy more. Consequently, American imports begin to rise and exports begin to fall; British imports begin to fall and exports begin to rise. The gold standard, through changing domestic money supplies and price levels, begins to correct the initial trade balance disequilibrium.

The change in the money supply that the gold standard sometimes requires has prompted some economists to voice the same argument against the gold standard that is often heard against the fixed exchange rate system; that is, it subjects domestic monetary policy to international instead of domestic considerations. In fact, many economists cite this as part of the reason many nations abandoned the gold standard in the 1930s. At a time when unemployment was unusually high, many nations with trade deficits felt that matters would only get worse if they contracted their money supplies to live by the edicts of the gold standard. We explore this question in greater detail in the next section.

WHERE WE'VE BEEN, WHERE WE ARE

Historians are quick to point out that we can only understand where we are if we first understand where we've been. With this in mind, we discuss a few key past and present events in U.S. international finance.

The Crack-up of the Gold Standard

From the 1870s to the 1930s, many nations tied their currencies to gold. The United States, for example, stood ready to exchange an ounce of gold for $20.67. For most of this period—roughly from the 1870s to the end of World War I—the gold standard worked well. Critics say that the gold standard worked well because there were few problems for it to solve. For example, during this time, no major trading country found itself with persistent balance of payments problems.

Then, after World War I, things began to change. Some countries (most notably the United States) began to break the rules of the gold standard by not contracting their money supplies to the extent called for by the outflow of gold. Under these circumstances, the gold standard could not restore balance of trade equilibrium.

In the 1920s, Great Britain and France tried to restore the gold standard. They did so, however, by setting the "wrong" exchange rates: The pound was overvalued and the franc was undervalued. This action led to trade surpluses in France and high unemployment and trade deficits in Great Britain. To maintain the gold standard, both countries would have had to change their money supplies significantly. The countries began to feel that it was not worth subjecting their domestic economies to such sharp changes in order to abide by the discipline of the gold standard.

As we noted earlier, the Great Depression was perhaps the straw that broke the back of the gold standard. In the face of widespread high unemployment, nations with trade deficits began to feel that abiding by the rules of the gold standard and contracting their money supplies to restore balance of trade equilibrium was too high a price to pay. So they went off the gold standard.

The Bretton Woods System

In 1944, once it appeared that the Allies were certain to win World War II, major negotiators from the Allied countries met in Bretton Woods, New Hampshire, to map out a new international monetary system. This system came to be known as the *Bretton Woods system*. It was based on fixed exchange rates and an international central bank called the **International Monetary Fund (IMF)**.[9] Under the Bretton Woods system, nations were expected to maintain fixed exchange rates (within a narrow range) by buying and selling their own currency for other currencies.[10] A nation experiencing a trade deficit could borrow international reserves from the IMF. It was expected that the nation that had borrowed reserves would, over time, generate a trade surplus with which it could pay off its loan. The IMF reserves were created by imposing a quota on each member nation—a fee based on the nation's trade and national income. Each member nation contributed 25 percent of its quota in gold or U.S. dollars and 75 percent in its own currency.

In the late 1960s, the IMF created a new international money to add to its international reserves fund. This was the **special drawing right (SDR).** In essence, SDRs are simply bookkeeping entries. However, once a country has an SDR account, it can use SDRs to settle a trade imbalance.

In the 1960s and early 1970s, the Bretton Woods system became strained at the seams. One of the major shortcomings of the system was that it encouraged speculative attacks on a currency. Suppose Great Britain is persistently running a trade

International Monetary Fund (IMF)
An international organization created by the Bretton Woods system to oversee the international monetary system. Although the Bretton Woods system no longer exists, the IMF does. It does not control the world's money supply, but it does hold currency reserves for member nations and makes loans to central banks.

Special Drawing Right
An international money, created by the IMF, in the form of bookkeeping entries; like gold and currencies, they can be used by nations to settle international accounts.

[9]The IMF is sometimes confused with the World Bank (or International Bank for Reconstruction and Development), although it is something different altogether. The World Bank, which was also part of the Bretton Woods agreement, was set up to provide long-term loans to assist developing nations in building roads, dams, and other capital projects that it was felt would contribute to their economic development.
[10]Actually, the Bretton Woods system was not an absolutely rigid fixed exchange rate system. Because it was not, it is sometimes referred to as the *adjustable peg system*. Exchange rates were set, and then a narrow band around each exchange rates was specified within which the exchange rate could move without central bank intervention. In addition, the IMF allowed for periodic realignment in exchange rates.

deficit and Germany is persistently running a trade surplus. Under these circumstances, speculators know that sooner or later Great Britain will have to devalue its currency, although government officials in Great Britain will probably deny this. Speculators will likely respond by selling the weak British pound (before it is devalued and they are left holding a bag full of less valuable pounds) and buying the strong currency—in our example, the German mark. Obviously, this speculative action will increase the supply of pounds on the foreign exchange market and cause the difference between the official price of pounds and the equilibrium price of pounds to increase. Thus, if the pound were overvalued before the speculative action, it is now even more overvalued; a bad situation has become worse.

This is, in fact, what happened to Great Britain in 1967. At the official price for a pound, the quantity supplied of pounds was greater than the quantity demanded of pounds. In short, the pound was overvalued, and Great Britain was faced with a combined current and capital account deficit. To maintain the official price (exchange rate), the Bank of England had to buy the excess supply of pounds. In doing this, though, it lost international reserves. By November 17, 1967, speculators began to suspect that despite IMF loans to Great Britain, the British pound would soon have to be devalued. They reasoned that Great Britain didn't have the reserves necessary to continue to maintain the official price of the pound. Speculators began to view a devaluation of the pound as (almost) certain and began to sell off pounds. This made the problem worse for the Bank of England because now, with more pounds on the foreign exchange market, it was forced to buy up more pounds to maintain the official price of the pound. On one day alone, the Bank of England had to buy $1 billion worth of pounds to keep the exchange rate from falling. Finally, the Bank of England realized that it could not continue to defend the pound successfully at its present official price, and soon after devalued the pound by 14 percent. This meant that the speculators who had sold $1 billion worth of pounds to the Bank of England collectively earned $140 million. How did they manage this? The dollars they had bought by selling pounds to the Bank of England had appreciated in value 14 percent. If they sold $1 billion worth of pounds, then they realized $140 million in profits (since 14 percent of $1 billion = $140 million). The Bank of England had found that defending its currency against speculative attack was expensive. Critics of the Bretton Woods system began to point out that any fixed exchange rate system has this failing; it can prompt speculative attacks on currencies.

In 1971, speculators began to speculate on the dollar. Before we can understand this action fully, we need to point out that the U.S. dollar was convertible into gold (for foreign governments and central banks only) at $35 an ounce. In the 1960s, the United States had witnessed an accelerating inflation that caused U.S. exports to become more expensive and U.S. imports to become less expensive. This difference in inflation rates between the United States and many other countries began to put pressure on exchange rates; more and more, it appeared that the dollar was overvalued at its official price. In short, there was a surplus of dollars. But this simply meant that some other currencies were undervalued and that there was an excess demand for them. According to the rules laid down under the Bretton Woods system, the countries whose currencies were in short supply had to buy up dollars and thus sell more of their currency to maintain exchange rates. For example, the German central bank, the Bundesbank, bought $2 billion of U.S. dollars between January and March 1971 to fulfill its obligation to keep the exchange rate fixed at 27 cents = 1 mark.

Now this meant that by buying dollars, the Bundesbank, and some other central banks, were increasing their holdings of dollars. But increasingly, central banks became reluctant to hold dollars. U.S. monetary authorities became worried because they knew that if central banks did demand gold (for dollars), the U.S. gold stock would be severely diminished if the United States maintained a $35 price for gold. Add to this the voiced anguish of many American exporters of goods who complained that they were being severely hurt by the overvalued dollar, and you knew something would soon have to happen.

It did. On Sunday evening, August 15, 1971, President Nixon addressed the nation and announced that the United States would no longer honor its IMF obligation to sell gold at $35 an ounce. Soon after, the U.S. dollar began to fluctuate in the foreign exchange market. The overvalued dollar soon depreciated against other major currencies. By 1973, the Bretton Woods system was dead.

The Current International Monetary System

Today's international monetary system is best described as a *managed flexible exchange rate system,* sometimes referred to more casually as a **managed float.** In a way, this is a rough compromise between the fixed and flexible exchange rate systems. The current system operates under flexible exchange rates, but not completely. Nations now and then intervene to adjust their official reserve holdings to moderate major swings in exchange rates. For example, the United States intervened in foreign exchange markets in 1978 to moderate the depreciation of the dollar. Recent intervention has involved coordinated efforts on the part of major industrial nations. In September 1985, the finance ministers of five industrial nations—France, Germany, Japan, Great Britain, and the United States—met at the Plaza Hotel in New York City and agreed to intervene in foreign exchange markets to achieve desired changes in exchange rates. At the time the meeting took place, the Group of Five (or G-5, as the countries came to be known) believed the dollar was overvalued and therefore agreed to achieve a depreciation of the dollar. In 1987, the Group of Five was joined by Canada and Italy and became known as the Group of Seven (G-7). At this time, the G-7 bought large quantities of dollars in the foreign exchange market in order to achieve appreciation of the dollar. The G-7 still periodically intervenes in foreign exchange markets to accomplish particular goals.

Proponents of the managed float system stress the following advantages:

1. It allows nations to pursue independent monetary policies. Under a (strictly) fixed exchange rate system, fixed either by agreement or by gold, a nation with a merchandise trade deficit might have to enact a tight monetary policy in order to retard inflation and promote its exports (see the discussion of the fixed exchange rate system). This would not be the case with the managed float. Its proponents argue that it is better to adjust one price—the exchange rate—than to adjust the price level to solve trade imbalances.

2. It solves trade problems without trade restrictions. As we stated earlier, with a fixed exchange rate system, nations sometimes impose tariffs and quotas to solve trade imbalances. For example, a deficit nation might impose import quotas so that exports and imports of goods will be more in line. With the current system, trade imbalances are usually solved through changes in exchange rates.

3. It is flexible and therefore can easily adjust to shocks. In 1973–74, the OPEC nations dramatically raised the price of oil, which resulted in many oil-importing nations running trade deficits. A fixed exchange rate system would have had a hard time accommodating such a major change in oil prices. The current system had little trouble, however. Exchange rates took much of the shock (there were

Managed Float

A managed flexible exchange rate system, under which nations now and then intervene to adjust their official reserve holdings to moderate major swings in exchange rates; this is today's international monetary system.

large changes in exchange rates) and thus allowed most nations' economies to weather the storm with a minimum of difficulty.

Opponents of the current international monetary system stress the following disadvantages:

1. It promotes exchange rate volatility and uncertainty and results in less international trade than would be the case under fixed exchange rates. Under a flexible exchange rate system, exchange rates are volatile and therefore make it risky for importers and exporters to conduct business; as a result, international trade is less than it would be under a fixed exchange rate system. Opponents of the current system often point to the sharp depreciation of the U.S. dollar in 1986. Proponents often report that a futures market in currencies exists that allows importers and exporters to shift the risk of fluctuations in exchange rates to others.

For example, if an American company wants to buy a certain quantity of a good from a Japanese company three months from today, it can contract today for the desired quantity of yen it will need, at a specified price; it will not have to worry about a change in the dollar price of yen over the next three months. There is, of course, a cost to this, but it is usually modest.

2. It promotes inflation. As we have seen, the monetary policies of different nations are not independent of one another under a fixed exchange rate system. For example, a nation with a merchandise trade deficit is somewhat restrained from inflating because this will worsen the deficit problem—it will make its goods more expensive relative to foreign goods and promote the purchase of imports. In its attempt to maintain the exchange rate, a nation with a merchandise trade deficit would have to enact a tight monetary policy.

Under the current system, a nation with a merchandise trade deficit does not have to concern itself with maintaining exchange rates or trying to solve its deficit problem through changes in its money supply. Opponents of the current system argue that this frees nations to inflate. They predict more inflation will result than under a fixed exchange rate system.

3. Changes in exchange rates alter trade balances in the desired direction only after a long time; in the short run, a depreciation in a currency can make the situation worse instead of better. It is often argued that soon after a depreciation in a trade-deficit nation's currency, the trade deficit will increase (not decrease, as was hoped). The reason is that import demand is inelastic in the short run: Imports are not very responsive to a change in price. Suppose Great Britain is running a trade deficit with the United States at the present exchange rate of $1.50 = £1. At this exchange rate, the pound is overvalued, and Great Britain (we assume) buys 2,000 television sets each with a price tag of $500 from the United States. Great Britain therefore spends £666,666 on imports of American television sets. Now suppose the overvalued pound begins to depreciate, say, to $1.25 = £1. Furthermore, in the short run, British customers only buy 100 fewer American television sets; that is, they import 1,900 television sets. At a price of $500 each, and at an exchange rate of $1.25 = £1, the British now spend £760,000 on imports of American television sets.

In the short run, then, a depreciation in the pound has widened the trade deficit because the percentage by which imports falls (5 percent) was less than the percentage by which the price of imports (in terms of pounds) increased (16.7 percent).[11] As time passes, imports will fall off more (it takes time for British buyers

---

[11]In other words, the demand for imports in the short run is highly price inelastic. As time passes, the price elasticity of demand for imports increases, and the trade deficit problem begins to be solved.

EXHIBIT 20–8
The J-Curve

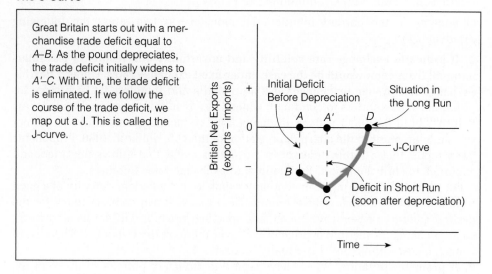

Great Britain starts out with a merchandise trade deficit equal to *A–B*. As the pound depreciates, the trade deficit initially widens to *A'–C*. With time, the trade deficit is eliminated. If we follow the course of the trade deficit, we map out a J. This is called the J-curve.

to shift from higher-priced American goods to lower-priced British goods), and the deficit will shrink. If we graph this phenomenon—namely, that a depreciation in a nation's currency widens the trade deficit in the short run and shrinks it in the long run—we obtain a **J-curve** (Exhibit 20–8).

In the exhibit, we have plotted time on the horizontal axis and British net exports on the vertical axis. Net exports = exports − imports; therefore, negative net exports imply a trade deficit (imports > exports). As we can see, before the depreciation of the pound, Great Britain is experiencing a trade deficit equal to $A - B$. Next, the pound is depreciated and the trade deficit widens to $A' - C$. The movement from B to C is the first part of the J-curve. Next, as time passes, the trade deficit begins to shrink. The British are, with time, moving from American imports to domestic goods. At point D, British net exports are zero (exports = imports). The movement from C to D is the second part of the J-curve. The J-curve is represented by the movement from B to C and from C to D.

J-Curve

The curve that shows a short-run worsening in the trade deficit after a currency depreciation, followed later by an improvement.

Question:

Does the J-curve phenomenon mean that a system of flexible exchange rates is undesirable?

Answer:

Some economists would say that if there is a J-curve phenomenon, changes in exchange rates are a rather crude way of solving a trade imbalance because in the short run they make things worse.

PART VI
INTERNATIONAL ECONOMICS:
THEORY AND POLICY

462

Balance of Payments

■ The balance of payments provides information about a nation's imports and exports, domestic residents' earnings on assets located abroad, foreign earnings on domestic assets, gifts to and from foreign countries, and official transactions by governments and central banks.

■ In a nation's balance of payments, any transaction that supplies the nation's currency in the foreign exchange market is recorded as a debit $(-)$. Any transaction that supplies a foreign currency is recorded as a credit $(+)$.

■ The three main accounts of the balance of payments are the current account, capital account, and official reserve account.

■ The current account includes all payments related to the purchase and sale of goods and services. The three major components of the account are exports of goods and services, imports of goods and services, and unilateral transfers.

■ The capital account includes all payments related to the purchase and sale of assets and to borrowing and lending activities. The major components are outflow of U.S. capital and inflow of foreign capital.

■ The official reserve account includes transactions by the central banks of various countries.

■ The merchandise trade balance is the difference between the value of merchandise exports and the value of merchandise imports. If exports are greater than imports, a nation has a trade surplus; if imports are greater than exports, a nation has a trade deficit. The balance of payments equals current account balance + capital account balance + official reserve balance + statistical discrepancy.

The Foreign Exchange Market and Flexible and Fixed Exchange Rates

■ The market in which currencies of different countries are exchanged is called the foreign exchange market. In this market, currencies are bought and sold for a price; an exchange rate exists.

■ If Americans demand British goods, they also demand British pounds and supply U.S. dollars. If the British demand American goods, they also demand U.S. dollars and supply British pounds. When the residents of a nation demand a foreign currency, they must supply their own currency.

■ Under flexible exchange rates, the foreign exchange market will equilibrate at the exchange rate where the quantity demanded of a currency equals the quantity supplied of a currency; for example, the quantity demanded of dollars equals the quantity supplied of dollars.

■ If the price of a nation's currency increases against a foreign currency, the nation's economy is said to have appreciated. For example, if the dollar price of a pound rises from $1.50 = £1 to $1.80 = £1, the pound has appreciated. If the price of a nation's currency decreases against a foreign currency, the nation's currency is said to have depreciated. For example, if the pound price of a dollar falls from 66 pence = $1 to 55 pence = $1, the dollar has depreciated.

■ Under a flexible exchange rate system, the equilibrium exchange rate is affected by a difference in income growth rates between countries, a difference in inflation rates between countries, and a change in (real) interest rates between countries.

■ Under a fixed exchange rate system, countries agree to fix the price of their currencies. The central banks of the countries must then buy and sell currencies to maintain the agreed-on exchange rate. If a persistent deficit or surplus in a nation's combined current and capital account exists at a fixed exchange rate, the nation has a few options to deal with the problem: devalue or revalue its currency, enact protectionist trade policies (in the case of a deficit), or change its monetary policy.

The Gold Standard

■ To have an international gold standard, nations must do the following: (1) Define their currencies in terms of gold. (2) Stand ready and willing to convert gold into paper money and paper money into gold at a specified rate. (3) Link their money supplies to their holdings of gold. The change in the money supply that the gold standard sometimes requires has prompted some economists to voice the same argument against the gold standard that is often heard against the fixed exchange rate system: It subjects domestic monetary policy to international instead of domestic considerations.

The Current International Monetary System

■ Today's international monetary system is described as a managed flexible exchange rate system, or managed float. For the most part, the exchange rate system is flexible, although nations do periodically intervene in the foreign exchange market to adjust exchange rates. Since it is a managed float system, it is difficult to tell if nations will emphasize the "float" part or the "managed" part in years to come.

■ Proponents of the managed flexible exchange rate system believe it offers several advantages: (1) It allows nations to pursue independent macroeconomic policies. (2) It solves trade problems without trade restrictions. (3) It is flexible and therefore can easily adjust to shocks. Opponents of the managed flexible exchange rate system believe it has several disadvantages: (1) It promotes exchange rate volatility and uncertainty, and thus results in less international trade than would be the case under fixed exchange rates. (2) It promotes inflation. (3) It corrects trade deficits only a long time after a depreciation in the currency; in the interim, it can make matters worse. This is the J-curve phenomenon.

Key Terms and Concepts

Balance of Payments	Current Account Balance	Fixed Exchange Rate System
Debit	Capital Account	Overvaluation
Credit	Capital Account Balance	Undervaluation
Current Account	Exchange Rate	Devaluation
Foreign Exchange Market	Flexible Exchange Rate System	Revaluation
Merchandise Trade Balance	Appreciation	International Monetary Fund (IMF)
Merchandise Trade Deficit	Depreciation	Special Drawing Right
Merchandise Trade Surplus	Purchasing Power Parity Theory	Managed Float
	Real Interest Rate	J-curve

1. The following foreign exchange information appeared in a newspaper:

	U.S. $ Equivalent		Currency per U.S. $	
	FRI.	THRS.	FRI.	THRS.
France (franc)	.1577	.1578	6.3410	6.3400
Japan (yen)	.007503	.007493	133.27	133.45
German (mark)	.5370	.5364	1.8563	1.8583

(a) Between Thursday and Friday, did the dollar appreciate or depreciate against the French franc? (b) Between Thursday and Friday, did the dollar appreciate or depreciate against the Japanese yen? (c) Between Thursday and Friday, did the dollar appreciate or depreciate against the German mark?

2. Suppose the United States and Greece are on a flexible exchange rate system. Explain whether each of the following events will lead to an appreciation or depreciation in the U.S. dollar and Greek drachma: (a) U.S. real interest rates rise above Greek real interest rates. (b) The Greek inflation rate rises relative to the U.S. inflation rate. (c) Greece puts a quota on imports of American radios. (d) Americans learn on the nightly news that terrorists at the Athens airport boarded a plane that they subsequently skyjacked with American citizens aboard. As a result, American tourism to Athens (Greece) drops off substantially.

3. Give an example that illustrates how a change in the exchange rate changes the relative price of domestic goods in terms of foreign goods.

4. Suppose the media report that the United States has a deficit in its current account. What does this imply about the U.S. capital account balance and official reserve account balance?

5. Suppose that Great Britain has a merchandise trade deficit and France has a merchandise trade surplus. Since the two countries are on a flexible exchange rate system, the franc appreciates and the pound depreciates. It is noticed, however, that soon after the depreciation of the pound, Great Britain's trade deficit grows instead of shrinks. Why might this be?

6. What are the strong and weak points of the flexible exchange rate system? What are the strong and weak points of the fixed exchange rate system?

7. Individuals do not keep a written account of their balance of trade with other individuals. For example, John doesn't keep an account of how much he sells to Alice and how much he buys from Alice. In addition, neither cities nor any of the 50 states calculate their balance of trade with all other cities and states. However, nations do calculate their merchandise trade balance with other nations. If nations do it, should individuals, cities, and states do it? Why?

8. Since every nation's balance of payments equals zero, does it follow that each nation is on an equal footing in international trade and finance with every other nation? Explain your answer.

9. Suppose your objective is to predict whether the British pound and the U.S. dollar will appreciate or depreciate on the foreign exchange market in the next two months. What information would you need to help you make your prediction? Specifically, how would this information help you predict the direction of the foreign exchange value of the pound and dollar? Next, explain how a person who could accurately predict exchange rates could become extremely rich in a short time.

PART

VII

ECONOMIC GROWTH, DEVELOPMENT, AND ALTERNATIVE ECONOMIC SYSTEMS

CHAPTER

21

ECONOMIC GROWTH AND DEVELOPMENT

WHAT THIS CHAPTER IS ABOUT

What would your life be like if you had been born in Ethiopia, India, or Tanzania instead of the United States? Most likely you wouldn't be driving a car because you wouldn't own one. You wouldn't have new clothes, a compact disc player, or a personal computer. You wouldn't go out to restaurants and movies regularly. You wouldn't be enrolled in a college or university studying economics! You largely have what you have—things that Ethiopians, Indians, and Tanzanians do not have because you were born to parents who live in a country that has experienced relatively more economic growth and development than most countries of the world. In this chapter, we examine the role economic growth and development play in a nation's life.

ECONOMIC GROWTH

■

Real Economic Growth
An increase from one period to the next in real GNP.

Per-Capita Real Economic Growth
An increase from one period to the next in per-capita real GNP, which is real GNP divided by population.

The term *economic growth* refers to either real economic growth or to per-capita real economic growth. **Real economic growth** is an increase from one period to the next in *real GNP*. **Per-capita real economic growth** is an increase from one period to the next in *per-capita real GNP,* which is real GNP divided by population.

Most economists think the per-capita measurement is more useful, since it, unlike absolute economic growth, tells us how much better or worse off the average person is in one period compared with another, assuming a given income distribution. For example, India has a higher real GNP than Norway. But it also has 171 times the population. It turns out that per-capita real GNP in Norway is approximately 50 times as high as per-capita real GNP in India.

Per-capita real economic growth is a relatively new phenomenon. In the preindustrial world, real economic growth often encouraged the population to increase beyond the increase in real GNP, and consequently people's standard of living fell. It was only in sixteenth-century England and the Netherlands that per-capita real economic growth first appeared on a sustainable basis. This means that before this time, a son's standard of living was much like his father's, his grandfather's, and so on back a few more generations. To get an idea of the changes that have occurred, just think of how much higher your standard of living is than that of persons who lived in the United States only 50 years ago.

Question:

Suppose the real GNP of country X is $1 billion and the population is 1,000,000 persons. The per-capita real GNP is $1,000. In country Y, the real GNP is $1 million and the population is 2,000 persons. The per-capita real GNP is $500. Does it necessarily follow that the average person in country X is better off than the average person in country Y (at least in material goods)?

Answer:

No, it does not. It could be that in country X one person has the entire real GNP, and in country Y the real GNP is spread evenly over the entire population. In short, per-capita real GNP does not tell us anything about the income distribution. This is not an argument against using the measure of per-capita real GNP, only against its misuse. As an example of its proper use, if for a given country and a given income distribution, the per-capita real GNP is higher in 1991 than in 1990, then it is accurate to say that the average person is better off in terms of material goods.

Growth in a Production Possibilities Frontier Framework

Growth can be seen in a production possibilities frontier (PPF) framework, as Exhibit 21–1 illustrates. On the horizontal axis, we have placed agricultural goods, and on the vertical axis, manufactured goods. There are two production possibilities frontiers: PPF_{1991} and PPF_{1996}. The distance between the two frontiers represents the increased productive capabilities that can, but may not, be realized by the economy. If the economy actually realizes these increased capabilities (and moves from a point on PPF_{1991} to a point on PPF_{1996}), then growth has occurred between 1991 and 1996. If it does not, then growth has not been realized. The

EXHIBIT 21–1
Economic Growth

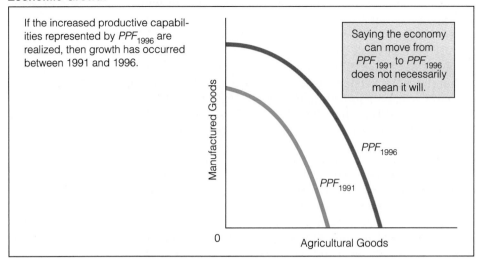

If the increased productive capabilities represented by PPF_{1996} are realized, then growth has occurred between 1991 and 1996.

Saying the economy can move from PPF_{1991} to PPF_{1996} does not necessarily mean it will.

Manufactured Goods

PPF_{1996}

PPF_{1991}

0

Agricultural Goods

latter case would be analogous to discovering a new field of oil or inventing a new technology and doing nothing about it. Potential growth exists, but actual growth is not realized.

Question:

Suppose country A experiences a 3 percent growth rate in real GNP each year for five years, and country B experiences a 6 percent growth rate in real GNP each year for five years. Does it follow that the residents of country B are better off in terms of material goods than the residents of country A?

Answer:

No, it doesn't. Think about this in terms of the *PPF* and per-capita real economic growth. First, the *PPF* for country B might be much closer to the origin than the *PPF* for country A. If this is the case, then fewer goods are produced in country B, even though it has the higher growth rate. Second, we need to know something about the populations of the two countries. It might be that the per-capita real GNP growth rate of country A is greater than the per-capita real GNP growth rate of country B, even though country B has witnessed greater real economic growth.

The United States and Japan: Shifting *PPF*s

Positive economic growth shows up as an outward shift in a country's production possibilities frontier. Let's look at the United States and Japan. Each country has been experiencing economic growth, which means each country's *PPF* has been shifting outward. Exhibit 21–2 shows how much each country's *PPF* has shifted outward for different periods and years. In the exhibit, a positive growth rate represents an outward shift in the country's production possibilities frontier. For most periods and years cited in the exhibit, the growth rate in Japan was greater than the growth rate in the United States.

What Factors Affect Growth?

Why do some countries experience economic growth while others do not? Why do some countries experience fast economic growth and others, slow economic growth? Is there a necessary factor for economic growth? For example, does a country need factor X before it can grow? Is there a sufficient factor for growth? If a country has factor Z, is that enough (sufficient) to guarantee growth?

Unfortunately, economists do not have answers to all these questions. No one theory of economic growth is universally accepted. But economists are agreed on a few factors that are linked to economic growth, although they differ as to how heavily each of the factors should be weighted. The factors are natural resources, capital formation, technological advances, and property rights structure.

Natural Resources. People often think that countries that have a plentiful supply of natural resources experience economic growth, whereas countries that are short on natural resources do not. In fact, some countries with an abundant supply of natural resources have experienced rapid growth (like the United States), and some have experienced no growth or only slow growth (like Bolivia and Ghana). Also, some countries that are short on natural resources, like Hong Kong, grow very fast. It appears that natural resources are neither a sufficient nor a necessary factor for growth: Nations rich in natural resources are not guaranteed economic growth, whereas nations poor in natural resources may grow. Having said all this, it is still more likely for a nation rich in natural resources to experience growth, *ceteris paribus.* For example, if Hong Kong had been blessed with much fertile soil instead of only a little, and many raw materials instead of almost none, it might have experienced more economic growth than it has.

Capital Formation. Capital formation includes two types of capital: physical and human. Physical capital, such as a tractor or a machine, and human capital, such as knowledge and skills, increase the ability of an individual to produce (that is, there is a predictable relationship between capital formation and labor productivity). For example, modern American farmers produce much more than their grandfathers largely because they have certain physical capital goods, such as tractors, that their grandfathers didn't have, and they know much more about the science of farming. In short, they possess more physical *and* human capital than their grandfathers.

Both physical and human capital formation do not come without cost. Tractors, computers, and factory machines do not fall from the sky. Education and knowl-

EXHIBIT 21-2
U.S. and Japanese Growth Rates in Real GNP, 1961-90
A positive growth rate represents an outward shift in a country's production possibilities frontier (*PPF*). As the exhibit shows, for most periods and specific years, Japan's *PPF* has been shifting outward by a greater percentage than the United States' *PPF*. Figures for 1990 are preliminary estimates.

	Growth Rates in Real GNP, 1961-90 (Percentage Change)										
COUNTRY	AVERAGE ANNUAL 1961-65	AVERAGE ANNUAL 1966-70	AVERAGE ANNUAL 1971-75	AVERAGE ANNUAL 1976-83	1984	1985	1986	1987	1988	1989	1990
Japan	12.4%	11.0%	4.3%	4.4%	5.1%	4.9%	2.5%	4.6%	5.7%	4.9%	6.1%
United States	4.6	3.0	2.2	2.5	6.8	3.4	2.7	3.4	4.5	2.5	0.9

SOURCE: Council of Economic Advisers, *Economic Report of the President, 1991* (Washington, D.C.: U.S. Government Printing Office, 1991).

edge are not obtained by snapping one's fingers. Sacrifices have to be made. To produce capital goods, which are not directly consumable, present consumption must be sacrificed. Robinson Crusoe, alone on an island fishing with a spear, must give up some of his present consumption of fish to weave a net (a physical capital good) with which he hopes to catch more fish.

If Crusoe gives up some of his present consumption, if he chooses not to consume now, he is in fact saving. There is a link between *non*consumption, or saving, and capital formation. As the savings rate increases, capital formation increases, and so does economic growth. Take the case of the United States and Japan. In the period 1961–90, Japan's per-capita real GNP growth rate was double that of the United States. Modern research indicates that Japan's higher per-capita real GNP growth rate is due to its higher savings rate, which is almost 75 percent higher than the U.S. savings rate.

Exhibit 21–3 makes this point. Suppose that in 1990, the production possibilities frontier was the same for both the United States and Japan. The United States decided to locate at point *A,* producing relatively more consumption goods and fewer investment goods than Japan, which decided to locate at point *B.* Because the two countries decided to produce a different investment-goods-to-consumption-goods ratio in 1990, they have different *PPF*s in 1998. Because Japan had a higher savings rate than the United States, which brought about greater investment in Japan than in the United States, it experienced greater growth than the United States.

Technological Advances. Technological advances make it possible to obtain more output from the same amount of resources. Compare the amount of work that can be done by a business that uses computers with the amount accomplished by a business that does not. The world has witnessed major technological advances in the past 100 to 200 years. Consider what your life would have been like if you

EXHIBIT 21–3
The Effect of Consumption/Investment Choices on Economic Growth

We assume that in 1990 both Japan and the United States occupy the same *PPF* but at different points. The United States is at point *A,* Japan is at point *B.* Japan saves and invests more than the United States; consequently, its *PPF* shifts outward farther.

Japan's *PPF*$_{1998}$ (because Japan chose point *B* in 1990)

U.S. *PPF*$_{1998}$ (because the United States chose point *A* in 1990)

PPF$_{1990}$ (for both Japan and the United States)

Investment Goods

Consumption Goods

B

A

0

had lived 200 years ago, around 1790. Most of the major technological achievements we take for granted today—the car, computer, telephone, electricity, mass production techniques—did not exist. It is sometimes said, and it is probably true, that a person living in the late 1700s had a living standard that was closer to the living standard of people living in the year 1 A.D. than of people living today.

Property Rights Structure.   Some economists have argued that per-capita real economic growth first appeared in those areas where a system of institutions and property rights had evolved that encouraged individuals to direct their human capital and energy to effective economic projects. Here *property rights* refers to the range of laws, rules, and regulations that define rights over the use and transfer of resources.

Consider two property rights structures: one in which people are allowed to keep the full fruits of their labor and one in which people are allowed to keep only one-half of the fruits of their labor. Many economists would predict that the first property rights structure would stimulate more economic activity than the second, *ceteris paribus.* Individuals will invest more, take more risks, and work harder when the property rights structure allows them to keep more of the fruits of their investing, risk taking, and labor.

Question:

Do economic growth rates matter that much in the long run? For example, suppose one country has a growth rate of 4 percent per year for 20 years and another country has a growth rate of 3 percent per year for 20 years. Will the total growth be different in the two countries over a period of 20 years?

Answer:

There will be a sizable difference. For example, in 1990, in the United States, a 1 percent higher annual growth rate represented approximately $54 billion worth of output. As far as growth over the long run is concerned, the example of compound interest illustrates what happens. If you put $100 into a savings account at a 10 percent annual interest rate, in a year you will have $110. And then if you keep the $110 in the savings account at the same annual interest rate, the following year you have $121. It takes only about 7 years to double your $100 savings. And, of course, the higher the interest rate is, the quicker your savings doubles. For instance, at an interest rate of 12 percent, your money doubles in approximately 6 years. It works the same way with growth rates. At a 4 percent growth rate (per year), it will take 18 years to double in size. At a 3 percent growth rate (per year), it takes 24 years to double—or 6 years longer. Thus, a 1 percent increase in the growth rate can mean a lot in the long run.

Follow-up Question:

How was the number of years calculated?

Answer:

We used the *Rule of 72*—a simple arithmetic rule for compound calculations. The Rule of 72, which is a rough rule of thumb, says that the time required for any variable to double is calculated by dividing its percentage growth rate into 72. For instance, an economy that experiences a 5 percent annual growth rate will take approximately 14.4 years ($72/5 = 14.4$) to double in size. The United States had an average annual growth rate in real GNP of 2.8 percent during the period 1986–90. If this annual growth rate were to continue, it would take 25.7 years ($72/2.8 = 25.7$) for the U.S. economy to double in size. During the same period, the Japanese average annual growth rate in real GNP was 4.7 percent. If this annual growth rate were to continue, it would take 15.3 years ($72/4.7 = 15.3$) for the Japanese economy to double in size.

When discussing economic growth, economists think in terms of tangibles and intangibles. The tangibles include natural resources, capital formation, and technological advancements. The intangibles include the property rights structure, which directly affects the incentives individuals have to apply the tangibles to the production of goods and services. No amount of resources, capital, and technology can do it alone. People must be motivated to put them all together; in addition, the degree of motivation matters to the result. In a world in which it is easy to think that only those things that occupy physical space matter, the economist is there to remind us that we often need to look further.

Productivity Slowdown

In the early 1970s, the United States began to experience a decline in real economic growth. This was noticed and recorded by many economists, in particular, by Edward Denison of the Brookings Institution. Denison calculated that the real national income growth rate was approximately twice as high for the United States in the period 1948–73 as it was in the period 1973–82.[1] This slowdown in economic growth appeared to be largely the result of a slowdown in labor productivity, as measured by output per hour of labor. But this, then, prompted individuals to ask what caused the slowdown in labor productivity. We note a few of the more frequently cited reasons here.

Decline in Capital per Hour Worked. We have discussed how labor, combined with capital goods, is more productive than labor alone. Recall that the farmer with a tractor is more productive than the farmer working alone. If we put capital goods on one hand and labor hours worked on the other, we can then look at one in terms of the other and speak of *capital per hour worked*. In the 1970s, the ratio of capital to labor hours worked began to decline. There were two reasons for this: (1) Growth of the capital stock slowed down. (2) Growth in labor hours worked speeded up. Thus, both components of the ratio were affected. The growth in labor hours worked increased because a large number of women moved from home activity into the labor force during the seventies.

   Why, however, did the growth of the capital stock decline? One economist, Martin Feldstein, argued that inflation and a tax system that did not adjust for inflation gains (but treated them instead as real gains) combined to overtax savings. As a result, saving, which is necessary for capital formation, was discouraged.

Decline in the Quality of the Labor Force. The early 1970s saw an increase in the number of women and young people who entered the labor force. As men-

[1]Edward Demison, *Trends in American Economic Growth, 1929–1982* (Washington, D.C.: Brookings Institution, 1985).

Do Special-Interest Groups Zap Productivity?

Economist Mancur Olson has proposed a theory that he and some others believe explains the productivity slowdown of the 1970s, among other things. Olson argues that when countries experience a long period of political stability, special-interest groups (or distributional coalitions, which often want to redistribute income from others to themselves) have an opportunity to grow and achieve political power. For example, labor union special-interest groups will use their increasing economic and political power to set wages and prevent employers from hiring nonunion labor, introducing labor-saving technology, and the like. Business-oriented special-interest groups will lobby government for preferential treatment in the form of subsidies, tariffs, and quotas.

Olson argues that the United States, having experienced a long period of

political stability, currently has powerful special-interest groups that can often accomplish their goals. In comparison, Japan and Germany, having lost World War II, had their societies turned upside down, and in the process once-powerful special-interest groups were dismantled; as yet these groups have not had the time to reestablish themselves and become as strong as their American counterparts. Olson implies that this gives the economic edge to Japan:

If the argument so far is correct, it follows that countries whose distributional coalitions have been emasculated or abolished by totalitarian government or foreign occupation should grow relatively quickly after a free and stable legal order is established. This can explain the postwar "economic miracles" in the nations that were defeated in World

War II, particularly those in Japan and West Germany.*

In the Olson theory, powerful special-interest groups reduce the economy's flexibility and slow down its ability to adapt to changing circumstances and technologies (they suffer, in Olson's words, from *institutional sclerosis*). For example, if demand in the economy falls, business- and labor-oriented special-interest groups will react slowly; thus, wages and prices are likely to stay fixed for some time, and unemployment will rise. Overall, the economy will not react smoothly and quickly to a new reality. National output and labor productivity will suffer.

*Mancur Olson, *The Rise and Decline of Nations: Economic Growth, Stagflation, and Social Rigidities* (New Haven, Conn.: Yale University Press, 1982), p. 75.

tioned earlier, many of the women entering the labor force had come from home activity. The young people were largely the "baby boomers" who were coming of age and getting their first jobs. Some economists contend that because these two groups initially lacked work experience, they pulled down the average quality of labor during this time and prompted the slowdown in labor productivity. Denison's studies, however, suggest that this played only a minor part in the slowdown of labor productivity.

Major Oil Price Increases. It is occasionally argued that the substantial oil price increases of the 1970s caused the relative price of labor compared with energy to decrease, prompting businesses to hire more labor and thus acquire less capital than they might ordinarily have acquired. Related to this, the sharp oil price increases caused much of the economy's capital stock to become obsolete. For example, many generators and gas-guzzling trucks had to be retired because high oil prices made them too costly to operate. Some say this reduction in the capital stock reduced labor productivity substantially. Others, like economist Michael Darby, believe that the energy crises and high oil prices played no role in the slowdown in labor productivity. In fact, Darby's work shows that there was no productivity slowdown. He notes that economists who use *output per hour of labor* as a measure of productivity fail to adjust for quality changes in labor and thus necessarily bias their results. In his work, Darby adjusted for quality changes in labor and concluded that hourly labor productivity has grown at a stable rate throughout the twentieth century.

Regulation.   The 1970s witnessed an increase in the number of government safety, environmental, and health regulations that affected businesses. Some maintain that since businesses were required to invest in equipment to meet these regulations, they could not invest as heavily in standard plant and equipment and this led to the slowdown in economic growth.

A Combination of Factors.   Economist Lester Thurow has argued that no single factor was decisive for the productivity slowdown, but that many factors together—inflation, regulation, oil price increases—all played a part. Thurow has compared the many-factor explanation of the productivity slowdown to "death by a thousand cuts."

Two Worries over Future Economic Growth

It would not be unreasonable for someone who has read this far to conclude that growth is good and no growth is bad. If you have this impression, it is because we have not yet painted the full picture. Not everyone believes growth is better than no growth, or that faster growth is better than slower growth.

Two worries commonly crop up in discussions of economic growth. One concerns the *costs* of growth. Some individuals argue that more economic growth comes with more pollution, more factories (and thus fewer open spaces), more crowded cities, more emphasis on material goods and getting ahead, more rushing around, more psychological problems, more people using drugs, more suicides, and so on. They argue for less growth instead of more.

Others maintain there is no evidence that economic growth (or faster as opposed to slower economic growth) causes all or most of these problems. They argue that growth brings many positive things: more wealth, less poverty, a society that is better able to support art projects and museums, less worry in people's lives (not having enough is a huge worry), and so forth. As for pollution and the like, such "undesirables" would be diminished if the courts were to establish and strictly enforce property rights—for example, in the rivers and the air (which are often the first to become polluted).

As you can no doubt see, the debate between those who favor more growth and those who favor less is not a simple one. Economists have become engaged in it, as have psychologists, biologists, sociologists, and many others. The debate promises to continue for a long time.

Another debate surrounds the issue of economic growth and the future availability of resources. Some people believe that continued economic and population growth threatens the very survival of the human race, since such growth will simply hasten the time when the world runs out of resources; inevitably, a time will come when there will be no more natural resources, no more clean air, no more pure water, no more land for people to live on comfortably. They urge social policies that will slow down growth and preserve what we have.

Critics of this position often charge that such "doomsday forecasts," as they have come to be called, are based on unrealistic assumptions, oversights, and flimsy evidence. For example, economist Julian Simon points out that, contrary to the doomsday forecasts, the quantity of arable land has increased in recent years owing to swamp drainage and land improvement, that there is not an inverse relationship between population growth and per-capita income growth, that the incidence of famine is decreasing, that we are not running out of natural resources, and that if and when scarcity of natural resources becomes a problem, rising relative prices of the resources will cause individuals to conserve them and stimulate economic activity to find substitutes.

Question:

It is easy to say that as oil reserves decline, for example, that the relative price of oil will rise, causing individuals to buy less oil and to search for a substitute for oil. But how can anyone be sure a good substitute will be found? Aren't the critics of the doomsday forecasts doing what they charge the doomsdayers with doing: simply making a claim instead of proving it?

Answer:

Probably some of them do this, and we need to watch out for it. But, then, the fact that someone can't come up with a substitute for *X* doesn't mean that a substitute won't one day be found. For example, it would have been hard for anyone living in eighteenth-century America to know that the car would one day be a substitute for the horse.

ECONOMIC DEVELOPMENT

■

In this section, we discuss the less-developed countries (LDCs), sometimes referred to as developing nations or third-world countries. Mainly, we are concerned with the question, Why are some nations poor?

The Problems of the Less-Developed Countries (LDCs): Why Some Nations Are Poor

Less-Developed Country (LDC)
A country with a low per-capita GNP.

A **less-developed country (LDC)** is a country with a low per-capita GNP. About three-quarters of the world's people live in LDCs.[2] Not all LDCs are alike; they differ in economic and political systems, culture, and ethnicity, to mention a few important factors.

To get some idea what a "low" per-capita GNP figure is, consider a few nations with "high" per-capita GNP figures. In 1987, Switzerland had a per-capita GNP of $27,300, the United States per-capita GNP was approximately $18,570, and Japan had a per-capita GNP of $19,410. Countries with low per-capita GNP figures include (to name only a few) Afghanistan, Bangladesh, Cambodia, China, Chad, Ethiopia, India, Nigeria, Pakistan, Somalia, Tanzania, Uganda, and Zambia. For example, in 1987, the per-capita GNP of India was $307, in China it was $438, and in Uganda it was $236. The developed nations, as a group, accounted for approximately 80 percent of the world's GNP in 1987; the LDCs for 20 percent. Per-capita GNP in the developed nations is, on average, approximately 12 times that in the LDCs.

Why has economic growth and development largely bypassed the people of the LDCs? Why are some nations so poor? Here are a few of the obstacles that some economists believe stifle economic development in the LDCs.

[2]When China and India have multiplied their per-capita incomes by about five times—to about where Greece is today—then three-quarters of the world's population will live in "rich" countries. Many experts think this will happen in less than 100 years.

Rapid Population Growth. It is commonly noticed that the population growth rate is higher in LDCs than in developed nations. The population growth rate in developed nations has been around one-half of 1 percent to 1 percent, whereas it has been around 2 to 3 percent for LDCs. The population growth rate is equal to the birthrate minus the deathrate. If in country X the birthrate is 3 percent in a given year, and the deathrate is 2 percent, the population growth rate is 1 percent.[3]

What has caused the relatively fast population growth rate in the LDCs? First, the birthrate tends to be higher than in developed nations. In countries where pensions, Social Security, and the like do not exist, and where the economy revolves around agriculture, children are often seen as essential labor and as security for parents in their old age. In this setting, people tend to have more children.

Second, in the past few decades in the LDCs, the deathrate has fallen, largely owing to medical advances. The combination of higher birthrates and declining deathrates explains why the population grows more rapidly in LDCs than in developed nations.

But is this faster population growth rate an obstacle to economic development? In Exhibit 21–4, many of the countries with the fastest-growing populations are relatively poorer on a per-capita basis than those countries with the slowest-growing populations. But this is still not proof that rapid population growth causes poverty. Many of the developed nations today witnessed faster population growth rates when they were developing than the LDCs do today.

Also, when we check population density (instead of population growth), there are a number of examples where high-density populations are much richer than low-density populations. Japan is more densely populated than India and has a higher per-capita income. The same is true for Taiwan vis-à-vis China.

Nonetheless, some still argue that rapid population growth, though not necessarily a deterrent to economic development, can stifle it. This is because in countries with fast-growing populations, the dependency ratio rises. The **dependency ratio** is the number of children under a certain age plus the number of the elderly (age 65 and over) divided by the total population. For example, if the number of

Dependency Ratio
The number of children under a certain age plus the number of the elderly (aged 65 and over) divided by the total population.

[3]In many cases, the birth- and deathrates are not given in percentage terms but in births or deaths per thousand. For example, the birthrate of country X is cited as "30 per thousand."

EXHIBIT 21–4
Some Countries with Fast and Slow Growing Populations
For the most part, countries with fast growing populations tend to be poorer than countries with slow-growing populations. There are exceptions, though. (Population figures are estimates.)

Some Countries with Fast-Growing Populations			Some Countries with Slow-Growing Populations		
	POPULATION IN 1989 (MILLIONS)	AVERAGE ANNUAL GROWTH RATE 1980–90 (PERCENT)		POPULATION IN 1989 (MILLIONS)	AVERAGE ANNUAL GROWTH RATE 1980–90 (PERCENT)
Qatar	0.5	7.7%	United States	248.0	0.9%
Saudi Arabia	16.1	5.0	Switzerland	6.6	0.4
Kuwait	2.0	4.2	Greece	10.0	0.4
Kenya	24.3	4.2	France	55.9	0.4
Bahrain	0.5	3.9	Czechoslovakia	15.6	0.3
Ivory Coast	11.6	3.6	Norway	4.2	0.3
Syria	12.0	3.6	Italy	57.5	0.2
Rwanda	7.3	3.6	Bulgaria	8.9	0.2
Iraq	18.0	3.5	United Kingdom	57.0	0.1
Ghana	14.8	3.5	Luxembourg	0.3	0.1
Equatorial Guinea	0.3	3.2	Hungary	10.5	−0.2

SOURCE: U.S. Bureau of the Census *Statistical Abstract of the United States, 1990* (Washington, D.C.: U.S. Government Printing Office, 1990).

children and elderly equals 500 and the total population is 1,500, the dependency ratio is 33 percent. The high dependency ratio in LDCs like India, Bangladesh, and Egypt puts added burdens on the productive working-age population.

Low Savings Rate. Economic growth and development requires investment, among other things. Capital formation increases labor productivity and economic growth. To accumulate capital, though, it is necessary to save; that is, to lower one's current consumption so that resources may be released for investment. It is generally argued that since living standards in the LDCs are barely above the subsistence level, and incomes must largely go for the necessities of life, there is little (if any) left over for saving. In short, LDCs are poor because they can't save and invest, but they can't save and invest because they are poor. Here we have what is usually referred to as the **vicious circle of poverty.**

    Critics charge that low (or subsistence) incomes cannot possibly be a permanent barrier to development since high (or above-subsistence) incomes were not always a feature of today's developed nations.

Cultural Differences. Do some of the LDCs have cultures that retard economic growth and development? Some people think so. For example, some cultures are reluctant to deviate from the status quo. People may think that things ought to stay the way they always have been; they view change as dangerous and risky. In these countries, it is not uncommon for a person's economic and social status to depend on who his parents were rather than on who he is or what he does; mobility is limited. In some cultures, the people are fatalistic—as measured by Western standards. They believe that a person's good or bad fortune in life is more dependent on fate than on how hard one works, or how much he or she learns, or how hard he or she strives to succeed.

Political Instability and Government Expropriation of Private Property. Individuals in both developed nations and LDCs sometimes do not invest in businesses in the LDCs because they are afraid either that the current leaders of an LDC will be toppled and thrown out of office or that the government might expropriate private property. Both political instability and the risk of government expropriation of private property substantially increase an investor's risk and therefore reduce total investment in a country. Probably the worst thing many governments of LDCs can do is to hint that they might nationalize industries. This usually scares off both domestic and foreign investors.

High Tax Rates. Some economists, like Alvin Rabushka, argue that high marginal tax rates (the *change* in a person's tax payment divided by the *change* in the person's taxable income) affect economic development. Rabushka undertook a study of the 1960–82 tax structures of 54 LDCs and categorized each LDC as a high-, low-, or medium-tax-rate nation. LDCs with top marginal tax rates of 50 percent or lower were classified as low-tax nations, whereas LDCs with top marginal tax rates of 50 percent or more that applied to incomes less than $10,000 were categorized as high-tax nations. Rabushka found that the nation with the lowest marginal tax rate, Hong Kong, had the highest growth rate in per-capita income during the period under study; low-tax nations overall had an average growth rate in per-capita income of 3.7 percent, whereas the high-tax nations had an average growth rate in per-capita income of 0.7 percent.

Vicious Circle of Poverty
The idea that countries are poor because they do not save (and invest) and that they cannot save (and invest) because they are poor.

Interview: Irma Adelman

Irma Adelman is one of the world's leading economists in the area of economic development. She has been a consultant to the United Nations, the World Bank, and numerous other national and international organizations. Adelman currently is at the University of California at Berkeley.

Why are some countries wealthy and others poor?

Historically, what mattered was whether a country had sufficient institutional development to benefit from the Industrial Revolution. Those countries that did not have the institutional conditions—either because of colonialism (e.g. India) or because of backwardness (e.g. Russia)—were unable to benefit from the revolution in technology. It was not a question of natural resources; in fact, most developing countries are, on the average, resource-rich rather than resource-poor. Even now, differences in economic performance among developing countries are much more a matter of institutional development policy choices.

Are there specific institutions that encourage development?

Yes; institutions that allow for factor mobility and political institutions that allow for a choice of policies that would be beneficial to the development of a modern industrial base.

Do you think the nations of Eastern Europe, the Soviet Union, and the People's Republic of China currently have the institutional development to make a major leap forward in economic growth and development?

No; this is what they are struggling with now. And by the way, I would distinguish between Eastern Europe and the U.S.S.R. In Eastern Europe, the human resources are still competitive with one another and eager to take the initiative, whereas in the Soviet Union, that is no longer true.

What do you predict will be the most pressing economic problem of less-developed countries in the mid-1990s?

I think it will be trade problems—specifically, trade barriers that exist in the developed world. And the other problem is ethnic-religious cleavages.

Is the latter problem insurmountable?

No one has developed a good method for handling ethnic-religious cleavages throughout history. And that is not a matter of development levels because we have some developed countries that are plagued with those problems.

Do you think the United States has a responsibility to less-developed countries?

Yes, it does. Its responsibility is to assist with a sensible development process and to use its influence to provide an international environment so that development is possible.

How do you think it is meeting this responsibility now?

On the aid front, very poorly; on the trade front, not too badly. The total amount of foreign assistance is small, and 80 percent of the foreign assistance is disbursed on political–strategic grounds. So there is very little that remains to be disbursed on economic and need criteria. Unfortunately, I don't see this changing. If anything, it is going to get worse.

Why worse?

The aftermath of the Gulf War.

You once said that "in countries in which you start out from a very unequal allocation of assets and opportunities, the market may work against reducing poverty." Why do you think things turn out this way given the condition you have specified?

One major reason is political. The wealthy capture the political apparatus and make sure that the government enacts policies that favor their interests. When the distribution of assets, including human assets, is not very uneven, industrialization eventually produces a middle class. And the middle class is capable of reorienting political policies in such a way that things are less unequal.

How would you describe the economic way of thinking?

Well, I am at odds with the general way of thinking in economics. Economists pretend that the way to approach problems is through hypothesis testing. But I believe that there are too many plausible hypotheses out there and we know too little to be able to formulate the hypotheses sharply enough so that hypothesis testing will, in general, be a fruitful approach.

What is an alternative to doing things the current way?

In statistics the approach goes by the name of exploratory data analysis. The approach applies fairly powerful statistical techniques to real-world data in such a way as to reduce the complexity of the data. Then one uses the results to help formulate hypotheses.

What got you interested in economics?

I hesitate to say because it sounds arrogant. My reason was that I wanted to benefit humanity. And my perception at the time was that economic problems were the most important problems that humanity has to face. That is what got me into economics and into economic development.

Why do you say it sounds arrogant?

Because it is arrogant to think that one person can make a real difference.

You said that "my perception at the time was that economic problems were the most important problems that humanity has to face." Has your perception changed?

Yes, a little bit. In the sense that I now recognize politicians can do a lot to change the situation—either for the better or the worse. But politics isn't my comparative advantage.

Question:

This approach to explaining why some nations are poor seems to be a "throw everything into the pot" approach—the poverty that some nations experience could be because of a low saving rate, and could be because of high population growth, and could be because of this and that. Aren't there some explanations that apply to all LDCs?

Answer:

This is one of the frustrations of research that we warned about earlier. Unfortunately, economists are not agreed on "the" reason why some nations are poor. It is not hard, however, to find *an* economist who will tell you what he or she thinks "the" reason is. Some economists might tell you that some nations are poor because they do not put free market practices into effect. Other economists will tell you that a very unequal wealth distribution retards economic development. With time and more and better research, we may be able to throw out a few of the things that are currently in the pot.

Fungibility

Fungibility
A term that is Latin in origin, meaning "such that any unit is substitutable for another." Fungibility means substitutable.

Fungibility is a key concept in economics. It comes from a Latin term that means "such that any unit is substitutable for another." In short, it simply means *substitutable*. For example, points in a basketball game are fungible. Team A plays team B in basketball and beats it by two points; the last two points are scored in the last second of the game by player Robinson, who is carried off the basketball court on the shoulders of his teammates. The headline in the newspaper the next day reads "Robinson Wins Game."

But what about player Petrie's two points in the first minute of the game? Had Petrie not gotten those two points, Robinson's two points would not have "won" the game. Why not then say that Petrie's two points were as important as Robinson's two points?

Well, that doesn't seem quite as exciting. But, nevertheless, it is true. Petrie's and Robinson's points are fungible: They are substitutable.

Money is fungible, too. Suppose Jack's parents hand over $200 to him and tell him to buy his textbooks with the money. Will the $200 actually be used to buy textbooks? Possibly, it will; Jack may take the $200 and buy his books. But possibly it won't. The $200 Jack's parents gave him can be used to buy clothes, and the $200 he earned last week can now be used to pay for his books. In the latter case, what did Jack's money really pay for—the books or the clothes? Since money is fungible, there is no sensible way to answer this question.

Now consider foreign aid. One government gives another government $100 million and makes the recipient government promise to use the money for project X. Is the money really used for project X? The answer is, not necessarily. Money, remember, is fungible. The $100 million might be used for project X, but then the recipient government has money it might have used for project X that it can now use on any project it wants.

Let's say country Z has $400 million to spend, and it would like to complete the following projects:

1. Build factories for $200 million.
2. Build roads and schools for $100 million.
3. Upgrade agriculture for $100 million.
4. Build a lavish palace for the leader of the country for $100 million.

Currently, the country can only complete projects 1–3.

Now the United States, say, gives $100 million to country Z and specifies that the money must be used to build roads and schools. So country Z does as the United States says. But now it has $100 million that can be used to build a lavish palace for the leader of the country. Did the U.S. money go for schools and roads or for a palace? Once again, money is fungible.

Question:

Is this an argument against the United States giving money to poor nations?

Answer:

No, it isn't. The point is simply that money given may not always be used for the purpose that the donor nation would prefer. However, the United States, or any other country for that matter, may decide that giving the money is preferable to not giving it, even though some of the money may be spent for purposes the donor has not intended.

The World Debt Crisis

Throughout the 1980s, there was much talk about a world debt crisis. Some of the LDCs—Mexico, Argentina, Brazil, the Philippines, Chile, and Nigeria, for example—had huge outstanding loans they were scheduled to repay to (mostly) Western banks, many of them in the United States. At the time, some people thought that the LDCs would default on the loans and that one major U.S. bank after another would fail.

How did this situation develop? Is the crisis over? What will happen? Most economists believe that the debt crisis had its origin in the quadrupling of oil prices by OPEC in 1973. After the price increase, the oil-rich nations began to run huge current account surpluses. The OPEC nations, in turn, deposited much of their oil money in U.S. banks. At the same time, many of the LDC oil-importing nations began to run deficits in their current accounts. The U.S. banks began to *recycle* the oil money to the LDCs. Some of this money went for worthwhile investment projects, some did not. For example, in some countries the borrowed funds were used for consumption rather than for investment.

In the late 1970s, some of the oil-exporting LDCs, such as Mexico, began to borrow huge sums from U.S. banks. Why did the U.S. banks extend them credit? Since oil prices were still rising, it looked as if Mexico and others would have no trouble paying off the loans. (If you are poor today, but your bank believes you will be rich tomorrow, then it will most likely be happy to extend you credit.) Then in 1981, the price of oil began to fall.

In August 1982, Mexico told Citibank of New York that it could not pay its loans on time. Other countries in a similar position began to follow suit. The list included both oil-importing LDCs, which had gotten into debt because of the rising price of oil in the 1970s, and oil-exporting LDCs, which had gotten into debt because of the falling price of oil in the early-to-mid 1980s. Lending banks were largely forced into *restructuring* and *rescheduling* the debt—extending the payback period, reducing interest payments, and so on. In this environment, LCDs have few funds to invest in new capital projects required for economic growth.

What the outcome will be largely depends on the state of the world economy (Will it grow enough so that debtor nations can export goods and earn the currency needed to meet their loan payments? Will it stagnate?) and the domestic economic policies that the LDCs with debt problems implement (Will they cut back on extravagant spending?). Some economists argue that the huge interest payments that some LDCs have to pay on their loans will prevent them from becoming developed nations for some time.

CHAPTER SUMMARY

Economic Growth

■ The term *economic growth* refers to either *real economic growth* or to *per-capita real economic growth*. Real economic growth is an increase from one period to the next in *real GNP*. Per-capita real economic growth is an increase from one period to the next in *per-capita real GNP,* which is real GNP divided by population.

■ Economists often argue that economic growth is dependent on a society's natural resources, rate of capital formation (physical and human), technological advances, and property rights structure. More natural resources, more and better capital goods and human capital, more and better technological advances, and a property rights structure that largely allows individuals to keep the fruits of their labor are thought to promote per-capita economic growth. This does not mean, however, that a nation with, say, many natural resources will necessarily experience faster per-capita economic growth than a nation with a few natural resources. There could be offsetting factors.

■ When calculating how long it will take a nation's economy to double in size, economists use the Rule of 72: To calculate the time required for any variable to double, divide its percentage growth rate into 72.

Productivity Slowdown

■ The decline in U.S. economic growth in the 1970s was largely caused by a slowdown in labor productivity which, it has been argued, was caused by one or more of the following: a decline in capital per hour worked, a decline in the quality of the labor force, major oil price increases, and regulation.

The Problems of the LDCs

■ Most economists cite one or more of the following problems as the reason(s) the LDCs are poor: rapid population growth rate (high dependency ratio), low savings rate, a culture that does not lend itself to economic growth, political instability and the threat of government expropriation of private property, and high tax rates.

Key Terms and Concepts

Real Economic Growth

Per-Capita Real
    Economic Growth

Less-Developed Country
    (LDC)

Dependency Ratio

Vicious Circle of
    Poverty

Fungibility

QUESTIONS AND PROBLEMS

1. Suppose the population growth rate of country X is 3 percent and the population growth rate of country Y is 0.5 percent. How long will it take before the population of each country has doubled?

2. How do you explain that some countries with plentiful natural resources are developed whereas others are less developed (LDCs)? How do you explain that some countries with few natural resources are developed whereas some countries with plentiful natural resources are less developed?

3. What is one of the major failings of "doomsday" forecasts?

4. Would you expect the birthrate in LDCs to go up or down as a result of per-capita economic growth and economic development?

5. If, before you had read this chapter, someone had asked you why the LDCs were poor and what they should do to promote economic development, what would you have said? What would you say now? Is there much difference between the two views? To what do you attribute the difference?

6. Absolute economic growth is about increasing the size of the economic pie. Per-capita economic growth is about increasing the size of the economic pie faster than the population is growing, so not only is there more but also there is more per person. Explain how different property rights structures might help or hinder both absolute and per-capita economic growth.

7. Some people argue that the LDCs will not grow and develop without foreign aid from developed countries. Other people say that foreign aid actually limits growth and development (they see it as a handout that distorts the incentive to produce) and propose in its place a reliance on foreign trade. In the real world, there is some of both. Do you think, however, that an increase in the aid-to-trade ratio (amount of foreign aid received divided by the amount of foreign trade) would decrease, increase, or leave unchanged the economic development of an LDC? What about a decrease? Explain your answers.

22

ALTERNATIVE ECONOMIC SYSTEMS: THEORY, PRACTICE, AND EVOLUTIONARY ASPECTS

WHAT THIS CHAPTER IS ABOUT

The bulk of this book has described the workings of the economic system that is best known as *mixed capitalism.* It is the economic system that, to different degrees, exists in the United States, Canada, Australia, and Japan, to name only a few countries. In this chapter, we discuss a few of the alternatives to mixed capitalism. The list includes *pure capitalism, command-economy socialism,* and *decentralized socialism.*

We also discuss the economies of the Soviet Union, China, and Japan.

ECONOMIC SYSTEMS AND SHARED ECONOMIC REALITIES

■

First, we define mixed capitalism and its alternatives and discuss the economic realities facing all economic systems. Then, we examine some of the similarities and differences of the various systems.

Mixed Capitalism and Its Alternatives

Mixed capitalism is an economic system characterized by largely private ownership of the factors of production, market allocation of resources, and decentralized decision making; most economic activities take place in the private sector, but government plays a substantial economic and regulatory role.

Pure capitalism is an economic system characterized by purely private ownership of the factors of production, market allocation of resources, and decentralized decision making; most economic activities take place in the private sector, and government plays a small role or no role at all in the economy.

Command-economy socialism is an economic system characterized by government ownership of the nonlabor factors of production, government allocation of resources, and centralized decision making; most economic activities take place in the public sector, and government plays a very large role in the economy.

Decentralized socialism is an economic system characterized by government ownership of the nonlabor factors of production, largely market allocation of resources, and decentralized decision making; most economic activities take place in the public sector, and government plays a major overseer role in the economy.

See Exhibit 22–1 for a review of the principal properties of the four economic systems outlined here.

Question:

Suppose seven countries are identified as mixed capitalist. Does it follow that the seven are mixed capitalist to the same degree?

Answer:

No, that is not exactly the case. An analogy is class grades. Suppose Jerry gets an 89 on a test and Trenton gets an 81. Both of them receive a B for a grade and thus

Mixed Capitalism
An economic system characterized by largely private ownership of the factors of production, market allocation of resources, and decentralized decision making; most economic activities take place in the private sector in this system, but government plays a substantial economic and regulatory role.

Pure Capitalism
An economic system characterized by private ownership of the factors of production, market allocation of resources, and decentralized decision making; most economic activities take place in the private sector, and government plays a small role or no role at all in the economy.

Command-Economy Socialism
An economic system characterized by government ownership of the nonlabor factors of production, government allocation of resources, and centralized decision making; most economic activities take place in the public sector, and government plays a very large role in the economy.

Decentralized Socialism
An economic system characterized by government ownership of the nonlabor factors of production, largely market allocation of resources, and decentralized decision making; most economic activities take place in the public sector, and government plays a major overseer role in the economy.

EXHIBIT 22–1
Four Economic Systems
The principal properties of four economic systems are summarized.

ECONOMIC SYSTEM	OWNERSHIP OF FACTORS OF PRODUCTION	ALLOCATION OF RESOURCES	DECISION MAKING	WHERE DO MOST ECONOMIC ACTIVITIES TAKE PLACE?	ROLE GOVERNMENT PLAYS IN THE ECONOMY
Mixed Capitalism	Largely private	Market allocation	Decentralized	Private sector	Plays a substantial economic and regulatory role
Pure Capitalism	Purely private	Market allocation	Decentralized	Private sector	Small or no role
Command-Economy Socialism	Government ownership of nonlabor factors of production	Government allocation	Centralized	Public sector	Very large role
Decentralized Socialism	Government ownership of nonlabor factors of production	Largely market allocation	Decentralized	Public sector	Major role

In all societies—no matter their economic system—there is no such thing as a free lunch.

both are B students. We can't really say which student is more of a B student, but we can say that Jerry, who is a B student, is a little closer to being an A student than Trenton, who is also a B student. Similarly, we might say that country X, with a mixed capitalist economic system, is closer to pure capitalism than country Y, or that country Y, with a mixed capitalist economic system, is closer to decentralized socialism than country X.

Shared Economic Realities

All economies share some features. We outline them here.

Scarcity. In Chapters 1 and 2, we introduced the concept of scarcity, which is the condition where wants outstrip the resources available to satisfy them. We already know that mixed capitalist economies must face up to the reality of scarcity. But what about pure capitalist, command-economy socialist, and decentralized socialist economies? Do they have to deal with scarcity? They certainly do. All economic systems must deal with scarcity. The people in the United States, the Soviet Union, the People's Republic of China, Japan, Venezuela, Saudi Arabia, and every other country in the world must grapple with it. What distinguishes economic systems is not that some economic systems have to deal with scarcity and others do not, but rather how different economic systems deal with scarcity.

Opportunity Cost, or No Free Lunch. We learned in earlier chapters that opportunity cost is a consequence of scarcity. It follows, therefore, that since all economic systems must deal with scarcity, all economic systems are faced with opportunity cost. In short, in all societies there is no such thing as a free lunch. This is the case in the United States, the Soviet Union, India, Chile, the People's Republic of China, and every other country.

Rationing Devices. Since all economic systems are faced with scarcity, all economic systems must ration goods. In the United States, for example, this is largely done through (dollar) price. Cars, houses, television sets, computers, toothbrushes, clocks, books, and much more are rationed by price. If, in some societies, money price is seen as a less than desirable rationing device, then some other rationing device must be put in its place. It may be first-come-first-served, political power, or something else, but in a world of scarcity, societies must always decide on a rationing device or devices.

The Law of Demand. Does the law of demand only hold for mixed capitalist economies and not for command-economy or decentralized socialist economies? It certainly does not. The law of demand holds for all economic systems. If the dollar price of television sets rises, Americans will buy fewer television sets, *ceteris paribus.* And if the ruble price of television sets rises, Russians will buy fewer television sets, *ceteris paribus.*

Rational Self-Interested Behavior. Rational self-interested behavior means to act in such a way as to maximize the difference between the benefits and costs as perceived by the individual. It is generally assumed that individuals all over the world, no matter what their economic system, exhibit this type of behavior.

What Goods will be Produced? How will the Goods be Produced? For Whom will the Goods be Produced? All economic systems must decide what goods will be produced, how the goods will be produced, and for whom the goods will be produced.

For example, will the economy produce more books or more fax machines? Implicit here is the question who decides what the economy produces. Will it be the marketplace, composed of millions of buyers and sellers, or a central government committee?

Once this question is answered, the economic system must decide how the goods will be produced. For example, will food staples be produced on private farms, or on large state-operated collective farms?

Finally, for whom are these goods produced? Are they produced for the people who pay the prices for them? Are they produced for whomever the government decides needs or should have them? Socialists often argue that capitalism produces houses for people who can pay the money prices for the houses and that socialism produces houses for people who need houses. Critics charge that socialism produces low-quality houses for people the government officials believe need houses and that need usually is linked to political party loyalty.

THINKING LIKE AN ECONOMIST

In our discussion of the shared economic realities of different societies, we noted that economists assume that individuals all over the world, no matter what their economic system, exhibit rational self-interested behavior. This does not mean, though, that individuals in different societies necessarily exhibit the same behavior because the costs and benefits of particular actions in different societies will be different. For example, in society A the costs of expressing one's opinion (say, about government political and economic policies) may be higher than the benefits and therefore an individual chooses not to express his opinions; whereas in society B the costs of expressing one's opinion are lower than the benefits and one does express his opinion. Is the individual in society A exhibiting rational self-interested behavior and the individual in society B not? Or are they both exhibiting rational self-interested behavior, while simply responding to a different configuration of costs and benefits? The economist will say it is the latter.

PURE CAPITALISM

Pure capitalism sometimes goes by the names *laissez-faire capitalism, anarcho-capitalism,* or *libertarianism.* Adherents to the pure capitalism position are usually referred to as *libertarians.* Libertarians either see a very limited role or no role at all for government. The former principally see government's role as protecting property rights and enforcing contracts. Some libertarians add the provision of national defense to this list. The latter argue that any government at all is too much government. They maintain that the free market is capable of providing roads, courts, police protection, and so forth. In this section we discuss the libertarians' case for pure capitalism.

Arguing the Pure Capitalism Case

For most libertarians, many public problems are caused by too much government. As a solution to these problems, libertarians usually recommend less government and greater reliance on the forces of the free market. Here are a few things libertarians say.

1. **Professional licensing.** Professional licensing reduces the supply of a service and increases its price. For example, because medical licensing makes it more difficult for individuals to become physicians and for nurses to compete directly with physicians, licensing increases the price of medical care. In a pure capitalist economy, professional licensing would not exist; that it largely does exist today is because government, by licensing certain trades, serves as the cartel enforcer of a special-interest group.

2. **Minimum wage law.** Minimum wage laws are a restraint on free trade. Setting a minimum wage guarantees that individuals whose present skills are worth less than the minimum wage will go unemployed. Individuals have the (natural) right to work for whatever wage they voluntarily agree to, and government, by passing a minimum wage law, prevents individuals from exercising this right in some instances. The minimum wage would not exist under pure capitalism.

3. **The U.S. Postal Service.** Private companies can and should be allowed to deliver first-class mail. Under pure capitalism, a number of competing mail services would deliver first-class mail, and such competition would drive prices down and quality up.

4. **Restraints on price.** All restraints on price, either price floors or price ceilings, reduce voluntary exchange to a level below that which would exist in a pure capitalist economy. Libertarians are against interest rate ceilings, minimum wages (as noted earlier), agricultural price supports, and rent controls.

5. **Discretionary fiscal and monetary policies.** Government intervention in the economy, via fiscal policy (taxing and spending policies) and monetary policy, often has negative effects—such as high interest rates, inflation, recession, and high unemployment. The free market is inherently stable and capable of equilibrating at full-employment output.

6. **The Federal Reserve.** The Federal Reserve System, the central bank of the United States, should be eliminated. It is an "engine of inflation," far too political, and the cause of unnecessary and harmful ups and downs in the economy. In monetary policy, libertarians usually favor an automatic monetary mechanism as opposed to a discretionary one. This translates into a monetary rule or a gold standard.

7. **Antitrust policy.** Government antitrust policy too often stifles market competition and is used to attack firms for no other reason than that they are big. Pure capitalism, which maximizes competitive forces, is the best antitrust policy. Firms are much more afraid of successful competitors than they are of government antitrust policy. In a related argument, libertarians maintain that antitrust policy is sometimes used by firms to limit their competition. For example, firm X, in competition with firm Y, may argue before the antitrust authorities against the merger between firm Y and firm Z. Too often, the authorities will accept the argument and a merger that possibly might increase productivity, reduce costs, and ultimately increase quality and lower price will not be permitted.

8. **Quotas and tariffs.** Quotas and tariffs increase prices and decrease exchange and only serve narrow special-interest groups. Neither would exist in a pure capitalist society.

9. **Social Security.** To libertarians, Social Security combines a compulsory savings program with a redistribution program—both of which they oppose. It is wrong to force people to save for old age (or anything else for that matter). How much one saves or doesn't save should be up to the individual. As to the redistributory aspect of Social Security, it is tantamount to theft for the government to reach into one person's pocket, take out money, and redistribute that money to someone else.

10. Welfare. Welfare is a forced redistribution program. In addition, in many instances, welfare programs produce outcomes contrary to the stated goals of the programs. For example, welfare often makes people more dependent on others and less likely to acquire work skills. Libertarians are in favor of voluntary charities.

A Critique of Libertarianism

The pure capitalism case, or libertarianism, has many critics. Here are some of the points the critics make:

1. Libertarians do not see the merit of using government's taxing, subsidy, and regulatory powers to adjust for third-party effects. In most exchanges, probably only two persons are affected—the person buying the good or service and the person selling the good or service. In some exchanges, however, there are *third-party effects,* whereby someone not involved in the exchange itself is nonetheless affected by it. Sometimes the third party is affected adversely by an exchange that others enter into: Say, company X produces steel that it sells to customers; in the process it generates pollution that harms people that live near the steel factory. And sometimes the third party is affected positively: Say, the university sells education to students; in the process it generates benefits for people who now reside in a community of well-educated individuals. Many economists argue that third-party effects should be taken into account, or adjusted for, and that government is the proper institution to do the adjusting—through regulation, taxes, subsidies, and so forth. For example, government might subsidize education so that the social benefits, not just the private benefits, are realized. In addition, sometimes the only way third-party effects *can* be adjusted for is through government. Thus, the choice is either letting government adjust or not adjusting at all.

2. Libertarians do not seriously consider complex exchanges. A simple exchange might be one person trading an apple for $1. A complex exchange may be millions of voters choosing a political candidate who has promised, if elected, to increase government spending on defense, education, or public assistance programs. The critics of libertarianism argue that some goods and services simply cannot be obtained through the free market, and therefore people naturally turn to the political "market" to obtain them. They criticize libertarians for not seeing that exchange comes in different varieties. Many libertarians would maintain that a complex exchange is not really an exchange at all. What about the person who votes against the candidate who is elected and raises spending on defense? Libertarians might question whether this voter is benefiting from the so-called complex exchange. If not, then it is not clear an exchange has taken place.

The words of economist James Buchanan are relevant here:

> Politics is a structure of complex exchange among individuals, a structure within which persons seek to secure collectively their own privately defined objectives that cannot be efficiently secured through simple market exchanges. . . . In the market, individuals exchange apples for oranges; in politics, individuals exchange agreed-on shares in contributions toward the costs of that which is commonly desired, from the services of the local fire station to that of the judge.[1]

3. Libertarians do not see the stabilizing effects of government monetary and fiscal policies. Most libertarians will say that they do not see the stabilizing effects of government monetary and fiscal policies because there are no stabilizing effects

[1]James Buchanan, "The Constitution of Economic Policy," *American Economic Review 77* (June 1987): 244.

to see. The critics argue otherwise, saying that since the economy does not always self-equilibrate at full-employment output, government management policies have a role to play.

KARL MARX (1818–83)

Karl Marx has played a major part in the development of socialist thought. Here we present a few of his major ideas.

The Basics of Marx's Thought

Few economists have had as much influence on the world as Karl Marx. In turn, Marx was influenced by the economist David Ricardo and the philosopher Georg Hegel, among others, in particular, by Ricardo's discussion of the labor theory of value and Hegel's dialectic.

Labor Theory of Value
Holds that the value of all commodities is equal to the value of the labor used in producing them.

The Labor Theory of Value. The **labor theory of value** holds that all value in produced goods is derived from direct and indirect (or embodied) labor. A man or woman working on a factory line is an example of direct labor. A machine, made by a man or woman, is an example of indirect, or embodied, labor.

Marx argued that the value of a commodity is determined by the *socially necessary labor time* embodied in the commodity. This is the sum of the direct and indirect (or embodied) labor necessary to produce socially desired commodities. (By using the adjective *socially,* Marx was able to differentiate between those goods that were genuinely desired by people—like shoes, coats, and houses—and those that were not—like sand castles on the beach.)

For example, if it takes 5 hours of socially necessary labor time to produce *X* and 10 hours to produce *Y,* then *Y* will be twice as valuable as *X.* Marx realized that labor was not all of equal quality, but he believed that skilled labor could be calculated as some multiple of unskilled labor.

Marx maintained that the labor, or labor power, capitalists purchase is itself a commodity, and thus its value (like that of commodities) is determined by labor time. Also, the value of labor power tends toward a subsistence wage, that is, the *labor time* necessary for the worker to earn the necessities consumed by the worker and his or her family.

Consider an example from Marx's time. Suppose a worker needs 2 shillings a day to subsist. Furthermore, suppose it takes 4 labor hours to produce the gold that is in 2 shillings. This means that the worker needs to work 4 hours to earn 2 shillings. Two shillings is the value of labor power—it is what workers would be paid for a day's work. But here is the sticking point: The workday is longer than 4 hours. It is 10 hours. In this case, the worker works a 10-hour day to earn 2 shillings (which is equal to 4 hours labor time), and the value produced by the worker in the 6 remaining hours is **surplus value** that the capitalist exploits from the worker.

Surplus Value
In Marxist terminology, the difference between the total value of production and the subsistence wages paid to workers.

Question:

Why couldn't the worker simply refuse to work more than 4 hours for 2 shillings? In short, why wouldn't the worker prevent the capitalist from exploiting him or her?

Answer:

Marx argued that capitalism creates a large *reserve army of the unemployed* and this excess supply of labor keeps wages at the subsistence level. For Marx, it was a matter of the worker working on the capitalist's terms or not working at all.

Dialectic. According to Hegel, knowledge and progress occur through a process of integrating opposing ideas or forces. An existing idea, or *thesis,* is at some point confronted with an opposing idea, *antithesis,* and there is a struggle of sorts. The outcome of the struggle is a *synthesis,* which in turn becomes the new thesis and the process starts again. Marx adapted Hegel's **dialectic** to explain the stages of economic development.

Dialectic
The method of logic based on the principle that an idea or event (thesis) generates its opposite (antithesis), leading to a reconciliation of opposites (synthesis).

Marx on Economic Development

Marx criticized many of his economic predecessors and contemporaries for not understanding that capitalism had emerged as a specific economic system, or mode of production, and through the dialectical process would eventually evolve into a different economic system. According to Marx, there are six stages of economic development through which a nation would progress:

■ *Primitive communism.* The first stage of economic development is characterized by common ownership of property, and people cooperate to earn a meager living from nature. People generally have to work all day simply to produce the bare necessities for survival. Under these conditions, there is no surplus value and thus no exploitation since both require workers to produce more than they need to consume for survival.

■ *Slavery.* At some point, the productive capabilities of people rise to such an extent that they are able to produce more than they need to consume for survival. Now slavery becomes a possibility; some people exploit others and garner the surplus value. Once this occurs, class conflict arises.

■ *Feudalism.* The economic actors in feudalism were lords and serfs, who, in Marx's view, had a relationship that was essentially the same as that between the slavemasters and slaves in the preceding stage of economic development. The serf was permitted to work a few days per week on the land allotted to him, but on other days he was required to till the lord's land.

■ *Capitalism.* Marx both disliked capitalism and marveled at its ability to greatly increase productivity and output. According to Marx, the means of production became more concentrated under capitalism. For him, the relationship between capitalist and worker was essentially the same as the relationship between slavemaster and slave and between lord and serf in earlier stages of economic development. The capitalist appeared to pay the worker for all the hours that he or she worked, but in reality only paid for a few hours and appropriated the value produced in the remaining hours to himself. Marx predicted intense class struggles under capitalism between the capitalists, or *bourgeoisie,* and the workers, or *proletariat.* He believed that capitalists would increasingly exploit the workers in the search for higher profits.

■ *Dictatorship of the proletariat, or socialism.* According to Marx, the intense class struggles under capitalism will eventually result in the state being used as an instrument of oppression by the capitalists against the workers. The workers will rise in revolt and overthrow the bourgeois state and establish in its place the dictatorship of the proletariat, in which the capital and land are owned by the proletarian government. Exploitation of the workers will cease.

■ *Pure communism.* The dictatorship of the proletariat eventually "withers away," only pure communism remains. In this stage of economic development, individuals produce according to their abilities and receive according to their needs. In pure communism, the highest stage of economic development, selfishness and greed are largely a thing of the past, and there is no need for a formal government apparatus.

The Critics of Marx

Here are some of the criticisms that have been levied against Marx's work:

1. The labor theory of value is faulty. Most contemporary economists agree that labor is not the sole source of value. They argue that land, capital, and entrepreneurship are independent factors of production and, like labor, are capable of creating value. Marxists sometimes retort that capital is ultimately created by labor, thus making it embodied labor. The critics agree that capital is *in part* past labor (and note that labor is paid its contribution to the production of capital), but they point out that capital is capable of creating value beyond the value of the labor employed to produce it.

2. There is no large reserve army of the unemployed. Marx maintained that capitalism produced a large reserve army of the unemployed that capitalists could use to hold wages down to a subsistence level. Massive unemployment has occurred under capitalism, but this has been the exception rather than the rule.

3. Most workers earn an above-subsistence wage. Here the critics argue that the competition for workers among business firms puts upward pressure on wages and causes firms to improve working conditions, shorten working hours, provide fringe benefits, and so forth.

4. Marxist revolutions have not appeared in the places Marx expected. Marx expected worker revolutions to appear in advanced capitalist nations where capitalism has had the longest time to develop, and the class conflict between capitalists and workers has had the longest time to intensify. According to Marx, countries such as Great Britain and the United States were far more likely to experience revolutions than countries such as Russia and China.

THE SOVIET ECONOMY: FROM COMMAND-ECONOMY SOCIALISM TO "IN TRANSITION"

■

Between 1985 and 1987, the Soviet economy evidenced growing problems: Growth rates were declining, there were few high-quality goods for consumers to buy, the scientific gap with the West was widening. In this environment, Soviet President Mikhail Gorbachev proposed two major reforms, which can be designated by the Russian terms *glasnost* and *perestroika*. **Glasnost** means greater openness in public discussions and the arts; **perestroika** means economic reform. The economic reforms are of particular interest to us.

The Soviet Union had been the primary example of a nation that practiced command-economy socialism. With the Gorbachev reforms, people began to wonder whether the Soviet Union would actually move away from command-economy socialism.

Glasnost
A Russian term popularly used to mean openness in public discussion and the arts.

Perestroika
A Russian term used to describe Soviet economic reform.

In August, 1991, communist hardliners waged a coup d'etat against Gorbachev. With Gorbachev under house arrest at his vacation home, Russian President and economic reform advocate, Boris Yeltsin, remained in the Russian republic's Parliament building and rallied large crowds to protest the military takeover. Coup leaders fled Moscow after they discovered that several military units would oppose the coup. Gorbachev was back in power in Moscow about 72 hours after he was first detained at his vacation home.

Immediately after the unsuccessful coup, Soviet President Gorbachev and Russian President Yeltsin forged a political alliance. Both men seemed committed to moving the Soviet economy away from command-economy socialism towards an economy where market forces and private property played a larger role than they had in the past. In the midst of their pursuit of economic reforms, many of the Soviet republics pushed for independence (independence was granted to the Baltic republics of Lithuania, Latvia, and Estonia in September, 1991), the Soviet economy witnessed an inflation rate of 250 percent, industrial production dropped substantially, and severe food shortages appeared imminent. So dire was the economic situation in the Soviet Union that many Soviet observers stated that another coup might be likely. This is the recent and fast-moving history of the Soviet Union.

We begin this section with a discussion of command-economy socialism, with particular reference to the Soviet economy. (In our description of the Soviet command economy, we continue to use the present tense, although events have already brought some changes.) We end with a discussion of the recent political and economic events in the Soviet Union—especially as they relate to the future of the Soviet economic system.

The Public and Private Sectors under Command-Economy Socialism

Under command-economy socialism, the private sector is very small; the public sector correspondingly large. This is simply another way of saying that most of what there is to be owned is owned by the central government—the state. For example, in the Soviet Union under command-economy socialism, the government owns and operates almost all the manufacturing, communication, transportation, and banking enterprises; wholesale and retail stores; and farms. A relatively few private farms (along with some garden plots), retail shops, and private personal services constitute the legal private sector. In addition to the legal private sector, command economies always have *black markets,* where goods are traded in violation of official regulations and prices. Still, the black market and the legal private sector together represent only a small percentage of the total economic activity in command economies.

Gosplan

In the Soviet Union under command-economy socialism, the central planning agency, or **Gosplan,** has the responsibility of drafting the economic plan for the Soviet economy. Gosplan does not, however, draft the economic plan without receiving input from the high Communist party officials in the Politburo (parliament), as well as supervision by the Council of Ministers, whose vice chairman is also the director of Gosplan.

Gosplan constructs two plans: a five-year (long-range) plan and a one-year (short-range) plan. The five-year plan allocates the nation's economic resources; it deter-

Gosplan
In the Soviet Union under command-economy socialism, the Soviet central planning agency that has the responsibility of drafting the economic plan for the nation.

mines how much goes to investment, how much to the military, how much to consumption, and so forth. The one-year plans are much more detailed than the five-year plans; they outline what each of the more than 200,000 Soviet enterprises under Gosplan's supervision is to produce, the amounts of labor and raw materials each will be allocated, the amount and type of machinery that will be installed, and so on.

To get a sense of how the process works, let's translate it to the American scene. If there were an American Gosplan, it would probably be located in Washington, D.C. The American Gosplan would then issue orders to General Motors, IBM, and other companies stating what each is to produce. For example, it might direct General Motors to produce 300,000 cars. In turn, Gosplan would direct the companies supplying General Motors to send so much steel, so much plastic, and so many tires to the company. It would also tell General Motors whether it could expect to have its factories updated, what type of new capital goods would be arriving, and other crucial information.

Allocating Resources: A Major Problem under Command-Economy Socialism

A planning agency's task is monumental; it must take the inputs of the economy and direct them into outputs in a manner consistent with the objectives set forth by the government leadership. This requires a careful balancing between output goals and available resources.

Suppose the planning agency sets as its annual goal the production of 100,000 units of X, 200,000 units of Y, and 300,000 units of Z. Next, it must allocate resources in such a way that it meets its goals. Suppose input W is necessary to the production of goods X, Y, and Z. The planning agency must then allocate input W so that 100,000 units of X, 200,000 units of Y, and 300,000 units of Z are produced. How will it know exactly how much input W to send to the enterprises producing goods X, Y, and Z? To know this, the planning agency needs to know how many units of W are required to make $1X$, $1Y$, and $1Z$.

Perhaps the planning agency thinks that 5 units of W are needed to make $1X$, 4 units of W are needed to make $1Y$, and 6 units of W are needed to make $1Z$. It therefore allocates 500,000 units of W to the enterprise producing good X ($5W$ for each of the required $100,000X$), 800,000 units of W to the enterprise producing good Y ($4W$ for each of the required $200,000Y$), and 1,800,000 units of W to the enterprise producing good Z ($6W$ for each of the required $300,000Z$). Although this sounds simple enough, several problems can easily arise.

First, the planning agency might incorrectly estimate the number of units of W that are required to make $1X$, $1Y$, and $1Z$. It could, say, overestimate the number of units of W required to produce good X and underestimate the number of units of W required to produce good Z. If this happens, then too many units of W will be sent to one enterprise and too few units of W will be sent to another.

Second, the number of units of input W required to make $1X$, $1Y$, and $1Z$ is likely to change over time. The quality of input W might fall so that more units will be needed to make $1X$. Will the planning agency know about this right away and adjust accordingly?

Third, the enterprise making W might require inputs from the enterprise that produces X before it can produce and ship W. Consider an enterprise that produces trucks. To produce trucks, the enterprise requires oil to generate the energy to run its plants. But, in turn, the enterprise producing oil needs trucks to move the oil to the truck factory. In such a situation, where one enterprise's production depends on another's, a failure by one enterprise to meet its production goals can make it impossible for other enterprises to meet their production goals, too.

Question:

First, if a U.S. enterprise fails to produce as expected, can't this make it impossible for other enterprises to meet their production goals, just as in the Soviet Union? After all, if firm X needs what firm Y produces and firm Y needs what firm Z produces, a slip-up by firm Z can prevent firms X and Y from producing as many units of their goods as they might want.

Answer:

Certainly, in the United States, one firm might be dependent on receiving supplies from another firm, but if it doesn't receive its supplies, it is more likely than its Soviet counterpart to locate substitute inputs. In the Soviet Union, if an enterprise doesn't receive the necessary inputs to make good X, the directors of the enterprise really have no incentive to locate substitute inputs. It is not the job of the directors of the enterprise to solve economic problems like this; it is the job of the planning agency. In the United States, however, the managers and owners of the business firm have an incentive to find substitute inputs because less output often means fewer dollars in their pockets.

The Case against Central Economic Planning

One of the major differences between individuals who favor pure capitalism and those who favor command-economy socialism is the issue of economic planning. The former are against central economic planning, and the latter are for it.

Critics advance two major arguments against central economic planning. First, economic plans, made by economic planners, cannot take into account as much relevant information as a market does; therefore, economic plans cannot coordinate economic activity or satisfy consumer demand as well as market forces. Consider an economic planning board, composed of 30 to 40 persons, that must decide how many houses, apartment buildings, buses, cars, and pizza parlors should be built within the next year. Where would the planners start? Would they know about people's changing demands for houses, apartment buildings, and the rest? Critics of economic planning argue that they would not. At best, the planners would be making a guess about what goods and services consumers would demand and how much they would buy at different prices. If they guess wrong, say the critics, resources will be wasted and demands will go unfulfilled. Private individuals, guided by rising and falling prices and by the desire to earn profits, are better at satisfying consumer demand. Economic planners risk little themselves when they draw up economic plans for others to follow (they don't put *their* money on the line), and therefore aren't as likely to avoid costly economic mistakes as are risk-taking entrepreneurs in a free market.

Second, economic planners mistakenly believe that the plans they construct will be followed by the members of society. Relevant here is Adam Smith's description of the economic planner or, as he called him, "the man of system":

> The man of system . . . seems to imagine that he can arrange the different members of a great society with as much ease as the hand arranges the different pieces upon a chess-

board. He does not consider that the pieces upon the chess-board have no other principle of motion beside that which the hand impresses upon them; but that, in the great chess-board of human society, every single piece has a principle of motion of its own, altogether different from that which the legislature might choose to impress upon it. If those two principles coincide and act in the same direction, the game of human society will go on easily and harmoniously, and is very likely to be happy and successful. If they are the opposite or different, the game will go on miserably, and human society must be at all times in the highest degree of disorder.[2]

Question:

Everybody uses plans. A person makes plans for his or her life, which include going to college, getting a job, and so forth. A business might draw up a plan for the next five years. If individuals and firms plan, why not societies? What do the critics of central economic planning say to this?

Answer:

They say that there is a major difference between the plan an individual or business firm makes and an economic plan for all of society. First, if an individual or a firm makes a plan that fails, only the individual or the firm suffers. For the most part, the rest of society is unaffected. This is not the case if a central economic plan (for all of society) fails. One mistake here can have major consequences for many people.

Second, if one person makes a personal plan, this does not prohibit others from making and following their own plans. But an economic plan that encompasses all of society just might do that. For example, a young woman with computer skills living in one part of a command-economy nation may want to move to another part. But whether she can realize her plan depends on whether her plan is consistent with the economic plan set down by the central authorities. It may be that the economic plan calls for technological development in the area of the country where the young woman lives and that she will be required to continue to live and work there.

EXHIBIT 22–2
Prices in the Soviet Union

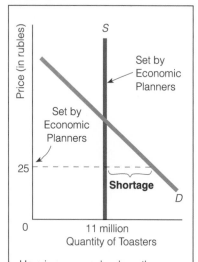

Here is an example where the wrong price is set. Planners set the ruble price for toasters too low; as a result, there is a shortage, and toasters are rationed by some combination of ruble price and waiting in line.

The Next Step: Supply and Demand

As we have seen, a planning agency determines the aggregate quantity of goods in a command economy; that is, how many radios, television sets, cars, refrigerators, toasters, and so forth will be provided. This is the supply side of the market. As we know, though, there is also a demand side to every market, and supply and demand together determine price.

Besides determining the supply of a particular good, the Soviet central planners under command-economy socialism also set its price. For example, they might decide that 11 million toasters will be produced this year and that each will sell for a price of 25 rubles. Unless 25 rubles is the equilibrium price, though, there will be either a surplus or a shortage of toasters. Exhibit 22–2 illustrates what happens when the price for toasters is set below the equilibrium price. A shortage of toasters results. In a market system, the price of toasters would be bid up to the equilibrium price, and the quantity demanded of toasters would equal the quantity supplied. But in the Soviet Union under command-economy socialism, it is illegal

[2]Adam Smith, *The Theory of Moral Sentiments* (Oxford: Oxford University Press, 1976), p. 234.

to bid up the ruble price of a good. So, instead, toasters are rationed by some combination of ruble price and waiting in line (that is, the rationing device, first-come-first-served).

Western travelers to the Soviet Union have observed long lines in front of some stores and no people at all in front of other stores. What accounts for this? Some prices are set below the equilibrium price, producing shortages and long lines of people, and some prices are set above the equilibrium price, producing surpluses and relatively empty stores. As long as price is centrally imposed, shortages or surpluses are likely to result. It would be most unusual if the planners could correctly guess the equilibrium price.

The Soviet Union in Transition

Currently, the Soviet Union is in transition. We describe some of the historical events of this transition period.

Gorbachev's Goal. In the late-1980s, Gorbachev's stated goal was to shift the Soviet Union from an overly centralized command system of management to a more flexible system incorporating some decentralization and choice. His desire was to increase efficiency and productivity by loosening the bureaucratic stranglehold on the economy. Most Western observers believed this meant that the Soviet leader wanted his country to adopt some market practices. Specifically, Gorbachev was proposing (a) the modernization of industry, (b) worker incentives, (c) a move towards the freer operation of supply and demand forces, and (d) more decentralized decision making.

Opposition to Reform. According to Soviet economist G. Povov, two main groups have opposed economic reform in the Soviet Union. First, there are the managers of state enterprises that have done well under the old system, satisfying their supervisors by using political skills they have cultivated over the years. Operating under the dictates of the marketplace would undermine their security and force them into new patterns of behavior. Second are the numerous workers who oppose economic reform because, under the old system, they are paid and guaranteed a job irrespective of the quality of their work.

Gorbachev's Problem. Gorbachev probably knew that the road to economic reform would not be easy. If the Soviet citizen was to accept the greater emphasis on supply and demand forces (especially when this meant he would have to pay higher prices for some goods), reduced job security, and the demand for harder and higher-quality work, then he had to see that he would get something for all this. Many Soviet citizens thought the reward would be higher pay and more consumer goods to buy. Without these two as the "carrot" to entice the Soviet citizens onward down the road of economic reform, the road for Gorbachev and his supporters was bound to be bumpy.

Eastern Europe. Nineteen eighty-nine (1989) was a revolutionary year. It was the year the Berlin Wall came down. One after the other, the nations of Eastern Europe toppled their communist governments. The new leaders of these countries proclaimed their intent to achieve political and economic freedom for their people (in varying degrees). Some commentators said that the upheavals in Eastern Europe could not have occurred had not Gorbachev earlier introduced glasnost and perestroika in the Soviet Union and had he not tacitly acceded to the desires of the peoples of Eastern Europe to free themselves from oppressive communist regimes.

Bad Economic News. In 1990, Soviet real GNP fell 6.4 percent and in 1991 it fell 17 percent. The inflation rate was 10 percent in 1990, and it had risen to 250 percent in 1991. When Soviet citizens were asked in a 1991 poll what the Soviet Union had to offer its citizens, 65 percent of the persons polled responded: "Shortages, waiting in lines, and a miserable existence."

We Ask Five Economists A Question. In early 1991, *before* the unsuccessful coup against Mikhail Gorbachev, we asked five well-known economists this question: **With recent economic and political changes in the Soviet Union and Eastern Europe, some people are suggesting this is an end of an era. Any thoughts on the subject?** This is what they had to say:

■ **Lester Thurow.** The post-World War II era is over. Capitalism beat communism. A new, as yet unnamed, era has begun. It will feature a contest between individualistic Anglo-Saxon capitalism and a more communitarian form of capitalism found in Germany and Japan.
■ **Gordon Tullock.** The world is not so much entering a new era as going back to an older one. Before 1914, there was no communism in the world. We had a set of nation states who frequently had bad relations with each other or had wars, but there was no crusading economic religion in existence which was attempting to change the world in its own direction. That period, retrospectively, was a good one, but not a period of perfect peace or total prosperity. That is what we seem to be entering into provided that Gorbachev's reforms are successful.
■ **John Kenneth Galbraith.** I think they will move [toward a market system] but I also think the passage is much more difficult than we had imagined. It is difficult essentially because of the lack of institutions and to some extent the lack of motivation. I believe the lack of motivation comes from having a history of relatively leisurely living.
■ **Milton Friedman.** The world is entering a new era but it is much too early to know how it will turn out. One thing is clear: communism in the Stalinist version is dead. But it is not clear that private free markets will emerge in Eastern Europe. That remains to be seen.
■ **James M. Bhuchanan.** The century-long ideological conflict between socialism and the market is no longer present, but there is no rebirth of laissez-faire. I find it hard to predict what will indeed emerge.

The Political and Economic Environment Shortly *Before* the (Unsuccessful) August 1991 Coup d'Etat. As we said earlier, there was an unsuccessful coup d'etat against Mikhail Gorbachev in August, 1991. The political and economic environment before the coup is best described as chaotic and uncertain. On the political front, several of the republics of the Soviet Union were vigorously pushing for independence. The hardliners in the Kremlin argued that the U.S.S.R. would have to be preserved, no matter the cost. Also, the hardliners could not forgive Gorbachev for introducing glasnost and perestroika. On the other hand, the democrats and reformers wanted independence for the republics pursuing this goal, and they were angry at Gorbachev for not working hard enough for political liberalization and economic reform. The leader of the political liberals and economic reformers was the president of the largest republic in the Soviet Union (Russia), Boris Yeltsin.
On the economic front, the Soviet Union was witnessing high inflation, a severe

drop in GNP, and a huge budget deficit. Many of the Soviet citizens were squarely behind greater political freedom, but their current experience with what they perceived as economic reform seemed less than favorable.

The Coup d'Etat and Yeltsin. In a matter of a few days, the hardliners coup d'etat against Milkhail Gorbachev had ended. Gorbachev returned to Moscow from his vacation home where he had been under house arrest. The man of the hour was not Gorbachev, however, but Boris Yeltsin, who had rallied the forces of liberalism and economic reform against the coup leaders.

The Political and Economic Environment Shortly *After* the August 1991 Coup d'Etat. Shortly after his return to Moscow, Gorbachev and Yeltsin forged a political alliance. The coup had been defeated and it seemed as if the victorious forces of political liberalism and economic reform had been finally thrust to center stage. In this environment, three of the (then) 15 republics of the Soviet Union were granted independence—Estonia, Latvia, and Lithuania. In this environment, Gorbachev no longer had to perform the political tightrope walk that he once performed between hardliners and reformers. But still the problems of the economy loomed large. There was both talk and some action among the remaining 12 republics to form a "common market" similar to that of the Economic Community (EC). The debate in the Soviet Union was waged between those who wanted to push hard and fast for radical economic change—which included selling state assets, strict fiscal and monetary discipline, private ownership of property on a wide scale, the decentralization of almost all government functions, freeing up most prices, and delegating responsibility for key economic affairs to the republics—and those who wanted a much more moderate and slower approach.

Yeltsin Proposes Commonwealth of Independent States: No More Soviet Union. In the midst of economic chaos in the Soviet Union, and Gorbachev's plea to maintain some solidarity within the Soviet state, Boris Yeltsin proposed a commonwealth of independent states with no central government. On Wednesday, December 11, 1991, Yeltsin won a decisive victory for his plan by persuading top military commanders that a post-Soviet commonwealth was the way to proceed. (Yeltsin also promised to raise all military salaries by 90%, effective January 1, 1992.) Under Yeltsin's commonwealth plan both Gorbachev's position as Soviet president, and the Soviet Union as we have come to know it, would perish. The move to create a commonwealth of independent states also coincided with Yeltsin's plan to move quickly toward a market economy.

What's Ahead?

Will the land mass we have known as the Soviet Union continue to be a union, or will it be a commonwealth of independent states? Will it join the ranks of market economies? In answer to the second question, we know that in the face of massive economic woes—high inflation, low production—it has made a first attempt. But the pace at which it will move toward privatization, free prices, and decentralization is unknown. Economic hardship, currently being felt by the Soviet citizenry, is often the soil in which radical changes can be made. Whether the radical changes will be back towards command-economy socialism—perhaps as a result of a successful coup in the future—or towards a market economy and a commonwealth, we don't know for sure. At minimum, the drama being played out continues to be worth watching, as its process and outcome will influence world events for years to come.

THE PEOPLE'S REPUBLIC OF CHINA

After the Communist (Maoist) takeover in 1949, the Chinese economy, using the Soviet economic system as a model, put command-economy socialism into effect, although Chinese economic planning was less centralized than Soviet planning.

In 1958, Mao Tse-tung instituted an economic plan known as the *Great Leap Forward,* which called for the development of heavy industry, a dramatic increase in output, and a more intensive use of labor. The plan was largely a failure. Goods were produced that no one wanted, large-scale projects (such as irrigation) were poorly planned, people were transferred from rural areas to the cities, and goods such as steel produced by unskilled workers in primitive work environments were of low quality. In Hunan province alone, 5,376 collectives were combined into 208 large people's communes with an average of 8,000 households in each. National income fell dramatically.

The next major Maoist attempt at national reconstruction was the *Cultural Revolution,* which began in 1966. This radical left movement aimed at remaking Chinese society in general and at eliminating all foreign influences from the country in particular. During the Cultural Revolution, teashops and private theaters were shut down; hand holding and kite flying were forbidden; the National Gallery of Fine Arts was closed, as were radio and television stations, newspapers, and magazines; and libraries were ransacked and books burned. (Mao disliked formal education. He once said, "The more books one reads, the stupider one becomes.") This was not an environment in which economic development could flourish. National income fell once again during the Cultural Revolution. Mao's death on September 9, 1976, ended the Cultural Revolution and opened the way for change.

The economic changes in China today are generally attributed to China's leader, Deng Xiaoping, who came to power shortly after Mao's death. These changes are examined next.

Bao gan dao hu

Bao gan dao hu means "contracting all decisions to the household." It is the essence of China's economic reforms in rural areas. China's collective farms are currently operated by households under the following system: (1) The government gives collectives specific production quotas that they must meet. (2) The government buys the quota-procured output at a fixed price. (3) Although the state owns the farmland, it is divided into small plots that are farmed by the households; households are allowed to contract with the collective to produce a share of the quota. (4) Once the households have met their quota-procurement responsibilities, they can produce and sell in the free market any output they want. These new agricultural reforms have led to a rise in agricultural output. For example, between 1978 and 1984 (a peak year), grain production increased 34 percent to 400 million tons. For a short while, China was a grain exporter instead of an importer.

A Shaky Free Market. Saying that China has adopted some free market practices does not mean that a free market practice put into effect today will not be abandoned tomorrow. For example, Hong Kong buys many of its pigs from Guangdong province in China. A few years ago, an increase in the demand for pigs in Hong Kong raised the price of pigs in Guangdong. Farmers in Hunan, the province north of Guangdong, saw the higher prices for pigs in Guangdong and started to ship their pigs there. As a result, the supply of pigs in Hunan decreased, and the price of pigs in Hunan increased. The provincial government in Hunan responded to the higher prices by banning the export of pigs raised in Hunan. When the press criticized this policy, the provincial government repealed its ban on exports and imposed an export tax on pigs instead. This policy had basically the same effect as the ban. Such interventions by provincial governments are thought to hamper the efficiency of the Chinese agricultural sector.

Unleashing Industry.   In 1978, Zhao Ziyang, the first secretary of the Communist party in Sichuan province, ordered that six Sichuan enterprises be partly freed from the central planning system. These enterprises, like the agricultural collectives, were first obligated to meet a state procurement target, after which they could produce according to the dictates of the marketplace. Since 1978, a few thousand enterprises have been allowed to operate under the same conditions as the original six Sichuan enterprises. In 1985, a truck-producing enterprise in China sold 55,000 of the 91,500 trucks it produced to the government and sold the remainder on the free market.

Leasing Bankrupt State-Owned Enterprises.   A few state-owned enterprises that were on the brink of bankruptcy have been leased to private citizens. In many cases, these private citizens have turned the enterprises around and have been able to keep some of the profit for their efforts.

Evading the system.   In China, large, well-managed enterprises are often required to meet larger production quotas than small, inefficient firms. Some commentators have noted that such a system actually penalizes the large, well-managed firms since they have to allocate many of their resources to fulfill government plans and thus have little left over to produce goods that can be sold on the free market. To get around this, many large, well-managed firms have either tried to hide some of their productive capacity (to look smaller) or to disguise their relative efficiency in production by failing to meet some contracts. (The reasoning here is that if government believes the enterprise is small and inefficient, it will look elsewhere to meet its production quotas, leaving the enterprise to produce for the market.)

Tian An Men Square, June 1989

Perhaps because of their new-found economic freedoms, and partly because of successes experienced by citizens of Eastern European nations, many Chinese began to demand greater political freedom. This desire for greater freedom coalesced in the mass rallies in Tian An Men Square in June 1989. Hundreds of thousands of demonstrators stood in the square and demanded (very moderate) political reforms. The Chinese government asked the demonstrators to leave, but they would not. Finally, the government ordered the army to disperse the protestors. Many hundreds of people were killed, scores more injured, as horrified viewers all over the world watched the carnage on their television screens.

What Next?

China has entered on a path of economic reform in the face of a resistance to political reforms. Whether reactionary politics will stifle economic reform, or economic reform will moderate reactionary politics, few people, if any, know at this time.

In March 1991, China's premier Li Peng, in a speech before the National People's Congress (China's legislature), said that China will continue to use central planning through the year 2000 and that enterprises will gradually be pushed into a market environment. Li stressed that as China cautiously moves forward with economic reforms, the Communist Party would not relax its hold on power.

THE JAPANESE ECONOMY
■

Japan is a country the size of Montana, with a population of 124 million people in 1991. It is also a country with the second largest market economy in the world (after the United States). In this section, we discuss the Japanese economy; in particular, the ways in which it differs from the U.S. economy.[3]

Savings

As we discussed in Chapter 21, there is a link between *non*consumption, or saving, and capital formation. As the savings rate increases, capital formation increases, and so does economic growth. For example, during the period 1961–90, the Japanese average annual growth rate in real GNP was approximately 6 percent, whereas during the same period in the United States, the average annual growth rate in real GNP was 3.3 percent. At these rates, the Japanese economy would double in size every 12 years, whereas the U.S. economy would double in size every 22 years.

Japan has a relatively high savings rate. To illustrate, savings as a percentage of disposable (after-tax) income has been around 5 percent in the United States in recent years, but it has been noticeably higher in Japan. There are probably a number of reasons for this.

1. Homebuyers are required to make a minimum downpayment of 40 percent of the purchase price of the home they buy which, since land is relatively scarce, is priced relatively high. As a consequence, households are required to save a large percentage of their income.
2. Social security benefits are relatively low and retirement age is rather young (55 to 60). Workers therefore must save for their old age.
3. It is a practice in Japanese firms to set a relatively low wage rate and offer large bonuses (based on profits) twice a year.
4. Japan's tax system allows substantial exemptions on interest income, thus stimulating saving.

Labor Market Considerations

Between 1962 and 1989, the average annual unemployment rate in the United States was 6.0 percent. In Japan, it was 1.8 percent.[4] During this period, Japan was consistently able to hold its unemployment rate below that of the United States, and without greater inflation.

---

[3]Much of the discussion in this section comes from Andrew Zimbalist, Howard J. Sherman, and Stuart Brown, *Comparing Economic Systems: A Political-Economic Approach* (San Diego: Harcourt Brace Jovanovich, 1989).

[4]It is natural to ask whether the Japanese define and measure unemployment as it is done in the United States. The answer is that there are minor methodological differences. However, a study by the Bureau of Labor Statistics reports that if Japan were to use the U.S. definition and measurement, its unemployment rate would nevertheless be unchanged: the upward and downward biases would cancel each other. Also, a study released by the Japanese embassy in Washington concluded that minor methodological differences lower the measured unemployment rate in Japan by only two-tenths of one percentage point.

Why has the Japanese unemployment rate consistently been lower than the U.S. unemployment rate? On the macro level, rapid economic growth, which Japan has had, brings with it a high demand for labor. On the micro level, the Japanese attribute it to lifetime employment and union–management cooperation, which we discuss next.

Lifetime Employment. Lifetime employment refers to the institutional setup in Japan where a person is guaranteed a job with a specific company until retirement. Lifetime employment does not cover all workers at all companies, nor does it always cover all workers at a given company. Still, it is a major feature of the Japanese economy.

There are some disadvantages to lifetime employment: It results in too many employees working in a company during an economic downturn and the retention of (sometimes) less than efficient workers. The advantages include lower worker turnover (which results in lower job training expenses), less worker resistance to technological change, and enhancement of worker loyalty to the firm.

Union–Management Cooperation. Approximately one-third of the Japanese labor force is unionized; moreover, Japanese unions and management commonly share the same goals and means to accomplish them. The founding slogan of the Nissan Company labor union was "Those who truly love their union, love their company." Some commentators argue that in Japan unions and management get along better than, say, U.S. unions and U.S. management, because Japanese management tries to cultivate a "family feeling" and "sense of loyalty" among workers. Several ways it does this is by offering lifetime employment, having a more equal distribution of income between managers and workers than in the United States (the gap between top management salaries in Toyota and worker salaries is less than the gap between top management salaries at General Motors and worker salaries), offering pay bonuses to workers, and regularly consulting with workers on how the company should be run.

Economic Policy-Making in Japan

In Japan, economic policy making, especially industrial policy making, is more in the hands of professional bureaucrats than the legislature. Two of the major economic bodies in the professional bureaucracy include the Ministry of Finance (MOF) and the Ministry of International Trade and Industry (MITI). One of the major duties of the MOF is to encourage banks to increase or decrease their lending to specific industries, largely identified by MITI.

MITI is the organization in Japan that largely forges Japan's **industrial policy**. Japanese industrial policy focuses on "watering the green spots": aiding those industries that are most likely to be successful in the world marketplace. The idea behind MITI "is that the private sector alone has insufficient vision, coordination, resources, and risk-bearing ability to conduct its affairs in an optimal manner. To alleviate bottlenecks, to avert overproduction, to anticipate market shifts, to develop and deploy unchartered technology, the government is needed to assist in the sharing of information, pooling of resources, and overall collaboration of efforts. As a result of the successful implementation of this approach, MITI has referred to the Japanese system as a *plan-oriented market economy*."[5]

The powers MITI has at its disposal to aid and guide certain industries are numerous. A few include (1) designating certain regions as industrial parks and

[5]Zimbalist, Sherman, and Brown, p. 52.

Industrial Policy
In Japan, the policy of "watering the green spots," or aiding those industries that are most likely to be successful in the world marketplace.

providing an infrastructure for the parks; (2) imposing trade barriers to protect firms; and (3) coordinating research efforts among firms in an industry.

The degree to which MITI has aided Japanese economic growth is controversial. Some economists maintain that MITI too often gets in the way of good ideas. For example, it mistakenly tried to discourage Japanese car manufacturers from competing in the world automobile market in the 1960s.

Others state that MITI has greatly benefitted the Japanese economy. For example, a key success seems to be in the semiconductor industry, an industry largely dominated by U.S. firms until MITI encouraged and aided Japanese firms. Currently, the Japanese supply almost 90 percent of the international semiconductor market.

Question:

Will the U.S. economy become more like the Japanese economy in the near future, or will the Japanese economy become more like the U.S. economy?

Answer:

That is hard to say. Critics of industrial policy in the U.S. believe that over time government policies are turned to the advantage of powerful interest groups and may actually retard economic performance instead of improve it. This fear is a powerful barrier to adopting MITI-type policies in the United States. It remains to be seen whether industrial policy will have these harmful effects in Japan as time passes. It is probably too early to say much more than this.

CHAPTER SUMMARY

Economic Realities and Economic Systems

■ The following hold for all economic systems: scarcity, opportunity cost (no free lunch), the need for a rationing device, the law of demand, and rational self-interested behavior. In addition, all economic systems must answer the following questions: What goods will be produced? How will the goods be produced? For whom will the goods be produced?

Pure Capitalism

■ Pure capitalism is an economic system characterized by private ownership of the factors of production, market allocation of resources, and decentralized decision making; most economic activities take place in the private sector, and government plays a small role or no role at all in the economy. The advocates of pure capitalism are often called libertarians.

■ Libertarians maintain that in a pure capitalist economy, none of the following would exist: government-granted professional licenses, minimum wage laws, only one firm that delivers first-class mail, restraints on price, discretionary fiscal and monetary policies, the Federal Reserve, antitrust policy, quotas, and tariffs, and compulsory saving or redistribution programs. Libertarians generally argue that whatever the government does, the private sector can do better and that some things the government does shouldn't be done and wouldn't be done by the private sector.

■ The critics of libertarianism state that libertarians (1) do not see the merit of sometimes allowing government to adjust for third-party effects through taxes, subsidies, and regulations; (2) do not seriously consider complex exchanges, and (3) do not see the stabilizing effects of government monetary and fiscal policies.

Karl Marx

■ Two major intellectual strands in Marx's thinking are the labor theory of value and the dialectical process. Marx argued that (1) the value of a commodity is determined by the *socially necessary labor time* embodied in it, and (2) history could be interpreted in terms of the dialectic, in which two opposing forces or ideas (the thesis and antithesis) form a synthesis that becomes the new thesis, thereby starting the process all over.

■ Marx identified the stages of economic development as primitive communism, slavery, feudalism, capitalism, the dictatorship of the proletariat, and pure communism.

■ The critics of Marx argue that the labor theory of value is faulty; there is no large reserve army of the unemployed as Marx predicted; contrary to Marx, most workers earn above-subsistence wages; and Marxist revolutions have not appeared in the places Marx expected.

The Soviet Economy: From Command-Economy Socialism to "In Transition"

■ Under command-economy socialism, the private sector is very small; the public sector correspondingly large.

■ Command economies make use of central planning agencies whose job it is to allocate the nation's resources. The critics of central planning argue that economic planners cannot take into account as much relevant information as a market does; therefore, economic plans cannot coordinate economic activity or satisfy consumer demand as well as market forces. Secondly, economic planners mistakenly believe that the plans they construct will be followed by the members of society.

■ Planning agencies in command economies set the prices of goods and services. Since planners rarely set prices at their equilibrium levels (because it is unlikely they could know what the equilibrium prices are without allowing the forces of supply and demand to operate), command economies commonly experience surpluses and shortages.

■ Currently the Soviet economy is in transition. Soviet President Mikhail Gorbachev's stated goal is to shift the Soviet Union from an overly centralized command system of management to a more flexible system incorporating some decentralization and choice. Russian President Boris Yeltsin has played a major part in spearheading the move towards an economy where market forces and private property play a major role. As of this writing (December, 1991), the Soviet economy is experiencing major economic problems: high inflation and sharply declining real GNP. In this setting, it is difficult to tell what will happen next. Some observers believe there may be a return to command-economy socialism and political repression; others believe that while the transition to an economy where market forces and private property play a major role will be arduous that nonetheless it will continue.

The Chinese Economy

■ After the Communist (Maoist) takeover in 1949, the Chinese economy, using the Soviet economic system as a model, put command-economy socialism into effect.

■ In 1958, Mao Tse-tung instituted an economic plan known as the Great Leap Forward. The next major Maoist attempt at national reconstruction was the Cultural Revolution, which began in 1966. Mao died in 1976.

- Currently the Chinese economy is experimenting with some economic reforms, mainly focused on implementing a few modified market practices.
- Perhaps because of their new-found economic freedoms, many Chinese began to demand greater political freedom. This resulted in mass rallies in Tian An Men Square in June 1989.

The Japanese Economy

- Japan has a relatively high savings rate. Savings as a percentage of disposable (after-tax) income has been around 5 percent in the United States in recent years, but it has been noticeably higher in Japan.
- Between 1962 and 1989, the average annual unemployment rate in the United States was 6.0 percent; in Japan, it was 1.8 percent.
- Lifetime employment, which does not cover all Japanese workers at all companies, is a major feature of the Japanese economy.
- MITI, the organization in Japan that largely forges Japan's industrial policy, has certain powers. A few include (1) designating certain regions as industrial parks and providing an infrastructure for the parks; (2) imposing trade barriers to protect firms; and (3) coordinating research efforts among firms in an industry.

Key Terms and Concepts

Mixed Capitalism	Decentralized Socialism	Glasnost
Pure Capitalism	Labor Theory of Value	Perestroika
Command-Economy Socialism	Dialectic	Gosplan
	Surplus Value	Industrial Policy

QUESTIONS AND PROBLEMS

1. Choose one of the fundamental economic realities that both the United States and the Soviet Union (under command-economy socialism) face, and explain the different ways by which the two economies would deal with it.
2. Socialists in the Soviet Union have remarked, in the past, that at least their economic plans maintain full employment, whereas capitalism cannot. What is the likely libertarian response?
3. Some people argue that capitalism and socialism are usually evaluated only on economic grounds, where capitalism has a clear advantage. But in order to evaluate the two economic systems evenhandedly, both should be evaluated on other factors as well—justice, fairness, the happiness of the people living under both systems, the crime rate, the standard of living of those at the bottom of the economic ladder, and much more. Do you think this is the proper way to proceed?
4. The *convergence hypothesis,* first proposed by a Soviet economist, suggests that over time the capitalist economies will become increasingly socialistic and the socialist economies will become increasingly capitalistic. Do you believe the convergence hypothesis has merit? What real-world evidence can you cite to prove or disprove the hypothesis?
5. Predict how mixed capitalism, pure capitalism, and command-economy socialism would each deal with the problem of pollution.
6. What are some of the advantages of industrial policy? the disadvantages?

Absolute Advantage The situation where a country can produce more of a good than another country can produce with the same quantity of resources.

Absolute Price The price of a good in money terms.

Abstraction The process (used in building a theory) of focusing on a limited number of variables to explain or predict an event.

Activists Persons who argue that monetary and fiscal policies should be deliberately used to smooth out the business cycle.

Adaptive Expectations Expectations that individuals form from past experience and modify slowly as the present and the future become the past (as time passes).

Aggregate Demand (*AD*) Curve A curve that shows the quantity demand of real GNP at different price levels, *ceteris paribus*.

Appreciation An increase in the value of one currency relative to other currencies.

Attainable Region Includes those points on and below the production possibilities frontier.

Automatic Fiscal Policy Changes in government expenditures or taxes that occur automatically without (additional) congressional action.

Bad Anything from which individuals receive disutility or dissatisfaction.

Balanced Budget Government expenditures equal tax receipts.

Balanced Budget Theorem A change in real GNP is equal to the change in government spending when government spending and taxes change by the same dollar amount and in the same direction.

Balance of Payments A periodic statement (usually annual) of the money value of all transactions between residents of one country and residents of all other countries.

Barter Exchanging goods and services for other goods and services without the use of money.

Base Year The year chosen as a point of reference or comparison for prices in other years; a benchmark year.

Black Market An illegal market. There are two varieties: one in which illegal goods are bought and sold and one in which goods are bought and sold at illegal prices.

Board of Governors The governing body of the Federal Reserve System.

Bond An IOU statement that promises to pay a certain sum of money (the principal) at maturity and also to pay periodic fixed sums until that date.

Budget Deficit Occurs when government expenditures (G) are greater than tax receipts (T): $G > T$.

Budget Surplus Occurs when government expenditures (G) are less than tax receipts (T): $G < T$.

Business Cycle Recurrent swings (up and down) in real GNP.

Capital Produced goods that can be used as inputs for further production, such as machinery, tools, computers, trucks, buildings, and factories.

Capital Account Includes all payments related to the purchase and sale of assets and to borrowing and lending activities. Components include outflow of U.S. capital and inflow of foreign capital.

Capital Account Balance The summary statistic for the outflow of U.S. capital and the inflow of foreign capital. It is equal to the difference between the outflow of U.S. capital and the inflow of foreign capital.

Capital Consumption Allowance or Depreciation The estimated amount of capital goods used up in production through natural wear, obsolescence, and accidental destruction.

Cash Leakage Occurs when funds are held as currency instead of being deposited into a checking account.

Ceteris Paribus The Latin term meaning "all other things held constant."

Choice The act of selecting among restricted alternatives.

Closed Economy An economy that does not trade goods and services with other nations.

Command-Economy Socialism An economic system characterized by government ownership of the non-labor factors of production, government allocation of resources, and centralized decision making; most economic activities take place in the public sector, and government plays a very large role in the economy.

Commercial Banks Privately owned, profit-seeking institutions that offer a wide range of services (checking accounts, savings accounts, loans) to customers.

Comparative Advantage The situation where a country can produce a good at lower opportunity cost than another country.

Complements Two goods that are used jointly in consumption. With complements, the demand for one rises as the price of the other falls (or the demand for one falls as the price of the other rises).

Complete Crowding Out The decrease in one or more components of private spending completely offsets the increase in government spending.

Consumer Price Index The most widely cited index number for the price level; the weighted average of prices of a specific set of goods and services purchased by a typical household.

Consumers' Surplus The difference between the price buyers pay for a good and the maximum or highest price they would have paid for the good. It is a dollar measure of the benefit gained by being able to purchase a unit of a good for less than one is willing to pay for it.

Consumption Household spending on consumer goods.

Continued Inflation A continued increase in the price level.

Contractionary Fiscal Policy Fiscal policy designed to decrease aggregate demand or aggregate supply.

Coupon Rate The percentage of the face value of the bond that is paid out regularly (usually quarterly or annually) to the holder of the bond.

Credit In the balance of payments, any transaction that either supplies a foreign currency or creates a demand for the nation's currency in the foreign exchange market.

Credit Market A market that channels funds from savers (lenders) to borrowers.

Crowding Out The decrease in private expenditures that occurs as a consequence of increased government spending or of the financing needs of the deficit.

Currency Includes coins and paper money.

Current Account Includes all payments related to the purchase and sale of goods and services. Components of the account include exports, imports, and net unilateral transfers abroad.

Current Account Balance The summary statistic for exports of goods and services, imports of goods and services, and net unilateral transfers.

Cyclical Unemployment Rate The difference between the unemployment rate and the natural unemployment rate.

Debit In the balance of payments, any transaction that either supplies the nation's currency or creates a demand for foreign currency in the foreign exchange market.

Decentralized Socialism An economic system characterized by government ownership of the non-labor factors of production, largely market allocation of resources, and decentralized decision making; most economic activities take place in the public sector, and government plays a major overseer role in the economy.

Demand The willingness and ability of buyers to purchase different quantities of a good at different prices during a specific time period.

Demand Curve The graphical representation of the law of demand.

Demand Curve for Money (Balances) Represents the inverse relationship between the quantity demanded of money balances and the price of holding money balances.

Demand Deposits A deposit of funds that can be withdrawn without restrictions and is transferable by check.

Demand Schedule The numerical tabulation of the quantity demanded of a good at different prices.

Dependency Ratio The number of children under a certain age plus the number of the elderly (aged 65 and over) divided by the total population.

Depreciation A decrease in the value of one currency relative to other currencies.

Devaluation An official governmental act that changes the exchange rate by lowering the official price of a currency.

Dialectic The method of logic based on the principle that an idea or event (thesis) generates its opposite (antithesis), leading to a reconciliation of opposites (synthesis).

Directly Related Two variables are directly related if they move in the same direction.

Discount Rate The interest rate the Fed charges depository institutions that borrow reserves from it.

Discretionary Fiscal Policy Deliberate changes of government expenditures and taxes to achieve particular economic objectives.

Disequilibrium A state of either surplus or shortage in a market.

Disequilibrium Price A price other than equilibrium price. A price at which quantity demanded does not equal quantity supplied.

Disposable Income (DI) That portion of personal income that can be used for consumption or saving. It is equal to personal income minus personal taxes (especially income taxes).

Disutility The dissatisfaction one receives (from the consumption of a bad).

Double Coincidence of Wants In a barter economy, a requirement that must be met before a trade can be made. It specifies that a trader must find another trader who is willing to trade what the first trader wants and at the same time wants what the first trader has.

Double Counting Counting a good more than once when computing GNP.

Dumping The sale of goods abroad at a price below their cost and below the price charged in the domestic markets.

Economics The science of scarcity: the science of how individuals and societies deal with the fact that wants are greater than the limited resources available to satisfy those wants.

Economic Analysis The process of applying economic tools and the economic way of thinking to real-world problems.

Economic Good A scarce good. A good where the amount available is less than people would want if it were given away at zero price.

Economic Problem The fact that there are not enough resources to produce enough goods to satisfy peoples' unlimited wants.

Economic Profit The difference between total revenue and total (opportunity) cost, including both its explicit and implicit components.

Efficiency In terms of production, the condition where the maximum output is produced with given resources and technology. Efficiency implies the impossibility of gains in one area without losses in another.

Efficiency Criterion Addresses the question of whether an alternative arrangement exists that can make at least one person better off without making anyone else worse off.

Efficiency Wage Models These models hold that it is sometimes in the best interest of firms to pay their employees higher than equilibrium wage rates.

Employment Rate The percentage of the noninstitutional adult civilian population that is employed: Employment rate = number of persons employed/number of persons in the noninstitutional adult civilian population.

Equation of Exchange An identity stating that the money supply times velocity must be equal to the price level times real GNP.

Equilibrium Equilibrium means "at rest." Equilibrium is the price–quantity combination in a market from which there is no tendency for buyers or sellers to move away. Graphically, equilibrium is the intersection point of the supply and demand curves.

Equilibrium Price (Market-clearing Price) The price at which quantity demanded of the good equals quantity supplied.

Equilibrium Quantity The quantity that corresponds to equilibrium price. The quantity at which the amount of the good buyers are willing and able to buy equals the amount sellers are willing and able to sell, and both equal the amount actually bought and sold.

Excess Reserves Any reserves held beyond the required amount. The difference between total reserves and required reserves.

Exchange rate The price of one currency in terms of another currency; for example, 1 dollar = 2 marks.

Expansionary Fiscal Policy Fiscal policy designed to increase aggregate demand or aggregate supply.

Expectations Effect The increase in the nominal interest rate due to a higher expected inflation rate.

Exports Total foreign spending on domestic (U.S.) goods.

Ex Ante Real Interest Rate The nominal interest rate minus the expected inflation rate.

Ex Post Real Interest Rate The nominal interest rate minus the actual inflation rate.

Face Value (Par Value) Dollar amount specified on the bond.

Fallacy of Composition The erroneous view that what is good or true for the individual is necessarily good or true for the group.

Federal Funds Market A market where banks lend reserves to one another, usually for short periods.

Federal Funds Rate The interest rate in the federal funds market; the interest rate banks charge one another to borrow reserves.

Federal Open Market Committee (FOMC) The 12-member policy-making group within the Fed. This committee has the authority to conduct open market operations.

Federal Reserve Notes Paper money issued by the Fed.

Final Good A good in the hands of its final user.

Fine-tuning The (usually frequent) use of discretionary monetary and fiscal policies to counteract even small undesirable movements in economic activity.

Fiscal Policy Changes in government expenditures and taxation in an effort to achieve particular macroeconomic goals, such as low unemployment, stable prices, economic growth, and so on.

Fixed Exchange Rate System The system where a nation's currency is set at a fixed rate relative to all other currencies, and central banks intervene in the foreign exchange market to maintain the fixed rate.

Fixed Investment Business purchases of capital goods, such as machinery and factories, and consumer purchases of new residential housing.

Flexible Exchange Rate System The system whereby exchange rates are determined by the forces of supply and demand for a currency.

Flow Variable A variable that can only be meaningfully measured over a period of time. GNP is a flow variable.

Foreign Exchange Market The market in which currencies of different countries are exchanged.

Fractional Reserve Banking A banking arrangement that allows banks to hold reserves equal to only a fraction of their deposit liabilities.

Free Good A good where the amount available is greater than the amount people want at zero price.

Frictional Unemployment The unemployment due to the natural "frictions" of the economy, caused by changing market conditions and represented by qualified individuals with transferable skills who change jobs.

Full Employment The condition that exists when the unemployment rate is equal to the natural unemployment rate.

Fungibility A term that is Latin in origin, meaning "such that any unit is substitutable for another." Fungibility means substitutable.

Glasnost A Russian term popularly used to mean openness in public discussion and the arts.

GNP Deflator The weighted average of prices of all goods and services produced in an economy.

Gold Standard The monetary arrangement whereby a nation backs its paper money totally or partially with gold.

Good Anything from which individuals receive utility or satisfaction.

Gosplan The Soviet central planning agency (under command-economy socialism) that has the responsibility of drafting the economic plan for the nation.

Government Expenditures, or Government Spending The total dollar amounts spent by federal, state, and local governments on final goods and services.

Gross National Product (GNP) The total market value of all final goods and services produced annually in an economy.

Gross Private Domestic Investment, or Investment The sum of all purchases of newly produced capital goods plus changes in business inventories. It also includes expenditures on new residential housing.

Imports Total domestic (U.S.) spending on foreign goods.

Income Effect (Micro) That portion of the change in the quantity demanded of a good that is attributable to a change in real income (brought about by a change in absolute price).

Income Effect (Macro) The increase in the real and nominal interest rates brought on by an increase in GNP.

Incomplete Crowding Out The decrease in one or more components of private spending only partially offsets the increase in government spending.

Independent Two variables are independent if as one changes, the other does not.

Industrial Policy In Japan, the policy of "watering the green spots," or aiding those industries that are most likely to be successful in the world marketplace.

Inefficiency In terms of production, the condition where less than the maximum output is produced with given resources and technology. Inefficiency implies the possibility of gains in one area without losses in another.

Inflation An increase in the price level.

Inflationary Gap The condition where the real GNP the economy is producing is greater than the natural real GNP, and the unemployment rate that exists is less than the natural unemployment rate.

Inflation Rate The annual percentage change in some price index—such as the CPI or GNP deflator.

Injection Any expenditure on (U.S.) goods and services besides consumption expenditures is considered an injection. In short, any nonconsumption expenditure.

Interest Rate Effect The changes in household and business buying as the interest rate changes.

Intermediate Good A good that is an input in the production of a final good.

International Monetary Fund (IMF) An international organization created by the Bretton Woods system to oversee the international monetary system. Although the Bretton Woods system no longer exists, the IMF does. It does not control the world's money supply, but it does hold currency reserves for member nations and makes loans to central banks.

International Trade Effect The change in foreign sector spending as the price level changes.

Inventory Investment Changes in the stock of unsold goods.

Inversely Related Two variables are inversely related if they move in opposite directions.

In-Kind Transfer Payments Transfer payments, such as food stamps, medical assistance, and subsidized housing, that are made in a specific good or service.

J-Curve The curve that shows a short-run worsening in the trade deficit after a currency depreciation, followed later by an improvement.

Junk Bonds Risky bonds that offer high coupon rates.

Labor The physical and mental talents people contribute to the production process.

Labor Theory of Value Holds that the value of all commodities is equal to the value of the labor used in producing them.

Laffer Curve The curve, named after Arthur Laffer, that shows the relationship between tax rates and tax revenues. According to the Laffer curve, as tax rates rise from zero, tax revenues rise, reach a maximum at some point, and then fall with further increases in tax rates.

Land All natural resources, such as minerals, forests, water, and unimproved land.

Law of Demand As the price of a good rises, the quantity demanded of the good falls, and as the price of a good falls, the quantity demanded of the good rises, *ceteris paribus*.

Law of Supply As the price of a good rises, the quantity supplied of the good rises, and as the price of a good falls, the quantity supplied of the good falls, *ceteris paribus*.

Leakage An outflow or withdrawal of expenditures from the spending stream. Any part of income that does not go to purchase (U.S.) goods and services is considered a leakage.

Less-Developed Country (LDC) A country with a low per-capita GNP.

Liabilities A debt of the business firm.

Liquid Asset An asset that can easily and quickly be turned into cash. Some assets are more liquid than others; that is, assets differ as to the degree of liquidity.

Liquidity Effect The decrease in the real and nominal interest rates due to an increase in the supply of loanable funds.

Liquidity Trap The horizontal portion of the demand curve for money.

Loanable Funds Funds that someone borrows and another person lends, for which the borrower pays an interest rate to the lender.

Long-Run Aggregate Supply Curve The long-run aggregate supply curve shows the real GNP the economy is prepared to supply at different price levels, assuming wage rates and all other input prices have fully adjusted to eliminate a recessionary or inflationary gap.

Long-Run Equilibrium The condition that exists in the economy when the real GNP being produced equals the natural real GNP and the unemployment rate that exists equals the natural unemployment rate. In long-run equilibrium, the quantity demanded of real GNP equals the (long-run) quantity supplied of real GNP. This condition is met at the intersection of the aggregate demand curve and the long-run aggregate supply curve.

Macroeconomics The branch of economics that deals with human behavior and choices as they relate to highly aggregated markets (such as the goods and services market) or the entire economy.

Managed Float A managed flexible exchange rate system, under which nations now and then intervene to adjust their official reserve holdings to moderate major swings in exchange rates; this is today's international monetary system.

Marginal Analysis Weighing additional benefits of a change against the additional costs of a change with respect to current conditions.

Marginal Tax Rate The change in a person's tax payment divided by a change in the person's taxable income: Δtax payment/Δtaxable income.

Market Any arrangement by which people exchange goods and services.

Medium of Exchange Anything that is generally acceptable in exchange for goods and services. A function of money.

Merchandise Trade Balance The difference between the value of merchandise exports and the value of merchandise imports.

Merchandise Trade Deficit The situation where the value of merchandise exports is less than the value of merchandise imports.

Merchandise Trade Surplus The situation where the value of merchandise exports is greater than the value of merchandise imports.

Microeconomics The branch of economics that deals with human behavior and choices as they relate to relatively small units—the individual, the firm, the industry, the single market.

Mixed Capitalism An economic system characterized by largely private ownership of the factors of production, market allocation of resources, and decentralized decision making; most economic activities take place in the private sector in this system, but government plays a substantial economic and regulatory role.

Monetary Base The sum of reserves and currency outside banks.

Monetary Policy The deliberate control of the money supply and credit conditions in an effort to achieve particular macroeconomic goals, such as low unemployment, stable prices, economic growth, and so on.

Monetary Rule Describes monetary policy that is based on a predetermined steady growth rate in the money supply.

Monetary Wealth The value of a person's monetary assets. *Wealth,* as distinguished from *monetary wealth,* refers to the value of all assets owned, both monetary and nonmonetary. In short, a person's wealth equals his or her monetary wealth (such as $1,000 cash) plus nonmonetary wealth (a car or a house).

Money Any good that is widely accepted for purposes of exchange.

Money Demand Line The graphical representation of the direct relationship between the quantity demanded of money and GNP.

(Money) Income The current-dollar amount of a person's income.

Money Market Accounts Accounts with banks (called money market deposit accounts, MMDA) or mutual fund companies (called money market mutual fund accounts, MMMF) that pay interest and offer limited check-writing privileges.

Money Multiplier Measures actual change in the money supply for a dollar change in the monetary base.

M1 Includes currency held outside banks + demand deposits + other checkable deposits + traveler's checks.

M2 Includes M1 + small-denomination time deposits + savings deposits + money market accounts + overnight repurchase agreements + overnight Eurodollar deposits.

National Debt The total sum of what the federal government owes its creditors.

National Income The sum of the payments to suppliers of the factors of production. It is equal to the compensation of employees + proprietors' income + corporate profits + rental income of persons + net interest.

Natural Rate Hypothesis The idea that in the long run, unemployment is at its natural rate. Within the Phillips curve framework, the natural rate hypothesis specifies that there is a long-run Phillips curve, which is vertical at the natural rate of unemployment.

Natural Real GNP The real GNP that is being produced at the natural unemployment rate.

Natural Unemployment Rate Unemployment caused by frictional and structural factors in the economy. Natural unemployment rate = frictional unemployment rate + structural unemployment rate. For some economists, this is the unemployment rate toward which the economy tends to return; it is the long-run average unemployment rate.

Net Exports Exports − imports.

Net National Product (NNP) GNP minus the capital consumption allowance.

Net Taxes Taxes minus transfer payments.

Nominal GNP The value of final goods and services produced in a given year in that year's prevailing market prices. The terms GNP, nominal GNP, and current-dollar GNP are used interchangeably.

Nominal Interest Rate The interest rate actually charged (or paid); the market interest rate. Nominal interest rate = real interest rate + expected inflation rate.

Nonactivists Persons who argue against the deliberate use of discretionary fiscal and monetary policies. They believe in a permanent, stable, rule-oriented monetary and fiscal framework.

Normal Good A good the demand for which rises (falls) as income rises (falls).

Normative Economics The study of "what should be" in economic matters.

One-Shot Inflation A one-time increase in the price level. An increase in the price level that does not continue.

Open Economy An economy that trades goods and services with other nations.

Open Market Operations The buying and selling of government securities by the Fed.

Opportunity Cost The most highly valued opportunity or alternative forfeited when a choice is made.

Overnight Eurodollar Deposits Dollar-denominated deposits in banks outside the United States.

Overnight Repurchase Agreements An agreement by a financial institution to sell short-term securities to its customers, combined with an agreement to repurchase them at a higher price at a specified future date.

Overvaluation A currency is overvalued if its price in terms of other currencies is above the equilibrium price.

Own Price The price of a good. For example, if the price of oranges is $1, this is (its) own price.

G–6

Perestroika A Russian term used to describe Soviet economic reform.

Personal Income (PI) The amount of income that individuals actually receive. It is equal to national income minus undistributed corporate profits, social insurance taxes, and corporate profits taxes, plus transfer payments.

Per-Capita Real Economic Growth An increase from one period to the next in per-capita real GNP, which is real GNP divided by population.

Phillips Curve A curve that originally showed the relationship between wage inflation and unemployment. Now it more often shows the relationship between price inflation and unemployment.

Policy Ineffectiveness Proposition (PIP) If (1) a policy change is correctly *anticipated,* (2) individuals form their expectations rationally, and (3) wages and prices are flexible, then neither fiscal policy nor monetary policy is effective at meeting macroeconomic goals.

Positive Economics The study of "what is" in economic matters.

Price Ceiling A government-mandated maximum price above which legal trades cannot be made.

Price Floor A government-mandated minimum price below which legal trades cannot be made.

Price Index A measure of the price level.

Price Level The weighted average of the prices of all goods and services.

Producers' Surplus The difference between the price sellers receive for a good and the minimum or lowest price for which they would have sold the good. It is a dollar measure of the benefit gained by being able to sell a unit of output for more than one is willing to sell it.

Production Possibilities Frontier Represents the possible combinations of two goods that an economy can produce in a certain period of time, under the conditions of a given state of technology, no unemployed resources, and efficient production.

Purchasing Power The quantity of goods and services that can be purchased with a unit of money. Purchasing power and the price level are inversely related: As the price level goes up (down), purchasing power goes down (up).

Purchasing Power Parity (PPP) Theory States that exchange rates between any two currencies will adjust to reflect changes in the relative price levels of the two countries.

Pure Capitalism An economic system characterized by private ownership of the factors of production, market allocation of resources, and decentralized decision making; most economic activities take place in the private sector, and government plays a small role or no role at all in the economy.

Quota A legal limit on the amount of a good that may be imported.

Ratex Short for rational expectations.

Rational Expectations Expectations that individuals form based on past experience and also on their predictions about the effects of present and future policy actions and events.

Rationing Device Something that is used to decide who gets what of available goods and resources. Price is a rationing device.

Real Balance Effect The change in the purchasing power of dollar-denominated assets that results from a change in the price level.

Real Business Cycle Theory The theory that business cycle contractions are generally brought about by aggregate supply changes that reduce the economy's capacity to produce.

Real Economic Growth An increase from one period to the next in real GNP.

Real GNP The value of the entire output produced annually in an economy, adjusted for price changes. It also can be defined as GNP (gross national product) valued in prices prevailing in the base year.

Real Income Income adjusted for price changes. A person has more (less) real income as the price of a good falls (rises), *ceteris paribus.*

Real Interest Rate The nominal interest rate adjusted for expected inflation; that is, the nominal interest rate minus the expected inflation rate.

Recession A decline in real GNP that lasts for two consecutive quarters (six months) or more.

Recessionary Gap The condition where the real GNP the economy is producing is less than the natural real GNP, and the unemployment rate that exists is greater than the natural unemployment rate.

Relative Price The price of a good in terms of another good.

Required-Reserve Ratio (r) A percentage of each dollar deposited that must be held on reserve (at the Fed or in the bank's vault).

Required Reserves The minimum amount of reserves a bank must hold against its deposits as mandated by the Fed.

Reserve Requirement The rule that specifies the amount of reserves a bank must hold to back up deposits.

Reserves The sum of bank deposits at the Fed and vault cash.

Revaluation An official governmental act that changes the exchange rate by raising the official price of a currency.

Savings Deposit A type of time deposit. In principle (though not always in practice), the depositor can be required to give advance written notice prior to withdrawal.

Scarcity The condition where our wants are greater than the limited resources available to satisfy those wants.

Shirking Behavior descriptive of a person who is putting forth less than the agreed-to effort when doing a job.

Shortage (Excess Demand) A condition in which quantity demanded is greater than quantity supplied. Shortages only occur at prices below equilibrium price.

Short-Run Aggregate Supply (SRAS) Curve Shows the real GNP producers will offer for sale at different price levels, *ceteris paribus.*

Short-Run Equilibrium In the economy, the condition that exists when the quantity demanded of real GNP equals the (short-run) quantity supplied of real GNP. This condition is met where the aggregate demand curve intersects the short-run aggregate supply curve.

Simple Deposit Multiplier The reciprocal of the required-reserve ratio, $1/r$.

Simple Quantity Theory of Money The theory that assumes that V and Q are constant and predicts that changes in M lead to strictly proportional changes in P.

Slope The ratio of the change in the variable on the vertical axis to the change in the variable on the horizontal axis.

Special Drawing Right An international money, created by the IMF, in the form of bookkeeping entries; like gold and currencies, they can be used by nations to settle international accounts.

Special-Interest Groups Subsets of the general population that hold (usually) intense preferences for or against a particular government service, activity, or policy. Often special-interest groups gain from public policies that may not be in accord with the interests of the general public.

Stagflation The simultaneous occurrence of high rates of inflation and unemployment.

Stock Variable A variable that can be meaningfully measured at a moment in time. For example, the nation's money supply is a stock variable.

Store of Value The ability of an item to hold value over time. A function of money.

Structural Unemployment Unemployment due to structural changes in the economy that eliminate some jobs and create others for which the unemployed are unqualified.

Substitutes Two goods that satisfy similar needs or desires. With substitutes, the demand for one rises as the price of the other rises (or the demand for one falls as the price of the other falls).

Substitution Effect That portion of the change in the quantity demanded of a good that is attributable to a change in its relative price.

Supply The willingness and ability of sellers to produce and offer to sell different quantities of a good at different prices during a specific time period.

Supply Schedule The numerical tabulation of the quantity supplied of a good at different prices.

Surplus (Excess Supply) A condition in which quantity supplied is greater than quantity demanded. Surpluses only occur at prices above equilibrium price.

Surplus Value In Marxist terminology, the difference between the total value of production and the subsistence wages paid to workers.

T-Account A simplified balance sheet that shows the changes in a bank's assets and liabilities.

Tariff A tax on imports.

Tax Base When referring to income taxes, the total amount of taxable income. The (average) tax rate × tax base = tax revenues.

Technology The body of skills and knowledge concerning the use of resources in production. An advance in technology commonly refers to the ability to produce more output with a fixed amount of resources or the ability to produce the same output with fewer resources.

The Federal Reserve System (the Fed) The central bank of the United States.

Theory An abstract representation of the real world designed with the intent to better understand that world.

Tie-in Sale A sale whereby one good can be purchased only if another good is also purchased.

Time Deposits Interest-earning deposits that have a stated maturity date and carry penalties for early withdrawal.

Trade Deficit The situation where the value of exports is less than the value of imports.

Trade-off A situation in which the attainment of something desirable necessarily implies the loss of something else desirable.

Transaction Costs The costs associated with the time and effort needed to search out, negotiate, and consummate an exchange.

Transfer Payments Payments that are not made in return for goods and services currently supplied.

Transmission Mechanism The routes or channels that ripple effects created in the money market travel to affect the goods and services market (represented by the aggregate demand and aggregate supply curves in the *AD–AS* framework).

Unattainable Region Includes those points above the production possibilities frontier.

Underground Economy Unreported exchanges that take place outside the normal recorded market channels. Some underground activities deal with illegal goods; others deal with legal goods and tax evasion.

Undervaluation A currency is undervalued if its price in terms of other currencies is below the equilibrium price.

Unemployment Rate The percentage of the civilian labor force that is unemployed: Unemployment rate = number of unemployed persons/number of persons in the civilian labor force.

Unit of Account A common measurement in which relative values are expressed. A function of money.

(Upward-sloping) Supply Curve The graphical representation of the law of supply.

U.S. Treasury Securities Bonds and bondlike securities issued by the U.S. Treasury when it borrows.

Utility The satisfaction one receives from the consumption of a good.

Velocity The average number of times a dollar is spent to buy final goods and services in a year.

Vicious Circle of Poverty The idea that countries are poor because they do not save (and invest) and that they cannot save (and invest) because they are poor.

"Voluntary" Export Restraint (VER) An agreement between two countries in which the exporting country "voluntarily" agrees to limit its exports to the importing country.

required reserve ratio, 277–78, 281
MV–PQ framework and, 307
in pure capitalism, 490
rational expectations and, 372
structure, 269–71
Feldstein, Martin, 475
Feudalism, 493
Final goods, **116**–17
Finance. *See* International finance
Fine-tuning, **338**, 363, 369
Fiscal policy, 94, **96**, 223, **224**–42. *See also*
specific types
activists vs. nonactivists, 338
automatic, 224
contractionary, 224
crowding out and, 230–35, 236, 242
demand-side, 227–36
discretionary, 224, 225–27
lags and, 235–36
domestic effects, 244, 245–46
expansionary, 224
international feedback effects, 244–45
in Keynesian theory, 225, 226, 227–30,
236, 242, 338
in new classical theory, 232–35, 370, 372
pure capitalism and, 490, 491
supply-side, 236–41, 242
Fisher effect, 299*n* 4
Fisher, Irving, 299, 324
Fixed exchange rate system, **450**, 464
Bretton Woods system, 458–60
central bank (Fed) and, 450–52
gold standard, 456–57
options under, 453–54
Fixed investment, **109**, 124
Flexible exchange rate system, **444**–50,
463–64
combined current/capital account,
749–50
equilibrium exchange rate in, 446–49
managed (current system), 460–62, 464
Flow variable, **115**, 308–9, **399**
Ford Gerald, 142
Ford, Henry, 187
Foreign aid, 483
Foreign exchange market, **440**, 463
credits and debits in, 438, 439
exchange rates in. *See* Exchange rate
Foreign sector, 97, 109, 151. *See also*
International finance; International
trade in four-sector economy, 112, 113
45° line, 25
Fractional reserve banking, **256**, 263, 274
Free good, **8**, 9, 21
Free lunch, no such thing as, 11, 488
Free trade
aggregate effects of, 421–26, 432, 433
agreements, 432
restrictions on, 428–31
Freund, Irwin, 184
Frictional unemployment, **156**–57, 360–61

Friedman, Milton, 15–16, 19, 293, 375,
377, 500
interview, 324–25
natural rate hypothesis, 363–66, 383–84,
386, 389, 396
permanent–income hypothesis, 220–22
Full employment, **158**
in classical theory, 179, 182, 186
in Keynesian theory, 185–86
Fungibility, **482**–83

Galbraith, John Kenneth, 500
Garn–St. Germain Act, 264
*General Theory of Employment, Interest
and Money, The* (Keynes), 183, 188
Glasnost, **494**, 499, 500
GNP deflator, 133, 134–37, **135**, 139, 144,
285, 289
Gold standard, **342**–44, 456–57, 464, 490
Good(s), **8**, 21
Gorbachev, Mikhail, 7, 494, 495, 499, 500,
501
Gordon, Robert, 339–40
Gosplan, **495**–96
Government
activists vs. nonactivists, 338–41
agricultural policies and programs, 80
bonds, 399–401, 402
in classical theory, 182, 208
in four-sector economy, 112, 113, 151
in Keynesian theory, 190, 194, 196–97,
208
as macroeconomic player, 97, 109
in monetarism, 323, 325
in new classical theory, 370, 372
political business cycle and, 389–92
privatization of functions, 406
regulation/restrictions, 59, 60. *See also*
Price ceilings; Price floors; Trade
restrictions
role in various economic systems, 487
in command-economy socialism,
495–99
in pure capitalism, 489–92
securities and the Fed, 276–77, 278
Government expenditures (spending), **97**,
109, 113, 126. *See also* Budget deficit;
National debt
business cycles and, 389
in classical economics, 226
and fiscal policy, 224, 226–27
crowding out and, 230–35
in Keynesian theory, 227–30
multiplier, 228–29
in GNP, 121, 151
inflation and, 292–93, 294–95
as an injection, 111
Graphs, 23–31
Great Depression, 95, 99, 101, 177, 183,
188, 210
gold standard and, 458

Keynesian explanation for, 207
monetarist explanation for, 319
Great Leap Forward (China), 502
Gross national product (GNP), **27**, 94, **103**,
115–24, 127, 130, 132. *See also*
Nominal GNP; Real GNP
deficits and debt as percentage of, 399
expenditure approach to measuring, 115,
120, 121–22, 124
income approach to measuring, 115, 120,
122–23, 124
limitations of, 120
national income and, 122–23
net national product and, 125
omissions from, 117–20
Gross private domestic investment, **97**,
109, 124–25, 126
net, 125*n* 7
Group of Five, 460
Group of Seven, 460

Hamermesh, Daniel, 12
Hamilton, Alexander, 325
Hasbrouck, Joel, 184
Hayek, Friedrich, 325
Hegel, Georg, 492, 493
Hoffman, Elizabeth, 66
Hong Kong, 433, 472, 480, 502
Household sector, 97, 109, 110, 133, 134,
151
in four-sector economy, 111–13
Human capital, and economic growth,
472–73
Hume, David, 324
Hussein, Saddam, 394

Imports, **97**, 113, 197. *See also*
International trade
distributional effects of, 424–26
of goods and services (in current
account), 438, 439, 440, 443
as a leakage, 111
restrictions on, 59. *See also* Trade
restrictions
tariffs on, 428–29
of United States (1990), 414
Imputed value, 118
Income, 114. *See also* Disposable income;
Income distribution; Income
inequality; Personal income; Real
income
approach to measuring GNP, 115, 120,
122–23, 124
and demand, 50
disposable, and consumption, 190, 191,
193, 219, 220
expectations of, and consumption, 194
growth rates and value of currency, 447
and money distinguished, 250
permanent-income hypothesis, 219–22
proprietors', in national income, 122

activist monetary policy and, 338–39
in the *AD–AS* framework, 188–89, 206–8
business cycle, 385–88, 396
criticisms of classical theory, 183–86, 188, 211–12
expansionary monetary policy and, 337–38
fiscal policy, 225, 226, 227–30, 236, 242
crowding out and, 230–32
government, role of, 190, 194, 196–97, 208
Great Depression, explanation of, 207
major tenets, 208
monetarism and, 318
multiplier in, 201, 203–5
new Keynesian ratex theory, 374
private economy, total expenditures in, 189–99
assumptions about, 189–90
consumption, 190–94, 199
investment, 194–97, 199
net exports, 197–99
on total expenditures, 188–89
and total production, 200–201, 202
transmission mechanism, 332–35, 344
Keynes, John Maynard, 7, 182–83, 184, 186, 188, 190, 195, 208, 220, 321, 374, 375
Kindleberger, Charles, 454
Knight, Frank, 325
Korea, 433
Kuwait crisis, 394–95

L, 254*n* 3
Labor, **34,** 114. *See also* Employment; Jobs
civilian labor force, 139, 140
decline in quality in 1970s, 475–76
market in Japan, 504–5
productivity. *See* Productivity
union. *See* Union
Labor theory of value, **492,** 494
Laffer, Arthur, 239, 241
Laffer curve, **239–41**
Lagging indicators, 387–88
Lags
activist monetary policy and, 339–40
discretionary fiscal policy and, 235–36
Laissez-faire, **182,** 208, 372
Laissez-faire capitalism. *See* Pure capitalism
Land, **34,** 114. *See also* Agriculture
Law of demand, **47,** 54
in all economic systems, 488
Law of diminishing marginal returns, 57
Law of increasing opportunity costs, **37–38,** 57
Law of supply, **54–57**
Leading indicators, 387–88
Leakage, **110–11,** 180–81
cash, 260
Leijonhufvud, Axel, 95, 210

Leisure, 118, 238–39
Lerner, Abba, 399
Less-developed countries, **478–82,** 485
Lewis, H. G., 19
Libertarianism, 489–91
critique of, 491–92
Licensing/license, 60
in pure capitalism, 490
Line graphs, 27–30
Line-item veto, 405
Li Peng, 503–4
Liquid asset, **254**
Liquidity effect, **298,** 299, 300
Liquidity trap, 333–**34,** 335, 337
Loanable funds
budget deficits and, 244–45
in new classical theory, 233–34
foreign, and crowding out, 231–32
Lobbyists/lobbying, 430*n* 3
Long run
aggregate supply curve, 156, **168,** 170, 172, 360–61
consumption function, 220, 221, 222
equilibrium, 160, 161, 162, 165, 167, **168,** 170, 171
Phillips curve, 366
Lucas, Robert, 366–67, 373

M1, **252–**53, 257, 275, 294
M2, **254–**55, 307
M3, 254*n* 3
McCabe, Kevin, 66
Macroeconomics, **20,** 22, 93, **94–**105
facts and questions in, 98–103, 105–6
categories, 94–96, 105
players, 96–98, 105
Madison, James, 325
Managed float, **460**
Mao Tse-tung, 502
Marginal propensity to consume, **190,** 191, 192, 219, 220, 228
Marginal propensity to save, **191,** 192
Marginal tax rate, **238**
aggregate supply and, 236, 238–39
Market, **47,** 61, 71. *See also* specific markets
goods and services, 331, 332
investment goods, 332
role in allocating resources in various economic systems, 487
Market basket (in CPI calculation), 133, 134
Market-clearing price. *See* Equilibrium price
Market demand curve, 48, 49
Market supply curve, 57, 58
Marshall, Alfred, 7, 61, 306
Marx, Karl, 492–94, 507
Medium of exchange, **250**
Meltzer, Allan, interview, 321
Merchandise trade balance, **440,** 441

Merchandise trade deficit, **440,** 461
J-curve, 462
Merchandise trade surplus, **440**
Microeconomics, **20,** 22
Mill, John Stuart, 179
Minimum wage, 81–82, 164, 165
in pure capitalism, 490
Ministry of Finance (Japan), 505
Ministry of International Trade and Industry (Japan), 505–6
Misery index, 142, 143
Mitchell, Wesley, 325
Mixed capitalism, 486, **487**
Monetarism, 178, 304, 308–26, 326–27
business cycles and, 389
classical monetary theory, 305–8
equation of exchange, 305–6
simple quantity theory of money, 306–8
Great Depression, explanation of, 319
and Keynesian theory, 318, 319
major tenets, 321, 323, 325
in *MV–PQ* framework, 317–18
stability of *k* and velocity in, 316–17
states of the economy, explanations of, 314–16
transmission mechanism, 335, 336, 344
Monetarists, 308
Monetary base, **273–**74, 275, 276*n* 6, 287, 282
Monetary policy, 94, **96,** 329, 330
activist case for, 338–39
business cycles and, 338–39
contractionary, 336*n* 2, 337, 349–50
expansionary, 336–38, 348–49
fixed exchange rates and, 453–54
gold standard and, 342–44
inflationary and recessionary gaps, 335–38
Keynesians on, 334
managed float system and, 460
monetary rule, 341–42
money market in, 330–31
in new classical theory, 370, 372
nonactivist case for, 338, 339–41
in an open economy, 348–50
in pure capitalism, 490, 491–92
transmission mechanisms in, 331–35
Monetary rule, **338,** 341–42, 389, 490
Monetary wealth, **148**
Money, 249, **250–**52, 265
contraction of, 261–62
demand curve for, 330, 333–34
demand for, 308–9, 310, 317, 320, 322, 327
expansion of, 257–61, 262–63, 266
functions of, 250–51
fungibility of, 482–83
origins of, 251
simple quantity theory, 305, 306–8
supply curve for, 330, 331